JUST SECURITY SERIES

Series Editor
RYAN GOODMAN

Perpetual War and International Law

JUST SECURITY

Series Editor
Ryan Goodman

Anne and Joel Ehrenkranz Professor of Law at New York University School of Law and co-editor-in-chief of Just Security

The *Just Security* book series from Oxford University Press tackles contemporary problems in international law and security that are of interest to a global community of scholars, policymakers, practitioners, and students. With each volume taking a particular thematic focus and gathering leading experts, the series aims to reflect on developments rigorously and critically in these areas of law, policy, and practice. Each volume will be accompanied by a series of shorter digital pieces in *Just Security*'s online forum at www.justsecurity.org, which tie the discussion to breaking news and headlines.

This series has been made possible through the extraordinary efforts of many individuals, including *Just Security* Postgraduate Fellow Haley Anderson and Oxford University Press editors John Louth, Merel Alstein, Robert Cavooris, Imogen Hill, Jacqueline Larabee, and Paulina dos Santos.

Perpetual War and International Law

Enduring Legacies of the War on Terror

Edited by

BRIANNA ROSEN

OXFORD
UNIVERSITY PRESS

OXFORD
UNIVERSITY PRESS

Oxford University Press is a department of the University of Oxford. It furthers the University's objective of excellence in research, scholarship, and education by publishing worldwide. Oxford is a registered trade mark of Oxford University Press in the UK and in certain other countries.

Published in the United States of America by Oxford University Press
198 Madison Avenue, New York, NY 10016, United States of America.

Library of Congress Cataloging-in-Publication Data
Names: Rosen, Brianna editor
Title: Perpetual war and international law : enduring legacies of the war on terror / [edited by] Brianna Rosen.
Description: New York : Oxford University Press, 2026. | Series: Just security | Includes bibliographical references and index.
Identifiers: LCCN 2025037484 (print) | LCCN 2025037485 (ebook) | ISBN 9780197748992 hardback | ISBN 9780197749005 paperback | ISBN 9780197749012 updf | ISBN 9780197749029 epub | ISBN 9780197749036 online
Subjects: LCSH: War (International law) | Aggression (International law) | Terrorism—Prevention—Law and legislation | Terrorism—Prevention—Law and legislation—United States | War finance—Law and legislation | War finance—Law and legislation—United States | Self-defense (International law) | Rule of law | LCGFT: Law materials
Classification: LCC KZ6385 .P49 2026 (print) | LCC KZ6385 (ebook) | DDC 341.6—dc23/eng/20250813
LC record available at https://lccn.loc.gov/2025037484
LC ebook record available at https://lccn.loc.gov/2025037485

DOI: 10.1093/oso/9780197748992.001.0001

The manufacturer's authorized representative in the EU for product safety is Oxford University Press España S.A. of Parque Empresarial San Fernando de Henares, Avenida de Castilla, 2 – 28830 Madrid (www.oup.es/en or product.safety@oup.com). OUP España S.A. also acts as importer into Spain of products made by the manufacturer.

Note to Readers
This publication is designed to provide accurate and authoritative information in regard to the subject matter covered. It is based upon sources believed to be accurate and reliable and is intended to be current as of the time it was written. It is sold with the understanding that the publisher is not engaged in rendering legal, accounting, or other professional services. If legal advice or other expert assistance is required, the services of a competent professional person should be sought. Also, to confirm that the information has not been affected or changed by recent developments, traditional legal research techniques should be used, including checking primary sources where appropriate.

(Based on the Declaration of Principles jointly adopted by a Committee of the American Bar Association and a Committee of Publishers and Associations.)

For the fallen, and for those who bear the enduring weight of what followed.

Contents

III. U.S. PERSPECTIVES ON THE WAR ON TERROR

IV. GLOBAL PERSPECTIVES ON THE WAR ON TERROR

Acknowledgments

This book is the product of a series of roundtables and workshops co-hosted by *Just Security* and the Oxford Institute for Ethics, Law and Armed Conflict. I am deeply grateful to all those who participated in these discussions and helped shape the project from its inception.

Many experts offered thoughtful and invaluable feedback on the structure and early drafts of the book's chapters: Fionnuala Ní Aoláin KC (Hon), Aslı Bâli, Tess Bridgeman, Richard Caplan, Neta Crawford, Federica D'Alessandra, Tom Dannenbaum, Laura Dickinson, Boyd van Dijk, Janina Dill, Mary Dudziak, Shaheed Fatima KC, Brian Finucane, Sir Lawrence Freedman KCMG, CBE, Rachel Goldbrenner, Pablo de Greiff, Scott Guggenheim, Luke Hartig, Oona Hathaway, Thomas Hegghammer, Rebecca Ingber, Harold Hongju Koh, Sarah Kreps, Eliav Lieblich, Samuel Moyn, Jelena Pejic, Stephen Pomper, Alka Pradhan, Aziz Rana, Ambassador Stephen Rapp, Mitt Regan, Hugo Slim, Sir Hew Strachan, Jessica White, and Sir Michael Wood KCMG, KC.

I owe a particular debt of gratitude to Audrey Balliette at *Just Security* for her assistance in preparing the final manuscript. Thanks also to the Fellows and Student Staff Editors who generously volunteered their time to review and standardize references, including Clara Apt, Isaac Buck, Jake Dow, Gwendolyn Strasberg Gardner, Wendy Leben, Jeremy Venook, and Siven Watts.

I am especially grateful to Ryan Goodman, the series editor, for his unwavering support of this project, and to Haley Anderson, without whom it would not have been possible. I would also like to thank Paulina dos Santos Major, Robert Cavooris, and the Oxford University Press editorial team for their care and professionalism in bringing this work to publication.

Finally, I extend my sincere appreciation to all the contributors for their intellectual generosity, moral clarity, and enduring commitment throughout this endeavor. Their insights reveal how law too often has enabled the expansion of contemporary warfare, even as it provides a foundation for reimagining restraint. The volume invites renewed attention to when and how wars should end, ultimately illuminating a path back to peace.

Contributors

Fionnuala Ní Aoláin KC (Hon), Regents Professor and Robina Chair in Law, Public Policy, and Society, University of Minnesota Law School; Professor of Law, Queen's University of Belfast, School of Law

Linda J. Bilmes, Daniel Patrick Moynihan Senior Lecturer in Public Policy, Harvard Kennedy School; Board of Directors, Belfer Center for Science and International Affairs

Tess Bridgeman, Senior Fellow and Visiting Scholar, Reiss Center on Law & Security, New York University School of Law; Co-Editor-in-Chief of *Just Security*

Andrew Clapham, Professor of Public International Law, Graduate Institute of International and Development Studies, Geneva

Federica D'Alessandra, Deputy Director Oxford Institute for Ethics, Law and Armed Conflict; British Academy Global Innovation Fellow, Carnegie Endowment for International Peace

Tom Dannenbaum, Frank Stanton Professor of Nuclear Security and Professor of Law, Stanford Law School; Senior Fellow, Freeman Spogli Institute for International Studies

Laura A. Dickinson, Lyle T. Alverson Professor of Law, The George Washington University School of Law

Anthony Dworkin, Senior Policy Fellow, European Council on Foreign Relations

Mary L. Dudziak, Asa Griggs Candler Professor of Law, Emory University School of Law

Pablo de Greiff, Senior Fellow and Director, Prevention Project, Center for Human Rights and Global Justice, School of Law, New York University

Adil Ahmad Haque, Distinguished Professor of Law and Judge Jon O. Newman Scholar, Rutgers Law School

Oona A. Hathaway, Gerard C. and Bernice Latrobe Smith Professor of International Law, Yale Law School

Harold Hongju Koh, Sterling Professor of International Law, Yale Law School

Alberto J. Mora, Senior Fellow, Carr-Ryan Center for Human Rights Policy, Harvard Kennedy School

Priyanka Motaparthy, Director, Center for International Human Rights, Northwestern University Pritzker School of Law

Radhya al-Mutawakel, Chairperson of Mwatana Organization for Human Rights

Faiza Patel, Senior Director, Liberty and National Security Program, Brennan Center for Justice

Brianna Rosen, Executive Director of the Oxford Programme for Cyber and Technology Policy, Blavatnik School of Government, University of Oxford; Senior Fellow, *Just Security*

Cheyney Ryan, Co-Chair of the Oxford Consortium of Human Rights; Emeritus Professor of Philosophy and Law at the University of Oregon

Timor Sharan, Founder and Director, Afghanistan Policy Lab

Elad Uzan, Departmental Lecturer at the Blavatnik School of Government, University of Oxford

Sir Michael Wood KCMG, KC, Barrister, Twenty Essex Chambers, London

Abbreviations

AQAP	al-Qaeda in the Arabian Peninsula
AQ Core	core al-Qaeda
AUMF	Authorization for Use of Military Force
CBO	Congressional Budget Office
CCF	continuous combat function
CCW	Convention on Certain Conventional Weapons
CIA	Central Intelligence Agency
DHS	Department of Homeland Security
DOD U.S.	Department of Defense
DOJ U.S.	Department of Justice
FBI	Federal Bureau of Investigation
FMF	Foreign Military Financing
FTO	foreign terrorist organization
GAO	Government Accountability Office
GGE	Group of Government Experts
GWOT	global war on terror
IAC	international armed conflict
IACHR	Inter-American Commission on Human Rights
ICC	International Criminal Court
ICCPR	International Covenant on Civil and Political Rights
ICJ	International Court of Justice
ICoC	International Code of Conduct
ICRC	International Committee of the Red Cross
ICTY	International Criminal Tribunal for the former Yugoslavia
IHL	international humanitarian law
IHRL	international human rights law
IO	international organization
JIAT	Joint Incidents Assessment Team
NGO	nongovernmental organization
NIAC	non-international armed conflict
NSC	National Security Council
NSEERS	National Security Entry-Exit Registration System
OCO	Overseas Contingency Operations
OEWG	Open-Ended Working Group
OLC	Office of Legal Counsel
PPBE	Planning, Programming, Budgeting, and Execution
PPG	Presidential Policy Guidance
PPM	Presidential Policy Memorandum

PRB	Periodic Review Board
PSOA	Private Security Offensive Actor
R2P	Responsibility to Protect
SIGAR U.S.	Special Inspector General for Afghanistan Reconstruction

I

INTRODUCTION

1
Still at War
Law and the Erosion of Restraint

Brianna Rosen

"Only the dead have seen the end of war."

– *George Santayana*[1]

Introduction

Contemporary conflicts have placed legal frameworks under great strain, testing the law's capacity to constrain violence. Interstate warfare has resurged as a defining feature of the international system, while conflicts involving non-state actors have become protracted and widespread.[2] Drawing on precedents set during the global "war on terror," states now claim greater latitude to use force against other states, armed groups, and even narcoterrorists. Meanwhile, advances in remote warfare and artificial intelligence have expanded the pace and scale of killing within and outside of recognizable battlefields. These features of contemporary warfare have given rise to the phenomenon of "perpetual war," that is, protracted violence lacking clearly defined conditions for resolution or termination.[3]

Perpetual wars encompass a broad spectrum of conflict ranging from conventional to asymmetric warfare, yet they share certain defining characteristics. Chief among these is the strategic ambiguity or implausibility of war aims, which makes decisive military victory unattainable. In such contexts, the mismatch between means and objectives produces conflicts that are, by design or default, unwinnable through force alone—thereby entrenching cycles of violence without

[1] George Santayana, Soliloquies in England and Later Soliloquies (1922).

[2] From the Russia-Ukraine War to conflicts in Gaza, Ethiopia, and Iran, the period since 2021 has emerged as one of the most violent epochs since the end of the Cold War. Siri Aas Rustad, Conflict Trends: A Global Overview, 1946–2023 (2024), https://cdn.cloud.prio.org/files/92a7aad5-3572-4886-9e9c-8aa155f1d0f4/Conflict_Trends-2024_DIGITAL.pdf?inline=true.

[3] The terms "perpetual war," "endless war," and "forever war" are used interchangeably throughout the volume. When capitalized, "Forever War" refers explicitly to the George W. Bush administration's declaration of a "Global War on Terrorism," also referred to as the "war on terror."

Brianna Rosen, *Still at War* In: *Perpetual War and International Law*. Edited by: Brianna Rosen, Oxford University Press. © Oxford University Press 2026. DOI: 10.1093/oso/9780197748992.003.0001

foreseeable end. Counterterrorism wars exemplify this logic, though interstate conflicts and civil wars similarly may fall within this paradigm.

The archetypal case of perpetual war is the global war on terror, a sprawling, open-ended conflict that the United States and its allies have waged continuously for nearly three decades. Also known as the "Forever War," the war on terror has persisted well beyond the end of conventional fighting in Afghanistan and Iraq.[4] Even after the U.S.-led withdrawal from Afghanistan in August 2021—America's "longest war"—the U.S. government maintained it was engaged in a global non-international armed conflict (NIAC) with al-Qaeda and an ever-expanding list of terrorist organizations designated as "associated forces."[5] As of this writing, that war continues, and the purported domestic legal basis for it—the 2001 Authorization for Use of Military Force (AUMF)—remains available to the executive branch as a source of domestic legal authority for military action against a broad and evolving range of targets. Relying on this authorization, the United States continues to conduct "over-the-horizon" operations—including drone strikes and special operations raids—in Afghanistan, Iraq, Somalia, Syria, Yemen, and elsewhere.[6] Although the threat of transnational terrorism has waxed and waned, the Obama administration's vision of a "tipping point"—the moment when the United States would transition from a war paradigm to a law enforcement model—has yet to materialize.[7]

The elusive tipping point in the war on terror has profound implications for global security. It marks a radical shift in the perception of war itself from an exceptional circumstance in which ordinary laws are suspended to a protracted condition in which states of emergency and the more permissive framework of international humanitarian law (IHL) apply continuously and indefinitely. What was once regarded as a time-bound response to an extraordinary threat has now been normalized, eroding the bedrock prohibition on the use of force and disrupting how legal rules ordinarily are designed to operate. With military action increasingly employed outside of recognizable battlefields, fundamental

[4] Between 2021 and 2023, the United States was involved in counterterrorism-related activities in at least seventy-eight countries, with U.S. troops in a combat role in five countries. *See* Costs of War Project, U.S. Counterterrorism Operations: Trends and Costs (Watson Inst. for Int'l & Pub. Aff., Brown Univ. 2023), https://watson.brown.edu/costsofwar/papers/2023/USCounterterrorismOperations.

[5] Transcript of Oral Argument at 79, United States v. Zubaydah, 595 U.S. 195 (2021) (No. 20-827).

[6] Brianna Rosen, *The Longest War Is Over the Horizon*, Just Security (Nov. 1, 2021), https://www.justsecurity.org/78818/the-longest-war-is-over-the-horizon/; Tess Bridgeman & Brianna Rosen, *Introduction to Symposium: Still at War—Where and Why the United States Is Fighting the "War on Terror,"* Just Security (Mar. 24, 2022), https://www.justsecurity.org/80800/introduction-to-symposium-still-at-war-where-and-why-the-united-states-is-fighting-the-war-on-terror/.

[7] Jeh Charles Johnson, General Counsel of the U.S. Department of Defense, Remarks before the Oxford Union (Nov. 30, 2012) (transcript available at https://ogc.osd.mil/Portals/99/Law%20of%20War/Practice%20Documents/GC%20Johnson%20-%20Oxford%20Union%20remarks%20-%20Nov%202012.pdf?ver=Tq48LfUJKY1Azg5QanM3yQ%3D%3D).

protections under international human rights law (IHRL) risk being disregarded or displaced altogether in how states conduct these operations. The costs and consequences of the war on terror, then, cannot be measured in terms of death and destruction alone. A more comprehensive accounting must interrogate how this war has reshaped legal precedents, political doctrines, and moral attitudes toward the use of force more broadly.

This volume examines the enduring legacies of the war on terror, looking back to understand how we arrived at this point, and forward to consider how such wars might finally end. Part II revisits the historical and conceptual foundations of perpetual war, tracing the evolution of the war paradigm in the pre- and post-9/11 eras. Part III offers a U.S.-focused analysis, examining mutually reinforcing dynamics between the domestic and foreign dimensions of perpetual war. Expanding the lens, Part IV offers a more global perspective, featuring insights from the United Kingdom, the European Union, Afghanistan, and Yemen. Part V reflects on the role of law in expanding counterterrorism warfare, drawing implications for global security and the future legal order. Finally, Part VI turns to the question of how the war on terror might end, exploring alternatives to the use of force and prospects for peace in an age of perpetual war.

In doing so, the volume makes two central contributions to the scholarly literature and policy discourse. First, it reveals how law has served both as an enabler and constraint on counterterrorism warfare, clarifying its dual role in shaping strategic, policy, and ethical frameworks. Second, the volume offers new insights into when and how counterterrorism wars should end, advancing the emerging *jus ex bello* literature. Notably, it provides the first sustained legal corollary to philosophical debates on the ethics of war termination. By bringing together leading legal scholars, philosophers, historians, and policy practitioners, the volume bridges disciplinary divides to provide a rare, integrated perspective on counterterrorism operations and the evolution of contemporary warfare.

Understanding Perpetual War

All wars, even those that span decades, eventually come to an end. History is replete with examples of conflicts that are open-ended and ill-defined.[8] Perpetual wars, then, are not merely long wars. The term, now firmly embedded in political rhetoric and public consciousness, denotes more than the duration of combat.

[8] The Hundred Years' War and Thirty Years' War are two salient historical examples. Since 1945, civil wars of all types tended to last between seven and twelve years. Alexander Bellamy estimates that 30 percent of ongoing "endless" wars today are connected to the war on terror. *See* Alexander Bellamy, *Ending Endless Wars, in* How to End a War: Essays on Justice, Peace, and Repair 111, 114–15 (Graham Parsons & Mark Wilson eds., 2023).

Yet the precise meaning of the term, and indeed of *war* itself, remains elusive; it is not a legal term of art in the United Nations (U.N.) Charter era, and there is no scholarly consensus on what constitutes war, let alone on what makes it perpetual. Lawyers measure the start of armed conflict in terms of crossing a threshold of gravity; philosophers weigh the morality of resorting to force against the prospects for success; and political scientists examine the scale and scope of violence. Perhaps we know a war when we see it, but that is hardly the case with perpetual war.

This chapter argues that perpetual war arises from the erosion of law as a meaningful constraint on the use of force. Far from being a question of duration or geography, the problem of perpetual war lies in the ambiguity of its objectives or the pursuit of ends unlikely to be achieved through force. David Rodin usefully distinguishes between "conceptually endless wars," in which war aims are undefined or unachievable, and "practically endless wars," whose objectives cannot be realized within normal policy planning cycles.[9] Alexander Bellamy locates the rise of perpetual war in "the changing nature of war and the attitudes that surround it," pointing to a deeper transformation in how societies understand and justify organized violence.[10] While claims about the changing character of war generally are overstated, advances in remote warfare and artificial intelligence have made it easier to initiate and sustain the use of force, lowering the threshold for violence and blurring the boundary between war and peace.[11]

The transformation of war from a state of emergency into an enduring feature of global politics is among the most consequential legacies of the post-9/11 era. What was initially framed as an extraordinary response to a terrorist attack has become widely institutionalized within legal, policy, and military doctrines, gradually weakening constraints on the use of force.[12] Along the way, the United States, as well as its allies and adversaries, have adopted increasingly elastic interpretations of international law that threaten to stretch, if not break, the legal system's capacity to constrain violence. That successive U.S. administrations have committed to waging a global armed conflict against terrorism indefinitely, regardless of the evolving threat landscape, raises the Orwellian prospect that

[9] David Rodin, *Forever Wars: Time and Value in War*, *in* How to End a War: Essays on Justice, Peace, and Repair 132 (Graham Parsons & Mark Wilson eds., 2023).

[10] Bellamy, *supra* note 8, at 120–21.

[11] Brianna Rosen, *AI and the Future of Drone Warfare: Risks and Recommendations*, Just Security (Oct. 3, 2023), https://www.justsecurity.org/89033/ai-and-the-future-of-drone-warfare-risks-and-recommendations/.

[12] Brianna Rosen, *Ending Perpetual War*, Just Security (Oct. 25, 2022), https://www.justsecurity.org/83749/ending-perpetual-war/.

"by becoming continuous war has ceased to exist" and therefore may never truly end.[13]

The second part of this volume explores the historical evolution and conceptual foundations of this transformation. In Chapter 2, Mary L. Dudziak opens with an exegesis of the view that perpetual war is a post-9/11 anomaly, situating its origins in a longer trajectory of American war-making since the Second World War. Her account reveals how permissive executive branch interpretations of international law, congressional abdication of its traditional war powers, and diminished public scrutiny have sustained a system in which conflicts proceed with few meaningful constraints. Foreshadowing Harold Hongju Koh's keynote chapter, Dudziak concludes with a powerful call for renewed civic engagement as a means of challenging and ending perpetual war.[14]

Cheyney Ryan continues this line of reasoning in a more philosophical vein in Chapter 3, arguing that the endlessness of war stems from its inherent aimlessness. Drawing on the tradition of political pacifism, Ryan challenges the belief that war can function as a rational instrument of politics, morality, or law, inviting deeper inquiry into justifications for resorting to force at the *jus ad bellum* level. Andrew Clapham picks up this thread in Chapter 4, reflecting on the legal and ethical consequences of framing counterterrorism operations as war. Raising themes that recur throughout the volume—particularly in subsequent chapters by Faiza Patel and Anthony Dworkin—Clapham illustrates how the adoption of the war paradigm lowers the threshold for the use of force and increases the risk of rights violations.[15]

These contributions offer a mutually reinforcing account of how war has become normalized and institutionalized, laying the foundation for the volume's broader inquiry. The authors show how the erosion of institutional checks, the philosophical incoherence of war as a strategic instrument, and the manipulation of legal categories have converged to blur the line between war and peace. The invocation of the war paradigm—irrespective of whether a formal state of armed conflict exists—produces a logic of exceptionalism, rendering acts that otherwise would be impermissible lawful and routine. The result is a structural realignment in which states repurpose legal and policy frameworks designed to limit war to sustain it, with profound implications for the role of law in constraining organized violence.

[13] *Id.*

[14] *See* Chapter 20 of this volume, "How to Finally End America's Forever War."

[15] *See* in this volume: Chapter 6, "Domestic Repercussions of the U.S. War on Terror," and Chapter 9, "Europe's Role in Perpetual War: From Counterpoint to Convergence."

Internalizing and Exporting the War Paradigm

The structural transformation in how wars are framed and fought reverberates far beyond the battlefield. Grasping this transformation requires close attention to the interplay between the domestic and global dimensions of perpetual war, as well as to the long-term costs and consequences of waging counterterrorism wars indefinitely. An underexplored area in the scholarly literature is the domestic-foreign nexus of perpetual war, where waging endless war abroad contributes to democratic backsliding at home that, in turn, legitimizes the erosion of global legal norms.

Part III of the volume addresses this gap by examining how the war paradigm has been internalized within the United States, resulting in decreased democratic oversight and the militarization of domestic policy. In Chapter 5, Linda J. Bilmes analyzes how the post-9/11 shift to debt-financed warfare and off-budget spending has eroded democratic oversight, allowing sustained military engagement with little public scrutiny or accountability. These themes continue in Chapter 6, where Faiza Patel examines the inward migration of the war paradigm, demonstrating how it has reshaped U.S. approaches to policing and the use of force domestically. In Chapter 7, Federica D'Alessandra and Alberto J. Mora reverse the lens, arguing that democratic backsliding at home has contributed to the weakening of global legal norms. Focusing on the legacy of torture at Guantánamo Bay, they show how permissive U.S. interpretations of international law have emboldened authoritarian regimes to follow suit.

Beyond setting precedents for authoritarian regimes, U.S. policies also have served as a lodestar for its allies and partners, many of whom have become increasingly willing to stretch the boundaries of international law. While public debate has centered on the United States, reflecting its outsized role in the war on terror, insufficient attention has been devoted to how precedents set in this conflict have shaped the use of force worldwide. Part IV therefore shifts focus from the United States to the United Kingdom, the European Union, and finally to the Middle East and North Africa.

The global export of U.S. counterterrorism practices invites deeper reflection on whether international law has fundamentally evolved in the post-9/11 era. In Chapter 8, Sir Michael Wood—drawing on his experience as principal Legal Adviser to the U.K. Foreign and Commonwealth Office during the initial years of the war on terror—makes the case that the law governing resort to force at the *jus ad bellum* level remains intact, notwithstanding policy efforts to stretch its contours. Nevertheless, Wood acknowledges a widening gap between legal principles and political practice, where justifications for the use of force against non-state actors risk undermining core constraints of the *jus ad bellum*. Offering a perspective that contrasts with other contributors in the volume—and serving as a counterpoint to Clapham's analysis—Wood introduces a critical note of caution against conflating policy with legal doctrine. He reminds us that much of the rhetoric surrounding the war on terror has no basis in law, setting the stage for a broader debate in the latter half of the volume about the resilience of international law in the face of evolving state practice.

State practice has shifted dramatically over time, as Anthony Dworkin argues in Chapter 9. While European governments initially resisted U.S. claims that it was engaged in a global armed conflict with non-state actors, they gradually embraced many of the same wartime practices, including status-based targeting in areas outside of active hostilities. This convergence enabled sustained military operations against non-state actors with few temporal or geographic limits. Allied acquiescence, Dworkin suggests, further entrenched the logic of perpetual war, leading to a deeper erosion of constraints on the use of force.

Shifting beyond Europe, the volume next turns to the Middle East and North Africa, the central theater of the war on terror. The U.S. withdrawal from Afghanistan, nearly two decades after the invasion in response to 9/11, marked a watershed moment in the conflict. President Joe Biden's declaration before the United Nations that the United States was "no longer at war" is cited by several contributors as emblematic of the dissonance between political rhetoric and reality.[16] Despite the formal end of large-scale combat operations, the war on terror has continued through drone strikes and special operations raids.[17] With the Taliban's return to power in August 2021, Afghanistan has once again become a haven for the very form of violent extremism that the war on terror sought to eradicate. The futility of the war on terror is brought into stark relief in Chapter 10, where Timor Sharan examines how U.S. counterterrorism policies inadvertently led to the destabilization and eventual collapse of the Afghan government. Sharan meticulously documents how the stated U.S. policy of using "money as a weapons system" empowered an Afghan kleptocratic elite, hollowed out state institutions, and hastened the Taliban's return to power.

Moving from an institutional to an individual perspective, Priyanka Motaparthy and Radhya al-Mutawakel in Chapter 11 illuminate the broader human costs of the war on terror. Drawing on firsthand testimonies collected in Yemen, the authors demonstrate how drone strikes devastated entire communities, deepened economic inequalities, and entrenched structural injustices. Echoing D'Alessandra and Mora, they argue that the absence of accountability in Yemen has undermined the rules-based order the United States

[16] Joseph R. Biden Jr., Remarks Before the 76th Session of the United Nations General Assembly (Sept. 21, 2021), https://it.usembassy.gov/remarks-by-president-biden-before-the-76th-session-of-the-united-nations-general-assembly/.

[17] Rosen, *supra* note 6.

claims to uphold. Ultimately, the legal and normative precedents established during the war on terror may be among its most corrosive legacies—a theme explored in greater depth in the penultimate part of the volume.

The Legal Expansion of War

At the time of writing, the United States has participated in a twelve-day war between Israel and Iran that threatened to engulf the broader region. On June 21, 2025, the United States took the unprecedented step of directly attacking Iranian territory, bombing nuclear facilities at Fordow, Natanz, and Esfahan.[18] The Trump administration conducted these strikes without congressional authorization, relying instead on purported Article II constitutional authority that permits the president, under narrow circumstances as commander-in-chief, to act unilaterally to defend U.S. forces.[19] From an international legal perspective, the United States did not seek authorization from the U.N. Security Council, instead claiming to have acted in "collective self-defense" of Israel—the legality of whose own actions is in grave doubt.[20] Both the domestic and international legal justifications for the U.S. strikes appear tenuous at best, laying bare how ineffective legal constraints on the use of force have become.[21]

This erosion can be traced to decades of national security lawyering during the war on terror, which has given the executive branch unparalleled power.[22] Relying on Article II authorities, as well as elastic interpretations of the 2001 and 2002 AUMFs, successive U.S. administrations have advanced increasingly strained legal justifications for the use of force absent congressional authorization or legitimate self-defense claims that would be widely accepted by most states (and absent U.N. Security Council authorization in all but the rarest of cases). U.S. presidents now invoke Article II with growing frequency, even in cases—such as the 2025 Iran strikes—where the risk of escalation almost certainly would rise to the level of "war in the constitutional sense" such that congressional authorization would be required.[23] At the same time, multiple

[18] Brianna Rosen, Tess Bridgeman, & Nima Gerami, *The Day After U.S. Strikes on Iran's Nuclear Program: A Policy and Legal Assessment*, Just Security (June 22, 2025), https://www.justsecurity.org/115234/policy-legal-iran-nuclear-strikes/.

[19] *Id.*

[20] Adil Ahmad Haque, *Indefensible: Israel's Unlawful Attack on Iran*, Just Security (June 19, 2025), https://www.justsecurity.org/115010/israel-unlawful-attack-iran-charter/.

[21] *See* Brian Finucane, *The Trump Administration's Flawed War Powers Report on Iran and the Need for a Congressional Rebuttal*, Just Security (June 24, 2025), https://www.justsecurity.org/115398/trump-justification-attacking-iran-congressional-rebuttal/.

[22] Oona A. Hathaway, *National Security Lawyering in the Post-War Era: Can Law Constrain Power?*, 68 UCLA L. Rev. 2 (2021).

[23] As Brian Egan and Tess Bridgeman explain, neither Article II authorities, nor the 2001 or 2002 AUMFs, provided domestic legal authority for the June 2025 U.S. strikes on Iran. *See* Brian Egan &

administrations have relied on the 2001 AUMF to target "terrorist" groups that did not exist when Congress passed it. Similarly, the executive branch consistently has invoked the 2002 AUMF authorizing force against Iraq to justify attacks against targets from other countries that presumably would not be covered under that congressional authority.[24] In short, the post-9/11 evolution of executive branch lawyering has enabled virtually unchecked authority to use force, and sporadic efforts from Congress to reclaim its traditional war powers thus far have failed to restore the democratic balance of power.

International law has fared little better. Legal innovations forged in the war on terror have seeped into other conflicts around the world from U.S. strikes against narcoterrorists in the Caribbean to the Russia-Ukraine War. Expansive "collective self-defense" arguments, for example—invoked in the 2022 Russian invasion of Ukraine and the 2025 U.S. strikes on Iran—are becoming a recurring feature in justifying the use of force absent any specific or temporally imminent threat to the state asserting it.[25] As Oona A. Hathaway warns, the precedents set in these conflicts have "the power to reshape the global legal order, transforming it from one governed by law to one governed by might."[26]

The penultimate part of this volume examines the role of law in enabling and sustaining perpetual war. In Chapter 12, Adil Ahmad Haque explores how legal indeterminacy—particularly regarding when hostilities begin or end, who may be lawfully targeted, and the geographic scope of conflict—has permitted the continuation of hostilities without clear limits. While IHL regulates the conduct of war, it neither authorizes the initiation or continuation of armed conflict nor directly requires its termination. Meanwhile, states have reinterpreted fundamental tenets of international law to prolong extraterritorial violence against non-state actors.

One of the most persistent legal ambiguities concerns the termination of armed conflicts, especially in the context of counterterrorism operations. To date, there is no settled view in international law on when parties to a NIAC, whether state or non-state actors, are legally obligated to cease hostilities.[27] In

Tess Bridgeman, *Top Experts' Backgrounder: Military Action Against Iran and U.S. Domestic Law*, JUST SECURITY (June 18, 2025), https://www.justsecurity.org/64645/war-powers-trump-iran-strikes/.

[24] The first Trump administration, for example, relied on the 2002 AUMF as part of the legal basis for the drone strike that killed Iranian General Qassem Soleimani in January 2020.

[25] JAMES A. GREEN, COLLECTIVE SELF-DEFENCE IN INTERNATIONAL LAW (2024).

[26] Oona A. Hathaway, *Trump's Strikes on Iran Were Unlawful. Here's Why That Matters*, N.Y. TIMES (June 23, 2025), https://www.nytimes.com/2025/06/23/opinion/international-world/trump-iran-strikes.html.

[27] For a discussion of this issue, *see* International Committee of the Red Cross, *Commentary of 2020: Article 3—Conflicts Not of an International Character*, *in* COMMENTARY ON THE THIRD GENEVA CONVENTION 45 (2021), https://ihl-databases.icrc.org/en/ihl-treaties/commentary/1949geneva-convention-iii/article-3.

legal and practical terms, identifying the end of a NIAC is particularly challenging due to the absence of clear legal standards, inconsistent state practice, and the complex conditions that typically shape conflict resolution. As Dustin Lewis, Gabriella Blum, and Naz Modirzadeh observe, "the current plurality of legal concepts of armed conflict, the sparsity of IHL provisions that instruct the end of application, and the inconsistency among such provisions thwart uniform regulation and frustrate the formulation of a comprehensive notion of when wars can, should, and do end."[28] The updated International Committee of the Red Cross (ICRC) Commentary to Article 3 of the First Geneva Convention offers some guidance, identifying factors such as the complete military defeat of one party or a "lasting cessation" of hostilities with no "real risk of resumption" as possible indicators of a conflict's end. However, the ICRC Commentary also makes clear that ceasefires, temporary lulls in fighting, or even formal peace agreements do not necessarily mark the legal conclusion of a NIAC.[29]

Tess Bridgeman unpacks this debate in Chapter 13, examining how evolving legal theories have enabled the United States to assert wartime authorities long after core al-Qaeda ceased to pose a strategic threat. Framing the discussion for the volume's conclusion on how counterterrorism wars end, Bridgeman explains why the "tipping point" standard—once articulated as a benchmark for ending hostilities with core al-Qaeda—has vanished, and how international law could help fill the void. Shifting from legal doctrines to the policy frameworks that sustain them, Laura A. Dickinson in Chapter 14 explores the evolution of executive branch lawyering related to the use of force outside areas of active hostilities. Calling for a reassessment of "legalistic policymaking," Dickinson urges the executive branch to curtail its wartime posture as a matter of both policy and law.

Building on these concerns, Oona A. Hathaway in Chapter 15 demonstrates how the erosion of U.S. legal constraints on unilateral presidential war power has undermined international law limits on the use of force. Ever-expanding U.S. claims of "self-defense," Hathaway argues, have weakened both congressional authority and prohibitions on the use of force under the U.N. Charter. These legal interpretations have reshaped global norms, allowing other states to exploit precedents and practices established during the war on terror. Rather than constraining counterterrorism warfare, expansive U.S. interpretations of international law have sustained it long after troop withdrawals from Afghanistan and Iraq.

[28] Dustin Lewis, Gabriella Blum, & Naz Modirzadeh, *Indefinite War: Unsettled International Law on the End of Armed Conflict*, Harvard Law Sch. Program on Int'l Law & Armed Conflict (Feb. 2017).

[29] International Committee of the Red Cross, *supra* note 27, at 522–26.

Reimagining War's End

The persistence of conflict beyond the last conventional front of the war on terror brings into focus pressing legal and ethical questions concerning when and how wars should end. When are states legally and morally required to end military action against terrorist groups? How can counterterrorism wars conclude justly when, in the absence of total defeat or annihilation, there is always a risk that hostilities will resume? Despite the gravity of these questions, they have received limited attention, even as protracted and unconventional conflicts have become pervasive in contemporary warfare.

International law and just war theory offer a foundation for grappling with the multifaceted challenges surrounding war termination. Given the law's relative indeterminacy on this issue, wars may be lawfully initiated and lawfully fought, yet still conclude in ways that are destabilizing or corrosive to the rule of law. By extension, a war fought for a just cause and in accordance with just war principles may nonetheless end unjustly. In either case, it is clear that wars do not end merely because *jus ad bellum* conditions cease to be fulfilled.[30] The U.S.-led war in Afghanistan, for example, arguably complied with *jus ad bellum* and *jus in bello* principles insofar as it was fought in self-defense and according to rules of engagement that were often more restrictive than what IHL required.[31] Yet it is a matter of debate whether that war ended when and how it should have.[32] The emerging philosophical literature that examines this debate—variously referred to as *jus ex bello* or *jus terminatio*—has no direct analogue in positive international law.[33] This body of work also remains underdeveloped relative to other theoretical domains, lagging behind even the nascent *jus post bellum* literature on how states might forge a just peace after war.[34]

The final part of the volume addresses these shortcomings, offering theoretical and policy guidance on ending perpetual war. In Chapter 16, Fionnuala Ní Aoláin provides a roadmap for reforming the global counterterrorism architecture. She urges states to move beyond security-centric approaches that

[30] A war, for example, might meet *jus ad bellum* criteria when it is launched, yet become disproportionate over time as cost assessments change, requiring a reassessment of whether it is permissible to continue fighting. Conversely, even when wars fail to meet *ad bellum* criteria at the outset, invading states nevertheless may have a moral obligation to stay and rectify the damage they have caused. *See* Cécile Fabre, *War Exit*, 125 Ethics 631 (2015).

[31] *See* Rodin, *supra* note 9, at 2.

[32] *See, e.g.*, Darrel Moellendorf, Jus Ex Bello *in Afghanistan*, 25 Ethics & Int'l Aff. 155–64 (2011); Richard Miller, *The Ethics of America's Afghan War*, 25 Ethics & Int'l Aff. 103–31 (2011).

[33] *See, e.g.*, David Rodin, *Ending War*, 25 Ethics & Int'l Aff. 359, 360 (2011); David Rodin, *The War Trap: Dilemmas of Jus Terminatio*, 125 Ethics & Int'l Aff. 674 (2015); and Fabre, *supra* note 30.

[34] For treatment of this issue, *see* Michael Walzer, *The Aftermath of War: Reflections on Jus Post Bellum*, *in* Ethics Beyond War's End (Eric Patterson ed., 2012).

enable counterterrorism abuses and instead adopt policies that empower civil society and strengthen the rule of law. Expanding on these insights, Pablo de Greiff in Chapter 17 advances a preventive interpretation of transitional justice, emphasizing its role in affirming norms, building civic trust, and addressing the structural drivers of terrorism. Together, these chapters propose forward-looking strategies that prioritize justice, legitimacy, and institutional reform as prerequisites for ending endless war.

Turning from practice to principle, Elad Uzan in Chapter 18 interrogates the normative threshold for ending counterterrorism wars from a risk distribution perspective. Drawing on the work of Gabriella Blum and David Luban, Uzan contends that counterterrorism wars must end once the risk to the defending population falls below an ethically acceptable level.[35] Noting that terrorism will always pose a risk that can never be reduced to zero, Uzan provides a framework for policymakers to determine whether hostilities against terrorist threats are morally permissible and the conditions under which those hostilities must cease.

Tom Dannenbaum advances a complementary legal argument in Chapter 19, where he presents a novel legal theory of *jus ex bello*. Challenging the presumption that international law is silent on war termination, Dannenbaum asks whether states are legally obligated to end hostilities once their conduct serves only to prolong, rather than resolve, armed conflict. Drawing on the *jus ad bellum* principles of necessity and proportionality, human rights law, and the normative imperative to pursue peace, Dannenbaum contends that international law already contains the basic foundations of such an obligation. He calls for further development of this legal regime to support a more robust framework for political decision-making on war termination.

The concluding keynote chapter of the volume presents precisely such a framework. In his *tour de force* analysis of both the causes and cures of the war on terror, former U.S. State Department Legal Adviser Harold Hongju Koh articulates concrete steps U.S. policymakers must take to transition from perpetual war to sustainable peace. After examining how the Forever War became entrenched through legal overreach, bureaucratic inertia, and evolving security threats, Koh proposes four practical policy strategies to end perpetual war. These strategies emphasize repealing and replacing outdated authorizations for the use of force, restoring meaningful interbranch legislative checks, disciplining defensive doctrines, and reshaping the national security bureaucracy to prioritize diplomatic and preventive tools. Koh concludes that ending the war on terror demands a fundamental reorientation of policymaking that treats war as an aberration and embraces legal restraint as a national security imperative.

[35] Gabriella Blum & David Luban, *Unsatisfying Wars: Degrees of Risk and the Jus ex Bello*, 125 Ethics 751 (2015).

Overall, the volume confronts the failure of international law to prevent the normalization and perpetuation of armed conflict in the post-9/11 era. Looking back to look forward, the chapters show how the expansion of executive power, elastic interpretations of international law, and precedents set in the war on terror have transformed war from an exceptional state of emergency into a near-permanent condition. In response, the volume offers detailed legal, ethical, and policy frameworks for ending perpetual war in theory and practice.

Georg Wilhelm Friedrich Hegel observed that "the owl of Minerva spreads its wings only with the coming of the dusk"—that wisdom arrives only on the verge of decline.[36] As the war on terror approaches the quarter-century mark and the rule of law faces mounting strain, that moment has arrived. Unless policymakers confront the enduring legacies of the war on terror and decisively change course, it may be too late to prevent further erosion of the legal order. The United States and its allies are still at war, and only a renewed commitment to restraint can restore international law as a credible limit on the use of force in an age of endless conflict. *Perpetual War and International Law* recognizes the gravity of this moment, navigates the legal, moral, and policy challenges it presents, and ultimately seeks to illuminate the path back to peace.

[36] GEORG WILHELM FRIEDRICH HEGEL, THE PHILOSOPHY OF RIGHT, at xxx (1896).

II

UNDERSTANDING PERPETUAL WAR

2

How Law, History, and Culture Enabled Perpetual War

Mary L. Dudziak

Introduction

The origins of Forever War are often thought to be in the aftermath of September 11, 2001, when well-organized teams of terrorists hijacked commercial aircraft filled with passengers and crashed them into the World Trade Center towers, the Pentagon, and a field in Pennsylvania. On that deadly and dreadful day, many Americans felt the terrorist attacks were an act of war and the United States must respond in a war-like fashion.[1] President George W. Bush framed the conflict in broad terms. "Our war on terror begins with al Qaeda, but it does not end there," he explained in an address to Congress and the American people. "It will not end until every terrorist group of global reach has been found, stopped and defeated."[2] With terrorism as the target of this war, it was defined at the outset as a war without end, for terrorism is an enduring tactic, not a nation or clan subject to conquer.[3] Nevertheless, Congress responded by passing the 2001 Authorization for Use of Military Force (AUMF) granting authority for what was now called the "war on terror."[4] In spite of the U.S.-led withdrawal from Afghanistan in 2021, U.S. military operations based on outdated congressional authorizations continue more than twenty years later.[5] September 11 was a

1 Thanks to Brianna Rosen and Sam Moyn for extremely helpful comments on an earlier version of this chapter. *See* Hannah Hartig & Carroll Doherty, *Two Decades Later, the Enduring Legacy of 9/11*, Pew Rsch. Ctr. (Sept. 2, 2011), https://www.pewresearch.org/politics/2021/09/02/two-decades-later-the-enduring-legacy-of-9-11/ [https://perma.cc/6KVD-N5HY]; September 11 in History: A Watershed Moment? 1–9 (Mary L. Dudziak ed., 2003).

2 George W. Bush, Address to a Joint Session of Congress and the American People (Sept. 20, 2001) (transcript available in the White House Archives), https://georgewbush-whitehouse.archives.gov/news/releases/2001/09/20010920-8.html [https://perma.cc/DX5T-WC98].

3 *See* Marilyn B. Young, *Ground Zero: Enduring War*, *in* September 11 in History, *supra* note 1, at 10–28.

4 Authorization for Use of Military Force, Pub. L. No. 107-40, 115 Stat. 224 (2001).

5 *See* Stephanie Savel, *The 2001 Authorization for Use of Military Force: A Comprehensive Look at Where and How It Has Been Used*, Costs of War, Watson Institute, Brown Univ. (Dec. 14, 2021), https://watson.brown.edu/costsofwar/files/cow/imce/papers/2021/Costs%20of%20War_2001%20AUMF.pdf [https://perma.cc/ECC5-MWWS].

Mary L. Dudziak, *How Law, History, and Culture Enabled Perpetual War* In: *Perpetual War and International Law*. Edited by: Brianna Rosen, Oxford University Press. © Oxford University Press 2026.
DOI: 10.1093/oso/9780197748992.003.0002

signal historical event, but it was not the beginning of Forever War, for American troops have been persistently deployed at U.S. bases around the world since World War II.[6] More broadly, if the timeline of U.S. war includes service under fire in forgotten conflicts large and small, ongoing U.S. war had been underway for most of the twentieth century.[7]

Casting the response to the al-Qaeda attacks as a "war" had significant long-term consequences within the United States and internationally. It divided the world into allies, enemies, and neutrals, undermining the broad international sympathy and solidarity that the attacks initially generated.[8] It thrust the United States—now referred to by American leaders as the "homeland,"[9] into a new era: a wartime. Wartimes traditionally are perceived to be discreet eras when safety and security are prioritized over individual liberty and presidential power is more expansive. These societal changes are tolerated both because of a fearful threat and because they are thought to be temporary. Traditionally, the end of wartime signaled the return of peacetime.[10] With persistent U.S. military engagement, however, there was no peacetime in which domestic security measures could be rolled back.

While the United States previously experienced sporadic terrorist attacks before 9/11, the only major wars involving an attack within American states (as opposed to U.S. territories) had occurred well over one hundred years before. American civilians within the continental United States had not personally experienced the close terror of war in generations.[11] During the long era since the American Civil War, civilians in other nations felt horror akin to what Americans in Manhattan experienced after the 9/11 attacks. Koreans fled from tanks entering their villages, and especially in the north, civilians suffered extensive casualties from aerial bombings. U.S. civilians, in contrast, read about the Korean War in the newspaper.[12] Young men in the United States were drafted to fight in the war in Vietnam, while American civilians saw snippets of it on

[6] *See, e.g.*, REBECCA HERMAN, COOPERATING WITH THE COLOSSUS: A SOCIAL AND POLITICAL HISTORY OF US MILITARY BASES IN WORLD WAR II LATIN AMERICA (2022).

[7] *See Instances of Use of United States Armed Forces Abroad, 1798–2023*, CONG. RSCH. SERV., (June 7, 2023), https://crsreports.congress.gov/product/pdf/R/R42738.

[8] *See* Elaine Tyler May, *Echoes of the Cold War: The Aftermath of September 11 at Home, in* SEPTEMBER 11 IN HISTORY, *supra* note 1, at 35–40.

[9] *See* Amy Kaplan, *Homeland Insecurities: Some Reflections on Language and Space*, 85 RADICAL HIST. REV. 82 (Winter 2003).

[10] *See* MARY L. DUDZIAK, WAR TIME: AN IDEA, ITS HISTORY, ITS CONSEQUENCES 15–17, 21–26 (2012).

[11] During World War II, Japan launched a single attack on the U.S. territory of Hawai'i, and the territories of Alaska, Guam, and especially the Philippines suffered more sustained warfare. The forty-eight U.S. states at the time did not experience military attacks. DANIEL IMMERWAHR, HOW TO HIDE AN EMPIRE: A HISTORY OF THE GREATER UNITED STATES 171–212 (2019).

[12] BRUCE CUMINGS, THE KOREAN WAR: A HISTORY (2010); Marilyn B. Young, *Hard Sell: The Korean War, in* MAKING THE FOREVER WAR: MARILYN YOUNG ON THE CULTURE AND POLITICS OF AMERICAN MILITARISM 39–65 (Mark Bradley & Mary L. Dudziak eds., 2021).

television.[13] In the 1990–91 Persian Gulf War, the visuals featured computerized images of "smart bombs," which Pentagon officials assured the U.S. public could precisely hit their targets, thereby minimizing civilian casualties now described as "collateral damage."[14] Throughout this period, as Tess Bridgeman and Oona A. Hathaway examine in this volume, presidential unilateral war powers expanded.[15] This was enabled in part by the isolation of U.S. civilians from the consequences of their wars, as war became a policy option, not a means of national survival.[16]

This chapter illustrates three aspects of law, culture, and politics that have enabled the perpetual war. First, the chapter shows how cultural understandings of "wartime" informed assumptions that conflicts were temporary. Second, it turns to the role of distant war in enabling U.S. domestic apathy once U.S. wars were fought far from the North American continent. Finally, the chapter demonstrates how law undermined Congress's ability to rein in presidential war power as the history of executive unilateralism became legal precedent for expansive presidential power.[17]

"Wartime" and the Culture of War

As post-9/11 conflicts in Afghanistan and Iraq continued, persistent war was in tension with the way most Americans conceptualized their country's history of military action. Traditionally, "war" and "peace" were thought of as separate states of existence, and war was thought to be time-limited, confined within wartimes and followed by peacetimes. In American history books, there was an entire "postwar" era after World War II, even though U.S. soldiers earned combat

[13] *See* BRUCE CUMINGS, WAR AND TELEVISION 83–101 (1994); Chester Pach Jr., *The War on Television: TV News, the Johnson Administration, and Vietnam*, *in* A COMPANION TO THE VIETNAM WAR 460–69 (Marilyn B. Young & Robert Buzzanco eds., 2002).

[14] Tim Weiner, *"Smart" Weapons Were Overrated, Study Concludes*, N.Y. TIMES (July 9, 1996), https://www.nytimes.com/1996/07/09/us/smart-weapons-were-overrated-study-concludes.html?smid=nytcore-android-share. On collateral damage, *see* NETA C. CRAWFORD, ACCOUNTABILITY FOR KILLING: MORAL RESPONSIBILITY FOR COLLATERAL DAMAGE IN AMERICA'S POST-9/11 WARS (2013).

[15] *See* Chapter 13, "The Vanishing 'Tipping Point' and the Problem of Perpetual War," and Chapter 15, "The Rise of "Self-Defense"—And the Fall of Constraints on the Use of Force," respectively.

[16] *See generally* Mary L. Dudziak, *Death and the War Power*, 30 YALE J.L. & HUMAN. 25 (2018).

[17] Others have powerfully argued that the law of armed conflict has enabled great violence in war. *See* JANINA DILL, LEGITIMATE TARGETS? SOCIAL CONSTRUCTION, INTERNATIONAL LAW AND US BOMBING (2015); SAMUEL MOYN, HUMANE: HOW THE UNITED STATES ABANDONED PEACE AND REINVENTED WAR (2021); JOHN FABIAN WITT, LINCOLN'S CODE: THE LAWS OF WAR IN AMERICAN HISTORY (2012). This chapter contributes to this literature by broadening the scope of law's deployment as a technology of war to include the expansion of unilateral presidential war power. This aspect of forever war is a focus of MARY L. DUDZIAK, GOING TO WAR: AN AMERICAN HISTORY (under contract, Oxford University Press).

service medals every year after 1945. The proclaimed "postwar" period was replete with military conflict.[18]

The idea of "forever war" captures the concern that wartimes no longer seem to have endings. The term first appeared in novels and scholarship during the Cold War years when the United States conceptualized the Korean War and other conflicts as part of an ongoing battle against communism, and as conflicts that lacked clear or victorious endpoints.[19] Forever war was featured more prominently in post-9/11 discourse.[20] Still, U.S. politics and culture largely hew to the outdated framing that wars are time-bound. As a result, when political leaders authorized the use of force, the long-term impact and costs of war were not widely recognized.[21]

The disconnect between the notion of wartime and the practice of ongoing war is one example of the way culture and ideas inform our understanding of what war is and how it should be regulated. Cultural ideas can have a profound impact on understandings of the threat, the way the enemy is conceptualized, and the very nature of war, as Andrew Clapham explores in Chapter 4.[22] When war is thought of as exceptional, departures from the usual rule of law are tolerated. When "peacetime" returns, regular forms of law are expected to re-emerge.[23] When war is instead persistent, war-related practices and policies, including military detention and secrecy, become embedded. There is no "peacetime" within which law is reset.[24]

Paradoxically, because wartime has become normal time, the public often pays little attention to it. Meanwhile, traditional ideas about war's assumed time-bound character have continued to inform political discourse and judicial decisions, despite the tension with current military practices.[25] The geographic distance of war from the American polity has enabled these dynamics, but distant war and civilian disengagement are not new in the twenty-first century.[26]

[18] *See* DUDZIAK, *supra* note 10, at 151–56.

[19] *See, e.g.*, JOE HALDEMAN, THE FOREVER WAR (1974) (science fiction novel); JAMES P. HARRISON, THE ENDLESS WAR: FIFTY YEARS OF STRUGGLE IN VIETNAM (1981) (social science critique of the U.S. role in Vietnam).

[20] Kelsey D. Atherton, *A Short Etymology of Forever War*, WARS OF FUTURE PAST, SUBSTACK (Sept. 28, 2020), https://athertonkd.substack.com/p/a-short-etymology-of-forever-war.

[21] *See generally* DUDZIAK, *supra* note 10. *See also* ROSA BROOKS, HOW EVERYTHING BECAME WAR AND THE MILITARY BECAME EVERYTHING (2016). On the global history of perpetual war, *see* LAUREN BENTON, THEY CALLED IT PEACE: WORLDS OF IMPERIAL VIOLENCE (2024).

[22] On the culture of war, *see generally* JOHN DOWER, CULTURES OF WAR (2010); MICHAEL SHERRY, THE SHADOW OF WAR (1995). *See also* ANDREW CLAPHAM, WAR (2021) (on the idea of war and its implications in international law); MOYN, *supra* note 17 (arguing that the idea that war is more humane helps entrench war).

[23] *See* DUDZIAK, *supra* note 10, at 15–16.

[24] *See* Mary L. Dudziak, *War and Peace in Time and Space*, 13 SEATTLE J. SOC. JUST. 381 (2014).

[25] *See id.* at 2–5.

[26] *See, e.g.*, Young, *supra* note 12, at 39–65.

Understanding that ongoing war did not originate in the post-9/11 era and that it has been a feature of U.S. history for some time, helps avoid mistaken assumptions about forever war's causality. The entrenchment of war as a feature of U.S. international activity also makes clear how urgent and difficult reform will be.

How the U.S. Polity Lost Touch with War

The starting point for understanding the history of U.S. civilian disengagement with war is the changing culture of American war since the Civil War—the last widespread military conflict within the continental United States. That war is often treated as one data point in the history of U.S. conflict despite the profound difference between war within one's own territory and war in other parts of the world. The Civil War was different in kind from subsequent large-scale U.S. wars. It was fought amid civilian homes, farms, and businesses.[27] Civilians were killed and displaced, as happens now in foreign war zones. Survivors were overwhelmed by the carnage. For decades afterward, human bones turned up in the cornfields.[28] The Civil War experience with death transformed the United States, historian Drew Gilpin Faust argues, creating "a veritable 'republic of suffering,'" as Frederick Law Olmsted put it. The broad-based experience with death would deeply impact American identity itself.[29]

Major twentieth-century U.S. wars are thought of as moments of national solidarity but did not generate a "republic of suffering"—deep engagement with war's suffering and death.[30] Instead, as the United States went to war on other continents, distant war generated a persistent problem: how to

[27] KEVIN M. WALKER, A GUIDE TO THE ANTIETAM FARMSTEADS 23–25 (2010); ANDREW WARD, THE SLAVES' WAR: THE CIVIL WAR IN THE WORDS OF FORMER SLAVES 95–96 (2008).

[28] J.S.P., *From the Battlefield*, THE MEDIA TRIB. (Oct. 9, 1862) (the writer identifies himself only by the initials "J.S.P"); D.R. Miller Farm, NAT'L PARK SERV., https://www.nps.gov/anti/learn/historyculture/d-r-miller-farm.htm (last visited Dec. 20, 2025).

[29] FAUST, REPUBLIC OF SUFFERING, xiii (2009); DAVID BLIGHT, RACE AND REUNION 6, 12–14, 18–30 (2002). To the extent that Civil War death affected the collective national experience, however, this impact did not extend to the deaths of Indigenous North Americans who do not figure in Faust's account. Instead, military efforts to brutally slaughter and eliminate them, for example, during the 1864 Sand Creek Massacre, show an especially dark side of Civil War era nation-building. *See* HELEN M. KINSELLA, THE IMAGE BEFORE THE WEAPON: A CRITICAL HISTORY OF THE DISTINCTION BETWEEN COMBATANT AND CIVILIAN (2011).

[30] *See* FAUST, *supra* note 29. Faust argues, in contrast to this chapter, that the Civil War dynamic was repeated in later wars, but her focus on the Civil War does not enable close consideration of the way distance from war's carnage affected civilian engagement. Works related to the culture of death in World War II, discussed in this chapter, instead illustrate the problem of civilian disengagement and the great difference between the culture of war death in these two wars.

mobilize American civilians to support wars conducted in other countries. Even during World War II, President Franklin D. Roosevelt worried civilians were not sufficiently committed to the war effort. That major war, for most American civilians, was an experience of domestic economic mobilization and war-related scarcity. It was not a direct experience with the war's violence.[31] Roosevelt addressed his concern about civilian mobilization by easing censorship of U.S. casualty photographs so that Americans at home could see dead U.S. soldiers in popular news magazines, which readers found to be shocking.[32] When soldiers returned home, their own memories of war clashed with widely held public understandings, and so they often refused to share their experience, historian Gerald Linderman found. As Cheyney Ryan demonstrates in Chapter 3 in the context of Vietnam, the result was a disjuncture between public understanding of the war and the soldier's lived experience.[33]

The military draft provided a connection between the American people and their wars. Its elimination after the war in Vietnam further lessened the direct costs of U.S. wars for most Americans, and some argue that bringing back the draft would be the most effective way to engage the U.S. public and generate broader political awareness of the effects of endless war.[34] Yet the absence of a draft did not create the problem of home-front disengagement. American leaders were concerned about waning public support even during World War II—a war in which 11,535,000 American men were drafted, and an additional 6,332,000 Americans volunteered.[35] A more fundamental characteristic of today's culture of war is not vulnerability to war service, but the fact that American war, fought on other continents, is an abstraction for the majority of the polity. It is something they may have strong views about but that they do not directly face. It is, of course, a relief and a privilege to be protected from the experience of destruction in war, but this enables an ability to ignore it. In this context, war is rarely a focus of American politics, and congressional authorization for war has been treated as if it were optional.

[31] On domestic mobilization, *see* James T. Sparrow, Warfare State: World War II Americans and the Age of Big Government (2013). Americans in Hawai'i, the Philippines, the Aleutian Islands, and Guam, in contrast, experienced the violence of war up close. *See also* Immerwahr, *supra* note 11, at 171–212.

[32] *See* George H. Roeder, The Censored War: American Visual Experience During World War Two 10–12 (1993); *Three Dead Americans on the Beach at Buna*, Life, Sept. 20, 1943, at 35; Dudziak, *supra* note 15, at 51–53.

[33] Gerald F. Linderman, The World within War: America's Combat Experience in World War II (1999).

[34] Andrew J. Bacevich, Breach of Trust: How Americans Failed Their Soldiers and Their Country (2013).

[35] *US Military Personnel (1939–1945)*, WWII Museum, https://www.nationalww2museum.org/students-teachers/student-resources/research-starters/research-starters-us-military-numbers.

The Erosion of Restraint

The constitutional requirement that Congress declares wars ideally builds in broad-based political engagement and debate on the question of whether to go to war. This process broke down in the twentieth century. The last time Congress formally declared war was during World War II.[36] Before those war declarations, public opinion about fully entering World War II was deeply divided, and Congress passed a series of neutrality acts to keep the country from getting embroiled in the conflict.[37] President Roosevelt bypassed Congress, however, drawing upon his commander-in-chief powers to fight what constitutional scholar Edward Corwin called "the war before the war," supplying war materiel to American allies. Ultimately, Corwin argues, "a 'shooting war' was precipitated without Congress having been consulted."[38] Then, on December 7, 1941, Japan attacked U.S. military installations in Hawaii, the Philippines, the Aleutian Islands, and elsewhere. As Emily Rosenberg illustrates, Roosevelt's dramatic address to the nation, focusing on Pearl Harbor in Hawaii, narrated that far-flung U.S. territory into the heart of American identity. Congressional opposition to war virtually evaporated with a nearly unanimous war declaration that the president needed to fully escalate American participation in the war.[39]

In the years after World War II, presidents have expanded executive power, relying on either congressional authorizations for the use of force or Article II authority under the U.S. Constitution.[40] The expansion of unilateral presidential power was enabled by congressional acquiescence, and this was a consequence of the fact that American civilians lost touch with the concrete reality of war, lessening the urgency of political restraint. Ultimately, as Brianna Rosen demonstrated in Chapter 1, law enabled the erosion of restraint as the practice of unilateral executive action became embedded in the law of presidential power.[41]

[36] Jennifer K. Elsea & Matthew C. Weed, *Declarations of War and Authorizations for the Use of Military Force: Historical Background and Legal Implications*, CONG. RSCH. SERV. (Apr. 18, 2014).

[37] *See* ROBERT A. DIVINE, THE ILLUSION OF NEUTRALITY (1962).

[38] EDWARD S. CORWIN, TOTAL WAR AND THE CONSTITUTION 22–25 (1946). *See also* DAVID REYNOLDS, FROM MUNICH TO PEARL HARBOR: ROOSEVELT'S AMERICA AND THE ORIGINS OF THE SECOND WORLD WAR 63–68 (2001); WALDO HEINRICHS, THRESHOLD OF WAR: FRANKLIN D. ROOSEVELT AND AMERICAN ENTRY INTO WORLD WAR II 3 (1988).

[39] *See* EMILY S. ROSENBERG, A DATE WHICH WILL LIVE: PEARL HARBOR IN AMERICAN MEMORY (2003).

[40] There are differences between scholars on whether the demise of war declarations was consequential. In an important account, Mariah Zeisberg focuses on the variety of ways that Congress supports war through appropriations, military draft authorization, and other legislative action. MARIAH ZEISBERG, WAR POWERS: THE POLITICS OF CONSTITUTIONAL AUTHORITY (2013). The moment of war authorization itself is a crucial political moment, however. Once troops have been deployed, Congress is often reluctant to rein in presidential overreach. *See* Bruce Ackerman & Oona Hathaway, *Limited War and the Constitution: Iraq and the Crisis of Presidential Legality*, 109 MICH. L. REV. 447 (2011).

[41] *See* Mary L. Dudziak, *The Gloss of War: Revisiting the Korean War's Legacy*, 122 MICH. L. REV. 149, 195–202 (2024).

The most dramatic example of unilateral presidential war power was the U.S. entry into war in Korea just five years after World War II. President Harry S. Truman sent American forces to the Korean War without asking Congress for war authorization and before the U.N. Security Council authorized a military response to repel North Korea's invasion of the South.[42] Truman justified his action by persistently claiming that the deadly conflict was not a "war"—even though over 1.5 million Americans would be drafted to serve in the conflict, 23,613 U.S. military personnel were killed, nearly 1.8 million wounded, and 4,817 missing in action.[43] How did this happen? In the rush of events at the beginning of the war, Truman's close aide George Elsey recalled, "[t]he President and his staff, and his other advisers, were too busy thinking of military action and United Nations action to try to cover up their tracks with Congressional resolutions. The President's motivation was to stop the aggression, not to prepare for future political skirmishes."[44] Truman treated Congress as a political foil, rather than a source of constitutional authority, and he departed from the tradition of formal war declarations for major foreign wars without giving the matter serious attention.[45]

Truman's action would be consequential. If a president could commit the United States to a large-scale war without a war declaration, smaller wars fit easily within the scope of the Korean War precedent, and all subsequent U.S. wars, with the exception of Vietnam, were smaller. Although presidents would later seek war authorizations in many circumstances, Korea served as precedent for massive use of force based on presidential power alone.

The impact of Truman's actions would be further fueled by an interpretive idea articulated during the Korean War. Supreme Court Justice Felix Frankfurter argued in his concurrence in the *Steel Seizure Case* that it was too narrow an approach to interpretation of the separation of powers "to confine it to the words of the Constitution and to disregard the gloss which life has written upon them."[46] Instead:

[42] Jane E. Stromseth, *Rethinking War Powers: Congress, The President, and the United Nations*, 81 Geo. L.J. 597, 598 (1993).

[43] *U.S. Military Casualties—Korean War Casualty Summary*, Defense Casualty Analysis System, https://dcas.dmdc.osd.mil/dcas/app/conflictCasualties/korea/koreaSum (last visited Jan. 19, 2024). The consequences of the war for Koreans—civilian and military—was much more deadly. *See* Paul Thomas Chamberlin, The Cold War's Killing Fields: Rethinking the Long Peace 104–30 (2019).

[44] Letter from George M. Elsey, Admin. Assistant to President, to Sen. Alexander H. Smith (July 16, 1950) (on file with the Harry S. Truman Library). There was robust discussion in early July by Truman and his advisers of whether to seek congressional authorization, but the president was reluctant to do so. *See* Larry Blomstedt, Truman, Congress, and Korea: The Politics of America's First Undeclared War 35–37 (2016). This episode is discussed in detail in Dudziak, *supra* note 41, at 173–88.

[45] *See* Dudziak, *id.* at 182.

[46] *Id.*

> [A] systematic, unbroken, executive practice, long pursued to the knowledge of the Congress and never before questioned, engaged in by Presidents who have also sworn to uphold the Constitution, making as it were such exercise of power part of the structure of our government, may be treated as a gloss on "executive Power" vested in the President by § 1 of Art. II.[47]

For Frankfurter, the distribution of powers in practice between the executive and legislative branches helped to reveal the contours of the constitutional distribution of power.[48] Under "gloss of history" or "historical practice"[49] analysis, the Korean War served as a template for presidents to unilaterally commit U.S. forces to conflicts as devastating as that war.[50] The Korean War also served as precedent for the idea that presidents could use military force to protect American "interests,"[51] informing subsequent rulings and constitutional interpretations within the executive branch. Presidents rely on actions of their predecessors as evidence of what the scope of presidential power is. The contours of this approach are fleshed out within the Office of Legal Counsel, and the office's opinions are often classified. Because of this, the role of "gloss of history" analysis in the expansion of presidential war power is deeply consequential, but often kept from public view.[52]

In contrast to Truman, President Lyndon B. Johnson sought congressional authorization for the next major American military engagement: the war in Vietnam and Indochina.[53] When Congress passed the 1964 Tonkin Gulf Resolution authorizing military action, it was both an example of the way the interbranch production of war authority could still work, but also the way Congress was complicit in the erosion of its own power. President Johnson took the occasion of a murky naval episode to ask Congress for war authority without waiting to sort out the ambiguities. He sought passage of a resolution that was, in the president's words, "as big as Grandma's nightshirt. It covered everything,"

[47] *Id.*

[48] Youngstown Sheet & Tube Co. v. Sawyer, 343 U.S. 579, 160 (1952) (Frankfurter, J., concurring) (also known as the Steel Seizure Case).

[49] The terms "gloss of history" and "historical practice" are used interchangeably. *See* Curtis A. Bradley, Historical Gloss and Foreign Affairs: Constitutional Authority in Practice (2024); Curtis A. Bradley, *Doing Gloss*, 84 U. Chi. L. Rev. 59 (2017).

[50] *See* Dudziak, *supra* note 41, at 197–98.

[51] *Id.* at 199–203. The U.S. "interest" that was thought to justify the use of force in Korea was safeguarding the new United Nations.

[52] *Id.* Mayze Teitler argues that "denying the public access to a body of secret opinions that shape government policy, and that reflect the government's understanding of its own power and the contours of individual rights, is fundamentally antidemocratic." Mayze Teitler, *The Office of Legal Counsel Discloses List of Classified Opinions in Important Step for Transparency*, Just Security (Dec. 21, 2023), https://www.justsecurity.org/90808/the-office-of-legal-counsel-discloses-classified-list-of-opinions-in-important-step-for-transparency/.

[53] *See generally* John Hart Ely, War and Responsibility: Constitutional Lessons of Vietnam and Its Aftermath (1993).

but Congress did not trim it down.[54] Presidential power under the resolution extended well beyond Vietnam, providing authority for military action on behalf of members of the Southeast Asia Defense Treaty, which included, among others, Thailand, Australia, New Zealand, Pakistan, and the Philippines.[55]

When President Richard M. Nixon expanded the war by ordering the invasion of Cambodia in 1970, his actions generated massive protests. The broad public reaction restricted the military choices Nixon believed he could make without generating even more extensive demonstrations.[56] In this way, the antiwar movement demonstrated that the American people retained an ability to restrain at least overt and expansive uses of the war power. Congress also acted, repealing the Tonkin Gulf Resolution in 1971.[57] These actions did not yet prompt withdrawal from Southeast Asia, however.[58]

Reflecting the country's turn against Nixon's actions in Vietnam and the region, Congress passed a landmark War Powers Resolution in 1973.[59] This did not result in a reset of constitutional power, however. Instead, the lesson drawn by later presidents was that their autonomy was contingent on avoiding the level of public antiwar sentiment that characterized the later years of the war in Vietnam. The end of the military draft in 1973, and the turn to all-volunteer armed forces, meant that the draft would no longer help motivate antiwar protest.[60] Meanwhile, behind the scenes, the Office of Legal Counsel eviscerated the intended restraints of the War Powers Resolution, interpreting limitations on presidential power as simply Congress's own interpretation of the Constitution. As such, congressional legal interpretation was not binding on the executive branch.[61] Oona A. Hathaway noted that "there's a good case to be made that this memo marks the beginning of the end of the War Powers Resolution."[62]

Presidents continued to be sensitive to the optics of war. When President George H.W. Bush ordered the use of force against Iraq in 1991 following Iraqi

[54] Fredrik Logevall, Choosing War: The Lost Chance for Peace and the Escalation of War in Vietnam 193, 196–205 (1999). *See also* Edwin E. Moïse, Tonkin Gulf and the Escalation of the Vietnam War (1996).

[55] Tonkin Gulf Resolution, H.J. Res. 1145, 88th Cong., 2d Sess., 78 Stat. 384 (1964) (repealed 1971).

[56] Carolyn Woods Eisenberg, Fire and Rain: Nixon, Kissinger, and the Wars in Southeast Asia (2023); Jeffrey Kimball, Nixon's Vietnam War (1998).

[57] Ely, *supra* note 53, at 32–34.

[58] *See* Logevall, *supra* note 54.

[59] War Powers Resolution, 50 U.S.C. §§ 1541–50 (1973).

[60] *See* Melvin Small, Antiwarriors: The Vietnam War and the Battle for America's Hearts and Minds at 1 (2002).

[61] *See* Mary L. Dudziak, *The Unhappy Legal History of the War Powers Resolution*, 6.2 Mod. Am. Hist. 270 (Aug. 7, 2023), https://www.cambridge.org/core/journals/modern-american-history/article/unhappy-legal-history-of-the-war-powers-resolution/F2CB327804389ED1EAA5A237F220785E.

[62] *See* Charlie Savage, *U.S. Discloses Decades of Justice Dept. Memos on Presidential War Powers*, N.Y. Times (Sept. 16, 2022), https://www.nytimes.com/2022/09/16/us/politics/war-powers-justice-dept-president.html (quoting Oona Hathaway).

leader Saddam Hussein's invasion of Kuwait, U.S. General Norman Schwarzkopf emphasized the role of technology in making war precise. "Smart" weapons were thought to herald a new age of warfare in which targets could be destroyed with less harm to civilians.[63] Eventually, technology, including the use of armed drones, enabled more force to be deployed without troops in harm's way. Drone wars would be harder for the media to cover than in earlier years when embedded journalists could describe the scene for Americans at home.[64] With the exception of major events, like the U.S.-led withdrawal from Afghanistan, ongoing war was rarely a major news event. A brave and media savvy Ukrainian president could capture the attention of the American public, but U.S. troops in conflict zones around the world largely went unnoticed.[65]

Conclusion: Restraining Endless War

Perpetual war was not inevitable but produced over time. Its trajectory in the United States is not a simple story of the rise of the imperial presidency. It has been enabled by civilian disengagement with distant war and aided by law, culture, and politics.

If political restraint has failed in part because of the disinterest of the American people, how might this be addressed? Public engagement with war is crucial to political reform, but public perception of American war has historically been shaped by the way leaders and the media narrate the story of war, and public discourse in the United States is heavily mediated by politics and interest. The Cold War era was a telling example of the way public understanding of international threats can be shaped and even manipulated.[66] Large Cold War conflicts required explaining. Why, for example, were Americans drafted to fight a war in Vietnam after France, the country's former colonizer with deep ties in the region,

[63] Malcolm W. Browne, *Invention That Shaped the Gulf War: The Laser-Guided Bomb*, N.Y. Times (Feb. 26, 1991), https://www.nytimes.com/1991/02/26/science/invention-that-shaped-the-gulf-war-the-laser-guided-bomb.html. President Bush unilaterally deployed troops to the Persian Gulf, but subsequently sought Congressional authorization before ordering the use of force. H.W. Brands, *George Bush and the Gulf War of 1991*, 34.1 Pres. Stud. Q. 113 (2004).

[64] *See* Chris Woods, *Understanding the Gulf Between Public and US Government Estimates of Civilian Casualties in Covert Drone Strikes*, *in* Drones and the Future of Armed Conflict: Ethical, Legal, and Strategic Implications 180 (David Cortright, Rachel Fairhurst, & Kristen eds., 2015).

[65] *See, e.g.*, Michael Birnbaum et al., *Zelensky Opens U.S. Visit with a Warning: "Evil Cannot Be Trusted,"* Wash. Post (Sept. 19, 2023), https://www.washingtonpost.com/world/2023/09/19/zelensky-united-nations-general-assembly/; Andrew J. Bacevich, Breach of Trust: How Americans Failed Their Soldiers and Their Country (2013).

[66] *See generally* Campbell Craig & Fredrik Logevall, America's Cold War: The Politics of Insecurity (2d ed. 2020).

had failed spectacularly at the same mission?[67] The argument was the domino theory—the idea that the advance of a communist-allied government, like Ho Chi Minh's in North Vietnam, would spread to communist domination and the global supremacy of the Soviet Union. Fear of communism—detached from actual national security threats—took hold within the United States, inflamed by political self-interest, and this deeply affected domestic culture and politics.[68]

Like the Cold War years, Americans now are encouraged to believe that their personal safety is assured by wars they cannot directly see or feel. Hyping security threats has again been a political ploy, as if patriotism requires support for deploying violence in foreign countries and increased securitization at home.[69] Meanwhile, remote killings help produce a new generation of enemies. To raise public awareness, and counter politically motivated fearmongering, a starting point might be to draw upon the insights of communications scholar Fred Turner, who has argued that confronting the trauma of war is the starting point for coming to terms with the violence it has wrought.[70]

Harold Hongju Koh's keynote contribution to this volume underscores the importance of public engagement, suggesting that "comprehensive public education" is needed to convince the public that war "is an unproductive means of achieving national ends."[71] Koh places his hope in the next generation, who might be persuaded to finally end the war on terror. Since the most dramatic twentieth-century effort to rein in U.S. war power—in Southeast Asia in the late 1960s and early 1970s—was led by young adults, Koh's focus on younger generations is understandable. It also leaves the older generation of policymakers—the ones designing and implementing contemporary endless war—off the hook.

The most effective way to educate the public that their security does not depend on endless war is ultimately not through the education of the next generation, but for *existing* American leaders to change the policy itself. This may seem politically risky—like questioning American militarism during the Cold War years. In war, however, Americans rely on the bravery of their soldiers. If ending perpetual war takes courage, that is the least that can be expected of the political leaders who send their fellow citizens to war.

[67] *See* Fredrik Logevall, Embers of War: The Fall of an Empire and the Making of America's Vietnam 445–534 (2014).

[68] *See, e.g.*, Ellen Schrecker, Many Are the Crimes: McCarthyism in America (1998); Elaine Tyler May, Homeward Bound: American Families in the Cold War Era (rev. ed. 2008).

[69] *See, e.g.*, Max Cleland (with Ben Raines), Heart of a Patriot: How I Found the Courage to Survive Vietnam, Walter Reed and Karl Rove (2009) (detailing the way Senator Max Cleland, a war hero and disabled veteran, was falsely accused by his political opponent of supporting al-Qaeda after he voted against some of President George W. Bush's war on terror initiatives).

[70] Fred Turner, Echoes of Combat: Trauma, Memory, and the Vietnam War (2001).

[71] Chapter 20 in this volume, "How to Finally End America's Forever War." *See also* Harold Hongju Koh, *Finally Ending America's Forever War, Part II: Prescription*, Just Security (Sept. 12, 2023), https://www.justsecurity.org/88164/finally-ending-americas-forever-war-part-ii-prescription/.

3

Endless War as Aimless War

Cheyney Ryan

"The War had won, and would go on winning."

– *Edmund Blundon*[1]

Introduction

The reflections that follow do not offer policy prescriptions for waging war in ways that will make it less endless or mitigate its endlessness. Indeed, recent historical experience suggests that the problem of endlessness is endemic to war as a social practice. If that is the case, then any serious discussion of ending perpetual war must be a discussion of ending war itself. This calls for a more fundamental rethinking than policy debates typically involve. Such rethinking warrants returning to the deeply skeptical perspective traditionally associated with pacifism.

In this chapter, I begin with some historical remarks on the problem of never-ending war and the responses it has elicited from those committed to liberal values. I discuss how what I call *political pacifism* emerged alongside more mainstream responses, grounded in the view that war's endlessness reflects its inherent aimlessness. I then step back to examine how the problem of aimlessness figures in current policy discussions, where it is often attributed to the personal failings of political leaders. From there, I turn to structural explanations for war's aimlessness, drawing in particular on Sir Michael Howard's distinction between "nationalized" and "post-nationalized" war. I suggest these dynamics support political pacifism's skepticism toward war as an "instrument of policy," and argue that such skepticism can already be found in the work of Carl von Clausewitz, the great theorist of war. I conclude with reflections on the central contrast between mainstream liberalism's reconciliation with war and the dissenting position of political pacifism.[2]

1 Edmund Blundon, The Mind's Eye 38 (1934), *cited in* Paul Fussell, The Great War and Modern Memory 13 (2000).

2 Parts of this discussion draw on views developed more extensively in my book, Cheyney Ryan, Pacifism as War Abolitionism (2024).

Cheyney Ryan, *Endless War as Aimless War* In: *Perpetual War and International Law.*
Edited by: Brianna Rosen, Oxford University Press.
DOI: 10.1093/oso/9780197748992.003.0003

"Neverendians"

In August 1972, a headline in the *New York Times* stated: "U.S. Aides in Vietnam See an Unending War." The article by Craig Whitney reported, "Two weeks after Henry A. Kissinger's surprise visit to Saigon, high-ranking American officials here are talking privately not of a breakthrough in the peace talks, but, rather, of the possibility of unending war."[3] That possibility had long been a source of dark humor among young Americans compelled to fight in Vietnam. When I was in Saigon in 1969 arranging to work for a medical project in Quang Ngai province, I was introduced to the term "short timer." A standard tour of duty was one year, and a "short timer" was someone approaching the end of that year. Someone joked that there was no term for a "long timer," or what previous wars had termed "in for the duration," since no one had any idea what "the duration" would be.[4]

World War I is the first war we know of where the problem of its never ending was part of its lived experience. It remains the reference point for any discussion of modern war as endless war. Paul Fussell observes in *The Great War and Modern Memory* that the major English memoirists all entertained the possibility of the war lasting forever. "One did not have to be a lunatic or a particularly despondent visionary to conceive quite seriously that the war would literally never end and would become the permanent condition of mankind," Fussell remarks. "The stalemate and the attrition would go on infinitely, becoming, like the telephone and the internal combustion engine, a part of the accepted atmosphere of the modern experience. Why indeed not, given the palpable irrationality of the new world?"[5] More generally, the prospect of endless war challenged the whole self-conception of western modernity as the agent of peace and progress. Fussell writes, "It was a hideous embarrassment to the prevailing Meliorist myth which had dominated the public consciousness for a century."[6] This is how it was regarded by many in the non-western world like Mohandas Gandhi and Rabindranath Tagore in India, who saw it as occasioning a fundamental reassessment of the spiritual emptiness at the heart of western politics.[7] They even

[3] Craig Whitney, *U.S. Aides in Vietnam See an Unending War*, N.Y. Times (Aug. 31, 1972), https://www.nytimes.com/1972/09/01/archives/us-aides-in-vietnam-see-an-unending-war.html.

[4] The association of the Vietnam War and endlessness has been a recurrent theme in the literature. *See* Leo Huberman, Vietnam: The Endless War (1971); James P. Harrison, The Endless War: Vietnam's Struggle for Independence (1989); Making Endless War: The Vietnam and Arab-Israeli Conflicts in the History of International Law (Brian Cuddy & Victor Kattan eds., 2023).

[5] Fussell, *supra* note 1, at 72.

[6] *Id.*, at 7.

[7] *See* Erez Manela, The Wilsonian Moment: Self-Determination and the International Origins of Anticolonial Nationalism (2007); Mishra Pankaj, From the Ruins of Empire: The Revolt Against the West and the Remaking of Asia (2012).

had a name for it, a "Neverendian"—someone who believed that the war would last forever.

Fussell suggests that the prospect of never-ending war has been with us ever since. "The idea of endless war as an inevitable condition of modern life would seem to have become seriously available to the imagination around 1916."[8] It did not vanish with the end of World War II—on the contrary. George Orwell's *1984*, envisioned during the war and published soon after, imagined a world in which war was "literally continuous" to the point that the whole distinction between war and peace "has ceased to exist."[9] Literary critic Alfred Kazin wrote that with "so many new wars on the horizon . . . '*the* war' [that is, World War II] soon became War anywhere, anytime—War that has never ended, War as the continued experience of twentieth-century man."[10] In the United States, the prospect was recognized as posing a significant challenge to liberalism. The nation's founders had seen endless war as an inherent threat to its republican arrangements. James Madison had remarked that "[n]o nation could preserve its freedom in the midst of continual warfare."[11] After World War I, many concluded that war and liberalism were simply incompatible. The *Nation* magazine's Oswald Garrison Villard wrote, "For war and liberalism to lie down together anywhere, at any time, with any excuse, means only one thing—disaster to liberalism."[12] After World War II, America's leading liberal pundit Walter Lippmann put it in apocalyptic terms. In *The Public Philosophy*, he announced that "[s]omething had gone very wrong in the liberal democracies." When "at long last and at exorbitant cost they had managed to defeat their enemies, they had been unable to make peace out of their victories. They were entangled in a vicious circle of wars that led to ever bigger and wider wars." Democracies could not survive such a condition of permanent war. Unless its origins were addressed, it portended a "catastrophic decline of Western society" if not "the fall of the West."[13] More recently, Sheldon Wolin has argued that America's experience of permanent war mobilization had "sunk deeply" into liberal values and practices to the point of eroding what was left of its democratic heritage.[14]

But the post–World War II era also witnessed the view that liberalism could not just survive amid endless war, but flourish. This liberal acquiescence was

[8] FUSSELL, *supra* note 1, at 74.

[9] GEORGE ORWELL, 1984, at 183 (1949).

[10] ALFRED KAZIN, BRIGHT BOOK OF LIFE 81 (1973), *cited in* FUSSELL, *supra* note 1, at 74.

[11] James Madison, *Political Observations, April 20, 1795*, FOUNDERS ONLINE, NAT'L ARCHIVES, https://founders.archives.gov/documents/Madison/01-15-02-0423.

[12] Oswald Garrison Villard, *Unsigned Editorial*, THE NATION (Nov. 8, 1920), *cited in* DAVID HENDRICKSON, THE REPUBLIC IN PERIL: AMERICAN EMPIRE AND THE LIBERAL TRADITION 147 (2017).

[13] WALTER LIPPMANN, THE PUBLIC PHILOSOPHY 5 (1955).

[14] SHELDON S. WOLIN, POLITICS AND VISION: CONTINUITY AND INNOVATION IN WESTERN POLITICAL THOUGHT 553 (2016).

exemplified in views like Arthur Schlesinger Jr.'s "Vital Center Liberalism." The conflict between liberalism and totalitarianism constituted "a *permanent crisis* which will test the moral, political and very possibly the military strength of each side" (emphasis added).[15] As such, war was the opportunity for liberalism to prove its mettle as a "fighting faith"; it was the arena in which liberal values could find their fullest expression in how they energized society to confront its challenges. The ethic of moderation that liberalism championed was now wedded to the most *im*moderate means of security, such that liberals proclaimed they would defend their ethic of moderation with nuclear holocaust, if need be. The argument continues. The post-9/11 era has seen repeated calls for a return to the "muscular" liberalism of the Cold War, against the (presumably) "98-pound weakling" liberalism of the "irresponsible left" in books such as Peter Beinart's *The Good Fight: Why Liberals—and Only Liberals—Can Win the War on Terror and Make America Great Again*.[16]

Mainstream liberalism has had two responses, then, to the problem of endless war. One is to embrace it as an opportunity for liberal values to show their mettle. I have elsewhere termed this *martial liberalism*.[17] The other acknowledges the tension between liberalism and war, but seeks to defuse it by reconfiguring the nature of war. I take this to be the project of *liberal internationalism*. Its vision is a legalistic one: it aims to depoliticize war by turning it into a legal instrument that is answerable to international and domestic law in ways that diminish threat to liberal values. This view recommends itself for its apparent realism in regarding war as a permanent feature of the political order. Our current age of endless war casts doubts on how truly realistic either of these approaches are in finding a place for liberal values in a world of ongoing conflict.

A third approach is political pacifism. It takes seriously Oswald Garrison Villard's insistence that *any* compromise with war is a disaster for liberalism, so our most cherished values require a more uncompromising rejection of war itself. A major reason pertains to the nature of war that manifests itself in its endlessness. This theme was introduced into American antiwar discourse by Randolph Bourne during World War I. At the time, liberals like John Dewey were championing America's involvement in the Great War, citing the noble aims it could achieve. For Dewey, war could be an "instrument of social purpose." Bourne replied that Dewey's mistake was imagining that war could be an "instrument" of anything at all. There was, in Bourne's words, an "inexorability" to modern war due to its "unbridled" character, by which he meant its fundamental

[15] Arthur Schlesinger Jr., Vital Center: The Politics of Freedom 9 (1949).

[16] *See* Peter Beinart, The Good Fight: Why Liberals—and Only Liberals—Can Win the War on Terror and Make America Great Again (2006).

[17] *See* Cheyney Ryan, The Chickenhawk Syndrome: War, Sacrifice, and Personal Responsibility (2009).

indifference to any aims we would impose on it—that rendered war fundamentally *promiscuous.* He wrote, "those of us who knew a real inexorable when we saw one . . . foresaw how quickly aims and purposes would be forgotten, and how flimsy would be any liberal control of events."[18]

In short, war's endlessness is a result of its aimlessness—which political pacifism claims is inherent in the nature of war itself, meaning that war cannot be contained, it can only be abolished. Let us explore this claim by considering first the problem of endlessness as aimlessness has arisen in mainstream discussions today.

"Bad Planning"

Since 9/11, and especially following the failures in Iraq, mainstream policymakers have increasingly confronted the persistent problem of poorly conceived and strategically incoherent U.S. military interventions. One of the more critical accounts is Donald Stoker's *Why America Loses Wars: Limited War and US Strategy from the Korean War to the Present.*[19] Stoker states flatly that western "elites and leaders" "do not understand how to think about waging wars, and thus don't wage them effectively" because they "lack the intellectual foundation to discuss war in a rational and logical manner." They are unconcerned with "winning" because, lacking any conception of a war's aims, they have no conception of what achieving them would mean. "Consistently, Western leaders don't know how to set clear political goals, don't understand how to conceptualize the wars they launch in pursuit of often fuzzy political objectives, and don't value victory—or tell their people what this means." As to why this happens, he surmises that "waging war in this manner is either an expression of ignorance or an example of dishonesty—intentional or not—on the part of political leaders."[20]

A more measured account is Gideon Rose's *How Wars End*, which stresses the failure to appreciate Clausewitz. His survey of conflicts from World War I through Afghanistan argues that they have all ended badly because "American leaders" have failed to reflect on their ultimate goals. "One of the striking findings of this study," he concludes, "is just how often leaders neglect Clausewitz's advice to think through clearly in advance just what a particular war is supposed to achieve." So he advises those in charge, "Define goals precisely."[21] But isn't this message rather obvious, especially when, as in the Iraq conflict, those leaders are

18 Randolph Bourne, War Is the Health of the State 67 (2015).
19 Donald Stoker, Why America Loses Wars: Limited War and US Strategy from the Korean War to the Present (2019).
20 *Id.* at 19–20.
21 Gideon Rose, How Wars End: Why We Always Fight the Last Battle 285 (2010).

mobilizing hundreds of thousands of soldiers, at an ultimate estimated cost of $2 trillion, not to mention the death and destruction brought? Rose acknowledges the point. "Surely, you might say, all this is nothing but common sense. And you would be right. But in war, as in life more generally, common sense is actually quite uncommon." Moreover, we all know that people are not especially rational. "Study after study has shown that the keys to proper weight control are eating limited portions of healthy food while getting regular exercise. But every year tens of millions of people follow fad diets of one kind or another, popping pills or eating only grapefruit in a quest for some magic bullet to whisk the pounds away . . . So it is understandable that national security policymakers, who are after all only human, often ignore even the most rudimentary best practices in their field."[22]

These claims are quite extraordinary. It is hard to imagine a more scathing indictment coming from the most diehard cynic about war. America does not just fight vague wars, it does so repeatedly, careening from one fuzzy conflict to the next. Its leaders engage in "bad planning" because they lack the ability "to discuss war in a rational and logical manner." They apparently have a totally flat learning curve, due to "ignorance" or "dishonesty." (Thomas Ricks notes in his aptly titled *Fiasco* that all the errors of the first Iraq War were repeated just a decade later in the second.) Their bungling into aimless conflicts is no different from those who would "whisk the pounds away" by following the "Hollywood Diet" in making pineapple the center of every meal. The authors of these jeremiads are not zealots from the War Resisters League or Peace Now. One (Rose) is a former editor of *Foreign Affairs* and National Security Council official under President Bill Clinton; the other (Stoker) is a longtime Professor of Strategy and Policy at the U.S. Naval War College.

Their import for received notions of just war is dire indeed. Just war thinkers have insisted that the aims of the war must be crystal clear from the start. Hugo Grotius insisted that they must be publicly declared so that "the whole human race as it were might judge the justness of it."[23] Emmerich de Vattel wrote in *The Law of Nations* that "whoever considers its terrible effects, its destructive and unhappy consequences, will readily agree that war should never be undertaken without the most cogent—i.e. *clear and incisive*—reasons."[24] More recently, Jean Elshtain stressed the same point. "Just war thinking also insists that war aims be made clear, that criteria for what is to count as success in achieving those aims be

[22] *Id.* at 286–88.

[23] Hugo Grotius, The Law of War and Peace 514 (1625).

[24] Emmerich de Vattel, The Law of Nations or the Principles of Natural Law Applied to the Conduct and Affairs of Nations and Sovereigns 573 (1852).

publicly articulated, and that negotiated settlement never be ruled out of court by fiat."[25] Judgments of what is necessary or proportionate in war, or whether the war must be fought at all, all follow from its aims. Plus, there is the question of what is owed to those who are asked to fight the war.

I still have my Vietnam War induction notice. It read: "Selective Service System: Order to Report for Induction," followed by "From the President of the United States," then "Greeting: You are hereby ordered for induction into the Armed Forces of the United States." After the 1971 release of *Pentagon Papers*, I imagined the notice continuing: "You will be sent to a war that a 7,000-page study by your own government has already determined is unnecessary and unwinnable." Given the appraisals of Rose and Stoker, one can imagine what a notice might say today: "We should advise you that the wars in which you will fight are regarded by leading authorities as having no clear purpose, no coherent strategy, and no conception of what 'ending' them might look like. Your leaders lack a coherent understanding of war aims because they lack even the most basic understanding of what 'war' is. (P.S. Thank you for your service.)" I put things personally to make a larger point about the role that war aims should play in a democratic culture. War aims do not just play an instrumental role guiding political and military decisions. They provide what John Rawls called "public reasons": they play a constitutive role in founding the community's shared projects, in this case war. As such, their role is a *dialogic* one: they provide the basis on which society makes claims on its citizens, and its citizens make claims on one another, as to the benefits and—especially in the case of war—the burdens of that shared project. The *failure* to make a war's aims clear undermines its internal legitimacy, whatever its justice might otherwise be. It is an insult to its citizenry, especially to those who fight; this is an aspect of what is now called *moral injury*. Its long-term upshot is to corrode the social fabric generally, as evidenced in the traumatic impact of the Vietnam War experience.

"The Day Of" Versus "The Day After"

Let me focus on Gideon Rose's specific complaint that policymakers ignore the lessons of Clausewitz. Accounts of the Iraq debacle typically begin with U.S. Army General Tommy Franks who, as Commander of the United States Central Command, oversaw the invasion. In his 2004 memoir, *American Soldier*—published as Iraq was rapidly spiraling into chaos—Franks proclaimed, with

[25] Jean Bethke Elshtain, *The Third Annual Grotius Lecture: Just War and Humanitarian Intervention*, 17 AM. U. INT'L L. REV. 1, 9 (2001), https://digitalcommons.wcl.american.edu/cgi/viewcontent.cgi?article=1211&context=auilr.

characteristic American self-assurance, that "[h]istory will record that America's strategy for fighting terrorism was a good strategy, that the plan for Operation Iraqi Freedom was a good plan—and that the execution of that plan by our young men and women in uniform was *unequalled in its excellence by anything in the annals of war*" (emphasis added). Subsequent commentary has reached a different conclusion: Thomas Ricks, for example, suggests that it was not merely a flawed plan but perhaps "the worst war plan in American history."[26]

What it failed to appreciate, according to Rose, was Clausewitz's insistence on the twofold character of war. Rose puts this in terms of a fixation on "war-as-combat." "Wars, we believe, are like street fights on a grand scale, with the central strategic challenge being how to beat up the bad guys." But this is only "half the story." It captures the extent to which war is "an act of force to compel our enemy to do our will," according to Clausewitz. Rose terms this the *destructive* side of war. But it ignores, or minimizes, what Rose terms the *constructive* side of war—what war seeks to achieve *by* defeating the enemy. This is what Clausewitz termed war as "an act of policy . . . simply a continuation of political intercourse, with the addition of other means." General Franks's plan was a good one for removing Saddam Hussein from power. But it was oblivious to what was to be achieved *by* removing Saddam Hussein from power, that is, what it meant to win the *war* as distinct from winning the *battle*. Specifically, as a war that was championed as remodeling the Middle East, it was oblivious to what arrangements of power would replace Saddam Hussein—the upshot being a power vacuum.

For Rose, the error was encapsulated in Franks's remark to the U.S. assistant secretary of defense on the eve of the war: "You pay attention to the day after, I'll pay attention to the day of." Andrew Bacevich has argued that this division of labor approach is a residue of the Vietnam War, where politicians were seen as meddling in military matters. It also reflected the institutional culture at the time. Franks's *American Soldier* makes clear that he regarded his political superiors as complete idiots, a judgment that was apparently reciprocated.[27] But the distinction of "day of vs. day after" is a bogus one "because political issues can permeate every aspect of war": how a war is fought must be determined by why a war is fought, as otherwise the fighting may be pointless or counterproductive or at worst an end in itself—as happened in the mother of all endless wars, World War I.

Rose dedicates his book "To the victims of bad planning," whose numbers, given that his indictment spans more than a century, must be very large indeed. Can the problem be this simple? Is it really an artifact of blundering leaders, or is it somehow endemic to the enterprise itself?

[26] *Id.* at 128–29.

[27] Andrew Bacevich, *A Modern Major General*, 29 New Left Rev., Sept.–Oct. 2004.

The Structure of Aimlessness

A starting point is to note that in the nineteenth century many held that the corporate nature of the modern state rendered talk of "war aims" meaningless. The influential British political philosopher T.H. Green wrote in his widely read *Lectures on the Principles of Political Obligation* (1883) that when people are killed in war, "(w)e may say that it is by the agency of the state, but what exactly does that mean?" By the "state," he noted, we must mean "the sovereign power in the state, but it is always difficult to say by whom that power is wielded." Indeed, "[i]t may be questioned whether there has ever been a war of which the origination could be truly said to rest with a definite person or persons"—such that we could intelligibly speak of its "aims." "No doubt there have been wars for which certain assignable individuals were specially blamable; but even in these cases the cause of the war can scarcely be held to be gathered up within the will of any individual, or the combined will of certain individuals."[28] For many international lawyers, Quincy Wright observed, war was considered an "event" rather than an "action" because the "aims" of any such "action" could not be identified due to "the complexity of the causes of war" in "the present state of international relations" and in "the difficulty of locating responsibility in the present regime of constitutional government."[29] Political philosopher Hannah Arendt felt that World War I dramatically confirmed the truth of this picture. She wrote, "[T]he unwillingness to resign oneself to the brutal fact that the agent of the war was actually nobody inspired the erection of the monuments to the 'unknown,' to all those whom the war had failed to make known and had robbed thereby, not of their achievement, but of their human dignity."[30] How, then, do we explain the ability of this impersonal, corporate entity—this Nobody—to mobilize whole societies for its efforts, especially the millions who fight and die?

The State as a "Patterned Mess"

Howard has argued that the answer lies in understanding the distinct character of what he terms "nationalized war." At the heart of such war is what he terms the "fusion" of the state and the nation, wherein the notion of the nation serves to personalize the state in ways that make talk of its having "aims" intelligible and the thought of "sacrificing" one's life for it compelling. Andreas Wimmer provides a way of unpacking this "fusion." He argues that it can be understood as

[28] T.H. Green, Lectures on the Principles of Political Obligation 121 (1883).

[29] Quincy Wright, *The Outlawry of War*, 19 Am. J. Int'l L. 76 (Jan. 1925); *see also Changes in the Conception of War*, 18 Am. J. Int'l L. 755 (Oct. 1924).

[30] Hannah Arendt, The Human Condition 181 (1958).

a type of contract. Drawing on Charles Tilly's account of states and war-making, he describes the transformation wrought by the rise of nationalism.

> Nationalism as a new principle of legitimacy emerged from Tilly's war-making western states. Increasing state centralization and military mobilization led to a new contract between rulers and ruled: the exchange of political participation and public goods against taxation and the military support by the population at large. The idea of the nation as an extended family of political loyalty and shared identity provided the ideological framework that reflected and justified this new compact. It meant that elites and masses should identify with each other and that rulers and ruled should hail from the same people.[31]

Michael Mann recounts the logic by which states were reconstituted as "primordial authority figures." "The state (Mother or Father) acted, personified by its statesmen, domiciled in the diplomatic buildings of its capital city. The nation-state also had sacred symbols, especially flags and anthems. The public parade produced behavior like that in churches: reverential posture (in this case, standing to attention) and strong emotions (tears in the eyes, stirrings in the chest). The nation-state was—and still is—*sacred*."[32] Its "interests" came to be regarded as "sacrosanct," higher hence incommensurable with more mundane interests and deserving of the highest sacrifice.

Talk of "war aims" sustains the illusion of one big family, joined by a common project. But the reality is different. For Arendt, war had no agent. Another view is that it does have an agent, but that agent is not sufficiently unified or homogeneous to have clear, concrete, and consistent "aims." Mann concludes his analysis of the state by portraying it as a "patterned mess" whose actions are the "unintended consequences of the interaction of overlapping, intersecting power networks."[33] Fusing the "nation" to the state only worsens the problem by adding something even more amorphous. Evoking Bourne's image of the rudderless ship, Mann claims that the problem is compounded by what he regards as "an institutional contradiction" at the heart of the modern state. On the one hand, the actions of states have massive consequences due to the enormous power structures they command. On the other hand, their decision-making processes are haphazard and disorderly if not chaotic, so that the modern state is "unitary

[31] Andreas Wimmer, Waves of War 18–19 (2013).

[32] Michael Mann, The Sources of Social Power Volume 2, The Rise of Classes and Nation-States, 1760–1914, at 745 (2012).

[33] In his study of World War I, The Sleepwalkers xxvi (2012), Christopher Clark writes that we speak of nations as if they were "compact, autonomous, discrete entities, like billiard balls on a table," while in truth "the sovereign structures that generated policy during the crisis were profoundly disunified"—to the point that we still debate where the major decisions come from.

in its consequences but polymorphous and factionalized in its structure."[34] In fact, Clausewitz can be understood as making a similar point. When he describes war as "political," he partly means that war is the pursuit of *policy* through means that aspire to rational calculation. But he also means that both the policies themselves and the means of pursuing them are expressions of politics—specifically, the ongoing struggle among social forces within the state. Christopher Bassford and Edward Villacres put the contradiction this way: "Clausewitz tells us that the conscious conduct of war (strategy, etc.) *should* be a continuation of rational calculation and policy, but also that war *inevitably* originates and exists within the chaotic, unpredictable realm of politics."[35]

This pertains to nationalized war of the type that emerged in the nineteenth century and came to fruition in World Wars I and II. Writing in 1979, Howard suggested that we were moving into a new era of *post*-nationalized war whose outlines were still to be determined. The demise of nationalized war partly resulted from the problem being discussed: citizens became disillusioned with wars fought for grandiose, amorphous aims lacking any specifics—like Vietnam. Wimmer's contract between the state and the nation was breaking down; people no longer regarded their nation-state as the "primordial authority figure," in Mann's words. Now one response might have been to reconfigure war aims so as to meet this concern. Instead, the response has been to reconfigure war in ways that disengage it from the citizenry. As Sir Michael put it, "War, in short, has once more been denationalized. It has become, as it was in the eighteenth century, an affair of states and no longer of peoples." The upshot is one of deep alienation. "On the one hand we have a new generation less inclined than their fathers of the World War era to acquiesce passively from patriotic motives in the activities of the State *apparat*." This was anticipated by Bourne in the waning stages of World War I. He wrote that we were learning "that patriotism is really a superfluous quality in war. The government of a modern organized plutocracy does not have to ask whether the people want to fight or understand what they are fighting for, but only whether they will tolerate fighting . . . [W]ar doesn't need enthusiasm, doesn't need conviction, doesn't need hope, to sustain it. Once maneuvered, it takes care of itself."

On the other hand, Howard observed, "the functionaries of that *apparat* may become increasingly impatient of measures of popular control no longer justified by a requirement for popular participation and that can only impede the efficient functioning of the machine in their charge." After all, the need to mobilize the nation once imposed certain demands on leaders to explain their actions.

[34] MANN, *supra* note 32, at 796.

[35] Christopher Bassford & Edward J. Villacres, *Reclaiming the Clausewitzian Trinity*, 25 PARAMETERS 9 (Autumn 1995).

But insofar as wars must still be "maneuvered," to use Bourne's term, the indeterminacy of war aims seems increasingly obscured by their very amorphousness—as in the case of the global "war on terror." Even when the threat is quite specific, the cause for which the war is fought must often be hyperventilated beyond all reasonable limits.

This tendency to inflate specific security threats into existential battles is not confined to the original theaters of the global war on terror. It now shapes the rhetoric and strategy surrounding new and ongoing conflicts around the world. Russia's invasion of Ukraine has been framed by U.S. leaders as a generational struggle to defend a "sacred" NATO alliance and uphold "eternal" stakes, invoking Cold War rhetoric that risks turning a finite crisis into an open-ended conflict.[36] Meanwhile, in Gaza, Israel appears to be repeating the strategic failures of past U.S. wars, launching a military campaign with no clear or realistic plan for what comes after.[37] As Clausewitz warned, without clarity about what a war is meant to accomplish, there can be no coherent strategy for achieving it—an insight that applies as urgently to the wars in Ukraine and Gaza today as to ongoing counterterrorism operations.

The Big Muddy

The idea that wars have determinate aims is implicit in the conception of war as an instrument of social policy, specifically an instrument of the state. This instrumentalist view of war is actually a relatively new picture historically, and its attractions are obvious. Especially as the technological powers of violence increase, it is disconcerting to imagine that wars are in truth just one big muddle. A popular antiwar song of the Vietnam War era portrayed that conflict as "Waist Deep in the Big Muddy."[38]

That war is inherently a "big muddy" is the starting point of the political pacifism I noted earlier, which holds that any linking of our cherished liberal values to war will ultimately betray them because it misconceives the nature of war. The liberal internationalist vision has sought to reconcile them by depoliticizing war, by making it an instrument of war rather than politics. This is an attractive vision,

[36] David E. Sanger, *On His Stops in Europe, Biden Adds to Talk of a New Cold War*, N.Y. Times (July 14, 2023), https://www.nytimes.com/2023/07/14/world/europe/on-his-stops-in-europe-biden-adds-to-talk-of-a-new-cold-war.html.

[37] Amos Harel, *Netanyahu's Stubborn Refusal to Discuss "The Day After" Also Endangers the Israeli Army's Achievements in Gaza*, Haaretz (Dec. 15, 2023), https://www.haaretz.com/israel-news/2023-12-15/ty-article/.premium/netanyahus-refusal-to-discuss-the-day-after-endangers-the-idfs-achievements-in-gaza/0000018c-69d3-de43-affd-fdd31add0000.

[38] Its recurring refrain is: "We were waist deep in the big muddy, and the big fool said 'Push on.'" Pete Seeger, Waist Deep in the Big Muddy and Other Love Songs (Columbia Records, 1967).

but it begs the question of whether war can be an instrument of anything at all. That it cannot, the political pacifist maintains, is one of the things demonstrated by our permanent era of war. So the focus should not be on depoliticizing war but on "de-bellicizing" politics, which is the aim of efforts to articulate nonviolent responses to contemporary conflicts.

4
Rethinking the War Paradigm

Andrew Clapham

Introduction

This chapter explores the functions that the word "war" performs in the context of the global "war on terror." At times, claims about being "at war" operate rhetorically, seemingly justifying the resort to armed force abroad. In other instances, the mere insertion of *war* as an adjective qualifies a target, thereby providing a quasi-legal rationale for the application of rules authorizing killing, detention, and destruction. Finally, framing a situation as a war shifts the state of mind to a war footing, engendering a special mindset.

Recall that there are still situations where certain laws apply only where there is a conflict that could properly be described as involving a formal international "State of War" between states, such as the Second World War. Such formal "States of War" or "Declared Wars," can be distinguished from other conflicts. While space does not permit a detailed examination of all the law contingent on a formal declaration of war—which varies across national jurisdictions and treaty frameworks—recalling the necessity of a Declared War to trigger specific rights and obligations under both national and international law is instructive.[1] This chapter cautions against assuming that the executive branch's invocation of a war on terror (or even a war on drugs and narco-terrorists) automatically entails the suspension of ordinary legal and moral rights. Moving beyond this framing, this chapter considers how the concept of war has evolved and influenced policy decisions concerning the targeting and detention of individuals suspected of terrorism.

To be clear, this chapter does not aim to provide a detailed legal analysis of the right to life as it intersects with the law of the United Nations (U.N.) Charter,

[1] For a useful overview, *see* Jennifer K. Elsea & Matthew C. Weed, Declarations of War and Authorizations for the Use of Military Force: Historical Background and Legal Implications (2014). For examples in the United Kingdom, *see* Andrew Clapham, War 193–293 (2021); for a definition of a formal State of War in international law, *see id.* at 31; and *see also* the discussion of the need for a Declared War to be permitted to use the death penalty under certain human rights treaties at 30–38. The Israeli Security Cabinet's approval of a war situation on October 8, 2023, affects certain powers under internal law but not necessarily international relations, *see id.* at 184–86.

Andrew Clapham, *Rethinking the War Paradigm* In: *Perpetual War and International Law.*
Edited by: Brianna Rosen, Oxford University Press. © Oxford University Press 2026.
DOI: 10.1093/oso/9780197748992.003.0004

international humanitarian law, and human rights law. This is a complex and well-trodden area expertly addressed elsewhere.[2] Rather, my objective is to explore how enduring notions of war and wartime enemies permeate the legal approaches adopted by states and theorists when confronting the contemporary challenges of counterterrorism.[3]

Killing in War

There is an abiding idea in public consciousness, and in most versions of just war theory, that killing in war is not murder. In wartime, it is presumed that soldiers have immunity from prosecution for what would otherwise be considered crimes. This tricky idea is captured by the former Nuremberg war crimes prosecutor Telford Taylor writing in his popular book *Nuremberg and Vietnam: An American Tragedy*:

> What is a "war crime"? To say that it is a violation of the laws of war is true, but not very meaningful. Wars consist largely of acts that would be criminal if performed in a time of peace—killing, wounding, kidnapping, destroying or carrying off other peoples' property. Such conduct is not regarded as criminal if it takes place in the course of war, because the state of war lays a blanket of immunity over the warriors.[4]

When one pauses to consider, the idea that a state of war can lay a blanket of immunity over warriors—including those who fire the first shot and engage in unprovoked aggression—seems rather odd and old-fashioned. Taylor provides a footnote explaining the authority for this proposition, writing: "This concept is very ancient; it is clearly stated by the 12th century compiler of canon law, Gratian: 'the soldier who kills a man in obedience to authority is not guilty of murder.'" This medieval notion of the soldier having immunity for killing

[2] *See especially* ZIV BOHRER, JANINA DILL, & HELEN DUFFY, LAW APPLICABLE IN ARMED CONFLICT (2020); THE LIMITS OF HUMAN RIGHTS (Bardo Fassbender & Knut Traibach eds., 2019); KATHARINE FORTIN, *Armed Groups and the DoD Manual: Shining a Light on Overlooked Issues*, *in* THE UNITED STATES DEPARTMENT OF DEFENSE LAW OF WAR MANUAL: COMMENTARY AND CRITIQUE 382 (Michael N. Newton ed., 2018); PRACTITIONERS' GUIDE TO HUMAN RIGHTS LAW IN ARMED CONFLICT (Darragh Murray ed., 2016); KENNETH WATKIN, FIGHTING AT THE LEGAL BOUNDARIES: CONTROLLING THE USE OF FORCE IN CONTEMPORARY CONFLICT (2016); and COUNTER-TERRORISM STRATEGIES IN A FRAGMENTED INTERNATIONAL LEGAL ORDER (Larissa Van Den Herik & Nico Schrijver eds., 2013).

[3] For the history of the idea of the "enemy" and the multiple strains of thought about what could be done to enemies, *see* BEATRICE HEUSER, WAR: A GENEALOGY OF WESTERN IDEAS AND PRACTICES, ch. 8 (2022).

[4] A.J.P. TAYLOR, THE ORIGINS OF THE SECOND WORLD WAR 19 (1971).

other soldiers survives in traditional moral philosophy. Philosophers adhering to traditionalist or orthodox just war theory subscribe to this exceptionalist view, distinguishing wars from "peacetime activity."[5] As Michael Walzer argues, "standard just war theory is untenable if we take wars and battles to be like street crimes and marital disputes."[6]

This exceptionalist position is increasingly difficult to justify in a world that accords significant weight to individual rights to life.[7] Another strand of just war theorists, known loosely as "revisionists," has challenged the notion that the mere fact of being in a state of war confers on combatants special immunities and liabilities that do not exist outside of war. However, this philosophical debate largely unfolds in a distinct domain—what philosophers such as Jeff McMahan term the "deep morality of war"—that is separate from legal considerations. McMahan concludes that, even if soldiers fight on the unjust side and therefore are morally culpable, they should nevertheless enjoy legal immunity from punishment solely for engaging in combat.[8]

What I wish to emphasize here is that, for some, there remains a traditional assumption that the exceptionalism associated with war justifies modern killings. These traditional ideas about war frequently are invoked to justify killing and detention in contexts such as the global war on terror, regardless of whether the laws of war formally apply or, where they do apply, whether those laws actually provide blanket immunity for such acts.

To illustrate, consider the 2020 killing of Iranian General Qassem Soleimani by the United States in Iraq. This incident can be analyzed through the lenses of potential violations of the U.N. Charter, human rights law, or compliance with the laws of war.[9] Yet some commentators bypass the complexities of international law and simply assert the legitimacy of killing in war. For example, Professor John Yoo, a former official in the U.S. Department of Justice, remarked on the killing: "The killing of the enemy in combat is protected by the laws of war. As Hugo Grotius, the father of modern international law, observed in 1646,

[5] *See* MICHAEL WALZER, JUST AND UNJUST WARS: A MORAL ARGUMENT WITH HISTORICAL ILLUSTRATIONS 338 (2015).

[6] *Id.*

[7] *See* CÉCILE FABRE, COSMOPOLITAN WAR, esp. chs. 2.2 & 5.5 (2012).

[8] JEFF MCMAHAN, *The Ethics of Killing in War*, 114 ETHICS 693, 730 (2004); for the view that soldiers fighting on the unjust side ought indeed to be held liable in law, *see* David Rodin, *The Moral Inequality of Soldiers: Why Jus In Bello Asymmetry Is Half Right*, *in* JUST AND UNJUST WARRIORS: THE MORAL AND LEGAL STATUS OF SOLDIERS 44, 52 (David Rodin & Henry Shue eds., 2008).

[9] *See, e.g.*, Ben Saul, *The Unlawful U.S. Killing of Ayman al-Zawahiri*, LAWFARE (Aug. 17, 2022), https://www.lawfaremedia.org/article/unlawful-us-killing-ayman-al-zawahri; Agnes Callamard, *The Targeted Killing of General Soleimani: Its Lawfulness and Why It Matters*, JUST SECURITY (Jan. 8, 2020), https://www.justsecurity.org/67949/the-targeted-killing-of-general-soleimani-its-lawfulness-and-why-it-matters/; *cf.* Stephen Jackson, *An Imperfect War: The Legality of the "Soleimani Strike" and Why the Biden Administration Should Adopt Its Precedent for Future Operations in Iraq and Afghanistan*, 11 PENN. ST. J.L. & INT'L AFF. 1, 34–107 (2022).

'it is permissible to kill an enemy.'"[10] While it is true that Grotius wrote something to this effect in the seventeenth century, such historical assertions should not uncritically guide contemporary practice. Grotius's notions—that many disputes could be settled by war and that all members of the opposing side become legitimate enemies—are no longer appropriate in the twenty-first century. Today, the U.N. Charter prohibits the resort to war except to self-defense; the law of armed conflict affords special protection to civilians; and the law of human rights safeguards individuals against arbitrary killing and ill treatment.

On reading Yoo's statement, I was prompted to examine the original passages in Grotius, which indeed characterize killing as a right of war and proclaim a right to kill or injure all who are found on enemy territory.[11] In context, Grotius held that—even if, as a matter of natural law, only the just side possesses a moral right to kill or seize property in response to wrongful acts—as a matter of state practice, the law of nations recognizes a permissive norm whereby both sides are allowed to "harm an enemy, both in his person and in his property" and remain immune from punishment "as a murderer or a thief."[12] According to Grotius, all enemy private property was likewise subject to capture and confiscation. Grotius, in turn, grounded this permissive stance in early authority. Citing Aristotle, he wrote: "On the authority of Aristotle also we read: 'The law is a sort of agreement, according to which things taken in war belong to those who take them.'"[13] As noted earlier, contemporary international law imposes strict limitations on who can be lawfully targeted and what may be lawfully seized during armed conflict.[14] Yet these ancient—indeed, antique—ideas about war continue to exert influence, not necessarily within formal legal reasoning, but at a more subconscious level, shaping assumptions and reactions. When military action is framed as a "war," the speaker often needs to do little more to elicit support or loyalty. The invocation of "war," by its very nature, presupposes that lives can be

[10] *The Soleimani Strike: The President Has the Constitution and Precedent on His Side*, NAT'L REV. (Jan. 7, 2020), https://www.nationalreview.com/2020/01/qasem-soleimani-strike-president-trump-has-constitution-precedent-on-his-side/. I am grateful to Francesca Iularo for highlighting this quote at the start of her chapter *Rights(I)*, *in* THE CAMBRIDGE COMPANION TO HUGO GROTIUS 243–74 (Randall Lesaffer & Janne E. Nijman eds., 2021).

[11] *See* HUGO GROTIUS, ON THE LAW OF WAR AND PEACE 349–54 (Stephen Neff ed., 2012) (bk. III, ch. 4, paras. 5 & 6) (square brackets in the original). I have used excerpts from Stephen Neff's student edition as the language is more accessible, and included the headings in bold, as they seem particularly relevant: *On the right of killing enemies in a public war, and on other violence against the person.* 5. "In general, killing is called a right of war." 6. *The right to kill and injure all who are in the territory of the enemy*... [this right to kill and injure the enemy in war] extends not only to those who actually bear arms, or are subjects of him that stirs up the war, but in addition to all persons who are in the enemy's territory. *See also* paras. 9 (women and children can be killed) and 18 (on assassins).

[12] *Id.*, bk. 3, ch. 4, para. 3.

[13] *Id.*, bk. 3, ch. 6, para. 2.

[14] JEAN-MARIE HENCKAERTS & LOUISE DOSWALD-BECK, CUSTOMARY INTERNATIONAL HUMANITARIAN LAW: RULES (2005); THE 1949 GENEVA CONVENTIONS: A COMMENTARY (Andrew Clapham, Paola Gaeta, & Marco Sassòli eds., 2015).

taken, individuals can be detained, and property may be destroyed. The rhetoric of war signals a time of exception or emergency—one in which constitutional protections and human rights may be curtailed, and in which allegiance and solidarity are presumed.

How, then, did the response to the events of September 11, 2001, come to be framed as a war against an enemy? Scholars have examined the ways in which President George W. Bush's rhetoric oscillated between a law enforcement paradigm and a war paradigm before ultimately settling on the latter.[15] In the 2004 State of the Union speech, for example, Bush stated:

> I know that some people question if America is really in a war at all. They view terrorism more as a crime—a problem to be solved mainly with law enforcement and indictments. After the World Trade Center was first attacked in 1993, some of the guilty were indicted, tried, convicted, and sent to prison. But the matter was not settled. The terrorists were still training and plotting in other nations, and drawing up more ambitious plans. After the chaos and carnage of September 11th, it is not enough to serve our enemies with legal papers. The terrorists and their supporters declared war on the United States—and war is what they got.[16]

In a more recent BBC documentary, Bush elaborated: "The first plane was an accident, the second an attack, the third was a declaration of war."[17] The idea that al-Qaeda—or Osama bin Laden specifically—had declared war on the United States is a recurring theme in various legal and rhetorical contexts. Often, reference is made to bin Laden's declaration in 1996, issued five years prior to the 9/11 attacks.[18] This 1996 declaration has, at times, even been invoked to argue

[15] *See* Adam Hodges, The "War on Terror" Narrative: Discourse and Intertextuality in the Construction and Contestation of Sociopolitical Reality (2011) (esp. at 24ff); for a brilliant exploration of the idea of war, *see* Mary L. Dudziak, War Time: An Idea, Its History, Its Consequences (2012).

[16] George W. Bush, Remarks by the President on the War on Terror (Jan. 20, 2004), https://georgewbush-whitehouse.archives.gov/news/releases/2004/01/20040120-7.html.

[17] 9/11: Inside the President's War Room (BBC One 2021).

[18] For a deeper look, see Mohammad-Mahmoud Ould Mohamedou's discussion of how the 1996 "Declaration of War" in turn referenced the United States "occupying the lands of Islam" and "the protracted blockade" after the 1991 Gulf War, and the "occupation of Jerusalem," and that such crimes committed by Americans were said in Bin Laden's Declaration to be "a clear declaration of war" by the United States: *see* Ould Mohamedou, Understanding Al Qaeda: The Transformation of War 70–71 (2007) (highlighting how parts of the U.S. administration decided they were at war with al-Qaeda without considering the war aims of al-Qaeda or the nature of any such war); *see also id.* at 52 & 12 (discussing that, "Al-Qaeda was pushing war forward more innovatively than its opponents," and referencing Hew Strachen, who has explained that "reciprocity is critical to any definition of war and all that follows"; *see also* Mohammad-Mahmoud Ould Mohamedou, A Theory of ISIS: Political Violence and the Transformation of the Global Order 54–55 (2018) (explaining that "Al Qaeda was pushing war forward more innovatively than its opponents" and it reinvented "terrorism as war").

that certain acts carried out before 9/11 fall within the framework of armed conflict, particularly for the purposes of war crimes prosecutions before the Military Commissions at Guantánamo Bay.[19] In any event, it is well known that on September 20, 2001, President Bush declared before Congress: "On September the 11th, enemies of freedom committed an act of war against our country."[20]

In fact, the existence of such a non-international armed conflict—and the applicability of the Geneva Conventions to such a conflict—is a matter of fact and is not contingent on any formal declaration of war by either party.[21] The question I wish to address is not whether states may lawfully use lethal force in particular circumstances under national or international law. Rather, the question we should consider is whether states ought to frame such actions through the paradigm of *war*. As Charles Garraway has shown, even where a state responds to terrorist attacks emanating from abroad, it may still do so within a "law enforcement paradigm,"[22] using its military in a manner consistent with that framework. The broader point is that we must consider the messaging sent to troops, to the public, and to one's perceived enemies when a government repeatedly invokes the language of war and frames its actions in terms of defeating an enemy, wherever that enemy may be. In my view, resorting to the language of war creates a domestic and international perception that certain forms of violence are now legitimate—acts that would otherwise be morally impermissible or constitute crimes in ordinary life.

It is worth recalling the case of British Army recruiter Fusilier Lee Rigby, who was fatally stabbed on the streets of London in 2013. At the time, the assailant issued a statement referencing the British military operations abroad. During the

[19] *See* the order of Judge Pohl: "In determining whether hostilities exist or do not exist, the enemy gets a vote. Whether Al Qaeda, the organization of unprivileged enemy belligerents to which the accused is alleged to be a member, considered itself to be at war with the United States on the date of the alleged law of war violations is a factor among many to be considered by the trier of fact and is as relevant as any judgments made or withheld by the President or the Congress." United States v. Al Nashiri, Order AE 104F, at 2 (Military Comm'n, Jan. 15, 2013), discussed along with other examples in CLAPHAM, *supra* note 1, at x.

[20] George W. Bush, Address to a Joint Session of Congress and the American People (Sept. 20, 2001), https://georgewbush-whitehouse.archives.gov/news/releases/2001/09/20010920-8.html.

[21] Note that a formal Declaration of War by one state on another state can in fact trigger the applicability of the four Geneva Conventions of 1949 even in the absence of fighting. Common Article 2 reads in part: "In addition to the provisions which shall be implemented in peacetime, the present Convention *shall apply to all cases of declared war* or of any other armed conflict which may arise between two or more of the High Contracting Parties, *even if the state of war is not recognized* by one of them." (emphasis added).

[22] "Most Common Article 3 conflicts are best dealt with under the law enforcement paradigm insofar as the use of force is concerned." *See* Charles Garraway, *The Law Applies, But Which Law? A Consumer Guide to the Laws of War*, *in* THE AMERICAN WAY OF BOMBING: CHANGING ETHICAL AND LEGAL NORMS, FROM FLYING FORTRESSES TO DRONES 87, 103 (Matthew Evangelista & Henry Shue eds., 2014); Charles Garraway, *Armed Conflict and Terrorist Organizations*, *in* COUNTER-TERRORISM STRATEGIES IN A FRAGMENTED INTERNATIONAL LEGAL ORDER 425, 452 (Larissa van den Herik & Nico Schrijver eds., 2013) (referencing Northern Ireland).

subsequent trial, defense counsel argued that the defendant "honestly believed he was fighting a war. He believed he was a soldier fighting that war. He only targeted a serving member of the British armed forces because they were engaged in fighting an unjust war on behalf of the State."[23] Regardless of the legal rules governing who may be lawfully targeted in an armed conflict, the idea of war itself exerts powerful influence. My argument is that invoking the war paradigm transforms not only the mindset of the state's armed forces but also the mindset of those on the opposing side. Declaring a "war" on terror, or on the so-called Islamic State may not change the legal framework, but it does profoundly shape how individuals on both sides perceive and justify the violence unleashed.

If we move away from the misguided but widely held belief that killing in war is automatically justified and instead consider the actual international law of armed conflict as it pertains to targeting, we find that the language of war is also invoked to expand the scope of what constitutes a targetable military objective. U.S. government statements, for instance, define legitimate military targets as including "objects that make an effective contribution to the enemy's war-fighting or war-sustaining capabilities."[24] Accordingly, "attacks have targeted ISIL-controlled oil infrastructure, tanker trucks, wells, and refineries, significantly reducing ISIL's oil production and the revenues that are used to support its armed operations."[25] This expansive interpretation of military objectives is not enshrined in any treaty. Nevertheless, by invoking the term "war" to justify such targeting, a form of incidental justification appears to be created along the war path. The implications extend beyond merely justifying killing and destruction; they signal to the adversary that infrastructure critical to financing the war effort—including buildings and transport—can and should be considered legitimate targets. As Marco Sassòli observes, "Such a broad interpretation

[23] R. v. Adebolajo & Anor., [2014] EWCA (Crim.) 2779, ¶ 17 (Eng. & Wales Ct. App. (Crim. Div.) Feb. 26, 2014) (Sweeney, J.). Both defendants were British nationals, according to the sentencing remarks of the judge: "You each converted to Islam some years ago. Thereafter you were radicalised and each became an extremist—espousing a cause and views which, as has been said elsewhere, are a betrayal of Islam and of the peaceful Muslim communities who give so much to our country. You decided, between you, and in order to advance your extremist cause, to murder a soldier in public in broad daylight and to do so in a way that would generate maximum media coverage, including getting yourselves killed by armed officers who would be bound to attend the scene in the aftermath of the murder—thereby expecting that you would become martyrs and each gain a place in paradise." Discussed in more detail in Clapham, *supra* note 1 at 270–72; the statements read at the scene of the crime sought to justify the murder as "retaliation for deaths in Muslim lands and to incite the removal of the Government in the United Kingdom." *R. v. Adebolajo & Anor.* at ¶ 13. The Court of Appeal examined the requirement that the prosecution had to prove that an element of the crime of murder is that the killing is within the "Queen's peace" and determined that this applied to the status of the victim and not the state of mind of the perpetrator.

[24] *Report on the Legal and Policy Frameworks Guiding the United States' Use of Military Force and Related National Security Operations*, White House 23 (2016), https://www.justsecurity.org/wp-content/uploads/2016/12/framework.Report_Final.pdf.

[25] *Id.* at 24.

might justify attacks on political, financial and economic targets (for instance, a country's main export industry, stock market or taxation authorities) or even psychological targets as long as such targets influence the capability of the enemy to continue the war."[26]

A final point concerning targeting and the use of lethal force relates to the notion that, once the right to self-defense is triggered, there is no further need to re-evaluate the degree of force employed to prosecute the war. It is assumed that adherence to the principles of armed conflict suffices. The 2016 White House Law and Policy Framework report, for example, argues that once an armed group has attacked the United States, there is no need to continuously reassess the necessity and proportionality of resorting to force from a *jus ad bellum* perspective. In effect, a single terrorist attack can trigger a prolonged expedition along the war path without further reflection on whether such a trajectory remains justified. The report states: "Once a State has lawfully resorted to force in self-defense against a particular actor in response to an actual or imminent armed attack by that group, it is not necessary as a matter of international law to reassess whether an armed attack is occurring or imminent prior to every subsequent action taken against that group, provided that hostilities have not ended."[27]

Whether this approach—outlined under the section "Application of the *Jus ad Bellum* in an Ongoing Armed Conflict"—complies with international law remains contested.[28] However, from an ethical and moral standpoint, it is untenable to hold that the invocation of self-defense exempts a state from ongoing considerations of proportionality and necessity so long as hostilities persist.[29] As the just war theorist Helen Frowe emphasizes, "Meeting the conditions of *jus ad bellum* is not a single judgment made before the start of a war, but rather an ongoing judgment that must be made throughout the war."[30]

26 Marco Sassòli, International Humanitarian Law: Rules, Controversies, and Solutions to Problems Arising in Warfare, para. 8.308 (2019).

27 *Report on the Legal and Policy Frameworks*, *supra* note 24, at 5. Note when considering the use of force against sovereign states the same report takes a different tack: "This does not mean the United States can strike wherever it chooses: the use of force in self-defense in an ongoing armed conflict is limited by respect for States' sovereignty and the considerations discussed above, including the customary international law requirements of necessity and proportionality when force could implicate the rights of other States." *Id.* at 11.

28 For a discussion of the different points of view concerning proportionality and necessity in self-defense in the context of hostilities with an armed group, *see* Christine Gray, International Law and the Use of Force 227–48 (4th ed. 2018); Adil A. Haque, *Necessity and Proportionality in International Law*, *in* The Cambridge Handbook of the Just War 255, 259–61 (Larry May ed., 2018); and Clapham, *supra* note 1, at 134–43.

29 I am grateful to Adil Haque for drawing out this issue during the June 2023 workshop for this book; the question is also explored by Tom Dannenbaum in Chapter 19 of this volume from a human rights perspective and in the context not only of proportionality during the armed conflict but also with a view to the obligation to ending it or exit the war *jus ex bello*.

30 Helen Frowe, *On the Redundancy of Jus ad Vim: A Response to Daniel Brunstetter and Megan Braun*, *in* Force Short of War in Modern Conflict: Jus ad Vim 197, 200 (Jai Galliott ed., 2019).

Unlawful Detention

The challenges to the lawfulness of detention in the wake of the 9/11 attacks are numerous and complex—too much so to fully address here.[31] Instead, my focus is on how judicial reasoning has often relied, at least in part, on assumptions rooted in wartime logic and the treatment of enemies. From the earliest challenges related to the detention of suspected al-Qaeda terrorists, U.S. federal judges have invoked the prosecution of German saboteurs captured on U.S. soil during the Second World War. This is especially significant given that those saboteurs were tried by a military commission hastily established by President Franklin D. Roosevelt.[32]

Of particular interest is a passage from the U.S. Supreme Court's decision in Ex parte *Quirin* (1941), which has been cited repeatedly in post-9/11 detention litigation. The Court held:

> An important incident to the conduct of war is the adoption of measures by the military command not only to repel and defeat the enemy, but to seize and subject to disciplinary measures those enemies who in their attempt to thwart or impede our military effort have violated the law of war.[33]

The language has since been invoked to support the claim that individuals labeled "unlawful combatants" may be lawfully detained and tried under the authority granted by Congress in the wake of 9/11. For example, in *Hamdi v. Rumsfeld* (2004), the Supreme Court relied on *Quirin* in holding:

> ... that detention of individuals falling into the limited category we are considering, for the duration of the particular conflict in which they were captured, is so fundamental and accepted an incident to war as to be an exercise of the "necessary and appropriate force" Congress has authorized the President to use. The capture and detention of lawful combatants and the capture, detention,

[31] *See* Helen Duffy, The "War on Terror" and the Framework of International Law (2d ed. 2015); Richard L. Abel, Law's Wars: The Fate of the Rule of Law in the U.S. "War on Terror" (2018); Duffy Amanda L. Tyler, Habeas Corpus in Wartime: From the Tower of London to Guantánamo Bay (2017); Claire Oakes Finkelstein & Harvey Rishikof, *Beyond Guantánamo: Restoring the Rule of Law to the Law of War*, Habeas Univ. of Pa., Ctr. for Ethics & the Rule of Law (2022); Anastasia Bradatanin, *Gul v. Biden: Habeas Corpus and the Associated Force Doctrine in Guantanamo Bay Litigation*, Lawfare (Nov. 14, 2022), https://www.lawfaremedia.org/article/gul-v-biden-habeas-corpus-and-associated-force-doctrine-guantanamo-bay-litigation (explaining a recent successful challenge in the U.S. Courts).

[32] *Proclamation No. 2561, Denying Certain Enemies Access to the Courts* (July 2, 1942), reproduced and discussed in Clapham, *supra* note 1, at 213–19.

[33] Ex parte *Quirin*, 317 U.S. 1, 28–29 (1942).

> and trial of unlawful combatants, by "universal agreement and practice," are "important incident[s] of war."[34]

The Court was aware that the law of war referenced in *Quirin* had developed out of a rather different set of facts and that the contemporary war on terror might evolve into something that would no longer justify detention as included within the authority to use force. As the *Hamdi* judgment cautioned:

> We understand Congress' grant of authority for the use of "necessary and appropriate force" to include the authority to detain for the duration of the relevant conflict, and our understanding is based on longstanding law-of-war principles. If the practical circumstances of a given conflict are entirely unlike those of the conflicts that informed the development of the law of war, that understanding may unravel.[35]

What has emerged, however, is use of the 2001 Authorization for Use of Military Force (AUMF), combined with *Quirin*'s wartime precedent, to justify the continued detention of a broad and evolving category of individuals as "law-of-war detainees." These are often held without charge and without a clearly defined endpoint. This shift—reliant on an expanded understanding of detention as an *incident to the conduct of war*—reflects how deeply the war paradigm has embedded itself into post-9/11 legal reasoning.

One such Guantánamo detainee—captured in 2001 in Pakistan and accused of having fought with al-Qaeda and the Taliban in Afghanistan—has recently challenged the legality of his continued detention on the grounds that the armed conflict in which he was allegedly involved has ended. Despite President Barack Obama's 2015 declaration that "our combat mission in Afghanistan is over, and America's longest war has come to a responsible and honourable end," U.S. lower courts held that ongoing counterterrorism operations against the Taliban and remnants of al-Qaeda continued to justify detention under the 2001 AUMF.[36] Although the Supreme Court declined to hear the appeal in 2019, Justice Stephen Breyer issued a statement drawing attention to the conceptual and legal

34 *Hamdi v. Rumsfeld*, 542 U.S. 507, 518 (2004), citing Ex parte *Quirin*, *supra* note 33, at 28, 30.
35 *Id.* at 521.
36 Similarly, inconclusive complaints under *habeas corpus* had been made in 2021 pointing out that "[f]irst, U.S. and allied military forces and personnel have left Afghanistan, and President Biden announced that '[t]he war in Afghanistan is now over,' and second, the PRB determined that 'continuing law of war detention is no longer necessary' for Mr. Paracha." *See* Paracha v. Biden, No. 21-2567 (PLF) (D.D.C. Nov. 12, 2021).

difficulties raised by indefinite detention based on outdated wartime reasoning. As he observed:

> al-Alwi faces the real prospect that he will spend the rest of his life in detention based on his status as an enemy combatant a generation ago, even though today's conflict may differ substantially from the one Congress anticipated when it passed the AUMF [2001 Authorization for Use of Military Force], as well as those "conflicts that informed the development of the law of war."[37]

In sum, it is time to acknowledge that the current conflict with al-Qaeda and so-called affiliated forces is not the type of conflict contemplated by the law of war in its classical formulation.[38] Interstate wars, as governed by international humanitarian law, authorize the detention of prisoners of war,[39] who must be released and repatriated upon the cessation of hostilities. Article 118 of the Geneva Convention, as well as customary international law, requires that "[p]risoners of war shall be released and repatriated without delay after the cessation of active hostilities."[40] Crucially, these rules apply only in international armed conflicts between states. Detention in non-international armed conflicts presents a very different legal and practical problem. Individuals detained in such conflicts are typically non-state actors from the country where they are being detained, and therefore there is no other state to which they can be repatriated. Moreover, states are reluctant to release such individuals, particularly when they are labeled as rebels or terrorists, in the absence of diplomatic arrangements or guarantees. Even where detainees have been found not to pose a continuing threat, few states have been willing to accept them for resettlement. The larger issue, however, is

[37] Al-Alwi v. Trump, 587 U.S. 1058, 1059 (2019); as part of the National Defense Authorization Act for Fiscal Year 2012, Congress includes authority for the armed forces to engage in such detention, *see* § 1021 (c)(1); for a discussion of these issues, *see* Curtis A. Bradley & Jack L. Goldsmith, *Obama's AUMF Legacy*, 110 AM. J. INT'L L. 628, 628–45 (2016).

[38] Some influential actors portrayed the terrorist attacks of 9/11 as somehow different from other forms of cross-border terrorist attacks and place the situation firmly on a war footing: "Today we are engaged in a war against terrorism—a war of survival—a war of necessity." This is different because the 9/11 attacks were perpetrated by "those who endeavor to destroy our values, our laws and the very order of the global community." William K. Lietzau, *Old Law, New Wars: Jus ad Bellum in an Age of Terrorism*, 8 MAX PLANCK Y.B. U.N. L. 383, 454 (2004). Interestingly the same author ten years later proposed an end to the war paradigm, *see* David Rose, *Why We Should Shut Down Guantanamo: Prison Camp's Jailer-in-Chief Makes Jaw-Dropping U-Turn and Says It Should Never Have Been Built*, MAIL ON SUNDAY (Aug. 3, 2013), https://www.dailymail.co.uk/news/article-2383672/Why-shut-Guantanamo-Prison-camps-jailer-chief-makes-jaw-dropping-U-turn-says-built.html ("The struggle with terrorism is not going to end. But we do have to end the legally cognizable armed conflict with Al Qaeda, a specific transnational group. Arguably, if the war aim of diminishing Al Qaeda's ability to mount a certain level of attack has been achieved, we could declare an end to hostilities and return to dealing with the threat as a law enforcement matter.").

[39] Geneva Convention Relative to the Treatment of Prisoners of War art. 21, Aug. 12, 1949, 6 U.S.T. 3316, 75 U.N.T.S. 135.

[40] Geneva Convention Relative to the Treatment of Prisoners of War art. 118, Aug. 12, 1949, 6 U.S.T. 3316, 75 U.N.T.S. 135; JEAN-MARIE HENCKAERTS & LOUISE DOSWALD-BECK, CUSTOMARY INTERNATIONAL HUMANITARIAN LAW: VOLUME I, RULES (2005) (discussing Rule 129(A)).

that while international law clearly provides a legal basis for internment in the context of international armed conflicts, it remains largely silent—or at best ambiguous—on the legal framework for detention during conflicts with non-state actors. This silence is being filled by a war paradigm stretched beyond its original doctrinal and ethical foundations.

Applying the prisoner of war regime by analogy is clearly no solution. When this issue has been examined in the U.K. courts, judges have not found that the United Kingdom was entitled to detain fighters in Afghanistan under international humanitarian law, preferring instead to base the legal authority for detention on the relevant U.N. Security Council Resolution.[41] In the absence of such a resolution, a state such as the United Kingdom would, under human rights law, need to have applicable domestic legislation establishing the legal basis for detention. The authority to detain individuals fighting for non-state actors should not, I would argue, be simply implied as "an incident to the conduct of war," or extrapolated from the law of war governing interstate conflicts, with no reference to individual rights.[42]

At the international level, in the context of detention at Guantánamo, the U.N. Working Group on Arbitrary Detention has concluded that the United States is in contravention of the Universal Declaration of Human Rights and the International Covenant on Civil and Political Rights due to its arbitrary detention of Abu Zubaydah.[43] The Working Group cited the U.S. government's claim that it may detain Zubaydah under "law of war" authority and congressional authorizations, but it ultimately found that he is "effectively a 'forever prisoner' with no forum to challenge, and seek to end, his arbitrary detention."[44] The Working Group recommended that the appropriate remedy would be to release Zubaydah.

Yet ongoing challenges to this policy, which allege violations of fundamental rights to liberty, are no longer adjudicated in U.S. courts strictly on the basis of statutory authority to detain, or indeed human rights law. Instead, courts now balance individual rights claims against the executive's asserted need to confront enemies in a time of "war." In April 2023, the U.S. Court of Appeals denied a petition from another Guantánamo detainee, Al-Hela, weighing his "liberty interest" against, in the court's words (citing *Hamdi v. Rumsfeld*), "the weighty and

[41] Serdar Mohammed v. Secretary of State for Defence, [2017] UKSC 2.

[42] *See further* LAWRENCE HILL-CAWTHORNE, DETENTION IN NON-INTERNATIONAL ARMED CONFLICT (2016); Andrew Clapham, *Detention and Prosecution as Described in the DoD Manual, in* THE UNITED STATES DEPARTMENT OF DEFENSE LAW OF WAR MANUAL: COMMENTARY AND CRITIQUE 282, 282–97 (Michael N. Newton ed., 2018); one might note in passing that the official Russian "Manual on International Humanitarian Law" states with regard to "internal armed conflicts" that "[i]ndividuals suspected of involvement in armed conflict are detained and transferred to law enforcement." Aleksei Romanovski (trans.), *Manual on International Humanitarian Law for the Armed Forces of the Russian Federation*, 99 INTL L. STUD. 813, para. 84 (2022).

[43] U.N. WORKING GRP. ON ARBITRARY DETENTION, Opinion No. 66/2022, para. 118, U.N. Doc. A/HRC/WGAD/2022/66 (Apr. 6, 2023).

[44] *Id.* at paras. 29, 30, & 43.

sensitive governmental interests in ensuring that those who have in fact fought with the enemy during a war do not return to battle against the United States."[45] This idea—that a war can continue long after active combat has ceased—was bolstered by the court's reliance on *Ludecke v. Watkins* (1948). As the court noted:

> Although American troops withdrew from Afghanistan in August 2021, Petitioner does not argue that the armed conflict out of which his detention arises has concluded, and because "[w]ar does not cease with a cease-fire order," the President's war powers "[are] not exhausted when the shooting stops." *Ludecke v. Watkins*, 335 U.S. 160, 167 (1948). We have no occasion here to consider whether, in circumstances in which an armed conflict may continue essentially in name only, the notion that a lengthy conflict supports a commensurately lengthy detention might give way.[46]

Ludecke concerned a German national protesting his deportation in 1946. In 1948, the Court deferred to the executive's determination about the individual's potential for "mischief," despite the absence of an active state of war.[47] However, three Justices dissented:

> The notion that the discretion of any officer of government can override due process is foreign to our system. Due process does not perish when war comes. It is well established that the war power does not remove constitutional limitations safeguarding essential liberties.[48]

The idea that war entitles the executive to detain people indefinitely, even after a conflict's end, is not the only troubling legacy of the "war path" when it comes to detainees. The notorious mistreatment of detainees at Abu Ghraib prison also illustrates the wartime mindset of those involved. In particular, the statements by Lynndie England—who was photographed in multiple degrading poses with detainees—reveal how she continues to view such treatment as justified: "They weren't innocent. They're trying to kill us, and you want me to apologize to them? It's like saying sorry to the enemy."[49] For her, treatment was framed in

[45] Abdulsalam Ali Abdulrahman Al-Hela v. Joseph R. Biden, No. 19-5079, at 21 (D.C. Cir. 2023) (citing *Hamdi v. Rumsfeld*, 542 U.S. 507, 531 (2004)).

[46] *Id.* at 46.

[47] Ludecke v. Watkins, 335 U.S. 160, 170 (1948); for some of the implications of this line of case law for the war powers exercised in the war on terror and the open-ended nature of the 2001 congressional authorization to use military force, *see* Stephen I. Vladeck, *Ludecke's Lengthening Shadow: The Disturbing Prospect of War Without End*, 11 Lewis & Clark L. Rev. 963, 963–96 (2007); *see also* Clapham, *supra* note 1, at 201–05.

[48] *Ludecke*, *supra* note 47, at 187.

[49] *Iraq War 10 Years Later: Where Are They Now? Lynndie England (Abu Ghraib)*, NBC News (Mar. 19, 2013), https://www.nbcnews.com/news/world/iraq-war-10-years-later-where-are-they-now-lynndie-flna1c8956499.

terms of reciprocity rather than an end in itself. England reportedly saw her behavior "as nothing" compared to what the enemy would do.[50]

Leaving the War Path

Descending down the war path is a tempting proposition. The executive branch may claim that more permissive standards for killing and detention apply in war than would otherwise be the case. There is a mistaken presumption that war entitles soldiers to kill, so long as they comply with the laws of war. This may have once been the case in the minds of the ancient philosophers, and may remain so for orthodox contemporary just war ethicists, but it now has to be considered against the background of an expectation that human rights will be respected and that state action will take place within the constraints of necessity and proportionality. It should not be enough to claim, "there's a war on." In international armed conflict, all deaths that flow from an act of aggression may be considered arbitrary deprivations of the right to life.[51] No killing on the aggressor side is justified as a matter of international law. Killing on behalf of the armed forces of the state that has been attacked must still occur within a framework of necessity and proportionality. Killing under a U.N.-authorized operation must be justified as necessary under the mandate to restore international peace and security.[52]

In armed conflicts against non-state actors—operations in the war on terror that meet the threshold for the application of international humanitarian law—it is not enough to designate the conflict as a war. The prisoner-of-war regime does not apply when fighting a non-state actor, and the use of force may appropriately be governed by a "law enforcement paradigm," even when fighting abroad.[53] Not all wartime law can be transposed to a war with an armed group. Even today, the U.S. law on seizing enemy property (as opposed to targeting) is confined to situations where there is an international armed conflict involving the United States and the armed forces of another state.[54] This law cannot be applied in any

[50] Mark Memmott, *Lynndie England: Abu Ghraib Abuses "Nothing" vs. What Enemy Would Do*, NPR (Aug. 5, 2009), https://www.npr.org/sections/thetwo-way/2009/08/lynndie_england_abu_ghraib_abu.html.

[51] U.N. Human Rights Comm., *General Comment No. 36, Article 6: Right to Life*, U.N. Doc CCPR/C/GC/36, ¶ 70 (Oct. 30, 2018). "States parties engaged in acts of aggression as defined in international law, resulting in deprivation of life, violate ipso facto article 6 of the Covenant." *See also* Eliav Lieblich, *The Humanization of Jus ad Bellum: Prospects and Perils*, 32 Eur. J. Int'l L. 579 (May 2, 2021).

[52] *See* Clapham, *supra* note 1 at 146–50.

[53] *See* Garraway, *supra* note 23; *see also* Chapter 20 of this volume, "How to Finally End America's Forever War," by Harold Hongju Koh, where he suggests that "[u]ltimately, ending perpetual war requires ending the mindset that enables it."

[54] *See, e.g.*, 50 U.S.C. § 1702 (a)(1)(C); *see also* Anton Moiseienko, *Trading with a Friend's Enemy*, 116 Am. J. Int'l L. 720 (2022).

so-called war on terror against non-state actors. Even where a terrorist attack rises to the level of what could be seen as an "armed attack," the response must still be confined to what is necessary and proportionate, including when the law of armed conflict applies and imposes additional prohibitions.[55]

To be clear, I am suggesting that the idea of war as an exceptional situation when ordinary rules no longer apply should have no place in our thinking. When it comes to detention, there may be specific rights for states to intern prisoners of war and civilian security detainees in an international armed conflict,[56] but, as a matter of law, the rest of the Geneva Conventions simply provide extra prohibitions on top of the limits that constrain the use of force as matters of necessity and proportionality. As regards killing, there is a tendency to suggest that war gives soldiers a "license to kill," or in Walzer's expression, an "equal right to kill."[57] In fact, this is today a misleading and dangerous idea.[58] At most, a member of a state's armed forces who distinguishes themselves from the civilian population will enjoy immunity from prosecution by the other side for merely participating in hostilities.[59] In the end, whatever the actual status of individual rights as a matter of law,[60] the wartime state of mind fosters not just a warrior mentality focused on eliminating the enemy but also a tendency to tilt the scales in favor of the state at the expense of individual rights and civil liberties.

Irrespective of whether the law of armed conflict applies, we should think carefully before declaring there is a state of war with an armed group, however tempting it might be to take advantage of all the deference and latitude that comes with the war paradigm. In particular, it can be especially inappropriate to consider that "enemy" targets contribute to "war-sustaining capabilities," to label private property "extraterritorial enemy property,"[61] or detainees as "law of war detainees."

[55] *See* Eliav Lieblich, *Internal Jus ad Bellum*, 67 Hastings L.J. 687, 742 (2016) ("Furthermore, the exceptions to right to life are limited by necessity and proportionality limitations, which mirror, to a large extent, the same limitations applying in external *jus ad bellum*.").

[56] *See* Geneva Convention Relative to the Treatment of Prisoners of War, Aug. 12, 1949, art. 21, 6 U.S.T. 3316, 75 U.N.T.S. 135; and Geneva Convention Relative to the Protection of Civilian Persons in Time of War, Aug. 12, 1949, arts. 42, 78, 6 U.S.T. 3516, 75 U.N.T.S. 287. Article 21 of the Third Geneva Convention 1949, and Articles 42 and 78 of the Fourth Geneva Convention.

[57] Walzer, *supra* note 5, at 41.

[58] *See* Clapham, *supra* note 1, at 265–74.

[59] *Id.*

[60] For detailed discussion, *see* Andrew Clapham, *The Complex Relationship between the 1949 Geneva Conventions and International Human Rights Law*, *in* The 1949 Geneva Conventions: A Commentary 701, 701–35 (Andrew Clapham, Paola Gaeta, & Marco Sassòli eds., 2015); Andrew Clapham, *Detention by Armed Groups under International Law*, 93 Int'l L. Stud. 1, 5–12 (2017).

[61] For an example of U.S. courts finding that "the President's power to wage war must also necessarily include the power to make extraterritorial enemy property designations because such designations are also an important incident of the conduct of war," *see* Clapham, *supra* note 1, at 219–22, citing *El-Shifa Pharm Indus v. United States* 378 F.3d 1346, 1364 (Fed. Cir. 2004), the case concerned the unsuccessful claim for compensation from a Sudanese pharmaceutical company.

In modern just war theory, increasing attention is being devoted to when it might be exceptionally justified to take life in war and how to reconcile such killing with the right to life.[62] International lawyers have also been grappling with these issues.[63] Given the increasing prominence of individual rights, even in times of war, the mere fact of being in a state of armed conflict with an armed group—or engaged in a war on terror—now seems insufficient justification for killing and detention. This chapter has sought to continue that inquiry and to challenge several assumptions about what law and morality should allow when states go to war. This challenge arises from recent practices that have relied on the mere idea of war to justify exceptional measures. In short, the idea of a war paradigm leading to exceptional powers has fostered a perceived immunity for states to engage in killing, destruction, prolonged arbitrary detention, and degradation—often with inadequate judicial oversight or accountability. Just as importantly, embarking on the war path leads to a state of mind that sees the enemy as undeserving of proper respect, and those nearby who disagree as the enemy within.

As this book goes to press, the signage at the U.S. Department of Defense is being changed to the Department of War, the Secretary of Defense is now introduced as the Secretary of War, and immigrants are being designated for deportation under the Alien Enemy Act (1798). Thinking about the war paradigm seems more essential than ever.

[62] Lionel K. McPherson, *Individual Self-Defense in War, in* The Cambridge Handbook of the Just War 135, 135–51 (Larry May ed., 2018); The Individualization of War: Rights, Liability, and Accountability in Contemporary Armed Conflict (Dapo Akande, Jennifer Welsh, & David Rodin eds., 2023).

[63] Ka Lok Yip, The Use of Force against Individuals in War under International Law: A Social Ontological Approach (2022); Lieblich, *supra* notes 51 and 55; Adil A. Haque, Law and Morality at War (2017); Lawrence Hill-Cawthorne, *supra* note 42.

III

U.S. PERSPECTIVES ON THE WAR ON TERROR

5

The "Ghost Budget"

How America Pays for Endless Wars

Linda J. Bilmes

Introduction

Historically, wars come to an end when one or both parties run out of "blood or treasure."[1] "Treasure" is an equal partner in this equation; hence, one of the central questions that arise during wartime is how each country will pay for the war. America's military history reflects this experience. During every major military conflict prior to 2001, the U.S. government raised taxes and cut domestic spending to pay for the costs of war. Every previous U.S. military conflict entailed considerable debate on how to identify resources to fund the conflict.[2] During wartime, U.S. presidents asked the public to support higher taxes and make financial sacrifices. At times, Congress invoked its "power of the purse," even withholding funds to end U.S. involvement in the fighting, as it did during the Vietnam War.

By contrast, after September 11, 2001, the United States financed the conflicts in Iraq, Afghanistan, and the nearby region entirely through debt and budgeted for these wars without increasing taxes or reducing nonwar spending. Such policies helped insulate most Americans from the painful costs of war, helping the United States remain on a perpetual war footing for more than two decades.

This chapter will explain how and why the United States severed the link between war policy and war funding. The main reasons include failed reforms in the congressional budgetary process, a more assertive military establishment, and unusual conditions in global capital markets. I will argue that breaking the link between war policy and war funding has decreased accountability for spending, reduced legislative control over policy, and removed an important constraint from waging war.

[1] The Formation of National States in Western Europe (Charles Tilly & Gabriel Ardant eds., 1975); Carolyn Webber & Aaron B. Wildavsky, A History of Taxation and Expenditure in the Western World (1986).

[2] Rosella Capella Zielinski, How States Pay for Wars (2016); Robert D. Hormats, The Price of Liberty: Paying for America's Wars (1st ed. 2007).

Linda J. Bilmes, *The "Ghost Budget"* In: *Perpetual War and International Law*. Edited by: Brianna Rosen, Oxford University Press. © Oxford University Press 2026. DOI: 10.1093/oso/9780197748992.003.0005

America's Post-9/11 Wars in Afghanistan and Iraq

The U.S. military campaigns in Afghanistan, Iraq, and neighboring areas from 2001 through 2021 (referred to as the "post-9/11 wars") were the longest and likely most expensive conflicts in U.S. history.[3] Estimates of the cost range from $2 trillion, using the narrowest definition of war spending, to nearly $8 trillion.[4] Joseph Stiglitz and I estimated the costs (in real terms) at over $4.5 trillion.[5]

How was it possible to sustain such an expense—which exceeded 1 percent of U.S. GDP for several years and reached peak spending levels during the 2008 financial crisis—while provoking almost no public debate over the cost?

The short answer is that the vast majority of the public neither fought in nor paid for the wars. Fewer than half of 1 percent of Americans were deployed to Iraq or Afghanistan, the lowest percentage in any foreign war in modern U.S. history.[6] There was no conscription, and private sector contractors supplied some 50 percent of the manpower.[7] In addition, the post-9/11 wars were funded differently than previous conflicts in two important respects. First, they were financed entirely by debt, which deferred costs to future taxpayers. Second, the war budget itself was structured in a way that allowed the government to avoid confronting the full cost of the conflict.[8] As military historian Andrew Bacevich commented in 2016:

[3] It is not possible to disaggregate total spending between Iraq and Afghanistan accurately due to the structure of appropriations, which in most cases funded personnel, equipment, weapons, and contracts that were deployed to some extent in both conflicts. Additionally, veteran disability benefits and medical care is categorized by year of service and condition, such that the level of benefits is calculated based on the cumulative disability resulting from multiple tours of duty, which were typically in different locations.

[4] BRENDAN W. MCGARRY & EMILY MORGENSTERN, CONG. RSCH. SERV., R44519, OVERSEAS CONTINGENCY OPERATIONS FUNDING: BACKGROUND AND STATUS 10–11 (2019), https://fas.org/sgp/crs/natsec/R44519.pdf; WATSON INST. FOR INT'L & PUBLIC AFFAIRS, http://watson.brown.edu/costsofwar/. Lower-bound estimates include only *direct* incremental costs, such as supplemental combat pay. Higher estimates also include *indirect* incremental costs, such as veterans' benefits, replacement of National Guard equipment, debt service, and loan forgiveness to coalition partners.

[5] JOSEPH E. STIGLITZ & LINDA J. BILMES, THE THREE TRILLION DOLLAR WAR: THE TRUE COST OF THE IRAQ CONFLICT (2008); Joseph E. Stiglitz & Linda J. Bilmes, *Estimating the Costs of War: Methodological Issues, with Applications to Iraq and Afghanistan*, *in* THE OXFORD HANDBOOK OF THE ECONOMICS OF PEACE AND CONFLICT (Michelle Garfinkel & Stergios Skaperdas eds., 2012).

[6] Approximately 0.43% of the adult U.S. population was deployed to the post-9/11 conflict, compared with 12% in World War II, 1.77% during the Korean War, and 1.5% during the peak years of fighting in Vietnam. Timothy Kane, *The Decline of American Engagement: Patterns in U.S. Troop Deployments* (Hoover Inst. Econ. Pol'y Working Group, Econ. Working Paper No. 16101, 2016).

[7] HEIDI M. PETERS & SOFIA PLAGAKIS, CONG. RSCH. SERV., R44116, DEPARTMENT OF DEFENSE CONTRACTOR AND TROOP LEVELS IN IRAQ AND AFGHANISTAN: 2007–2018 1 (2019) [https://perma.cc/SH3X-YMHZ].

[8] The *budgeting* for the wars refers to the cycle during which funds are planned, requested, justified, evaluated, authorized, appropriated, apportioned, obligated, and executed to fund the conflict. Such money may be enacted in the regular annual budget (the "base" budget), in supplemental

> We don't feel the pain of casualties and we are not required to pay for anything, so people just don't care. If taxes were increased linked to continued military involvement it would cause people to re-engage their attention. Politicians would realize this is an issue.[9]

The combination of *budgetary* policies (exempting war spending from budget limits and appropriating funds in supplemental bills outside the annual budgetary process), *funding* policies (paying for war operations without taxes or offsetting cuts), and *financing* methods (relying wholly on debt) established what I have termed a "Ghost Budget."

I coined the term "Ghost Budget" based on the widespread use of the word "ghost" in government reports on the post-9/11 wars, referring to alleged people, places, or projects that turned out to be phantoms, and where funds vanished. The U.S. Special Inspector General for Afghanistan Reconstruction (SIGAR) has written about "ghost" projects that appeared only on paper, as well as "ghost workers" and "ghost schools."[10] The Pentagon acknowledged the rampant problem of "ghost" soldiers and "ghost" police in Afghanistan in numerous reports.[11]

Post-9/11 war spending gradually evolved into a permanent second defense war chest, with minimal oversight, which has endured despite the end of the Iraq and Afghanistan wars and has been repurposed to pay for unrelated military activities.

spending bills, or both. The budget process can be conducted "on-budget" (within congressional spending limits and calculated against the total surplus or deficit) or "off-budget," exempt from budget caps and pay-as-you-go limits and not counted against the total budget surplus or deficit. Allen Schick, The Federal Budget: Politics, Policy, Process (1995).

[9] Linda J. Bilmes, The "Ghost Budget": Explaining US Budgetary Deviations in the Post-9/11 Wars, 2020; interview with Andrew J. Bacevich, Professor Emeritus of Hist. and Int'l Relations, Boston Univ. (Sept. 23, 2016).

[10] In 2008, the U.S. Congress established the Office of the Special Inspector General for Afghanistan Reconstruction (SIGAR) to provide "independent and objective oversight" of the $144 billion in U.S.-funded Afghanistan reconstruction projects and activities. Since then, it has conducted hundreds of audits and investigations to detect and prevent waste, fraud, and abuse, as well as performance assessments and other reporting. SIGAR, Contract Oversight Capabilities of the Defense Department's Combined Security Transition Command—Afghanistan (CSTC-A) Need Strengthening (2009) [https://perma.cc/UJ6M-DA69]; SIGAR, Schools in Herat Province: Observations from Site Visits at 25 Schools (2016) [https://perma.cc/ENM6-RG3X]; SIGAR, Good Performers Initiative: Status of Seven Completed Projects in Khost Province, Afghanistan (2017) [https://perma.cc/6XQS-8HQT]; SIGAR, Schools in Paktrika Province, Afghanistan: Observations from Site Visits at 6 Schools (2019) [https://perma.cc/RK84-QEXJ].

[11] *See, e.g.*, Letter from Jedidiah P. Royal, Deputy Assistant Sec'y of Def. for Afg., Pak. and Cent. Asia, to John Sopko (Oct. 3, 2016) (regarding DOD efforts to eliminate "ghost personnel" from the Afghan National Security Forces (ANSDF)).

Table 5.1 Taxes and Spending Cuts During America's Wars

	War of 1812	Civil War	Spanish American War	World War I	World War II	Korea War	Vietnam War	Gulf War	Post-9/11 Wars
Tax Increase	YES	YES	YES	YES	YES	YES	YES	YES	NO
Nonwar Budget Cuts	YES	YES	YES	YES	YES	YES	YES	YES	NO

How Did America Pay for Previous Wars?

All U.S. wars prior to 9/11 were paid for by taxes and budget cuts enacted specifically to cover costs of the conflict (see Table 5.1).[12] One-third of World War I costs and one-half of the costs of World War II were funded by higher taxes.[13] These practices were path-dependent on previous practices. For example, U.S. President Woodrow Wilson decided to raise taxes to defray World War I costs after studying tax policy during the American Civil War.[14]

In previous wars, many lawmakers were concerned with the distribution of the fiscal burden and that the public perceived their decisions as being fair.[15] During World War I, Democrats in Congress advocated using war taxes to redistribute income, arguing that fighting the war required "conscription of wealth" as well as "conscription of men."[16] President Wilson argued that corporations benefited from the war through increased demand for their products and hence should be taxed more heavily.[17] To make higher income taxes palatable to voters, Congress raised corporate income taxes from 1 percent at the start of the war to 12 percent and enacted an excess corporate profits tax, as well as increasing income tax rates for individuals.[18]

[12] Louis Fisher, Congressional Abdication on War and Spending (2000); Hormats, *supra* note 2; Sarah E. Kreps, Taxing Wars: The American Way of War Finance and the Decline of Democracy (2018); Richard M. Miller, Funding Extended Conflicts: Korea, Vietnam, and the War on Terror (2007); Zielinski, *supra* note 2.

[13] Hormats, *supra* note 2; Kreps, *supra* note 12.

[14] Steven R. Weisman, The Great Tax Wars: Lincoln to Wilson: The Fierce Battles over Money and Power That Transformed the Nation (2002).

[15] William G. Howell, Saul P. Jackman, & Jon C. Rogowski, The Wartime President: Executive Influence and the Nationalizing Politics of Threat (2013); Weisman, *supra* note 14.

[16] Hormats, *supra* note 2 at 120.

[17] Weisman, *supra* note 14.

[18] Top marginal rates were raised to 77%, but only 13% of the population paid income taxes at the time. Weisman, *supra* note 14.

Wilson appealed to citizens to buy war bonds, in what he called "capitalizing patriotism."[19] He viewed Liberty Bonds not only as sound economic policy (to curb consumption and reduce the likelihood of inflation) but also as a way for ordinary people to support the war effort.

During World War II, President Franklin D. Roosevelt described paying taxes as "not a sacrifice" but a "privilege."[20] He raised taxes on business, imposed a "wealth tax," raised inheritance taxes, and expanded the number of income taxpayers to roughly 80 percent of the workforce by 1945.[21]

The budgeting and financial decisions for U.S. wars in Korea and Vietnam largely followed this pattern.[22] U.S. President Harry Truman pledged to make the country "pay as we go" for the Korean War and to distribute the burden fairly across society. As he declared in a radio and television address in September 1950:

> There is only one sensible way to do this [pay for our increased defenses]. It is the plain, simple, direct way. We should pay for them as we go, out of taxes. There are very good reasons for this. To the extent that we finance our defense effort out of taxes now, we will avoid an increase in the national debt.[23]

Truman pushed three major tax bills to fund the war through Congress. This legislation increased corporate tax rates from 38 percent to 45 percent, and raised taxes on cars, alcohol, and gasoline, as well as other excise taxes. He raised top marginal income tax rates to 92 percent, while increasing median rates from 22 percent to 27 percent.[24] He gave more than two hundred speeches in support of his "pay as we go" approach.[25] He abandoned his domestic spending plans, deeming them too costly. Consequently, the nation ended the war with a lower national debt than when it began.[26]

War funding was a central issue in waging the Vietnam War and a key factor in determining its outcome. Congress repeatedly sparred with Presidents Lyndon

[19] HORMATS, *supra* note 2 at 122.

[20] President Franklin D. Roosevelt, Fireside Chat (Dec. 9, 1941), https://www.presidency.ucsb.edu/node/210419.

[21] Thomas Piketty & Emmanuel Saez, *Income Inequality in the United States, 1913–1998*, 118 Q.J. ECON. 1 (2003).

[22] KREPS, *supra* note 12; MILLER, *supra* note 12; ZIELINSKI, *supra* note 2.

[23] President Harry S. Truman, Radio and Television Address to the American People Following the Signing of the Defense Production Act (Sept. 9, 1950) [https://perma.cc/XS6M-E6VZ].

[24] Letter from L. Laszio Ecker-Racz to Walter F. George (July 25, 1950) (on file with the Harry S. Truman Presidential Library & Museum); The Tax Foundation, *U.S. Federal Individual Income Tax Rates History, 1862–2013 (Nominal and Inflation-Adjusted Brackets)* (2013) [https://perma.cc/M4BB-UPG4].

[25] American Bar Association, *The Revenue Act of 1950*, 3 BULLETIN (A.B.A. SECTION OF TAX'N) 8 (1950). Congress designated these tax increases temporary, set to expire in 1953.

[26] Thomas Piketty, Emmanuel Saez, & Gabriel Zucman, *Distributional National Accounts: Methods and Estimates for the United States*, 133 Q.J. ECON. 553 (2018).

B. Johnson and Richard M. Nixon over war appropriations and taxes.[27] Many aspects of the war made Vietnam increasingly unpopular with the public, including the military draft, the high casualty toll, and the bombing of innocent civilians overseas. Yet the question of how to *pay* for the war and the trade-offs between military and domestic spending were key to the debate.

Johnson began his presidency confident that the United States could fund both the Vietnam War and his ambitious domestic agenda, but he feared that the war might become too expensive.[28] As he said in January 1964: "I gotta figure out how to pay for these fucking wars and keep my commitment to feed, educate and care for the people of this country."[29] Johnson was extremely reluctant to raise taxes for the war because he thought doing so would be unpopular. But his advisers convinced him there was no alternative, due to rising inflation.[30] Eventually, Johnson announced in 1967 that he intended to "borrow a part of it, tax a part of it, and save a part of it."[31] He imposed a tax surcharge on individual and corporate taxes, with an exemption for the two lowest brackets of income, that raised top marginal rates to 75 percent.[32]

As Johnson predicted, the plan set off a firestorm. Polls showed public opinion was against the tax by a margin of 65 percent to 25 percent.[33] Ultimately, the fight over the war tax forced Congress to examine how the conflicts were being financed and provided the leverage for Congress to terminate the fighting.[34] On May 15, 1973, Congress voted to cut off funding for the bombing of Cambodia and thereafter refused to fund the South Vietnamese military.[35] This action effectively ended America's involvement in the war.

In summary, although decision makers faced unique political, national security, and economic issues in each conflict, the United States adhered to certain norms when it came to war funding. First, the U.S. president and his advisers played an active role in formulating the fiscal strategy and debated a range of options to raise war funds, including postponing domestic investments, issuing war bonds, raising

27 Louis Fisher, The Politics of Shared Power: Congress and the Executive (4th ed. 1998); Allen Schick, Congress and Money: Budgeting, Spending, and Taxing (1980).

28 Francis M. Bator, *No Good Choices: LBJ and the Vietnam/Great Society Connection*, 32(3) Diplomatic Hist. 309 (June 2008).

29 Lloyd C. Gardner, Pay Any Price: Lyndon Johnson and the Wars for Vietnam (1995).

30 Bilmes, *supra* note 9; interview with Francis Bator, Lucius N. Littauer Professor of Pol. Econ., Harv. Univ. (July 12, 2017).

31 President Lyndon B. Johnson, The President's News Conference on the Tax Message (Aug. 3, 1967), https://www.presidency.ucsb.edu/documents/the-presidents-news-conference-the-tax-message.

32 President Lyndon B. Johnson, Annual Message to the Congress on the State of the Union (Jan. 10, 1967), https://www.presidency.ucsb.edu/node/238176.

33 "Harris Release for Monday," Feb. 24, 1967, WHCF 5-2 (3)—BOX 31 (1967).

34 Fisher, *supra* note 12.

35 *See* Memorandum from President Gerald Ford to Congress (Jan. 8, 1975) (asking congressional leaders for assistance to provide ammunition to the South Vietnamese).

taxes, and using deficit spending.[36] Congress responded to these proposals and made direct trade-offs between war spending and nonwar expenditures.[37]

Second, the bulk of war spending (after an initial period) was requested through the regular defense budget, with only lesser amounts of supplemental appropriations. This ensured that war funding was subject to scrutiny and oversight within the executive branch broadly, the Department of Defense (DOD) narrowly, and the congressional appropriations process. The executive branch even weighed in on smaller-scale decisions, such as whether the DOD was permitted to shift funds from nonwar accounts into war funds.[38]

Third, the president requested tax increases for the explicit purpose of funding military actions. Since Congress is required to authorize all taxes, this meant that the congressional fiscal committees (Senate Finance Committee and House Ways and Means Committee) were *obliged* to hold hearings on the financing of the wars. The committees devoted a significant level of attention to the question of how to fund the wars. In turn, the media reported on these developments and the subject of war costs remained in public view.

Paying for the Post-9/11 Wars

The post-9/11 wars diverged markedly from this pattern in both financing and budgeting. For the first time since the Revolutionary War, the United States relied almost exclusively on debt financing. There were no tax increases or budget cuts enacted to offset war costs.[39] *In addition* to the financial deviation, this was also the first time that Congress employed "emergency" and "contingency" funding over many years, rather than integrating war monies into the base defense budget and the regular budget processes after the initial period.

In his essay *Perpetual Peace* (1795), Immanuel Kant's fourth principle for states to exist in peace is that they should not incur debt to wage wars. He argued that running out of resources is a key constraint on wars. The Ghost Budget provided the ability to keep borrowing and spending for more than two decades and thus was a critical enabler in sustaining military activity over a prolonged period.[40]

[36] Federal budgeting was governed by the Budget and Accounting Act of 1921, which assigned the president the lead role in planning, formulating, and requesting budgets and established the Bureau of the Budget (now OMB) within the EOP. Reviews of the Truman and Johnson archives show that the presidents were engaged in this function. Hormats, *supra* note 2; Miller, *supra* note 12; Zielinski, *supra* note 2.

[37] Hormats, *supra* note 2; Webber & Wildavsky, *supra* note 1; Zielinski, *supra* note 2.

[38] Louis Fisher, The Politics of Shared Power: Congress and the Executive (3rd ed. 1993).

[39] Hormats, *supra* note 2; Kreps, *supra* note 12.

[40] Bilmes, *supra* note 9.

Table 5.2 Mentions of War Funding Policies in Hearings of the Fiscal Authorizing Committees during the Korean, Vietnam, and Post-9/11 Wars

		Korea (1950–53)	Vietnam (1965–73)	Post-9/11 (2001–18)
Senate Finance Committee	Total Hearings	55	134	681
	Relevant Hearings*	9	10	20
	Mentions	5	7	1
	Percentage of Mentions	56%	70%	5%
		–	–	–
House Ways & Means Committee	Total Hearings	49	200	612
	Relevant Hearings	7	19	47
	Mentions	5	14	7
	Percentage of Mentions	71%	74%	15%

*Excludes hearings on procedures and rules.

My original research, based on data mining thousands of historical documents and interviewing dozens of senior administration and military officials, shows that the lack of debate over war finance stifled conversation over the value of the war itself. Compared with earlier wars, presidents made fewer public speeches about the wars and seldom talked about their cost.[41] Congress held fewer hearings, and there was far less oversight over the spending itself.[42] For example, the Senate and House fiscal committees mentioned war costs in a much smaller fraction of hearings than they did during the Korean and Vietnam conflicts (see Table 5.2).[43]

The Ghost Budget contained three anomalies in war funding that transformed the relationship between war policy and war funding: (1) use of emergency spending; (2) the Overseas Contingency Operations (OCO) budget; and (3) debt financing.

Emergency Spending

For the first decade of the Afghanistan and Iraq conflicts, the United States used "emergency" appropriations, which are typically reserved for one-off crises such

[41] For example, the number of times President Bush mentioned war costs in his budget transmittal memos was only 13% of the number of mentions during Truman and Johnson administrations.

[42] BILMES, *supra* note 9.

[43] Data-mined from congressional hearing records.

as floods and hurricanes. Emergency spending is defined in statute as "unanticipated . . . sudden . . . urgent . . . unforeseen . . . and temporary."[44] It is exempt from regular rules, because the intent is to disburse money quickly in situations where delay would be harmful.[45]

In March 2003, the United States invaded Iraq, an operation that deployed over 130,000 U.S. military personnel alongside troops from more than thirty countries.[46] By 2009, there were 187,200 U.S. "boots on the ground" in Afghanistan and Iraq, supported by a similar number of military contractors, and the United States was occupying nearly five hundred military bases across Iraq.[47]

Despite this entrenched presence, Congress continued to enact "emergency supplemental" funding for the entire first decade (FY 2001–11) of what President George W. Bush termed the "Global War on Terror" (GWOT).[48] These type of appropriations had never been used to fund such a large, extended conflict.[49] As shown in Figure 5.1, it marked a deviation from past conflicts, when war funding had migrated to the base budget as soon as there was a partial projection of costs.[50]

The result was what former Defense Secretary Robert Gates termed a "culture of endless money" inside the Pentagon.[51] War spending was specifically excluded from congressional budget limits. The Pentagon used the special war budget to buy upgrades, services, and new equipment that were in some cases barely related to Iraq or Afghanistan. Consequently, by 2009 the Pentagon budget grew to its highest level since the Second World War (see Figure 5.1).[52]

44 Balanced Budget and Emergency Deficit Control Act of 1985, Pub. L. No. 99-177 § 250(c)(20–21) (codified as amended at 2 U.S.C. § 900).

45 David Weiler & Brian Callanan, *War Budgeting Strategies: Case Studies of the Gulf War and the Iraq War*, at 37 (Harv. L. Sch. Fed. Budget Pol'y Seminar, Briefing Paper No. 39, 2008) [https://perma.cc/6MNB-CMJA]; Stephen Daggett, Cong. Rsch. Serv., RS22926, Costs of Major U.S. Wars (2010), https://fas.org/sgp/crs/natsec/RS22926.pdf.

46 The initial invasion on March 20, 2003, included 160,000 troops, including those from the United States (130,000), the United Kingdom (38,000), and smaller numbers from other participating countries. Joyce Battle, *The Iraq War—Part I: The U.S. Prepares for Conflict, 2001*, Nat'l Sec. Archive (Sept. 22, 2010) [https://perma.cc/TM2W-6X25].

47 Amy Belasco, Cong. Rsch. Serv., RL33110, The Cost of Iraq, Afghanistan, and Other Global War on Terror Operations Since 9/11 (2014), https://sgp.fas.org/crs/natsec/RL33110.pdf.

48 The term GWOT was used to refer to military operations in Afghanistan, Iraq, and surrounding areas beginning in 2001 until when President Obama replaced it with "Overseas Contingency Operations."

49 Hormats, *supra* note 2.

50 Stephen Daggett, Cong. Rsch. Serv., RS22455, Military Operations: Precedents for Funding Contingency Operations in Regular or in Supplemental Appropriations Bills (2006), https://fas.org/sgp/crs/natsec/RS22455.pdf.

51 Daniel Dombey & Jeremy Lemer, *Pentagon's "Endless Money" Era Ends*, Fin. Times (Aug. 9, 2010), https://www.ft.com/content/316ba40c-a40a-11df-a872-00144feabdc0.

52 Brendan W. McGarry & Emily Morgenstern, Cong. Rsch. Serv., R44519, Overseas Contingency Operations Funding: Background and Status 10–11 (2019), https://fas.org/sgp/crs/natsec/R44519.pdf.

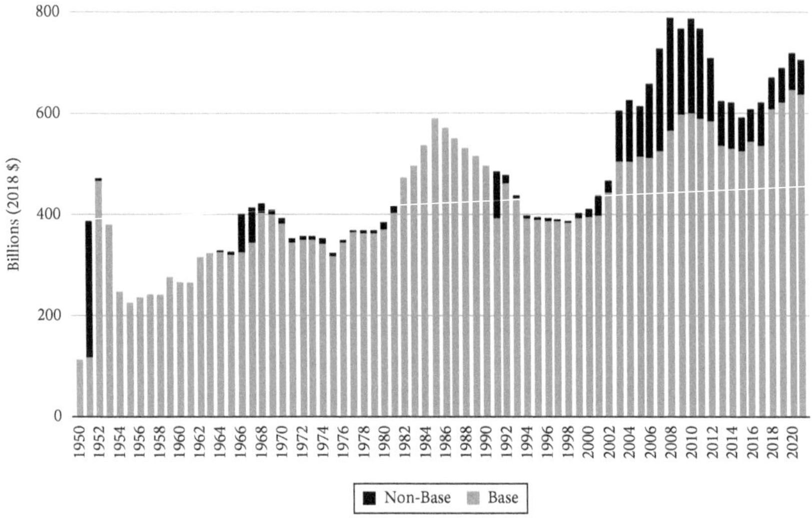

Figure 5.1 Base and Supplemental Funding in DOD Budget, FY 1950–FY 2022

The "emergency" designation provided benefits to all the key stakeholders. It helped the president present an artificially low federal budget deficit because he did not have to include war funding in his annual defense budget request. This helped the George W. Bush administration uphold the pretense that the wars would be over shortly and pursue its electoral pledge to cut taxes, despite the growing cost of the war.[53] Congress was freed from the need to find offsetting budget cuts elsewhere in the budget. Legislators could pay for rising entitlement spending while also providing extra funding for the war.[54]

Within the Pentagon, emergency money was convenient. It avoided the lengthy internal budget justification process (Planning, Programming, Budgeting, and Execution (PPBE))[55] and was placed in the "Operations and Maintenance" account, which has few restrictions on how it may be spent, providing the Pentagon with even greater autonomy.[56]

[53] Bilmes, *supra* note 9.

[54] Entitlement spending refers to mandatory appropriations for programs such as Social Security that are based on a set formula and do not require annual legislative approval.

[55] PPBE system is a strategic planning process for allocating resources among DOD military departments that originated under Secretary Robert McNamara in 1961. *See, e.g.*, Brendan W. McGarry, Cong. Rsch. Serv., R47178, DOD Planning, Programming, Budgeting, and Execution (PPBE): Overview and Selected Issues for Congress 14 (2022), https://crsreports.congress.gov/product/pdf/R/R47178.

[56] Belasco, *supra* note 47; Bilmes, *supra* note 9.

The Overseas Contingency Operations Budget

After a decade of emergency spending, President Barack Obama (who had criticized this policy as a candidate) replaced it with a slightly different mechanism named "Overseas Contingency Operations" in 2011.[57] The OCO money required the president to submit a "placeholder" estimate of war costs during the annual budget cycle but nevertheless continued to be regarded as an extra infusion of money, distinct from regular defense spending. The same year, Congress enacted the Budget Control Act of 2011, which set modest spending limits on some discretionary government spending but exempted GWOT/OCO funds.[58]

This funding pattern endured through 2021, adding a sizable boost to the Pentagon budget every year (see Figure 5.2).[59] Consequently, the Pentagon became dependent on OCO and used it to pay for various missions outside of Iraq and Afghanistan. For example, OCO funded $26 billion for the European Reassurance Initiative, launched in 2014 after the Russian annexation of Crimea, to "bolster the security and capacity of U.S. allies and partners" in Europe.[60] The OCO fund was flexible enough to enable the Pentagon to secure many items on its wish list that had been rejected by Congress previously.[61] The DOD practiced an "arbitrage" strategy of requesting desired items through OCO in order to secure them more easily.[62]

Financing

When President George W. Bush took office in January 2001, the federal budget was already in deficit. He slashed taxes in 2001 and again in 2003, as the United States invaded Iraq. Taxes were cut yet again in 2017 under President Donald J. Trump. Consequently, instead of financing the wars through some

[57] Most government records use the term OCO to refer to the entire GWOT/OCO budget stream since 9/11. *See, e.g.*, McGarry & Morgenstern, *supra* note 4.

[58] *Id.* at 6–10.

[59] Off. of the Under Sec'y of Def. (Comptroller), Dep't of Def., National Defense Budget Estimates 2001–2021.

[60] Paul Belkin & Hibbah Kaileh, Cong. Rsch. Serv., IF10946, The European Deterrence Initiative: A Budgetary Overview (2021); Todd Harrison, *The Enduring Dilemma of Overseas Contingency Operations Funding*, Defense 360 (Jan. 11, 2017), https://defense360.csis.org/enduring-dilemma-oco-funding/.

[61] Bilmes, *supra* note 9.

[62] Tai Fukumoto & Patrick Sharma, *The Two-Tiered Defense Budget: The Base Budget and Overseas Contingency Operations* 18–19 (Harv. L. Sch. Fed. Budget Pol'y Seminar, Briefing Paper No. 53, 2015) [https://perma.cc/U78Q-HL8X].

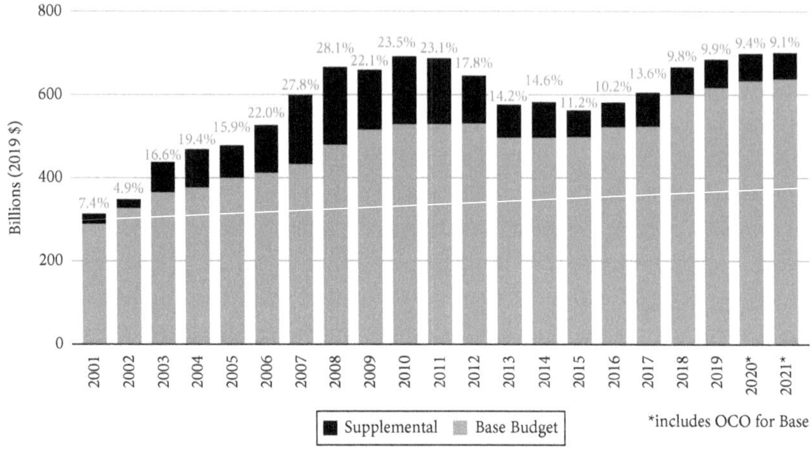

Figure 5.2 OCO Supplemental War Funding on Top of the DOD Base Budget

combination of higher taxes, fees, dedicated war bonds, borrowing, and monetary expansion, the post-9/11 wars were financed almost entirely by borrowing.[63]

Americans paid a much lower tax rate during the post-9/11 wars compared not only to earlier wars but also to the beginning of the period. For example, in FY 2001 (the year the United States invaded Afghanistan) a household earning $300,000 would have paid a 39.1 percent top marginal tax rate (see Figure 5.3).[64] By 2018, that rate had fallen to 35 percent. By contrast, a household with the *equivalent* income during the Korean and Vietnam wars would have paid a top marginal rate of 71 percent in 1953 and 61 percent in 1973 (adjusting for the tax code).[65]

Federal taxes declined from 18.8 percent of GDP in 2001 to 16 percent of GDP at the start of 2020, while federal debt held by the public rose from $3.4 trillion to $17.2 trillion during the same period.[66] War spending contributed at least $2.2 trillion in direct outlays to this total debt.[67]

[63] McGarry & Morgenstern, *supra* note 4; Hormats, *supra* note 2; Kreps, *supra* note 12; Stiglitz & Bilmes, The Three Trillion Dollar War, *supra* note 5.

[64] Piketty, Saez, & Zucman, *supra* note 26; The Tax Foundation, *supra* note 24; Fed. Reserve Bank of St. Louis, U.S. Dep't of the Treasury, U.S Individual Income Tax: Tax Rates for Regular Tax: Highest Bracket (2020), https://fred.stlouisfed.org/series/IITTRHB.

[65] There were twenty-six separate tax brackets in the 1950s and thirty-six during the Vietnam War, compared with six to seven during the post-9/11 period. Hence, the number of households in the top 92% during the Korean War was small. This chart has adjusted for these differences, and state tax effects, based on data from Piketty & Saez, *supra* note 21, and Piketty, Saez, & Zucman, *supra* note 26.

[66] Fed. Reserve Bank of St. Louis, U.S. Dep't of the Treasury, Federal Receipts as Percent of Gross Domestic Product (2024), https://fred.stlouisfed.org/series/FYFRGDA188S; Fed. Reserve Bank of St. Louis, U.S. Dep't of the Treasury, Federal Debt Held by the Public (2024), https://fred.stlouisfed.org/series/FYGFDPUN.

[67] Including $200 billion in debt service for borrowing attributable to war spending.

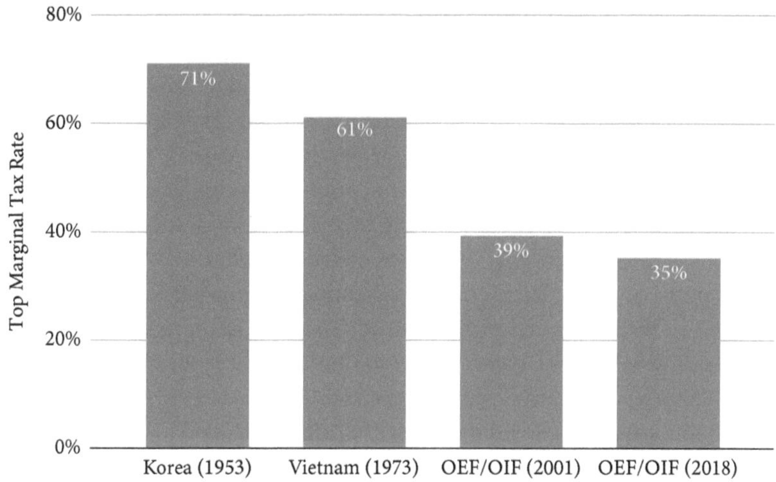

Figure 5.3 Wartime Federal Tax Rate for a Household Earning $300,000 (in 2001 Dollars)
Note: OEF/OIF is Operation Enduring Freedom (Afghanistan)/Operation Iraqi Freedom

The absence of taxes had a profound impact on how the public viewed the wars. As Sarah Kreps has shown, the public *experiences* debt differently from paying taxes. Taxes are tangible and painful, which makes people pay close attention to what they are being used for. The public is more attentive to the costs and the duration of a conflict if it is financed through taxation. Kreps argues that the debt financing severs this relationship, since the public no longer associates the value of war with the level of taxation.[68]

Why Did the Ghost Budget Emerge?

The Ghost Budget was the biggest budgetary anomaly in U.S. history. My research has identified three primary drivers of this phenomenon: congressional budget dysfunction, military assertiveness, and unusual economic conditions.

Congressional Budget Dysfunction

A critical factor in the rise of the Ghost Budget was the breakdown of the legislative budget process following budget reforms enacted in 1974. For most of the twentieth century, the U.S. president had dominated the budget process.

[68] Kreps, *supra* note 12.

Toward the end of the Vietnam War, President Richard Nixon refused to disburse billions of dollars in funds that Congress had appropriated for domestic programs. Congress forced Nixon to sign the "Budget and Impoundment Control Act," which aimed to reclaim congressional power over the budget.

Most budget experts of all political stripes agree that since then, the budget system has become less capable of reconciling competing demands and more prone to fiscal crises. Prior to 1974, the federal government had *never* ceased operations for lack of funding. Since then, it has "shut down," completely or partially, twenty-two times. It has only passed annual appropriations on time in four years (1977, 1989, 1995, and 1997). Instead, Congress has mostly enacted short-term spending measures ("continuing resolutions") that replicate the prior year's budget. There have been 205 continuing resolutions since 1997.[69]

Given this volatility, the military began to view Congress as unreliable when it came to funding the troops. The solution was to continue using "emergency" OCO funding, which was shielded from the budgetary dysfunction in Congress. This became the default method for funding the wars.

Institutional Military Assertiveness

The second factor was the desire of the defense establishment to secure an increase in defense spending after 2001.[70]

During the 1990s, President Bill Clinton capitalized on the post–Cold War "peace dividend" to reduce military spending and personnel. By September 11, 2001, military spending as a percentage of GDP had fallen to a post–World War II low of 2.9 percent—approximately one-fifth of the postwar peak of 14.4 percent in 1953.[71] This policy helped produce a fiscal surplus in the years 1998–2001. However, the defense cuts were unpopular within defense and defense contractor circles, what President Dwight D. Eisenhower termed the "military-industrial complex."[72] Even before the 9/11 attacks, a vocal group of conservatives was urging the United States to peg defense spending at 4 percent of GDP regardless of any specific national security threats.[73]

69 Cong. Rsch. Serv., R46595, Continuing Resolutions: Overview of Components and Practices (2025), https://www.congress.gov/crs-product/R46595.

70 Bilmes, *supra* note 9.

71 *See* Off. of Mgm't & Budget, Summary of Receipts, Outlays, and Surpluses or Deficits: 1789–2022 (2017).

72 President Dwight D. Eisenhower, Farewell Radio and Television Address to the American People (Jan. 17, 1961) [https://perma.cc/C6KF-PCQ7] (warning against "the acquisition of unwarranted influence, whether sought or unsought, by the military-industrial complex" and stating that "the potential for the disastrous rise of misplaced power exists, and will persist"); Bilmes, *supra* note 9.

73 Mackenzie Eaglen, *Four Percent for Freedom: The Need to Invest More in Defense—Selected Writings*, Heritage Found. (Sept. 25, 2007) [https://perma.cc/MD56-6M4M].

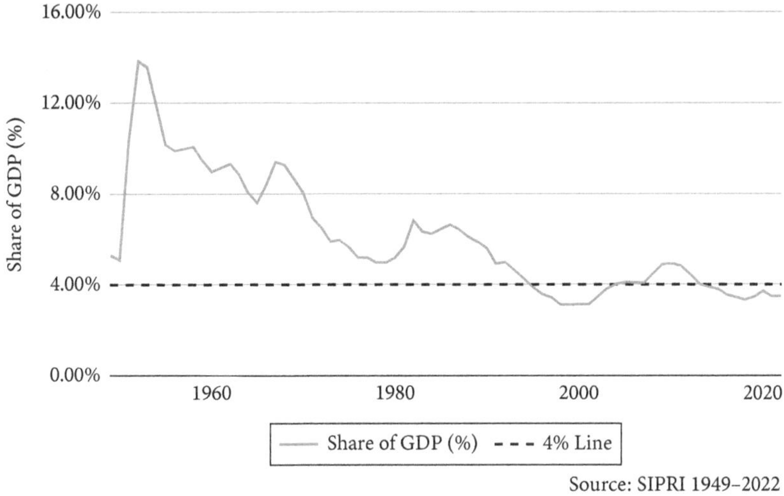

Figure 5.4 U.S. Defense Spending as Percentage of GDP, 1950–2020

Following the U.S. invasion of Afghanistan, the downward budget trend in the military was reversed. Between FY 2001 and FY 2017, the Pentagon budget grew by more than $1 trillion. The infusion of supplemental cash through emergency and OCO war money brought the total DOD budget back to 4 percent of GDP by 2005[74] and kept it there through 2014 (see Figure 5.4).[75]

The DOD tried to shift as much spending as possible into OCO, as there was less risk of Congress or the president rejecting it and fewer restrictions on how it could be spent.[76] Even better, OCO money required far less justification than ordinary defense expenditures. For example, in FY 2010, the Pentagon spent 23.5 percent of the total military budget to pay for OCO/wartime expenditures, but the annual defense budget estimate (which was over two hundred pages long and submitted just four months prior to the beginning of the FY 2010 fiscal year on October 1, 2009) contained *zero* pages of justification details (see Table 5.3).[77]

[74] McGarry & Morgenstern, *supra* note 4.

[75] Off. of the Under Sec'y of Def. (Comptroller), Dep't of Def., National Defense Budget Estimates for FY 2020, tbl. 2-1 (2019); Off. of Mgmt. and Budget, Historical Table 3.1—Outlays by Superfunction and Function: 1940–2029 (2024).

[76] Bilmes, *supra* note 9.

[77] Off. of the Under Sec'y of Def. (Comptroller), Dep't of Def., National Defense Budget Estimates 2005–2019.

Table 5.3 Pages of the DOD Budget Submission Devoted to OCO (Sample of Years)

Budget Year	Total No. of Pages in DOD Budget Submission	No. of Pages for War Budget Justification	% of Pages on OCO War Budget Justification	Estimated % of DOD Budget for OCO Spending
FY 2005	227	3	1.3%	15.8%
FY 2010	209	0	0	23.5 %
FY 2015	275	14	5.0 %	11.2%
FY 2019	109	8	7.3 %	10.0%

Atypical Economic Environment

The post-9/11 wars took place during a period of historically low interest rates and low inflation. Consequently, the U.S. Treasury was able to borrow trillions of dollars to pay for the wars—and simultaneously finance the tax cuts of 2001 and 2003—without having any material effect on the amount of debt service being repaid through the annual budget. Taking inflation into account, real interest rates (rates minus inflation) during the post-9/11 period started at 1.75 percent in 2002 and plummeted to 0.65 percent after 2008, a sixty-year low.[78]

By FY 2017, total public debt had more than tripled, but debt service payments as a percentage of annual budget outlays had *decreased* to 6.6 percent, compared to 8.5 percent of federal budget outlays in FY 2002. In terms of cash outlays, the United States paid only slightly more in interest payments in FY 2017 than it had in FY 2002 ($268 billion versus $232 billion in 2018 dollars). This meant that the public did not see tangible evidence of mounting war costs in the annual budget, so from a cost point of view, the war seemed almost invisible.[79]

In this environment, there was no worry that such spending would spark inflation, and the money being spent on the war may also have provided a form of stimulus for the economy. These conditions allowed the United States to avoid the traditional war-funding model of raising taxes and cutting spending that had been applied in previous wars.

Implications for Perpetual War

As Kant predicted, the ability to keep borrowing and spending with minimal oversight produced an Orwellian outcome in which the United States was always

[78] FED. RES. BANK OF MINNEAPOLIS, REAL INTEREST RATES OVER THE LONG RUN (2016) [https://perma.cc/F4SC-W8PA].

[79] BILMES, *supra* note 9.

fighting a war somewhere in the wider Iraq/Afghanistan region. The OCO budget extended far beyond the immediate operational needs of the wars themselves, with the Pentagon and its defense contractors incentivized to keep the conflicts going. Had war funding reverted to the normal budget process, with all the accompanying trade-offs, approval, and oversight requirements, Congress might have been forced to confront the question of whether the gains from the wars were worth the huge continuing cost.

The foregoing analysis has several implications. First, post-9/11 war costs were materially higher than they otherwise would have been. The combination of deferred spending, weak oversight, elastic definition of war costs, and the ready availability of funding relaxed the pressure to contain military spending. Years of "free money" accustomed the military to operating without effective budget constraints. Unsurprisingly, much of the wartime expenditures were highly wasteful. The Iraq, Afghanistan, and Pentagon inspectors general and the Wartime Contracting Commission all documented large-scale waste, profiteering, corruption, and "ghost" spending (money spent on nonexistent activities). OCO accounts could not even be submitted for audits, as they contained significant material weaknesses and discrepancies, particularly related to contingency contracts.[80]

Private defense contractors, who supplied 50 percent of the workforce, were key beneficiaries of the Ghost Budget. The DOD lacked any clear framework for determining which functions could be turned over to private companies efficiently. Defense stocks outperformed the stock market overall by nearly 60 percent during the Afghanistan War, fueled by the surge in war spending and a wave of consolidation in the industry.[81]

Second, the Ghost Budget weakened the main lever through which Congress maintains control of a war, namely, its control of the purse. The U.S. Constitution grants Congress both the power to declare wars and the power to fund them through the appropriations process. These are the principal levers that Congress has to control war policy,[82] with the appropriations process providing the most leverage.[83] The Ghost Budget facilitated paying for a long series of wars in ways that

[80] BILMES, *supra* note 9; ANN FLORINI, THE RIGHT TO KNOW: TRANSPARENCY FOR AN OPEN WORLD (2007); CHRISTOPHER KINSEY & MALCOLM HUGH PATTERSON, CONTRACTORS AND WAR: THE TRANSFORMATION OF US EXPEDITIONARY OPERATIONS (2012); COMM'N ON WARTIME CONTRACTING, TRANSFORMING WARTIME CONTRACTING: CONTROLLING COSTS, REDUCING RISKS (2011) [https://perma.cc/CEW8-NWPC]; HEIDI PELTIER, THE COMMERCIALIZATION OF THE US MILITARY POST-9/11: IMPLICATIONS FOR NATIONAL SECURITY, THE FEDERAL BUDGET, AND LABOR MARKETS (2020); SIGAR, CORRUPTION IN CONFLICT: LESSONS FROM THE U.S. EXPERIENCE IN AFGHANISTAN (2016) [https://perma.cc/FD97-MHTR]; F. MATTHEW WOODWARD, CONG. BUDGET OFF., FUNDING FOR OVERSEAS CONTINGENCY OPERATIONS AND ITS IMPACT ON DEFENSE SPENDING (2018) [https://perma.cc/JTG7-TAG8].

[81] Linda J. Bilmes, *Where Did the $5tn Spent on Afghanistan and Iraq Go? Here's Where*, GUARDIAN (LONDON) (Sept. 11, 2021), https://www.theguardian.com/commentisfree/2021/sep/11/us-afghanistan-iraq-defense-spending.

[82] FISHER, *supra* note 12; Weiler & Callanan, *supra* note 45.

[83] FISHER, *supra* note 12; LOUIS FISHER, PRESIDENTIAL WAR POWER (3d rev. ed. 2013).

diminished the role of the legislative branch, creating a vacuum that enabled the military bureaucracy to gain control.[84] In Congress, the question of whether war funding was necessary shifted over time to the question of "how big" the OCO budget should be.

Third, the Ghost Budget contributed to the increasing militarization of U.S. foreign policy. The surge in military spending and the ready availability of funds for new defense programs encouraged the United States to see the world through a "Pentagon lens" where military intervention became the preferred foreign policy option.[85] Roughly 92 percent of emergency supplemental OCO funding after 2001 was awarded to the DOD, even for activities such as postwar reconstruction that are not traditionally under the DOD's purview.[86] This precluded any serious debate over whether the rapid increase in military spending and the accompanying shift of power to the Pentagon was the optimal way to promote U.S. national security. This approach has endured despite evidence that natural security threats can and do arise from nonmilitary sources, such as the COVID-19 pandemic and climate change.

Even though direct U.S. military engagement in Iraq and Afghanistan is largely over, the legacy of the Ghost Budget continues.[87] OCO was absorbed into the defense base budget following the U.S. withdrawal from Afghanistan in 2021, creating a permanent increase to ongoing spending. But, in FY 2022, it was revived as a mechanism to help pay for U.S. military assistance to Ukraine. A combination of emergency appropriations, presidential budget "drawdown" authority, minimal oversight, accounting tricks, debt finance, heavy reliance on contractors, and Foreign Military Financing (FMF)—in short, a new Ghost Budget—has been used to fund military and security assistance to Ukraine, Israel, and the Middle East region.[88] Such methods have been criticized by standard

[84] Aaron Martin, Paying for War: Funding U.S. Military Operations Since 2001 (2011) (Ph.D. dissertation, Pardee Rand Graduate School) [https://perma.cc/G4HH-3QF3]; Fukumoto & Sharma, *supra* note 62.

[85] Carl Conetta, *Forceful Engagement: Rethinking the Role of Military Power in US Global Policy*, PROJECT ON DEFENSE ALTERNATIVES (2008); ALASDAIR ROBERTS, THE COLLAPSE OF FORTRESS BUSH: THE CRISIS OF AUTHORITY IN AMERICAN GOVERNMENT (2008); BILMES, *supra* note 9.

[86] Note: Of the remaining appropriations, approximately 8% went to the State Department and USAID, with less than 1% to the Department of Homeland Security and the U.S. Coast Guard. MCGARRY & MORGENSTERN, *supra* note 4.

[87] The United States has spent $11.2 billion on assistance and refugee programs for Afghanistan since the U.S. withdrawal in August 2021. SIGAR, QUARTERLY REPORT TO THE UNITED STATES CONGRESS (Jan. 30, 2024). As of February 16, 2024, approximately 2,400 U.S. military personnel were still deployed in Iraq and 800 in Syria. Between October 2023 and February 2024, U.S. personnel in Iraq were attacked more than 60 times by Iran-backed groups, and the United States conducted air strikes in Iraq and Syria. CHRISTOPHER M. BLANCHARD, CONG. RSCH. SERV., IN12309, IRAQ: ATTACKS AND U.S. STRIKES REOPEN DISCUSSION OF U.S. MILITARY PRESENCE (Feb. 16, 2024).

[88] In June 2023, the Pentagon reported that it had overestimated the value of the weapons sent to Ukraine by $6.2 billion resulting in a surplus that it will use for future security packages. Matthew Adams, *Pentagon Overestimated Cost of Weapons Sent to Ukraine by $6.2 Billion*, STARS AND STRIPES (June 23, 2023), https://www.stripes.com/theaters/us/2023-06-20/ukraine-military-aid-rus

government inspection agencies, such as the Government Accountability Office (GAO), for lacking sufficient oversight and monitoring.[89]

The Ghost Budget playbook effectively means that spending constraints are no longer a serious deterrent to war. Although support for the wars in both Ukraine and Israel has encountered domestic political opposition, the objections are almost entirely related to partisan electoral politics during a presidential election year.[90] There is little, if any, focus on the total sum of funding or the financing mechanisms. The Biden administration has even justified its request for new emergency supplemental overseas military spending as a boost for American business. As President Joe Biden stated in February 2024, "While this bill sends military equipment to Ukraine, it spends the money right here in the United States of America in places like Arizona, where the Patriot missiles are built; and Alabama, where the Javelin missiles are built; and Pennsylvania, Ohio, and Texas, where artillery shells are made."[91]

This budgetary and financial structure has become addictive for both the Pentagon and its private contractors. For the Pentagon, it enables military programs to sidestep the unpredictable path of the congressional budget process, with its repeated cycle of threatened government shutdowns and stopgap funding bills. For the contractors, who now play a critical and permanent role in military operations, it is an important source of steady revenues and profits that is protected with powerful congressional lobbying operations.

The Ghost Budget phenomenon is occurring at a time of growing geopolitical tensions and a decisive shift among global powers toward a mood of perpetual war. Evidence of this new ethos is widespread. Sweden's military commander-in-chief General Micael Bydén asked the Swedish population to mentally prepare for the possibility of war.[92] British Army chief General Sir Patrick Sanders called for Britain to train a "citizen army" and observed that the British people are part of a new "prewar generation" who may have to prepare themselves to fight in a

sia-pentagon-10498388.html. Additionally, Israel has been able to take advantage of FMF to buy U.S. weapons directly from manufacturers without public disclosure. Senators Elizabeth Warren, Bernard Sanders, Martin Heinrich, Jeffrey Merkley, Tim Kaine, Letter to The Honorable Joseph R. Biden Jr., 4 (Dec. 5, 2023).

89 U.S. Gov't Accountability Off., GAO-24-106289, Ukraine: DOD Should Improve Data for Both Defense Article Delivery and End-Use Monitoring (2024).

90 In October 2023, the Biden administration proposed $106 billion in supplementary emergency appropriations, which included $61.4 billion for Ukraine, primarily for weapons and to support military intelligence; with the remainder for military assistance to Israel, Indo-Pacific, humanitarian aid, and border enforcement. The Senate enacted a bill for $95 billion without the border component.

91 Jamie Stengle & Josh Boak, *Biden Wants People to Know Most of the Money He's Seeking for Ukraine Would Be Spent in US*, Associated Press (Feb. 20, 2024), https://apnews.com/article/biden-ukraine-johnson-factories-aid-62cbb83a184fd14b1573e25a73475767.

92 Paul Kirby, *Swedish Alarm After Defence Chiefs' War Warning*, BBC News (Jan. 10, 2024), https://www.bbc.com/news/world-europe-67935464.

war.[93] Sales of U.S. arms and military equipment to foreign governments reached a record high of $238 billion in 2023, as governments restock arsenals.[94] *The Economist* magazine, in a feature heralding the new global arms build-up, said the world is "tooling up" for a new global arms race, with global defense spending likely to rise by $200 billion to $700 billion per year and noted that Ukraine and Israel could provide a "battle lab for new ideas."[95]

The increasingly dangerous global environment means that effective oversight, transparency, and control of defense spending have become more important than ever. Congress needs to wrest back its critical role in U.S. war-making if we are to ensure that the mistakes of the past two decades are not repeated in the future.

[93] Jonathan Beale & Doug Faulkner, *Britain Must Train Citizen Army, Military Chief Warns*, BBC News (Jan. 24, 2024), https://www.bbc.com/news/uk-68086188; *see also* House of Commons Defence Committee, Ready for War?, 2023–4, HC 26 (UK).

[94] Mike Stone, *US Arms Exports Hit Record High in Fiscal 2023*, Reuters (Jan. 29, 2024).

[95] *The Cost of the Global Arms Race*, Economist (May 23, 2023), https://www.economist.com/international/2023/05/23/the-cost-of-the-global-arms-race.

6
Domestic Repercussions of the U.S. War on Terror

Faiza Patel

Introduction

Too often U.S. overseas conflicts result in diaspora minority communities at home being systematically suppressed and treated as internal enemies. Negative group characteristics are assigned to these communities and permeate security, policymaking, and press circles, making it easy to disregard their rights and interests. Because the government often uses national security as a justification for laws and policies affecting minorities, courts are generally reluctant to intervene. Perhaps the most infamous example of this propensity was the internment of some 125,000 Japanese Americans[1] after the attack on Pearl Harbor, a policy that was upheld by the U.S. Supreme Court in the 1944 case of *Korematsu v. United States*.[2] Dissenting from the Court's decision, Justice William Francis Murphy rejected the government's claim that Japanese Americans posed a security threat. Rather, they were "condemned because they are said to be 'a large, unassimilated, tightly knit racial group, bound to an enemy nation by strong ties of race, culture, custom and religion.'"[3] The government's attitude, in the crude words of an Army general in command of U.S. forces on the West Coast, was: "A Jap's a Jap. They are a dangerous element, whether loyal or not."[4]

Since the 9/11 attacks, Muslim Americans have been treated as a "dangerous element." The home front of the U.S. "war on terror" launched with roundups, detentions, and interrogations of thousands of Muslims in the United States, and the establishment of a registry of men from twenty-five countries, twenty-four of

[1] Margaret Crable, *Japanese Americans Were Forcibly Imprisoned in Camps During World War II. We Finally Know All Their Names*, USC Dornsife (Sept. 26, 2022), https://dornsife.usc.edu/news/stories/names-of-japanese-americans-forcibly-imprisoned/.

[2] Korematsu v. United States, 323 U.S. 214 (1944).

[3] *Korematsu*, 323 U.S. at 237 (1944) (Murphy J., dissenting) (quoting J.L. DeWitt, Final Report: Japanese Evacuation from the West Coast, 1942 (1943)).

[4] T.A. Frail, *The Injustice of Japanese-American Internment Camps Resonates Strongly to This Day*, Smithsonian Mag. (Jan. 2017), https://www.smithsonianmag.com/history/injustice-japanese-americans-internment-camps-resonates-strongly-180961422/.

Faiza Patel, *Domestic Repercussions of the U.S. War on Terror* In: *Perpetual War and International Law*. Edited by: Brianna Rosen, Oxford University Press.
DOI: 10.1093/oso/9780197748992.003.0006

which were majority Muslim.[5] The George W. Bush administration built a domestic surveillance system allowing the Federal Bureau of Investigation (FBI) to scrutinize anyone it considered a national security threat, with virtually no protections against religious and ethnic discrimination.[6] Muslim Americans were treated as "international" as opposed to domestic terrorists based on the theory that they sympathized with alien ideologies rather than any operational affiliation with a foreign terrorist group.[7] These policies and practices have persisted for more than two decades, under both Democratic and Republican administrations, with courts mostly acquiescing.

More recently, President Donald J. Trump built on this discriminatory foundation in his first term, banning people from several predominantly Muslim countries from traveling to the United States.[8] The ban was upheld by the U.S. Supreme Court, even in the face of overwhelming evidence that it was motivated by animus.[9] The second Trump administration has gone much further, increasingly targeting all immigrants—not just those from Muslim-majority countries—by playing on and heightening societal fears of terrorism and foreigners. In the first three months of his term, President Trump issued three executive orders claiming that migrants coming across the country's southern border are invading the United States, bringing drugs and crime in their wake.[10] This so-called "invasion" is the legal and rhetorical hook for the administration to ignore constitutional constraints. At the same time, the Trump administration is casting its immigration agenda as part of the terrorism threat that the United States has focused on for the last two decades.[11] Drug cartels have been designated as terrorist groups,[12] with senior administration officials asserting that individuals deemed to be "terrorists" have no claim to due process.[13] Permanent

[5] *See infra* text accompanying notes 17–31.

[6] *See infra* text accompanying notes 32–40.

[7] *See infra* text accompanying notes 48–50.

[8] *See, e.g.*, Exec. Order No. 13769, 82 Fed. Reg. 8977 (Jan. 27, 2017); Proclamation No. 9645, 82 Fed. Reg. 45161 (Sept. 24, 2017).

[9] Trump v. Hawaii, 585 U.S. 667 (2018).

[10] Exec. Order No. 14159, 90 Fed. Reg. 8443 (Jan. 20, 2025); Proclamation No. 10888, 90 Fed. Reg. 8333 (Jan. 20, 2025); Proclamation No. 10903, 90 Fed. Reg. 13033 (Mar. 14, 2025).

[11] According to Tricia McLaughlin, spokesperson for the Department of Homeland Security (DHS), Venezuelans deported to El Salvador "are actually terrorists, human rights abusers, gangsters and more." Andrew Goudsward & Ted Hesson, *Trump Officials Push Immigrant Gang Message, But Sometimes Don't Back It Up in Court*, REUTERS (Apr. 14, 2025), https://www.reuters.com/world/us/trump-officials-push-immigrant-gang-message-sometimes-dont-back-it-up-court-2025-04-13/. Stephen Miller, the White House Chief of Staff, similarly said, "we're going to continue to send foreign terrorist aliens to El Salvador as well as to many other countries." America (@America), X (formerly TWITTER) (Apr. 14, 2025), https://x.com/america/status/1911810520581021778 [https://perma.cc/C7LL-5MYT].

[12] Foreign Terrorist Organization Designations of Tren de Aragua, Mara Salvatrucha, Cartel de Sinaloa, Cartel de Jalisco Nueva Generacion, Carteles Unidos, Cartel del Noreste, Cartel del Golfo, and La Nueva Familia Michoacana, 90 Fed. Reg. 10030 (Feb. 20, 2025).

[13] *See, e.g.*, Stephen Miller (@StephenM), X (formerly TWITTER) (Mar. 24, 2025), https://x.com/StephenM/status/1904320253473026192 [https://perma.cc/4LA3-WQBD] ("Dear marxist judges: if an illegal alien criminal breaks into our country the only 'process' he is entitled to is deportation").

residents and student visa holders who participated in pro-Palestinian protests have been abruptly stripped of their status because their speech "aligns" with the terrorist group Hamas.[14]

The Republican-majority Congress has failed to serve as a check on these blatant abuses of power. It remains to be seen whether the courts and the public will serve as an effective bulwark against Trump's expansive claims of presidential authority and degradation of constitutional rights. Early court decisions have blocked some of the administration's efforts,[15] but most of these critical issues will ultimately be decided by the U.S. Supreme Court.[16] Only then will the limits of the war and terrorism framework advanced by the Trump administration be fully understood.

The Domestic Front of the War on Terror

Detention, Interrogation, and Registration of Muslims

Days after the 9/11 attacks, federal authorities began rounding up and imprisoning Muslim men, seeking anyone who might have a connection to terrorist activities, no matter how attenuated.[17] In the first two months after the attack, over twelve hundred people nationwide were detained,[18] some for as long as eight months,[19] in conditions that the Department of Justice's Inspector General found "unnecessarily severe"[20] with a pattern of "physical and verbal abuse."[21] A legal challenge to the program was unsuccessful.[22]

Also in late 2001, FBI agents, working with state and local police, began interviewing men who had recently entered the United States from Muslim-majority countries. Over the next two years, the government identified 7,602

[14] *See infra* text accompanying notes 95–108.

[15] Nia Prater & Margaret Harmann, *Trump's Biggest Court Losses: How Judges Are Blocking His Agenda*, N.Y. MAG. (Mar. 27, 2025), https://nymag.com/intelligencer/article/trump-court-losses.html.

[16] At the time of this writing, the Trump administration has already filed a record of ten emergency applications to the Supreme Court seeking to overturn lower court decisions. Abbie VanSickle, *At the Supreme Court, the Trump Agenda Is Always an "Emergency,"* N.Y. TIMES (Apr. 10, 2025), https://www.nytimes.com/2025/04/10/us/politics/supreme-court-trump-emergency.html.

[17] *See* Gary Fields & Noreen Nasir, *Muslims Recall Questionable Detentions That Followed 9/11*, ASSOCIATED PRESS (Oct. 4, 2021), https://apnews.com/article/immigration-africa-canada-religion-asia-bf725e0016e88eef2abc73bedd0c5718.

[18] OFF. OF THE INSPECTOR GEN., U.S. DEP'T OF JUST., THE SEPTEMBER 11 DETAINEES: A REVIEW OF THE TREATMENT OF ALIENS HELD ON IMMIGRATION CHARGES IN CONNECTION WITH THE INVESTIGATION OF THE SEPTEMBER 11 ATTACKS 1, no. 2 (June 2023).

[19] *Id.* at 182.

[20] *Id.* at 164.

[21] *Id.* at 182.

[22] Turkmen v. Ashcroft, 589 F.3d 542 (2d Cir. 2009).

men who had entered the United States on non-immigrant visas for "voluntary" interviews.[23] No terrorism plots were discovered,[24] but many people were deported for minor visa violations.[25]

In 2002, the George W. Bush administration rolled out the National Security Entry-Exit Registration System (NSEERS) for males over the age of sixteen from twenty-five countries,[26] twenty-four of which were majority Muslim.[27] They were required to register with a local immigration office, where they were interrogated, fingerprinted, and photographed.[28] Federal district and appeals courts uniformly rejected lawsuits challenging NSEERS on equal protection grounds, and no appeal was taken to the U.S. Supreme Court.[29] The program never identified any terrorists,[30] but it continued for a decade until the Obama administration delisted the countries the program covered.[31]

[23] U.S. Gov't Accountability Off., GAO-03-459, Homeland Security: Justice Department's Project to Interview Aliens after September 11, 2001 (2003), https://www.gao.gov/assets/gao-03-459.pdf. As of March 2003, the government had interviewed almost half of those identified. *Id.* Though the interviews were technically voluntary, those identified for interviews "worried about repercussions, such as future INS denials for visa extensions or permanent residency, if they refused." *Id.* at 5.

[24] David Cole, *Are We Safer?*, N.Y. Rev. of Books (Mar. 9, 2006), https://www.nybooks.com/articles/2006/03/09/are-we-safer/.

[25] Immigr. Pol'y Ctr., Targets of Suspicion: The Impact of Post-9/11 Policies on Muslims, Arabs and South Asians in the United States 10 (May 2004), https://www.americanimmigrationcouncil.org/sites/default/files/research/Targets%20of%20Suspicion.pdf.

[26] Registration and Monitoring of Certain Nonimmigrants, 67 Fed. Reg. 52584 (Aug. 12, 2022).

[27] Press Release, *Center for Constitutional Rights, National Security Entry-Exit Registration Systems (NSEERS) Freedom of Information Act (FOIA) Request* (Apr. 15, 2019), https://ccrjustice.org/home/what-we-do/our-cases/national-security-entry-exit-registration-system-nseers-freedom.

[28] *See supra* note 26. They were also required to complete a departure check at a designated departure port on the same day that they were leaving the U.S. for overseas travel. U.S. Immigration and Customs Enforcement, Special Registration Procedures for Visitors and Temporary Residents 1, https://www.ice.gov/doclib/nseers/srindividuals.pdf.

[29] *See, e.g., id.*; Kandamar v. Gonzales, 464 F.3d 65 (1st Cir. 2006); Ali v. Gonzales, 440 F.3d 678 (5th Cir. 2006); Zafar v. U.S. Att'y Gen., 461 F.3d 1357 (11th Cir. 2006); Shaybob v. Att'y Gen., 189 Fed. Appx. 127 (3d Cir. 2006); Hadayat v. Gonzales, 458 F.3d 659 (7th Cir. 2006); Malik v. Gonzales, 213 Fed. Appx. 173 (4th Cir. 2007). Rajah v. Mukasey, 544 F.3d 427 (2d Cir. 2008).

[30] Chris Rickerd, *Homeland Security Suspends Ineffective, Discriminatory Program*, ACLU (May 6, 2011), https://www.aclu.org/news/speakeasy/homeland-security-suspends-ineffective-discriminatory-immigration-program; Nadeem Muaddi, *The Bush-era Muslim Registry Failed. Yet the US Could Be Trying It Again*, CNN (Dec. 22, 2016), https://www.cnn.com/2016/11/18/politics/nseers-muslim-database-qa-trnd/index.html (noting that NSEERS "didn't result in a single terrorism conviction").

[31] Removing Designated Countries from the National Security Entry-Exit Registration System (NSEERS), 76 Fed. Reg. 23830 (Apr. 28, 2011). The regulatory framework remained in place until December 2016, when it was finally withdrawn in the last days of the Obama administration. Removal of Regulations Relating to Special Registration Process for Certain Nonimmigrants, 81 Fed. Reg. 94231 (Dec. 23, 2016).

Expansive New Domestic Surveillance Authorities and Programs

In the name of counterterrorism, the George W. Bush administration built an expansive domestic surveillance architecture which has been used to target Muslim Americans for the last two decades. In doing so, the administration turned its back on the lessons of the 1970s investigations conducted by a specially convened Senate committee known as the Church Committee, which catalogued how unfettered domestic intelligence authorities could be abused.[32] Most notably, the committee documented the FBI's efforts to surveil, disrupt, and neutralize a broad range of domestic protest groups and their leaders, including Dr. Martin Luther King Jr.[33]

The Church Committee's findings resulted in significant reforms, including the establishment of internal Department of Justice guidelines that restricted the FBI's authority to conduct open-ended domestic intelligence investigations.[34] Since 9/11, however, the Justice Department has progressively loosened these rules. Formalizing what the FBI had already been doing since the early 2000s, guidelines issued in 2008 provide that an agent can open an investigation so long as their purpose is to protect against criminal or national security threats or to collect foreign intelligence.[35] Since no factual predicate is required, this has often resulted in fishing expeditions which assigned suspicion based on faith and background. For example, in 2009, the FBI's Detroit field office sought permission to open an investigation evaluating the threat posed by terrorist groups in Michigan, which it justified on the theory that "[b]ecause Michigan has a large Middle Eastern and Muslim population, it is prime territory for attempted radicalization and recruitment by these terrorist groups."[36]

An internal FBI manual implementing the 2008 guidelines reflected similar assumptions. It allowed the targeting of communities that possess the same "religion-based characteristics or practices" as a terrorist group,[37] and the

[32] *See* FINAL REPORT ON SELECT COMM. TO STUDY GOVERNMENT OPERATIONS WITH RESPECT TO INTELLIGENCE ACTIVITIES, BOOK II, S. REP. NO. 94-755 (1976).

[33] *Id.* at 7, 11 (1976).

[34] EDWARD LEVI, U.S. DEP'T OF JUST., THE ATTORNEY GENERAL'S GUIDELINES FOR DOMESTIC FBI OPERATIONS (Nov. 4, 1976); *see also* EMILY BERMAN, BRENNAN CTR. FOR JUST., DOMESTIC INTELLIGENCE: NEW POWERS, NEW RISKS 10–12 (2011), https://www.brennancenter.org/our-work/policy-solutions/domestic-intelligence-new-powers-new-risks.

[35] U.S. DEP'T OF JUST., THE ATTORNEY GENERAL'S GUIDELINES FOR DOMESTIC FBI OPERATIONS § II (2008), https://www.justice.gov/archive/opa/docs/guidelines.pdf [https://perma.cc/4UTL-YSLC]; BERMAN, DOMESTIC INTELLIGENCE, *supra* note 34, at 21–22.

[36] Azmat Khan, *FBI Criticized for Collecting Racial and Ethnic Data*, FRONTLINE (Oct. 21, 2011), https://www.pbs.org/wgbh/frontline/article/fbi-criticized-for-collecting-racial-and-ethnic-data/ (citing a 2009 memorandum from the Detroit FBI field office obtained by the ACLU).

[37] FBI, DOMESTIC INVESTIGATIONS AND OPERATIONS GUIDE 27 (Dec. 16, 2008), https://www.eff.org/sites/default/files/filenode/FBI_guidelines/domestic_investigations_and_operations_guide_part1.pdf.

collection of information regarding ethnic and racial behaviors "reasonably believed to be associated with a particular criminal or terrorist element of an ethnic community."[38] The manual embraced the view that if the members of a particular terrorist group shared a certain characteristic (such as the Muslim faith), then anyone who shared that characteristic was a fair target of suspicion. The FBI was specifically permitted to map the "locations of concentrated ethnic communities" as well as to collect "the locations of ethnic-oriented businesses and other facilities" because "members of certain terrorist organizations live and operate primarily within a certain concentrated community of the same ethnicity."[39] The agency "mapped" many minority groups, including Arab and Muslim Americans in Michigan.[40] Other law enforcement agencies, most famously the New York City Police Department, have also engaged in this practice.[41]

Some of the FBI's surveillance of Muslim-American communities was carried out by spies who infiltrated mosques, student groups, and community organizations.[42] The Bureau has reportedly built an enormous network of informants—fifteen thousand as of 2017.[43] These spies have been the lynchpin of the government's counterterrorism strategy. According to data collected by reporter Trevor Aaronson, in the two decades after the 9/11 attacks, around 50 percent of terrorism prosecutions involved informants.[44]

The FBI's informants infiltrate religious communities and pursue ordinary Muslim Americans, not suspected criminals. They often seek to trigger, rather than to discover, criminal activity. Craig Monteilh, for example, infiltrated mosques in Orange County, California, disguised as a French Syrian convert

[38] *Id.* at 33.

[39] *Id.* at 32. All of these same provisions, verbatim, are contained in the 2024 version of the manual, which is the most recent one publicly available. FBI, Domestic Investigations and Operations Guide §§ 4.2–4.3 (Feb. 27, 2024).

[40] *ACLU EYE on the FBI: The FBI Is Engaged in Unconstitutional Racial Profiling and Racial "Mapping,"* ACLU (Oct. 20, 2011), https://www.aclu.org/sites/default/files/field_document/aclu_eye_on_the_fbi_alert_-_fbi_engaged_in_unconstitutional_racial_profiling_and_racial_mapping_0.pdf.

[41] *See, e.g.*, Adam Goldman & Matt Apuzzo, *NYPD Muslim Spying Led to No Leads, Terror Cases*, Associated Press (Aug. 21, 2012), https://www.ap.org/ap-in-the-news/2012/nypd-muslim-spying-led-to-no-leads-terror-cases; *Factsheet: The NYPD Muslim Surveillance Program*, ACLU (June 17, 2013), https://www.aclu.org/other/factsheet-nypd-muslim-surveillance-program.

[42] *See, e.g.*, Leila Rafei, *How the FBI Spied on Orange County Muslims and Attempted to Get Away With It*, ACLU (Nov. 8, 2021), https://www.aclu.org/news/national-security/how-the-fbi-spied-on-orange-county-muslims-and-attempted-to-get-away-with-it; Rozina Ali, *The "Herald Square Bomber" Who Wasn't*, N.Y. Times (updated June 15, 2023), https://www.nytimes.com/2021/04/15/magazine/fbi-international-terrorism-informants.html.

[43] Trevor Aaronson, *The FBI Gives Itself Lots of Rope to Pull In Informants*, Intercept (Jan. 31, 2017), https://theintercept.com/2017/01/31/the-fbi-gives-itself-lots-of-rope-to-pull-in-informants/.

[44] Ali, *"Herald Square Bomber," supra* note 42. Trevor Aaronson & Margot Williams, *Trial and Terror*, Intercept (updated June 14, 2023), https://trial-and-terror.theintercept.com/.

named Farouk al-Aziz.[45] He claims the FBI tasked him with taking "the real pulse of the Muslim community in America."[46] Starting in 2006, he spent time praying in the area's mosques and making friends among the community, but soon started asking people what they thought about Osama bin Laden and the need to take revenge for the United States' killing of Muslims in Afghanistan and Iraq. Wary and scared, mosque leaders reported Monteilh as potentially dangerous to the FBI, unaware that the Bureau had sent him to their mosque.[47]

The FBI also has access to foreign intelligence tools when investigating Muslim Americans because it considers them to be international—rather than domestic—terrorists on the theory that they are inspired by foreign terrorist ideologies, even if they have no operational connections to foreign terrorist organizations.[48] These individuals are labeled "homegrown violent extremists" to distinguish them from "domestic violent extremists" (e.g., white supremacists) whose ideas are considered all-American.[49] This allows the government to apply counterterrorism tools designed for use against hostile foreign agents against Muslim Americans residing solely in the United States.[50] For example, the FBI used foreign intelligence surveillance orders between 2002 and 2008 to monitor the electronic communications of five Muslim men, all of whom had led highly public, outwardly exemplary lives. They included high-level officials in the White House and Department of Homeland Security (DHS), attorneys and organizers of civil rights organizations, and academics.[51]

These programs and policies are just a few examples of the suspicion and suppression that Muslim Americans have faced in the post-9/11 era. And,

[45] Trevor Aaronson, *Spy in Disguise: An FBI Informant's Unlikely Role in Upcoming Supreme Court Case on Surveillance of Muslims*, Intercept (Sept. 12, 2021), https://theintercept.com/2021/09/12/fbi-informant-surveillance-muslims-supreme-court-911/.

[46] Paul Harris, *The Ex-FBI Informant with a Change of Heart: "There Is No Real Hunt. It's Fixed,"* Guardian (Mar. 20, 2012), https://www.theguardian.com/world/2012/mar/20/fbi-informant.

[47] *Id.*

[48] *See Confronting the Rise of Domestic Terrorism in the Homeland: Hearing Before the H. Comm. on Homeland Security*, 116 Cong. 1 (2019) (statement of Michael C. McGarrity, Assistant Director, Counterterrorism Division, FBI) (noting that the difference between "international" and "domestic" terrorism is that international terrorism includes individuals "inside the United States" who are "inspired" by "global jihad").

[49] *Worldwide Threats to the Homeland: Hearing Before the S. Comm. on Homeland Security and Governmental Affairs*, 118th Cong. 2–3 (2020) (statement of Christopher A. Wray, Director, FBI) (explaining that domestic violent extremists work "in furtherance of ideological goals stemming from domestic influences" while homegrown violent extremists are "inspired by" foreign terrorist organizations. For further discussion of this issue, *see Brennan Center Submits Comments for PCLOB's Forum on Domestic Terrorism*, Brennan Ctr. for Just. (updated July 11, 2022), https://www.brennancenter.org/our-work/research-reports/brennan-center-submits-comments-pclobs-forum-domestic-terrorism.

[50] *See generally* Shirin Sinnar, *Separate and Unequal: The Law of "Domestic" and "International" Terrorism*, 177 Mich. L. Rev. 1333 (2019).

[51] *See* Glenn Greenwald & Murtaza Hussain, *Under Surveillance: Meet the Muslim-American Leaders the FBI and NSA Have Been Spying On*, Intercept (July 9, 2014), https://theintercept.com/2014/07/09/under-surveillance/.

as discussed below, they are excluded from the protection of federal rules prohibiting the FBI from profiling on the basis of race, religion, ethnicity, and similar traits.

Exclusion from Protections Against Profiling

In 2003, the George W. Bush administration published guidance prohibiting federal law enforcement agencies from racial and ethnic profiling.[52] It did not cover religion or national origin and exempted national security and border investigations.[53] The Obama administration issued the next version of the guidance in 2014, expanding the prohibition to cover religious and national origin discrimination, but essentially recreating the national security and border loopholes.[54]

The most recent set of rules, issued by the Biden administration in 2023, continue to allow consideration of characteristics such as race and religion in national security cases.[55] According to an example in the guidance, if a terrorist group located in Southeast Asia consisting predominantly of a particular ethnic group releases poison gas in an area frequented by American tourists, the FBI is permitted to recruit informants of that ethnic group in the United States. The Bureau must have relevant and trustworthy information tying the group to overseas activity and on its ethnic make-up, but does not need evidence connecting those it is targeting in the United States with any criminal activity or security threats. Their shared ethnicity with the foreign group is enough.[56] The guidance—and this example in particular—thus validates long-standing biased practices, such as the FBI's scrutiny of diaspora Muslim communities in the wake of violence overseas, which has sowed fear and confusion among many.[57]

[52] CIVIL RIGHTS DIV., U.S. DEP'T OF JUST., GUIDANCE REGARDING THE USE OF RACE BY FEDERAL LAW ENFORCEMENT AGENCIES (June 2003).

[53] *Id.* at 2.

[54] U.S. DEP'T OF JUST., GUIDANCE FOR FEDERAL LAW ENFORCEMENT AGENCIES REGARDING THE USE OF RACE, ETHNICITY, GENDER, NATIONAL ORIGIN, RELIGION, SEXUAL ORIENTATION, OR GENDER IDENTITY 2, n.2 (2014); *see* Faiza Patel, *Recreating the Old Loopholes: Thoughts on the Revised Guidance for Federal Law Enforcement*, LAWFARE (Dec. 23, 2014), https://www.lawfaremedia.org/article/recreating-old-loopholes-thoughts-revised-guidance-federal-law-enforcement.

[55] U.S. DEP'T OF JUST., GUIDANCE FOR FEDERAL LAW ENFORCEMENT AGENCIES REGARDING THE USE OF RACE, ETHNICITY, GENDER, NATIONAL ORIGIN, RELIGION, SEXUAL ORIENTATION, GENDER IDENTITY, AND DISABILITY (2023); Faiza Patel & Harsha Panduranga, *A Roadmap for Implementing Rules on Racial Profiling*, JUST SECURITY (Aug. 25, 2023), https://www.justsecurity.org/87722/a-roadmap-for-implementing-rules-on-racial-profiling/.

[56] The guidance also requires other information (e.g., travel to southeast Asia), but this hardly bears on threat and is instead common among the relevant diaspora community. U.S. DEP'T OF JUST., GUIDANCE FOR FEDERAL LAW ENFORCEMENT, *supra* note 55, at 10.

[57] *See, e.g.*, Prem Thakker & Daniel Boguslaw, *FBI Targets Muslims and Palestinians in Wake of Hamas Attack, Civil Rights Advocates Warn*, INTERCEPT (Oct. 13, 2025), https://theintercept.com/2023/10/13/palestinians-muslims-fbi/; Mazin Sidahmed, *FBI's Pre-election Sweep of Muslim*

Three iterations of the Justice Department's rules against profiling over almost two decades demonstrate that the United States' commitment to banning racial profiling—a practice that it recognizes is ineffective and invidious—does not apply when it comes to national security investigations which often target Muslim Americans.[58]

Overbroad Material Support Laws

In the last two decades, terrorism cases have mostly been brought under 18 U.S. Code § 2339B, which prohibits providing material support or resources—such as training, property, expert advice, and transport—to a designated foreign terrorist organization (FTO).[59] Under the Anti-terrorism and Effective Death Penalty Act of 1996, the Secretary of State has broad power to designate any entity a "foreign terrorist organization."[60] As of this writing, seventy-seven entities are designated as FTOs,[61] which must be published in the Federal Register.[62]

An individual can be prosecuted under this statute even if they have no intention of supporting the violent or terrorist activities of an FTO, so long as they are aware that the entity has been designated as such.[63] According to the Supreme Court's decision in *Holder v. Humanitarian Law Project*, providing a terrorist group with conflict resolution training could qualify as material support if carried out in coordination with the designated group.[64] The Court accepted the

Americans Raises Surveillance Fears, GUARDIAN (Jan. 16, 2017), https://www.theguardian.com/us-news/2017/jan/16/fbi-muslim-americans-visits-surveillance-cair.

[58] CIVIL RIGHTS DIV., GUIDANCE (2003), *supra* note 52, at 1; U.S. DEP'T OF JUST., GUIDANCE (2014), *supra* note 54, at 1–2; U.S. DEP'T OF JUST., GUIDANCE (2023), *supra* note 55, at 2, 5.

[59] 18 U.S.C. § 2339B. Federal law also prohibits providing material support for any one of a set of enumerated terrorism-related offenses. 18 USC § 2339A. CHARLES DOYLE, CONG. RESEARCH SERV., R41333, TERRORIST MATERIAL SUPPORT: AN OVERVIEW OF 18 U.S.C. § 2339A AND § 2339B (2023) ("The material support statutes, 18 U.S.C. § 2339A and § 2339B, have been among the most frequently prosecuted federal anti-terrorism statutes"). *See also* Domestic Terrorism Prosecutions Outnumber International, TRAC REP. (Sept. 21, 2017), https://perma.cc/ZM6U-YTKF (stating that § 2339B was the most commonly filed lead charge in federal terrorism cases in 2017); KAREN J. GREENBERG, CENT. ON NAT'L SECURITY AT FORDHAM U. SCH. OF L., THE AMERICAN EXCEPTION: TERRORISM PROSECUTIONS IN THE UNITED STATES—THE ISIS CASES 28 (2017).

[60] The Secretary of State can designate an entity as an FTO if: the entity is a foreign organization; the entity engages in terrorist activity, terrorism, or material support of terrorism, or retains the capacity and intent to engage in terrorism; and the terrorist activity or terrorism threatens the security of U.S. nationals or U.S. national security. Antiterrorism and Effective Death Penalty Act of 1996, Pub. L. No. 104-132, § 302, 110 Stat. 1248 (1996) (codified as amended at 8 U.S.C. § 1189(a)(1)).

[61] Bureau of Counterterrorism, U.S. Department of State, Foreign Terrorist Organizations (accessed Apr. 15, 2025), https://www.state.gov/foreign-terrorist-organizations.

[62] 8 U.S.C. § 1189(a)(2)(A)(ii).

[63] Holder v. Humanitarian Law Project, 561 U.S. 1, 16 (2010) ("Congress plainly spoke to the necessary mental state for a violation of § 2339B, and it chose knowledge about the organization's connection to terrorism, not specific intent to further the organization's terrorist activities").

[64] *Id.* at 24–25.

Obama administration's argument that this interpretation of the material support laws is required because all humanitarian assistance to designated terrorist groups is "fungible" with other, more pernicious, types of support, such as lethal aid.[65]

While the material support statute explicitly allows for independent advocacy, and the Court in *Humanitarian Law Project* clarified that independent advocacy for a terrorist group is protected by the U.S. Constitution's First Amendment, material support laws have been used to criminalize what seems like pure speech uncoordinated with an FTO.[66] For example, in 2011, Tarek Mehanna was convicted of material support based in part on evidence that he viewed, translated, and disseminated al-Qaeda propaganda on his own volition. The prosecution never established that Mehanna had been in contact with al-Qaeda, let alone that he received instructions from them.[67]

Two decades after the 9/11 attacks, the domestic counterterrorism infrastructure that treats Muslim Americans as dangerous elements remains in place. The Trump administration has now identified immigrants as an adjacent and much larger set of dangerous elements, deporting many while eroding due process rights. In doing so, President Trump is displaying an increasingly dismissive attitude toward constitutional rights, relying on broad national security rationales of the type that were accepted by the courts and the public as part of the war on terror.

The War on Immigrants

The war on terror was always an amorphous idea, but it did encompass the U.S. invasions of Afghanistan and Iraq.[68] The United States is not currently at war with Mexico, Venezuela, or any other countries that are major sources of migration. But treating migration as an invasion enables Trump to more easily undertake his deportation agenda and tees up the possibility of actual military

65 *Id.* at 31.

66 18 U.S.C. § (g)(6); *id.* at 24.

67 United States v. Mehanna, 735 F.3d 32 (1st Cir. 2013); Alex Abdo, *Rhetorical Support Is Not "Material Support,"* ACLU (Dec. 26, 2012), https://www.aclu.org/news/free-speech/rhetorical-support-not-material-support; Rachel Levinson-Waldman, *The Narrowing of Tarek Mehanna's Liberties Has Consequences for Us All*, Brennan Ctr. for Just. (May 15, 2012), https://www.brennancenter.org/our-work/analysis-opinion/narrowing-tarek-mehannas-liberties-has-consequences-us-all.

68 Stephanie Savell, Watson Institute for International and Public Affairs at Brown University, United States Counterterrorism Operations 2018–2020 (Feb. 2021), https://watson.brown.edu/costsofwar/files/cow/imce/papers/2021/US%20Counterterrorism%20Operations%202018-2020%2C%20Costs%20of%20War.pdf. The Costs of War Project identifies eighty-five countries where the U.S. government has carried out counterterrorism operations in 2018, 2019, and/or 2020, which have grown out of President George W. Bush's "Global War on Terror." Forty-two of the eighty-five countries have a majority Muslim population.

operations. When faced with questions about individuals who appear to have been wrongly targeted and deported, the administration has simply labeled them terrorists, implying that no further inquiry is warranted.[69]

On March 14, 2025, Trump issued a proclamation invoking the Alien Enemies Act of 1798,[70] which allows the president to summarily detain and deport enemy aliens during times of war, invasion, or predatory incursion.[71] The proclamation makes two key findings. First, it claims that Tren de Aragua (TdA)—designated as an FTO in February 2025—is conducting an invasion or predatory incursion into the United States, citing "drug trafficking" and "mass illegal migration" as examples of TdA's "irregular warfare" in the country.[72] Second, the proclamation attempts to tie TdA to the Venezuelan government, claiming that the gang has infiltrated its military and law enforcement and coordinates with another cartel sponsored by the Venezuelan president.[73] It instructs the Attorney General and the Secretary of Homeland Security to apprehend and deport Venezuelan nationals alleged to belong to TdA.[74]

Five Venezuelan nationals in U.S. immigration custody filed suit in the District of Columbia challenging the proclamation the day after it was issued.[75] As an emergency hearing on their claims was proceeding, the Trump administration sent three planes carrying 261 people to El Salvador's Terrorism Confinement Center, infamous for its brutal conditions, seemingly violating the district court's order blocking such removals.[76] While the lower courts blocked the administration's use of the Alien Enemies Act,[77] a majority of the Supreme Court found that the case should have been brought as a habeas petition in Texas where

[69] *See supra* note 11.

[70] Proclamation No. 10903, *supra* note 10.

[71] 50 U.S.C. § 21.

[72] *See supra* note 12; Proclamation No. 10903, *supra* note 10.

[73] Proclamation No. 10903, *supra* note 10. In April 2025, U.S. intelligence agencies produced an internal memorandum that undermined the administration's argument that the Venezuelan government directs TdA. The memorandum concluded: "While Venezuela's permissive environment enables TDA to operate, the Maduro regime probably does not have a policy of cooperating with TDA and is not directing TDA movement to and operations in the United States." Nat'l Intelligence Council, Off. of the Dir. of Nat'l Intelligence, SOCM 2025-11374, Venezuela: Examining Regime Ties to Tren de Aragua 2 (2025); *see also* Charlie Savage & Julian E. Barnes, *Spy Agencies Do Not Think Venezuela Directs Gang, Declassified Memo Shows*, N.Y. Times (May 6, 2025), https://www.nytimes.com/2025/05/05/us/trump-venezuela-gang-ties-spy-memo.html.

[74] Proclamation No. 10903, *supra* note 10, at 13034.

[75] Class Action Complaint & Petition for Writ of Habeas Corpus, J.G.G. v. Trump, No. 25-cv-766 (D.D.C. Mar. 15, 2025), ECF No. 1.

[76] *See, e.g.*, Nicholas Riccardi & Regina Garcia Cano, *Trump Administration Deports Hundreds of Immigrants Even as a Judge Orders Their Removals to Be Stopped*, Associated Press (Mar. 17, 2025), https://apnews.com/article/trump-venezuela-el-salvador-immigration-dd4f61999f85c4dd8bcaba7d4fc7c9af; *see also* Luke Broadwater et al., *A Judge Ordered Deportation Planes to Turn Around. The White House Didn't Listen*, N.Y. Times (Apr. 8, 2025), https://www.nytimes.com/2025/03/17/us/politics/timeline-trump-deportation-flights-el-salvador.html.

[77] Order, J.G.G. v. Trump, No. 25-5067, 2025 WL 914682 (D.C. Cir. Mar. 26, 2025) (per curiam), *aff'g*, Minute Order, J.G.G. v. Trump, No. 25-cv-766, 2025 WL 890401 (D.D.C. Mar. 15, 2025).

the men were being held.[78] The Court did not opine on whether the administration could use the Alien Enemies Act in the absence of an actual invasion, but did require the government to provide adequate notice and an opportunity to contest their removal under the law.[79] At the time of writing, two habeas cases have already been initiated, one in Texas and another in New York. They have been brought on behalf of a class consisting of noncitizens in immigration custody who could be deported pursuant to the proclamation.[80] In both, federal judges have issued orders prohibiting the government from removing plaintiffs from the United States as they parse the legal basis for the government's actions.[81]

The due process requirements imposed by the Supreme Court are significant. It has become abundantly clear that the Trump administration whisked people off to El Salvador without any notice or opportunity to contest the government's view of their deportability. This has resulted in serious errors. The administration concedes it erroneously deported an El Salvadoran national named Kilmar Armando Abrego Garcia who had established a well-grounded fear of persecution if he returned to his country.[82] But it refuses to bring Abrego Garcia back, claiming that he is a member of the MS-13 gang, which the State Department recently designated as an FTO.[83] The Supreme Court ruled that the administration must "facilitate" Abrego Garcia's return, but thus far it does not appear that the administration intends to comply.[84] Instead, the White House claims that it cannot bring Abrego Garcia back because he is under the sovereign authority of El Salvador[85]—seemingly ignoring the fact the U.S. government is paying $6 million annually to send prisoners there.[86] The use of an overseas prison to avoid intervention from American courts echoes the George W. Bush administration's

[78] Trump v. J. G. G., No. 24A931, 2025 WL 1024097 (U.S. Apr. 7, 2025) (per curiam).

[79] *Id.* at *2.

[80] Class Petition for Writ of Habeas Corpus & Class Complaint for Declaratory and Injunctive Relief, J.A.V. v. Trump, No. 25-cv-072, 2025 WL 1064009 (S.D. Tex. Apr. 9, 2025), ECF No. 1; Class Petition for Writ of Habeas Corpus & Class Complaint for Declaratory and Injunctive Relief, G.F.F. v. Trump, No. 25-cv-2886 (S.D.N.Y. Apr. 8, 2025), ECF No. 1.

[81] Temporary Restraining Order, *J.A.V.*, 2025 WL 1064009, ECF No. 12; Order Granting Temporary Restraining Order, *G.F.F.*, No. 25 Civ. 2887, ECF No. 31.

[82] Defendants' Memorandum of Law in Opposition to Plaintiffs' Emergency Motion for Temporary Restraining Order at 3, Abrego Garcia v. Noem, No. 25-cv-951, 2025 WL 1014261 (D. Md. Mar. 31, 2025).

[83] Noem v. Abrego Garcia, No. 24A949, 2025 WL 1077101, at *1 (U.S. Apr. 10, 2025); *see supra* note 12.

[84] *Abrego Garcia*, 2025 WL 1077101, at *1.

[85] Michael Collins et al., *Federal Judge Directs US to Return Deported Maryland Man "as Soon as Possible,"* USA Today (Apr. 11, 2025), https://www.usatoday.com/story/news/nation/2025/04/11/abrego-garcia-deportation-ruling-federal-judge/83041374007/ ("the Justice Department has said it has no authority to return the Maryland father to the United States because he is in a foreign country").

[86] Cecilia Vega, *U.S. Sent 238 Migrants to Salvadoran Mega-Prison; Documents Indicate Most Have No Apparent Criminal Records*, CBS News (Apr. 6, 2025), https://www.cbsnews.com/news/what-records-show-about-migrants-sent-to-salvadoran-prison-60-minutes-transcript/.

attempt to avoid judicial review of its detention of people captured in the conflict with al Qaeda at the U.S. naval base in Guantánamo Bay.

The invasion theory also features in another proclamation which is premised on the constitutional clause requiring the federal government to protect the states against invasions.[87] The order essentially forbids migrants from invoking their right to asylum under the Immigration and Nationality Act on the theory that this is necessary to protect the states against invasion from migrants.[88] Anticipating potential military action, another executive order directs the Secretary of Defense to draw up plans for the military to repel "forms of invasion including unlawful mass migration, narcotics trafficking, human smuggling and trafficking, and other criminal activities."[89]

President Trump has also drawn on specific tools that are the hallmarks of the war on terror. Acting pursuant to an executive order,[90] the Secretary of State designated eight criminal groups, including the Venezuelan TdA, MS-13, and six Mexican groups as FTOs.[91] Given the broad scope of the material support laws discussed earlier, this designation could be used to prosecute a range of people who have nothing to do with drug cartels, from asylum seekers who may have had no choice but to pay cartels to bring them across the border, to churches that provide shelter to migrants.[92] And, while the presence or absence of an FTO designation is not directly related to armed conflict, it could help support a future case for going to war against foreign terrorists—just as the United States invaded Afghanistan for harboring Osama bin Laden.

Anti-Muslim animus has long been part of Trump's anti-immigrant posture and policies. After he was elected in 2015—in words strikingly similar to his current rhetoric about immigrants generally—Trump said that Muslims represent an "extraordinary influx of hatred and danger coming into our country"[93] and banned travel from several Muslim majority countries, a step the administration took again in its second term in June 2025.[94]

[87] Proclamation No. 10888, *supra* note 10; U.S. Const. art. IV, § 4.

[88] Proclamation No. 10888, *supra* note 10. Under the Immigration and Nationality Act, "[a]ll noncitizens physically present in the U.S., irrespective of their status, have the right to apply for asylum. 8 U.S.C. § 1158(a)(1). *See also* Refugee and Immigr. Ctr. for Education and Legal Services v. Noem, No. 25-cv-306 (D.D.C. filed Feb. 3, 2025).

[89] Exec. Order No. 14167, 90 Fed. Reg. 8613 (Jan. 20, 2025).

[90] Exec. Order No. 14157, 90 Fed. Reg. 8439 (Jan. 20, 2025).

[91] *See supra* note 12.

[92] *See* Rachel Levinson-Waldman, *The Dangerous Sweep of Trump's Plan to Designate Cartels as Terrorist Organizations*, Just Security (Feb. 5, 2025), https://www.justsecurity.org/107400/trump-plan-cartels-terrorist-organizations/.

[93] Jenna Johnson, *Trump Calls For "Total and Complete Shutdown of Muslims Entering the United States,"* Wash. Post (Dec. 7, 2015), https://www.washingtonpost.com/news/post-politics/wp/2015/12/07/donald-trump-calls-for-total-and-complete-shutdown-of-muslims-entering-the-united-states/.

[94] *See supra* text accompanying notes 8–9.

During his second term, Trump has used allegations of support for terrorist groups and antisemitism as a cudgel to silence pro-Palestinian speech. When campaigning for president, he promised to "immediately deport" foreign students protesting the war in Gaza.[95] As instructed in two executive orders, the State Department and DHS have launched an ideological deportation campaign. The first order, on keeping foreign terrorists out of the United States, asks the Secretary of State to recommend actions against foreign nationals who undermine Americans' constitutional rights, including rights to freedom of speech and the free exercise of religion.[96] The second order, on combating antisemitism, instructs the secretaries of State and DHS to find ways "prosecute, remove, or otherwise hold to account" those who perpetrate "unlawful anti-Semitic harassment and violence."[97] The administration's actions go far beyond punishing any type of illegal activity and instead target pro-Palestinian speech, as it has conceded.

The first salvo of this campaign came on March 8, 2025, when federal immigration enforcement agents arrested Mahmoud Khalil, a permanent resident and Columbia University graduate who was a prominent leader of pro-Palestinian protests on the university's campus.[98] He was quickly transferred to a detention facility in Louisiana.[99] In support of its decision to detain Khalil, the government has not cited any criminal activity.[100] Rather it is mainly relying on a rarely used provision of the immigration law, which allows the Secretary of State to remove foreigners because allowing them to remain in the country "would have potentially serious adverse foreign policy consequences."[101] The administration argues

[95] Simone Weischselbaum, *Trump's Plan to Quell Protests: "Deport Pro-Hamas Radicals,"* NBC News (Aug. 13, 2024, 12:19 PM), https://www.nbcnews.com/news/trumps-plan-quell-protests-deport-hamas-radicals-rcna166168.

[96] Exec. Order No. 14161, 90 Fed. Reg. 8451 (Jan. 20, 2025).

[97] Exec. Order No. 14188, 90 Fed. Reg. 8847 (Jan. 29, 2025).

[98] Eliza Shapiro, *Immigration Authorities Arrest Pro-Palestinian Activist at Columbia*, N.Y. Times (Mar. 9, 2025), https://www.nytimes.com/2025/03/09/nyregion/ice-arrests-palestinian-activist-columbia-protests.html.

[99] Michael Wilson et al., *How a Columbia Student Activist Landed in Federal Detention*, N.Y. Times (Mar. 17, 2025), https://www.nytimes.com/2025/03/16/nyregion/mahmoud-khalil-columbia-university.html.

[100] Chloe Atkins, *Government's Case against Mahmoud Khalil Is Reliant on Tabloid Accounts, Review of Evidence Shows*, NBC News (Apr. 15, 2025), https://www.nbcnews.com/news/us-news/governments-case-mahmoud-khalil-shaky-reliant-tabloid-accounts-review-rcna201254.

[101] In its initial court filings, the government cites 8 U.S.C. § 1227(a)(4)(C)(i). Respondents' Memorandum of Law in Support of their Motion to Dismiss or to Transfer the Case at 2, Khalil v. Joyce, No. 25-cv-1963 (D.N.J. Mar. 12, 2025) ECF 31. In a later brief filed by the government, it included a new allegation against Khalil—that he failed to disclose certain information on his green card application, violating immigration law. Respondents' Opposition to Petitioner's Motion for Release Under Lucas v. Hadden and Mapp v. Reno at 32, Khalil v. Joyce, No. 25-cv-1963 (D.N.J. Mar. 23, 2025) ECF 99. Khalil is also separately defending against removal proceedings in immigration court, where the judge recently ruled that he could be deported. *See* Jonah E. Bromwich, *Immigration Judge Rules Khalil Can Be Deported, but Legal Hurdles Remain*, N.Y. Times (Apr. 11, 2025), https://www.nytimes.com/2025/04/11/nyregion/khalil-jena-deportation-ruling.html. Unlike regular federal court judges, immigration judges are administrative judges in the Department of Justice and do

that allowing Khalil's advocacy on behalf of Palestinians undermines its foreign policy goal of combating antisemitism around the world.[102]

The government is using the same grounds to detain and deport other students as well.[103] Rumeysa Ozturk, a Fulbright scholar pursuing a PhD at Tufts University, was picked up outside her home and sent to an immigration detention facility in Louisiana. According to a DHS spokesperson, she had engaged in "activities in support of Hamas," an apparent reference to an op-ed she co-wrote for a school newspaper criticizing the university's response to a call to divest from companies with ties to Israel.[104] Another foreign student, Badar Khan Suri, was similarly picked up and sent to Louisiana, with DHS accusing him of "spreading Hamas propaganda" and "promoting antisemitism on social media."[105] He was also described as having "close connections to a known or suspected terrorist," an apparent reference to his wife, whose father was formerly an adviser to deceased Hamas leader Ismail Haniyeh.[106]

Statements from the president and senior administration officials clearly show that their intent is to target people who express pro-Palestinian views, whose sentiments they repeatedly describe as "pro-Hamas," "pro-terrorist," "antisemitic," and even anti-American.[107] The focus on speech has become even more apparent with DHS's recent announcement that it will screen the social media accounts of those applying for permanent resident status, including

not have the authority to rule on the constitutionality of the Immigration and Nationality Act. Matter of C-, 20 I. & N. Dec. 529, 532 (BIA 1992). The immigration judge's decision can be appealed up to the Board of Immigration Appeals (another Justice Department entity) and then up to the federal court of appeals.

[102] *See* Lauren Mascarenhas & Gloria Pazmino, *Newly-Released Memo from Rubio Details Government's Only Evidence in Effort to Deport Mahmoud Khalil*, CNN (Apr. 10, 2025), https://www.cnn.com/2025/04/10/us/mahmoud-khalil-evidence-deadline/index.html (quoting a memo submitted to immigration court by Secretary of State Marco Rubio, which said that it is U.S. foreign policy to "combat anti-Semitism around the world and in the United States, in addition to efforts to protect Jewish students from harassment and violence in the United States").

[103] *See, e.g.*, Petition for Writ of Habeas Corpus and Complaint at 2, Suri v. Trump, No. 25-cv-480 (E.D. Va. Mar. 18, 2025); First Amendment Petition for Writ of Habeas Corpus and Complaint at 8, Ozturk v. Trump, No. 25-cv-10695 (D. Mass. Mar. 28, 2025).

[104] Gloria Pazmino et al., *What We Know about the Tufts University PhD Student Detained by Federal Agents*, CNN (Mar. 28, 2025), https://www.cnn.com/2025/03/27/us/rumeysa-ozturk-detained-what-we-know/index.html.

[105] Hank Sanders & Zolan Kanno-Youngs, *D.H.S. Detains a Georgetown University Academic*, N.Y. Times (Mar. 19, 2025), https://www.nytimes.com/2025/03/19/us/politics/georgetown-suri-detained.html.

[106] *Id.*

[107] *See, e.g.*, Donald J. Trump (@realDonaldTrump), Truth Social (Mar. 10, 2025), https://truthsocial.com/@realDonaldTrump/posts/114139222625284782; Lisa Rozner & Ali Bauman, *Protest to Support Columbia University Activist Mahmoud Khalil Leads to Arrests at New York City Hall*, CBS News (Mar. 12, 2025), https://www.cbsnews.com/newyork/news/mahmoud-khalil-protest-arrests-at-city-hall/ (quoting White House Press Secretary Karoline Leavitt, who said that the "administration is not going to tolerate individuals having the privilege of studying in our country and then siding with pro-terrorist organizations that have killed Americans").

foreign students and foreigners affiliated "with educational institutions linked to antisemitic activity," for speech that it regards as anti-Semitic.[108]

Conclusion

Muslim Americans, many of whom are immigrants, have borne the brunt of the domestic front of the war on terror, from its early detentions and interrogations to the systemized surveillance of their communities and the stigma of suspicion. The war paradigm provided the framework within which national security programs and policies targeting Muslim Americans were developed and validated. The Trump administration is now stretching the idea of war even more, extending it to an immigrant invasion that simply does not exist in the hopes that courts will once again defer to the executive branch's judgment. The administration's prolific use of the terrorism label to tar protestors and migrants draws on Americans' post-9/11 acceptance of departures from constitutional norms to shut down calls for proof and process. Whether these tactics will be successful remains to be seen, but it is a chilling reminder of the enduring legacies of the war on terror that persist today.

[108] Press Release, *U.S. Citizenship and Immigration Services, DHS, DHS to Begin Screening Aliens' Social Media Activity for Antisemitism* (Apr. 9, 2025), https://www.uscis.gov/newsroom/news-releases/dhs-to-begin-screening-aliens-social-media-activity-for-antisemitism.

7

Assessing the Legacy of U.S. Torture in an Era of Geostrategic Competition

Federica D'Alessandra and Alberto J. Mora

Introduction

Amid a shifting geopolitical and global security environment, and an intensified great power competition between the United States and its rivals, it might be tempting to think of foreign policy in realpolitik terms and treat normative agendas, including accountability, as peripheral. This might arguably be even more so for accountability issues that some consider to be already resolved and not needing re-examination. One example of this is the torture program the George W. Bush administration authorized in 2002 as part of its response to the 9/11 attacks. The program allowed the Central Intelligence Agency (CIA) to capture and detain al-Qaeda suspects and transfer (i.e., "render") them for interrogation to "black sites"—secret prisons located in other jurisdictions, often operating well beyond the law. At these sites, prisoners would be subjected to "enhanced interrogation techniques"—a euphemism indicating brutal interrogation tactics, often amounting to torture—to extract information relating to their alleged al-Qaeda links or plans to wage future attacks.[1] At least 119 individuals were unlawfully rendered, with 39 of them confirmed to have been tortured under the program at nine different sites. For a period of time, analogous authorities (i.e., "counter-resistance interrogation techniques")[2] were also conferred to the Department of Defense (DOD), with some detainees held and interrogated in facilities operated by U.S. armed forces in Afghanistan, in Iraq, and at Guantánamo Bay, resulting in serious allegations against DOD and

[1] Senate Select Comm. on Intelligence, *Committee Study of the Central Intelligence Agency's Detention and Interrogation Program, together with Foreword by Chairman Feinstein and Additional and Minority Views*, S. Rep. No. 113-288 (2014), https://www.intelligence.senate.gov/sites/default/files/publications/CRPT-113srpt288.pdf.

[2] U.S. Senate Armed Servs. Comm., *Inquiry into the Treatment of Detainees in U.S. Custody*, Executive Summary at xii (2008), https://www.armed-services.senate.gov/imo/media/doc/Detainee-Report-Final_April-22-2009.pdf.

Federica D'Alessandra and Alberto J. Mora, *Assessing the Legacy of U.S. Torture in an Era of Geostrategic Competition* In: *Perpetual War and International Law*. Edited by: Brianna Rosen, Oxford University Press.
 DOI: 10.1093/oso/9780197748992.003.0007

CIA personnel.[3] Perhaps the most infamous of these sites is the still-operating prison at the U.S. naval base in Guantánamo Bay,[4] where 780 men are confirmed to have been detained, and dozens more suspected to have been rendered.[5] Despite terminating the use of brutality in interrogations in 2009 with Executive Order (E.O.) 13491,[6] President Barack Obama was criticized for failing to close Guantánamo and hold officials responsible for torture accountable.[7] Though parts of the U.S. government have intermittently pursued internal oversight or other forms of investigation, most reviews either paint an incomplete picture or remain classified. To this day, no U.S. administration has released a public, in-depth assessment of the policy costs and strategic consequences of the decision to employ interrogation techniques that amounted to torture.

More than two decades later, a legal review and policy assessment of U.S. torture remains urgent for many reasons. At a minimum, an assessment would draw and crystallize lessons learned to inform future U.S. policy, potentially feeding into ongoing debates on reforming the U.S. military justice system.[8] A final review of U.S. torture would also present strategic benefits, particularly in the current geopolitical climate in which U.S. rivals are deliberately weaponizing past instances of wrongful American conduct as part of a broader strategy in pursuing their own geostrategic objectives and hegemonic ambitions. Indeed, in the current geopolitical landscape, foreign policy debates regularly feature "whataboutism" tactics that confront states violating the rules anchoring the current global order, which the United States shaped and has benefitted from ever since. Such debates have also become "a proxy debate about the very value and universality of such norms and principles."[9] This is especially true

[3] *The Road to Abu Ghraib*, Human Rights Watch (2004), https://www.hrw.org/report/2004/06/09/road-abu-ghraib.

[4] Between 2001 and 2005, Alberto J. Mora was General Counsel of the U.S. Navy. Although he was not in the chain of command for operational matters, in late 2002, he learned of allegations of abuse from the Naval Criminal Investigative Service (NCIS), which was integrated into the operational unit at Guantánamo. Upon investigation, he discovered that "Counter-Resistance Interrogation Techniques" were being administered against detainees and that they had been authorized by then–Secretary of Defense Donald Rumsfeld under guidance offered by the Office of Legal Counsel in the DOJ, in what would become known as the "torture memos." For more background on the efforts of Mora and others within the administration to bring the abuse to an end, *see* Jane Mayer, *The Memo*, New Yorker (Feb. 27, 2006), https://www.newyorker.com/magazine/2006/02/27/the-memo.

[5] *Supra* note 1.

[6] Exec. Order No. 13,491, Ensuring Lawful Interrogations, 74 Fed. Reg. 4893 (Jan. 22, 2009).

[7] Adam Serwer, *Obama's Legacy of Impunity for Torture*, Atlantic (Mar. 12, 2018), https://www.theatlantic.com/politics/archive/2018/03/obamas-legacy-of-impunity-for-torture/555578/.

[8] *See, e.g.*, Geoffrey S. Corn & Rachel E. VanLandingham, *Strengthening American War Crimes Accountability*, 70 Am. U. L. Rev. 309 (2020), https://aulawreview.org/blog/strengthening-american-war-crimes-accountability/.

[9] Sophie Eisentraut, *Standard Deviation: Views on Western Double Standards and the Value of International Rules*, Munich Security Brief, Issue 1 (Sept. 2024), https://securityconference.org/assets/02_Dokumente/01_Publikationen/2024/MunichSecurityBrief_1_2024_Standard_Deviation.pdf.

for long-politicized human rights and accountability issues, which are particularly vulnerable in the current geopolitical climate.[10] In today's geostrategic landscape, human rights abuses by the United States and its allies have indeed become strategic vulnerabilities, serving as ammunition to adversaries seeking to undermine U.S. legitimacy and—in the case of hegemony-seeking, near-peer competitors—are used as political and rhetorical leverage in their quest to rewrite international rules in a way that could restack the world order against U.S. interests.

Against this background, identifying appropriate ways to address past instances of wrongful conduct would benefit the United States in constructively navigating shifting geopolitics. This would deprive adversaries of the opportunity to shield themselves from accountability by accusing western countries of "hypocrisy" and "double standards" for frequently deviating from their own foreign policy principles.[11] We argue that addressing its legacy of torture would be a "low risk, high reward" first step for the United States toward achieving this objective. In fact, a genuine and transparent review of U.S. torture more specifically would also directly benefit a range of U.S. policy goals and objectives, particularly in support of global accountability efforts. To begin with, it would directly address ongoing U.S. government concerns about potential exposure of U.S. personnel before the International Criminal Court (ICC), alleviating an important point of tension with the Court and directly supporting U.S. policy in Ukraine. Indeed, using Russia's war crimes against Ukraine as an example, this chapter discusses how reluctance to address the enduring legacy of torture from the "war on terror" continues to undermine U.S. policy objectives, strain international relations, and fuel narratives that undermine the United States' standing at a pivotal geopolitical moment.

The Costs and Consequences of Torture

Before announcing E.O. 13491, President Obama instructed his legal, intelligence, and national security advisers to probe the impacts of "enhanced" interrogation on intelligence gathering. The CIA told then–National Security Advisor Susan Rice that these techniques had been "effective in providing intelligence and has been a key reason why al-Qaeda has failed to launch a spectacular attack in the West since September 11."[12] Yet specialists, lawmakers, and (at times) the

[10] Federica D'Alessandra, *Conceptualizing Great Power Perpetrators*, 18 Genocide Stud. & Prevention: Int'l J. 151, 151–89 (2024), https://doi.org/10.5038/1911-9933.18.1.1949.

[11] Eisentraut, *Standard Deviation*, *supra* note 9.

[12] *Effectiveness of the CIA Counterterrorist Interrogation Techniques*, CIA (June 13, 2016).

CIA itself have concluded the opposite,[13] or at least conceded that it is "unknowable" whether brutality aided the collection of actionable intelligence.[14] But even if agreeing with the CIA's assessment of the potential usefulness of torture, it is imperative to simultaneously ask, at what cost?

The public may never understand the full implications of the U.S. government's decision to authorize torture in the aftermath of 9/11. The closest the American public has come to understanding the program's scope was the Senate Select Committee on Intelligence report's Executive Summary, released in 2014 amid a partisan battle over an alleged "effort to discredit the CIA and the Bush administration."[15] Even if the full report were released, it would likely only scratch the surface of the detrimental impact that torture has had on U.S. national security, foreign policy, and counterterrorism efforts. Given that no U.S. administration has ever commissioned a public, systematic review of the geopolitical price of torture, many civil society groups have attempted to quantify and qualify the costs at home and abroad.[16] The results are staggering.

The U.S. government's decision to utilize torture was found to have "greatly damaged [its] national security, incited extremism in the Middle East, hindered cooperation with U.S. allies, exposed American officials to legal repercussions, undermined U.S. diplomacy, and offered a convenient justification for other governments to commit human rights abuses."[17] Researchers also found that reports of abuse provoked an immediate surge in foreign terrorist fighters joining al-Qaeda (and later ISIS) in Afghanistan and Iraq; made recruiting local allies more challenging amid tensions with local U.S. collaborators; impeded interoperability among coalition forces in the war on terror; and exposed the United States to legal and reputational damage while hindering core foreign policy, defense, and security objectives.[18]

[13] *Panetta Review* (2009) (unpublished) (on file with the CIA) (noting that the CIA has distanced itself from the findings, calling the review incomplete and cursory, and has blocked its release under FOIA).

[14] Brian Murphy, *CIA Chief: "Unknowable" Whether Ordinary Interrogation Would Bring Same Intel Gains*, Wash. Post (Dec. 11, 2014), https://www.washingtonpost.com/world/national-security/cia-director-impossible-to-assess-gains-from-enhanced-interrogations/2014/12/11/8ba972e0-8160-11e4-9f38-95a187e4c1f7_story.html.

[15] Mark Mazzetti, *CIA Report Found Value of Brutal Interrogation Was Inflated*, N.Y. Times (Jan. 20, 2015), https://www.nytimes.com/2015/01/21/world/cia-report-found-value-of-brutal-interrogation-was-inflated.html.

[16] *The Strategic Consequences of the U.S. Use of Torture*, Harvard Kennedy Sch. Carr Ctr. for Hum. Rts. Pol'y (Oct. 7–8, 2016), https://projects.iq.harvard.edu/files/tortureconference/files/tortureconferenceagendafinaloctober_13_2016.pdf.

[17] Douglas A. Johnson, Alberto Mora, & Averell Schmidt, *The Strategic Costs of Torture*, Foreign Aff. (Jan. 1, 2016), https://www.foreignaffairs.com/united-states/strategic-costs-torture.

[18] The abuse of prisoners in U.S. military custody was investigated by the Senate Armed Services Committee and its findings were published on December 2008 in a report entitled *Inquiry Into the*

Criminal investigations have been opened against former U.S. officials in Switzerland, France, Germany, Spain, Italy, and elsewhere, with a flurry of cases also reaching the European Court of Human Rights.[19] The United Nations, too, has criticized the United States for breaching its human rights obligations, and called for the closure of Guantánamo.[20] Of the 780 confirmed detainees held in Guantánamo, only eight men were convicted, with four convictions being subsequently reversed.[21] The existence of such sites has undermined the United States' leadership and reputation worldwide, with authoritarian regimes—including China, Russia, and Iran—accusing the United States of "hypocrisy" and "double standards."[22] At a minimum, continued secrecy around the torture program has contributed directly to the failure to deliver even a small measure of justice for 9/11 victims. It led to the creation of the Guantánamo military commissions, which have failed to deliver fair trials in accordance with due process standards. Throughout the proceedings, the U.S. government insisted on withholding evidence concerning the torture the defendants had been subjected to, while it sought to use evidence obtained through torture of said defendants in their own prosecution. This is not only a deeply concerning precedent; it has directly contributed to fifteen of the men who were subject to torture still languishing at Guantánamo in arbitrary detention without adequate medical care.[23] To this day, the legacy of torture continues to concretely hinder key U.S. objectives on the global stage.

Treatment of Detainees in U.S. Custody. Among the unanimous findings of the committee was that the abuse of prisoners "damaged our [the U.S.] ability to collect accurate intelligence that could save lives, strengthened the hand of our enemies, and compromised our moral authority." *See supra* note 2.

[19] *Secret Detention Sites*, Eur. Ct. H.R. (Mar. 2024), https://www.echr.coe.int/documents/d/echr/fs_secret_detention_eng.

[20] *Guantánamo Bay: "Ugly Chapter of Unrelenting Human Rights Violations"—U.N. Experts*, U.N. Off. of the High Comm'r for Human Rights (Jan. 10, 2022), https://www.ohchr.org/en/press-releases/2022/01/Guantánamo-bay-ugly-chapter-unrelenting-human-rights-violations-un-experts.

[21] *Guantánamo Bay Top Facts*, Reprieve U.K., https://reprieve.org/uk/campaign/Guantánamo/faq/#:~:text=In%20total%2C%20only%208%20men,being%20charged%20with%20a%20crime.

[22] Tom O'Connor, *Cuba Slams 20 Years of US "Occupation," "Abuses" at Guantánamo Bay, U.N. Calls for Closure*, Newsweek (Jan. 11, 2022), https://www.newsweek.com/cuba-slams-20-years-US-occupation-abuses-Guantánamo-bay-un-calls-closure-1668249; Thomas Grover, *Russia Condemns United States for Human Rights Record*, Reuters (Oct. 22, 2012), https://www.reuters.com/article/uk-russia-usa-humanrights/russia-condemns-united-states-for-human-rights-record-idUKBRE89L14K20121022; *The United States' Arbitrary Detention at Home and Abroad: Truth and Facts*, Ministry of Foreign Aff. of the People's Republic of China (Mar. 29, 2023), https://www.mfa.gov.cn/eng/wjbxw/202303/t20230329_11050809.html.

[23] The number of detainees currently held at Guantánamo is up to date as of October 9, 2025. On the ongoing conditions of their detention, *see Footnote to 2023 SRCT Report*, U.N. Off. of the High Comm'r for Human Rights, https://www.ohchr.org/en/press-releases/2023/06/un-counterterrorism-expert-concludes-visit-united-states-and-guantanamo.

"Reciprocity" Concerns and Accountability for Russia's Crimes in Ukraine

Under the Biden administration, U.S. foreign policy supported Ukraine following Russia's 2022 full-scale invasion, with varying degrees of bipartisan support for holding Russian leaders accountable.[24] Supporting Ukraine has led the U.S. government to make previously unlikely policy choices, such as endorsing the creation of a special aggression tribunal[25] and the ICC's investigation into Russian war crimes.[26] Yet, in March 2023, reports emerged that the DOD was seeking to block the Biden administration from sharing evidence of Russian atrocities gathered by U.S. intelligence with the ICC. The report followed a cabinet-level Principals Committee meeting of the White House National Security Council on February 3, in which Secretary of Defense Lloyd Austin reportedly lodged his objections, despite the fact that "[t]he rest of the administration, including intelligence agencies and the State and Justice Departments, favors giving the evidence to the court."[27] In a May 11 congressional hearing, the secretary confirmed his opposition, citing "concerns about reciprocity going forward" and "about the protection of U.S. military personnel."[28]

The story broke just before the ICC Prosecutor, Karim Khan, issued an arrest warrant against Russian President Vladimir Putin for war crimes that include the deportation of hundreds of thousands of children from Russian-occupied Ukrainian territories.[29] Addressing the Pentagon's position, retired U.S. Generals Philip Breedlove, Ben Hodges, and Wesley Clark penned a joint editorial a few days later arguing in favor of U.S.-ICC cooperation.[30] Pursuant to the Court's evidentiary and procedural rules, filing the indictment and

[24] Antony J. Blinken, *Press Statement: Crimes Against Humanity in Ukraine* (Feb. 18, 2023), https://www.state.gov/crimes-against-humanity-in-ukraine/.

[25] *Ambassador Van Schaack's Remarks on the U.S. Proposal to Prosecute Russian Crimes of Aggression*, U.S. Dep't of State Office of Global Criminal Justice (Mar. 27, 2023), https://www.state.gov/ambassador-van-schaacks-remarks/.

[26] Todd Buchwald, *Unpacking New Legislation on US Support for the International Criminal Court*, Just Security (Mar. 9, 2023), https://www.justsecurity.org/85408/unpacking-new-legislation-on-us-support-for-the-international-criminal-court/.

[27] Charlie Savage, *Pentagon Blocks Sharing Evidence of Possible Russian War Crimes with Hague Court*, N.Y. Times (Mar. 8, 2023), https://www.nytimes.com/2023/03/08/us/politics/pentagon-war-crimes-hague.html.

[28] Adam Keith, *Is the Pentagon Relenting?: A Close Study of Opposition to the Int'l Criminal Court's Ukraine Investigation*, Just Security (July 12, 2023), https://www.justsecurity.org/87231/is-pentagon-opposition-to-the-international-criminal-courts-ukraine-investigation-relenting/.

[29] *Situation in Ukraine: ICC Judges Issue Arrest Warrants Against Vladimir Vladimirovich Putin and Maria Alekseyevna Lvova-Belova*, International Criminal Court (Mar. 17, 2023), https://www.icc-cpi.int/news/situation-ukraine-icc-judges-issue-arrest-warrants-against-vladimir-vladimirovich-putin-and.

[30] Philip Breedlove, Wesley Clark, & Ben Hodges, *Why Isn't the Pentagon Helping the International Court Prosecute Putin?*, Defense One (May 23, 2023), https://www.defenseone.com/ideas/2023/05/why-isnt-pentagon-helping-international-court-prosecute-putin/386681/.

unsealing the arrest warrant against Putin only required the ICC Prosecutor to satisfy his case to a "reasonable grounds" standard.[31] U.S. government cooperation might, however, be crucial to effectively prosecute Putin and prove his guilt beyond a reasonable doubt. Evidence linkage between a suspect and the crimes with which they are charged is notoriously difficult, particularly for international war crimes in which defendants are charged with command responsibility for subordinates' conduct. Prosecuting "conduct of hostilities violations," that is, breaches of the laws of war, such as the indiscriminate targeting of civilians or disproportionate casualties/damage, is equally difficult.[32] The value of U.S. cooperation is therefore beyond question: U.S. intelligence was indeed key in many cases before other international tribunals over the last twenty-five years.[33]

U.S.-ICC cooperation on the Russia-Ukraine case is even more crucial given the unprecedented nature of the arrest warrant against Putin: the first issued against a *sitting* head of state of a country that is not a member of the Court, without referral by the United Nations (U.N.) Security Council.[34] Beyond benefiting the case itself, supporting the ICC investigation also strategically benefits U.S. interests. Indeed, when the White House eventually announced it would override the DOD and cooperate with the Court, U.S. allies and partners applauded the decision as it fully aligned with shared values and signaled the United States' continued leadership against Russian aggression.[35] Why, then, would the Pentagon object to this outcome?

Neither Russia nor the United States is a State Party to the Rome Statute. Both have long maintained they do not recognize the ICC's jurisdiction over the nationals of non-State Parties, even if they commit war crimes, crimes against humanity, or acts of genocide in a territory that is otherwise under the jurisdiction of the Court, such as Ukraine. The Pentagon may believe acknowledging such jurisdiction could potentially expose U.S. officials who served in the war on terror. Importantly, such views do not appear exclusive to the DOD. Rather, they reflect broader concerns within the U.S. government on the matter, begging the

[31] Rome Statute of the ICC art. 53, 58, at 24, 27, https://www.icc-cpi.int/sites/default/files/RS-Eng.pdf; ICC, *Rules of Procedure and Evidence* rule 48: Determination of Reasonable Basis to Proceed with an Investigation under Article 15, para. 3, at 18, https://www.icc-cpi.int/sites/default/files/Publications/Rules-of-Procedure-and-Evidence.pdf.

[32] Carolin Wuerzner, *Mission Impossible? Bringing Charges for the Crime of Attacking Civilians or Civilian Objects Before International Criminal Tribunals*, 90 *Int'l Rev. of the Red Cross* 872 (Dec. 2008), https://international-review.icrc.org/sites/default/files/irrc-872-5.pdf.

[33] Clint Williamson, *The Role of the United States in International Criminal Justice*, 25 Penn State Int'l L. Rev. 4, Art. 7 (2008), http://elibrary.law.psu.edu/psilr/vol25/iss4/7.

[34] *Supra* note 31.

[35] Federica D'Alessandra, *Pursuing Accountability for the Crime of Aggression Against Ukraine*, 5 Revue Européenne du Droit (2023), https://geopolitique.eu/en/articles/pursuing-accountability-for-the-crime-of-aggression-against-ukraine/.

question: To what extent can U.S. officials be criminally prosecuted by the ICC for torture committed under the George W. Bush administration?

Real or Perceived Risk: U.S. Exposure Before the International Criminal Court

The November 2017 filing by then–ICC Prosecutor Fatou Bensouda requesting authorization to investigate the conflict in Afghanistan provides a starting point to understand what allegations concern U.S. officials. The Prosecutor's request focused on crimes against humanity and war crimes allegedly committed by members of the Taliban, and members of the Afghan security forces, with particular emphasis upon large-scale, systematic torture.[36] According to the American Society of International Law's 2021 report of a Presidential Task Force, alleged crimes by U.S. personnel, "while serious, are substantially more limited" and concern "allegations of torture and other detainee abuse (principally in the period of 2003–04)," not "allegations regarding combat operations by U.S. armed forces," with the Prosecutor identifying seventy-eight instances of such allegations: fifty-four involving U.S. armed forces and twenty-four involving CIA personnel.[37]

The Prosecutor also found that alleged mistreatment by DOD personnel was "inflicted on a relatively small percentage of all persons detained by U.S. armed forces . . . [and] also appear[s] to have occurred during a limited time period, after which the use of all brutal interrogation techniques by U.S. armed forces worldwide was formally rescinded" and that alleged DOD abuses were committed "pursuant to authorized interrogation policies adopted *locally*," with no evidence of "headquarters level" policy to approve the abuse. By contrast, allegations concerning the CIA, despite affecting fewer victims, were more "systematic" in nature (i.e., not isolated incidents) and were the product of a "*policy* to obtain actionable intelligence," pursuant to the CIA's rendition and enhanced interrogation program (in Afghanistan and in "black sites" located in other ICC States Parties, such as NATO allies Poland, Romania, and Lithuania).[38] The Pentagon's concerns around exposure of U.S. personnel before the ICC are thus narrow but

[36] Situation in Afghanistan, ICC-02/17-12, Prosecutor's Provision of Additional Information Pursuant to Pre-Trial Chamber III's *Order to the Prosecutor to Provide Additional Information* (ICC-02/17-8), para. 12 (Dec. 12, 2017); Situation in Afghanistan, OTP Application to Investigate, para. 189, at 255–57.

[37] ASIL ICC Task Force Report, *Recent ICC Developments Relevant to Its Relationship with the United States: The Situation in Afghanistan*, para. 3, https://www.asil-usc-task-force.org/report/05-recent-icc-developments-relevant-to-its-relationship-with-the-united-states/the-situation-in-afghanistan/.

[38] Emphasis added. *See id.*, paras. 219, 228, 355.

deep, and linger precisely because the United States has not comprehensively and transparently investigated what happened.

Under the Rome Statute's "complementarity regime," the ICC can only intervene when the state(s) with primary jurisdiction are "unwilling or unable" to themselves investigate the alleged conduct.[39] Evaluating whether a state is "unwilling or unable" remains challenging,[40] but the Court's jurisprudence has clarified key points of interpretation.[41] "Unwillingness and inability" arises only after a formal investigation is opened by the state in question. For a case to be considered "under investigation" by the interested state, the latter must take steps to ascertain whether the same individual is responsible for the same conduct under scrutiny by the Court. If the state in question does activate such steps, the case remains inadmissible, "unless the decision resulted from the unwillingness or inability of the State genuinely to prosecute." Crucially, once the interested state initiates such investigative steps, but decides not to prosecute, the burden shifts to the ICC prosecutor, if they still want to pursue the case, to demonstrate the state is unwilling or unable.[42] This implicitly acknowledges the Court's deference to the authority and discretion of functioning domestic legal systems, such as the United States.

In a 2018 speech, then–National Security Advisor John Bolton emphasized the importance of using the U.S. judicial system to prosecute American citizens, stating: "We believe in the rule of law, and we uphold it. We don't need the ICC to tell us our duty or second-guess our decisions."[43] Ambassador Bolton would have been correct except for one crucial point: in the case at hand, the United States has *not* upheld the rule of law by genuinely and transparently probing the conduct in question or holding those responsible accountable. Had the United States already done so, the ICC Afghanistan investigation would have never posed a perceived threat to either CIA or DOD personnel.

Importantly, in 2021, the ICC Prosecutor announced his office would "deprioritize" allegations against U.S. personnel from the Afghanistan inquiry, given that "the worst crimes in terms of gravity and scale and extent seem to be committed by the so-called Islamic State [in] Khorasan and also the Taliban."[44]

[39] Rome Statute art. 17(1)(a)(b).

[40] Frédéric Mégret, *What Is an "Unwilling" or "Unable" Jurisdiction Under Article 17 of the Rome Statute? Lessons from International Law's Theories of "Denial of Justice,"* Québécois Rev. of International Law (2005), https://papers.ssrn.com/sol3/papers.cfm?abstract_id=1277523.

[41] Case Matrix Network, *ICC Commentary on the Rome Statute*: pt. 2, arts. 11–21, https://www.casematrixnetwork.org/index.php?id=336.

[42] *Id.*

[43] John Bolton, *Full Text of John Bolton's Speech to the Federalist Society*, Al Jazeera, para. 42, https://www.aljazeera.com/news/2018/9/10/full-text-of-john-boltons-speech-to-the-federalist-society.

[44] Situation in Afghanistan, *Statement of the Prosecutor of the International Criminal Court, Karim A.A. Khan QC, Following the Application for an Expedited Order Under Article 18(2) Seeking*

The decision was harshly criticized,[45] but opened a crucial window for the United States to *remove exposure concerns* by doing what is required under international law and its domestic legal framework: reviewing the seventy-eight cases of alleged war crimes identified by the Court or, if it has already done so, making public both the process and outcomes of said review, including why U.S. authorities might have declined to file charges where warranted.[46] Doing so could have eliminated concerns about exposing U.S. personnel to the ICC, laying the foundation for a more productive future relationship. Though politically challenging domestically, such a review would have also served U.S. public and strategic interests, while directly countering "whataboutism" attempts by Russia and other U.S. adversaries to deflect from their own abuses.[47]

Indeed, when attacking the ICC in response to the arrest warrant against Putin, the Kremlin deployed retaliatory actions reminiscent of those adopted by previous U.S. administrations concerning the Afghanistan investigation,[48] such as the first Trump administration's decision to revoke U.S. visas, freeze U.S.-based assets, and impose sweeping sanctions on Court officials pursuant to a distorted application of U.S. counterterrorism sanctions.[49] Clearly, Russia's accusations of American hypocrisy obscure the lack of parallelism between the scope of crimes alleged against U.S. personnel and against Russian troops—for whom disregard for civilian life and brutality have been a historic part of armed forces doctrine.[50] Nevertheless, the lasting reputational damage suffered

Authorization to Resume Investigations in the Situation in Afghanistan (Sept. 27, 2021), https://www.justsecurity.org/79136/uncertain-future-for-the-iccs-investigation-into-the-cia-torture-program/.

[45] Julian Elderfield, *Uncertain Future for the ICC's Investigation into the CIA Torture Program*, Just Security (Nov. 12, 2021), https://www.justsecurity.org/79136/uncertain-future-for-the-iccs-investigation-into-the-cia-torture-program/.

[46] It is important to acknowledge that, although the United States remains under a legal obligation to *investigate* allegations of torture by any U.S. personnel, it is arguably unlikely that investigations would have led to any charges being filed, given federal statutes of limitations on non-capital torture offenses. The possible exception being acts of torture resulting in *death*, which would however require evidencing a material nexus between the alleged acts of torture and the resulting death(s). Such requirements are extremely hard to substantiate in general and would arguably be even more so at this stage, given the time that has since lapsed from the alleged conduct and result.

[47] Eliav Lieblich, *Whataboutism in International Law*, 65 Harv. Int'l L.J. 2 (2024), https://ssrn.com/abstract=4609679.

[48] Ketrin Jochecová, *Russia Blasts Back at ICC Over Putin Arrest Warrant*, Politico (Mar. 20, 2023), https://www.politico.eu/article/putin-russia-icc-criminal-case-moscow-ukraine-war/.

[49] White House, *Executive Order on Blocking Property of Certain Persons Associated with the International Criminal Court* (June 11, 2020), https://trumpwhitehouse.archives.gov/presidential-actions/executive-order-blocking-property-certain-persons-associated-international-criminal-court/. *See generally* Beth Van Schaack, *The Int'l Criminal Court Executive Order: Global Reactions Compiled* (Sept. 1, 2020), https://www.justsecurity.org/72256/the-intl-criminal-court-executive-order-global-reactions-compiled/.

[50] Max Fisher, *Russia's Brutality in Ukraine Has Roots in Earlier Conflicts*, N.Y. Times (Mar. 18, 2022), https://www.nytimes.com/2022/03/18/world/europe/russia-military-strategy-bombing-cities.html.

by the United States plays directly into Russia's hands and obscures America's long history of constructive engagement with the ICC. This extends well beyond Ukraine, and includes global and ICC accountability efforts in Libya, Uganda, the Democratic Republic of the Congo, Nigeria, the Central African Republic, Venezuela, and Myanmar, among others.[51]

A Ripe Opportunity, if Seized

Beyond clearly distancing itself from the approach embraced by Russian officials, there are also other reasons why the U.S. government would have benefited from probing allegations of torture domestically. First, doing so would have aligned U.S. conduct with that of allies and partners that have also faced the Court's scrutiny. British troops, for example, came under ICC investigation in the context of the 2003 invasion and occupation of Iraq, for conduct allegedly amounting to war crimes such as murder, torture, and other forms of ill treatment and prisoner abuse. In December 2020, the ICC Prosecutor announced her decision to close the probe that had initially been terminated in 2006, but reopened in 2014. In an unprecedented report, she confirmed the allegations, highlighting how "several levels of institutional civilian supervisory and military command failures contributed to the commission of crimes against detainees by UK soldiers in Iraq" and denouncing presumed cover-up attempts by British authorities. She nevertheless found that there was insufficient evidence to say that the United Kingdom's ongoing investigations were not genuine,[52] deciding to close the ICC probe and allow the justice process to play out domestically.

In another example of complementarity at play, with U.S. assistance, Ukraine is itself investigating and preparing to try domestically hundreds of thousands of alleged international crimes committed by mid- and low-ranking perpetrators, both Russian and Ukrainian nationals,[53] hence allowing the ICC investigation to focus on the most responsible perpetrators in the Kremlin's top echelon. Russian authorities have instead initiated bogus criminal proceedings and issued arrest warrants against both the ICC Prosecutor and the three judges who approved ICC warrants against Putin and two of his top generals, including the defense minister, among others.[54] It seems evident that Ukraine's approach is smart, for it

[51] *Supra* note 36, at 13–24.

[52] ICC Office of the Prosecutor, *Situation in Iraq/UK Final Report* (Dec. 9, 2020), at paras. 113, 371, 408, 432, 504.

[53] *Ukraine Probing over 122,000 Suspected War Crimes, Says Prosecutor*, Reuters (Feb. 23, 2024), https://www.reuters.com/world/europe/ukraine-probing-over-122000-suspected-war-crimes-says-prosecutor-2024-02-23/.

[54] ICC Press Release, *Situation in Ukraine: ICC Judges Issue Arrest Warrants Against Sergei Kuzhugetovich Shoigu and Valery Vasilyevich Gerasimov* (June 25, 2024), https://www.icc-cpi.int/news/situation-ukraine-icc-judges-issue-arrest-warrants-against-sergei-kuzhugetovich-shoigu-and.

further underscores the stark contrast between Ukraine as a law-abiding nation (if one still facing many rule of law challenges) on the one hand, and the lawlessness of Russian conduct on the other.

In addition, a U.S. domestic probe would have served as a beneficial example for Israeli allies, whose leadership—specifically, the prime and former defense ministers—are also facing ICC arrest warrants for alleged crimes of starvation, willful killing, persecution, and indiscriminate attacks against Palestinians in Gaza, alongside now-dead Hamas leaders Mohammed Deif, Yahya Sinwar, and Ismail Haniyeh, for war crimes and crimes against humanity—including murder, extermination, the taking of hostages, sexual violence, torture, and other inhumane acts.[55] The unprecedented decision has been highly polarizing and faced harsh criticism by both U.S. and Israeli officials. They denounced the move as drawing false moral equivalence between a democratic nation acting in self-defense and the terrorists and "mass murderers" who attacked it, in addition to asserting that the ICC lacks jurisdiction.[56]

Concerningly, in February 2025, the second Trump administration signed an executive order issuing financial sanctions and visa restrictions on ICC officials conducting investigations concerning U.S. personnel and allies, including Israel.[57] Meanwhile, the U.S. House of Representatives passed the Illegitimate Court Counteraction Act, which would make it illegal for U.S. persons to transact with many ICC officials.[58] Rather than doubling down on this path, the U.S. government should instead seize the opportunity to advocate with Israeli allies that cooperating with ICC proceedings (as Israel has done so far with independent proceedings before the U.N. International Court of Justice)[59] would certainly be more beneficial, both to Israel's global standing and to its assertions that its military operations in Gaza fully comply with the laws of war.[60] Even better would be for Israeli authorities to initiate genuine investigations domestically, as Israel's

[55] *Statement of ICC Prosecutor Karim A.A. Khan KC: Applications for Arrest Warrants in the Situation in the State of Palestine*, ICC (May 20, 2024), https://www.icc-cpi.int/news/statement-icc-prosecutor-karim-aa-khan-kc-applications-arrest-warrants-situation-state.

[56] Sam Cabral, *Netanyahu Denounces Bid to Arrest Him over Gaza War*, BBC News (May 20, 2024), https://www.bbc.co.uk/news/articles/cmllykpwgdyo.

[57] White House, *Imposing Sanctions on the International Criminal Court* (Feb. 6, 2025), https://www.whitehouse.gov/presidential-actions/2025/02/imposing-sanctions-on-the-international-criminal-court/.

[58] Adam Keith, *Sweeping ICC Sanctions Bill Would Harm Victims, U.S. Interests*, Just Security (July 17, 2024), https://www.justsecurity.org/97770/icc-sanctions-bill-harm/.

[59] *See, e.g.*, *Application of the International Convention on the Elimination of All Forms of Racial Discrimination (Georgia v. Russia)*, International Court of Justice (May 17, 2024), https://www.icj-cij.org/sites/default/files/case-related/192/192-20240517-ora-01-00-bi.pdf.

[60] Matthew H. Gillett, *Between Rhetoric and Effects: The ICJ Provisional Measures Order in South Africa v. Israel*, Just Security (Mar. 14, 2024), https://www.justsecurity.org/91728/between-rhetoric-and-effects-the-icj-provisional-measures-order-in-south-africa-v-israel/.

Attorney General suggested,[61] which could entirely remove Israel's exposure concerns before the ICC. Indeed, had the U.S. government initiated a domestic probe of torture allegations, it would have the chance today to not only argue for the benefits of such an approach but to actually demonstrate them. In the case of the United States at least, it is unlikely that investigations might lead to criminal prosecutions, given the statute of limitations has now passed for noncapital torture offenses.[62] Nevertheless, undertaking a domestic review of allegations would have still offered significant benefits.

The Geopolitics of Accountability

In the current geopolitical climate, the United States will need to "walk the talk" if it is to sustain global leadership and achieve its international objectives. Against the current backdrop of increasing instability and a shift to multipolarity, new geopolitical groupings have already begun to emerge.[63] The many global challenges confronting the United States today require sustaining international cooperation rather than shifting toward isolationism.[64] Cross-national collaboration is essential in all policy domains, particularly for human-centered agendas such as global accountability matters, which U.S. geostrategic competitors are actively targeting as part of broader efforts aimed to "renegotiate" international legal rules pursuant to a "revisionist" vision that opposes U.S. interests and values.[65]

To achieve its objectives, the United States must therefore look beyond its closest allies to partners in other regions, where significant grievances persist around perceptions of "western double standards."[66] In this new era of geostrategic competition, the importance of "productive power"—an actor's ability to shape narratives and credibly advance certain propositions over others—is only destined to grow.[67] Thus, failing to uphold transparency, consistency, and accountability is actively detrimental to U.S. objectives and credibility on the world stage today.[68] Having engaged in torture during the war on terror,

[61] Toi Staff, *Netanyahu Weighing Various Commissions of Inquiry to Stave Off Legal Action at ICC*, The Times of Israel (August 16, 2024), https://www.timesofisrael.com/netanyahu-weighing-various-commissions-of-inquiry-to-stave-off-legal-action-at-icc/.

[62] *Supra* note 43.

[63] Aaron Friedberg, *A World of Blocs*, Center for Strategic & International Studies (Apr. 6, 2023), https://www.csis.org/analysis/world-blocs.

[64] Condoleeza Rice, *The Perils of Isolationism: The World Still Needs America—and America Still Needs the World*, Foreign Aff (Aug. 20, 2024), https://www.foreignaffairs.com/united-states/perils-isolationism-condoleezza-rice.

[65] *Supra* note 9.

[66] *Id.*

[67] *Supra* note 10.

[68] Dmitry Gorenburg, *Strategic Messaging: Propaganda and Disinformation Efforts*, in *Russia's Global Reach: A Security and Statecraft Assessment* (Graeme P. Herd ed., 2021), https://www.mar

the United States' continued reluctance to reckon with its legacy has now become counterproductive across a variety of other policy domains, hindering efforts to strengthen the international legal rules underpinning the world order that has sustained the United States' role, values, and leadership for nearly a century.

Conclusion

This chapter assesses the ongoing legacy of U.S. torture through a legal review and policy assessment, addressing its costs and strategic consequences in the current geopolitical landscape. While there are legitimate reasons to maintain a degree of secrecy and confidentiality with respect to many of the details a full assessment would unveil, understanding and learning from the past is foundational to inform future U.S. policy. At a minimum, the U.S. government should consider publicly releasing a redacted version of the full 2014 report by the U.S. Senate Select Committee on Intelligence investigating the CIA torture program, as well as information as viable on investigations carried out by other U.S. government agencies, including the DOD and the Department of Justice (DOJ).

Given that the American public have yet to hear the full truth about the torture program and its implications, doing so could directly benefit U.S. public interest, helping restore much-needed public trust and confidence in the U.S. government and its institutions, as well as the sacred principles of transparency and open governance by which they are democratically bound. Even former Attorney General Eric Holder, whose DOJ oversaw a 2011 CIA investigation led by Special Counsel John Durham—which concluded with no charges being filed—has called for the public release of investigation details, acknowledging that transparency can only benefit U.S. public trust in the integrity of the process.[69] Admittedly, the Durham investigation was itself carried out under a very narrow mandate which leaves ample scope for a much broader assessment of the program, its legality, its policy costs, and strategic implications.[70]

As we have argued, the most powerful incentive for such a review, more than twenty years later, would be to directly support assimilating key lessons learned to benefit future U.S. policy. The U.S. government would have the

shallcenter.org/en/publications/marshall-center-books/russias-global-reach-security-and-statecraft-assessment/chapter-15-strategic-messaging-propaganda-and.

[69] Ryan Devereaux, *Holder's Too Late Calls for Transparency on DOJ Torture Investigation*, INTERCEPT (Oct. 15, 2015), https://theintercept.com/2015/10/15/holder-too-late-calls-for-transparency-on-doj-torture-investigation/.

[70] Robert Chesney, *DOJ Announces Full Criminal Investigation into Deaths of Two Detainees in Relation to CIA Interrogation*, LAWFARE (Aug. 4, 2023), https://www.lawfaremedia.org/article/doj-announces-full-criminal-investigation-deaths-two-detainees-relation-cia-interrogation.

opportunity to repudiate the use of torture as both counterproductive and contrary to U.S. values, duties, and interests. Furthermore, a review might address U.S. government concerns about exposing officials who served in the war on terror to ICC jurisdiction. So long as it is genuine and transparent, the ICC would have to defer to U.S. authorities on any criminal matters arising from the assessment, removing this point of tension between the United States and the Court. Additionally, undertaking such a review would signal that the U.S. government is willing to hold itself accountable and learn from the past. This could go a long way in restoring elements of trust and confidence in U.S. leadership around the world, immediately benefiting a range of U.S. objectives, especially those relating to human rights protections and global accountability.

Importantly, this review should be part and parcel of much-needed broader efforts aimed to rebalance the errors and excesses the U.S. government pursued post-9/11 in the name of national security,[71] including a return to the constitutionally mandated sphere of concurrent authority over foreign affairs "under presidential management, but bounded by the checks provided by congressional consultation and judicial review."[72] Ultimately, choosing transparency and accountability is strategically advantageous to the United States by sustaining public trust amid a global crisis of democracy and building the partnerships needed to uphold rule of law principles within a changed geopolitical landscape.

[71] Oona Hathaway, *War Unbound: Gaza, Ukraine, and the Breakdown of International Law*, Foreign Aff. (July 16, 2024), https://www.foreignaffairs.com/ukraine/war-unbound-gaza-hathaway; Oona Hathaway, *For the Rest of the World, the U.S. President Has Always Been Above the Law*, Foreign Aff. (July 16, 2024), https://www.foreignaffairs.com/united-states/rest-world-us-president-has-always-been-above-law.

[72] Harold Hongju Koh, The National Security Constitution in the 21st Century 2 (2024).

IV

GLOBAL PERSPECTIVES ON THE WAR ON TERROR

8

The War on Terror and the *Jus Ad Bellum*

Sir Michael Wood KCMG, KC

Introduction

This chapter may seem somewhat out of place in the present volume. As is often the case when U.S. lawyers discuss the international use of force, other contributors mostly address U.S. law and politics. This is not said by way of criticism. U.S. foreign relations law is of great importance, and not only for U.S. lawyers.[1] The point is simply that the discussion tends to relegate questions of public international law governing recourse to force (*jus ad bellum*) to the background. International law, insofar as it is considered, is seen through the prism of U.S. politics. Some U.S. practitioners, however, especially those in the State Department or in the National Security Council, do engage seriously with the *jus ad bellum*, including in "legal diplomacy" with their colleagues in other countries,[2] or to persuade allies to join the United States in action whose legality they may find questionable.[3] This contribution does not aspire to join in the debates about U.S. law or politics; instead, it focuses on a particular aspect of the *jus ad bellum*: whether, and if so when, there is an international legal obligation to terminate armed conflict. This is considered against the background of the so-called global "war on terror" following 9/11, and recourse to force against non-state actors more generally, matters which are discussed by others in this volume and which seem to be central to the questions they raise about "perpetual" or "forever" war.

Some words of caution are in order. To begin with, it seems desirable to stress the importance of a careful use of terminology. For lawyers, at least, words matter. Clear and precise language is crucial to persuasive legal discourse. Publicists do no service to the law by employing obscure or even made-up

[1] *See, e.g.*, Sean Murphy & Edward Swaine, The Law of U.S. Foreign Relations (2023).

[2] On legal diplomacy, *see* John B. Bellinger III, *Luncheon Address: International Legal Public Diplomacy*, 83 Int'l L. Stud. 205 (U.S. Naval War Coll. 2007).

[3] A high-profile but by no means unique example occurred when the U.K. Attorney General visited Washington in January 2003 in order to hear U.S. views on the legality of invading Iraq. *See* William Taft, *The Bush (43rd) Administration—William H. Taft IV (2001–2005)*, *in* Shaping Foreign Policy in Times of Crisis. The Role of International Law and the State Department Legal Adviser 133 (Michael Scharf & Paul Williams eds., 1999).

Sir Michael Wood KCMG, KC, *The War on Terror and the* Jus Ad Bellum In: *Perpetual War and International Law*. Edited by: Brianna Rosen, Oxford University Press. © Oxford University Press 2026.
DOI: 10.1093/oso/9780197748992.003.0008

words, or ambiguous terms, which do not illuminate but confuse. Examples in the present context include "war on terror" and, I venture to suggest, "perpetual" or "forever" war. It sometimes seems to be sufficient to come up with a new term and weave around it some novel theory, of little interest beyond a narrow circle of writers, who proceed to debate the matter endlessly among themselves. In this regard I cannot do better than recall Jan Klabbers's words at the 2018 European Society of International Law Annual Conference:

> International law, in the academy, is no longer about what states do, but has become about what international lawyers do. We have lost touch with legal practice, and the discipline has become transfixed by methodological debates, . . . Instead of the fragmentation of international law being a concern, we should be worried about the fragmentation of international lawyers.[4]

A second note of caution concerns the suggestion that:

> Practitioners may have the luxury (if such it be) of only thinking about the here and now—about the case in front of them. But the more detached observer of the subject may feel some compulsion to try and identify trends, to speculate about the way matters are developing.[5]

That is not really the case. Practitioners, at least those advising governments, should (and for the most part probably do) take account of the effect of what states say and do on the development of the law, including customary international law.[6] In any event, it is essential that writers be clear about their purpose: do they seek to state existing law (*lex lata*) or to make policy proposals for what the law should be, in other words, proposals for developing the law or for entirely new law. Lawyers campaigning for certain policies seem particularly prone to blurring this distinction. The present contribution addresses the law as it is, not the law as some might wish it to be; nor does it address what might be termed "legal policy," which is covered in depth by Tess Bridgeman and Laura A. Dickinson in Chapters 13 and 14 of this volume, respectively.

[4] Jan Klabbers, *On Epistemic Universalism and the Melancholy of International Law*, keynote address to the European Society of International Law and 2018 Melland Schill lecture (2018), *in* 29 Eur. J. Int'l L. 1057, 1062 (Nov. 2018). I cited this and similar remarks in lectures delivered in 2020: *see* Michael Wood, International Law in Practice (2020), *in* Courses of the Summer School on Public International Law, Vol. XI, Int'l & Comp. L. Rsch. Center, especially at 27–31 (2020), https://iclrc.ru/storage/publication_pdf/35/%D0%A6%D0%9C%D0%A1%D0%9F%D0%98_%D0%A2%D0%BE%D0%BC_XI_13.01.2022_1689325409.pdf.

[5] Maurice Mendelson, *The Formation of Customary International Law*, 272 Recueil des Cours 155, 390 (1998).

[6] *See generally* Omri Sender & Michael Wood, Identification of Customary International Law (2024).

Third, some writers attach undue significance to government statements. They are all too ready to read novel legal positions into what is sometimes no more than political speech. They might ignore the context, and even the actual words used. Yet government statements are often intentionally worded so as to avoid taking clear legal positions; only rarely, outside litigation or a parliamentary or other inquiry, do governments make careful statements on questions of international law. For example, to express understanding or even support for another state's use of force is not necessarily to suggest that it is lawful. It seems, by now, to be generally agreed that the use by the United States and others of expressions such as "war on terror" or "global war on terror" was little more than political rhetoric, and misleading rhetoric at that.

What is more controversial is the influence, if any, of the 9/11 terrorist attacks and the responses thereto (by the United States and other states, as well as the United Nations) on the *jus ad bellum*. Much has been said and written about the intervention in Afghanistan launched on October 7, 2001 (Operation Enduring Freedom)[7] and subsequent actions against terrorists, such as the attacks on al-Qaeda,[8] and more generally on the use of force in self-defense against non-state actors.[9] But the discussion does not seem to have much to say about the legal implications of the term "war on terror" as such (except sometimes when considering the application of the *jus in bello*). That may itself be significant.

After these introductory remarks, the next section recalls briefly the broad elements of the *jus ad bellum*. This is followed by aspects of the law on the use of force against non-state actors, including terrorist groups. The penultimate section considers the notions of "perpetual" or "forever war" and in particular when and how wars end, before concluding.

The *Jus Ad Bellum*

Before turning to the global "war on terror" (GWOT) and the notion of perpetual war, it seems desirable to recall the broad and largely uncontested—among practitioners, at least—outlines of the *jus ad bellum*.[10] This is particularly so

[7] Michael Byers, *The Intervention in Afghanistan—2001*, *in* THE USE OF FORCE IN INTERNATIONAL LAW: A CASE-BASED APPROACH 625, 625–38 (T. Ruys, O. Corten, & A. Hofer eds., 2018).

[8] *See* Christopher Greenwood, *International Law and the "War Against Terrorism,"* 78 INT'L AFF. 301 (2002); C. Greenwood, *War, Terrorism and International Law*, 56 CURRENT LEGAL PROBS. 505 (2003), *reprinted in* CHRISTOPHER GREENWOOD, ESSAYS ON WAR IN INTERNATIONAL LAW 409–32 (2006).

[9] Among a wide literature, *see* MARY ELLEN O'CONNELL, CHRISTIAN J. TAMS, & DIRE TLADI, SELF-DEFENCE AGAINST NON-STATE ACTORS (2019).

[10] *See, among the vast literature*, INTERNATIONAL LAW ASSOCIATION, COMMITTEE ON THE USE OF FORCE, *Final Report on Aggression and the Use of Force*, SYDNEY CONFERENCE (2018). For recent writings, *see* RUSSELL BUCHAN & NICHOLAS TSAGOURIAS, REGULATING THE USE OF FORCE IN

given the many distortions of legal aspects of the GWOT[11] and the complexities often seen by some writing about counterterrorism operations. There is still no agreed definition in international law of "terrorism" or "international terrorism" or their derivatives.[12] The difficulties caused by this lack of definition, and the corresponding lack of definition of the term "counterterrorism," are highlighted elsewhere in this volume.[13]

The international use of force gives rise to acute political controversies, which may be reflected in disagreements among lawyers, who are sometimes rather simplistically seen as being divided into one of two camps: strict "dogmatists" and flexible "realists." This overlooks the fact that a practicing lawyer's main task is to apply the law as it is, in as neutral a way as he or she can.

The use of force is governed by international law in two ways: first, by the rules regulating recourse to force (the *jus ad bellum*), and second, by the rules concerning the methods employed when using force, or international humanitarian law, otherwise referred to as the law of armed conflict or the *jus in bello*. International human rights law and international criminal law may also play a role to some degree. This contribution focuses on the *jus ad bellum*.

The *jus ad bellum* is a dynamic area of international law, with a great deal of state practice; indeed, at times there seems to be almost daily practice.[14] The rules of the *jus ad bellum* are to be found in treaty provisions and in customary international law. Judgments of the International Court of Justice (ICJ) are a subsidiary means for determining the rules but need to be approached with some caution when they are case specific.

Exceptions to the Prohibition on the Use of Force

The prohibition of the threat or use of armed force is set forth in Article 2(4) of the United Nations (U.N.) Charter:

INTERNATIONAL LAW (2021); C. HENDERSON, THE USE OF FORCE AND INTERNATIONAL LAW (2d ed. 2024).

[11] The present author, who was Legal Adviser to the U.K. Foreign and Commonwealth Office from 1999 to 2006, used to think that it might also have been called GWOL (the Global War on Law).

[12] Efforts within the U.N. General Assembly to agree on a comprehensive convention against international terrorism have been ongoing since 1996, without success. *See also* Gilbert Guillaume, *Terrorisme et le droit international*, 215 RECUEIL DES COURS 287 (1989); TERRORISM AND INTERNATIONAL LAW (R. Higgins & M. Flory eds.,1997).

[13] *See* Fionnuala Ní Aoláin's contribution to this volume in Chapter 16, "Alternative Approaches to Counterterrorism."

[14] *See, e.g.*, the practice discussed in various blogs, as well as that gathered in the *Digest of State Practice* section of the JOURNAL ON THE USE OF FORCE AND INTERNATIONAL LAW (2014–present).

> Members shall refrain in their international relations from the threat or use of force against the territorial integrity or political independence of any state, or in any other manner inconsistent with the Purposes of the United Nations.[15]

The U.N. Charter contains two exceptions to the prohibition on the use of force: forcible measures taken or authorized by the Security Council under Chapter VII of the U.N. Charter, and force used in the exercise of the inherent right of individual or collective self-defense, the latter being part of customary international law and recognized in Article 51 of the U.N. Charter. The use of force upon request or with the consent of the territorial state ("intervention by invitation") does not fall within the prohibition in Article 2(4) of the U.N. Charter and is not a true exception.[16]

Under the U.N. Charter, primary responsibility for the maintenance of international peace and security is conferred upon the Security Council. The General Assembly only has the power to make recommendations. Chapter VII of the Charter provides that if the Security Council determines the existence of any threat to the peace, breach of the peace, or act of aggression, it may decide what measures shall be taken to maintain or restore international peace and security. Article 42 provides that the Council may take such action by air, sea, or land forces as may be necessary for that purpose. Under this provision, the Council may itself use force or authorize its use by others.

When Chapter VII was drafted, it was envisaged that armed forces would be made available to the Council by U.N. members and that these forces would operate under U.N. command. In practice, the Charter's collective security system has not generally operated in this way.[17] Since Iraq's invasion of Kuwait in 1990, the Council has tended to authorize one or more U.N. members to use "all necessary means" to achieve a particular objective. The limits of the authorization must be respected, as force beyond those limits will be unlawful unless justified on some other ground. Deciding what is within the limits of an authorization may be challenging, given the difficulty in interpreting Security Council resolutions, which reflect political compromise.[18]

The second exception to the prohibition on the use of force, the right of self-defense, is an inherent right of states recognized by Article 51 of the U.N. Charter:

[15] U.N. Charter art. 2, para. 4.

[16] A committee of the International Law Association has been studying "military assistance on request" since 2018.

[17] Erika De Wet & Michael Wood, *Collective Security*, MAX PLANCK ENCYCL. OF PUB. INT'L L. (2023).

[18] On the interpretation of Security Council resolutions, *see Accordance with International Law of the Unilateral Declaration of Independence in Respect of Kosovo*, Advisory Opinion, 2010 I.C.J. 402, 442, 94.

> Nothing in the present Charter shall impair the inherent right of individual or collective self-defense if an armed attack occurs against a Member of the United Nations, until the Security Council has taken the measures necessary to maintain international peace and security. Measures taken by Members in the exercise of this right of self-defense shall be immediately reported to the Security Council and shall not in any way affect the authority and responsibility of the Security Council under the present Charter to take at any time such action as it deems necessary in order to maintain or restore international peace and security.[19]

As the ICJ has observed, Article 51 of the Charter "may justify a use of force in self-defense only within the strict confines laid down therein. It does not allow the use of force by a State to protect perceived security interests beyond these."[20]

As stated in Article 51, the right of self-defense exists "if an armed attack occurs against a Member of the United Nations." The meaning of "armed attack" has been the subject of much debate.[21] It is widely thought to include a limited use of force to rescue nationals abroad. Despite what the ICJ has said about "mere frontier incidents" not rising to the level of an "armed attack,"[22] state practice suggests that small-scale border attacks involving the use of force are not excluded from the concept of an "armed attack" and may give rise to the right of self-defense, subject always to the conditions of necessity and proportionality. Otherwise there may be a gap, since reprisals involving the use of force are undoubtedly unlawful,[23] though politicians often—understandably but wrongly—use the language of retaliation or punishment.

It remains controversial whether the armed attack requirement means that an armed attack must have commenced,[24] or whether action may be taken in anticipation of an armed attack. Those supporting anticipatory self-defense nevertheless accept that only an imminent attack will justify the use of force in anticipatory self-defense and that there must be a reasonable and objective basis for concluding that an armed attack is imminent. Questions may arise as to what "imminence" means in today's world. The imminence criterion may

[19] U.N. Charter art. 51.

[20] *Armed Activities on the Territory of the Congo (Dem. Rep. Congo v. Uganda)*, Judgment, 2005 I.C.J. 168, 223–24, 148.

[21] *See* Adil Ahmad Haque, *The United Nations Charter at 75: Between Force and Self-Defense—Part One*, Just Security (June 24, 2020), https://www.justsecurity.org/70985/the-united-nations-charter-at-75-between-force-and-self-defense-part-one/.

[22] *Military and Paramilitary Activities in and against Nicaragua (Nicaragua v. United States of America)*, Judgment, 1986 I.C.J. 14, 103–04, 195.

[23] For a discussion, *see* Buchan & Tsagourias, *supra* note 10 at 43–50.

[24] Some supporting this position stretch the notion of occurrence: for Dinstein the attack had occurred provided it is on its way even if it had not reached the target. Yoram Dinstein, War, Aggression and Self-Defence 614 (6th ed. 2017).

need to be applied somewhat more flexibly in the face of new circumstances and new threats, including threats from non-state actors, given that in some circumstances the attack could become a reality at any moment and without warning. It has been suggested that this cannot be assessed solely in temporal terms. Nevertheless, a preemptive use of force to avert a non-imminent attack is not lawful.

Other possible exceptions to the prohibition on the use of force have been put forward (including a right to use force to avert an overwhelming humanitarian catastrophe); these remain controversial. States propounding novel justifications for the use of force should exercise caution since they might in future find their claims cited against themselves.

The prohibition on the use of force is widely accepted as a rule of *jus cogens* (a peremptory norm of general international law from which no derogation is permitted),[25] and a violation of the prohibition may amount to aggression. Fifty years ago, the U.N. General Assembly drew up a definition of aggression, but it was merely recommended to the Security Council.[26] Another definition of "crime of aggression" (together with a definition of "act of aggression") was added to the Rome Statute of the International Criminal Court (ICC), by amendments adopted at Kampala in 2010.[27] The amendments entered into force in 2017, but as of February 2024 had only been ratified or accepted by less than one-third of the States Parties to the Rome Statute.[28] These definitions are for the purpose of the Statute only and are not to be interpreted as limiting or prejudicing in any way existing or developing rules of international law for purposes other than the Rome Statute.[29]

It has sometimes been suggested that the international law on recourse to force is inadequate to meet modern challenges. The U.N. General Assembly rejected that view in its 2005 World Summit Outcome:

> We reaffirm that the relevant provisions of the Charter are sufficient to address the full range of threats to international peace and security. We further reaffirm the authority of the Security Council to mandate coercive action to maintain and restore international peace and security. We stress the importance of acting in accordance with the purposes and principles of the Charter.[30]

[25] *See* Annex, Int'l L. Comm'n, *Draft Conclusions on Identification and Legal Consequences of Peremptory Norms of General International Law (Jus Cogens)* (2022).

[26] *See* UNGA Resolution 3314 (XXIX) of 14 December 1974.

[27] Rome Statute of the ICC art. 8 *bis*, as amended by Resolution RC/Res. 6 of the Review Conference of the Rome Statute, June 11, 2010.

[28] As of September 2025, 49 of the 125 States Parties to the Rome Statute had accepted the Kampala amendments on the definition of the crime of aggression.

[29] This was expressly agreed in an understanding adopted in Kampala.

[30] G.A. Res. 60/1, 79, U.N. GAOR, 60th Sess., Supp. No. 1, U.N. Doc. A/RES/60/1 (Sept. 16, 2005).

My conclusion at the time was that, however much the world might have changed following 9/11, the international law on the use of force had not changed.[31] That remains my view and, I believe, is the view of most states and practitioners.

International Law and the Use of Force Against Terrorist Groups

Having set out briefly the essentials of the international law on the use of force, this chapter now turns to the so-called global "war on terror" and then to the notion of perpetual or forever war. In fact, none of these terms has any particular legal meaning or significance in international law.

Expressions such as "war on terrorism," "war on terror," and "global war on terror" are generally used in a nonlegal sense. Politicians use the rhetoric of war in all kinds of contexts, far removed from armed conflict—the war on drugs or obesity, for example.[32] Thus when asked in November 2001 whether the United Kingdom was legally at war, a foreign office minister (Baroness Amos) explained:

> The term "the war against terrorism" has been used to describe the whole campaign against terrorism, including military, political, financial, legislative and law enforcement measures.[33]

The United States is on record in similar terms: in 2006, the State Department Legal Adviser observed:

> We do not believe we are in a legal state of war with every terrorist everywhere in the world. Rather, the United States uses the term "global war on terrorism" to mean that all countries must strongly oppose, and must fight against, terrorism in all its forms, everywhere around the globe.[34]

In other words, the term is used in a political, not a legal sense.[35] State officials may find it politically attractive to use terms such as "terrorists," "terrorism," or

[31] *See* Michael Wood, *Terrorism and the International Law on the Use of Force*, *in* Research Handbook on International Law and Terrorism 180, 180–91 (Ben Saul ed., 2d ed. 2020); *see also* Sir Michael Wood, *International Law and the Use of Force: What Happens in Practice?*, U.N. Audiovisual Library of Int'l Law (Nov. 5, 2015), https://legal.un.org/avl/ls/Wood_PS.html.

[32] Michael Wood & Eran Sthoeger, The UN Security Council and International Law 131 (2022).

[33] U.K. Parl. Deb. (HL), 22 Nov. 2001, col. WA153 (written answers), available at https://publications.parliament.uk/pa/ld200102/ldhansrd/vo011122/text/11122w01.htm.

[34] *See* John B. Bellinger III, *Legal Issues in the War on Terror*, London School of Economics (Oct. 31, 2006), available at https://2009-2017.state.gov/s/l/2006/98861.htm.

[35] Greenwood put it well: "References to the attacks as 'acts of war', like the subsequent talk of a 'war on terrorism', are understandable in political terms but are not to be taken as referring to the

"the (global) war on terrorism," but these too add little to legal clarity. Much has been said and written about the international law relating to the use of force against non-state actors, including terrorist groups.[36] The main questions seem to be whether the right of self-defense applies at all in response to attacks by non-state actors; if so, whether there is a right of "anticipatory self-defense"; and, if so, how the imminence requirement applies in relation to attacks by terrorist groups.

When and How Should Wars End?

Terms like "perpetual war" and "forever war" seem to be of recent origin and aimed at conveying the notion of a single everlasting armed conflict. Yet even if in theory such a conflict might exist, in practice there has been no such thing. There have been lengthy armed conflicts or, more commonly, lengthy series of armed conflicts, both of an international and non-international nature (such as the Hundred Years' War, the Wars of the Roses, and the Thirty Years' War). Such conflicts may have seemed to be indefinite at the time, but they do in fact end. Perpetual war may be no more than a convenient term to convey a concern that a conflict has lasted too long and should come to an end.

Both "war" and "perpetual war" raise questions for a lawyer. First, is "war" the best term in modern international law? It would be more usual nowadays for lawyers to speak of "armed conflict."[37] The old technicalities surrounding the meaning of "war" are scarcely relevant in the Charter era. Then there is a need to distinguish between international armed conflict and non-international armed conflict, as well as situations below the threshold of armed conflict. And are we considering a single armed conflict or several conflicts? If the latter, as was the case with the global war on terror in the early 2000s, we surely need to consider them individually, since to conflate several conflicts may lead to confusion and muddled thinking.

Quite a lot has been written about how wars end or, more accurately in today's world, how armed conflicts end.[38] This may be by peace treaty or other agreement, a decision of the U.N. Security Council, unconditional surrender, a cease-fire, truce or pause, or simply a cessation of hostilities. Less has been written, by

concept of war in international law." Greenwood, *International Law and the "War Against Terrorism,"* *supra* note 8 at 306.

[36] *See, e.g.*, Self-Defence Against Non-State Actors, *supra* note 9.

[37] *See* Andrew Clapham, War 1–40 (2021); Yoram Dinstein, *supra* note 24, at 7.

[38] Sydney Bailey, How Wars End: The United Nations and the Termination of Armed Conflict 1946–1964 (1982).

lawyers at any rate, about when armed conflicts should end, a key gap that Tom Dannenbaum seeks to fill in Chapter 19 of this volume. Perhaps this is because the latter is usually a matter of policy or politics, and normally requires assent by all parties to the conflict. Indeed, while the issue may be framed as a legal question, that does not mean it is entirely determined by law, though the law may be relevant.

Limitations on the Use of Force

The elementary proposition that the *jus ad bellum* permits the use of force in certain circumstances, but those circumstances import limits, seems to answer the question of limitations on the use of force insofar as it concerns public international law. So we should look in turn at the two exceptions to the prohibition of the use of force described earlier.

Any authorization of the use of force by the U.N. Security Council may be limited in various ways. First, force may be expressly time-limited by the Security Council itself. Second, the purpose of the authorization will itself be defined and thus limited by the Security Council resolution. Moreover, force may be used only if it is necessary to achieve the purposes laid down by the Security Council. While such authorizations are by no means always clear, to put it mildly, they are to be interpreted in good faith in accordance with their terms. And the Council may of course change or terminate the authorization.

Turning to self-defense, according to Article 51 of the Charter, the use of force in exercise of the inherent right of individual or collective self-defense is only permitted "until the Security Council has taken the measures necessary to maintain international peace and security."[39] The question whether the Council has taken such measures depends on how effective the Council's measures are, an assessment of which would seem to be, at least in the first place, for the state or states acting in self-defense. More importantly in practice, self-defense must be limited to what is necessary and proportionate. There is much practice and learning on these key conditions, which may require that the armed conflict end, though this might entail a mixed political and legal judgment.

Conclusion

This chapter is an attempt to suggest that matters are not as obscure as some writers would have us believe. The *jus ad bellum* is relatively easy to state, even

[39] U.N. Charter art. 51.

if it is not always easy to apply to the facts (assuming one knows the facts, which commentators often do not).

A number of important questions arise in connection with the use of force against terrorist groups, ranging from the exercise of the inherent right of self-defense against non-state actors, to how the criterion of imminence may apply in such cases. To introduce notions such as "global war on terror" or "perpetual" or "forever" war, whatever their interest may be to international relations experts, adds unnecessary complications to the legal debate. In international law, these expressions have no particular meaning or significance.

9

Europe's Role in Perpetual War

From Counterpoint to Convergence

Anthony Dworkin

Introduction

The global "war on terror" was a U.S. construct, but it evolved in the broader context of European legal policymaking, as U.S. allies also wrestled with how to respond to transnational terrorism. Conventional wisdom holds that European countries provided a more principled counterpoint to the United States by adhering to a traditional view of armed conflict and treating terrorism outside areas of active hostilities as a law enforcement matter.[1] European governments denied that there could be a global armed conflict against non-state groups and therefore rejected the legal claims underpinning many U.S. drone strikes and the detention regime at Guantánamo Bay. While they cooperated in some cases with U.S. operations, these divergent views constrained European support and helped prompt limited changes in U.S. policies on targeted killing due to the influential nature of the transatlantic partnership.[2]

This account has elements of truth. European legal positions differed from those adopted by the United States in meaningful ways, and this had some impact on European-U.S. cooperation and on the evolution of U.S. policy. Yet this vision of Europe's role significantly understates the extent to which the posture of the United States and of the most militarily active European countries regarding the use of armed force against terrorist groups became progressively

[1] *See, e.g.*, the comments of the former EU Counter-Terrorism Coordinator Gilles de Kerchove distinguishing the European Union's "more traditional approach" from the U.S. "war on terror narrative" based around the notion of "an overarching global armed conflict against Al-Qaeda and/or the IS," and arguing that "in the EU, the balance between security and human rights remains." *Interview with Gilles de Kerchove*, 103 Int'l. Rev. Red Cross 51, 54 (2021). *See also* Jörg Monar, *The EU's Approach Post-September 11: Global Terrorism as a Multidimensional Law Enforcement Challenge*, 20 Cambridge Rev. Int'l Aff. 267, 268 (2007); Gilles de Kerchove & Christiane Höhn, *Counter-Terrorism and International Law Since 9/11, Including in the EU-US Context*, 16 Y.B Int'l Humanitarian L. 267, 269 (2013); Eliza Manningham-Buller, *Securing Freedom: Terror*, BBC Reith Lecture (Sept. 6, 2011), https://downloads.bbc.co.uk/rmhttp/radio4/transcripts/2011_reith3.pdf.

[2] Laura T. Dickinson, *National Security Policymaking in the Shadow of International Law*, 2021 Utah L. Rev. 629, 652–70 (2021).

Anthony Dworkin, *Europe's Role in Perpetual War* In: *Perpetual War and International Law*.
Edited by: Brianna Rosen, Oxford University Press.
DOI: 10.1093/oso/9780197748992.003.0009

more closely aligned in the years after September 11, 2001. While rejecting the notion of a global armed conflict against al-Qaeda and affiliated groups, France, the United Kingdom, and other European countries not only supported many U.S. drone strikes but also embraced the targeted killing of terrorist suspects, often carried out with armed drones, and accepted the open-ended detention of members of armed groups.[3] The evolving nature of terrorist groups, the threat to Europe from attacks organized overseas, and changes in the way the United States characterized some of its military operations contributed to a growing convergence between U.S. and European counterterrorist practices.

These developments should prompt a reassessment of the assumptions underlying many critiques of the U.S. campaign against terrorist groups since 9/11. Critics of the United States often focus on the disputed notion of a global armed conflict as the foundation of the most problematic aspects of the war on terror, including the use of practices associated with battlefield conditions in anomalous contexts and the seemingly endless nature of the authority that the United States claims to target and detain enemy fighters.[4] But European countries that rejected the idea of a global armed conflict nevertheless have conducted targeted killings outside of conventional battlefields and persisted in drawn-out, low-intensity military campaigns against armed groups.[5]

The record of European countries suggests that a complete reckoning with the problematic actions associated with counterterrorism wars will involve questioning some of the legal positions on which European countries and the United States have agreed. In particular, to rein in the expansive and temporally open-ended targeting and detention practices that these wars have involved, it is essential to reconsider the extent of the authority that states possess to use force in such conflicts. We can most plausibly locate the root of the expansive targeting and detention of alleged terrorists since 9/11 in the assumption shared by European and American governments that the existence of a non-international armed conflict (NIAC) in itself gives authority for a state involved to target or detain members of the armed forces of opposing non-state groups on the basis of their status. This assumption has solidified into a transatlantic consensus in the past two decades, yet it remains legally unconvincing and dangerous in its implications. In place of this consensus, we need a new reflection on

[3] *See infra* notes 26–62 and accompanying text.

[4] On the former point, *see e.g.*, Marco Sassòli, *Use and Abuse of the Laws of War In the War on Terrorism*, 22 MINN. J.L. & INEQUALITY 195 (2004); on the latter point, *see* Marko Milanovic, *Accounting for the Complexity of the Law Applicable to Modern Armed Conflicts*, *in* COMPLEX BATTLESPACES: THE LAW OF ARMED CONFLICT AND THE DYNAMICS. OF MODERN WARFARE 33, 51 (Christopher M. Ford & Winston S. Williams eds., 2019) (arguing that the difficulty of fixing an end to NIAC "becomes greater by an order of magnitude if the question is asked with respect to the global NIAC with Al-Qaeda and its affiliates, the 'forever war' . . . ").

[5] This is particularly true of France and the United Kingdom. *See infra* notes 26–58 and accompanying text.

how to understand the limits on the state's authority for the use of force in NIAC, which, I argue, arise from the operation of human rights law.[6] In the wake of the October 7 terrorist attacks by Hamas against Israel and Israel's military response, it is more critical than ever to revisit the legal framework governing conflicts between states and non-state groups.

Europe's Critical Distance from the Early War on Terror

After a U.S. drone strike on alleged al-Qaeda members in Yemen in November 2002—the first such action outside the conventional war zone in Afghanistan—Sweden's foreign minister Anna Lindh described the attack as "a summary execution that violates human rights."[7] Few, if any, serving European officials were to repeat such a strong public comment on targeted killings by U.S. forces in the ensuing years. Instead, European governments showed a marked reluctance to criticize U.S. drone strikes, in contrast to their earlier condemnation of targeted killings carried out by Israel.[8] Europe seemingly was unwilling to charge a close security partner with violations of international law, or to draw any more attention to questions about the lawfulness of U.S. actions. Nevertheless, European countries refrained from officially endorsing the legality of U.S. drone strikes in countries such as Pakistan, Somalia, and Yemen, and some opposition politicians continued to criticize them in the strongest terms.[9]

Moreover, extensive background conversations with legal officials in European countries in the years after 2008 indicate that some of the views underlying Lindh's comments about the legality of U.S. drone strikes were widely shared.[10] European officials disagreed with the U.S. position that an armed conflict without territorial limitation could exist between the United States and al-Qaeda, the Taliban, and "associated forces." Instead, they largely maintained that a NIAC—which they agreed encompassed any conflict between a state and non-state actor—must be confined to a specific theater or region of

[6] *See infra* notes 76–81 and accompanying text.

[7] Walter Pincus, *Missile Strike Carried Out with Yemeni Cooperation*, WASH. POST (Nov. 6, 2002), https://www.washingtonpost.com/archive/politics/2002/11/06/missile-strike-carried-out-with-yemeni-cooperation/db580142-c920-4fec-95cf-24c90b29b8de/.

[8] ANTHONY DWORKIN, EUROPEAN COUNCIL ON FOREIGN RELATIONS, DRONES AND TARGETED KILLING: DEFINING A EUROPEAN POSITION 2 (2013); JESSICA DORSEY & CHRISTOPHE PAULUSSEN, INTERNATIONAL CENTER FOR COUNTER-TERRORISM, TOWARDS A EUROPEAN POSITION ON ARMED DRONES AND TARGETED KILLING: SURVEYING EU COUNTERTERRORISM PERSPECTIVES 5 (2015); Elisabeth Schweiger, *"Targeted killing" and the Lack of Acquiescence*, 32 LEIDEN J. INT'L. L. 741 (2019).

[9] *Political Leaders Call Obama "Assassin" for Use of Drones*, COPENHAGEN POST (July 25, 2012), https://cphpost.dk/2012-07-25/general/political-leaders-call-obama-assassin-for-use-of-drones/.

[10] DWORKIN, *supra* note 8, at 7–10; ANTHONY DWORKIN, EUROPEAN COUNCIL ON FOREIGN RELATIONS, EUROPE'S NEW COUNTER-TERROR WARS 10–14 (2016).

hostilities.[11] While officials were unwilling to define precisely how far such an armed conflict could extend, at least some U.S. drone strikes appeared to fall outside of any armed conflict so defined.[12] This meant that there could be no authority for such strikes from the perspective of international humanitarian law (IHL), and a more restrictive set of rules would govern the state's targeting practices, drawn from human rights law and the right of self-defense. This position was articulated by Swedish Foreign Minister Carl Bildt in an answer to a question in Parliament in June 2013: "If a drone attack—or an attack with any other weapon—does not take place in the context of an armed conflict, the laws of war do not apply. States' ability to lawfully use force against individuals is thus sharply curtailed. The premise is that a suspect must be arrested and brought to justice in accordance with the procedural safeguards applicable under Human Rights Law."[13]

Despite this stance, European countries cooperated in various ways with U.S. drone operations. For example, European countries reportedly shared intelligence for drone strikes, allowed U.S. bases in their countries to be used to track potential targets, and participated in joint operations planning.[14] Danish citizen Morten Storm claimed he had used his access to jihadist circles in Yemen to help U.S. agents track and kill the radical cleric Anwar al-Awlaki in 2011 with the knowledge of Danish intelligence services.[15] However, these alleged links proved embarrassing for the states concerned. The British and German governments faced lawsuits over their support for U.S. drone strikes, while the Danish Parliament's Legal Affairs Committee questioned the government for its role in Awlaki's killing.[16]

[11] For a public statement of this position, see the written statement of the Security Policy Department of the Ministry of Foreign Affairs of the Netherlands that "the Netherlands does not consider it possible that a non-international armed conflict (NIAC) can exist without finite geographical boundaries," quoted in DORSEY & PAULUSSEN, *supra* note 8, at 33. *See also* Dickinson, *supra* note 2, at 654–59.

[12] For a statement from a French government legal official indicating that non-international armed conflict need not be confined within the boundaries of a single state, *see* Nicolas Hervieu, *Entretien avec Claire Landais, Directrice des affaires juridiques du Ministère de la Défense*, 7 REVUE DES DROITS DE L'HOMME [online] (June 5, 2015), https://journals.openedition.org/revdh/1309#quotation.

[13] Quoted in DORSEY & PAULUSSEN, *supra* note 8, at 41.

[14] AMNESTY INTERNATIONAL, DEADLY ASSISTANCE: THE ROLE OF EUROPEAN STATES IN US DRONE STRIKES 36–75 (2018); Namir Shabibi & Jack Watling, *Exclusive: How the UK Secretly Helped Direct Lethal US Drone Strikes in Yemen*, VICE NEWS (Apr. 7, 2016), https://www.vice.com/en/article/exclusive-how-the-uk-secretly-helped-direct-lethal-us-drone-strikes-in-yemen/; Herbert Gude, *German Jihadist Killed in US Drone Attack*, SPIEGEL INT'L (Apr. 30, 2012), https://www.spiegel.de/international/world/german-citizen-killed-in-us-air-strike-after-joining-the-jihad-a-830585.html.

[15] Joby Warrick, *Danish Former Jihadist Claims to Have Aided U.S. Attack on al-Qaeda Leader Anwar al-Awlaki*, WASH. POST (Oct. 10, 2012), https://www.washingtonpost.com/world/national-security/danish-former-jihadist-claims-to-have-aided-us-attack-on-al-qaeda-leader-anwar-al-awlaki/2012/10/10/0735efd8-131d-11e2-a16b-2c110031514a_story.html.

[16] Jennifer Gibson, *The US's Covert Drone War and the Search for Answers: Turning to European Courts for Accountability*, *in* EUROPEAN CENTER FOR CONSTITUTIONAL AND HUMAN RIGHTS, LITIGATING DRONE STRIKES: CHALLENGING THE GLOBAL NETWORK OF REMOTE KILLING 102

Moreover, European states took steps to limit their involvement with U.S. actions and protect their officials from being held liable for actions that did not conform with the European interpretation of international law. The former U.K. Security and Intelligence Coordinator Sir David Omand signed a letter with other public figures in 2014 calling on the government to disclose "the guidance and restrictions concerning the passing or use of UK intelligence" that could be used in U.S. drone strikes, in order to "reassure an anxious public that the UK government will protect personnel from inadvertent collusion in counter-terrorism operations contrary to our understanding of the law."[17] The German Interior Ministry reportedly instituted a policy of not allowing its domestic intelligence agency to pass information to the United States that could be used for drone strikes on German citizens.[18]

U.S. officials acknowledged European concerns. As President Barack Obama's counterterrorism adviser, John Brennan, said in 2011, "The effectiveness of our counterterrorism activities depends on the assistance and cooperation of our allies . . . But their participation must be consistent with their laws, including their interpretation of international law."[19] Brennan argued that, in practice, U.S. and European views were not as far apart as might be thought, as the United States often conducted strikes away from the battlefield on the basis of what it perceived as an imminent threat.[20] Two years later, President Obama codified and extended this approach of discretionary restraint in the Presidential Policy Guidance (PPG) governing drone strikes outside areas of active hostilities, policy guidance that was revived in a modified form in President Joe Biden's Presidential Policy Memorandum (PPM).[21] Some European officials interpreted the changes, in part, as a response to European concerns.[22]

(2017); Amrit Singh & Jessica Scholes, *Denmark, the CIA, and the Killing of Anwar al-Awlaki*, Open Society Justice Initiative (Apr. 30, 2014), https://www.justiceinitiative.org/voices/denmark-cia-and-killing-anwar-al-awlaki.

[17] Kiran Stacey, *Publish Guidance on Lethal Drone Strikes, Says Former GCHQ Chief*, Fin. Times (Nov. 26, 2014), https://www.ft.com/content/c9a38848-73ea-11e4-92bc-00144feabdc0.

[18] Holger Stark, *Germany Limits Information Exchange with US Intelligence*, Spiegel Int'l (May 17, 2011), https://www.spiegel.de/international/germany/drone-killing-debate-germany-limits-information-exchange-with-us-intelligence-a-762873.html.

[19] John O. Brennan, Assistant to the President for Homeland Sec. & Counterterrorism, Remarks to the Harvard Law School Program on Law & Security: Strengthening our Security by Adhering to our Values and Laws (Sept. 16, 2011), https://obamawhitehouse.archives.gov/the-press-office/2011/09/16/remarks-john-o-brennan-strengthening-our-security-adhering-our-values-an.

[20] *Id.*

[21] White House, *Fact Sheet: U.S. Policy Standards and Procedures for the Use of Force in Counterterrorism Operations Outside the United States and Areas of Active Hostilities* (May 23, 2013), https://obamawhitehouse.archives.gov/the-press-office/2013/05/23/fact-sheet-us-policy-standards-and-procedures-use-force-counterterrorism.

[22] Dorsey & Paulussen, *supra* note 8, at 19.

A similar process took place with respect to the U.S. detention regime at Guantánamo Bay. Even leaving aside the "black sites" program of secret detention and torture of the early years of the war on terror, which Federica D'Alessandra and Alberto J. Mora examine in Chapter 7 of this volume, many European officials viewed the mere existence of Guantánamo as a violation of fundamental legal principles. The British Law Lord, Lord Steyn, described it in 2003 as a "legal black hole."[23] While some European countries cooperated with the black sites program and were reportedly involved in the interrogation of prisoners at Guantánamo, they took steps to avoid handing prisoners to the United States who could end up at the detention camp.[24] Obama referred to international condemnation of Guantánamo and the European refusal to transfer prisoners who could be sent there when discussing his policy of not taking additional prisoners to the site and his goal of closing it, even as his administration continued to argue in court that the detention regime was justified as part of a continuing armed conflict.[25]

The Turn in European Policy

While the Obama administration debated how to accommodate European concerns, developments were underway that would lead to significant changes in European policy.[26] The European rejection of U.S. legal claims was rooted in the view that NIACs had to be confined to a limited geographical space. But where terrorist groups were participating in internal armed conflicts against western partners, counterterrorist strikes could be presented as a military action in support of host state forces. Some European support for U.S. drone strikes, while covert, appears to have been justified in this way. In a revealing passage in his memoirs, former British Prime Minister David Cameron wrote that, in Pakistan, "the terrorists were assisting the Taliban against the government in neighbouring Afghanistan, and so were legitimate targets of the U.S. drone programme. So we could support that."[27] Cameron adds that al-Qaeda operatives in Yemen were also legitimate targets because the United States was helping the government

[23] Johan Steyn, *Guantanamo Bay: The Legal Black Hole*, 53 INT'L & COMPAR. L.Q. 1, 1 (2004).

[24] Sibylle Scheipers, *Closing Guantanamo: Is Europe Ready?*, 51 SURVIVAL 5, 6 (2009).

[25] President Barack Obama, Remarks by the President at the National Defense University, Washington D.C. (May 23, 2013), https://obamawhitehouse.archives.gov/the-press-office/2013/05/23/remarks-president-national-defense-university; Respondent's Memorandum Regarding the Government's Detention Authority Relative to Detainees Held at Guantánamo Bay, In re: Guantánamo Bay Detainee Litig., Misc. No. 08-0442, at 1 (D.D.C. Mar. 13, 2009).

[26] For a detailed account of these developments, on which the following section draws, *see* DWORKIN, *supra* note 10.

[27] DAVID CAMERON, FOR THE RECORD 598 (2019).

against a terrorist insurgency.[28] The German Federal Administrative Court ruled in 2020, in a case examining the role of the U.S. Ramstein Air Base in Germany in drone strikes in Yemen, that these strikes took place in the context of a NIAC between al-Qaeda in the Arabian Peninsula and the Islamic State of Iraq and Syria (ISIS) and the U.S.-supported Yemen government, and therefore their legality should be assessed under IHL.[29]

In the years after 2011, more of the areas where jihadist groups were active became the sites of local armed conflicts as hostilities between these groups and host state forces widened. The armed groups involved in these conflicts pursued a hybrid strategy, combining terrorist attacks with more conventional insurgency. In response, European governments came to intervene in cooperation with local authorities, employing techniques that were often remarkably similar in practice to U.S. operations.

In its original incarnation, al-Qaeda had been reluctant to seize and occupy territory.[30] But in 2012, a collection of jihadist groups seized control of large parts of northern Mali, and the following year launched an offensive into the center of the country. In 2014, ISIS broke out of the foothold it had established in Syria and captured a significant part of Iraq, including the city of Mosul. An ISIS affiliate in Libya took advantage of the country's disorder to establish a sizable area of control around Sirte.[31] In Yemen, al-Qaeda in the Arabian Peninsula evolved from a small organization primarily focused on western targets to an insurgent movement able to control territory and challenge state authorities.[32]

In the face of these developments, European countries became involved in military campaigns designed to roll back the armed groups' advances. Because the action in which Europeans took part had a counterinsurgent character, it did not seem to contravene the European claim that terrorism outside war zones should be treated as a law enforcement matter. As a German official put it, "a classic terrorist group should not be a target of military operations, but if the group is creating military forces, then it becomes a target for military operations."[33] In 2013, France launched the military campaign Operation Serval to prevent jihadist groups from overrunning Mali. Several European countries joined the coalition of countries conducting a campaign against ISIS in 2014.

[28] *Id.*

[29] Federal Administrative Court (Germany), Judgment of 25 November 2020 – BVerwG 6 C 7.19 § 72.

[30] United States Institute of Peace, The Jihadi Threat: Isis, al-Qaeda, and Beyond 19 (2016); William McCants, The ISIS Apocalypse 64–69 (2016).

[31] Cameron Glenn, *Libya's Islamists: Who They Are—And What They Want*, Wilson Center (Aug. 8, 2017), https://www.wilsoncenter.org/article/libyas-islamists-who-they-are-and-what-they-want.

[32] International Crisis Group, Yemen's al-Qaeda, Expanding the Base 6 (2017).

[33] Dworkin, *supra* note 10, at 2.

But European countries did not limit themselves to conventional counterinsurgency tactics in these campaigns. Confronting groups that combined insurgency and terrorist attacks, including attacks against European targets, European forces also waged hybrid campaigns. Alongside classic military engagements, they conducted operations that resembled counterterrorist strikes of the form that the United States had been carrying out for the previous decade. France's Operation Serval quickly succeeded in its initial mission of recapturing territory that had been seized by jihadist groups.[34] These groups had not been destroyed, however, and they repositioned themselves across neighboring states and continued to mount terrorist attacks.[35] In response, France announced a new iteration of its intervention, Operation Barkhane, that would extend the fight against armed groups across these countries with the consent of the states involved.[36]

According to French government lawyers, France believed that the armed conflict between Mali, supported by France, and jihadist groups allowed it to target fighters on the territory of neighboring states, as these engagements took place "within an indisputable operational continuum."[37] Much of Barkhane consisted of attempts to track and kill these groups' members as they moved across a large expanse of barely governed territory. In the words of French Defense Minister Jean-Yves Le Drian, France was "pursuing counterterrorism across the whole of the Sahel-Saharan strip."[38]

As part of Barkhane, French forces carried out a series of strikes against clearly identified targets, including a long roster of high-profile members of most of the region's jihadist groups.[39] France also at times carried out "signature strikes" against individuals who were thought to display the characteristics of members of armed groups.[40] Yet these actions did little to reduce the activity of jihadist groups in the region. As a result, French operations appeared potentially open-ended, though they have been radically scaled back following a series of coups in Sahel states that led to demands for the withdrawal of French

[34] Sergei Boeke & Bart Schuurman, *Operation "Serval": A Strategic Analysis of the French Intervention in Mali, 2013–2014*, 38 J. Strategic Stud. 801, 813–16 (2015).

[35] Nathaniel Powell, *Why France Failed in Mali*, War on the Rocks (Feb. 21, 2022), https://warontherocks.com/2022/02/why-france-failed-in-mali/; Andrew Lebovich, *The Hotel Attacks and Militant Realignment in the Sahara-Sahel Region*, 9 CTC Sentinel 22 (2016).

[36] *François Hollande's African Adventures*, Economist (July 21, 2014), https://www.economist.com/europe/2014/07/21/francois-hollandes-african-adventures.

[37] Hervieu, *supra* note 12.

[38] David Revault d'Allones, Les Guerres du Président 149–50 (2015, passage translated by author).

[39] Christophe Châtelot, *How France Was Driven Out of the Sahel*, Le Monde (Sept. 5, 2023), https://www.lemonde.fr/en/france/article/2023/09/05/how-france-was-driven-out-of-the-sahel_6124522_7.html.

[40] Rebecca Mignot-Mahdavi, *Frappe de Bounti: la France conduit-elle des « frappes signatures » au Sahel?*, Revue des Droits de l'Homme: Actualités Droits-Libertés (Apr. 19, 2021), https://journals.openedition.org/revdh/11718.

troops.[41] France's record in the Sahel shows how the distinction between counterinsurgency and counterterrorism operations can blur in a context of regional disorder, and how the legal framework of a geographically contained armed conflict can provide the foundation for an expansive, low-intensity, and drawn-out campaign of strikes against a range of terrorist groups.

By contrast, European forces participated in high-intensity military campaigns in Iraq and Syria designed to recover and hold territory that had been captured by ISIS. Yet this conflict was also hybrid. Alongside its conventional military operations in the region, ISIS tried to encourage radicalization and to organize attacks on European territory. To counter this activity, some European countries carried out or supported targeted strikes that were often disconnected from military action on the ground. In August 2015, for example, Britain launched a drone strike in Raqqa, Syria, that killed the British jihadist Reyaad Khan and two other men. According to British security services, Khan had tried to recruit British members for ISIS and organize attacks in the United Kingdom.[42] At the time he was killed, the U.K. government was conducting operations against ISIS in Iraq, but not in Syria. British Prime Minister David Cameron told the House of Commons that the action was "a targeted strike to deal with a clear, credible and specific terrorist threat to our country at home."[43]

Despite the apparent clarity of this statement, the full account of the legal basis for the strike that the British government presented was more complicated. The government argued that the use of force was justified both as an act of individual self-defense against an imminent threat to the United Kingdom and as part of the collective self-defense of Iraq against an armed group that operated across the Iraq-Syria border.[44] Government lawyers relied on the existence of an armed conflict "taking place in Syria and crossing over into Iraq" in which the fighters killed in the attack were participants to deflect calls for a judicial review of the action.[45] But Cameron's memoirs suggest that, for him, the attack was part of an effort to supplement the U.S. program of counterterrorist drone strikes.[46] Cameron

[41] On the open-ended nature of France's military campaign, *see* Rebecca Mignot-Mahdavi, *Rethinking Direct Participation in Hostilities and Continuous Combat Function in Light of Targeting Members of Terrorist Groups*, 105 Int'l. Rev. Red Cross 1028, 1029–31 (2022); on the scaling back of the French campaign, *see* Cyril Bensimon et al., *The Insurmountable Failure of France's Strategy in the Sahel*, Le Monde (Nov. 4, 2023), https://www.lemonde.fr/en/international/article/2023/11/04/the-insurmountable-failure-of-france-s-strategy-in-the-sahel_6226447_4.html.

[42] Intelligence and Security Committee of Parliament, UK Lethal Drone Strikes in Syria 7–11, HC1152 (Apr. 26, 2017).

[43] David Cameron, *Syria: Refugees and Counter-Terrorism, Prime Minister's Statement to the House of Commons* (Sept. 7, 2015), https://www.gov.uk/government/speeches/syria-refugees-and-counter-terrorism-prime-ministers-statement.

[44] UK Parliament Joint Committee on Human Rights, HL Paper 141/HC 574, The Government's Policy on the Use of Drones for Targeted Killing 41–42 (2016).

[45] *Id.* at 31.

[46] Cameron, *supra* note 27, at 599.

also wrote that the United Kingdom had worked "hand in glove" with the United States to track other British jihadists such as Junaid Hussain and Mohammed Emwazi, who were killed in American drone strikes.[47] Later in 2015, the United Kingdom formally began military operations in Syria against ISIS, and British drone strikes against ISIS fighters were significantly stepped up.[48] Although ISIS lost its last territorial base in 2019, the United Kingdom's counter-ISIS operation remained active long after that; U.K. forces carried out a drone strike against an alleged ISIS fighter in Syria as recently as June 2024.[49]

France did not acknowledge any strikes against individual fighters in Iraq or Syria. But according to media reports, French special forces worked with local forces to identify and kill French citizens who had joined ISIS.[50] France reportedly provided the names and coordinates of up to thirty French citizens to Iraqi forces, with the aim of preventing the individuals from returning to France, where authorities would be obliged to handle them within the criminal justice system.[51] Assuming the reports are accurate, these actions seem more like targeted killings under the cover of armed conflict than conventional counterinsurgency operations. French media reports also describe a preparatory note for a meeting at the Élysée in November 2015 recommending that strikes designed to kill French jihadists should be described as being aimed at training camps as part of an effort "to avoid further debate on the issue of targeted strikes/extrajudicial executions."[52]

In conversations with two French journalists for a book published in 2016, French President François Hollande admitted to having ordered at least four targeted killings.[53] The journalist Vincent Nouzille claims that the true number of French targeted killings between 2013 and 2016 was at least forty.[54]

[47] *Id.* at 598.

[48] Chris Cole, *Operation Without End: Time to halt UK's Now Decade-Long Air War in Iraq and Syria*, DRONE WARS (Aug. 12, 2024), https://dronewars.net/2024/08/12/operation-without-end-time-to-halt-uks-now-decade-long-air-war-in-iraq-and-syria/#more-19342.

[49] UK MINISTRY OF DEFENSE, *RAF Air Strikes in Iraq and Syria: January to December 2024* (Dec. 16, 2024), https://www.gov.uk/government/publications/british-forces-air-strikes-in-iraq-monthly-list/raf-air-strikes-in-iraq-and-syria-january-to-april-2024.

[50] Tamer El-Ghobashy, Maria Abi-Habib, & Benoit Faucon, *France's Special Forces Hunt French Militants Fighting for Islamic State*, WALL ST. J. (May 29, 2017), https://www.wsj.com/articles/frances-special-forces-hunt-french-militants-fighting-for-islamic-state-1496090116.

[51] *Id.*

[52] Gérard Davet & Fabrice Lhomme, *Comment Hollande autorise "l'exécution ciblée" de terroristes*, LE MONDE (Jan. 4, 2017, 8:49PM), https://www.lemonde.fr/societe/article/2017/01/04/comment-hollande-autorise-l-execution-ciblee-de-terroristes_5057421_3224.html (translation by author).

[53] *Id.*

[54] *François Hollande et "Le Permis de Tuer,"* LE MONDE [extracts from VINCENT NOUZILLE, ERREURS FATALES] (Jan. 4, 2017), https://www.lemonde.fr/police-justice/article/2017/01/04/francois-hollande-et-le-permis-de-tuer_5057277_1653578.html. However, the director of France's military intelligence service denied that France had conducted targeted killings of high-value targets: *see* Pierre Alonso, *Les zones d'ombre de la guerre contre l'EI*, LIBÉRATION (Dec. 25, 2016), https://www.liberation.fr/planete/2016/12/25/les-zones-d-ombre-de-la-guerre-contre-l-ei_1537445/.

Such killings apparently did not require the cover of counterinsurgency operations: French operatives had killed or captured nearly one hundred jihadists in the Sahel between 2008 and 2013, according to Nouzille, before the formal beginning of military operations there.[55] Nevertheless, following the launch of France's wars in the Sahel and Levant, Nouzille wrote that the boundaries between covert operations and publicly acknowledged military operations had become "more porous."[56]

While European countries moved closer to U.S. practices, the United States began to frame some of its counterterrorism operations in a different light. As the fight between al-Shabaab and the Somali government intensified, U.S. forces began advising and training Somali soldiers in 2013. From 2016, the United States began characterizing most of its strikes as "collective self-defense" of partner forces.[57] The fight against the Islamic State branch in Libya also acquired a territorial dimension. In 2016, Italy agreed to a long-standing U.S. request for permission to carry out strikes in Libya with drones launched from the Sigonella air base in Sicily, although Italy specified that such strikes could only be used to defend U.S. forces.[58]

European countries also claimed the right to detain suspected fighters captured in their counterterrorism wars under the laws of war. French forces held people in the Sahel before turning them over to local authorities.[59] However, the European vision of a series of discrete armed conflicts in specific locations would not have allowed them to hold captives outside the theater of hostilities, as the United States did in Guantánamo. But the European approach produced its own deformations: European citizens could be targeted as fighters in theater, yet had to be treated as criminal suspects if they returned home. As the area held by ISIS was recaptured by local forces, above all by the Kurdish-led Syrian Democratic Forces, many Europeans who had joined the group were taken prisoner.[60] While Kurdish authorities were eager to hand them back to their countries of origin, most European states were reluctant to take them—preferring instead to leave them as wartime captives in theater rather than bringing them home to face

55 *François Hollande*, *supra* note 54.

56 Alonso, *supra* note 54 (quoting from VINCENT NOUZILLE, TUEURS DE LA REPUBLIQUE, author's translation).

57 INTERNATIONAL CRISIS GROUP, OVERKILL: REFORMING THE LEGAL BASIS FOR THE U.S. WAR ON TERROR 14 (2021).

58 Gordon Lubold & Julian E. Barnes, *Italy Quietly Agrees to Armed U.S. Drone Missions over Libya*, WALL ST. J. (Feb. 22, 2016), https://www.wsj.com/articles/italy-quietly-agrees-to-armed-u-s-drone-missions-over-libya-1456163730.

59 *To Respect and Ensure Respect for IHL: Interview with Representatives of the French Ministry for the Armed Forces and Ministry of Europe and Foreign Affairs*, 103 INT'L REV. RED CROSS 843, 847–49 (2021).

60 Thomas Renard & Rik Coolsaet, *From Bad to Worse: The Fate of European Foreign Fighters and Families Detained in Syria, One Year after the Turkish Offensive*, EGMONT INSTITUTE (Oct. 2020), https://www.egmontinstitute.be/app/uploads/2020/10/SPB130_final.pdf?type=pdf.

trial or be set free.[61] Nearly six years after ISIS's last stronghold was recaptured, experts estimate that several hundred ISIS fighters and family members from Europe remain in indefinite detention in the Kurdish enclave in Syria.[62]

The Lessons of Europe's Counterterror Wars

The record of European action against international terrorism in the period since 9/11 shows that the widely held view that European countries pursued a more restrained and rights-compliant approach to military operations against terrorist groups is misleading. It is true that European countries insisted that armed conflicts could only exist against armed groups in geographically confined locations. Nevertheless, France, the United Kingdom, and other countries found ways to carry out or support targeted strikes against terrorists outside conventional military engagements, to prolong campaigns of strikes over several years, and to acquiesce in the indefinite detention of fighters and members of their families. These developments suggest that it is necessary to look beyond the United States' disputed assertion of a global NIAC and consider some legal positions on which the United States and its European allies agreed, to fully address the basis of expansive military actions that western countries have taken in their extended counterterrorism campaigns.

While the United States and European countries disagreed on significant aspects of the legal framework governing operations against terrorist groups overseas, the years after 9/11 saw a growing convergence between them (as well as other countries) on the key question of the authority to target or detain members of armed groups in a NIAC.[63] At the beginning of this period, there was considerable debate over these fighters' legal status, and in particular whether they should be treated as civilians, who could be targeted under IHL only while taking direct part in hostilities, or instead as full-time members of an organized armed group who could be targeted at any time under IHL, in the same way as

[61] Michael Birnbaum, *Months After the Fall of ISIS, Europe Has Done Little to Take Its Fighters*, WASH. POST (June 20, 2019), https://www.washingtonpost.com/world/europe/after-caliphate-collapsed-europe-has-done-little-to-take-back-those-who-joined-isis/2019/06/20/4bab9cc2-8bc4-11e9-b6f4-033356502dce_story.html; *Syrian Kurds Say They Cannot Hold Foreign Jihadists Indefinitely*, REUTERS (Sept. 20, 2018), https://www.reuters.com/article/us-mideast-crisis-syria-foreign-fighters/syrian-kurds-say-they-cannot-hold-foreign-jihadists-indefinitely-idUSKCN1M02LN/.

[62] Xenia Tourki, *Thomas Renard: Europe Faces Rising Terror Threat as Jihadists Exploit Syrian Crisis*, IN-CYPRUS (Jan. 12, 2025), https://in-cyprus.philenews.com/international/thomas-renard-europe-faces-rising-terror-threat-as-jihadists-exploit-syrian-crisis/.

[63] Stephen Pomper, *Toward a Limited Consensus on the Loss of Civilian Immunity in Non-International Armed Conflict: Making Progress through Practice*, 88 INT'L. LEGAL STUD. 182, 187–89 (2012).

the state's armed forces.[64] After the International Committee of the Red Cross (ICRC) issued its Interpretive Guidance on the Notion of Direct Participation in Hostilities in 2009, suggesting that members of organized armed groups who performed a continuous combat function (CCF) thereby forfeited their status as civilians, European states, alongside the United States, embraced a status-based "membership" approach to targeting.[65]

Disagreements persist about how membership of an armed group should be defined: the United States supports a broader test of "functional membership" that includes those who perform support tasks which normally would be performed by members of state armed forces, while some European countries rely on the narrower CCF test.[66] However, there is broad agreement on the principle of status-based targeting of members of organized armed groups. There are signs that a similar process of convergence has taken place on the subject of detention. Several European countries as well as the United States have claimed authority under IHL to detain members of organized armed groups until the end of hostilities on the basis of their status, building in part on the European Court of Human Rights' decision in *Hassan*.[67] These claims represented a departure from earlier state practice, which recognized human rights law as the applicable framework governing detention, as evidenced by the record of derogations during internal armed conflict.[68] These positions on status-based targeting and detention provided the basis for the actions described in the earlier parts of this chapter.

Some scholars have argued that the answer to these developments lies in a stricter understanding of how IHL applies in such counterterrorism wars. In particular, scholars have made a persuasive case that there needs to be greater precision in determining when NIACs end, as Tess Bridgeman and Tom

[64] *See, e.g.*, INTERNATIONAL COMMITTEE OF THE RED CROSS, SUMMARY REPORT: SECOND EXPERT MEETING ON THE NOTION OF DIRECT PARTICIPATION IN HOSTILITIES 20–23 (2004), available at https://www.icrc.org/sites/default/files/external/doc/en/assets/files/other/2004-07-report-dph-2004-icrc.pdf.

[65] Pomper, *supra* note 63, at 187–90; Eliav Lieblich, *The Law of Warfare: 1989–2022*, at 21–24 (Mar. 14, 2022), *in* CAMBRIDGE HISTORY OF INTERNATIONAL LAW (VOL. XII): INTERNATIONAL LAW SINCE THE END OF THE COLD WAR (Eyal Benvenisti & Dino Kritsiotis eds., *forthcoming*), available at SSRN: https://ssrn.com/abstract=4057088.

[66] OFF. OF GEN. COUNS., U.S. DEP'T OF DEF., DEPARTMENT OF DEFENSE LAW OF WAR MANUAL § 5.7.3.2 (June 12, 2015) (updated July 2023); BUNDESMINISTERIUM DER VERTEIDIGUNG (Germany), LAW OF ARMED CONFLICT MANUAL § 1308 (May 2013).

[67] Hassan v. United Kingdom (2014) ECtHR App. No. 29750/09; LAWRENCE HILL-CAWTHORNE, DETENTION IN NON-INTERNATIONAL ARMED CONFLICT 160 (2016); *To Respect and Ensure Respect*, *supra* note 59 (note that the French position expressed in this interview is that detention is justified under IHL for imperative reasons of security; nevertheless, it is grounded in IHL in a way that seems to exclude the application of human rights law).

[68] HILL-CAWTHORNE, *supra* note 67, at 165–73.

Dannenbaum do in this volume.[69] It could also be suggested that, in some of the cases mentioned above, the individuals targeted as terrorist threats should not be considered to be taking a direct part in hostilities, and are therefore not liable to attack under IHL. But the ICRC Interpretive Guidance is clear that acts directed against the civilian population of a party to the conflict may amount to direct participation in hostilities, and it is hard to believe that states will readily give up this claim.[70]

In any case, such arguments do not resolve the wider problem of grounding a state's entitlement to target or detain individuals merely on the existence of an armed conflict, when this is a factual matter that the state itself can influence through its use of military force. Given the difficulty of defeating armed groups through the use of force alone, there is a danger that states conducting military campaigns against such groups may end up pursuing open-ended campaigns at a low level that nevertheless plausibly meets the threshold of armed conflict.[71] Indeed, as Derek Jinks pointed out, if we set the existence of NIAC as the threshold for allowing states to pursue status-based targeting and detention of members of organized armed groups, displacing the more restrictive standards of human rights law, it opens the way for ill-motivated states "to bootstrap into a more favourable international legal framework" by initiating or maintaining hostilities above a certain level of intensity.[72]

In the context of the hostilities between Israel and Hamas in Gaza, the risks of allowing the continuation of hostilities to legitimize military conduct that does not violate IHL are clear.[73] At the time of this writing, with Hamas refusing to release its hostages and leave Gaza, Israel has committed to keep fighting until it has destroyed the organization as a military and governing force in the territory.[74] The apparent impossibility of achieving this goal without causing even greater levels of death and destruction among the Palestinian population—and

[69] *See* Chapter 13, "The Vanishing 'Tipping Point' and the Problem of Perpetual War," and Chapter 19, "Forever War and the *Jus Ex Bello*, respectively, in this volume; *see also* Benjamin R. Farley & Anka Pradhan, *Establishing a Practical Test for the End of Non-international Armed Conflict*, 106 Int'l Rev. Red Cross 1157 (2024).

[70] Nils Melzer, International Committee of the Red Cross, Interpretive Guidance on the Notion of Direct Participation in Hostilities Under International Humanitarian Law 49 (2009).

[71] On the prolonged duration of irregular wars, *see* Laia Balcells & Stathis N. Kalyvas, *Does Warfare Matter? Severity, Duration, and Outcomes of Civil Wars*, 58 J. Conflict Resol. 1390, 1398–1402 (2014).

[72] Derek Jinks, *International Human Rights Law in Time of Armed Conflict*, *in* The Oxford Handbook of International Law in Armed Conflict 656, 669 (Andrew Clapham & Paola Gaeta eds., 2014).

[73] Adil Ahmad Haque, *Enough: Self-Defense and Proportionality in the Israel-Hamas Conflict*, Just Security (Nov. 6, 2023), https://www.justsecurity.org/89960/enough-self-defense-and-proportionality-in-the-israel-hamas-conflict/.

[74] Mehul Srivastava & Neri Zilber, *Israel Readies Plans for Occupation of Gaza*, Fin. Times (Mar. 24, 2025), https://www.ft.com/content/40127b12-62e4-4f3f-8723-d1821332b0d6.

perhaps not even then—raises urgent questions about the legitimacy of Israel's war goals, amid fears that the conflict could become "Israel's forever war."[75]

What is missing in the emerging understanding of status-based targeting and detention in NIACs is consideration of the extent of and limits to the state's justification for the use of force.[76] Arguably, without some restriction limiting the use of force in NIAC to what is necessary and proportionate to a legitimate and limited end, as the *jus ad bellum* provides in international armed conflicts (IACs), military campaigns against armed groups easily may become overexpansive and self-perpetuating. It is doctrinally anomalous to ground a state's entitlement to target or detain members of an armed group in the factual existence of an armed conflict rather than in a justification rooted in the threat that the group and its members pose to the state and its citizens.[77] On this basis, I have argued that we should see human rights (specifically the right to life and the right to liberty) as defining the limits of the state's authority to target and detain members of armed groups both outside and during NIAC, so that even acts of targeting and detention that comply with IHL would not be authorized if they are not necessary and proportionate to prevent a threat to life and security.[78] Like the *jus ad bellum*, the role of human rights in setting a framework for the use of force against non-state groups applies not only to the initial resort to force but continuously throughout the conflict.[79]

The emerging western consensus on status-based targeting, and to some degree status-based detention, has come at the expense of consideration of the justification for the state's use of force in NIAC. Logically, the question of whether IHL treats fighters of armed groups as civilians directly participating in hostilities or as members of an organized armed group comparable to the state's armed forces

[75] David E. Rosenberg, *Why Gaza Is Israel's Forever War*, Foreign Pol'y (Jan. 9, 2025), https://foreignpolicy.com/2025/01/09/gaza-israel-forever-war/; Keith Gessen, *Is This Israel's Forever War?*, New Yorker (Apr. 13, 2024), https://www.newyorker.com/news/the-weekend-essay/is-this-israels-forever-war; Amos Harel, *Amid a Hamas Resurgence in Gaza, Netanyahu's Promise of "Total Victory" Remains Elusive*, Haaretz (Mar. 28, 2025), https://www.haaretz.com/israel-news/2025-03-28/ty-article/.premium/amid-a-hamas-resurgence-in-gaza-netanyahus-promise-of-total-victory-remains-elusive/00000195-db49-df6d-abff-db6f63d20000. Note that the conflict in Gaza probably qualifies both as a NIAC and an IAC, and thus raises complex questions about the interplay between the legal regimes governing the use of force in each case, which I leave aside here.

[76] Eliav Lieblich, *Internal Jus ad Bellum*, 67 Hastings L.J. 687 (2016); Anthony Dworkin, *Individual, Not Collective: Justifying the Resort to Force against Members of Non-State Armed Groups*, 93 Int'l Legal Stud. 476 (2017).

[77] Adil Ahmad Haque, *Human Rights in Armed Conflict, Part II*, Just Security (Nov. 23, 2016), https://www.justsecurity.org/34815/human-rights-armed-conflict-part-ii/; Lieblich, *supra* note 76; Dworkin, *supra* note 76. For a contrary argument, *see* Anne Quintin, The Nature of International Humanitarian Law: A Permissive or Restrictive Regime? 270–88 (2020).

[78] Dworkin, *supra* note 76, at 491–97.

[79] Eliav Lieblich, *On the Continuous and Concurrent Application of ad Bellum and in Bello Proportionality*, *in* Necessity and Proportionality in International Peace and Security Law 41 (Claus Kreß & Robert Lawless eds., 2021).

is distinct from the question of whether human rights law continues to impose restrictions in NIACs beyond those contained in IHL. However, it seems plausible that the consolidation of state doctrine behind a status-based approach to targeting and detention within IHL helped entrench the idea that *nothing* stood in the way of the state's authority to target members of organized armed groups at any time in NIAC or detain them until the end of hostilities. The coalescing of official views around the membership approach to individuals belonging to organized armed groups was rooted in a vision of NIACs that emphasized their commonalities with IACs, where the state's authority to target or detain enemy combatants at any time is broadly accepted.[80] However, the analogy between NIACs and IACs ignores the role that the *jus ad bellum* plays in IACs to set limits on when and to what extent the use of force is justified.[81] Unless a comparable framework for NIACs is recognized, the state's authority to target and detain enemy fighters becomes unmoored from any justification based on the ends for which that force is used.

Taken as a whole, a consideration of the European counterterrorism wars of recent decades alongside the U.S. War on Terror suggests the need to revisit assumptions about the legal basis for the use of force in NIACs. As long as we accept that the existence of an armed conflict between a state and one or more organized armed groups allows states to target members of that group at any time or detain them until the end of hostilities based on their status, the stage is set for expansive campaigns of targeted killings and open-ended detention regimes. To rein in the risks of perpetual war, it is essential to reintroduce the requirement that the use of force is permitted only insofar as it is necessary and proportionate to the state's legitimate security goals, as determined through the operation of international human rights law.

[80] However, *see* MELZER, *supra* note 70, at 78–82; Ryan Goodman, *The Power to Kill or Capture Enemy Combatants*, 24 EUR. J. INT'L L. 819 (2013).

[81] Kevin Jon Heller, *The Use and Abuse of Analogy in IHL*, *in* THEORETICAL BOUNDARIES OF ARMED CONFLICT & HUMAN RIGHTS 232 (Jens Ohlin ed., 2016).

10

How the War on Terror Entrenched Corruption

The Corrosive Legacy of U.S. Intervention in Afghanistan

Timor Sharan

Introduction

The collapse of the Afghan government to the Taliban and subsequent U.S. military withdrawal from the country in August 2021 marked the failure of two decades of fighting to root out terrorist and fundamentalist groups and establish an effectively functioning state. In the aftermath of the withdrawal, the United States blamed corrupt Afghan political leaders for the Taliban's return to power. Yet, as this chapter argues, the U.S. strategy of wielding financial power to wage counterinsurgency warfare—what has been referred to as "money as a weapons system"—was a key driver of corruption in Afghanistan. By infusing billions of dollars for military contracts and buying the allegiances of local elites and communities, the United States inadvertently created an ecosystem that significantly increased the level and scope of corruption in Afghanistan, ultimately contributing to the downfall of the Afghan Republic.

This chapter examines the political economy of the U.S.-led war in Afghanistan and the implications for the "war on terror." First, I demonstrate how the U.S. military weaponized the financial system as a principal element of its counterinsurgency strategy. Next, I explore how this strategy and the huge flow of international patronage and military spending exacerbated and entrenched systematic corruption and fostered the establishment of a kleptocratic class, leading to the "hollowing out" of the Afghan state. Corruption became more decentralized and prevalent, permeating all levels of Afghan society, polity, and economy, moving away from its traditionally tightly managed hierarchical structure. I conclude with a brief reflection on the implications of the U.S.-led withdrawal for Afghanistan and the broader region.

Timor Sharan, *How the War on Terror Entrenched Corruption* In: *Perpetual War and International Law*. Edited by: Brianna Rosen, Oxford University Press. © Oxford University Press 2026.
DOI: 10.1093/oso/9780197748992.003.0010

Weaponizing the Financial System

From the outset, the U.S. approach to the war in Afghanistan was to leverage its financial power to secure quick gains. General David Petraeus, then the U.S. Armed Forces Commander in Afghanistan and principal architect of the U.S. counterinsurgency strategy, stated in 2008 that "money is my most important ammunition in this war," advocating for its use as a "weapons system" to undermine the enemy's financial resources and secure the loyalty of the political elite.[1] Drawing from the perceived success of this approach in Iraq, Petraeus emphasized the necessity of injecting substantial funds into Afghanistan through various programs aimed at winning the "hearts and minds" of local actors. Subsequently, an official military handbook was published explicitly encouraging army commanders to utilize financial resources and military contracts to curry favor with local actors and gain influence.[2]

In the years that followed, international spending and financial resources became the principal instrument of military power in Afghanistan, taking precedence over direct engagement with the adversary. Indeed, U.S. financial spending eclipsed a staggering $2.3 trillion in Afghanistan over the course of two decades.[3] With minimal due diligence, effective oversight, or accountability, much of the U.S. war spending was extravagant, irresponsible, and ultimately counterproductive to efforts aimed at stabilizing the country and eradicating terrorism.[4]

Massive U.S. and allied military spending and contracting significantly contributed to the entrenchment of corruption in Afghanistan. U.S. military contracts such as the Host Nation Trucking (HNT) agreement—a $2.16 billion contract providing logistical support to NATO—became mechanisms for wielding money as a weapon, rewarding warlords and political elites in exchange

[1] Renanah Miles Joyce & Brian Blankenship, *Money as a Weapons System: The Promises and Pitfalls of Foreign Defense Contracting*, Cato Institute (June 3, 2020), https://www.cato.org/policy-analysis/money-weapons-system-promises-pitfalls-foreign-defense-contracting.

[2] Ctr. for Army Lessons Learned, Commander's Guide to Money as Weapons System: Tactics, Techniques, and Procedures, No. 09-27 (Apr. 27, 2009), https://apps.dtic.mil/sti/pdfs/ADA597458.pdf.

[3] Watson Inst. for Int'l and Public Affairs, Brown Univ., *Human and Budgetary Costs to Date of the U.S. War in Afghanistan, 2001–2022* (Aug. 2021), https://watson.brown.edu/costsofwar/figures/2021/human-and-budgetary-costs-date-us-war-afghanistan-2001-2022.

[4] *See* Sarah Chayes, Thieves of State: Why Corruption Threatens Global Security (2015); Kate Clark, *The Cost of Support to Afghanistan: New Special Report Considers the Causes of Inequality, Poverty, and a Failing Democracy*, Afg. Analyst Network (May 29, 2020), https://www.afghanistan-analysts.org/en/reports/economy-development-environment/the-cost-of-support-to-afghanistan-new-special-report-considers-the-causes-of-inequality-poverty-and-a-failing-democracy/; Jonathan Goodhand, *Corrupting or Consolidating the Peace? The Drug Economy and Post-Conflict Peacebuilding in Afghanistan*, *in* Corruption and Post-Conflict Peacebuilding: Selling the Peace? (Dominik Zaum & Christine Cheng eds., 2012); Gretchen Peters, Seeds of Terror: How Heroin Is Bankrolling the Taliban and al Qaeda (2009); Astri Suhrke, When More Is Less: The International Project in Afghanistan (2012).

for the security and safety of U.S. logistical supplies.[5] These logistics and security contractors often charged exorbitant fees for their services. By 2009, U.S. military contracts were financing between six thousand and eight thousand truck shipments per month. International military spending and aid effectively became the biggest creditors of "rent" for Afghanistan by large margins.[6] U.S. funds permeated all levels of Afghan polity and society, fostering an environment ripe for embezzlement, fraud, and favoritism. At the peak of the American military engagement, from 2009 to 2012, the United States operated over 800 small, medium, and large military bases across the country serving 120,000 U.S. troops, excluding contractors.[7]

Over the years, the Special Inspector General for Afghanistan Reconstruction (SIGAR)—established in 2008 to provide the U.S. Congress with independent and objective oversight of aid for reconstruction programs—produced numerous damning reports on U.S. aid expenditures, excluding military-run programs and contracts.[8] A SIGAR report from October 2020, published before the Afghan government's collapse, estimated that the United States had lost a staggering $19 billion in development programs due to waste, fraud, and abuse since the start of the war.[9]

Instead of winning "hearts of minds," military spending exacerbated socio-economic disparities and divisions within Afghan society. While southern and southeastern Afghanistan—where most of the insurgency war was concentrated—received substantial aid, more secure areas, including the Central Highlands, received little to none. Indeed, many of the poorest rural areas in Afghanistan received only sporadic international assistance, primarily in the form of subsistence items such as cooking oil or wheat.[10] International aid and U.S. military programs

[5] *See* STAFF OF H. SUBCOMM. ON NAT'L SEC. AND FOREIGN AFF., 111TH CONG., WARLORD, INC.: EXTORTION AND CORRUPTION ALONG THE U.S. SUPPLY CHAIN IN AFGHANISTAN (2010) [hereinafter WARLORD, INC.].

[6] *See* Clark, *supra* note 4; CHAYES, *supra* note 4; TIMOR SHARAN, INSIDE AFGHANISTAN: POLITICAL NETWORKS, INFORMAL ORDER AND STATE DISRUPTION (2022).

[7] Megan Minnion, *United Nations Development Programme, Economy Built Around ISAF and Impact of Withdrawal* (2013) (unpublished report).

[8] *See* SPECIAL INSPECTOR GENERAL FOR AFGHANISTAN RECONSTRUCTION (SIGAR), CORRUPTION IN CONFLICT: LESSONS FROM THE US EXPERIENCE IN AFGHANISTAN (2016), https://www.sigar.mil/interactive-reports/corruption-in-conflict/index.html; SIGAR, UPDATE ON THE AMOUNT OF WASTE, FRAUD, AND ABUSE UNCOVERED THROUGH OVERSIGHT WORK BETWEEN JANUARY 1, 2018, AND DECEMBER 31, 2019 (2020), https://www.sigar.mil/pdf/special%20projects/SIGAR-21-05-SP.pdf.

[9] UPDATE ON THE AMOUNT OF WASTE, FRAUD, AND ABUSE, at 3. This oversight mandate of course did not include the massive amounts of money going into the pockets of foreign contractors, consultants, and aid workers, who were paid ludicrously more than their resumes and eventual job performances could justify. This kind of "legal" corruption has often been overlooked when calculating waste in Afghanistan.

[10] *See* SUHRKE, *supra* note 4; PAUL FISHSTEIN & ANDREW WILDER, FEINSTEIN INT'L CTR., TUFTS UNIV., WINNING HEARTS AND MINDS? EXAMINING THE RELATIONSHIP BETWEEN AID AND SECURITY IN AFGHANISTAN (2012).

to win hearts and minds also created perverse incentives to sustain violence at the local level. Interviews with business leaders in Kabul in September 2016 revealed that one Afghan airline was paying the Taliban to deliberately intimidate travelers in Taliban-controlled provinces to encourage people to book flights to leave.[11] Most commonly, a U.S. congressional report found that many Afghan businesses were paying off local Taliban commanders and illegal armed groups as the most efficient way to operate while managing security risks.[12] The same report found that some of these proceeds were then channeled to the Taliban and local tribes as protection money to deter attacks on NATO convoys.

The strategy of using money as a weapons system continued despite mounting evidence that corruption and insurgency intensified in areas where military spending increased. In a reviews of U.S. expenditures and development aid, scholars have found that what international forces considered their most important program for winning hearts and minds—reconstruction work at the provincial level, Provincial Reconstruction Teams (PRTs), and other stabilization initiatives—consistently received negative feedback from Afghans, rather than generating goodwill toward the United States.[13] Rather than winning over the population, these initiatives led to a decline in trust in the state and reinforced the Taliban's narrative that the Afghan government was corrupt and incapable of delivering social justice.[14]

The result was widespread corruption in Afghanistan. Historically, while petty corruption had been a routine part of daily life, involving relatively small sums and limited scope, major instances of corruption—often termed "grand theft"—were more structured and typically confined to higher levels of hierarchy. However, with the sustained influx of U.S. contracts and funds, the nature of corruption changed dramatically. It became more decentralized and prevalent as political and business figures in various provinces became increasingly dependent on U.S. financial support, leading to diminished accountability throughout the chain of command.

This systemic corruption is underscored by data from Transparency International's Corruption Perceptions Index (CPI).[15] Since 2007, Transparency

[11] Interview with the Chief Financial Operating Officer of an Afghan Airline Company, Kabul (Sept. 2016).

[12] Warlord, Inc., *supra* note 5.

[13] *See* Fishstein & Wilder, *supra* note 10.

[14] Barbara J. Stapleton, *A Means to What End? Why PRTs Are Peripheral to the Biggest Political Challenges in Afghanistan*, 10 J. Mil. & Strategic Stud. 1 (2007). Robert M. Perito, U.S. Inst. Of Peace, The U.S. Experience with Provincial Reconstruction Teams in Afghanistan: Lessons Identified (2005).

[15] Adele Harmer, Katherine Haver, & Mirwais Wardak, Transparency Int'l, Collective Resolution to Enhancing Accountability and Transparency in Emergencies: Afghanistan Report (2017).

Table 10.1 Afghanistan's Corruption Perception Index (2005–21)

Year	Position
2005	117/158
2007	172/179
2009	179/180
2011	180/182
2013	175/175
2015	166/167
2017	177/180
2019	173/180
2021	174/180

International—the world's most widely cited corruption perception survey—has consistently listed Afghanistan among the countries perceived to have the highest levels of corruption globally, an issue that has persisted for more than two decades.[16] As shown in Table 10.1, Afghanistan was comparatively better off in 2005, before the major influx of international funds, ranked 117 out of 158 countries. However, as U.S. military spending escalated, there was a marked deterioration in perceived levels of corruption. In Transparency International's 2021 CPI, Afghanistan was ranked 174th out of 180 countries (see Table 10.1).[17] This data suggests that systemic corruption became deeply entrenched and largely unaddressed throughout the period.

Consolidating a Criminal State and a Kleptocracy

The international flow of money and subsequent rise of pervasive corruption led to the emergence of a criminal state in Afghanistan. International rent sustained

[16] For the latest report that had data on Afghanistan before the collapse, *see* TRANSPARENCY INT'L, CORRUPTION PERCEPTION INDEX 2020 (2020), https://images.transparencycdn.org/images/CPI2020_Report_EN_0802-WEB-1.pdf.

[17] *See Our Work in Afghanistan*, TRANSPARENCY INT'L, https://www.transparency.org/en/countries/afghanistan, and the Corruption Perception Index 2017 (https://www.transparency.org/en/cpi/2005). This ranking was collected using the data from the Corruption Perception Index over the years for Afghanistan. Note that Afghanistan was not evaluated in 2006 or any year prior to 2005. Additionally, the methodology for calculating the Corruption Perceptions Index was revised in 2012, transitioning from a scale of 10 points (with 10 indicating less corruption) to a scale of 100 points (with 100 indicating more corruption).

an extensive patronage system through which Afghan President Hamid Karzai and his successor Ashraf Ghani built vast networks by appointing allies ministers, provincial and district governors, mayors, judges, attorney generals, and thousands of other roles within the system. Afghan nongovernmental organizations, media, and political elites inadvertently become entangled in—and dependent on—the complex ecosystem created by American financial flows for their survival.[18] Controlling access to international spending and donor aid became the primary economic incentive for political networks, overshadowing efforts to establish legitimate tax-based economic activities.[19]

This strategy of weaponizing money turned human rights abusers, criminals, and narcotics traffickers into partners in the war on terror.[20] Many jihadists that the United States helped to empower in post-2001 Afghanistan had long-standing ties to criminal organizations dating back to the 1980s.[21] With the infusion of international funds and the existing criminal networks forged in the war economy of the 1990s, organized crime and political elites jointly seized control of the Afghan state and economy.[22] In 2010, a U.S. congressional inquiry found that the United States had protected and financed regional strongmen and local militia leaders in Afghanistan through military contracts and civic outreach initiatives.[23] Consequently, a new kleptocratic class emerged in Afghanistan.

The Kabul Bank crisis of 2010 exposed the extent of state capture in Afghanistan. Due to fraud, embezzlement, and mismanagement by bank officials, the bank lost $900 million.[24] It was the primary channel for processing the $1.5 billion payrolls for the Afghan security forces and hundreds of thousands of government employees. Considered too big to fail, the bank was bailed out using U.S. taxpayer money. Investigations revealed that the bank began as a Ponzi scheme, as one western diplomat familiar with the bank's dealings put it,

[18] *See* Sharan, *supra* note 4.

[19] Khyber Farahi & Scott Guggenheim, U.S. Inst. of Peace, Pathways for Post-Peace Development in Afghanistan (2020).

[20] Warlord, Inc., *supra* note 5.

[21] *See* Antonio Giustozzi, War, Politics and Society in Afghanistan, 1978–1992 (2000); Goodhand, *supra* note 4; Dipali Mukhopadhyay, Carnegie Endowment for Int'l Peace, Warlords as Bureaucrats: The Afghan Experience (2009).

[22] *See* Internal Kroll Memorandum emailed to the Governor of Da Afghanistan Bank on Kabul Bank Loans for Shares and Capital Injections (June 4, 2012); *UAE's Azizi Records $350m Home Sales at Cityscape*, Arabian Bus. (Sept. 17, 2017), https://www.arabianbusiness.com/interviews/property/property-news/378657-uaes-azizi-records-350m-home-sales-at-cityscape.

[23] *See* Warlord, Inc., *supra* note 5.

[24] *See* Inside Afghanistan, *supra* note 6; Martine van Bijlert, *The Kabul Bank Investigations: Central Bank Gives Names and Figures*, Afg. Analyst Network (May 2, 2011), https://www.afghanistan-analysts.org/en/reports/economy-development-environment/the-kabul-bank-investigations-central-bank-gives-names-and-figures/. *See also* Emma Graham-Harrison, *Afghan Elites Ransacked $900m from Kabul Bank, Inquiry Finds* (Nov. 28, 2012), https://www.theguardian.com/world/2012/nov/28/afghan-elite-ransacked-kabul-bank.

for the Afghan kleptocratic class.[25] Nearly all the key Afghan elites and criminal networks held stakes in the collapsed Kabul Bank, including the brother of then-President Karzai and the brother of Karzai's first vice president.[26]

By 2019, at least two-thirds of Afghan parliamentarians—including the speaker, deputy speakers, and heads of all House committees (except one)—had either direct questionable involvement in the illicit economy or were linked to it through family members.[27] Notably, over forty parliamentary members were implicated in unlawful activities related to mining sector extraction.[28] The security ministries, heavily influenced by the U.S. military and embassy through funding and appointments, were thoroughly captured by corrupt officials—most of whom had direct links to American subcontractors. An assessment from the Afghan Ministry of Interior (MoI) described the ministry as having become a "honeycomb" for a faction of Afghan political elites from a particular province, who used it as a conduit for extortion and intimidation against rivals.[29] The MoI generated enormous revenues from various sources, including the illicit drug trade, licensing, and kickbacks from businesses. International military contracts, rents, and perks became the primary means of survival for Afghan elites and criminal groups.

In November 2023, the U.S. Treasury Department's Office of Foreign Assets Control sanctioned Mir Rahman Rahmani, the former Speaker of the Lower House, the third most powerful position in Afghan government (2018–21); his son, Ajmal Rahmani; and forty-four associated entities under the Human Rights Accountability Act for allegedly misappropriating millions of dollars from U.S. government–funded fuel contracts intended to support Afghan security forces.[30] Between 2018 and 2022, Ajmal Rahmani, using a Cyprus passport and

[25] *See* Alissa J. Rubin & Rod Nordland, *Afghan Elite Borrowed Freely from Kabul Bank*, N.Y. Times (Mar. 28, 2011), https://www.nytimes.com/2011/03/29/world/asia/29kabulbank.html.

[26] *See* Internal Kroll Memorandum emailed to the Governor of Da Afghanistan Bank on Allocation of the Loan Book (June 4, 2012).

[27] *See* Inside Afghanistan, *supra* note 6.

[28] *See* Timor Sharan & Srinjoy Bose, *Political Networks and the 2014 Afghan Presidential Election: Power Restructuring, Ethnicity, and State Stability*, 16 Conflict, Sec. & Dev. 613 (2016).

[29] *See* Timor Sharan, *What Went Wrong: The 2021 Collapse of Afghan National Security Forces*, Afg. Analyst Network (Dec. 15, 2022), https://www.afghanistan-analysts.org/en/reports/war-and-peace/what-went-wrong-the-2021-collapse-of-afghan-national-security-forces/.

[30] *See* Press Release, *U.S. Treas. Dep't, Treasury Targets Transnational Corruption* (Dec. 11, 2024), https://home.treasury.gov/news/press-releases/jy1973. Mir Rahman Rahmani is a jack-of-all-ideologies figure who began as a communist-era army official, turned into a jihadist commander during the civil war, and finally transformed into a democratic parliamentarian and capitalist in the post-2001 era. By 2018, he and his son, Ajmal Rahmani, had grown so wealthy and powerful that they could secure the ultimate layer of political protection: running for the Lower House themselves. Many accused them of essentially buying their seats, allegedly purchasing each vote for up to $50—a significant sum considering that a daily-wage laborer in Kabul would earn less than $4 a day, if fortunate enough to find work.

Cypriot holding companies, acquired real estate in Germany valued at 197 million euros (over $210 million).[31]

By 2014, they had become two of the richest oligarchs in Afghanistan, monopolizing the supply of fuel to NATO through dubious and opaque companies.[32] Despite American knowledge of their corruption, both father and son were elected to the Afghan Parliament in 2018 and enjoyed political protection. Figures like Mir Rahman Rahmani (local commanders-cum-contractors) and his son Ajmal Rahmani (translators-cum-contractors) grew extremely wealthy in post-2001 Afghanistan as the result of the U.S. strategy of using money as a "weapons system." They evolved into a new class known as the "9/11 millionaires," acting as gatekeepers and middlemen to international military forces.[33]

The Hollowing Out of the Afghan State

The ill-conceived U.S. strategy of weaponizing its money in the war on terror ultimately undermined its core mission: the establishment of robust Afghan state institutions. Years of persistent corruption hollowed out of state structures, including critical security agencies. In 2020, a SIGAR assessment of four southern provinces found that between 50 percent and 70 percent of personnel assigned to police facilities and checkpoints were "ghost officers"—deceased individuals whose positions were still paid for, while commanding officers and generals collected their paychecks.[34] As Linda J. Bilmes notes in this volume, this rampant corruption stands as one of the enduring legacies of the war on terror.[35]

By 2013, some U.S. policymakers viewed corruption as the Afghan Republic's greatest existential threat, eclipsing even the Taliban. In his 2014 Senate testimony, General John Allen warned—seven years before the Republic's collapse—that "[f]or too long, we focused our attention solely on the Taliban . . . They are an annoyance compared to the scope and the magnitude of corruption with which you must contend."[36] Yet despite such warnings, successive U.S. administrations

[31] *See* von Johannes Bauer, Marta Orosz, & Salim Sadat, *Der Fall Rahmanis: Was wird aus seinen millionenschweren Immobilien?*, ZDF (June 28, 2024), https://www.zdf.de/politik/frontal/usa-sanktionen-gegen-afghanischen-investor-immobilien-deutschland-korruption-youtube-100.html.

[32] *See* Inside Afghanistan, *supra* note 6.

[33] Christina Wilkie, *"9/11 Millionaires" and Mass Corruption: How American Money Helped Break Afghanistan*, CNBC (Nov. 5, 2021), https://www.cnbc.com/2021/09/10/9/11-millionaires-and-corruption-how-us-money-helped-break-afghanistan.html.

[34] SIGAR, Quarterly Report to the United States Congress (July 30, 2020).

[35] *See* Chapter 5, "The 'Ghost Budget': How America Pays for Endless Wars."

[36] *A Transformation: Afghanistan Beyond 2014: Hearing Before the S. Foreign Rels. Subcomm. on Near Eastern and Central Asian Affairs*, 114th Cong. 28 (2004) (testimony of Gen. John Allen).

largely maintained the status quo, allowing the conflict to drag on. As one analyst succinctly put it, they "avoided accountability and dodged reprisals that could have changed the outcome or shortened the conflict. Instead, they chose to bury their mistakes and let the war drift."[37]

Corruption weakened Afghanistan's state institutions, eroded public trust, and deepened governance challenges, thereby hindering the development of robust state institutions, democratization, and financial independence. According to the Asia Foundation Survey, between 74 percent and 84 percent of Afghans viewed corruption as a major problem from 2006 to 2019.[38] Corruption further marginalized reform-minded groups and civil society voices pushing for a more open and inclusive society. The result was a legitimacy deficit and diminished public confidence as U.S. funding distorted incentives within the Afghan state and economy, entrenching corrupt practices. This meant that the state was unable to fulfill essential functions, such as providing security, delivering services, and upholding the rule of law.

The Taliban effectively capitalized on widespread discontent by reinforcing the narrative that they were fighting an unjust and corrupt regime. They presented themselves as a cleaner alternative, promising swift and straightforward justice.[39] This message resonated with many in rural Afghanistan, disillusioned by the government's perceived inefficiency and graft, boosting the Taliban's image and aiding their recruitment efforts.

In pursuing short-term objectives, the United States and Afghan elites neglected the critical long-term task of building resilient state structures through comprehensive state-building. This oversight led to a fragmented landscape of unstable power centers and elites rather than a unified national framework. While promoting democratization and women's rights to domestic and international audiences, the United States compromised deeper processes of institutionalization and democratization. This approach undermined efforts to combat corruption and uphold justice, all in the name of achieving political stability and order. As a result, robust institutions capable of enforcing the rule of law, ensuring justice, providing effective governance, and fostering sustainable economic growth failed to take root.

[37] Julian Borger, *The Afghanistan Papers Review: Superb Exposé of a War Built on Lies*, GUARDIAN (Sept. 5, 2021), https://www.theguardian.com/books/2021/sep/05/the-afghanistan-papers-review-craig-whitlock-washington-post.

[38] *Afghanistan in 2019: A Survey of the Afghan People*, ASIA FOUNDATION, 22 (2019), https://reliefweb.int/report/afghanistan/survey-afghan-people-afghanistan-2019.

[39] *See* ADAM BACZKO, THE TALIBAN COURTS IN AFGHANISTAN: WAGING WAR BY LAW (2023).

Conclusion

Corruption played a central role in the collapse of the Afghan Republic, deeply entrenched by two decades of flawed U.S. military intervention that prioritized leveraging financial resources for short-term gains. The United States and other international donors inadvertently trapped large segments of the Afghan government and society in a cycle of dependency on their funding. This reliance permeated every layer of society, fueling extortion of civilians and severely undermining the state's legitimacy and efficacy. Consequently, a kleptocratic elite emerged, fostering widespread corruption and criminality that significantly weakened the Afghan state.

The misuse of financial power allowed Afghan political leaders to evade their responsibilities, prioritizing short-term objectives over the essential task of building a strong, unified state structure. This led to a fragmented landscape dominated by unstable power centers and self-serving elites rather than a cohesive national framework. Efforts to establish transparent and accountable governance were sidelined, marginalizing reformist elements striving for a more open and inclusive society. The erosion of trust between the Afghan elite and broader society further eroded the state's legitimacy, which the Taliban skillfully exploited, paving the way for their return.

The collapse of the Afghan Republic has left a lasting impact on the country, shaping its trajectory to this day. The Taliban's military takeover has plunged Afghanistan into a profound humanitarian and human rights crisis, with the most vulnerable—especially women and girls—bearing the greatest burden. It has also jeopardized domestic and regional stability, raising concerns that Afghanistan could once again become a haven for international terror groups such as al-Qaeda, Tehrik-i-Taliban Pakistan, the Islamic Movement of Uzbekistan, and the East Turkistan Islamic Movement. The Taliban's resurgence and consolidation of power offer a troubling model for other groups to follow, with serious implications for regional and global security in the years ahead.

11

"Nobody Wanted to Hear Us"

Systemic Civilian Harm in Yemen

Priyanka Motaparthy and Radhya al-Mutawakel

Introduction

On March 14, 2017, two men were riding a motorcycle on their way to Moujan, a remote village in the Abyan governorate of Yemen where they lived.[1] Moujan was a tiny community of about sixty-five homes, with no electricity or running water. Salem Ahmed Saleh Bileidi, thirty-four, and his nephew, Hadi Ali Ahmed Bileidi, twenty-eight, had gone to a neighboring area to purchase groceries and supplies for their families. Salem was a schoolteacher in the local school, and Hadi worked as a fisherman and mechanic; both also traded honey to earn income and support their families.

At about 6 p.m., Salem's and Hadi's relative received a phone call from another village resident. The two men had been killed in an airstrike directly targeting their motorbike, he learned. Family members wanted to retrieve their bodies immediately, but they were afraid to travel, fearing another strike. Instead, people living near the site took remnants of Salem and Hadi's bodies to a local hospital.

Their deaths came as a tremendous shock. According to investigations conducted by Mwatana for Human Rights, the Yemeni human rights organization co-founded by one of the authors, both men were civilians, and no one knew why the United States had targeted and killed them.

The strike happened during a period of intensified U.S. airstrikes in Yemen, as Department of Defense (DOD) spokespeople announced strikes in Abyan that week.[2] However, the United States did not formally acknowledge it had carried

[1] *Death Falling from the Sky*, Mwatana for Human Rights 128 (Mar. 23, 2021), https://www.mwatana.org/posts-en/death-falling-from-the-sky.

[2] Terri Moon Cronk, *U.S. Detects, Tracks Multiple North Korea Missile Launches*, U.S. Dep't of Defense News (Mar. 6, 2017), https://www.defense.gov/Explore/News/Article/Article/1103997/us-detects-tracks-multiple-north-korea-missilelaunches/.

Priyanka Motaparthy and Radhya al-Mutawakel, *"Nobody Wanted to Hear Us"* In: *Perpetual War and International Law*. Edited by: Brianna Rosen, Oxford University Press. © Oxford University Press 2026.
DOI: 10.1093/oso/9780197748992.003.0011

out this strike until four years later, in response to a letter both authors of this chapter sent to the Pentagon.[3]

Unfortunately, Hadi and Salem's story is not unique. We have spent years advocating for the rights of civilians like them, who were killed in U.S. drone operations, airstrikes, or counterterrorism ground raids in Yemen. One of the authors has spent over a decade speaking to families who lost loved ones in these operations, documenting their cases and efforts to seek justice since 2013.[4] These interviews and investigations required traveling to remote areas of Yemen—areas neglected by Yemeni authorities for decades. Families had little ability to advocate for themselves or obtain answers, since the Yemeni government rarely advocated on their behalf, and they did not know how to reach the U.S. authorities responsible.

Since 2019, the authors have worked together to present cases of civilian harm to the U.S. government, and specifically to the DOD. We have conveyed families' requests for acknowledgment their loved ones were civilians and their desire to see accountability for their deaths. In response, the U.S. government has often continued to insist it killed combatants in the vast majority of cases, while refusing to look beyond its internal records and include external sources of information in their investigations.

Hadi al-Bileidi's father expressed his frustration at being unable to challenge the U.S. determination that his son was a combatant. "We tried more than once to make our voice heard . . . asking the U.S. to come and check . . . but nobody wanted to hear us," he said. Many families share his frustration.

In this chapter, we examine the U.S. government's failure to fully grasp the costs and consequences of more than two decades of lethal operations in Yemen, as well as the failure to provide amends for civilian harm, with a brief overview of U.S. military involvement in Yemen. Next, we examine the physical, psychological, and economic costs of U.S. lethal operations. Finally, we consider U.S. policy responses to civilian harm in Yemen and draw conclusions about the broader failure of the U.S. government to be held accountable to victims, survivors, and the public.

[3] *See* Columbia Law School Human Rights Clinic and Mwatana for Human Rights, *U.S. Military Admits Killed One Civilian in Yemen after NGO Investigations, but Refuses to Provide Remedy*, Colum. L. S. Human Rights Institute (June 3, 2023), https://hri.law.columbia.edu/cls-clinic-and-mwatana-human-rights-welcome-new-civilian-casualty-acknowledgment-us-military-call.

[4] *See* Amrit Singh, *Death by Drone: Civilian Harm Caused by U.S. Targeted Killings in Yemen*, Mwatana for Human Rights and The Open Society Justice Initiative (May 2, 2015), https://cdn.prod.website-files.com/621cfefe2b950d85b2a1e2d1/647321905f6b9006c01664a8_death-drones-report-en.pdf; *see also U.S. Drone Strikes and Raids*, Mwatana, https://www.mwatana.org/subjets-en/u-s-drone-strikes-and-riads.

U.S. Lethal Operations and Military Support in Yemen

The United States carried out its first acknowledged drone strike in Marib, Yemen, in November 2002.[5] A CIA-operated Predator drone struck a vehicle on a remote desert road, killing six men, including suspected members of al-Qaeda accused of participating in the October 2000 USS *Cole* bombing.[6] The strike was considered an extreme measure at the time. However, the U.S. program of killing terrorism suspects abroad has now lasted through four successive U.S. administrations, spanning at least eight countries.[7] Since the operation in Marib, the United States has conducted at least four hundred to five hundred strikes in Yemen alone, according to independent monitoring groups.[8] During the first half of the Obama administration, the United States accelerated the pace of drone strikes compared to the George W. Bush administration.[9] Under the first Trump administration, the program expanded yet again, widening both geographic scope and the range of groups that it permitted the U.S. to target.[10] In particular, the administration loosened the rules regulating air strikes outside of active war zones and granted authority to conduct these strikes to lower levels of command.[11]

U.S. operations also expanded from those announced against al-Qaeda in the Arabian Peninsula (AQAP) to encompass operations against the Islamic State in Yemen. While the Biden administration never officially acknowledged carrying out operations against al-Qaeda in the Arabian Peninsula or the Islamic State in Yemen, a January 2023 airstrike that reportedly killed suspected members of

[5] *U.S. Predator Kills 6 Al Qaeda Suspects*, ABC News (Nov. 5, 2002), https://abcnews.go.com/WNT/story?id=130027&page=1.

[6] *Id.*

[7] Stephanie Savell, *United States Counterterrorism Operations Under the Biden Administration, 2021–2023*, The Costs of War Project (Nov. 2023), https://watson.brown.edu/costsofwar/files/cow/imce/papers/2023/US-CounterterrorismOperations_2021-2023.pdf; Stephanie Savell, *The 2001 Authorization for Use of Military Force: A Comprehensive Look at Where and How It Has Been Used*, The Costs of War Project (Dec. 14, 2021), https://watson.brown.edu/costsofwar/files/cow/imce/papers/2021/Costs%20of%20War_2001%20AUMF.pdf.

[8] *America's Counterterrorism Wars: The War in Yemen*, New America Foundation, https://www.newamerica.org/international-security/reports/americas-counterterrorism-wars/the-war-in-yemen/ (last visited Mar. 26, 2024); *U.S. Forces in Yemen*, Airwars, https://airwars.org/conflict/us-forces-in-yemen/ (last visited Mar. 26, 2024).

[9] Micah Zenko, *Obama's Final Drone Strike Data*, Council on Foreign Relations (Jan. 20, 2017), https://www.cfr.org/blog/obamas-final-drone-strike-data.

[10] Michael Laris, *Trump Administration to Allow Quick and Dramatic Expansion of Drone Use*, Wash. Post (Oct. 25, 2017), https://www.washingtonpost.com/local/trafficandcommuting/trump-administration-establishing-innovation-zones-for-widespread-drone-use/2017/10/25/a004b400-b990-11e7-9e58-e6288544af98_story.html; Hina Shamsi, *Trump's Secret Rules for Drone Strikes and Presidents' Unchecked License to Kill*, Just Security (May 3, 2021), https://www.justsecurity.org/75980/trumps-secret-rules-for-drone-strikes-and-presidents-unchecked-license-to-kill/.

[11] Charlie Savage & Eric Schmitt, *Trump Poised to Drop Some Limits on Drone Strikes and Commando Raids*, N.Y. Times (Sept. 21, 2017), https://www.nytimes.com/2017/09/21/us/politics/trump-drone-strikes-commando-raids-rules.html.

al-Qaeda showed distinctive damage typically caused by a Hellfire R9X drone, known to be used only by U.S. forces.[12]

Since 2015, the United States has also supported the Saudi and Emirati–led coalition in Yemen, including by refueling coalition aircraft engaged in military operations during the early years of the conflict, providing intelligence and training to coalition forces, and selling weapons to members of the coalition (including military aircraft and parts, and precision-guided munitions).[13] In September 2014, the Ansar Allah armed group (the Houthis) and forces loyal to Yemen's former president Ali Abdullah Saleh took control of the capital, Sana'a, by force. In March 2015, Saudi Arabia, together with the United Arab Emirates (UAE), led a military coalition of states to intervene in the armed conflict in Yemen on behalf of Yemen's internationally recognized government under President Abdu Rabu Mansour Hadi. Between 2015 and 2021, the United States supplied more than $54.6 billion worth of military support to Saudi Arabia, including training and "advisory services."[14]

Following the October 7, 2023, attacks in Israel and subsequent war in Gaza, the United States and the United Kingdom have conducted direct strikes on Houthi targets, responding to attacks the group carried out on U.S. and other ships passing through the Red Sea shipping channel.[15] The Houthis escalated such attacks following Israel's military operations in Gaza.

Costs and Consequences of Civilian Harm

Civilian harm stemming from U.S. lethal operations has been well documented by Mwatana and other human rights organizations, as well as by journalists,[16] United Nations (U.N.) experts,[17] and independent research

[12] Ahmed El-Haj & Jon Gambrell, *Mystery Yemen Drone Strike Renews Questions over U.S. Campaign*, Associated Press (Feb. 10, 2023), https://apnews.com/article/al-qaida-ayman-zawahri-united-states-government-military-technology-yemen-860d86430603dc36ea786e72e09438c1.

[13] Joyce Sohyun Lee, Meg Kelly, & Atthar Mirza, *Saudi-led Airstrikes in Yemen Have Been Called War Crimes. Many Relied on U.S. Support.* Wash. Post (June 4, 2022), https://www.washingtonpost.com/investigations/interactive/2022/saudi-war-crimes-yemen/.

[14] U.S. Gov't Accountability Off., GAO-22-105988, *Yemen State and DOD Need Better Information on Civilian Impacts of U.S. Military Support to Saudi Arabia and the United Arab Emirates* (June 2022), https://www.gao.gov/assets/gao-22-105988.pdf.

[15] Jim Garamone, *U.S., U.K. Launch Strikes Against Houthi Targets in Yemen to Protect Red Sea Shipping*, U.S. Dep't of Defense (Feb. 4, 2024), https://www.defense.gov/News/News-Stories/Article/Article/3665898/us-uk-launch-strikes-against-houthi-targets-in-yemen-to-protect-red-sea-shipping/.

[16] Azmat Khan, *The Human Toll of America's Air Wars*, N.Y. Times (Dec. 19, 2021), https://www.nytimes.com/2021/12/19/magazine/victims-airstrikes-middle-east-civilians.html.

[17] Christoph Heyns (Special Rapporteur on extrajudicial, summary or arbitrary executions), *Report of the Special Rapporteur on extrajudicial, summary or arbitrary executions*, U.N. Doc. A/68/382 (Sept. 13, 2013), https://docs.un.org/en/A/68/382.

institutions.[18] The United Kingdom, the Netherlands, and Australia also have acknowledged responsibility for killing or injuring civilians in their operations against the Islamic State, either in Iraq or Syria.[19] Yet understanding the broader costs and consequences—beyond civilian deaths and injuries—is vital to fully evaluate the impact of civilian harm in Yemen. These costs and consequences include not only deaths, injuries, and destruction of property but also psychological and economic harms.

Physical and Psychological Harms

Communities who live in areas frequently impacted by U.S. counterterrorism operations, whether drones, conventional airstrikes, or ground raids, live with the fear that one day, out of the blue, an unexpected attack may strike, depriving civilians of their lives and safety, as well as their homes and livelihoods. The sudden, shocking nature of these killings leaves families angry and bewildered years, even decades, after the initial harm occurs. In 2013, Hussein Nasser Abu Bakr al-Khushm, the father and cousin of two (young) men killed in a U.S. drone strike, described to one of the authors how the sudden, unexpected nature of their deaths psychologically impacted him and his family:

> The news fell on our ears like a thunderbolt. I got motionless.... Until this moment, I'm unable to figure out what happened to my son and cousin.... Why? Why did they kill my son Sanad and my cousin Ahmed Saleh Abu Bakr?[20]

Researchers and medical studies have found that unexpected, sudden, and violent deaths are particularly traumatic for families.[21] This trauma is frequently

[18] Neta C. Crawford & Catherine Lutz, *Human Cost of Post 9/11 Wars: Direct War Deaths in Major War Zones*, The Costs of War Project (Sept. 1, 2021), https://watson.brown.edu/costsofwar/files/cow/imce/papers/2021/Costs%20of%20War_Direct%20War%20Deaths_9.1.21.pdf.

[19] Gavin Williamson (U.K. Secretary of State for Defence), *Counter-Daesh Operations: Statement made on 2 May 2018* (May 2, 2018), https://questions-statements.parliament.uk/written-statements/detail/2018-05-02/HCWS665; Netherlands Ministry of Defence, *Minister on Visit to Iraq: Peace and Security in Interest of Entire Middle East* (Nov. 11, 2022), https://english.defensie.nl/latest/news/2022/11/30/minister-on-visit-to-iraq-peace-and-security-in-interest-of-entire-middle-east; Australian Ministry of Defence, *Potential Involvement in Civilian Casualty Incident in Mosul, 13 June 2017* (Jan. 31, 2019), https://www.defence.gov.au/news-events/releases/2019-01-31/potential-involvement-civilian-casualty-incident-mosul-13-june-2017.

[20] *Supra* note 4, at 46.

[21] Lesley Wexler & Jennifer K. Robbennolt, *Designing Amends for Lawful Civilian Casualties*, 42 Yale J. Int'l L. 121 (2017).

compounded when they are unable to get information about why the deaths occurred.[22]

Communities who live in areas frequently impacted by U.S. counterterrorism operations live in fear that one day, out of the blue, they too will suffer unexpected harm. Those living in communities impacted by drone strikes have described the long-term psychological effects in a variety of ways. Musa Ahmed Ali al-Jarraah, a fifteen-year-old boy who was seriously injured by shrapnel, told Mwatana he regularly experienced panic and disturbed sleep after he was injured:

> When I hear aircraft flying in the air, it makes me panic and try to hide in any place. I constantly have nightmares of U.S. aircraft attacking us: such nightmares disturb me while asleep.[23]

Another resident of the same village, Moqbel Abdullah Ali al-Jarraah, described the impact on the community.

> We used to feel safe in our village and never expected to be the target of such an attack . . . . [Now,] fear still haunts everyone, and everyone gets more scared whenever we hear the sound of aircraft flying in the atmosphere. Everyone is afraid, men, women and children.[24]

In 2013, Dr. Peter Schaapveld, a clinical and forensic psychologist, traveled to Yemen to assess the impact of lethal strikes on communities in Aden, Yemen. He described what he found as a "psychological emergency" and that in nearly all of those he interviewed, particularly children, trauma was triggered by an airstrike.[25] He found that children he "examined were suffering from attachment disorders (either clinging to parents or behaving in an aloof, disconnected manner, essentially withdrawing). They also exhibited a severe fear of noise, a lack of concentration, a loss of interest in pleasurable activities and infrequent or nonexistent school attendance."[26] Schaapveld also found that some of the children would urinate involuntarily due to fear when they heard aircraft. These psychological effects continued years after the attack, he said.[27]

[22] *Id.*
[23] *Supra* note 4 at 74.
[24] *Id.*
[25] *Drones: No Safe Place for Children*, Reprieve (Mar. 2013), https://reprieve.org/wp-content/uploads/sites/2/2015/04/2013_04_04-PUB-drones-no-safe-place-for-children.pdf.
[26] *Id.*
[27] *Id.*

Economic Harms

In many cases, U.S. lethal strikes killed primary earners in a family—individuals who farmed, earned money abroad, or otherwise provided for large numbers of dependents. Strikes also destroyed the source of an individual or family's livelihood. In some cases, this was a vehicle the family depended on to help earn money. In others, U.S. airstrikes destroyed beehives, or left people afraid to engage in farming or other income-generating activities.

In several cases, in the aftermath of strikes or operations, those directly affected or other community members fled their area, suffering displacement for months or years. The prospect of remaining in an area where they previously felt safe due to their civilian status, and lack of involvement in conflict, turned grim after a loved one was killed in a seemingly random strike. Fearing further attacks, these families became displaced from their home and communities, moving into less secure living situations and new communities that could offer little support. In doing so, they lost prior sources of income and valuable community ties they relied upon in times of hardship. The long-term economic harms of these strikes and other attacks persisted for years.

Frequently, these lethal strikes and operations had devastating effects on women that were largely overlooked. When men who served as the primary earners for their family were killed, women became the sole carer for all dependents, responsible for finding ways to financially support them in traditional societies where they had little earning power. The long-term economic harms of these strikes and other attacks persisted for years.

U.S. Policy Responses and Shortcomings

U.S. policymakers, and at times Yemeni officials, have justified strikes and other counterterrorism operations in the name of promoting safety and stability for Yemenis.[28] Yet more than two decades after the first known U.S. strike, AQAP remains present in Yemen, carrying out acts of violence and destabilizing regions of the country. Meanwhile, communities harmed by both AQAP and U.S. counterterrorism operations continue to live in poverty, in some cases suffering mass

[28] *See, e.g.*, President Barack Obama, Remarks by the President at the National Defense University (May 23, 2013), https://obamawhitehouse.archives.gov/the-press-office/2013/05/23/remarks-president-national-defense-university ("In Yemen, we are supporting security forces that have reclaimed territory from AQAP"); *also* Jeff Mason, *Obama Praises Yemeni Leader, Makes No Mention of Guantanamo*, REUTERS (Aug. 1, 2013), https://www.reuters.com/article/2013/08/01/us-yemen-usa-idUSBRE9701H420130801/ (". . . these threats are not only transnational in nature, but also cause severe hardship and prevent the kind of prosperity for the people of Yemen themselves.").

displacement. They lack schools, proper roads, reliable electricity, and in some locations, running water.[29]

People interviewed by Mwatana repeatedly expressed skepticism at the U.S. approach which, in their experience, focused exclusively on violence and military action, at the expense of programs to better support communities harmed by extremist groups. The father of a civilian killed in a U.S. drone strike in the Hadramout governorate in 2013 said, "They just kill. They don't know what havoc their missiles have caused. They are unaware of the suffering they create for our families."[30]

Many of the civilians harmed by U.S. lethal operations reflected on this harm as an extreme form of discrimination, in which the United States failed to recognize the value of their lives, and their inalienable human rights, due to their poverty, remote location, and position of relative powerlessness. One resident shared his view that "America is testing its lethal inventions in our poor villages, because [it] cannot afford to do so at any place where human life has value."[31]

For more than two decades, numerous in-depth investigations, studies, and reports have found that U.S. military targeting is plagued by the misidentification of targets, "confirmation bias" that leads U.S. officials to interpret inconclusive data as supporting the conclusion individuals should be targeted, and by flawed or incorrect intelligence.[32] These studies include external journalistic investigations, nongovernmental organization (NGO) reports, studies by DOD employees, and studies commissioned by the DOD.[33]

The United States often attributes stark differences in how NGOs, humanitarian groups, and journalists count civilian harm, versus U.S. military records, to differences in the type of information each group can access. In particular, the United States has regularly argued that its confidential intelligence, which the public cannot independently evaluate, ensures that its own counts of civilian harm are more accurate than those of external groups.[34]

[29] *Supra* note 1, at 56, 129.

[30] Radhya al-Mutawakel, Testimony at the hearing on the use of drones and the fight against terrorism—the impact on Human Rights, held by The European Parliament (Sept. 25, 2017) (transcript available at Mwatana), https://www.mwatana.org/posts-en/speech-by-radhya-about-drones).

[31] *Id.*

[32] *Supra* note 18; *The Hidden US War in Somalia; Civilian Casualties from Air Strikes in Lower Shabelle*, Amnesty Int'l (Mar. 20, 2019), https://www.amnesty.org/en/documents/afr52/9952/2019/en/; Larry Lewis, Joint and Coalition Operational Analysis, Reducing and Mitigating Civilian Casualties: Enduring Lessons (Apr. 12, 2013), https://info.publicintelligence.net/JCOA-ReducingCIVCAS.pdf; Michael McInerny et al., *Understanding Civilian Harm in Raqqa and Its Implications for Future Conflicts*, Rand Corporation (Mar. 31, 2022), https://www.rand.org/pubs/research_reports/RRA753-1.html.

[33] *Id.*

[34] *See, e.g.*, U.S. Dep't of Defense, *CY2022 Annual Report on Civilian Casualties in Connection with United States Military Operations*, at 10 (Apr. 25, 2024), https://media.defense.gov/2024/Apr/25/2003449887/-1/-1/0/CY2022-ANNUAL-REPORT-ON-CIVILIAN-CASUALTIES-IN-U.S.-MILITARY-OPERATIONS.PDF. The report states: "Although such information [used by NGOs and media outlets] can be valuable, this information alone can be incomplete or inaccurate. DoD

However, in our own experience reporting civilian harm to the DOD, the U.S. military regularly fails to adequately consider external groups' reporting, take into account important sources of evidence, or give credence to information that goes beyond internal military records and sources. In 2019 and 2020, Mwatana and the Columbia Law School Human Rights Clinic, our respective organizations, sent reports to the DOD of thirteen U.S. counterterrorism operations that, according to our evidence, killed or injured civilians.[35] We asked for their review of and response to these cases, in-depth investigations of these incidents, and where warranted, accountability and redress.

The reports included extensive documentation of these incidents, including personal identity documents of those killed and injured, documents verifying civilian employment or status as a student, statements from interviews with witnesses and community members, photographs, videos, and expert analysis of weapon fragments found at the sites of airstrikes.

The United States Central Command, responding to this information, acknowledged only one new civilian death. While the military acknowledged killing a civilian, the acknowledgment shared no information about how a lethal operation, an apparent "targeted killing," in fact killed the wrong individual. Further, the military refused to apologize for his death, to further investigate whether any negligence or wrongdoing took place in the operation that claimed his life, or to pay either redress or amends to his grieving family.

The response also dismissed Mwatana and Columbia's documentation of eleven incidents of civilian harm. Mwatana, through thorough investigations of these incidents, had found not only that civilians were killed and injured in these cases but that there was no clear military target either nearby or at the site struck.[36] However, the U.S. military concluded that all of those killed in these eleven incidents were "combatants," without providing clear information about who they believed they had killed, what criteria the military used to determine these individuals were "combatants" and targetable under international law, or any factual evidence as to why they were legal targets.[37]

The lack of transparency around much of the criteria and legal standards for these attacks, as well as the factual circumstances when civilian deaths are reported, have largely shielded those responsible from political accountability—from having to meaningfully answer for the circumstances under which civilians

assessments seek to incorporate all available information, including information provided by NGOs and IOs [international organizations], as well as additional information and tools that are not available to other organizations—such as operational planning data and intelligence sources."

[35] *Supra* note 1, at 144–53.
[36] *Supra* note 3.
[37] *Id.*

were killed. And there has been no investigation beyond internal, closed-door military investigations, let alone legal inquiries, into these deaths.

In 2022, the Pentagon announced a new policy, the Civilian Harm Mitigation and Response Action Plan (CHMR-AP), which sets forth new commitments to learn lessons from civilian harm incidents and provide a more robust response.[38] In December 2023, the DOD issued an additional new policy, an instruction on civilian harm, setting forth new procedures and responsibilities for mitigating and responding to civilian harm incidents.[39] However, the new policies do not require the United States to consider past harms, though their harmful impact has not been addressed, and families still wait for answers. In addition, the policies contain only passing references to accountability, with little information on what accountability will mean in practice.

The failure to hold anyone accountable for civilian deaths and harm caused by U.S. operations in Yemen does not only impact those most directly harmed. U.S. military shortcomings, inadequate investigations, and accountability failures were apparently passed along to coalition partners as well.[40] While the United States provided to coalition partners, notably Saudi Arabia and the UAE, significant training on targeting, civilian harm mitigation, and human rights, this training had no discernible results in reducing civilian harm.[41]

For example, the United States helped the Saudi-led coalition develop the Joint Incidents Assessment Team (JIAT)—the coalition body responsible for investigating reported violations of international humanitarian law and apparent war crimes—and determining whether civilians were killed or international law violated in specific incidents.[42] Yet flaws apparent in the DOD's own investigation processes, including insufficient investigations that solely considered coalition military records, poor transparency, and an absence of clear commitments to amends or redress, featured in JIAT's findings as well. JIAT findings largely exonerated coalition forces, only on rare occasions finding "mistakes," but always concluding that coalition forces had complied with the laws of war.[43] Commenting on the JIAT, U.N. human rights head Zeid Ra'ad al-Hussein noted, "the minimal efforts made towards accountability over the past year are insufficient to respond to the gravity of the continuing and daily violations."[44]

[38] U.S. Dep't of Defense, *Civilian Harm Mitigation and Response Action Plan* (Aug. 25, 2022), https://media.defense.gov/2022/Aug/25/2003064740/-1/-1/1/CIVILIAN-HARM-MITIGATION-AND-RESPONSE-ACTION-PLAN.PDF.

[39] U.S. Dep't of Defense, *Instruction on Civilian Harm Mitigation and Response* (Dec. 21, 2023), https://www.esd.whs.mil/Portals/54/Documents/DD/issuances/dodi/300017p.pdf.

[40] *Supra* note 12, at 32.

[41] *Id.*

[42] *Id*, at 21.

[43] Stephen Kalin, *Saudi Coalition Investigates Own Air Strikes, Clears Itself*, Reuters (Sept. 12, 2017), https://www.reuters.com/article/us-yemen-security-investigation-idUSKCN1BN2O6/.

[44] Press Release, Office of the High Commissioner for Human Rights, UN High Commissioner for Human Rights Zeid Ra'ad Al Hussein highlights human rights concerns around the world in an

Conclusion

The United States has been conducting lethal operations in Yemen for more than two decades. What was once extreme and exceptional has now been reaffirmed by four successive U.S. presidents, and these operations have continued in Yemen and around the world. Countless civilians have been killed, and only a handful of deaths have been officially acknowledged. Much remains to be done to ensure that Yemeni civilians will no longer be killed in the name of countering terrorism in the future.

More than six years have passed since Hadi al-Bileidi and his uncle Salem were killed on a routine trip to buy groceries. It is not too late for his father's voice, and those of the many others harmed in U.S. operations, to be heard. The costs and consequences of U.S. lethal operations in Yemen and beyond continue to have wide-ranging reverberations. These harms set an example of impunity for countries around the world to critique, and in other cases, to emulate. U.S. policy continues to rest on the assumption that these killings, largely impacting families in rural areas with little ability to advocate for their rights, have few costs and require only a minimal response. However, we have found that the failure to recognize and account for the significant costs to these families and communities have wide-ranging and long-term effects.

To begin addressing past harms, there are vital steps the United States should take. More expansive and detailed disclosures, in the name of truth-telling and providing solace to the families who lost their loved ones suddenly, would be a first step. A thorough examination of whether targeting officers followed the laws of war, one that could be reviewed by external parties, would be another. Finally, apologies and amends, or redress where appropriate, would provide some measure of justice to those whose lives were immeasurably changed.

address to the 36th session of the Human Rights Council in Geneva (Sept. 11, 2017), https://www.ohchr.org/en/press-releases/2017/09/un-high-commissioner-human-rights-zeid-raad-al-hussein-highlights-human.

V

LEGAL AND POLICY DIMENSIONS

12
Filling the Void
Law, Policy, and Morality at War

*Adil Ahmad Haque**

Introduction

When the United States killed Lotfi Hassan Misto in a 2023 drone strike in Syria, officials claimed he was a senior al-Qaeda figure.[1] He was, in fact, a civilian. Over the last two decades, U.S. military operations have repeatedly misidentified civilians as members of armed groups and directly targeted them, declined to take precautions to avoid killing them, or failed to consider whether the expected loss of their lives is excessive in relation to the military advantage anticipated from the planned attack. These failures are often dismissed as tragic mistakes or intelligence failures, but they are symptoms of something deeper: the breakdown of legal and moral restraints in an era of endless war.

Perpetual war creates ambiguities concerning the initiation and termination of hostilities, who may be lawfully targeted and when, and the geographic scope of conflict, among other issues. In particular, international humanitarian law (IHL) regulates how war is fought, not when it begins or ends. Meanwhile, the law governing the use of force, the *jus ad bellum*, remains state-centric, ambiguous, and increasingly interpreted by powerful states to justify sustained, extraterritorial violence against non-state actors. These legal structures enable and normalize perpetual war.

Faced with the permissiveness and vagueness of law, policymakers turn to moral reasoning or policy frameworks to guide action. In areas where the law is indeterminate, open to interpretation, or still emerging, moral principles and policy rules may help reduce legal ambiguities. Moral reasoning plays a critical role in interpreting and developing international law, yet in the context of perpetual war, it is often either distorted by strategic self-interest or sidelined

* Special thanks to Brianna Rosen for her many improvements to this essay.

[1] Omar Nezhat et al., *U.S. Officials Walk Back Claim Drone Strike Killed Senior al-Qaeda Leader*, Wash. Post (May 18, 2023), https://www.washingtonpost.com/world/2023/05/18/pentagon-drone-strike-syria-civilian-al-qaeda/.

Adil Ahmad Haque, *Filling the Void* In: *Perpetual War and International Law*. Edited by: Brianna Rosen, Oxford University Press. © Oxford University Press 2026. DOI: 10.1093/oso/9780197748992.003.0012

entirely, leaving policymakers to fill the void with policy discretion rather than principled constraint. Policy, for its part, is flexible and instrumental—capable of incorporating legal and moral considerations, but just as easily dispensing with them. In short, while neither law, morality, nor policy can constrain war on its own, the convergence of all domains is essential to restoring restraint.

This chapter examines how international law, morality, and policy interact in shaping the rules of modern warfare, particularly in the counterterrorism context. It proceeds in three parts. The first section analyzes the legal gaps that enable the initiation and indefinite continuation of hostilities against non-state actors, focusing on how expansive U.S. interpretations of the *jus ad bellum* and IHL contribute to the normalization of violence. The second section turns to the moral frameworks that are used to interpret or supplement legal rules. The final section explores how remote warfare and the bureaucratization of targeting decisions have widened the gap between law, morality, and policy in practice. Ultimately, the chapter calls for reimagining how law reflects moral responsibility, how moral reasoning is disciplined by legal principles, and how policy must be bound by both.

Legal Ambiguity and Perpetual War

International humanitarian law broadly defines civilians as all persons who are not members of the armed forces of a party to an armed conflict, and narrowly provides that civilians lose their general legal protection only if and for such time as they take a direct part in hostilities.[2] International law requires armed forces to do everything feasible to verify that persons are not civilian but are instead military prior to attack, and to consider or presume that persons are civilian in case of doubt.

The United States adopts a broad interpretation of membership in an armed group as well as direct participation in hostilities. After U.S. forces misidentified Afghan aid worker Zemari Ahmadi as a member of the Islamic State and killed him, two other adults, and seven children in 2021, U.S. officials attributed the misidentification to "confirmation bias" and claimed not to have seen the children until it was too late.[3] If U.S. forces did everything feasible to verify that Ahmadi was not civilian but military—if they looked for evidence inconsistent with civilian status, rather than evidence consistent with membership in an

[2] Protocol (I) Additional to the Geneva Conventions of 12 Aug. 1949, and Relating to the Protection of Victims of International Armed Conflicts, June 8, 1977, 1125 U.N.T.S. 3, 26 (art. 50).

[3] *Air Force Inspector General's Findings of Errant Drone Strike in Kabul on Aug. 29. 2021*, WASH. POST (Nov. 3, 2021), https://www.washingtonpost.com/context/air-force-inspector-general-s-findings-of-errant-drone-strike-in-kabul-on-aug-29-2021/a7d9edaf-b8d3-497b-9be1-8db427ca7cf6/.

armed group—perhaps ten lives would have been spared. We will never know. Two years later, the United States finally endorsed the verification rule as well as a presumption of civilian status for persons and objects, though not the rule of doubt as commonly understood.[4]

There is a more fundamental reason why U.S. forces kill civilians, namely that U.S. forces carry out many military operations in many countries over many years. "Perpetual," "endless," or "forever" war is the ultimate explanation for most death, injury, and displacement suffered by civilians at the hands of U.S. forces over the last twenty years and with no end in sight.

International law fails to end endless war for many reasons. International humanitarian law is, for the most part, a prohibitive body of rules that constrain the conduct of hostilities whenever they occur and the treatment of vulnerable groups wherever they may be. International humanitarian law neither authorizes the initiation or continuation of armed conflict, nor directly requires its termination. The prohibitive nature and constraining function of IHL enables it to equally apply to all sides of every armed conflict, but leaves it with little to say about when armed conflicts must end.

The international law regulating the use of armed force between states does not extend to armed force between states and non-state actors as such. The general prohibition of interstate armed force also falls away with the consent of the state on whose territory force is used. As a result, international law does not directly regulate the initiation or endless continuation of armed conflicts between states and non-state actors on their own territory, or between states and non-state actors on the territory of another state that consents to outside intervention. Legal regulation, if any, arises indirectly, from the application of international human rights law.

In April 2016, in the final months of the Obama administration, the United States took the position that:

> In some cases, international law does not require a State to obtain the consent of the State on whose territory force will be used. In particular, there will be cases in which there is a reasonable and objective basis for concluding that the territorial State is unwilling or unable to effectively confront the non-State actor in its territory so that it is necessary to act in self-defense against the non-State actor in that State's territory without the territorial State's consent. For example, in the case of ISIL in Syria, as indicated in our Article 51 letter, we could act in self-defense without Syrian consent because we had determined that the Syrian

[4] *See* Adil Ahmad Haque, *Ambiguity in the Conduct of Hostilities*, JUST SECURITY (May 10, 2018), https://www.justsecurity.org/56087/ambiguity-conduct-hostilities/. For the recent change, *see* U.S. DEP'T OF DEF., LAW OF WAR MANUAL §§ 5.5.3, 5.4.3.2 (July 2023).

regime was unable or unwilling to prevent the use of its territory for armed attacks by ISIL.[5]

Moreover, the United States took the position that, "once a State has lawfully resorted to force in self-defense against a particular armed group following an actual or imminent armed attack by that group, it is not necessary as a matter of international law to reassess whether an armed attack is imminent prior to every subsequent action taken against that group, provided that hostilities have not ended."[6] The combination of these legal positions entails that the prohibition of armed force between states permits the initiation and endless continuation of cross-border military operations by states against non-state actors, without the consent of the territorial state, subject only to a standard of unwillingness or inability that remains as underspecified today as when it was first proposed.

These U.S. legal positions have no basis in the text or drafting history of the United Nations (U.N.) Charter, which concerns self-defense against armed aggression by another state.[7] These U.S. legal positions also have no firm or settled basis in subsequent state practice in the application of the Charter, or in customary international law. Some states reject the basic position that states may use armed force against non-state actors in the territory of a nonconsenting state. Even U.S. allies seem to reject the further position that states may use armed force in the absence of an ongoing or imminent armed attack.[8] The combined position which licenses perpetual war remains an international outlier.

Law and Morality

When law is vague, ambiguous, incomplete, or inconsistent, moral considerations come into play. International law invites moral considerations into legal reasoning in various ways.[9] International law provides that a treaty

[5] Brian Egan, *International Law, Legal Diplomacy, and the Counter-ISIL Campaign: Some Observations*, 92 Int'l L. Stud. 235 (2016).

[6] *Id.*

[7] Adil Ahmad Haque, *The United Nations Charter at 75: Between Force and Self-Defense—Part One*, Just Security (June 24, 2020), https://www.justsecurity.org/70985/the-united-nations-charter-at-75-between-force-and-self-defense-part-one/; Adil Ahmad Haque, *The United Nations Charter at 75: Between Force and Self-Defense—Part Two*, Just Security (June 24, 2020), https://www.justsecurity.org/70987/the-united-nations-charter-at-75-between-force-and-self-defense-part-two/; Adil Ahmad Haque, *"Clearly of Latin American Origin": Armed Attack by Non-State Actors and the UN Charter*, Just Security (Nov. 5, 2019), https://www.justsecurity.org/66956/clearly-of-latin-american-origin-armed-attack-by-non-state-actors-and-the-un-charter/.

[8] Adil Ahmad Haque, *Self-Defense Against Non-State Actors: All Over the Map*, Just Security (Mar. 24, 2021), https://www.justsecurity.org/75487/self-defense-against-non-state-actors-all-over-the-map/.

[9] Adil Ahmad Haque, *The Inner Logic of International Law*, *in* Philosophy and International Law: Contestations and Extensions (David Lefkowitz & Andreas Føllesdal eds., forthcoming).

shall be interpreted in light of its object and purpose. If the object and purpose of a treaty is to promote a moral aim or respect a moral value, then legal interpretation requires moral reasoning. International humanitarian law treaties aim to protect the victims of armed conflict and ensure respect for the human person.[10] The best legal interpretation of these treaties will reflect these moral aims. A defective legal interpretation will lead to a result which is manifestly absurd or unreasonable in moral terms.

Customary international law reflects the attempt by states to arrive at a shared view of how all states should act, irrespective of their policy aims and even when contrary to their national interests. This shared view generates obligations whose breach constitutes a wrongful act that incurs responsibility and justifies demands for reparation and (in some cases) countermeasures. In these ways, customary international law presents itself as morally legitimate, its rules as morally justified, its obligations as moral obligations, and its consequences as morally deserved. By claiming, or presupposing, its own legitimate moral authority, customary international law invites moral considerations into its formation and evolution.

Customary international law is a moral practice. There are no secondary rules providing for the interpretation of customary rules in light of their object and purpose, but there are also no secondary rules excluding moral considerations from the clarification and progressive development of customary law. Since moral considerations apply to all human beings, even state officials, prior to and independently of law, state officials legally may and practically must invoke moral considerations as they converge on a shared view of how all states must act.

The legal rules constraining the conduct of hostilities exemplify the moral aim of protecting civilians and respecting their humanity. This moral aim gives these legal rules a coherent background for interpretation, narrows the scope of reasonable disagreement, and infuses legal disputes with moral force. Interpreters make moral arguments for or against possible legal positions, disputing which position will best protect civilians or place unfair burdens on combatants.

Human well-being and human dignity are universal and basic values. The ability to bring them to bear on practical questions is a basic competence of moral agency. Our shared grasp of the moral values at stake in legal debates partly explains why apparent violations of IHL both draw and sustain our collective attention.

[10] Protocol (I) Additional to the Geneva Conventions of 12 Aug. 1949, and Relating to the Protection of Victims of International Armed Conflicts, June 8, 1977, 1125 U.N.T.S. 3, 6–7 (Preamble); Protocol (II) Additional to the Geneva Conventions of 12 Aug. 1949, and Relations to the Protection of Victims of Non-International Armed Conflicts, June 8, 1977, 1125 U.N.T.S. 609, 611 (Preamble).

In contrast, the law governing the use of armed force is generally understood as a state-centric body of law that aims to preserve the territorial integrity and political independence of sovereign equals from the most extreme form of coercive interference. This body of law protects individual human beings only indirectly, contingently, and conditionally. Under this body of law, the legality of armed force against non-state actors depends on the consent of the territorial state—not on the consequences for individual human beings.

Most of us today do not believe that states possess intrinsic moral value or enjoy fundamental moral rights. We tend to believe that states are legal constructs that are instrumentally valuable insofar as they contribute to human well-being, or derivatively valuable insofar as they reflect the efforts of their peoples to achieve collective self-determination. Legal interpretation through moral reasoning remains possible, but must take a different form.

Moral reasoning may deploy a "domestic analogy," treating the state as a moral person with moral rights and duties, legitimate interests, and a capacity for autonomous choice. This form of "as if" moral reasoning accepts the moral premise or presupposition that apparently underlies this body of law, and reasons from that moral premise or presupposition to moral conclusions. We deploy this form of moral reasoning every time we transpose self-defense criteria of imminence, necessity, and proportionality from the domain of individual morality and ordinary criminal law to the international plane. We reason about what states may or may not do in self-defense by analogy to what individuals may or may not do in self-defense. Critics of the U.S. "unwilling or unable" position argue that a state cannot forfeit its protection from armed force except by its own wrongful conduct. If the actions of a non-state actor are not attributable to the state in whose territory it operates, then the "innocent state" retains its right against armed force on its territory.[11] The territorial state is like an innocent bystander, and there is no moral reason for law to prefer the rights of the intervening state over the rights of the territorial state.

The basic problem with this analogical approach is that legal fictions have no moral status, and a false moral premise supports no true moral conclusion. The problem intensifies when the government of the territorial state is neither a responsible fiduciary of its people nor the instrument of their collective self-determination. In these cases, the morality of cross-border armed force against non-state actors seems to turn not on the crossing of borders but on the rights and welfare of the human beings who may be immediately harmed by the armed force or saved from later harm at the hands of the non-state actor.[12]

[11] Dire Tladi, *The Nonconsenting Innocent State: The Problem with Bethlehem's Principle 12*, 107 Am. J. Int'l L. 570 (2013).

[12] Eliav Lieblich, *Self-Defense Against Non-State Actors and the Myth of the Innocent State*, *in* Global Governance and Human Rights (Nehal Bhuta & Rodrigo Vallejo eds., 2024).

Alternatively, moral reasoning may take an instrumental or consequentialist form. If states are not moral persons, then the law governing the use of armed force has no inner logic worth unpacking. Instead, its rules should be treated as tools to achieve good outcomes and avoid bad outcomes over the long term. We see this approach deployed by those who reject the U.S. "unwilling or unable" position on the grounds that its general acceptance by states will result in so much error, arbitrariness, and abuse that the costs of its adoption will far exceed the benefits. The basic problem with such rule-consequentialist arguments is not so much that the long-term consequences of a rule's general acceptance can never be predicted with confidence. Instead, the basic problem is that an individual faced with a moral choice between killing some and possibly saving others, or sparing some and possibly leaving others to die, needs a compelling moral reason to follow a legal rule rather than make their own moral judgment. It is no answer that general acceptance of the rule—by other people in other places and at other times—will yield better consequences over the long term. The individual may fairly reply, "What is that to me, here and now?"

There is a mismatch between the state-centric legal regime governing the initiation, continuation, and termination of armed conflict and the person-centric moral principles that underlie and animate our concerns with perpetual war. We are left to invoke legal rules whose moral force we privately question, or instead resort to pure moral argument without the orientation provided by a morally sound legal framework.

How Policy Can Promote Law's Moral Function

We see glimmers of a way forward. Tom Dannenbaum argues that the core concepts of force and armed attack can be understood in terms of harm to individual human beings.[13] Eliav Lieblich argues that a state's consent to military intervention is constrained by its obligations to respect the human rights of its own citizens. The U.N. Human Rights Committee concludes that armed aggression violates the human right to life of every individual person it kills.[14] I have argued that the right of self-defense may not be exercised at disproportionate total cost to civilians.[15] Taken together, contributions like these point toward a

[13] Tom Dannenbaum, The Crime of Aggression, Humanity, and the Soldier (2018).

[14] Hum. Rts. Comm., General Comment No. 36 on International Covenant on Civil and Political Rights, art. 6: Right to Life, U.N. Doc. C/GC/36 (2019).

[15] Adil Ahmad Haque, *Enough: Self-Defense and Proportionality in the Israel-Hamas Conflict*, Just Security (Nov. 6, 2023), https://www.justsecurity.org/89960/enough-self-defense-and-proportionality-in-the-israel-hamas-conflict/.

"humanization of the *jus ad bellum*" that narrows the gap between state-centric law and person-centric morality.[16]

Law purports to reflect moral considerations, but not to perfectly mirror moral standards. If moral standards were clear in content and easy in application, there would be no need for law except perhaps to provide incentives for compliance to those unmoved by moral concerns. The main contribution that law makes to our moral lives—the moral service it provides—is to help us conform to our moral obligations more closely than we would if we relied on our own moral judgment, which is too often confounded by uncertainty and led astray by temptation and fear.[17]

The battlefield is a domain of low information and high emotion. It is no place for fine-grained determinations of moral responsibility for unjust threats, moral liability to defensive harm, or close calls between greater and lesser evils. Even morally motivated fighters may find their moral judgments skewed by concern for their own safety, partiality toward comrades and fellow citizens, and wishful thinking regarding the consequences of their actions. Impartial weighing of available evidence, and due diligence to make more evidence available, may be tempting to cut short due to stress, fear, or exhaustion.

International humanitarian law guides fighters through the fog of war by setting out clear and narrow criteria for civilian status and loss of civilian protection, and by requiring exhaustive target verification and restraint in cases of doubt. These legal rules preempt moral judgment distorted by motivated reasoning and other cognitive biases that systematically incline fighters toward violating their moral obligations to civilians and other vulnerable groups.

Given the moral function of IHL, it is perhaps not surprising that the rise of remote warfare has placed new pressures on the law's integrity. Extended surveillance with drones and satellites creates the illusion of full information, while bureaucratic processes and formalized targeting cycles encourage the conceit of cool judgment. The killing of Ahmadi and nine other civilians followed eight hours of remote surveillance by a targeting cell a thousand miles away in Qatar. Yet U.S. officials attributed the killings to confirmation bias, communication breakdowns, stress, and risk to ground forces.[18] Remote warfare reproduces familiar risks of error, with similarly devastating effects.

[16] Eliav Lieblich, *The Humanization of* Jus ad Bellum: *Prospects and Perils*, 32 EUROPEAN J. INT'L L. 579 (2021).

[17] ADIL AHMAD HAQUE, LAW AND MORALITY AT WAR (2017).

[18] Lt. Gen. Sami D. Said, Inspector General, U.S. Air Force, *Pentagon Press Secretary John F. Kirby and Air Force Lt. Gen. Sami D. Said Hold a Press Briefing* (Nov. 3, 2021), https://www.defense.gov/News/Transcripts/Transcript/Article/2832634/pentagon-press-secretary-john-f-kirby-and-air-force-lt-gen-sami-d-said-hold-a-p/ ("[T]hree days prior, such an attack took place, where we lost 13 soldiers—or lost 13 members and a lot of Afghan civilians. We are one day from the exfil, so the ability for defense had declined. We're concentrated in one location, with a lot of threat streams indicating imminent attacks that looked similar to the attack that happened three days prior. So you

The decision to initiate, continue, or terminate military operations against non-state actors is typically made by groups, over time, gathering and analyzing information, discussing and debating options and risks, before coming to a final decision. This deliberative process breeds false confidence. The benefits of high information and low stress are offset by groupthink, group polarization, and other distortions of collective decision-making invisible to group members themselves. It is easy for decision makers to convince themselves that they will make better decisions by relying on their own collective judgment than by following international law. True, *other* officials of *other* states regularly make disastrous decisions regarding the use of armed force, and perhaps it would be better if *they* followed international law. But what is that to *us*? Let others follow the rules. We are exceptional. For us, the decision to resort to armed force or continue armed conflict is a matter, not of law, but of policy.

Policy is an open-ended category of practical thought, and need not exclude legal or moral considerations. Policy differs from law and morality in its form, not its content. Policy is the domain of hypothetical imperatives and instrumental reasoning. Tell me your aims, and I will tell you how to achieve them. Tell me your preferences, and I will tell you how to maximize their satisfaction. Legal and moral considerations enter into policymaking, or do not, as policymakers wish. If policymakers trust their own judgment more than the law's directives, then policy will assign law a subordinate role in decision-making, instead of law's categorical mandates setting the limits of policy discretion.

Policy can promote law's moral function, rather than undermine it, by distilling law's general rules into specific directives. International humanitarian law addresses all fighters, regardless of rank or role, education or experience, in the same general terms. Rules of engagement and policy frameworks can be tailored to young soldiers in the field, targeting cells far from danger, or senior officials at home, with varying levels of simplicity and complexity. Policy should aim to help individuals conform to their legal obligations, just as—and because—law should aim to help individuals conform to their moral obligations.

The United States tends to adopt permissive interpretations of IHL, which it then supplements with policy constraints.[19] For example, while the U.S. Department of Defense rejects a legal rule of doubt, the U.S. Army and Marine Corps, "as a matter of practice due to operational and policy reasons, generally take a more restrictive view than required under LOAC. In cases of doubt whether a person or object is a military objective, Soldiers and Marines should

can imagine the stress on the force is high and the risk to force is high, and not appreciating what I'm about to say through that lens I think would be inappropriate.").

[19] Adil Ahmad Haque, *Targeted Killing Under Trump: Law, Policy, and Legal Risk*, JUST SECURITY (Feb. 10, 2017), https://www.justsecurity.org/37636/targeted-killing-trump-law-policy-legal-risk/.

consider that person or object as a civilian or civilian object."[20] While it is not entirely clear why the United States adopts policies but will not accept law, it is possible that the United States wishes to reserve the right to set its targeting policies aside in large-scale military operations against near-peer adversaries.[21] If the United States finds itself in direct armed conflict with Russia or China, perpetual war will be the least of our concerns. Such a war will end itself. It must never begin. The danger is that policymakers will convince each other that they know better than the law.

In the end, the moral argument for a restrictive interpretation of the law governing the use of force is straightforward, even obvious. The use of force is almost always a mistake, except when an armed attack occurs or an impartial group of states collectively determines that force is necessary to maintain international peace and security. Left free to decide for themselves when force is warranted by long-term threats, strategic rivalries, regional tensions, or domestic disorder, states will fall into error, arbitrariness, and abuse, violating their own fundamental moral obligations not to kill, maim, or dispossess individual human beings except to prevent comparable or greater harm to others. This is what history shows and our current predicament confirms. In the resort to force, as in the conduct of armed conflict, law, morality, and wise policy demand restraint.

[20] Dep't of the Army & U.S. Marine Corps, The Commander's Handbook on the Law of Land Warfare, FM 6-27/MCTP 11-10C, para. 2-54 (2019).

[21] Lt. Gen. Charles Pede & Col. Peter Hayden, *The Eighteenth Gap: Preserving the Commander's Legal Maneuver Space on "Battlefield Next."* Mil. Rev., Mar.–Apr. 2021, at 6.

13

The Vanishing "Tipping Point" and the Problem of Perpetual War

*Tess Bridgeman**

> *"The AUMF is now nearly 12 years old. The Afghan war is coming to an end. Core al Qaeda is a shell of its former self. Groups like AQAP must be dealt with, but in the years to come, not every collection of thugs that labels themselves al Qaeda will pose a credible threat to the United States. Unless we discipline our thinking, our definitions, our actions, we may be drawn into more wars we don't need to fight, or continue to grant Presidents unbound powers more suited for traditional armed conflicts between nation states."*
>
> *– President Barack Obama, Speech at National Defense University, May 23, 2013*

Introduction

Multiple U.S. presidents spanning Democratic and Republican administrations have expressed a desire to end the "forever" wars that began with the terrorist attacks on September 11, 2001.[1] Each of them, however, has simultaneously

* Tremendous thanks to Siven Watts, Isaac Buck, Wendy Leben, Jake Dow, and Clara Apt for their assistance, and to Brianna Rosen, Tom Dannenbaum, Ryan Goodman, Oona Hathaway, Harold Hongju Koh, Rebecca Ingber, Stephen Pomper, and Mitt Regan for their invaluable comments on earlier versions of this chapter.

[1] *See, e.g.*, Barack Obama, President of the U.S., Remarks by the President at the National Defense University (May 23, 2013) [hereinafter Obama Remarks at NDU], https://obamawhitehouse.archives.gov/the-press-office/2013/05/23/remarks-president-national-defense-university ("But this war, like all wars, must end. That's what history advises. That's what our democracy demands."); Barack Obama, President of the U.S., Statement by the President on Afghanistan (Oct. 15, 2015), https://obamawhitehouse.archives.gov/the-press-office/2015/10/15/statement-president-afghanistan ("As you are well aware, I do not support the idea of endless war . . . ."); Donald Trump, President of the U.S., President Donald J. Trump's State of the Union Address (Feb. 5, 2019), https://trumpwhitehouse.archives.gov/briefings-statements/president-donald-j-trumps-state-union-address-2/ ("As a candidate for President, I pledged a new approach. Great nations do not fight endless wars."); Donald Trump, President of the U.S., Remarks by President Trump at the 2020 United States Military Academy at West Point Graduation Ceremony (June 13, 2020), https://trumpwhitehouse.archives.gov/briefings-statements/remarks-president-trump-2020-united-states-military-acad

Tess Bridgeman, *The Vanishing "Tipping Point" and the Problem of Perpetual War* In: *Perpetual War and International Law*. Edited by: Brianna Rosen, Oxford University Press. © Oxford University Press 2026.
DOI: 10.1093/oso/9780197748992.003.0013

implemented counterterrorism policies that rely on maintaining a state of armed conflict. More than two decades on, the conflict has expanded significantly, encompassing numerous groups that did not yet exist at the time of the 9/11 attacks. Afghanistan is no longer the geographic locus of active hostilities. And while new threats have emerged, "core" al-Qaeda (or "AQ Core"), the group responsible for the 9/11 attacks, reached its "historical nadir,"[2] according to the executive branch, and "probably lacks the capability" to attack the United States.[3]

Despite the fundamentally changed nature of the conflict, recent U.S. administrations have continued the decades-old counterterrorism strategies they inherited. Key to these strategies are status-based targeting and detention policies that are lawful only during armed conflict, due to the relatively permissive nature of the law of armed conflict, also known as international humanitarian law (IHL), as compared with peacetime legal frameworks.[4] To scaffold the furthest reaches of its expansive counterterrorism strategies, the executive branch has crafted a series of novel domestic and international legal theories, with minimal oversight by Congress and the courts. Those theories at one point included the initial sketches of a viable endpoint to the war. But as it stretches

emy-west-point-graduation-ceremony/ ("We are ending the era of endless wars."); Joseph Biden, President of the U.S., Remarks by President Biden on the Way Forward in Afghanistan (Apr. 14, 2021), https://bidenwhitehouse.archives.gov/briefing-room/speeches-remarks/2021/04/14/remarks-by-president-biden-on-the-way-forward-in-afghanistan/ ("I have concluded that it's time to end America's longest war . . . And it's time to end the forever war."); Joseph Biden, President of the U.S., Remarks by President Biden Before the 76th Session of the United Nations General Assembly (Sept. 21, 2021), https://bidenwhitehouse.archives.gov/briefing-room/speeches-remarks/2021/09/21/remarks-by-president-biden-before-the-76th-session-of-the-united-nations-general-assembly/ ("[W]e close this period of relentless war . . . .").

2 Press Release, Christine Abizaid, Director, National Counterterrorism Center, 9/11 Statement from National Counterterrorism Center Director Christy Abizaid (Sept. 11, 2023) [hereinafter Abizaid Statement], https://www.dni.gov/index.php/nctc-newsroom/3725-9-11-statement-from-national-counterterrorism-center-christy-abizaid.

3 Dep't of Def., Department of Defense Report on Use of Military Force and Support of Partner Forces for the Following Periods: January 1, 2020, to June 30, 2020; July 1, 2020, to December 31, 2020; and January 1, 2021, to June 30, 2021, 5, 7–8 [hereinafter Section 1285 Reports], https://www.justsecurity.org/wp-content/uploads/2023/09/1285-Reports-.pdf. *See also Annual Threat Assessment to the Homeland: Hearing Before the S. Comm. on Homeland Sec. and Gov't Aff.*, 118th Cong. (2023) (statement for the record of Christine Abizaid, Director, National Counterterrorism Center), https://www.dni.gov/index.php/newsroom/congressional-testimonies/congressional-testimonies-2023/3735-nctc-director-christine-abizaid-statement-for-the-record-senate-committee-on-homeland-security-and-government-affairs. *See also Threats to the Homeland: Hearing Before the S. Comm. on Homeland Sec.*, 117th Cong. (2022) (statement for the record of Christine Abizaid, Director, National Counterterrorism Center), https://www.hsgac.senate.gov/wp-content/uploads/imo/media/doc/Testimony-Abizaid-2022-11-17.pdf.

4 *See, e.g.*, Marko Milanovic, *The End of Application of International Humanitarian Law*, 96 Int'l Rev. of the Red Cross 163, 185 (2014), https://international-review.icrc.org/sites/default/files/irrc-893-milanovic.pdf (describing how the United States "cast the Al Qaeda threat and the US response thereto as a 'war' for both domestic and international purposes, in order to get the detention and targeting authority that it thought it needed and avoid having its hands tied by any applicable rules of domestic constitutional law as well as international human rights law").

into its third decade, any meaningful legal standard for reaching the so-called "tipping point" that would mark this conflict's end now seems to have vanished.

This chapter examines the international law governing when non-international armed conflicts (NIACs), such as the one between the United States and al-Qaeda, end. Next, I explain two catalysts for the development of legal theories that expand and perpetuate conflict: locating domestic authority for the use of military force against new armed groups in the decades-old authorizing statute for the conflict with AQ Core—the 2001 Authorization for Use of Military Force (AUMF)[5]—and the perceived need for continued detention authority at Guantánamo Bay. These drivers paved the way for an expansive new legal theory advanced in defensive detention litigation under which the conflict continues until *any* hostilities the executive deems to be authorized by the 2001 AUMF have ceased—even if those hostilities are conducted by distinct groups, operating independently, and in diverse geographic locations. Use of this approach in the context of U.S. counterterrorism wars risks perpetual conflict overclassification and undermines the crucial distinction between war and peace. It allows the United States to claim continued wartime authorities vis-à-vis an extraordinarily broad range of groups, even though the existence of a state of armed conflict with some of them (including AQ Core itself) may be in serious doubt. It also calls into question whether the "tipping point" standard the United States once articulated for when its conflict with AQ Core will cease has been rendered meaningless. The chapter concludes with a brief discussion of how international law might fill the void, particularly if these issues are addressed outside of the defensive litigation context.

International Law on the Temporal Scope of Non-International Armed Conflict

The temporal scope of application of IHL in NIACs is a complex and evolving area.[6] It is often described as indeterminate, given "the relevant treaties provide no clear answer,"[7] while the law on the threshold for the commencement of a NIAC, which defines when IHL applies in the first instance, is more settled.

[5] Authorization for Use of Military Force, Pub. L. No. 107-40, 115 Stat. 224 (2001) [hereinafter 2001 AUMF].

[6] *See* Nathalie Weizmann, *The End of Armed Conflict, the End of Participation in Armed Conflict, and the End of Hostilities: Implications for Detention Operations under the 2001 AUMF*, 47 Colum. Hum. Rts. L. Rev. 204, 209–20 (2016); Julia Grignon, *The "General Close of Military Operations" as the Benchmark for the Declassification of Armed Conflicts and the End of the Applicability of International Humanitarian Law*, 59 Can. Y.B. Int'l L. 80 (2021); Julia Grignon, *The "General Close of Military Operations" and the End of Armed Conflicts*, West Point Lieber Inst. (Sept. 21, 2022), https://lieber.westpoint.edu/general-close-military-operations-end-of-armed-conflicts/.

[7] Milanovic, *supra* note 4, at 164.

A comprehensive accounting of NIAC initiation and cessation is beyond the scope of this chapter, but a brief overview can elucidate clearer aspects of the legal framework and highlight where ambiguity persists.[8]

To start, Common Article 3 of the Geneva Conventions applies for the duration of "conflicts not of an international character" (non-international armed conflicts, or NIACs), but it does not define the threshold for determining whether such a conflict exists or has ceased. The Appeals Chamber of the International Criminal Tribunal for the former Yugoslavia (ICTY) introduced a two-part standard for application of Common Article 3 in its *Tadić* Interlocutory Decision on Jurisdiction,[9] which "has been widely accepted as reflecting custom."[10] First, hostilities must be "protracted," which the ICTY has added "refers more to the intensity of the armed violence than to its duration."[11] To reach the minimum level of "intensity," the violence must exceed that which would be characteristic of an internal disturbance or riot, necessitating the use of military force rather than law enforcement. Second, the non-state actor(s) involved must demonstrate a minimum level of "organization" to be considered a party to armed conflict, such that they are capable of conducting hostilities and acting under a command structure.

Turning to NIAC cessation, in certain contexts the law is fairly clear. For example, as the International Committee of the Red Cross (ICRC) explains in its updated commentary on Common Article 3, armed conflicts may end through military defeat or complete dissolution or demobilization of one or more parties

[8] For an overview of the initiation of NIACs, *see generally* David E. Graham, *Defining Non-International Armed Conflict: A Historically Difficult Task*, 88 INT'L L. STUD. 43 (2012). For an overview of when NIACs end, *see generally* Dustin A. Lewis et al., *Indefinite War: Unsettled International Law on the End of Armed Conflict* §§ 5, 7, 8 (Harv. L. Sch. Program on Int'l L. & Armed Conflict, Working Paper No. 17-16, 2017), https://papers.ssrn.com/sol3/papers.cfm?abstract_id=2923413 [hereinafter PILAC Study].

[9] Prosecutor v. Tadić, Case No. IT-94-1-AR72, Decision on the Defence Motion for Interlocutory Appeal on Jurisdiction (Int'l Crim. Trib. for the Former Yugoslavia Oct. 2, 1995).

[10] Milanovic, *supra* note 4, at 179. The International Committee of the Red Cross (ICRC) embraced this de facto approach to determining the existence of a NIAC in its 2016 updated commentary on Common Article 3. INT'L COMM. OF THE RED CROSS, COMMENTARY ON THE FIRST GENEVA CONVENTION 389–90 (2d ed. 2016), https://ihl-databases.icrc.org/en/ihl-treaties/gci-1949/article-3/commentary/2016#_Toc465169867 [hereinafter GCI 2016 Commentary]. *See also id.* 423 (quoting ICRC, *How Is the Term "Armed Conflict" Defined in International Humanitarian Law?*, Opinion Paper, March 2008, 5, https://www.icrc.org/en/doc/assets/files/other/opinion-paper-armed-conflict.pdf) ("Non-international armed conflicts are *protracted armed confrontations* occurring between governmental armed forces and the forces of one or more armed groups, or between such groups arising on the territory of a State [party to the Geneva Conventions]. The armed confrontation must reach a *minimum level of intensity* and the parties involved in the conflict must show a *minimum of organisation*."). *But see* Michael J. Adams & Ryan Goodman, *De Facto and De Jure Non-international Armed Conflicts: Is It Time to Topple Tadić?*, JUST SECURITY (Oct. 13, 2016), https://www.justsecurity.org/33533/de-facto-de-jure-non-international-armedconflicts-time-topple-tadic/.

[11] Weizmann, *supra* note 6, at 211 (citing Prosecutor v. Haradinaj, Case No. IT-04-84-T, Judgment, 49 (Int'l Crim. Trib. for the Former Yugoslavia Apr. 3, 2008)).

to the conflict.[12] On the other end of the spectrum, a state of armed conflict is clearly ongoing if armed confrontations among organized parties are occurring at least at the intensity that would satisfy reaching the NIAC threshold in the first instance.

But what does international law say about cessation of a NIAC when these factors are not present but the fighting tempo has considerably decreased? Or situations in which at least one party's intent or capability to conduct hostilities is genuinely in question, but not known with certainty by the other belligerent(s)? What does IHL say about this murky middle ground that increasingly characterizes today's conflicts? A growing body of expert commentary has attempted to elucidate frameworks that fill in these gaps, while generally acknowledging the law remains unsettled.[13] What follows is a brief overview of two compelling approaches.[14]

Filling the Gaps on NIAC Cessation

First, the "reverse *Tadić*" or "two-way-ratchet theory" holds that a NIAC terminates when either the armed group's level of organization or the intensity of violence "falls below the threshold necessary for the NIAC to have existed in the first place."[15] In short, "[f]or IHL to apply, its thresholds of application must continue to be satisfied at any given point in time."[16] The legal clarity of the reverse *Tadić* test is appealing. However, in conflicts where the intensity of fighting fluctuates, or "lulls" temporarily bring the violence below the intensity threshold, this approach could create a confusing and potentially destabilizing "revolving door of applicability and non-applicability of IHL."[17] Such fluctuations were

[12] GCI 2016 Commentary, *supra* note 10, 489–96. History is replete with examples of these scenarios, including in conflicts with at least one party characterized by the other side as a terrorist organization. For a recent example, *see* Gul v. Biden, 573 F. Supp. 3d 148, 153 (D.D.C. 2021) (discussing peace agreement between "Hezb-E-Islami Gulbuddin (HIG), a force that was [previously] associated with al Qaeda," and the government of Afghanistan). *See also* Milanovic, *supra* note 4, at 180.

[13] *See* PILAC Study, *supra* note 8, at 96–108 (distilling scholarship); *id.* at 96 (postulating "four theories on the vanishing point of the application" of IHL in NIACs, while cautioning that "these theories may be over- or under-inclusive" and "[n]one has attained consensus in either law or commentary"; "none, on its own, presents a sufficiently totalizing theory to address all the normative, practical, and legal concerns that may arise with respect to the discontinuance of the application of IHL to NIAC").

[14] For two additional theories, *see id.* at 100–03 (discussing the "state-of-war-throwback theory," which holds that NIAC ends "upon the achievement of a peaceful settlement between the formerly-warring parties," and the "no-more-combat-measures theory," which posits that NIAC ends "upon the general close of military operations as characterized by the cessation of actions of the armed forces with a view to combat").

[15] PILAC study, *supra* note 8, at 97.

[16] Milanovic, *supra* note 4, at 170.

[17] PILAC study, *supra* note 8, at 97–98.

exemplified in Afghanistan, where a "fighting season" roughly corresponded to seasonal changes in weather.[18] One can easily envision other such scenarios.

Accounting for these difficulties, Marko Milanovic posits that a NIAC can terminate if "hostilities . . . fall below the threshold of 'protracted armed violence' with a certain degree of permanence and stability so as to enable us to establish that the hostilities have, in fact, ended."[19] Nathalie Weizmann likewise describes a "risk of resumption" factor in determining whether a NIAC no longer meets the *Tadić* intensity or organization thresholds.[20]

By adding the risk of resumption factor, this theory begins to overlap with a second useful approach, which avoids the "oscillation" problem by considering a NIAC to end when "there is no reasonable risk of hostilities resuming."[21] The ICRC embraced a version of this approach in its updated Common Article 3 commentary, explaining that "a lasting cessation of armed confrontations without real risk of resumption will undoubtedly constitute the end of a NIAC."[22] The commentary elaborates that "the lasting absence of armed confrontations between the original Parties to the conflict may indicate—depending on the prevailing facts—the end of that [NIAC], even though there might still be minor isolated or sporadic acts of violence."[23]

The specific context and "prevailing facts" will matter in determining the likelihood that hostilities might resume. Thus, "[i]t is impossible to state in the abstract how much time without armed confrontations needs to pass" to conclude the NIAC has ceased.[24] A number of factors could be sufficient to reach this conclusion, including one that addresses the murky "petering out"

[18] *Id.* at 99.

[19] Milanovic, *supra* note 4, at 180. More broadly, he construes the theory as a "general principle," allowing that "departures" from the general rule may sometimes be warranted. *Id.* at 170 ("[U]nless there is a good reason of text, principle or policy that warrants an exception, the application of IHL will cease once the conditions that triggered its application in the first place no longer exist.").

[20] Weizmann, *supra* note 6, at 224 ("The risk of resumption can be evaluated by examining all the facts on the ground, including declarations by all sides, ground maneuvers, steps towards disarmament, demobilization and reintegration, and whether any measures have been taken to reach a peaceful settlement.").

[21] PILAC study, *supra* note 8, at 100. *See also* Derek Jinks, *The Temporal Scope of Application of International Humanitarian Law in Contemporary Conflicts* 3 (Harv. Program on Humanitarian Pol. & Conf. Rsch., Background Paper, 2003), https://hhi.harvard.edu/sites/g/files/omnuum6866/files/humanitarianinitiative/files/session3.pdf (suggesting NIAC ends when "there is no probability of a resumption of hostilities in the near future").

[22] GCI 2016 Commentary, *supra* note 10, 491 (arguing the situation would "equate to a peaceful settlement of the conflict, even without the conclusion or unilateral pronouncement of a formal act such as a ceasefire, armistice or peace agreement").

[23] *Id.* 494. The ICRC's 2024 Opinion Paper on the definition of armed conflict further supports this view. *See "How Is the Term 'Armed Conflict" Defined in International Humanitarian Law?* 19 (Int'l Comm. of the Red Cross, Opinion Paper, 2024), https://www.icrc.org/sites/default/files/document_new/file_list/armed_conflict_defined_in_ihl.pdf.

[24] GCI 2016 Commentary, *supra* note 10, 492. *See also* PILAC study, *supra* note 8, at 100 (The standard turns on the "reasonableness . . . of the threat of further hostilities," which is "admittedly vague.").

problem: or where to draw the line when there is an "increasing duration of the period without hostilities."[25]

The U.S. "Tipping Point" Approach

The United States has not publicly expressed a view that appears to nudge customary international law toward any particular approach to NIAC termination in general. It has, however, explained its view on one way the specific conflict with al-Qaeda might end.[26] A 2016 White House report, citing earlier speeches by President Obama, lays out this view, which the Trump and Biden administrations maintained as a baseline:

> At a certain point, the United States will degrade and dismantle the operational capacity and supporting networks of terrorist organizations like al-Qa'ida to such an extent that they will have been effectively destroyed and will no longer be able to attempt or launch a strategic attack against the United States. At that point, there will no longer be an ongoing armed conflict between the United States and those forces.[27]

This formulation invokes the "tipping point" articulated by then–General Counsel of the Department of Defense (DOD) Jeh Johnson in a speech at the Oxford Union in 2012:

> [T]here will come a tipping point—a tipping point at which so many of the leaders and operatives of al Qaeda and its affiliates have been killed or captured, and the group is no longer able to attempt or launch a strategic attack against the United States, such that al Qaeda as we know it, the organization that

25 GCI 2016 Commentary, *supra* note 10, 495 (listing other factors including "implementation of a peace agreement or ceasefire" and "implementation of disarmament, demobilization and/or reintegration programmes").

26 *See* THE WHITE HOUSE, REPORT ON THE LEGAL AND POLICY FRAMEWORKS GUIDING THE UNITED STATES' USE OF MILITARY FORCE AND RELATED NATIONAL SECURITY OPERATIONS 11 (Dec. 2016) [hereinafter 2016 White House Frameworks Report], https://s3.documentcloud.org/documents/3232529/Framework-Report-Final.pdf (The United States has long rejected the possibility of a peaceful settlement to its conflict with al-Qaeda. The Obama administration stated that the "unconventional" hostilities against al-Qaeda "presumably will not come to a conventional end." Al-Qaeda is "highly unlikely to disarm and sign instruments of surrender," and there is "little chance that there will be an agreement to end these hostilities.").

27 *Id.* at 12–13 (citing Obama Remarks at NDU, *supra* note 1; Jeh C. Johnson, Gen. Couns., Dep't. of Def., Speech at the Oxford Union: The Conflict Against Al Qaeda and Its Affiliates: How Will It End? (Nov. 30, 2012) [hereinafter Johnson OU Speech], https://www.lawfaremedia.org/article/jeh-johnson-speech-oxford-union#_ftn1).

> our Congress authorized the military to pursue in 2001, has been effectively destroyed.
>
> At that point, we must be able to say to ourselves that our efforts should no longer be considered an "armed conflict" against al Qaeda and its associated forces; rather, a counterterrorism effort against individuals who are the scattered remnants of al Qaeda, or are parts of groups unaffiliated with al Qaeda, for which the law enforcement and intelligence resources of our government are principally responsible, in cooperation with the international community—with our military assets available in reserve to address continuing and imminent terrorist threats.[28]

This appears to have been the authoritative U.S. position ever since. Notably, while it uses terms like "effectively destroyed," it does not require that *all* violence have ceased—rather, it envisions that "scattered remnants" of al-Qaeda and its affiliates would remain, but would be addressed through peacetime legal frameworks. This is appropriate given the nature of al-Qaeda and other terrorist organizations, which often splinter into new organizations that may lack the requisite level of organization or intensity of violence against the United States sufficient to sustain a NIAC. The reference to inability to conduct "a strategic attack" (as opposed to a lower level of violence) further confirms this point.

If the United States were to opine in a way that did nudge (or seek to reflect) custom,[29] it could situate this existing formulation fairly comfortably within either of the two theories described earlier. Reaching the "tipping point" of inability to launch a strategic attack, for example, could be understood as one means of satisfying the "no-reasonable-risk-of-resumption" theory. (This would be but one sufficient way to meet the standard, and others could also be offered.) Reaching the "tipping point" could also be sufficient to satisfy the "two-way-ratchet" standard on the intensity prong at minimum, and likely the organization prong as well.

Under any of these formulations, the standard for conflict termination may have already been met with respect to AQ Core, which the United States defined in 2016 as "the senior leaders and cadre of the organization based in Afghanistan and Pakistan who were primarily responsible for planning and carrying out"

[28] Johnson OU Speech, *supra* note 27, at 6 ("But, now that efforts by the U.S. military against al Qaeda are in their 12th year, we must also ask ourselves: how will this conflict end?").

[29] The United States has been an early mover, if not the first mover, in stating its view of customary international law and using legal diplomacy and transparency to push its crystallization in certain other conflict-related contexts. However, this generally occurs when doing so is perceived to expand operational flexibility. Two examples include advancing the unable or unwilling and elongated imminence theories in the law of self-defense, the latter of which is the subject of Oona A. Hathaway's contribution to this volume, Chapter 15, "The Rise of 'Self-Defense'—And the Fall of Constraints on the Use of Force."

the 9/11 attacks.[30] Based on U.S. government reports and public statements, it is hard to discern active hostilities in the past few years. AQ Core's decline was already evident in 2013, when President Obama declared the group "a shell of its former self."[31] That decline has continued. The Biden administration stated prior to removing U.S. forces from Afghanistan in September 2021 that "Al-Qa'ida probably lacks the intent and capability for attacks abroad."[32] Withdrawal from Afghanistan made armed clashes with the remnants of AQ Core even less likely. Since then, the United States is known to have launched two isolated strikes against AQ Core, killing a "senior al-Qaeda leader" in Syria in 2021[33] and the organization's head Ayman al-Zawahiri in Kabul in 2022.[34] Al-Qaeda apparently did not respond with its own attacks. In September 2023, President Biden's National Counterterrorism Center Director stated: "[A] new intelligence assessment states al-Qa'ida is at its historical nadir in Afghanistan and Pakistan, and its revival is unlikely. It has lost target access, leadership talent, group cohesion, rank-and-file commitment, and an accommodating local environment."[35]

While certainly not an intentional pronouncement of the legal end of armed conflict, these official statements and reports, taken together, would seem to indicate that AQ Core, at present, can "no longer . . . attempt or launch a strategic attack against the United States"—the 2016 White House formulation for when the conflict with al-Qaeda will have ceased.[36]

With AQ Core at its "nadir," no locus of hostilities in Afghanistan, no recent attacks on the part of AQ Core, an "eviscerated"[37] organizational structure, and its "revival [] unlikely," it would seem difficult to make the case that a NIAC vis-à-vis AQ Core persists. Why, then, does the United States claim that its decades-old conflict is ongoing?

[30] *See* 2016 White House Frameworks Report, *supra* note 26, at 5 n.21.

[31] Obama Remarks at NDU, *supra* note 1.

[32] *See* Section 1285 Reports, *supra* note 3, at 14 (adding that al-Qaeda "suffered leadership losses after years of counterterrorism pressure").

[33] Press Release, *U.S. Central Command, U.S. Strike in the Vicinity of Suluk, Syria, Oct. 22, 2021* (Oct. 22, 2021), https://www.centcom.mil/MEDIA/STATEMENTS/Statements-View/Article/2820408/us-strike-in-the-vicinity-of-suluk-syria-oct-22-2021/#:~:text=Statement%2C%20attributable%20to%20U.S.%20Army,using%20an%20MQ%2D9%20aircraft.

[34] Shane Harris et al., *U.S. Kills al-Qaeda Leader Ayman al-Zawahiri in Drone Strike in Kabul*, Wash. Post (Aug. 1, 2022), https://www.washingtonpost.com/national-security/2022/08/01/zawahiri-al-qaeda-killed/.

[35] Abizaid Statement, *supra* note 2. Abizaid also stated, "[I]t is important that we continue to" "sustain[] a Core counterterrorism effort—tailored to the challenges of the time." *Id.* Another assessment by a "senior administration official" likens the remaining militants to "a nursing home for AQ seniors." David Ignatius, *In Afghanistan, the Taliban Has All but Extinguished al-Qaeda*, Wash. Post (Sept. 14, 2023), https://www.washingtonpost.com/opinions/2023/09/14/al-qaeda-afghanistan-taliban-destroyed/.

[36] *See* Johnson OU Speech, *supra* note 27.

[37] *See* Jennifer Daskal & Stephen I. Vladeck, *After the AUMF*, 5 Harv. Nat'l Sec. J. 115, 121 (2014) ("The entity that attacked the United States on September 11, 2001—what is often described as 'al Qaeda Core'—has been effectively eviscerated.").

Drivers of Perpetual Conflict: Detention, Associated, and Successor Forces

Despite repeated efforts to move beyond the post-9/11 era, the United States remains entangled in a conflict whose legal boundaries have steadily expanded. Evolving interpretations of detention authority, along with the concepts of "associated" and "successor" forces, have helped sustain perpetual war.

Detention

The position that the United States remains in armed conflict with AQ Core appears premised, in part, on the consequences for detention operations at Guantánamo Bay should the conflict cease. Although several administrations have sought to close the facility, the United States continues to hold about fifteen men there in connection with the conflict.[38] Under IHL, the nine men in the military commissions system may continue to be prosecuted, and serve sentences, following the end of hostilities.[39] But the United States has long acknowledged that detention would need to wind down as to any other detainees at the "cessation of active hostilities," which may occur at the same time as NIAC ends[40] or even prior to the end of armed conflict.[41]

A plurality of the U.S. Supreme Court in *Hamdi v. Rumsfeld* confirmed this understanding when it explained in 2004 that the detention authority conferred

[38] Sarah Almukhtar et al., *The Guantánamo Docket*, N.Y. Times (updated Dec. 11, 2023), https://www.nytimes.com/interactive/2021/us/guantanamo-bay-detainees.html.

[39] *See* Int'l Comm. of the Red Cross, Protocol Additional to the Geneva Conventions of 12 August 1949, and relating to the Protection of Victims of Non-International Armed Conflicts (Protocol II), 8 June 1977, Commentary of 1987, 4493 (1987) [hereinafter Additional Protocol II Commentary], https://ihl-databases.icrc.org/en/ihl-treaties/apii-1977/article-2/commentary/1987?activeTab= ("[M]easures restricting people's liberty, taken for reasons related to the conflict, should cease at the end of active hostilities, i.e., when military operations have ceased, except in cases of penal convictions."). Note the number may be fewer than ten, as some who are charged may not be triable due to their previous torture or for other reasons. *See, e.g.*, Ellen Knickmeyer, *A 9/11 Defendant is Ruled Unfit for Trial after a Medical Panel Finds Torture Left Him Psychotic*, Associated Press (Sept. 22, 2023), https://apnews.com/article/guantanamo-911-torture-psychotic-011de316d14d2093a57b6bbd1901499a.

[40] The U.S. DOD's concept of "cessation of active hostilities" in its *Law of War Manual* closely resembles the "no-reasonable-risk-of resumption" standard for end of NIAC. *See* Office of Gen. Couns., Dep't of Def., Law of War Manual § 9.37.2 (2023), https://media.defense.gov/2023/Jul/31/2003271432/-1/-1/0/DOD-LAW-OF-WAR-MANUAL-JUNE-2015-UPDATED-JULY%202023.PDF. ("[Cessation of active hostilities] is the complete end of the fighting with clearly no probability of resumption of hostilities in the near future."); *see also* Al-Bihani v. Obama, 590 F.3d 866, 874 (D.C. Cir. 2010) ("The Conventions, in short, codify what common sense tells us must be true: release is only required when the fighting stops.").

[41] *See* Weizmann, *supra* note 6, at 233.

by the 2001 AUMF is bounded by the "clearly established principle of the law of war that detention may last no longer than active hostilities."[42] Given the petitioner in that case, U.S. citizen Yaser Hamdi, had been captured fighting with the Taliban in Afghanistan, the hostilities at issue were between U.S. forces and that group (the Taliban), in that location (Afghanistan). As Justice Stephen Breyer later explained, Hamdi feared that due to "the 'unconventional nature' of the 'war on terror,' there was a 'substantial prospect' that detention for the 'duration of the relevant conflict' could amount to 'perpetual detention.'"[43] But in 2004, there were still troops on the ground in Afghanistan, fighting directly with the Taliban, in a conflict that could be expected to end. At that point, "the war authorities that flow from the 2001 AUMF [would terminate] without further congressional action."[44] In turn, status-based detention authority would cease. Litigation brought by Guantánamo detainees challenging the legality of their detention in federal courts (habeas litigation) still proceeds against the background of this important IHL principle.

A full accounting of responsible ways to close Guantánamo is beyond the scope of this chapter,[45] but as of this writing the U.S. executive branch is not pursuing a closure policy. This creates pressure for government national security lawyers to argue that the relevant hostilities have not, in fact, ceased. But decades after *Hamdi* and over three years after withdrawal from Afghanistan, a key question before habeas courts is what the relevant hostilities are for determining the lawfulness of continuing detention today.

To understand how the executive branch has addressed that question, we must examine legal innovations that successively expanded the scope of the conflict. Both concern the 2001 AUMF, passed by Congress days after 9/11 to authorize force against those who "planned authorized, committed, or aided" the 9/11 attacks (widely understood as al-Qaeda), "or harbored" those responsible (the Taliban in Afghanistan), "in order to prevent any future acts of international terrorism against the United States by such nations, organizations, or persons."[46]

[42] Hamdi v. Rumsfeld, 542 U.S. 507, 520 (2004) (citing Geneva Convention (III) Relative to the Treatment of Prisoners of War, art. 118, Aug. 12, 1949 6 U.S.T. 3316, 3406 ("Prisoners of war shall be released and repatriated without delay after the cessation of active hostilities.")).

[43] Al-Alwi v. Trump, 901 F.3d 294, 299 (D.C. Cir. 2018), *cert. denied*, 139 S. Ct. 1893 (2019).

[44] Tess Bridgeman, *How to Ensure New Congressional War Authorization Is Not a Blank Check*, Just Security (Apr. 20, 2018), https://www.justsecurity.org/55147/stop-congressional-war-authorization-blank-check/.

[45] *See* Ian Moss, *There Is a Way to Close Guantanamo*, Just Security (Jan. 11, 2022), https://www.justsecurity.org/78166/there-is-a-way-to-close-guantanamo/.

[46] *See* 2001 AUMF, *supra* note 5, at § 2a.

"Associated" and "Successor" Forces

Having inherited a war that extended beyond AQ Core and the Taliban, the Obama administration faced a choice: wind down the war—or those aspects of it that extended beyond the parties active in the Afghanistan-Pakistan region who were responsible for the 9/11 attacks—or attempt to tie the further penumbras of the conflict to international law. It chose the latter. In doing so, it innovated legal concepts that have enabled further expansion of the war on what has become a perpetually renewing basis.[47] Specifically, as part of its effort to tether the armed conflict to international law and to statutory authority,[48] and in contrast to the prior administration, the United States under President Obama began to describe what had been called the "Global War on Terror" (GWOT) as an armed conflict governed by IHL. But in order to encompass groups beyond AQ Core and the Taliban (those described in the 2001 AUMF), it conceived of the scope of the conflict as one "against al-Qa'ida, the Taliban, and *associated forces*."[49]

The basic theory of "associated forces" is that Congress must have intended the 2001 AUMF to authorize armed force against groups who are "co-belligerents" (as that term would purportedly be understood under international law[50]) of AQ Core or the Taliban. This is so, the theory goes, even if those groups had no connection to the 9/11 attacks and were formed after those attacks occurred (which reads the purpose clause and the specification of actors entirely out of the statute).[51]

The Obama administration crafted the following legal test to determine when an armed group constitutes an "associated force": "First, the entity must be an organized, armed group that has entered the fight alongside al-Qa'ida or the Taliban. Second, the group must be a co-belligerent with al-Qa'ida or the Taliban in hostilities against the United States or its coalition partners."[52] It is not clear

[47] *See* Curtis A. Bradley & Jack L. Goldsmith, *Obama's AUMF Legacy*, 110 Am. J. Int'l L. 628, 629 (2016) (describing how, where law on NIAC was unsettled, "the administration often adopted interpretations that supported presidential discretion and flexibility, and thus that enhanced rather than constrained the administration's authority to take action under the AUMF").

[48] *See, e.g.*, Respondents' Memorandum Regarding the Government's Detention Authority Relative to Detainees Held at Guantánamo Bay at 1–2, *In re* Guantánamo Bay Detainee Litigation (D.D.C. Mar. 13, 2009) (Misc. No. 08-442).

[49] 2016 White House Frameworks Report, *supra* note 26, at 6 (emphasis added).

[50] *See* Rebecca Ingber, *Co-Belligerency*, 42 Yale J. Int'l L. 67 (2017); Daskal & Vladeck, *supra* note 37, at 123 ("A key difference is that Congress declared war against the United States' co-belligerent enemies in World War II, whereas the Executive Branch has, since 2001, read co-belligerents into the AUMF without ever going back to Congress for subsequent authorization. In fact, it has refused to publicly acknowledge what groups qualify as associated forces . . . .").

[51] Congress rejected a broader formulation proposed by the Bush administration. *See* Bradley & Goldsmith, *supra* note 47, at 630 ("Congress rejected the Bush administration's request for a broader authority to 'deter and preempt any future acts of terrorism or aggression against the United States' and gave it instead the more targeted authority to use force against entities connected to 9/11.").

[52] *See* 2016 White House Frameworks Report, *supra* note 26, at 4.

whether the intensity threshold for the existence of a NIAC is subsumed in the "entered the fight" or "in hostilities" portions of this test, or whether otherwise meeting the "associated forces" test essentially bypasses those requirements.[53]

Successive U.S. administrations have used this test to apply the 2001 AUMF to, at least, "certain other terrorist or insurgent groups affiliated with al-Qa'ida or the Taliban in Afghanistan; al-Qa'ida in the Arabian Peninsula [in Yemen]; al-Shabaab [in Somalia]; individuals in Libya who are part of al-Qa'ida; [and] al-Qa'ida in Syria."[54] Congress and lower federal courts have embraced the notion of associated forces in the context of detention of noncitizens.[55] Neither, however, has determined that each of the specific groups the executive classifies as "associated forces" are so as a factual matter, in part because that list is often treated as classified, and in part because Guantánamo habeas litigation has long been the only avenue for judicial review of the executive's interpretation of the 2001 AUMF's scope.[56]

A second interpretive shift that expanded the scope of the conflict was bringing the Islamic State of Iraq and Syria (ISIS, also known as ISIL) within the scope of the 2001 AUMF under a novel theory classifying the group as a "successor force" of AQ Core.[57] This innovation was born of the urgency to find

[53] Milanovic, *supra* note 4, at 187 ("One simply cannot aggregate all terrorist acts motivated by Islamic fundamentalism coupled with professed allegiance to Al Qaeda all across the world in order to satisfy the twofold intensity and organization test. Nor does it seem justifiable to depart from the *Tadić* criteria in the case of Al Qaeda but continue applying them rigorously to 'normal', common NIACs.").

[54] Office of Legal Adviser, Dep't of State, Digest of United States Practice in International Law 730 (2017), https://www.state.gov/digest-of-united-states-practice-in-international-law-2017.

[55] *See* National Defense Authorization Act for Fiscal Year 2012, Pub. L. No. 112-81, § 1021(a), 125 Stat. 1298, 1562 (2011); Al-Adahi v. Obama, 613 F.3d 1102, 1102 (D.C. Cir. 2010) ("The government may therefore hold at Guantanamo and elsewhere those individuals who are 'part of' al-Qaida, the Taliban, or associated forces."); Khan v. Obama, 655 F.3d 20, 23 (D.C. Cir. 2011) ("We have held that the AUMF grants the President authority (inter alia) to detain individuals who are 'part of forces associated with Al Qaeda or the Taliban.'").

[56] Brian Finucane, *Putting AUMF Repeal into Context*, Just Security (June 24, 2021), https://www.justsecurity.org/77088/putting-aumf-repeal-into-context/ ("[F]or most of the past two decades the complete inventory of enemies U.S. forces are fighting or authorized to fight under the 2001 AUMF has been a secret."). For a critique of keeping the list of "associated forces" secret, *see* Jack Goldsmith, *DOD's Weak Rationale for Keeping Enemy Identities Secret*, Lawfare (July 26, 2013), https://www.lawfaremedia.org/article/dods-weak-rationale-keeping-enemy-identities-secret.

[57] Brianna Rosen and I have explained the highly controversial nature of this interpretive move. *See* Tess Bridgeman & Brianna Rosen, *Still at War: The United States in Syria*, Just Security (Apr. 29, 2022), https://www.justsecurity.org/81313/still-at-war-the-united-states-in-syria/. *See also* Ryan Goodman & Shalev Roisman, *Assessing the Claim that ISIL Is a Successor to Al Qaeda—Part 1 (Organizational Structure)*, Just Security (Oct. 1, 2014), https://www.justsecurity.org/15801/assessing-isil-successor-al-qaeda-2001-aumf-part-1-organizational-structure/ ("[T]he available public record contradicts more than it supports the successor model."); Robert Chesney, *The 2001 AUMF: From Associated Forces to (Disassociated) Successor Forces*, Lawfare (Sept. 10, 2014), https://www.lawfaremedia.org/article/2001-aumf-associated-forces-disassociated-successor-forces (chronicling the "stunning" nature of this decision "from a legal perspective"); Bradley & Goldsmith, *supra* note 47, at 629 ("[T]he administration significantly extended the scope and duration of the AUMF by interpreting it to apply to the Islamic State.").

domestic legal authorization for counter-ISIS military operations as the group swept across Syria and Iraq in 2014, and the tempo of operations made it untenable to rely solely on the U.S. president's Article II authority, as had been done for more limited operations in the lead-up to the full-scale military campaign against the group.[58]

If not for the need for domestic authorization (the White House later proposed an ISIS-specific AUMF, but it never became law[59]), there would have been no need for a "successor forces" theory to join AQ Core and ISIS under the 2001 AUMF. Unlike earlier "associated forces," there was a clear basis under international law for using force against ISIS independent of any notions of "co-belligerency"—collective self-defense of Iraq.[60] Moreover, the organization and intensity NIAC thresholds were easily crossed by the summer of 2014 with respect to ISIS. But in the absence of an ISIS-specific AUMF, the group was lumped together with AQ Core for *domestic* law purposes, even though AQ Core and ISIS had themselves been engaged in armed clashes *against each other*.[61] As a 2021 report relying on extensive interviews of executive branch officials describes, "none of the senior executive branch lawyers involved in the deliberations thought that the application of the 2001 AUMF to ISIS was the best interpretation of the law, particularly because of the split between ISIS and al-Qaeda."[62] Nevertheless, "confronted with leaders who felt an urgent imperative to continue battling ISIS, and who did not want to be beholden to Congress for authorisation, these lawyers took the view that [application to ISIS] was a 'legally available' interpretation of the AUMF."[63]

Like the "associated forces" innovation before it, this "successor forces" interpretive claim opened a veritable Pandora's box, as ISIS grew at tremendous speed and spawned global affiliates. It is unclear whether the executive believes the United States is now in conflict with some or all of these affiliates due to its initial NIAC with ISIS in Iraq and Syria,[64] or whether each must meet the

58 Bridgeman & Rosen, *supra* note 57.

59 *See* Administration of Barack Obama, Draft Joint Resolution to Authorize the Limited Use of the United States Armed Forces Against the Islamic State of Iraq and the Levant (Feb. 11, 2015), https://obamawhitehouse.archives.gov/sites/default/files/docs/aumf_02112015.pdf.

60 The United States claimed a right of both individual and *collective* self-defense, based on Iraq's request for assistance. *See* Brian Egan, Legal Adviser, U.S. Dep't of State, Speech at the Annual Meeting of the American Society of International Law (Apr. 1, 2016).

61 *See, e.g.*, Daniel L. Byman & Jennifer R. Williams, *ISIS v. Al Qaeda: Jihadism's Global Civil War*, Brookings Inst. (Feb. 24, 2015), https://www.brookings.edu/articles/isis-vs-al-qaeda-jihadisms-global-civil-war/ (explaining conflict between AQ Core and ISIS).

62 Overkill: Reforming the Legal Basis for the U.S. War on Terror, Int'l Crisis Group (Sept. 17, 2021), https://www.crisisgroup.org/united-states/005-overkill-reforming-legal-basis-us-war-terror.

63 *Id.*

64 For example, is the United States in armed conflict with "ISIS-Khorasan Province, ISIS-West Africa, ISIS-Sahel, ISIS-Libya, ISIS-Somalia, ISIS-Yemen, ISIS-DRC, ISIS-East Asia Province, [and] ISIS-Mozambique," or does it view them as "a single undifferentiated entity"? *See* Heather Brandon-Smith & Brian Finucane, *Opaque Transparency on the Use of Force: Observations on the 2022 "1264"*

"associated forces" test. No limiting principle has been articulated to suggest that the United States would *not* consider the "associated force" of a "successor force" to be party to the same expanding conflict. It is also possible that the United States views some or all of these groups as "part of" ISIS—that is, as "a single organized group."[65]

In sum, for purposes of finding *domestic* law authorization to use force against terrorist groups beyond those described in the 2001 AUMF (AQ Core and the Taliban), the United States has loosely grouped many organized armed groups into what it now terms "an ongoing armed conflict" [singular],[66] from ISIS in Iraq and Syria to "al-Shabaab, an associated force of al-Qa'ida" in Somalia, among others.[67]

The Conflict-Perpetuating Effect of Aggregating Hostilities of "Associated" and "Successor" Forces

We can now return to the questions of which hostilities are relevant for purposes of determining whether (a) there has been a "cessation of hostilities," or (b) the thresholds for the end of NIAC have been reached. This issue has gained importance in part because of the disconnect between the affiliations of the remaining detainees at Guantánamo (generally, AQ Core) and the groups the United States still occasionally strikes (such as ISIS in Syria and al Shabaab in Somalia[68]). The situation has prompted some to ask: "With Afghanistan no longer serving as the likely ground for extensive conflict between the United States and AQ and ISIS-K" and the passage of time without significant fighting, "could operations against AQ/ISIS affiliates in Somalia, Sahel countries, and others be aggregated to operations

Report, JUST SECURITY (Mar. 14, 2023), https://www.justsecurity.org/85448/opaque-transparency-on-the-use-of-force-observations-on-the-2022-1264-report; Brian Finucane, *Key Takeaways from September 28 House Foreign Affairs Committee Hearing on AUMF Reform*, JUST SECURITY (Oct. 4, 2023), https://www.justsecurity.org/89148/key-takeaways-from-september-28-house-foreign-affairs-committee-hearing-on-aumf-reform/.

[65] Finucane, *supra* note 64 ("In response to a question . . . about the standards by which the executive branch determines which groups were covered by the 2001 AUMF, DOD General Counsel Caroline Krass explained that it views ISIS 'as itself being a single organized group.' ").

[66] *See, e.g., Reclaiming Congress's Article I Powers: Counterterrorism AUMF Reform: Hearing Before the House Comm. on Foreign Aff.*, 118th Cong. 1–2 (2023) (joint statement of Christopher Maier, Assistant Sec'y of Defense for Special Operations and Low-Intensity Conflict, Dep't of Def., & Caroline Krass, Gen. Couns., Dep't of Def.), https://www.documentcloud.org/documents/23995972-hmtg-118-fa00-wstate-maierc-20230928/?responsive=1&title=1.

[67] *Id.* at 2–3.

[68] *Id.*

in Afghanistan for the purposes of sustaining the *Tadić* protracted armed conflict requirement?"[69]

The short answer, based on the prevailing view of IHL, is no. The controversial expansion of the 2001 AUMF into essentially an umbrella domestic authorizing statute for war against all of these organized armed groups[70] should not be understood as an international law matter to collapse all hostilities against terrorist groups into one large NIAC.[71] While a full discussion of controversial U.S. assertions regarding the global geographic scope of conflict is not needed here,[72] it is important for our purposes to distinguish between the "where" and the "who." A situation in which one NIAC spans multiple countries could potentially exist, but "only . . . where the individuals against which the State uses force in those several countries are *actually members of the same non-State group*."[73]

Even *if* each of the "associated" and "successor" forces (for AUMF purposes) are considered to be part of one NIAC spanning multiple locations and myriad parties—rather than forming multiple NIACs, which is the better view—these organized armed groups, operating in different parts of the globe and with different aims and strategies, do not lose their individual identities. AQ Core is not ISIS in Syria and Iraq, which is not AQAP, and so on.[74] Individual parties to NIAC(s), whether understood for *domestic* law purposes as "associated" or

[69] Steve Szymanski & Chris Koschnitzky, *Afghanistan 2021: Reflections from the Stockton Center for International Law's Workshop*, West Point Lieber Inst. (Jan. 24, 2022), https://lieber.westpoint.edu/afghanistan-2021-reflections-stockton-center-workshop/.

[70] *See* Bradley & Goldsmith, *supra* note 47, at 628 ("The transformation of the AUMF from an authorization to use force against the 9/11 perpetrators who planned an attack from Afghanistan into a protean foundation for indefinite war against an assortment of terrorist organizations in numerous countries is one of the most remarkable legal developments in American public law in the still-young twenty-first century.").

[71] ISIS, for example, should not be understood to be in the same NIAC with the United States as AQ Core. *See, e.g.*, Sasha Radin, *Global Armed Conflict? The Threshold of Extraterritorial Non-International Armed Conflicts*, 89 Int'l L. Stud. 696, 723–24 (2013), https://digital-commons.usnwc.edu/cgi/viewcontent.cgi?article=1047&context=ils ("It is a well-accepted view that separate conflicts may exist in parallel. Consequently, multiple conflicts may exist side-by-side in the same region.") (internal citations omitted).

[72] For an overview, *see* Weizmann, *supra* note 6, at 215–19. For acknowledgment of disagreement regarding the U.S. view, *see* John O. Brennan, Assistant to the President for Homeland Sec. and Counterterrorism, Remarks at the Harvard Law School Program on Law & Security: Strengthening our Security by Adhering to our Values and Laws (Sept. 16, 2011), https://obamawhitehouse.archives.gov/the-press-office/2011/09/16/remarks-john-o-brennan-strengthening-our-security-adhering-our-values-an ("[O]thers in the international community—including some of our closest allies and partners—take a different view of the geographic scope of the conflict . . . .").

[73] Christof Heyns et al., *The International Legal Framework Regulating the Use of Armed Drones*, 65 Int'l Comp. L.Q. 791, 807 (2016) ("[T]he violence can only be part of the same armed conflict if it is *between the same parties*.") (emphasis added); *see also* Noam Lubell, Extraterritorial Use of Force Against Non-State Actors 101, 120 (2010) ("If numerous incidents round the world classified as terrorism could be attributed to *the same entity* then one could argue that the threshold for conflict has been crossed.") (emphasis added).

[74] Milanovic, *supra* note 4, at 186 ("[T]he existing legal framework does not seem to allow for a construction as amorphous as a planet-wide NIAC, particularly one in which a loose terrorist network such as Al Qaeda is treated as a single organizational entity and belligerent party.").

"successor" forces or something else entirely, remain segregable unless they actually merge.[75] In determining when IHL ceases to apply, the conflict ends as to any one of the parties involved when the threshold for NIAC termination is reached *as to that party*[76] (should it dissolve, be defeated, make peace, or the like), even if it continues vis-à-vis others.[77]

In sum, the majority view in IHL is that *Tadić*'s organization and intensity thresholds (or whatever other threshold is used to determine whether IHL still applies) must be met by each party to the NIAC, and a belligerent cannot impute its hostilities with *other* parties onto each other to reach a level of intensity that does not, in fact, exist.[78]

The Aggregation Theory and Its Drawbacks

A view has recently emerged, however, that "aggregation" of violence across distinct armed groups for purposes of measuring the intensity threshold is permissible in some circumstances. Competing variants of this theory have been posited, featuring different analyses of which acts of violence should count and what level of coordination across the groups should be required.[79] The concern

[75] *Gul v. Biden*, 573 F. Supp. 3d at 165 ("[A]llied forces maintain separate identities.") (citing Int'l Comm. of the Red Cross, Commentary of 2020 on the Third Geneva Convention, art. 118, at C.2, 4452).

[76] *See* Radin, *supra* note 71, at 724 (2013) ("Strictly speaking, it is the hostilities that take place between the specific parties to the conflict that must surpass a level of sporadic violence."). As an international law matter, it would be odd to claim that the conflict with AQ Core goes on because later-commenced conflicts continue with other distinct groups. This understanding is also consistent with the innovation of the "associated" and "successor" forces concepts themselves—if all of the armed groups were actually one entity that could function as a single party to armed conflict (essentially, as part of AQ Core), there would have been no need to employ these new concepts.

[77] For an explanation in the context of the U.S. NIACs against al-Qaeda and "associated forces," *see* Gul v. Biden, 573 F. Supp. 3d 148, at 164 ("The commentary to the Geneva Conventions makes clear that '[t]he obligation to release and repatriate prisoners of war arises as soon as active hostilities between the Detaining Power and the Power on which the prisoners depend have ceased.' That is true even though '[a]ctive hostilities might . . . cease bilaterally between two belligerent Parties[] before the general close of military operations and even though active hostilities continue *with other Parties to the conflict*.' Even if a force's allies or associates continue fighting, once 'the Power on which the prisoner[] depend[s]' has withdrawn from active hostilities, the duty to repatriate is triggered.") (internal citations omitted).

[78] Szymanski & Koschnitzky, *supra* note 69 (as of January 2022, explaining "the actual strike frequency is more probative for a *Tadić* assessment. Even if it is conceded that a limited [over-the-horizon] air campaign alone may satisfy the 'minimum intensity' *Tadić* threshold, the five-month dearth undermines the argument that the present de facto intensity level in Afghanistan is sufficient."); Milanovic, *supra* note 4 at 187 ("One simply cannot aggregate all terrorist acts motivated by Islamic fundamentalism coupled with professed allegiance to Al Qaeda all across the world in order to satisfy the twofold intensity and organization test. Nor does it seem justifiable to depart from the Tadić criteria in the case of Al Qaeda but continue applying them rigorously to 'normal', common NIACs.").

[79] *See* Chiara Radaelli, *A Common Enemy: Aggregating Intensity in Non-International Armed Conflicts*, Int'l Comm. of the Red Cross Humanitarian L. & Policy Blog (Apr. 22, 2021),

driving this theory is that, in some situations, it can be difficult to "disentangle the level of violence by each of the armed groups involved."[80] This leads to a risk of "under-classification" of NIAC—a situation that looks and feels like armed conflict on the ground, but is not categorized as such because it is impossible to tell whether the individual groups involved meet the intensity threshold.[81] Coordination among the groups and common geography are key elements in this regard.[82] As one aggregation proponent explains with respect to the latter, "if two groups are based in two different regions, it would not be hard to assess the level of violence separately, even if they are members of the same coalitions. Accordingly, it is submitted that a geographical continuum is necessary to aggregate intensity."[83]

The aggregation approach raises a number of concerns. In some contexts, it gives rise to a serious risk of "States try[ing] to 'overclassify' a situation as an armed conflict in order to apply IHL even where it does not apply."[84] Overclassification is particularly problematic in the counterterrorism context, as "[t]he more permissive rules of IHL governing the use of force seem to offer an attractive alternative to the law enforcement paradigm for counterterrorist operations."[85]

Aggregation also introduces the problem of what to do when the threshold for NIAC termination seems to be met for one of the parties but not others—a problem that does not arise under the majority approach. Even some who argue for developing an aggregation approach to determine when a conflict *begins* see danger in using it to determine when conflict *ends*, arguing instead that when the threshold for NIAC termination is reached as to any one party "it seems

https://blogs.icrc.org/law-and-policy/2021/04/22/common-enemy/; Jann K. Kleffner, *The Legal Fog of an Illusion: Three Reflections on "Organization" and "Intensity" as Criteria for the Temporal Scope of the Law of Non-International Armed Conflict*, 95 Int'l L. Stud. 161 (2019); Jelena Nikolic et al., *Aggregated Intensity: Classifying Coalitions of Non-State Armed Groups*, Int'l Comm. of the Red Cross Humanitarian L. & Policy Blog (Oct. 7, 2020), https://blogs.icrc.org/law-and-policy/2020/10/07/aggregated-intensity-classifying-coalitions-non-state-armed-groups/.

[80] Nikolic et al., *supra* note 79.

[81] *See, e.g.*, *id.* (citing complex situations in Syria, Democratic Republic of the Congo, Central African Republic); Gloria Gaggioli & Pavle Kilibarda, *Counterterrorism and the Risk of Over-Classification of Situations of Violence*, 103 Int'l Rev. of the Red Cross no. 916-917, 231 (2021) ("[T]hese . . . theoretical constructions [are] driven by the desire to facilitate conflict classification in situations where the facts are difficult to ascertain.").

[82] Radin, *supra* note 71, at 725 (explaining circumstances when "it can be difficult to isolate the specific group that conducted each attack and to assign to a particular group some of the indicative factors used to ascertain that the intensity requirement is fulfilled . . . given the shared territory. In a way, the common territory serves to link the violence undertaken by these various armed groups.").

[83] Radaelli, *supra* note 79.

[84] Marco Sassòli, *The Implementation of International Humanitarian Law: Current and Inherent Challenges*, 10 Y.B. of Int'l Humanitarian L. 45, 50 (2007).

[85] Gaggioli & Kilibarda, *supra* note 81.

reasonable to conclude that [other affiliated group] is not party to the NIAC anymore," regardless of the remaining level of intensity as to other parties.[86]

Can the developing aggregation theory be applied to the U.S. conflict(s) with AQ Core and others? First, despite its gaining traction among some important stakeholders, it would be premature to consider the aggregation approach as established law. Second, proponents of the theory generally apply it only when the facts on the ground make it difficult to disentangle violence committed by various armed groups, as when multiple actors are involved in fighting in the same geographic area. And third, the groups involved must be acting in "a coalition, objectively and effectively demonstrating a collective approach of the fighting."[87] According to the ICRC, a "shared ideology" or existence of a "common enemy" would not be sufficient to determine the existence of a coalition for purposes of aggregating intensity. "Rather, factual indicators must be considered, including . . . , the establishment of a coordination structure, the sharing of operational tasks, the existence of common standard operating procedures and/or rules of engagement, the coordination of simultaneous attacks against the opposing party and the conduct of joint military operations."[88]

Thus, even *if* the aggregation theory commanded the status of custom (it does not), it is fairly clear that the U.S. NIAC(s) with "al-Qaeda, the Taliban, and associated forces, including ISIL" do not present a scenario where it would be appropriate to apply it. The actors lack both geographic proximity and the factual indicators of true coalition status (with some AUMF-covered groups at times in conflict with each other). More fundamentally, there is no underclassification risk. Instead, there is a serious risk of *over*classification. It is just such a scenario that has been unfolding.

The U.S. Position in Habeas: Unbounded Aggregation and the End of the Tipping Point

During the first Trump administration and the Biden administration, the United States quietly developed a breathtakingly capacious theory of aggregation in the context of Guantánamo habeas litigation. It requires parsing because U.S. briefs generally appear careful not to speak to any one group in isolation when stating a legal standard for the existence of ongoing hostilities, but rather refer to

[86] Radaelli, *supra* note 79 ("When a NIAC is classified on the basis of aggregated violence, should its end be assessed cumulatively? It is suggested that this should not be the case and that the end of the conflict should be determined using the fragmented approach.").

[87] Nikolic et al., *supra* note 79.

[88] ICRC, *How Is the Term "Armed Conflict" Defined in International Humanitarian Law?*, Opinion Paper, March 2008, 17, https://www.icrc.org/en/doc/assets/files/other/opinion-paper-armed-conflict.pdf.

"al-Qaida and associated forces" jointly. Moreover, many key facts are redacted for classification purposes. And to be sure, not all of the concepts being advanced are new.[89] But from what is publicly available, it seems the executive has been aggregating hostilities across different armed groups, in different corners of the world, without regard to whether the groups are acting in coalition with each other. Instead, the only fact that appears meaningful in the government's analysis is whether the groups are each deemed by the executive to be covered by the 2001 AUMF *for domestic law purposes*. Indeed, to demonstrate ongoing hostilities between the United States and al-Qaeda in recent habeas litigation, the United States has relied on its use of armed force against groups that have themselves been in open armed conflict *against al-Qaeda* (ISIS).[90]

The Department of Justice's December 2022 filing in the case of Tofiq Nasser Awad al-Bihani, who is detained on the basis that he is "part of al-Qaida,"[91] illustrates the breadth of the aggregation being employed. "[I]n recent months," it states, "U.S. forces conducted an air strike against a high-value *al-Shabaab* target and remain prepared to conduct air strikes against ISIS and al-Shabaab."[92] It adds that "a small number of U.S. military personnel continue to be deployed to *Yemen* to conduct operations" against AQAP and ISIS, and that in December 2022, "U.S. forces *in Syria* conducted a raid that successfully targeted two senior ISIS officials."[93] None of these relate to the group to which al-Bihani allegedly belonged, nor the locations in which that group had fought—they have in

[89] The United States has long claimed the AUMF is not geographically bound, for example. *See, e.g.*, Rahim v. Trump, 486 F. Supp. 3d 350, 356–57 (D.C. Dist. 2020) (agreeing with the government that "the original conflict in Afghanistan metastasizing across the globe" to new groups would further justify continued detention rather than undermine it). At the same time, the United States greatly relied on the ongoing conflict in Afghanistan in particular. *See, e.g.*, Al Odah v. United States, 62 F. Supp. 3d 101, 110 (D.C. Cir. 2014) (agreeing with the government that a habeas petition is not ripe because "the events that could entitle Petitioner to relief, that he be detained unlawfully upon the cessation of hostilities in Afghanistan, have not yet occurred").

[90] *See, e.g.*, Qassim v. Biden, No. 1:04-cv-01194, 2023 U.S. Dist. LEXIS 173537 (D.D.C. Sept. 27, 2023) (adopting the U.S. position on ongoing hostilities as embraced in prior cases, including *Paracha* and *Rahim*); Rahim v. Biden, No. 1:09-cv-01385, 2023 U.S. Dist. LEXIS 168832 (D.D.C. Sept. 21, 2023); Husayn v. Austin, No. 1:08-cv-01360, 2024 U.S. Dist. LEXIS 183377 (D.D.C. Oct. 8, 2024) (denying defendant's motion for an order requiring immediate release and repatriation); Paracha v. Biden, No. 1:04-cv-02022, 2022 U.S. Dist. LEXIS 133035 (D.D.C. July 1, 2022) (denying defendant's second petition for habeas corpus and other relief).

[91] Government Response to Petition for Writ of Habeas Corpus at 2, Al-Bihani v. Biden, No. 1:22-cv-02845, 2022 U.S. Dist. Ct. Motions LEXIS 467120 (D.D.C. Dec. 16, 2022) (arguing that Petitioner "is lawfully detained by the United States at Guantanamo Bay under AUMF as 'part of al-Qaida,' thereby justifying his continued law-of-war detention while hostilities against al-Qaida *and associated forces* remain ongoing") (emphasis added) (internal citation omitted).

[92] *Id.* at 24 (emphasis added).

[93] *Id.* (emphases added). Oddly, this section leads with "U.S. personnel remain postured outside Afghanistan to address threats to the U.S. interests *that may arise* from inside Afghanistan" (emphasis added), which could indicate there are currently *not* threats that would necessitate the use of military force. *See id.*

common only the executive's view that each group is covered by the 2001 AUMF for domestic law purposes.

In its filing of April 28, 2023, the government updated its list of "hostilities under the 2001 AUMF" (again lumping together all organized armed groups it deems covered by the 2001 AUMF), which it describes as "plainly ongoing."[94] The brief cites examples only regarding ISIS in Syria and al-Shabaab in Somalia:

> Indeed, since Respondents' initial filing on December 16, 2022, several other high-profile, publicly reported military operations against Al Qaeda and associated forces reinforce the ongoing nature of hostilities authorized by the 2001 AUMF. *See* Navy Times, "Key Islamic State leader killed in US military operation in Somalia," Jan. 30, 2023 (detailing special forces raid in Northern Somalia that killed senior ISIS leader Bilal al-Sudani) . . . ; Military Times, "First AFRICOM airstrike of the year kills 30 al-Shabab militants," Jan. 23, 2023 (US airstrikes supporting Somali ground troops kills 30 al-Shabab fighters and destroys three vehicles) . . . ; CENTCOM Press Release, "ISIS Senior Leader Killed and Four U.S. Servicemembers Wounded in Helicopter Raid in Northeastern Syria," Feb. 17, 2023 (helicopter raid killing a senior ISIS leader in Northeastern Syria) . . . .
>
> Thus, . . . hostilities remain ongoing.[95]

For its part, the judiciary has thus far embraced the conflation of hostilities with a party to a NIAC with hostilities involving any armed group identified by the executive as falling within the domestic statute authorizing what are arguably several NIACs (involving multiple parties). At a bare minimum, those organized armed groups that have been in open hostilities with each other (ISIS and al-Qaeda) cannot be collapsed into one party, at least absent an attempt to show that they have formed a true coalition. Yet the argument now goes: "Detention under the law of war" is permitted "until the end of the hostilities authorized by the [AUMF]"[96]—as opposed to the end of hostilities with the relevant belligerent party.

This argument confuses the "where" with the "who." It conflates the geography-based notion that the AUMF has no borders (a "where" force may be used question) with the proposition that hostilities with any group covered by the AUMF are sufficient to find that cessation has not occurred vis-à-vis any

[94] Government Sur-reply in Opposition to Petition for Writ of Habeas Corpus at 13–14, Al-Bihani v. Biden, No. 1:22-cv-02845 (D.D.C. Apr. 28, 2023).

[95] *Id.*

[96] Rahim v. Biden, No. 1:09-cv-01385, 2023 U.S. Dist. LEXIS 168832, at *3 (citing *Al-Alwi*, 901 F.3d at 294).

other group (a "who" force may be used against question, regardless of where they are located).

Defensive Litigation and Judicial Deference

Two dynamics that push the U.S. government's view toward this position merit mention: the litigation posture through which the question arises and the highly deferential attitude of federal courts.[97] First, defensive litigation in the national security realm often leads the executive branch to take broader positions on the scope of its own authority than it otherwise might—say, in a high-level speech or presidential document—for reasons that have been explored at length elsewhere.[98] It engages the strong tendency in executive branch national security lawyering to avoid legal interpretations that constrain executive power or set outer boundaries that might reduce future flexibility.[99]

Second, this effect combines with wide deference from the courts to yield broad legal positions that have staying power once they become judicially endorsed. As Rebecca Ingber explains:

> With some critical exceptions over the course of the last decade—notable mainly for their rarity—U.S. courts tend to defer broadly to the executive in areas of wartime authority, foreign policy, and national security. This means that the executive's interpretation of its legal authority in a given case . . . is given enormous weight and often becomes the law of the land.[100]

Deference has been particularly wide in Guantánamo habeas litigation in general, and specifically on the issue of the cessation of hostilities. Indeed, contrary to the role played by federal courts in past U.S. conflicts,[101] habeas courts are quite comfortable deferring to the executive on the dispositive facts that dictate

[97] Rebecca Ingber, *Interpretation Catalysts and Executive Branch Legal Decisionmaking*, 38 Yale. J. Int'l L. 359 (2013).

[98] *Id.* at 379 (explaining how in a defensive litigation posture "nearly all forces align to push the executive to advocate an expansive view of its own authority, to defend past action, and to request a judgment in favor of the government on the broadest possible grounds so as to preserve executive flexibility to the greatest possible extent").

[99] For an excellent discussion of these factors and others that entrench and expand executive power, *see* Rebecca Ingber, *The Obama War Powers Legacy and the Internal Forces that Entrench Executive Power*, 110 Am. J. Int'l L. 680 (2016).

[100] Ingber, *supra* note 97, at 378–79.

[101] *See, e.g.*, Oona Hathaway, Paulina Perlin, & Beatrice Walton, *Al-Alwi and the Unraveling of Detention Authority at the End of Active Hostilities*, Just Security (Feb. 6, 2018), https://www.justsecurity.org/51896/al-alwi-unraveling-detention-authority-active-hostilities/ (summarizing cases from the Civil War to World War II in which federal courts found facts to determine whether a state of armed conflict had commenced or had ended and noting a Guantánamo habeas ruling that "the President's position, while relevant, is not the only evidence that matters") (internal citations omitted).

what law applies. Courts have consistently found that "[t]he determination of when hostilities have ceased is a political decision," and "defer to the Executive's opinion on the matter, at least in the absence of an authoritative congressional declaration purporting to terminate the war."[102] This deference has put the executive in complete control of deciding whether to flip the switch between application of IHL and peacetime legal rules, without meaningful review of its factual assertions *or*, in turn, the legal framework it is applying to determine which facts are relevant to that consequential determination. In doing so, they have rubber-stamped the conflation of when hostilities cease as to a particular armed group, with the question of whether any hostilities continue, anywhere, with any armed group the executive deems covered by the 2001 AUMF.[103]

Disciplining Our Definitions: Aggregation and NIAC Termination

The global aggregation of hostilities by any group covered by the 2001 AUMF for purposes of maintaining that hostilities with AQ Core remain ongoing presents a serious overclassification problem. It allows continued status-based targeting and detention not just against AQ Core but also *any* group the executive classifies as an "associated" or "successor" force now or in the future, so long as any other such group remains "on the battlefield."

Moreover, who counts as a force covered by the 2001 AUMF is determined unilaterally by the executive branch in secret with no meaningful check by its coequal branches of government.[104] With a conflict that has already lasted longer than any other in U.S. history, consistent overclassification seriously undermines the imperative distinction between war and peace.

The "perpetual war" that the last three U.S. presidents have disclaimed a desire to pursue, and warned would imperil our democracy, is all but ensured by this approach.[105] Justice Breyer urged in 2014, and again in 2019, that it was time to "confront the difficult questions left open by *Hamdi*" regarding "the outer boundaries

[102] Rahim v. Biden, No. 1:09-cv-01385, 2023 U.S. Dist. LEXIS 168832, at *9 (citing Al-Bihani v. Obama, 590 F.3d 866, 874 (D.C. Cir. 2010)).

[103] *See Al-Alwi*, 901 F.3d 294 ("[I]f the 'life of a statute' conferring war powers on the Executive 'is defined by the existence of a war, Congress leaves the determination of when a war is concluded to the usual political agencies of the Government.'") (quoting *Ludecke v. Watkins*, 335 U.S. 160, 169 n.13 (1948)). *See also* Rahim v. Biden, No. 1:09-cv-01385, 2023 U.S. Dist. LEXIS 168832, at *12–13 (citing *Al-Alwi*, 901 F.3d at 300 and Paracha v. Biden, 2022 WL 2952493, at *6) ("Accordingly, the Court concludes that hostilities between the United States and Al Qaeda are ongoing, regardless of any 'change in the form of hostilities.'").

[104] *See* Finucane, *supra* note 64.

[105] *See* Obama Remarks at NDU *supra* note 1 ("[I]n the absence of a strategy that reduces the wellspring of extremism, a perpetual war—through drones or Special Forces or troop deployments—will prove self-defeating, and alter our country in troubling ways.").

of war powers," given the "real prospect" that detention could go on for a lifetime. He cautioned that "today's conflict may differ substantially from the one Congress anticipated when it passed the AUMF, as well as those 'conflicts that informed the development of the law of war.'"[106] This, in turn, renews with urgency the potential "unraveling" of the "understanding" that this conflict is susceptible to being governed by IHL at all, as Justice Sandra Day O'Connor warned in *Hamdi*.

Framing the GWOT as an armed conflict governed by IHL, including its permissive features (status-based detention) and constraints (ending detention at the cessation of active hostilities), may have moored the conflict to the rule of law for a time. But new legal theories have been consistently facilitating its conversion back into a perpetual GWOT, uncoupled from the self-defense justification of 9/11 and with few domestic or international law constraints (with those that remain essentially self-judged by the executive).

Thus far, the U.S. executive branch, its lawmakers, and its courts have not found a way to heed President Obama's admonition that we "may be drawn into more wars we don't need to fight, or continue to grant Presidents unbound powers more suited for traditional armed conflicts between nation states," "unless we discipline our thinking, our definitions, our actions."[107] Any one of the political branches has the ability to do so.

The executive may decide to prioritize the larger policy goals of winding down "legacy" wars and reducing reliance on policy strategies of the past given a new and different threat landscape. Congress may decide its Article I war powers must be reasserted given the increased entrenchment of Article II power. Should the Supreme Court take up the question, it might conclude that federal courts in habeas proceedings should look to whether hostilities with the relevant group have ceased, as *Hamdi* laid out, rather than continuing to allow the lower courts' conflation of all groups the executive has determined fall under the 2001 AUMF. It is not too late to reach the "tipping point," or any of the other viable formulations in this still-crystallizing branch of IHL, to ensure this conflict, like all others, must some day come to an end.

[106] Al-Alwi v. Trump, 139 S. Ct. 1893, 1894 (2019) (mem.) ("In my judgment, it is past time to confront the difficult question left open by *Hamdi*. See Boumediene v. Bush, 553 U. S. 723, 797–798 (2008) ('Because our Nation's past military conflicts have been of limited duration, it has been possible to leave the outer boundaries of war powers undefined. If, as some fear, terrorism continues to pose dangerous threats to us for years to come, the Court might not have this luxury')"); *id.* ("As a consequence, al-Alwi faces the real prospect that he will spend the rest of his life in detention based on his status as an enemy combatant a generation ago, even though today's conflict may differ substantially from the one Congress anticipated when it passed the AUMF, as well as those 'conflicts that informed the development of the law of war.'") (citing *Hamdi*, 542 U. S. at 521 (plurality opinion)).

[107] Obama Remarks at NDU, *supra* note 1; *see also* Harold Hongju Koh, *How to End the Forever War?, Remarks at the Oxford Union* (May 7, 2013), *in* Just Security, https://www.justsecurity.org/wp-content/uploads/2013/10/Koh-Oxford-How-to-End-the-Forever-War.pdf ("[I]f we are too loose in who we consider to be 'part of' or 'associated with' Al Qaeda going forward, then we will always have new enemies, and the Forever War will continue forever.").

14

Legalistic Policy and Limits to the Global War Paradigm for Counterterrorism

Laura A. Dickinson

Introduction

In August 2021, President Joe Biden withdrew all U.S. armed forces from Afghanistan and declared that the war there had come to an "end."[1] Yet the U.S.-led global "war on terror" continues today. In ongoing operations against al-Qaeda in Afghanistan, the Islamic State of Iraq and Syria (ISIS), al-Shabaab in Africa, and elsewhere, the United States is using lethal force in a variety of contexts. For these operations, the United States maintains the view that it is still at war and that the laws of war apply. Strikingly, the United States has maintained this stance even with respect to operations in Afghanistan. U.S. officials have argued that, regardless of President Biden's August 2021 statement, the armed conflict against al-Qaeda and "associated forces" continues both in Afghanistan and worldwide.[2] As a legal matter, the United States continues to cling to a global war paradigm in the counterterrorism context.

As I have written elsewhere,[3] the United States' assertion that it is engaged in a global armed conflict against terrorist groups is highly contested. Some European allies of the United States, for example, hold a more geographically and temporally confined view of extraterritorial counterterrorism operations that gives greater prominence to international human rights law (IHRL) and the *jus ad bellum*.[4] Faced with these differences regarding the scope of the conflict, and therefore the applicability of the law of armed conflict, the United States has

[1] President Joseph R. Biden Jr., U.S., Remarks by President Biden on the End of the War in Afghanistan (Aug. 30, 2021), https://www.whitehouse.gov/briefing-room/speeches-remarks/2021/08/31/remarks-by-president-biden-on-the-end-of-the-war-in-afghanistan/.

[2] *See* Laura A. Dickinson, *Still at War, The Forever War Legal Paradigm in Afghanistan*, Just Security (Apr. 14, 2022), https://www.justsecurity.org/81110/still-at-war-the-forever-war-legal-paradigm-in-afghanistan/.

[3] *See generally* Laura A. Dickinson, *National Security Policymaking in the Shadow of International Law*, 2021 Utah L. Rev. 629 (2021), https://papers.ssrn.com/sol3/papers.cfm?abstract_id=3872681.

[4] *See, e.g.*, Anthony Dworkin's contribution to this volume in Chapter 9, "Europe's Role in Perpetual War: From Counterpoint to Convergence."

Laura A. Dickinson, *Legalistic Policy and Limits to the Global War Paradigm for Counterterrorism*
In: *Perpetual War and International Law*. Edited by: Brianna Rosen, Oxford University Press.
 DOI: 10.1093/oso/9780197748992.003.0014

embraced what I have called "legalistic policies" governing the use of lethal force in extraterritorial counterterrorism operations.[5] Such policies adopt more stringent limits on the use of force—echoing the spirit, if not the letter of IHRL—but only as a matter of policy. These policies are "legalistic" in the sense that they are structured like international legal rules, with complex interpretive judgments required from military and civilian lawyers. Among other things, the use of these policies helps the United States smooth over differences with its allies regarding the requirements that international law imposes, both within and outside zones widely recognized as conflict areas.[6]

Nevertheless, even as successive U.S. administrations have embraced such policies, the United States has still chosen not to pull back from the war paradigm in the counterterrorism context strictly as a matter of law. Indeed, although the Biden administration championed human rights in other domains, it failed to rein in the war framework. Instead, it imposed more stringent rules than international humanitarian law (IHL) requires, but only through a set of policies articulated in the Presidential Policy Memorandum Governing Direct Action Counterterrorism Operations Outside Areas of Active Hostilities (PPM).[7] Furthermore, although the administration made public a redacted version of the PPM following Freedom of Information Act litigation,[8] it was not transparent about the precise policy approach it followed as an operational matter. At the time of this writing, the second Trump administration has appeared to adopt a somewhat similar policy[9] even as there is no sign it plans to pull back from the global war paradigm for counterterrorism as a matter of law. Indeed, with no demonstrated legal basis, the second Trump administration has now *expanded* the war paradigm to include Latin American drug trafficking gangs it has designated as terrorist organizations.[10]

This chapter evaluates the United States' ongoing embrace of the "legalistic policy" approach to extraterritorial counterterrorism operations.[11] First,

[5] Dickinson, *National Security Policymaking*, *supra* note 3, at 636.

[6] *See id.* at 673–74.

[7] Presidential Policy Memorandum Governing Direct Action Counterterrorism Operations Outside Areas of Active Hostilities (declassified on June 29, 2023) [hereinafter PPM] https://int.nyt.com/data/documenttools/savage-nyt-foia-biden-presidential-policy-memo-ct-direct-action-rules/91583cea8267d704/full.pdf.

[8] *See* Charlie Savage, *Biden Rules Tighten Limits on Drone Strikes*, N.Y. Times (July 1, 2023), https://www.nytimes.com/2023/07/01/us/biden-drone-strikes.html.

[9] *See* Charlie Savage, *Trump Relaxes Limits on Counterterrorism Strikes Outside Conventional War Zones*, N.Y. Times (March 1, 2025), https://www.nytimes.com/2025/03/01/us/politics/counterterrorism-drone-strikes.html.

[10] *See* Carol Rosenberg, Charlie Savage, and Eric Schmitt, *U.S. Kills 3 on Boat Suspected of Smuggling Drugs for Colombian Rebels*, N.Y. Times (Oct. 19, 2025), https://www.nytimes.com/2025/10/19/us/politics/trump-military-boat-strike-colombia.html; Michael Schmitt, *Striking Drug Cartels Under the Jus ad Bellum and the Law of Armed Conflict*, Just Security (Sept. 10, 2025), https://www.justsecurity.org/120235/drug-cartels-jus-ad-bellum-loac/.

[11] For further discussion of legalistic policies and their distinctive features, *see* Dickinson, *National Security Policymaking*, *supra* note 3, at 670; Laura A. Dickinson, *Extraterritorial*

I describe the reasons the legalistic policy approach emerged, as well as some of the policies implemented and maintained across multiple administrations. Second, I examine why successive U.S. administrations did not retreat from the global war paradigm and instead continued to embrace a policy approach with respect to direct action—that is, the killing or capture of terrorist targets. Finally, I highlight the risks of this approach and conclude that the United States should rethink its continued application of the war paradigm to counterterrorism operations.

The "Legalistic Policy" Approach

In the decades following the 9/11 terrorist attacks, the United States has, across multiple administrations, taken a broad view of the armed conflicts with al-Qaeda, ISIS, and "associated forces." As U.S. military operations against these groups spread around the world, the United States found itself in tension with some of its allies as well as some international organizations (IOs) and nongovernmental organizations (NGOs) that resisted both the idea of a global "war on terror" and the essentially global applicability of IHL to target and detain terrorist suspects beyond the "hot" battlefields of Afghanistan, Iraq, and Syria.[12] Legislators, human rights groups, and civil society actors likewise urged the U.S. executive branch to move toward adopting an IHRL framework for extraterritorial counterterrorism operations. In addition, the United States, as compared to many allies, IOs, and NGOs, interpreted IHL differently and adopted a distinct view of the relationship between IHRL and IHL even within traditional battlefields.[13]

Faced with these pressures, the United States developed a series of extraterritorial counterterrorism policies that adopted many of the norms embodied in IHRL and the *jus ad bellum*, but without accepting that these norms applied as a matter of law. As I have earlier noted, these policies brought the United States closer to its allies in practice, even if not as a matter of official legal interpretation.[14]

Counterterrorism: Policymaking v. Law, Just Security (July 15, 2021), https://www.justsecurity.org/77357/extraterritorial-counterterrorism-policymaking-v-law/.

[12] *See* Dickinson, *National Security Policymaking*, *supra* note 3, at 652–59.

[13] *See id.* at 673; *see also* Annie Shiel et al., *U.S. Lethal Strikes Program Continues to Violate International Human Rights Law*, Just Security (Oct. 27, 2023), https://www.justsecurity.org/89781/us-lethal-strikes-program-continues-to-violate-intl-human-rights-law/.

[14] *See* Dickinson, *National Security Policymaking*, *supra* note 3, at 673–74; *see also* Dworkin, *supra* note 4.

One such policy was the Obama-era Presidential Policy Guidance (PPG) entitled "Procedures for Approving Direct Action Against Terrorist Targets Located Outside the United States and Areas of Active Hostilities."[15] The PPG provided higher standards for the use of lethal force than IHL would require as a matter of law.[16] For example, the PPG established a preference for capture of a terrorism target rather than the use of lethal force[17] (although there is debate[18] regarding whether this is indeed required by IHL). In addition, in any lethal force operation, the PPG required "near certainty" that civilians would not be killed, as well as a "near certainty" that the identified target was in fact present.[19] The PPG also made clear that the targets of lethal force had to pose a "continuing, imminent threat."[20]

Another Obama-era policy was contained in the procedures governing the review of Guantánamo detainees by Periodic Review Boards (PRBs). As initially set out in Obama's Executive Order (E.O.) 13567,[21] PRBs were an administrative process that evaluated the threat posed by the detainee at least every six months, allowed detainees to present information to the PRB, and permitted them to be represented both by a lawyer and a government-provided personal representative. As a matter of domestic law, some of these PRB procedures[22] have now been codified, but the initial E.O. established PRBs "as a discretionary matter."[23]

These standards move in the direction of IHRL (although to be sure they do not fully implement IHRL rules), but they were implemented as a matter of policy, rather than law.[24] For example, under most interpretations, IHRL would not allow the premeditated use of lethal force against a specific individual, unless strictly necessary to prevent imminent harm. The preference for capture and the "near certainty" elements of the PPG, combined with the requirement of a continuing, imminent threat to U.S. persons, therefore approximate the IHRL necessity standard and are more stringent than IHL targeting principles. Under IHL, there is typically a lower threshold for the use of lethal force, because IHL permits such force so long as a commander follows applicable IHL rules, such as

15 Presidential Policy Guidance, *Procedures for the Use of Force in Counterterrorism Operations Outside the United States and Areas of Active Hostilities* (May 23, 2013) (redacted) [hereinafter PPG], https://www.justice.gov/oip/foialibrary/procedures_for_approving_direct_action_against_terrorist_targets/download.

16 *See* Dickinson, *National Security Policymaking*, *supra* note 3, at 661–64.

17 *See* PPG, *supra* note 15, at §§ 4B, 5A.

18 *See* Ryan Goodman, *The Power to Capture or Kill Enemy Combatants*, 24 Eur. J. Int'l L. (2013).

19 *See* PPG, *supra* note 15, at §§ 4B, 5A.

20 *Id.* at §§ 3A, 4A.

21 Exec. Order No. 13,567, Periodic Review of Individuals Detained at Guantánamo Bay Naval Station Pursuant to Authorization to Use Military Force, 76 Fed. Reg. 13, 277 (Mar. 10, 2011).

22 *See* Periodic Review Secretariat, U.S. Dep't of Defense, The Periodic Review Board, https://www.prs.mil/About-the-PRB/.

23 Exec. Order No. 13,567, *supra* note 21.

24 *See* Dickinson, *National Security Policymaking*, *supra* note 3, at 660–69.

those on military necessity, distinction, proportionality, precautions, and unnecessary suffering. Proportionality requires that a commander consider whether the expected harm to civilians and civilian objects is "excessive" compared to the anticipated direct and concrete military advantage—a standard that would generally be easier to meet than IHRL's strict necessity rule or the "near certainty" elements of the PPG.

In the case of military detention, the PRB procedures for Guantánamo detainees arguably exceed what the United States has said IHL requires.[25] These procedures still do not fully satisfy the requirements of IHRL, which would mandate much more stringent due process for these detainees, such as a right to a lawyer at no cost and the right to be brought within an independent judicial body to be charged within a reasonable period or released. (Both IHL and IHRL also mandate humane treatment of detainees, but IHRL generally imposes more stringent requirements as well). Nevertheless, even if the PRB procedures do not fully satisfy IHRL, they at least nod in the direction of human rights. They also nod toward an interpretation of IHL that such review is mandatory as a matter of law.

Such policies have been somewhat durable across U.S. administrations. The first Trump administration, although much more secretive than the Obama administration, nonetheless retained many of the PPG's core elements, even while jettisoning others, in its policy guidance, "Principles, Standards, and Procedures for U.S. Direct Action Against Terrorist Targets" (PSP).[26] For example, the Trump successor policy omitted the requirement to establish "near certainty" that a terrorist target was present before lethal force could be used, and it also allowed decision-making by actors at lower levels of authority. But the Trump administration policy retained the preference for capture and the standard of "near certainty" that civilians would not be harmed in a lethal force operation, although the policy allowed decision makers to water down the capture preference and to deviate from the "near certainty" standard where "necessary" (reportedly, Trump administration officials applied the standard to women and children, but not men).[27] Additionally, at least on paper, the first Trump administration retained key elements of the PRB process, even those not codified in

[25] *See id.*, at 664–69.

[26] Presidential Policy Guidance, *Principles, Standards, and Procedures for U.S. Direct Action Against Terrorist Targets* (redacted) (2017) [hereinafter PSP], https://int.nyt.com/data/documenttools/trump-psp-drone-strike-rules-foia/52f4a4baf5fc54c5/full.pdf/; *see also* Charlie Savage, *Trump's Secret Rules for Drone Strikes Outside War Zones Are Disclosed*, N.Y. TIMES (May 1, 2021), https://www.nytimes.com/2021/05/01/us/politics/trump-drone-strike-rules.html.

[27] *See* Savage, *supra* note 26 ("While [the Trump Administration] kept [the near certainty] rule for women and children, it permitted a lower standard of merely 'reasonable certainty' when it came to civilian adult men.").

domestic law, although some commentators have claimed the administration did not implement the procedures in a robust fashion.[28]

Subsequently, the Biden administration developed its own use of force policy outside areas of active hostilities: the PPM.[29] Like the policies of the previous administrations, the PPM retained the preference for capture and the standard of "near certainty" that civilians would not be harmed.[30] In addition, the PPM[31] restored the Obama-era requirement of decision-making at more senior levels that had been delegated down in the Trump-era policy. Indeed, the Biden administration policy generally required advance approval by the president before an individual could be targeted, although exceptions were permitted. As to the level of confidence required that a specific individual had to be present before they could be targeted, the PPM left that standard redacted and therefore unclear. Some commentators speculated that it left in place the lower, Trump-era PSP "reasonable certainty standard" rather than restoring the higher "near certainty" standard from the Obama-era PPG.[32] The PPM also did not govern strikes by U.S. forces stationed abroad, either in self-defense or in the collective self-defense of partner forces, a significant carveout, given examples of extensive self-defense strikes in Somalia and elsewhere.[33]

The Biden administration also reinvigorated implementation of the PRB policy applicable to counterterrorism detainees at Guantánamo Bay. During the first Trump administration, the policy existed on paper but stalled in practice.[34] The Biden administration initiated multiple PRB reviews to assess whether detainees no longer posed a continuing threat and could therefore be transferred out of Guantánamo.[35]

At the time of this writing, the second Trump administration appears to have reverted to the policy framework for drone strikes and special operations raids

[28] *See* Benjamin R. Farley, *Who Broke Periodic Review at Guantánamo Bay*, Lawfare (Oct. 15, 2018), https://www.lawfareblog.com/who-broke-periodic-review-guantanamo-bay.

[29] PPM, *supra* note 7.

[30] *Id.* at 3E.

[31] For excellent discussions of the PPM, *see* Luke Hartig, *The Biden Drone Playbook: The Elusive Promise of Restrained Counterterrorism*, Just Security (Oct. 17, 2022), https://www.justsecurity.org/83586/assessing-bidens-counterterrorism-rules/; Oona Hathaway, *Biden's New Counterterrorism Policy Guidance Further Entrenches the Forever War*, Just Security (Oct. 11, 2022), https://www.justsecurity.org/83487/bidens-new-counterterrorism-policy-guidance-further-entrenches-forever-war/; and Brianna Rosen, *Ending Perpetual War*, Just Security (Oct. 25, 2022), https://www.justsecurity.org/83749/ending-perpetual-war/.

[32] *See* Charlie Savage, *Biden Rules Tighten Limits on Drone Strikes*, N.Y. Times (July 1, 2023), https://www.nytimes.com/2023/07/01/us/biden-drone-strikes.html.

[33] Oona Hathaway & Luke Hartig, *Still at War: The United States in Somalia*, Just Security (Mar. 21, 2022), https://www.justsecurity.org/80921/still-at-war-the-united-states-in-somalia/.

[34] *See* Dickinson, *National Security Policymaking*, *supra* note 3, at 669.

[35] *See* Carol Rosenberg, *Two More Guantánamo Detainees Are Cleared for Transfer to Other Nations*, N.Y. Times (June 17, 2021), at https://www.nytimes.com/2021/06/17/us/politics/guantanamo-detainees-transfer.html.

it adopted in the first administration, granting greater autonomy to military commanders in the field and permitting a lower level of certainty in verifying terrorist targets.[36] It has also repurposed Guantánamo Bay for expanded immigration detention, including plans to house thousands of noncitizen detainees, while continuing to hold approximately fifteen terrorism suspects under the original post-9/11 authorities.[37]

Embracing the War Paradigm

All the policies described here are "legalistic."[38] To some degree, they borrow legal categories from international law, particularly IHRL. Congress has now incorporated elements of these policies into domestic law, such as key pieces of the PRB process.[39] They are presented with clauses and standards that sound more like law than policy. And lawyers are needed to interpret their terms. In other words, lawyers' judgments and recommendations are essential to implementing these policies, just as they are to evaluating the legality of operations under international law.

From an executive branch perspective, national security policies have several key benefits when compared to an approach that would incorporate more robust human rights (or *jus ad bellum*) requirements as a matter of law. As outlined earlier, such policies can bridge differences with allies, including international and host nation partners, and address the concerns of IOs and NGOs as well, by implementing a more human-rights-oriented approach. But crucially, they do so without locking the government into legal commitments. In the targeting context, these policies provide an opportunity to implement standards that approximate IHRL and/or *jus ad bellum* elements embraced by those who adopt a more limited view of the scope of existing armed conflict. For example, a policy might mandate that U.S. officials fulfill IHRL or *jus ad bellum* requirements as a matter of policy even when officials have concluded that such requirements do not apply as a matter of law; or a policy might impose a higher standard for some IHL or *jus ad bellum* elements than the United States has accepted as a matter of law. In short, policies provide key interoperability and normative benefits with many partners while enabling the United States to retain flexibility in complex counterterrorism environments.

36 *See* Rosenberg et al., *supra* note 10.

37 *The Guantánamo Docket*, N.Y. Times, (Oct. 16, 2025), https://www.nytimes.com/interactive/2021/us/guantanamo-bay-detainees.html; *see also* Carol Rosenberg, *U.S. Emptied Migrant Detention Space at Guantánamo*, N.Y. Times (Oct. 17, 2025), https://www.nytimes.com/2025/10/17/us/politics/guantanamo-migrants-deported.html.

38 Dickinson, *National Security Policymaking*, *supra* note 3, at 670.

39 *See id.* at 665.

Further, policies can explicitly incorporate room for officials to deviate from standards, or, if necessary, revise their terms entirely in secret and without public debate. The executive branch can eschew or change policies if they prove problematic. Adopting such policies can also bridge differences *within* the executive branch—for example, between officials who advocate for a broader role for IHRL and those who see IHL as dominant. A large investment in training U.S. armed forces in IHL, without a corresponding training program in IHRL, adds to this institutional reliance on IHL as the dominant framework, even as these policies incorporate IHRL norms more flexibly.

Finally, from a human rights perspective, these policies have the practical impact of making the United States more aligned with human rights norms in its day-to-day counterterrorism operations. In the period leading up to the adoption of the original PPG, for example, it is possible that if the human rights community had pushed for a full-throated legal embrace of IHRL in the extraterritorial counterterrorism context, the effort would have failed. And in litigation, attempts to implement IHRL could backfire because if a court formally rejected the applicability of IHRL in favor of IHL—for example, in the litigation related to Guantánamo detainees—the human rights community would lose leverage to encourage future administrations to adopt more protective policies. Thus, one might see the adoption of legalistic policies as providing important, pragmatic human rights victories with tangible positive consequences on the ground. Moreover, even though U.S. administrations can theoretically change such policies, they are at least somewhat durable in practice, as demonstrated by the fact that some form of the policy guidance on direct action has endured now through three Democratic and Republican administrations and the beginning of a fourth.

These pragmatic benefits notwithstanding, the withdrawal of U.S. armed forces in Afghanistan and the sheer length of time that the United States has been engaged in counterterrorism armed conflict around the globe suggest it is long past time for a new evaluation of the policy approach in this context. Does the United States still consider itself to be waging a forever war against terrorist groups in Afghanistan? The answer so far appears to be yes.[40] Indeed, the United States continues to rely on "over-the-horizon" capabilities against terrorist groups in Afghanistan and beyond.[41] Furthermore, successive U.S. administrations have not declared the end of the forever war as a *legal* paradigm. To the contrary, the U.S. government maintains its position that it is engaged in a broad, ongoing, and transnational armed conflict against al-Qaeda and associated forces, and

[40] Biden, *supra* note 1.
[41] Brianna Rosen, *The Longest War Is Over the Horizon*, JUST SECURITY (Nov. 21, 2022), https://www.justsecurity.org/78818/the-longest-war-is-over-the-horizon/.

that the dominant international legal framework governing extraterritorial operations against these groups is therefore IHL.[42]

In my view, this approach has been driven at least in part by ongoing detention practices at Guantánamo Bay, since the only justification under international law for detaining terrorism suspects for years without charge or trial is in the context of an ongoing armed conflict.[43] Even after troop withdrawals from Afghanistan, U.S. officials in legal proceedings brought by Guantánamo detainees continued to argue that the global non-international armed conflict against terrorist groups was ongoing. For example, in its response to a habeas petition filed by Saifullah Abdullah Paracha, a Pakistani citizen held briefly in Afghanistan and then transferred to Guantánamo in 2004, Biden administration lawyers argued in October 2021—after the withdrawal from Afghanistan—that "the United States remains in active hostilities against al-Qaeda and its associated forces, including in Afghanistan."[44] In subsequent pleadings in the same litigation, the administration similarly argued that "the record evidence demonstrates that hostilities against al-Qaida and associated forces have not ceased, whether in Afghanistan or elsewhere." And in briefing materials filed in October 2021 in response to the habeas petition[45] of Assadullah Harun Gul, an Afghan citizen held at Guantánamo since 2007, the administration argued there is a "current ongoing conflict against al-Qaida and associated forces in areas of Africa and the Middle East, including Afghanistan . . . [and] U.S. forces remain engaged in active hostilities with al-Qaida and associated forces in these regions."[46] (Both detainees have since been released,[47] and in Gul's case the release was pursuant to a court order concluding that his detention was in fact unlawful).[48]

[42] *See* Dickinson, *Still at War*, *supra* note 2.

[43] Under IHRL, by contrast, prolonged detention of this nature would violate the detainees' fundamental human rights. *See* Dickinson, *National Security Policymaking*, *supra* note 3, at 644–45.

[44] Paracha v. Biden, Case No. 1:21-cv-2567-PLF, *Respondents' Return to Petition for Habeas Corpus and Response to Petition for Other Relief*, at 6 (Oct. 25, 2021), https://www.justsecurity.org/wp-content/uploads/2022/04/Paracha-response-to-habeas-claim-post-Afghanistan-withdrawal-25-Oct-2021.pdf.

[45] A petition for a writ of habeas corpus is used to invoke the U.S. constitutional right not to be unlawfully imprisoned. For more information on the history of this constitutional right, *see* https://constitutioncenter.org/the-constitution/articles/article-i/clauses/763.

[46] Gul v. Biden, Case No. 16-cv-1462 (APM), *Respondents' Supplemental Opposition in Response to Petitioner's Request for Renewed Consideration of the Motion for Immediate Release*, at 13 (Oct. 1, 2021), https://www.justsecurity.org/wp-content/uploads/2022/04/Gul-v.-Biden_response-to-Habeas-Claim_1-Oct-2021.pdf.

[47] *See, e.g.*, Carol Rosenberg, *U.S. Releases Guantánamo's Oldest Prisoner*, N.Y. Times (Oct. 29, 2022), https://www.nytimes.com/2022/10/29/us/politics/oldest-prisoner-gitmo-terrorism.html; Carol Rosenberg, *U.S. Repatriates Afghan Detainee Whose Detention Was Unlawful*, N.Y. Times (June 24, 2022), https://www.nytimes.com/2022/06/24/us/politics/guantanamo-afghan-prisoner-released.html.

[48] Gul v. Biden, Case No. 16-cv-01462 (APM), *Memorandum Opinion*, Oct. 18, 2021 (D. D.C.), https://int.nyt.com/data/documenttools/haroon-habeas-2021-rulings/abd03abacfaf0151/full.pdf.

In short, despite political statements signaling the contrary, the forever war continues as a legal matter. Although the Biden administration sought to impose greater constraints on direct action outside of "hot" battlefields as a policy matter,[49] it did not take the opportunity to restrict the war paradigm as a matter of law. The second Trump administration has since relaxed some elements of the Biden-era policy even as it has continued others,[50] and it has likewise continued to apply a war paradigm as a matter of law. Thus, U.S. administrations from both parties have continued to embrace a policy approach to counterterrorism operations while remaining on a war footing from a legal perspective. Accordingly, we must ask what is next, both for the war paradigm as a matter of international law and for these legalistic national security policies.

Weighing the Risks

The return to power of the Trump administration offers an important moment to reweigh the benefits and risks of what I have termed the policy approach to extraterritorial counterterrorism that consists of human rights–informed principles applied as a matter of policy outside areas of active hostilities, layered over a continuing embrace of a global war paradigm as a matter of international law. Although this policy approach certainly confers many benefits, as described earlier, it also carries significant risks. In my view, it is time for the U.S. executive branch to rethink those benefits and risks and consider whether it is time to pull back from the war paradigm as a matter of law. Furthermore, it is important for this discussion to take place in a relatively transparent way. For example, in producing the PPM, it is unclear whether U.S. officials in the Biden administration considered pulling back from the war paradigm or just assumed, as they rewrote the policy, that the policy approach would continue. To be sure, it seems unlikely that the second Trump administration would engage in such a process, and, as noted earlier, it is to the contrary *expanding* the war paradigm with a dubious legal rationale. Indeed, the failure of the Biden administration to rein in the global war paradigm may have paved the way for this expansion by normalizing the idea of perpetual, global war. Nonetheless, it is important to begin to discuss the benefits of limiting the global war paradigm as a matter of law, and to delineate a process for doing so, in the event that a U.S. administration is inclined to initiate such a process in the future.

49 *See* Charlie Savage, *White House Tightens Rules on Counterterrorism Drone Strikes*, N.Y. Times (Oct. 7, 2022), https://www.nytimes.com/2022/10/07/us/politics/drone-strikes-biden-trump.html.

50 Rosenberg et al., *supra* note 10.

Here, I do not propose to map out just where the boundaries of the war paradigm ought to lie as a matter of international law, nor to argue that the United States should necessarily replace it with an IHRL approach. Rather, I identify the risks of continuing to use this policy approach. I then suggest that, at a minimum, the executive branch should debate internally whether it is time to pull back to some degree from the global war paradigm as a matter of international law and, ideally, make some public statement about the result of that debate. Finally, I highlight a few of the significant challenges related to pulling back from the war paradigm, though I emphasize that it is important to squarely confront those challenges rather than continuing the policy approach without debate and as a matter of institutional inertia.

What are the risks of the policy approach I have described? First, policies can create muddiness and confusion about what the law actually is. It is often hard to tell where law ends and policy begins. This muddiness can impede understanding and development of the law, as well as create ambiguities about whether the United States is creating customary international law when it acts according to policy.

Second, the United States—and other countries as well—have at least some strategic, as well as moral, incentives to forgo legalistic policies in favor of the stricter laws they may reflect. For example, to the extent that the United States is essentially abiding by IHRL rules in extraterritorial counterterrorism operations outside areas of active hostilities, but not committing to them as being legally binding, a policy approach reduces the opportunity for the United States to encourage states not following such principles to embrace a human rights approach. Because the adoption of policy implies flexibility and discretion, it can be harder to encourage another state to follow the same policy than to follow established rules of international law. Moreover, if the United States were to consider applying IHRL to some extraterritorial counterterrorism operations as a matter of law, it should be noted that it is not the straitjacket often portrayed by its critics and can offer considerable flexibility in counterterrorism contexts.[51] To be sure, in applying IHRL as a matter of law to extraterritorial counterterrorism operations, the United States would need to overcome long-standing views about the limited scope of IHRL obligations extraterritorially,[52] and retreating from the global war paradigm might not actually result in an expanded use of IHRL, but rather greater reliance on the *jus ad bellum* for use-of-force operations.[53]

[51] *See, e.g.,* Dickinson, *National Security Policymaking, supra* note 3, at 659–60; *see also* Kenneth Watkin, Fighting at the Legal Boundaries: Controlling the Use of Force in Contemporary Armed Conflict 121–34 (2016).

[52] For a detailed discussion of this issue, *see* Dickinson, *Still at War, supra* note 2.

[53] *Id.*

Third, abiding by IHRL as a matter of law in some extraterritorial counterterrorism operations outside areas of active hostilities, rather than following a policy that merely reflects IHRL principles, would give the United States greater scope to shape how that body of law is applied to counterterrorism operations and to engage with institutions—such as the Human Rights Committee and other human rights treaty bodies—that seek to apply IHRL to U.S. activities abroad, with or without U.S. participation.

Fourth, the secrecy around the implementation of these policies can lead to self-serving interpretations by executive branch officials that water down their terms.[54] To be sure, states are often not transparent about their interpretations of international law, but the application of policy creates even more confusion about which law states are applying, thereby weakening calls for clarity about legal interpretation. And a policy is more vulnerable to subsequent reinterpretation or case-by-case backsliding than a legal interpretation would be (though, as described earlier, even policy determinations can be somewhat sticky from one administration to another). And, as long as the United States maintains that these policies are discretionary, it gives other states cover if they fail to apply to IHRL in their own operations.

Perhaps most importantly, a policy approach helps to perpetuate and normalize an ever-expanding global war paradigm. The policy approach described here allowed successive administrations to smooth over differences with allies, IOs, and NGOs, making it easier for the United States to continue perpetuating the war paradigm as a matter of law. As Andrew Clapham discusses in this volume, that approach is not an inevitability—it is a choice. Indeed, as he points out, states can respond to terrorist attacks both by using ordinary criminal courts to prosecute suspects and by complying with IHRL in responding extraterritorially.[55] By failing to take steps to limit the war paradigm, the Biden administration may have made it easier for the second Trump administration to expand this paradigm to drug-trafficking gangs and potentially others—by perpetuating the idea of a long-running global war that expands to encompass more and more terrorist groups. Thus, it is high time to at least reconsider whether this paradigm is useful or necessary as the United States proceeds through its third decade of post-9/11 counterterrorism activities. Instead of masking our approach through policy guidance, we should revisit the fundamental question of how to conceptualize ongoing counterterrorism operations within the framework of international law.

At the very least, a future U.S. executive branch that is inclined to grapple with this problem should launch an internal process to study the circumstances under which it would be appropriate to curtail the global war paradigm as a matter

[54] *See* Shirin Sinnar, *Rule of Law Tropes in National Security*, 129 Harv. L. Rev. 1566 (2016).
[55] *See* Chapter 4 of this volume, "Rethinking the War Paradigm," by Andrew Clapham.

of international law, and in the process define some potential benchmarks for doing so. (A parallel process under domestic law, as other contributors to this volume have argued,[56] is also important.) Such a process should consider the circumstances under which the legal war paradigm might end, perhaps in some geographic regions outside areas of active hostilities. For example, the withdrawal of all U.S. armed forces from a territory, such as the withdrawal in Afghanistan, might be one such benchmark or factor. Another factor might be the degree to which a particular terrorist group has been degraded or destroyed in that territory. The ongoing military detention by the United States of individuals who fought in or are citizens of that territory might be another factor. Such a process should also consider which international legal paradigm or paradigms would apply to ongoing counterterrorism operations in that region if the war paradigm were curtailed. Thus, for use-of-force operations, the *jus ad bellum* would likely apply, and there would be a question about whether IHRL should govern as a matter of law.[57] For detention operations, there would be similar questions about whether IHRL would apply.[58] And overall, such a process should explicitly weigh the risks and benefits of continuing to apply a policy approach that layers human rights principles as a matter of policy over a global war paradigm as a matter of law.

There are, of course, significant obstacles to the U.S. executive branch reaching the conclusion that the war paradigm should be curtailed, and IHRL should be applied as a matter of international law, rather than policy. To begin with, the extent to which terrorist groups have reconstituted and rebuilt would likely make executive branch actors reluctant to conclude that the armed conflict is over between the United States and any particular group. But just because this might be a challenge does not mean that the United States should refrain from setting benchmarks as to the circumstances under which this might occur.

Another highly significant obstacle is the continuing military detention of counterterrorism suspects at Guantánamo, because ongoing detention without criminal charges could only have a legal basis under IHL. Perhaps the process I have suggested would result in the conclusion that transfer of all law-of-war detainees from Guantánamo is a precondition for reining in the global IHL paradigm. This is particularly true for those who fought in Afghanistan or who are Afghan citizens. Yet, due to restrictions in U.S. law prohibiting transfer to the United States, such transfers must be to third-party states, which is an ongoing

[56] *See* Chapter 13 of this volume, "The Vanishing 'Tipping Point' and the Problem of Perpetual War," by Tess Bridgeman.
[57] *See, e.g.*, Dickinson, *Still at War*, *supra* note 2.
[58] *Id.*

challenge, even for detainees cleared for transfer.[59] And for the three detainees not cleared for transfer, yet not charged within the military commissions system, the prospects for them to leave Guantánamo are even slimmer. (Some experts have, to be sure, suggested that plea agreements and transfers could be a viable option even for these three.)[60] But there may be other approaches to preserve flexibility at Guantánamo while embracing a more limited view of the scope of the armed conflict. For example, there may be geographic locations other than Afghanistan that are not areas of active hostilities and are locations where no Guantánamo detainees fought or were captured or are citizens—the United States might be able to determine that such locations (assuming other factors were met as well) could fall outside the global war paradigm, even if detainees linked to other areas remained at Guantánamo. Or, there might be some terrorist groups that are sufficiently destroyed or degraded, and that lack detainees at Guantánamo, such that the United States could determine that the armed conflict has ended with regard to those particular terrorist groups, even if detainees linked to other terrorist groups remained at Guantánamo. In such cases, the presence of some detainees at Guantánamo would not necessarily dictate the need for a war paradigm globally.

Yet another obstacle is the long-standing U.S. posture that IHRL obligations do not generally apply extraterritorially.[61] Even though the global consensus seems to be moving away from the U.S. position,[62] it would require a significant shift for the United States to embrace IHRL as applicable as a matter of law to extraterritorial counterterrorism operations outside areas of active hostilities. And the second Trump administration has thus far reduced the U.S. emphasis on

[59] *See* James E. Baker & Laura Dickinson, *The Future of the U.S. Military Commissions at Guantánamo: Legal and Policy Issues*, Just Security (May 8, 2018), https://www.justsecurity.org/55865/future-u-s-military-commissions-legal-policy-issues/.

[60] *See, e.g.*, Ian Moss, *There Is a Way to Close Guantánamo*, Just Security (Jan. 11, 2022).

[61] For example, in its recent submission to the Human Rights Committee regarding Article 2(1) of the International Covenant on Civil and Political Rights, which provides that each "State Party . . . undertakes to respect and to ensure to all individuals within its territory and subject to its jurisdiction the rights recognized in the present Covenant," *see* International Covenant on Civil and Political Rights art. 2, Dec. 19, 1966, 999 U.N.T.S. 171, the United States did not change its "longstanding position" that "Article 2(1) creates obligations for a State Party only with respect to individuals who are both within the territory of the State Party and within that State Party's jurisdiction." Human Rights Committee, *Fifth Periodic Report submitted by the United States of America Under Article 40 of the Covenant pursuant to the Optional Reporting Procedure*, at 4 (para. 14), CCPR/C/USA/5, Nov. 11, 2021. After considering the U.S. Report, in its concluding observations the Human Rights Committee observed, "It . . . regrets that the State party maintains the position that the Covenant does not apply with respect to individuals who are under its jurisdiction but outside its territory, despite the divergent interpretation of article 2(1) of the Covenant that may be found in the Committee's established jurisprudence, the jurisprudence of the International Court of Justice and State practice." Human Rights Committee, *Concluding Observations on the Fifth Periodic Report of the United States of America*, at 2 (para. 4), CCPR/C.USA/CO/5.

[62] *See* Michael N. Schmitt, *Big Data: International Law Issues Below the Armed Conflict Threshold*, *in* Big Data and Armed Conflict: Legal Issues Above and Below the Armed Conflict Threshold 29–54 (Laura A. Dickinson & Edward W. Berg eds., 2024).

human rights compliance in many contexts.[63] Nevertheless, if a future U.S. administration were more open to such an approach, the United States could perhaps change its position incrementally, for example, by focusing on IHRL obligations regarding detention rather than the use of force. With respect to extraterritorial detention, the weight of international opinion is especially strong that IHRL applies because state agents have control over individuals.[64] In my view, the United States should at least consider advancing the ball further in this domain.

Overall, the United States must begin to reweigh the risks and benefits of the policy approach and consider deeply and thoroughly the circumstances under which it might make sense to rein in the war paradigm as a matter of law. It is also worth noting the significant obstacles to doing so. Such a process is sorely needed to ensure that sheer inertia and bureaucratic path dependence do not perpetuate endless war.

[63] *See* Adam Taylor, *Rubio Recasts Long-Held Beliefs with Cuts to Human Rights Reports*, Wash. Post (Aug. 12, 2025), https://www.washingtonpost.com/national-security/2025/08/12/rubio-human-rights-reports/.

[64] *See* Dickinson, *National Security Policymaking*, *supra* note 3, at 647–48.

15

The Rise of "Self-Defense"—And the Fall of Constraints on the Use of Force

*Oona A. Hathaway**

Introduction

The last several decades have witnessed a dramatic decline in the capacity of the U.S. Congress to constrain the president's unilateral decisions to send the United States to war. That erosion of congressional authority has accelerated since the terrorist attacks of September 11, 2001. Today, Congress's ability to limit the exercise of presidential decisions to deploy force abroad is highly constrained. Presidents of both parties have expansively interpreted presidential authority to make decisions to use force, and Congress has proven unable or unwilling to insist on playing its formal constitutional role in response. Courts, meanwhile, have stood back and allowed this accretion of power to take place unabated. On the rare occasion that they have been asked to intervene, courts have almost always refused, relying on a variety of justiciability doctrines.[1] As a result, the

* My thanks to participants in the 2022 Chicago-Virginia Foreign Relations Roundtable for their feedback on this chapter. With permission, this chapter reprints in significant part, Oona A. Hathaway, *How the Erosion of U.S. War Powers Constraints Has Undermined International Law Constraints on the Use of Force*, 14 Harv. Nat'l Sec. J. 335 (2023).

[1] For example, the U.S. District Court for the District of Columbia found that the suit brought by the father of Anwar al-Aulaqi challenging al-Aulaqi's targeting by the U.S. Department of Defense could not go forward because the plaintiff lacked standing and his claims were non-justiciable under the political question doctrine. Al-Aulaqi v. Obama, 727 F. Supp. 2d 1, 49–50 (D.D.C. 2010). The same court dismissed a suit by a member of the armed forces who challenged the legality of the U.S. military operations against ISIS. Smith v. Obama, 217 F. Supp. 3d 283 (D.D.C. 2016) (dismissing on standing and political question grounds), *order vacated, appeal dismissed on other grounds sub nom.* Smith v. Trump, 731 F. App'x 8 (D.C. Cir. 2018) (per curiam) (vacated on mootness grounds, because Captain Smith had by then tendered an unqualified resignation from active duty). In addition, a line of cases has all but foreclosed the idea that an individual member of Congress or group of members can assert legislative standing to maintain a suit against a member of the executive branch. *See, e.g.*, Kucinich v. Obama, 821 F. Supp. 2d 110, 125 (D.D.C. 2011); Raines v. Byrd, 521 U.S. 811, 829–30 (1997); Chenoweth v. Clinton, 181 F.3d 112, 117 (D.C. Cir. 1999); Campbell v. Clinton, 203 F.3d 19, 23–24 (D.C. Cir. 2000). For a more complete list of cases through 2012, *see generally* Michael John Garcia, Cong. Rsch. Serv., RL30352, War Powers Litigation Initiated by Members of Congress Since the Enactment of the War Powers Resolution (2012), https://sgp.fas.org/crs/natsec/RL30352.pdf [https://perma.cc/2QS6-ALEZ]. The courts were not always so reluctant to reach the merits of such cases, but that changed in the 1970s and 1980s. *See* Carlin Meyer, *Imbalance of Powers: Can Congressional Lawsuits Serve as Counterweight?*, 54 U. Pitt. L. Rev. 63, 84 (1992).

Oona A. Hathaway, *The Rise of "Self-Defense"—And the Fall of Constraints on the Use of Force*
In: *Perpetual War and International Law*. Edited by: Brianna Rosen, Oxford University Press.
 DOI: 10.1093/oso/9780197748992.003.0015

president today has had unprecedented free rein to decide when, where, and how to deploy armed force on behalf of the United States.

During the last two decades, one of the most notable trends to result from this largely unbridled presidential power over the decision to go to war is an ever-expanding reliance on the principle of "self-defense." The reliance on self-defense by the president serves two purposes: It allows the president to paper over weaknesses in the congressional authorizations for use of force with a general reference to the president's Article II powers to defend the nation. It also offers a justification for the use of force under international law—specifically the Article 51 self-defense exception to the United Nations (U.N.) Charter's general prohibition on unilateral resort to force by states.[2]

This chapter argues that ever-expanding U.S. claims of "self-defense" have had the effect, perhaps unintended, of eroding the international law prohibition on the use of force more broadly. The prohibition on the unilateral resort to force by states under the 1945 U.N. Charter was designed to be highly restrictive, undergirding the creation of a new legal order in which might no longer made right. Article 51 offered a very limited exception to states to resort to force without Security Council authorization in cases where a state had come under an "armed attack."[3] Enabled by the loose limits on presidential war powers, the United States has gradually expanded its claims to self-defense under Article 51. The consequence has been not only erosion of congressional authority to constrain unilateral presidential decisions to deploy military force but also erosion of the *international law* limits on unilateral resort to force. After all, the United States, which drafted the U.N. Charter and holds one of five permanent seats on the U.N. Security Council, has played an outsized role in the creation and evolution of international law during the entire postwar era. Hence, whenever the United States makes novel or marginal claims to the right to use force under international law in "self-defense" or "collective self-defense" under Article 51, it offers up arguments to other states that may wish to capitalize on the legal space that the United States claims create. In this way, the erosion of U.S. law constraining unilateral presidential war power has had a direct effect—and a

For more on the dynamics that have led to few constraints on presidential power over national security decisions, *see* Oona A. Hathaway, *National Security Lawyering in the Post-War Era: Can Law Constrain Power?*, 68 UCLA L. Rev. 2 (2021).

[2] *Compare* U.N. Charter art. 2(4) (requiring all members to refrain from "the threat or use of force"), *with* U.N. Charter art. 51 (noting that "[n]othing in the present Charter shall impair the inherent right of individual or collective self-defence").

[3] U.N. Charter art. 51; *see* Adil Ahmad Haque, *The United Nations Charter at 75: Between Force and Self-Defense—Part One*, Just Security (June 24, 2000), https://www.justsecurity.org/70985/the-united-nations-charter-at-75-between-force-and-self-defense-part-one/ [https://perma.cc/H8YF-65K8].

corrosive one—on the international law constraining the use of force under the U.N. Charter.

The chapter begins by documenting the erosion of U.S. constitutional constraints on the power of the president to wage war. It then examines the impact of this erosion on interpretations of Article 51 of the U.N. Charter—which provides that states may respond in self-defense or collective self-defense to an armed attack. It concludes by calling on Congress to reassert its war powers—not simply to defend its proper constitutional role but also to stem the erosion of international legal limits on the use of armed force.

The Erosion of Constitutional Constraints on Presidential War Powers

Over the course of the last century, presidential war powers have expanded to the point that today the president effectively exercises significant unilateral authority over decisions to use military force—at least in cases where there are no major deployment of ground troops. The U.S. Congress has not approved a use of force since 2002, when it authorized the president to invade Iraq.[4] And yet the United States certainly has not been at peace in the two decades since. In 2001, Congress authorized the United States to go to war against those who carried out the 9/11 attacks and any nation, organization, or persons that harbored them.[5] Even though it halted major combat operations in Afghanistan in 2021,[6] the U.S. military has continued battling insurgent and terrorist forces in the country.[7] And the United States has continued to battle the insurgent groups that emerged in Iraq after the U.S. invasion.[8] The U.S. government has also used force against extremist groups outside Iraq and Afghanistan. The United States reportedly has recently had active missions in around 20 countries, including most prominently in Afghanistan, Somalia, Yemen, Syria, and Libya.[9]

[4] Authorization for Use of Military Force Against Iraq Resolution of 2002, Pub. L. No. 107-243, 116 Stat. 1498 (2002) [hereinafter 2002 AUMF].

[5] Authorization for Use of Military Force, Pub. L. No. 107-40, 115 Stat. 224 (2001) [hereinafter 2001 AUMF].

[6] Joseph Biden, President of the U.S., Remarks by President Biden on the End of the War in Afghanistan (Aug. 31, 2021), https://www.whitehouse.gov/briefing-room/speeches-remarks/2021/08/31/remarks-by-president-biden-on-the-end-of-the-war-in-afghanistan/ [https://perma.cc/3QGG-YEDM].

[7] Laura Dickinson, *Still at War: The Forever War Legal Paradigm in Afghanistan*, Just Security (Apr. 14, 2022), https://www.justsecurity.org/81110/still-at-war-the-forever-war-legal-paradigm-in-afghanistan/ [https://perma.cc/2QTP-3J62].

[8] Crispin Smith, *Still at War: The United States in Iraq*, Just Security (May 18, 2022), https://www.justsecurity.org/81556/still-at-war-the-united-states-in-iraq/ [https://perma.cc/67U4-4996].

[9] Annika Lichtenbaum, *U.S. Military Operational Activity in the Sahel*, Lawfare (Jan. 25, 2019), https://www.lawfareblog.com/us-military-operational-activity-sahel [https://perma.cc/8QQL-75PQ]; Greg Myre, *The Military Doesn't Advertise It, But U.S. Troops Are All Over Africa*, NPR

None of these military operations has been separately authorized by Congress, even though the U.S. Constitution provides that Congress has the power to "declare War, grant Letters of Marque and Reprisal, and make Rules concerning Captures on Land and Water," as well as "raise and support Armies" and "provide and maintain a Navy."[10] Instead, they are grounded in capacious readings of the congressional 2001 and 2002 Authorizations for Use of Military Force (AUMFs),[11] together with an expansive interpretation of the president's Article II authority to use force unilaterally.[12] As a result, the vast majority of

(Apr. 28, 2018), https://www.npr.org/sections/parallels/2018/04/28/605662771/the-military-doesnt-advertise-it-but-u-s-troops-are-all-over-africa [https://perma.cc/3WJW-5TJ8]; Stephanie Savell, *The 2001 Authorization for Use of Military Force: A Comprehensive Look at Where and How It Has Been Used*, Watson Inst. Int'l & Pub. Aff., Brown Univ. (Dec. 14, 2021), https://watson.brown.edu/costsofwar/files/cow/imce/papers/2021/Costs%20of%20War_2001%20AUMF.pdf [https://perma.cc/Z2HX-DD5T]; Nick Turse & Alice Speri, *How the Pentagon Uses a Secretive Program to Wage Proxy Wars*, The Intercept (July 1, 2022), https://theintercept.com/2022/07/01/pentagon-127e-proxy-wars/ [https://perma.cc/3HAY-L832]. For additional detail, see *Just Security*'s "Still at War" symposium featuring articles examining U.S. operations in Yemen (Luke Hartig & Oona Hathaway), the Sahel (Brian Finucane), Syria (Tess Bridgeman & Brianna Rosen), and Somalia (Oona Hathaway & Luke Hartig). Tess Bridgeman & Brianna Rosen, *Introduction to Symposium: Still at War—Where and Why the United States Is Fighting the "War on Terror,"* Just Security (Mar. 24, 2022), https://www.justsecurity.org/80800/introduction-to-symposium-still-at-war-where-and-why-the-united-states-is-fighting-the-war-on-terror/ [https://perma.cc/3WK7-97U7].

[10] U.S. Const. art. I, § 8, cls. 11–13. There are several other relevant grants of authority to Congress in the Constitution. *See id.* cl. 14 (authority to make rules regulating land and naval forces); *id.* cls. 15, 16 (authority relating to raising and providing for militias); *id.* cl. 18 (authority to "make all Laws which shall be necessary and proper for carrying into Execution the foregoing Powers, and all other Powers vested by this Constitution in the Government of the United States").

[11] *See, e.g.*, Stephen W. Preston, U.S. Dep't of Defense Gen. Couns., The Legal Framework for the United States' Use of Military Force Since 9/11, Speech Before the Annual Meeting of the American Society of International Law (Apr. 10, 2015), https://www.defense.gov/News/Speeches/Speech/Article/606662/the-legal-framework-for-the-united-states-use-of-military-force-since-911/ [https://perma.cc/F8QZ-B43U] (providing an explanation for the Obama administration's use of force in Syria against ISIS based on an expansive reading of the 2001 AUMF). Some claim that Congress continues to vote to pay for the wars through authorizing the military budget and that is enough, but the War Powers Resolution specifically provides that "[a]uthority to introduce United States Armed Forces into hostilities or into situations wherein involvement in hostilities is clearly indicated by the circumstances shall not be inferred . . . from any provision of law . . . including any provision contained in any appropriation Act" unless it specifically authorizes such action. War Powers Resolution, Pub. L. No. 93-148, § 8, 87 Stat. 555, 558 (1973).

[12] *See, e.g.*, Memorandum from Steven A. Engel, Assistant Att'y Gen., Office of Legal Counsel, Re: April 2018 Airstrikes Against Syrian Chemical-Weapons Facilities (May 31, 2018), https://www.justice.gov/olc/opinion/file/1067551/download [https://perma.cc/9ARA-ZT9D]; Memorandum from Caroline D. Krass, Principal Deputy Assistant Att'y Gen., Office of Legal Counsel, to Eric Holder, Att'y Gen., Re: Authority to Use Military Force in Libya (Apr. 1, 2011) [hereinafter Libya OLC Memo], https://www.justice.gov/sites/default/files/olc/opinions/2011/04/31/authority-military-use-in-libya.pdf [https://perma.cc/3PUW-4DTN]. For critiques of these claims, *see* Jack Goldsmith & Oona Hathaway, *Bad Legal Arguments for the Syria Strikes*, Lawfare (Apr. 14, 2018), https://www.lawfareblog.com/bad-legal-arguments-syria-airstrikes [https://perma.cc/3VUM-NCZE]; Jack Goldsmith & Oona Hathaway, *The Downsides of Bombing Syria*, Just Security (Apr. 10, 2018), https://www.justsecurity.org/54698/downsides-bombing-syria/ [https://perma.cc/Y99D-E45K]; Spencer Ackerman et al., *Syria Missile Strikes: US Launches First Direct Action Against Assad*, The Guardian (Apr. 7, 2017), https://www.theguardian.com/world/2017/apr/06/trump-syria-missiles-assad-chemical-weapons [https://perma.cc/3E6J-BNPN]; Cory Booker & Oona

members of Congress have never voted to authorize a military operation. When the 2002 authorization for war against Iraq was enacted, only 12 of the 100 current senators and 44 of the 435 representatives were in office.[13] The failure of Congress to be actively engaged in decisions about when and whether the United States should be at war means there has been little democratic accountability for two decades of constant war-making,[14] which has cost trillions of dollars and hundreds of thousands of lives.[15]

One reason for the erosion of effective congressional constraints on the president's power to unilaterally wage war was the fateful decision of the authors of the War Powers Resolution to tie the reporting requirements and the automatic withdrawal provisions in the resolution not to "war" or "armed conflict," but to "hostilities." The House report on the War Power Resolution explained that the word was "substituted for the phrase *armed conflict* during the subcommittee drafting process because it was considered to be somewhat broader in scope . . . . *[H]ostilities* also encompasses a state of confrontation in which no shots have been fired, but where there is a clear and present danger of armed conflict."[16] Perhaps because the meaning was self-evident to those involved, the

Hathaway, *A Syria Plan that Breaks the Law*, N.Y. Times (Jan. 23, 2018), https://www.nytimes.com/2018/01/23/opinion/syria-tillerson-constitution-trump.html [https://perma.cc/V5HS-T7ZF].

[13] Calculations by the author, based on the information available at *Senate Seniority List: 118th Congress*, United States Senate Periodical Press Gallery, https://www.periodicalpress.senate.gov/senate-facts/senate-seniority/ [https://perma.cc/K3DM-24CS] (last visited July 8, 2024), and at *Terms of Service for Members of the House of Representatives in the 118th Congress*, House of Representatives History, Art & Archives (July 8, 2024), https://clerk.house.gov/member_info/Terms_of_Service.pdf/ [https://perma.cc/HV3B-F4AN].

[14] Some argue that presidential elections offer sufficient accountability. However, direct accountability is only effective during a president's first term. Moreover, presidential elections are multi-issue elections. *See, e.g.*, Pew Rsch. Ctr., 2016 Campaign: Strong Interest, Widespread Dissatisfaction 31–40 (2016), https://www.pewresearch.org/politics/wp-content/uploads/sites/4/2016/07/07-07-16-Voter-attitudes-release.pdf [https://perma.cc/6952-R6QQ] (examining the many issues that mattered to voters in the 2016 presidential election).

[15] *Costs of War: Human Cost of Post-9/11 Wars*, Watson Inst. Int'l & Pub. Aff., Brown Univ. (Sept. 2021), https://watson.brown.edu/costsofwar/figures/2021/WarDeathToll [https://perma.cc/DGW4-EVCH] (documenting roughly 900,000 lives lost due to post-9/11 wars); *Costs of War: Economic Costs*, Watson Inst. Int'l & Pub. Aff., Brown Univ. (Sept. 2021), https://watson.brown.edu/costsofwar/costs/economic [https://perma.cc/FKV4-5M8W] (documenting $8 trillion in costs through Fiscal Year 2022 for post-9/11 wars).

[16] *See* H.R. Rep. No. 93-287, at 23 (1973), available at https://ufdc.ufl.edu/AA00022638/00001/images/30 [https://perma.cc/FQ7B-AAZQ]. Interestingly, the explanation given by the House report is at some odds with the common use of the term "hostilities" at the time—which was to refer to active fighting, as opposed to the legal state of war (which could begin after hostilities began and end before they were concluded). It is unclear whether the authors of the House Report understood this. The Senate report reflected this more common understanding of the term, stating, "The essential purpose of the bill, therefore, is to reconfirm and to define with precision the constitutional authority of Congress to exercise its constitutional war powers with respect to 'undeclared' wars [i.e., hostilities] and the way in which this authority relates to the constitutional responsibilities of the President as Commander-in-Chief." S. Rep. No. 93-220, at 2 (1973), available at https://congressional-proquest-com.ezp-prod1.hul.harvard.edu/congressional/result/congresultpage:pdfevent?

term was not a subject of significant debate during the many hearings on the proposed legislation,[17] nor was it defined in the legislation. That has since left it open to wildly differing interpretations. The problem has been exacerbated by the unwillingness of the courts to weigh in, relying instead on justiciability doctrines to avoid reaching the merits. That has often left the executive branch as the only source of public legal opinions on war powers—issued in the form of Office of Legal Counsel memoranda or testimony and speeches by executive branch lawyers.[18]

What is sometimes referred to as "historical gloss"[19]—the shaping of the law through practice—has contributed to the erosion of the congressional role in authorizing uses of force. Over the course of the decades following the passage of the resolution, administrations of both parties have adopted strained interpretations of "hostilities." Many presidents evaded the consultation, reporting, and mandatory withdrawal provisions by arguing that military operations were not hostilities, even when they plainly were. For instance, according to the administration of President Ronald Reagan, the invasion of Grenada did not qualify as hostilities and so was not subject to the War Powers Resolution.[20] That incident was far from unique. In 1993, John Hart Ely observed:

> Repeatedly—as in the final stages of the war in Indochina, the botched 1980 attempt to free our hostages in Iran, the tragic 1982–83 commitment of our troops to Lebanon, the 1983 invasion of Grenada, the Gulf of Sidra incident of March 1986, the bombing of Tripoli a month later, the 1987–1988 Persian Gulf naval war against Iran, and the 1989 invasion of Panama—the president filed either no report at all or a vague statement pointedly refusing to identify itself as a Section 4(a)(1) "hostilities" report.[21]

rsId=18641ADD345&pdf=/app-bin/gis-serialset/8/a/9/2/13017-3_srp220_from_1_to_38.pdf&uri=/app-gis/serialset/13017-3_s.rp.220 [https://perma.cc/WV4R-RTSJ].

[17] The many hearings on the resolution use the term repeatedly, but there appears to be very little debate over its meaning. There was, by contrast, significant debate over the relative constitutional authorities of Congress and the president over the initiation, conduct of, and termination of hostilities. *See generally* Congress, the President, and War Powers: Hearings before the Subcomm. on Nat'l Sec. Pol'y and Sci. Dev. of the Comm. on Foreign Aff., 91st Cong. 2nd Sess. (June–Aug. 1970).

[18] *See* Hathaway, *supra* note 1.

[19] *See* Curtis A. Bradley, Historical Gloss and Foreign Affairs: Constitutional Authority in Practice (2024); Mary L. Dudziak, *The Gloss of War: Revisiting the Korean War's Legacy*, 122 Mich. L. Rev. 149 (2023).

[20] Stuart Taylor Jr., *Legality of Grenada Attack Disputed*, N.Y. Times (Oct. 26, 1983), https://www.nytimes.com/1983/10/26/world/legality-of-grenada-attack-disputed.html [https://perma.cc/V2EC-E5P6].

[21] John Hart Ely, War and Responsibility: Constitutional Lessons of Vietnam and Its Aftermath 49 (1993).

The War Powers Resolution was grievously ailing when the Obama administration dealt what was arguably a death blow in 2011 by not seeking congressional authorization to continue military operations in Libya past the sixty-day limit—and defending that decision as consistent with the War Powers Resolution.[22] Notwithstanding an extensive bombing campaign that precipitated the end of the Muammar Ghaddafi regime, the administration asserted its military operations were not "hostilities." Speaking for the administration, State Department Legal Adviser Harold Hongju Koh stated that "hostilities" is "an ambiguous standard, which is nowhere defined in statute."[23] He contended that, because the mission was limited, exposure of U.S. armed forces was limited, risk of escalation was limited, and the military means the United States was using were limited, the Libya operation did not amount to hostilities and thus the constraints in the War Powers Resolution did not apply. It later emerged that there had been a rare schism among lawyers in the administration on the issue, and President Obama had sided with Koh and White House counsel Robert Bauer over Department of Defense General Counsel Jeh Johnson and acting head of the Justice Department's Office of Legal Counsel Caroline Krass, who argued that the resolution required the president to terminate or scale back the mission after sixty days.[24]

A 2019 Senate hearing on war powers reform reflected ongoing uncertainty about the meaning of the term "hostilities." Senator Tom Udall asked the acting State Department Legal Adviser Marik String whether the U.S. disabling of an Iranian drone counted as hostilities under the War Powers Resolution. String responded that his office had not yet made a determination—a puzzling answer

[22] For a contemporaneous critique, *see* Bruce Ackerman & Oona Hathaway, *Obama's Illegal War*, Foreign Pol'y (June 1, 2011), https://foreignpolicy.com/2011/06/01/obamas-illegal-war-2/ [https://perma.cc/E5U3-B8ZF]; Bruce Ackerman & Oona Hathaway, *The Constitutional Clock Is Ticking on Obama's War*, Foreign Pol'y (Apr. 6, 2011), https://foreignpolicy.com/2011/04/06/the-constitutional-clock-is-ticking-on-obamas-war/ [https://perma.cc/7WJ7-R32P]; Bruce Ackerman & Oona Hathaway, *It's Not Up to the President to Impose a No-Fly Zone over Libya*, Huffington Post (Mar. 9, 2011), https://www.huffpost.com/entry/no-fly-zone-libya_b_833426 [https://perma.cc/KP56-6N29].

[23] *Libya and War Powers: Hearing Before the S. Comm. on Foreign Rels.*, 112th Cong. 1–14 (2011) (statement of Harold Koh, Legal Adviser, U.S. Dep't. of State), https://2009-2017.state.gov/documents/organization/167452.pdf [https://perma.cc/3J27-STJU]. Two months earlier, the DOJ Office of Legal Counsel (OLC) had issued an opinion concluding that "the President had the constitutional authority to direct the use of force in Libya because he could reasonably determine that such use of force was in the national interest." It further decided that he "was not constitutionally required to use military force in the limited operations under consideration." Both conclusions stretched the unilateral authority of the president to authorize the use of military force far beyond previous limits. Libya OLC Memo, *supra* note 13.

[24] Charlie Savage, *2 Top Lawyers Lost to Obama in Libya War Policy Debate*, N.Y. Times (June 17, 2011), https://www.nytimes.com/2011/06/18/world/africa/18powers.html [https://perma.cc/5J9G-SR5D]; Adam Serwer, *Koh Defends His Interpretation of the War Powers Act*, American Prospect (June 29, 2011), https://prospect.org/article/koh-defends-interpretation-war-powers-act/ [https://perma.cc/2TMT-2QQU].

given that, if it did, it would trigger war powers reporting obligations. Senator Mitt Romney then asked how the Trump administration defined the term "hostilities" under the War Powers Resolution. String responded that he could only discuss that in a closed (classified) setting.[25]

There are signs that many members of Congress think that the word "hostilities" has a broader meaning than the Obama and Trump administrations gave it. In April 2019, House lawmakers passed a measure that would have used the War Powers Resolution to force an end to U.S. participation in the conflict in Yemen.[26] Part of what was intriguing about the draft resolution was the way in which it defined hostilities.[27] It found that "since March 2015, members of the United States Armed Forces have been introduced into hostilities between the Saudi-led coalition and the Houthis, *including providing to the Saudi-led coalition aerial targeting assistance, intelligence sharing, and mid-flight aerial refueling*."[28] And it specifically stated that "[f]or purposes of this resolution, in this section, the term 'hostilities' includes in-flight refueling of non-United States aircraft conducting missions as part of the ongoing civil war in Yemen."[29] The definition of hostilities in this resolution is a far cry from the definition offered by the Obama administration during the debate over the 2011 U.S. intervention in Libya. Yet even in this case where Congress was able to muster the votes to attempt to claw back power, it was ineffective—Trump vetoed the effort to bring an end to U.S. support for the Saudi-led coalition's war in Yemen. A recent draft resolution on the war in Yemen similarly defined hostilities broadly, and it was pulled by its sponsors before a vote due in part to opposition from the Biden administration over its definition of the term.[30] The result of this narrow interpretation of hostilities by successive U.S. administrations has turned the constitutional order on its head—requiring Congress to muster supermajorities in

[25] *Reviewing Authorities for the Use of Military Force: Hearing Before S. Comm. on Foreign Rels.*, 115th Cong. 20 (2019), https://www.foreign.senate.gov/download/transcript-072419 [https://perma.cc/PE7R-R9W6].

[26] *See* Missy Ryan, *After Yemen Vote, Question Remains: When Is the U.S. at War?*, WASH. POST (Apr. 5, 2019), https://www.washingtonpost.com/world/national-security/after-yemen-vote-question-remains-when-is-the-us-at-war/2019/04/05/08dbdcb6-57b4-11e9-9136-f8e636f1f6df_story.html?utm_term=.5de6fba7deb8 [https://perma.cc/T3ZK-U87Y].

[27] A joint resolution to direct the removal of United States Armed Forces from hostilities in the Republic of Yemen that have not been authorized by Congress, S.J. RES. 7, 116th Cong. (2019), https://www.congress.gov/bill/116th-congress/senate-joint-resolution/7/text [https://perma.cc/FL27-QJLE].

[28] *Id.* (emphasis added).

[29] *Id.* A similar resolution was introduced and then withdrawn by Senator Bernie Sanders in 2022, apparently due to White House opposition. Ryan Grim & Ken Klippenstein, *Bernie Sanders Pulls Yemen War Powers Resolution Amid Opposition from White House*, INTERCEPT (Dec. 13, 2022), https://theintercept.com/2022/12/13/bernie-sanders-yemen-war-white-house/ [https://perma.cc/6YAM-UFF2].

[30] *See* Gunar Olsen, *So Much for Biden's Promise to End U.S. Support for the War in Yemen*, NEW REPUBLIC (Dec. 23, 2022), https://newrepublic.com/article/169699/biden-pledge-yemen-hostilities-saudi [https://perma.cc/VKN8-RGWY].

both houses to *stop* U.S. involvement in a war rather than requiring the president to seek the support of Congress to start one.

The one situation in which most would agree the War Powers Resolution does apply is a situation in which significant commitments of ground forces are involved (though even then there are those who would argue the president can act without Congress).[31] Due to the changing nature of warfare, however, such wars are now unusual. Instead, force is deployed from the air, often by remotely piloted aircraft, or in the form of cyber interventions, small footprint special operations, or warfare "by, with, and through" partners.[32] Hence, the result of years of decline in the role of Congress in decisions to use force abroad is that today the president is almost entirely unconstrained in waging war abroad.

The Expansion of "Self-Defense"

A major consequence of the erosion of Congress's war powers is the expansion of the self-defense exception to the U.N. Charter's prohibition on the use of military force. Because of the United States' geopolitical role and its ability to articulate its legal positions broadly and forcefully, this shift has affected not only the law as applied to the United States but also international law on a global scale.

This section begins with a brief description of the original understanding of Article 51 of the U.N. Charter, showing that the self-defense exception to the Charter's prohibition on force was, at its inception, understood to be duly narrow. It then proceeds to show how successive U.S. administrations have gradually expanded the aperture of this exception following the September 11 attacks, stretching interpretations of self-defense beyond recognition. Today, the uses of the exception by the United States and those who have followed its interpretation bear little resemblance to its original narrow meaning. As a result, the exception now threatens to undermine the prohibition on force it was once meant to support.

[31] John Yoo authored an opinion for the Office of Legal Counsel arguing that President George W. Bush could invade Iraq without congressional authorization. Though his torture memos were withdrawn by the office, this opinion remains on the books and thus binding executive branch precedent. Memorandum from Jay S. Bybee, Assistant Att'y Gen., to Alberto Gonzales, Counsel to the President, Re: Authority of the President Under Domestic and International Law to Use Military Force Against Iraq (Oct. 23, 2002), https://www.justice.gov/d9/olc/opinions/2002/10/31/op-olc-v026-p0143_0.pdf [https://perma.cc/Y545-E2NP] ("The President possesses constitutional authority to use military force against Iraq to protect United States national interests. This independent constitutional authority is supplemented by congressional authorization in the form of the Authorization for Use of Military Force Against Iraq Resolution.") (signed by Jay Bybee, but known to have been authored by John Yoo).

[32] For more on modern warfare, *see* Oona Hathaway et al., *Congressional Oversight of Modern Warfare: History, Pathologies, and Proposals for Reform*, 63 WM. & MARY L. REV. 137 (2021).

Text and Original Understanding of Article 51

Article 51 of the U.N. Charter reads as follows:

> Nothing in the present Charter shall impair the inherent right of individual or collective self-defence if an armed attack occurs against a Member of the United Nations, until the Security Council has taken measures necessary to maintain international peace and security. Measures taken by Members in the exercise of this right of self-defence shall be immediately reported to the Security Council and shall not in any way affect the authority and responsibility of the Security Council under the present Charter to take at any time such action as it deems necessary in order to maintain or restore international peace and security.[33]

By its express terms, Article 51 created a narrow exception for individual and collective self-defense where a U.N. member state has suffered an "armed attack." The *travaux préparatoires* support this plain reading. At the Dumbarton Oaks conference, the Chinese delegation asked "whether it would be possible under the document for either member or non-member states to use force unilaterally under the claim that such action was not inconsistent with the purposes of the Organization." The answer was no: "[E]xcept in cases of self-defense, no unilateral use of force could be undertaken without the approval of the council."[34] There could be no doubt that *all* uses of military force would be covered by the prohibition. Self-defense, moreover, was permitted only if there had been an "armed attack." The delegates, after all, were well aware of the dangers of blurred lines between defensive and aggressive war. Indeed, it was precisely such concerns that had persuaded the authors of the Kellogg-Briand Pact not to include an express exception for self-defense at all. But that exclusion had proven paralyzing when Japan invaded Chinese Manchuria, leaving the world unsure how to respond.[35] The authors of the Charter, having learned that lesson, decided to include an express self-defense exception but make it narrow in scope. They chose the term "armed attack" specifically to avoid defining aggression, believing "armed attack" to be less likely to cause definitional problems.[36]

[33] U.N. Charter art. 51.

[34] Memorandum from Edward Stettinius Jr., Under Secretary of State, to Cordell Hull, Secretary of State, Re: Progress Report on Dumbarton Oaks Conversations—Thirty-seventh Day (Oct. 2, 1944), https://history.state.gov/historicaldocuments/frus1944v01/d491 [https://perma.cc/HRQ4-Q2ZV]. For more on the negotiating history, *see* Haque, *supra* note 4; TOM RUYS, "ARMED ATTACK" AND ARTICLE 51 OF THE UN CHARTER: EVOLUTIONS IN CUSTOMARY LAW AND PRACTICE 126–249 (2010).

[35] OONA A. HATHAWAY & SCOTT J. SHAPIRO, THE INTERNATIONALISTS: HOW A RADICAL PLAN TO OUTLAW WAR REMADE THE WORLD 160–62 (2017).

[36] Memorandum by Mr. Robert W. Hartley of the United States Delegation of a Conversation Held at San Francisco, Saturday, May 12, 1945, *in* 1 US Department of State, Foreign Relations of the United States 1945, General: The United Nations (New York, 1967), https://history.state.gov/

There is a strong textual argument that the Article 51 exception is so narrow that not all uses of force in violation of Article 2(4) amount to an "armed attack" under Article 51. After all, Article 2(4) prohibits any "use of force," whereas Article 51 allows for self-defense only in response to an "armed attack."[37] Subsequent interpretations of Article 51 by the International Court of Justice (ICJ) have largely affirmed this narrower reading, including by defining "armed attack" as a "grave violation" of Article 2(4)'s prohibition on the use of force.[38] Moreover, the text of the Charter makes clear that only states are prohibited from uses of force under Article 2(4) ("All Members shall refrain") and only states have a right to self-defense and collective self-defense in response to an armed attack under Article 51 ("if an armed attack occurs against a Member of the United Nations").[39]

While there is a strong case that the original understanding of Article 51 was narrow, there is little doubt that this understanding has come under intense pressure—much of it resulting from the U.S. executive branch's increasingly aggressive interpretations of the exception. The United States is far from alone in offering stretched interpretations of Article 51. But as a key author and advocate of the Charter, a permanent member of the Security Council, and a state that

historicaldocuments/frus1945v01/d224 [https://perma.cc/MCU8-SHCZ] (noting that John Foster Dulles stated that "the United States proposal attempted to define aggression in terms of 'armed attack' and in this way it was hoped to avoid the problem of trying to define aggression as such").

[37] The United States is unusual in taking the position that the threshold for an Article 2(4) violation and a right of self-defense under Article 51 are one and the same. *See* Harold Hongju Koh, Legal Adviser, U.S. Dept. of State, International Law in Cyberspace, Remarks at USCYBERCOM Inter-Agency Legal Conference (Sept. 18, 2012), https://2009-2017.state.gov/s/l/releases/remarks/197924.htm [https://perma.cc/24DW-33SR] ("the United States has for a long time taken the position that the inherent right of self-defense potentially applies against *any* illegal use of force") (emphasis in original).

[38] *See, e.g.*, Mil. & Paramilitary Activities in & Against Nicaragua (Nicaragua v. United States), 1986 I.C.J. 14, 356 ¶ 191 (June 27); Oil Platforms (Iran v. United States), 2003 I.C.J. 161, 353 ¶ 64 (Nov. 6); Legal Consequences of the Construction of a Wall in the Occupied Palestinian Territory, 2004 I.C.J. 136, 194 ¶ 139 (July 9) [hereinafter Wall Advisory Opinion]; *cf.* Armed Activities on the Territory of the Congo (Democratic Republic of the Congo v. Uganda), 2005 I.C.J. 168, 223 ¶ 147 (Dec. 19) (finding that the "legal and factual circumstances for the exercise of a right of self-defence by Uganda against the DRC were not present," but declining to reach the question of whether self-defense extends to defense against non-state actors, perhaps signaling openness to such arguments in the future).

[39] There is some debate whether Article 51 should be read in light of the customary law of self-defense at the time it was drafted. Reading Article 51 in this way would allow for some actions in self-defense in the absence of an armed attack if an armed attack is imminent and there is no alternative course of action to avert the attack, a principle drawn from the 1837 *Caroline* incident. D.W. Bowett, Self-Defense in International Law 58–59 (2009) (1958); *see also* Albert B. Corey, The Crisis of 1830–1842 in Canadian-American Relations 61–69 (1941); Craig Forcese, Destroying the Caroline: The Frontier Raid that Reshaped the Right to War 9–55 (2018); Martin A. Rogoff & Edward Collins Jr., *The Caroline Incident and the Development of International Law*, 16 Brook. J. Int'l L. 493, 494–95 (1990); R.Y. Jennings, *The Caroline and McLeod Cases*, 32 Am. J. Int'l L. 82, 82–92 (1938).

holds itself out as committed to the rule of law with capacity to issue detailed legal justifications for its use of force decisions, the United States has an outsized impact on global understanding of the reach and limits of the self-defense exception. As its interpretation of the exception expands, other states follow. The rest of this section traces that evolution.

Preemptive Self-Defense (the "Bush Doctrine")

President George W. Bush's administration claimed the United States had the option to take preemptive action to counter a "sufficient threat to our national security."[40] In the case of significant threats, the United States could respond "even if uncertainty remains as to the time and place of the enemy's attack."[41] Indeed, in the lead-up to the Iraq War, John Yoo wrote an opinion of the Department of Justice's Office of Legal Counsel that claimed congressional authorization of the war was unnecessary: "Although the Administration might welcome an expression of Congressional support for any military action the Executive Branch may decide to take against Iraq, such a resolution is unnecessary as a matter of constitutional law," because, he claimed, "the President has the authority to initiate the use of force to protect the United States."[42] This assertion was met with

[40] George W. Bush, President of the U.S., U.S. National Security Strategy: Prevent Our Enemies from Threatening Us, Our Allies, and Our Friends with Weapons of Mass Destruction, West Point (June 1, 2002), https://2001-2009.state.gov/r/pa/ei/wh/15425.htm [https://perma.cc/DW5T-SAJ5].

[41] The White House, The National Security Strategy of the United States of America 15 (2002), https://2009-2017.state.gov/documents/organization/63562.pdf [https://perma.cc/4QMT-CBS4]. This view was also reflected in opinions issued by the Office of Legal Counsel during the Bush administration. *See, e.g.*, Memorandum from John C. Yoo, Deputy Assistant Att'y Gen., & Robert J. Delahunty, Special Couns., to Alberto R. Gonzales, Counsel to the President, & William J. Haynes II, Gen. Couns., Dep't. of Def., Authority for Use of Military Force to Combat Terrorist Activities Within the United States 1 (Oct. 23, 2001), https://nsarchive2.gwu.edu//torturingdemocracy/documents/20011023.pdf [https://perma.cc/Z8HW-SQ99] (concluding that the president has authority to "deploy military force against terrorist threats within the United States").

[42] Memorandum from John C. Yoo, Deputy Assistant Att'y Gen., Re: Specter/Harkin Joint Resolution Calling for Congress to Vote on a Resolution for the Use of Force by the United States Armed Forces Against Iraq 1–2 (July 23, 2002), https://www.justice.gov/sites/default/files/olc/legacy/2010/06/04/olc-memo-07232002.pdf [https://perma.cc/V6M3-MS6V]; *see also* Memorandum from John C. Yoo, Deputy Assistant Att'y Gen., Re: Authorization for Use of Military Force Against Iraq Resolution of 2002 1 (Oct. 21, 2002), https://www.justice.gov/sites/default/files/olc/legacy/2009/08/24/memo-military-force-iraq.pdf [https://perma.cc/HHL7-BYYJ] ("We have no constitutional objection to Congress expressing its support for the use of military force against Iraq. . . . We have long maintained, however, that resolutions such as H. J. Res. 114 are legally unnecessary."); Bybee, Re: Authority of the President Under Domestic and International Law to Use Military Force Against Iraq, *supra* note 32, at 143 ("Using force against Iraq would be consistent with international law because it would be authorized by the United Nations Security Council or would be justified as anticipatory self-defense."); Memorandum from John C. Yoo, Deputy Assistant Att'y Gen., Re: Effect of a Recent United Nations Security Council Resolution on the Authority of the President under International Law to Use Military Force Against Iraq 199 (Nov. 8, 2002), https://www.justice.gov/d9/olc/opinions/2002/11/31/op-olc-v026-p0199_0.pdf [https://perma.cc/42DD-4YBX] ("We emphasize at the outset that U.N. Security Council authorization is not a necessary precondition under

significant criticism at the time.[43] It later became clear that this idea of anticipatory, or preemptive, self-defense was not limited to weapons of mass destruction. Conventional weapons, if sufficiently concerning, could prompt a preemptive response as well.[44]

The embrace of preemptive self-defense came to be known as the "Bush Doctrine."[45] President Bush's successor, President Barack Obama, ran for office in part based on a more constrained view of presidential war powers. But once in office, Obama never renounced the expansive vision of self-defense that Bush had espoused. Indeed, he surprised his supporters and detractors alike by taking steps to expand it, as the following sections will make clear.[46] Tellingly, while the Obama administration retracted John Yoo's infamous legal opinions on torture, Yoo's equally problematic legal opinions on the use of force still stand.

Self-Defense Against Non-State Actors

Before September 11, 2001, self-defense under Article 51 was generally believed to apply only "in the case of an armed attack by *one State against another State*."[47] Although a number of states had filed Article 51 letters in which they cited both state and non-state actor threats, relatively few states had exclusively cited non-state actor threats in Article 51 letters filed before 2001.[48]

international law for the use of force. . . . Under the doctrine of anticipatory self-defense, the United States may use force against Iraq if the President determines the use of force would be necessary due to an imminent threat, and a proportional response to that threat.").

[43] *See, e.g.*, Christian Henderson, *The Bush Doctrine: From Theory to Practice*, 9 J. CONFLICT & SEC. L. 3, 24 (2004) ("It is clear that the Bush Doctrine has the potential to shatter the legal regulation of the use of force. . . . Putting too much power in the hands of individual states when making decisions on the use of pre-emptive force is potentially very dangerous . . .").

[44] *Id.* at 12–22.

[45] *See, e.g.*, *id.* (describing "Bush Doctrine"); Carlos L. Yordan, *America's Quest for Global Hegemony: Offensive Realism, the Bush Doctrine, and the 2003 Iraq War*, 53 THEORIA: J. OF SOC. & POL. THEORY 125 (2006) (same); Mackubin Thomas Owens, *The Bush Doctrine: The Foreign Policy of Republican Empire*, FOREIGN POL'Y RSCH. INST. (2009), https://apps.dtic.mil/sti/tr/pdf/ADA596721.pdf [https://perma.cc/L7PZ-6WMY].

[46] *See generally* Noura S. Erakat, *New Imminence in the Time of Obama: The Impact of Targeted Killings on the Law of Self-Defense*, 56 ARIZ. L. REV. 195 (2014); Bruce Ackerman, *Is Obama Enabling the Next President to Launch Illegal Wars?*, ATLANTIC (Aug. 24, 2016), https://www.theatlantic.com/politics/archive/2016/08/obama-illegal-wars/497159/ [https://perma.cc/N2DK-ZX2Z].

[47] Monica Hakimi, *Defensive Force against Non-State Actors: The State of Play*, 91 INT'L L. STUD. SER. U.S. NAVAL WAR COL. 1, 4–5 (2015) (citing Wall Advisory Opinion); Wee Yen Jean, *The Use of Force against Non-State Actors: Justifying and Delimiting the Exercise of the Right of Self-Defence*, 9 SING. L. REV. 1, 3 (2017).

[48] *See Annex: HLS PILAC Catalogue of Communications to the Security Council of Measures Taken by United Nations Member States in Purported Exercise of the Right of Self-Defense: October 24, 1945 Through December 31, 2018*, *in* DUSTIN A. LEWIS ET. AL, QUANTUM OF SILENCE: INACTION AND *JUS AD BELLUM*, HARV. L. SCH. PROJECT ON INT'L L. AND ARMED CONFLICT (2019), https://dash.harvard.edu/bitstream/handle/1/40931878/Quantum%20of%20Silence%202019.pdf?isAllowed=y&seque

After September 11, 2001, non-state aggressors were more frequently treated as direct targets of self-defensive force by states.[49] The United States in its Article 51 letter notifying the Security Council of its self-defense operations in Afghanistan after the 9/11 attacks indicated that it was responding to the "ongoing threat . . . posed by the Al-Qaeda organization" made possible by the Taliban's willingness to allow Afghanistan to be used as a base of operation.[50] A subsequent letter signed by the United Kingdom similarly indicated that it was engaging in collective self-defense "against targets we know to be involved in the operation of terror."[51] Before the end of the year, Canada, France, Australia, Germany, New Zealand, and Poland had issued Article 51 letters that echoed the United States, relying explicitly or implicitly on an international law right of self-defense and collective self-defense against the non-state actors responsible for the September 11 attacks.[52] A number of other Article 51 letters filed by states against other non-state actors followed in the next few years, and, indeed, Article 51 letters citing

nce=1 [https://perma.cc/2KXN-8TA9] [hereinafter *HLS PILAC Catalogue*]. Israel filed the most such letters, the first of which it filed on November 16, 1966. U.N. SCOR, 21st Sess., 1320th mtg. U.N. Doc. S/PV.1320 (Nov. 16, 1966), https://digitallibrary.un.org/record/581598/files/S_PV-1320-EN.pdf?ln=en [https://perma.cc/6W7S-YDMJ]. Iran also filed several such letters, the first of which it filed on May 25, 1993. U.N. SCOR, 48th Sess. U.N. Doc. S/25843 (May 25, 1993), https://digitallibrary.un.org/record/167123/files/S_25843-EN.pdf?ln=en [https://perma.cc/56DC-J7ZQ]. Other states cited the right to self-defense against non-state actors only rarely. For example, Portugal filed such a letter on September 29, 1971. U.N. SCOR, 26th Sess. U.N. Doc. S/10343 (Sept. 29, 1971), https://digitallibrary.un.org/record/494391/files/S_10343-EN.pdf?ln=en [https://perma.cc/EJE2-EVBH]. Kazakhstan, Kyrgyzstan, Russia, and Tajikistan submitted a joint letter in 1993. U.N. SCOR, 48th Sess. U.N. Doc. S/26290 (Aug. 11, 1993), https://digitallibrary.un.org/record/171757/files/A_48_304--S_26290-EN.pdf?ln=en [https://perma.cc/PFT2-828Y].

[49] As Christian Marxsen and Anne Peters put it, "while States did defend themselves against non-State actors by military means, these hardly triggered any international legal debate. . . . This changed significantly with the terrorist attacks of 9/11 in 2001 and with the subsequent military interventions. These events are often seen as constituting a 'true turning point' in the debate on the international law of self-defence." Christian Marxsen & Anne Peters, *Introduction: Dilution of Self-Defense and its Discontents*, *in* SELF-DEFENSE AGAINST NON-STATE ACTORS 2–3 (Ellen O'Connell, Christian J. Tams, & Dire Tladi eds., 2019).

[50] Letter from the Permanent Representative of the United States of America to the United Nations addressed to the President of the Security Council, U.N. Doc. S/2001/946 (Oct. 7, 2001), https://documents-dds-ny.un.org/doc/UNDOC/GEN/N01/567/85/PDF/N0156785.pdf?OpenElement [https://perma.cc/9RF8-5FCE]; *see* Jutta Brunnee & Stephen J. Toope, *Self-Defence against Non-State Actors: Are Powerful States Willing but Unable to Change International Law?*, 67 BRIT. INST. INT'L & COMP. L. 263, 269 (2018). The U.S. letter followed Security Council resolutions that mentioned the inherent right of self-defense before condemning the terrorist attacks. S.C. Res. 1368 (Sept. 12, 2001); S.C. Res. 1373 (Sept. 28, 2001).

[51] Letter from the Chargé d'affaires of the Permanent Mission of the United Kingdom to the United Nations addressed to the President of the Security Council, U.N. Doc. S/2001/947 (Oct. 7, 2001), https://digitallibrary.un.org/record/449477/files/S_2001_947-EN.pdf?ln=en [https://perma.cc/K9F2-DQLZ].

[52] *HLS PILAC Catalogue*, *supra* note 49.

the right of self-defense against non-state actors have become common in the years since.[53]

The United States and some of its allies soon endorsed what has come to be referred to as the "unwilling or unable" doctrine—the claim that action against a non-state threat is justified so long as the state in which the non-state actor resides is "unwilling or unable" to suppress the threat.[54] The doctrine originated much earlier—during the Nixon administration, which claimed that self-defense was permissible whenever the neutral state "cannot or will not" prevent the unneutral use of its territory to justify expanding its military campaign against North Vietnamese forces in Cambodia.[55] At last count, thirteen states either explicitly or implicitly endorse the "unwilling or unable doctrine," six have objected to it, and ten have made ambiguous expressions.[56] Latin American states, including Brazil and Mexico, have voiced opposition to the unwilling or unable doctrine,[57] and the Community of Latin American and Caribbean States

[53] In 2002, Rwanda cited a right of individual self-defense against the Democratic Republic of the Congo and "ex-Forces armées rwandaises (ex-FAR) and Interahamwe," Letter from the Permanent Representative of Rwanda to the United Nations addressed to the President of the Security Council, U.N. Doc. S/2002/420 (Apr. 15, 2002), https://documents-dds-ny.un.org/doc/UNDOC/GEN/N02/333/83/PDF/N0233383.pdf?OpenElement [https://perma.cc/V6H6-X6RE]. In 2003, Cote d'Ivoire cited a right of individual self-defense against "[r]ebel forces," Letter from the Permanent Representative of Cote d'Ivoire addressed to the President of the Security Council, U.N. Doc. S/2003/510 (Apr. 28, 2003), https://digitallibrary.un.org/record/493559/files/S_2003_510-EN.pdf?ln=en [https://perma.cc/8J5R-YTKV]. In 2004 and 2005, Israel cited a right of individual self-defense against "Hezbollah and Ahmed Jibril's Popular Front for the Liberation of Palestine (PFLP)," Letter from the Chargé d'affaires of the Permanent Mission of Israel to the United Nations addressed to the Secretary-General and the President of the Security Council, U.N. Doc. A/58/837-S/2004/465 (June 8, 2004), https://digitallibrary.un.org/record/523012/files/A_58_837--S_2004_465-EN.pdf?ln=en [https://perma.cc/RJP3-UJD8]; "the terrorist organization Hamas," Letter from the Chargé d'affaires of the Permanent Mission of Israel to the United Nations addressed to the Secretary-General and the President of the Security Council, U.N. Doc. A/60/382-S/2005/609 (Sept. 28, 2005), https://digitallibrary.un.org/record/557436/files/A_60_382--S_2005_609-EN.pdf?ln=en [https://perma.cc/6KPN-WLZ8]; "al-Aqsa Martyrs Brigade," Letter from the Permanent Representative of Israel to the United Nations addressed to the Secretary-General and the President of the Security Council, U.N. Doc. A/60/580-S/2005/756 (Dec. 5, 2005), https://digitallibrary.un.org/record/561975/files/A_60_580_S_2005_756-EN.pdf?ln=en [https://perma.cc/NUK3-GVTS]. For additional Article 51 letters against non-state actors, *see HLS PILAC Catalogue*, *supra* note 49. *See generally* Marxsen & Peters, *supra* note 50.

[54] Elena Chachko & Ashley Deeks, *Which States Support the "Unwilling and Unable" Test?*, LAWFARE (Oct. 10, 2016), https://www.lawfareblog.com/which-states-support-unwilling-and-unable-test [https://perma.cc/V64L-DAFA].

[55] Kevin Jon Heller, *The Earliest Invocation of "Unwilling or Unable,"* OPINIO JURIS (Mar. 19, 2019), http://opiniojuris.org/2019/03/19/the-earliest-invocation-of-unwilling-or-unable/ [https://perma.cc/P3XW-R63H] (attributing the insight to a doctoral dissertation by military historian Brian Cuddy).

[56] Chachko & Deeks, *supra* note 55.

[57] Pablo Arrocha Olabuenaga, *An Insider's View of the Life-Cycle of Self-Defense Reports by U.N. Member States*, JUST SECURITY (Apr. 2, 2019), https://www.justsecurity.org/63415/an-insiders-view-of-the-life-cycle-of-self-defense-reports-by-u-n-member-states/ [https://perma.cc/K4XQ-D4BZ] (describing "Latin American disquiet with the 'Unable or Unwilling' doctrine"); Alex Moorehead, *Brazil's Robust Defense of the Legal Prohibition on the Use of Force and Self Defense*, JUST SECURITY (Apr. 20, 2018), https://www.justsecurity.org/55126/brazils-robust-defense-legal-prohibition-force/ [https://perma.cc/J9Y2-SQPR].

has expressed unease with the use of Article 51 to justify counterterrorism operations.[58] The vast majority of states, however, have not expressed a position on the "unwilling or unable" doctrine—and it remains controversial outside the U.S. government, even if it is widely accepted within.[59] Controversially, the United States appears to take silence on the issue as acquiescence, while others challenge that inference.[60]

The assertion that Article 51 permits states to use armed force against non-state actors in a nonconsenting state is in tension with the ICJ's decision in *Nicaragua v. United States*, which held that an "armed attack" could include aggression by "armed bands, groups, irregulars, or mercenaries," but only if they were sent "by or on behalf of a state."[61] In 2004, the ICJ, in its Advisory Opinion on the *Legal Consequences of the Construction of a Wall in the Occupied Palestinian Territory*, affirmed that "Article 51 of the Charter . . . recognizes the existence of an inherent right to self-defense in the case of armed attack by *one State against another State*."[62] More recently, in *Democratic Republic of the Congo v. Uganda*, the ICJ rejected the claim that Uganda had an Article 51 right of self-defense against a non-state group within the Democratic Republic of the Congo (DRC) because it failed to establish that the non-state group had sufficient ties to the government of the DRC.[63]

[58] Statement by the Permanent Mission of El Salvador to the United Nations on Behalf of the Community of Latin American and Caribbean States (CELAC), Measures to Eliminate International Terrorism (Oct. 3, 2018), http://statements.unmeetings.org/media2/19408950/el-salvador-on-behalf-of-celac-e-.pdf [https://perma.cc/7SC3-UBDG] ("We take note with concern of the increase in the number of letters to the Security Council under Article 51 of the Charter submitted by some States in order to have recourse to the use of force in the context of counter-terrorism, most of the times 'ex post facto'. We reiterate that any use of force which is not in compliance with the UN Charter is not only illegal, it is also unjustifiable and unacceptable. Further consideration should be given in an open and transparent debate on this issue.").

[59] For more on the disconnect between government national security lawyers and public understanding of the law, *see generally* Hathaway, *supra* note 1. For more on the unwilling or unable doctrine, *see generally* Gabriella Blum & John C.P. Goldberg, *The Unable or Unwilling Doctrine: The View from Private Law*, 63 HARV. INT'L L.J. 63 (2022); Dawood I. Ahmed, *Defending Weak States Against the "Unwilling or Unable" Doctrine of Self-Defense*, 9 J. INT'L L. & INT'L RELS. 1, 14 (2013); Tess Bridgeman, *When Does the Legal Basis for U.S. Forces in Syria Expire?*, JUST SECURITY (Mar. 14, 2018), https://www.justsecurity.org/53810/legal-basis-u-s-forces-syria-expire/ [https://perma.cc/L7WR-JXZX].

[60] For more on how to read silence, *see HLS PILAC Catalogue*, *supra* note 49. Mexico takes a very different view from the United States on both the legality of the "unwilling or unable" test and on how best to read silence. *See generally* Naz K. Modirzadeh & Pablo Arrocha Olabuenaga, *A Conversation Between Pablo Arrocha Olabuenaga and Naz Khatoon Modirzadeh on the Origins, Objectives, and Context of the 24 February 2021 "Arria-formula" Meeting Convened by Mexico*, 8 J. USE OF FORCE & INT'L L. 291 (2021).

[61] Wee Yen, *supra* note 48, at 3.

[62] Wall Advisory Opinion, *supra* note 39, at ¶ 139 (emphasis added).

[63] *Armed Activities on the Territory of the Congo*, *supra* note 39, at ¶¶ 146–47; *see also* Stephanie A. Barbour & Zoe A. Salzman, *The Tangled Web: The Right of Self-Defense Against Non-State Actors in the* Armed Activities *Case*, 40 N.Y.U. J. INT'L L. & POL. 53, 55 (2008). Interestingly, the ICJ declined to address the question of whether there could have been a right of self-defense against a non-state actor. *Armed Activities on the Territory of the Congo*, *supra* note 39, at ¶ 147.

Nonetheless, for much of the last two decades, the United States and United Kingdom have publicly pressed the claim that military force against non-state aggressors like al-Qaeda is permissible under Article 51. Former U.K. Legal Adviser Daniel Bethlehem outlined the U.S., U.K., and other allied governments' legal position in a 2012 *American Journal of International Law* article published under Bethlehem's own name, though widely understood to be based on conclusions reached in government-to-government talks known as the "West Point Group."[64] That article articulated a set of principles that have come to be referred to as the "Bethlehem Principles." The first principle provides: "[S]tates have a right of self-defense against an imminent or actual armed attack by non-state actors."[65] The eleventh and twelfth principles state that the requirement for consent by the host state does not operate where the host state is colluding with the non-state actor "or otherwise unwilling" to restrain its activities, nor does it apply when "there is a reasonable and objective basis for concluding the third state is unable to effectively restrain the armed activities of the nonstate actor."[66] Part of what was notable about the principles, moreover, was the purpose of publishing them: Bethlehem acknowledged that they "do not reflect a settled view of any state," but nonetheless indicated that "[t]he hope . . . is that the principles may attract a measure of agreement about the contours of the law relevant to the actual circumstances in which states are faced with an imminent or actual armed attack by nonstate actors."[67] In other words, the project was self-consciously aimed at development and evolution of the international law of self-defense.

The effort met with some resistance.[68] Elizabeth Wilmshurst and Sir Michael Wood (who was, like Bethlehem, formerly U.K. Legal Adviser), argued in response to Bethlehem that "there are some respects in which the new principles risk departing from international law"—noting that Principles 11 and 12 "remain

[64] Interview by Russell Riley, Presidential Oral Histories Project, with John Bellinger III, Legal Adviser to the Dep't of State (Apr. 20, 2013), https://millercenter.org/the-presidency/presidential-oral-histories/john-bellinger-iii-oral-history-part-ii [https://perma.cc/S8JK-CLS4] (describing the "West Point Group" meetings, which led to what came to be known as the Bethlehem principles).

[65] Daniel Bethlehem, *Self-Defense Against an Imminent or Actual Armed Attack by Nonstate Actors*, 106 Am. J. Int'l L. 770, 776 (2012); *see also* Themis Tzimas, *Self-Defense by Non-State Actors in States of Fragmented Authority*, 24 J. Conflict & Sec. L. 175, 179 (2019) ("[W]hile on the one hand self-defense constitutes a state-centric right, on the other hand, and given that it is part of the collective security system, we cannot fail to take into account the ongoing transformations in relation to the incursion . . . of non-state actors in the wider framework of collective security . . . .").

[66] Bethlehem, *supra* note 66, at 776.

[67] *Id.* at 773.

[68] *See, e.g.*, Dire Tladi, *The Use of Force in Self-Defence against Non-State Actors, Decline of Collective Security and the Rise of Unilateralism: Whither International Law?*, *in* Self-Defense Against Non-State Actors 89 (Ellen O'Connell, Christian J. Tams, & Dire Tladi eds., 2019) ("There are those arguing vociferously for an expansion of this right to such an extent that States would be free to use force in the territory of that State, without that State's consent or without attribution of the conduct of the non-State actors to that State. Terrorism, as heinous as it certainly is, does not offer sufficient reason to depart from the constraints placed by international law.").

controversial."[69] Some scholars objected to the "unwilling or unable" doctrine as inconsistent with existing law. Adil Haque, for example, argues that the U.N. Charter's text, context, and purpose indicate that it does not permit "one State (say, the United States or Turkey) to use armed force on the territory of another State (say, Syria), without the territorial State's consent, targeting a non-State actor."[70]

Even as the unwilling or unable doctrine remains contested, the United States has openly relied on it to justify expansive and long-standing uses of force. In doing so, the United States has bypassed the need to establish that there had been an "armed attack" or to demonstrate ties to a sponsoring sovereign state. For example, in 2014, the United States submitted an Article 51 letter to the Security Council justifying its use of force against ISIS in Syria and Iraq on the grounds that states had the "inherent right to individual and collective self-defense . . . when the government of the State where the threat is located is unwilling or unable to prevent the use of its territory for . . . [terrorist] attacks."[71] It has continued to use force against ISIS in Syria now for nearly a decade. It has relied on this same theory to justify other uses of force as well, including, most recently, in an Article 51 letter to the United Nations justifying strikes against a facility in eastern Syria used by Iran-backed militia groups.[72]

The U.S. approach has influenced not only other states' stated legal policy but even their targeting policies and practices. Following ISIS attacks in 2015, France stated that its military action in Syria, which had previously been justified as collective self-defense, could now also be characterized as individual self-defense.[73]

[69] Elizabeth Wilmshurst & Michael Wood, *Self-Defense against Nonstate Actors: Reflections on the "Bethlehem Principles,"* 107 Am. J. Int'l L. 390, 393 (2013).

[70] Adil Ahmad Haque, *"Clearly of Latin American Origin": Armed Attack by Non-State Actors and the UN Charter*, Just Security (Nov. 5, 2019), https://www.justsecurity.org/66956/clearly-of-latin-american-origin-armed-attack-by-non-state-actors-and-the-un-charter/ [https://perma.cc/H4WR-53ED].

[71] Letter from the Permanent Representative of the United States of America to the United Nations addressed to the Secretary-General, U.N. Doc. S/2014/695 (Sept. 23, 2014), https://www.securitycouncilreport.org/atf/cf/%7B65BFCF9B-6D27-4E9C-8CD3-CF6E4FF96FF9%7D/s_2014_695.pdf [https://perma.cc/LJH4-6B4T].

[72] Letter from the Permanent Representative of the United States of America addressed to the President of the Security Council, U.N. Doc. S/2022/647 (Aug. 26, 2022), https://www.justsecurity.org/wp-content/uploads/2022/09/8.26.2022-Art.-51-Letter-Syria.pdf [https://perma.cc/6DDA-VGAK]. For a review of "international law questions raised" by the letter, *see* Tess Bridgeman & Brian Finucane, *Tit-for-Tat Hostilities in Syria: War Powers and International Law Implications*, Just Security (Sept. 8, 2022), https://www.justsecurity.org/82979/tit-for-tat-hostilities-in-syria-war-powers-and-international-law-implications/ [https://perma.cc/QG66-LBPL].

[73] Identical letters dated September 8, 2015 from the Permanent Representative of France to the United Nations addressed to the Secretary-General and the President of the Security Council, U.N. Doc. S/2015/745 (Sept. 9, 2015), [https://perma.cc/JV42-FV9P] ("By resolutions 2170 (2014), 2178 (2014) and 2199 (2015) in particular, the Security Council has described the terrorist acts of Islamic State in Iraq and the Levant (ISIL), including abuses committed against the civilian populations of the Syrian Arab Republic and Iraq, as a threat to international peace and security. Those acts are also a direct and extraordinary threat to the security of France.").

French military forces participating in the operation emulated the U.S. approach to targeting in counterterrorism operations. In an interview, a French drone pilot who had participated in French armed drone operations from the Niamey air base in Niger described the French use of drones and, in particular, their increased use to engage in "anticipatory" self-defense in the Sahel.[74] The operator received training in the United States on how to operate the drone,[75] and the legal policies under which he was operating were similarly modeled on U.S. legal policy for counterterrorism operations in the Middle East—including the broad U.S. understanding of permissible "self-defense."[76]

"Collective Self-Defense" on Behalf of Non-State Actor Partners

The United States' latest step in the expansion of self-defense is the new assertion that the right of collective self-defense includes not only actions in defense of state actors but actions in defense of *non-state actors* as well. While this view has not yet been openly embraced by other states, the invocation of "collective self-defense" in such contexts by the United States could, over time, once again shift the scope of what is considered permissible under international law.

The use of collective self-defense in the context of non-international armed conflicts is far from new. For example, the United States relied almost entirely on "collective self-defense" of Somali counterparts to justify strikes against al-Shabaab from as early as 2015. In characterizing the strikes as defensive in nature, U.S. forces were able to circumvent policy restrictions that would otherwise have applied.[77] Indeed, the International Crisis Group quotes a U.S. official explaining that "[c]ollective self-defense is really close air support without authorization."[78] The rationale allowed military forces on the ground to get "ahead of what Washington had blessed or thought it had blessed" and allowed more expansive strikes than would otherwise have been permitted under the 2001 AUMF.[79]

[74] *Testimony of French Drone Operator: Anticipatory Strikes in the Sahel*, EUR. F. ON ARMED DRONES (Feb. 16, 2022), https://www.efadrones.org/testimony-of-a-french-drone-operator-anticipatory-strikes-in-the-sahel/ [https://perma.cc/G6CK-FKUV].

[75] Interview by Alexandre Jubelin with Lieutenant-Colonel Romain, French Air Force officer and drone operator (Apr. 9, 2021), https://www.efadrones.org/wp-content/uploads/2022/02/Drone-strike-in-the-Malian-desert_interview-in-English-2.pdf [https://perma.cc/RQ3M-YZEJ].

[76] *See generally* Rebecca Mignot-Mahdavi, *Drones Programs, the Individualization of War and the* Ad Bellum *Principle of Proportionality*, *in* NECESSITY AND PROPORTIONALITY IN INTERNATIONAL PEACE AND SECURITY LAW (Claus Kreß & Robert Lawless eds., 2020).

[77] This is well described in *Overkill: Reforming the Legal Basis for the U.S. War on Terror*, INT'L CRISIS GROUP (Sept. 17, 2021), https://www.crisisgroup.org/united-states/005-overkill-reforming-legal-basis-us-war-terror [https://perma.cc/6T94-6XPH].

[78] *Id.*

[79] *Id.* President Biden's Presidential Policy Memorandum does not require White House approval "for strikes carried out in self-defense, such as the so-called collective self-defense of partner

Using collective self-defense to extend authorities to use force is not new, then. But what is new is the extension of this "collective self-defense" justification to encompass not only state partner forces but non-state actor partners as well. The novel theory that collective self-defense could be undertaken on behalf of non-state actor partners first became public in 2017, when the United States announced military operations in defense of the Syrian Democratic Forces (SDF), a coalition of ethnic militia and antigovernment groups operating in North and East Syria with which the United States had partnered since 2015. On June 18, 2017, the United States shot down a manned Syrian regime SU-22 aircraft that had "dropped bombs near SDF fighters south of Tabqah"—a city in north-central Syria near Raqqa.[80] This was in response to an attack by Syrian forces on Ja'Din, an SDF-controlled town, "wounding a number of SDF fighters and driving the SDF from the town."[81] It is unclear if any U.S. service members were at risk, and the U.S. Department of Defense press release on the strike did not reference their presence. Instead, it stated, "At 6:43 p.m., a Syrian regime SU-22 dropped bombs near SDF fighters south of Tabqah and, in accordance with rules of engagement and *in collective self-defense of Coalition partnered forces*, was immediately shot down by a U.S. F/A-18E Super Hornet."[82]

Perhaps recognizing the extraordinary step it had taken—attacking the military forces of a country in its *own territory* in order to defend an unlawful organized armed non-state actor group—the press release went on to connect the attack to the ongoing self-defense mission in Syria: "[T]he Coalition's mission is to defeat ISIS in Iraq and Syria. The Coalition does not seek to fight Syrian regime, Russian, or pro-regime forces partnered with them, but will not hesitate to defend Coalition or partner forces from any threat."[83] It further argued that "[t]he Coalition presence in Syria addresses the imminent threat ISIS in Syria poses globally. The demonstrated hostile intent and actions of pro-regime forces

forces." Charlie Savage, *White House Tightens Rules on Counterterrorism Drone Strikes*, N.Y. Times (Oct. 7, 2022), https://www.nytimes.com/2022/10/07/us/politics/drone-strikes-biden-trump.html [https://perma.cc/9EST-BFUN]; Presidential Policy Memorandum Governing Direct Action Counterterrorism Operations Outside Areas of Active Hostilities 2, https://int.nyt.com/data/documenttools/savage-nyt-foia-biden-presidential-policy-memo-ct-direct-action-rules/91583cea8267d704/full.pdf [https://perma.cc/H5PA-3XVE] (declassified in part by John Powers, June 29, 2023).

80 Press Release No. 20170618-02, *U.S. Central Command, Coalition Defends Partner Forces from Syrian Fighter Jet Attack* (June 18, 2017), https://www.centcom.mil/MEDIA/PRESS-RELEASES/Press-Release-View/Article/1217892/coalition-defends-partner-forces-from-syrian-fighter-jet-attack [https://perma.cc/4SYJ-BYDA].

81 *Id.* There was an identical press release published the next day. Press Release, *CJTF-OIR, Coalition Defends Partner Forces from Syrian Fighter Jet Attack* (June 19, 2017), https://www.centcom.mil/MEDIA/NEWS-ARTICLES/News-Article-View/Article/1217917/coalition-defends-partner-forces-from-syrian-fighter-jet-attack [https://perma.cc/NY4Q-HZ8C].

82 *Id.* (emphasis added).

83 *See* Press Release No. 20170618-02, *supra* note 81.

toward Coalition and partner forces in Syria conducting legitimate counter-ISIS operations will not be tolerated."[84]

The incident was an inflection point in the Syrian conflict. In response, the Russian Ministry of Defense suspended its use of the U.S.-Russia deconfliction line, calling the U.S. strike "a blatant breach of the international law" and "military aggression" against the Syrian regime.[85] Russian Deputy Foreign Minister Sergei Ryabkov said the U.S. strike "has to be seen as a continuation of America's line to disregard the norms of international law" and suggested that it was an "act of aggression."[86] Australia suspended airstrikes in Syria in response to what appeared to be a very real threat of escalation.[87]

The June 18 shoot-down was the first time a U.S. "warplane downed a manned aircraft since 1999," during the NATO intervention in Kosovo,[88] and it was the first time the United States justified force under international law as "collective self-defense of Coalition partnered forces" where that partner was a non-state actor and no U.S. service members were apparently at risk.[89] In early August 2017, the State Department offered a more detailed legal justification for the June 18 incident in a letter to Senator Bob Corker.[90] First, the State Department justified the strike under domestic law, citing the 2001 AUMF as providing "authority to use force to defend U.S., Coalition, and partner forces engaged in the campaign to defeat ISIS to the extent such use of force is a necessary and appropriate

[84] *Id.*

[85] *See, e.g.*, Russian Ministry of Defense, *Statement of the Russian Defence Ministry Concerning Downing of the Syrian Su-22 Near the Town of Resafa*, FACEBOOK (June 19, 2017), https://www.facebook.com/mod.mil.rus/posts/1943173689258711:0 [https://perma.cc/9S4B-FPX7]; Michael R. Gordon & Ivan Nechepurenko, *Russia Warns U.S. After Downing of Syrian Warplane*, N.Y. TIMES (June 19, 2017), https://www.nytimes.com/2017/06/19/world/middleeast/russia-syria.html [https://perma.cc/44UA-JGKX]; *U.S. Aviation Actions Against Syrian Armed Forces Are Gross Violation of Int'l Law, Military Aggression—Russian Defense Ministry*, INTERFAX (June 19, 2017), https://interfax.com/newsroom/top-stories/27770 [https://perma.cc/3ZDZ-CHM3].

[86] Patrick Wintour & Julian Borger, *Russia Warns US Its Fighter Jets Are Now Potential Target in Syria*, GUARDIAN (June 19, 2017), https://www.theguardian.com/world/2017/jun/19/russia-target-us-led-coalition-warplanes-over-syria [https://perma.cc/5MXA-KDSB].

[87] *Australia Suspends Air Strikes in Syria—Government*, REUTERS (June 20, 2017), https://www.reuters.com/article/mideast-crisis-syria-australia-idUSS9N1J304U [https://perma.cc/GT9D-YBMG].

[88] Ryan Browne, *New Details on US Shoot Down of Syrian Jet*, CNN (June 21, 2017), https://www.cnn.com/2017/06/21/politics/us-syria-russia-dogfight/index.html [https://perma.cc/DW8Y-URBT].

[89] *See* Press Release No. 20170618-02, *supra* note 81.

[90] Letter from Charles Faulkner, Bureau of Leg. Aff., U.S. Dep't of State, to Bob Corker, Chair, S. Comm. on Foreign Rels. (Aug. 2, 2017), available at https://www.politico.com/f/?id=0000015d-a3bf-d43a-a3dd-b3bf14170000 [https://perma.cc/LT8V-RMCZ]. Note that Charles Faulkner, the author of this State Department letter, came under scrutiny in summer 2019 for his background as an arms-industry lobbyist and his role in the Trump administration decision to "sell weapons to Saudi Arabia and the United Arab Emirates without seeking legislative approval." Edward Wong & Catie Edmondson, *Democrats to Scrutinize Ex-Lobbyist's Role in Trump's Arms Sales to Gulf Nations*, N.Y. TIMES (June 11, 2019), https://www.nytimes.com/2019/06/11/us/politics/democrats-charles-faulkner-arms-sales.html [https://perma.cc/BJ7L-2GUE].

measure in support of counter-ISIS operations."[91] Second, the State Department justified the use of force under international law, explaining that the United States "is using force in Syria against al-Qa'ida and associated forces, including ISIS, and is providing support to Syrian partners fighting ISIS, such as the Syrian Democratic Forces, in the collective self-defense of Iraq (and other States) and in U.S. national self-defense."[92]

In February 2018, the United States again cited the "defense of Coalition and partner forces" to justify "defensive strikes" against Syrian pro-regime forces.[93] These justifications are notable because they indicate the U.S. government believed it could lawfully use force against Syria in *collective* self-defense of the SDF. That position is not limited to Syria. An exchange of letters between Senator Tim Kaine and Secretary of Defense James Mattis in 2017 and 2018 made clear just how much the administration had come to rely on collective self-defense as a justification for the use of military force.[94] In response to a request from Senator Kaine for a description of "the legal and policy differences between self-defense and collective self-defense," the Department of Defense explained that "collective self-defense . . . means extension of U.S. unit self-defense to foreign or irregular partner forces or person."[95] That extends, the Department maintained, not only to responses to attacks but to imminent threats, as well: "The collective self-defense supplemental rule of engagement, when approved, permits U.S. forces to defend partner forces from attack or an imminent threat of attack with necessary and appropriate force."[96] Senator Kaine rightly responded to these broad claims by expressing alarm that the Department "believes that, by merely designating a group as a partner force, it can respond with military action to protect that partner force and its property if threatened by any group—even one that poses no direct threat to the United States, its Armed Forces or persons, nor is covered by an AUMF."[97] Nonetheless, in the years since, the United States has reflexively relied on "collective self-defense" in an array of circumstances that similarly push far beyond the historic boundaries of Article 51.[98]

[91] Letter from Charles Faulkner, *supra* note 90.

[92] *Id.*

[93] Press Release No. 20180208-01, *U.S. Central Command, Unprovoked Attack by Syrian Pro-regime Forces Prompts Coalition Defensive Strikes* (Feb. 8, 2018), https://www.centcom.mil/MEDIA/PRESS-RELEASES/Press-Release-View/Article/1435188/unprovoked-attack-by-syrian-pro-regime-forces-prompts-coalition-defensive-strik/ [https://perma.cc/XW8W-N6LB].

[94] Letter from Senator Tim Kaine to Secretary of Defense James Mattis (Oct. 2, 2018), https://www.scribd.com/document/390037794/Kaine-Presses-Trump-Administration-on-the-Expansive-Use-of-Collective-Self-Defense-to-Justify-Military-Action-That-Bypasses-Congress.

[95] *Id.*

[96] *Id.*

[97] *Id.*; *see also* Elvina Pothelet, *U.S. Military's Collective Self-Defense of Non-State Partner Forces: What Does International Law Say*, JUST SECURITY (Oct. 26, 2018), https://www.justsecurity.org/61232/collective-self-defense-partner-forces-international-law-say/ [https://perma.cc/AJ24-KWM4].

[98] *See, e.g.*, Hathaway & Hartig, *Still at War: Somalia*, *supra* note 9.

These decisions to stretch the scope of Article 51 have been made, moreover, without any affirmative approval from Congress. As Senator Kaine's response pointed out, the use of force in defense of partner forces is often not authorized by Congress. It appears that the administration assumes that they are nonetheless not subject to war powers reporting or a requirement to seek authorization. The justification appears to be that the underlying operations are justified by the 2001 AUMF. The defense of partner forces in those operations then are justified as "self-defense," and thus, they apparently maintain, fall within the president's own Article II powers and do not require congressional approval. Of course, all of this is speculation because no formal legal memos articulating these positions have been released to the public. Rather, one can only glean the evolving legal positions from speeches, press releases, and occasional public statements.[99]

In a somewhat ironic twist, the latest evolution of U.S. legal policy has brought it into nearly direct conflict with a state that has emulated its long-standing position on self-defense against non-state actor forces. In 2019, Turkey—a NATO ally of the United States—launched an assault on Kurdish forces in northern Syria, an incursion it justified by "the right of self-defense as outlined in Article 51 of the UN Charter, to counter the imminent terrorist threat, to ensure Turkey's border security, to neutralize terrorists."[100] The non-state actor forces Turkey attacked were some of the very same the United States had used force to defend based on its own claims of "collective self-defense."[101] NATO allies thus found themselves on opposite sides of a conflict—one state (Turkey) using claims of self-defense under Article 51 to attack the SDF, the very same group the other state (the United States) claimed a right to defend under Article 51.

Perhaps even more concerning, Russian President Vladimir Putin attempted to claim a right to act in the "collective self-defense" of the "independent" eastern regions of Ukraine when he initiated Russia's war in Ukraine on February 24, 2022. The day Russia launched the first attack, its Permanent Representative to the United Nations notified the U.N. Secretary-General that the military action was "taken in accordance with Article 51 of the UN Charter in the exercise of the right of self-defence."[102] In explanation, he appended a speech Putin had made to

[99] For more on the pathologies of the National Security lawyering process, *see* Hathaway, *supra* note 1.

[100] Letter from the Permanent Representative of Turkey to the United Nations addressed to the President of the Security Council, U.N. Doc. S/2019/804 (Oct. 9, 2019), https://daccess-ods.un.org/tmp/8213402.62889862.html [https://perma.cc/77CZ-6J3M].

[101] *See* Oona Hathaway, *Turkey Is Violating International Law. It Took Lessons from the U.S.*, WASH. POST (Oct. 22, 2019), https://www.washingtonpost.com/outlook/2019/10/22/turkey-is-violating-international-law-it-took-lessons-us/ [https://perma.cc/66VV-Q3E2].

[102] Letter from the Permanent Representative of the Russian Federation to the United Nations addressed to the Secretary-General, U.N. Doc. S/2022/154 (Feb. 24, 2022), https://documents-dds-ny.un.org/doc/UNDOC/GEN/N22/268/16/PDF/N2226816.pdf?OpenElement [https://perma.cc/EF6U-3XZZ].

the Russian people earlier in the day. "The People's Republics of Donbass turned to Russia with a request for help . . ." he stated. "In this regard, in accordance with Article 51 (chapter VII) of the UN Charter, . . . I have decided to conduct a special military operation."[103] Russia thus attempted to use the language of self-defense, and the expanded scope of Article 51, to justify a blatantly illegal invasion. The attempt at justification was met with widespread skepticism,[104] as it should have been, but that Russia even considered the argument worth making reveals how flexible Article 51 has come to be seen.

"Collective Self-Defense" of the "Free Flow of Commerce"

The erosion of constraints on the use of force has continued apace. The very latest innovation has been an assertion by the United States of a right to conduct strikes to "disrupt and degrade the capabilities of Iranian-backed Houthi militia to conduct their reckless and destabilizing attacks against U.S. and international vessels lawfully transiting the Red Sea."[105] The "collective action," taken together with several partner states, goes a step beyond already existing assertions of self-defense. The United States has justified actions against Houthi "storage facilities, missile systems and launchers, air defense systems, and radars" as lawful defense of "lives and the free flow of commerce in one of the world's most critical waterways."[106] The assertion of a right of defense is thus not limited to U.S. forces or even to partner forces (whether state or non-state) but to the more amorphous "free flow of commerce." The "international shipping" that the military operations defended included some U.S. ships but certainly was not limited to them. The assertion, then, is a breathtaking claim to a right to defend the world's waterways against any and all threats—notably without authorization of the U.N. Security Council. In doing so, the United States and its international partners are effectively asserting police powers over international waterways the world over.

The executive branch is doing so, moreover, without seeking congressional authorization for these ongoing military operations—operations that could, it is important to note, bring the United States into closer confrontation with Iran, which backs the Houthis. Rather than seek authorization, the executive branch has adopted yet another novel interpretation of the War Powers Resolution to

[103] *Id.*
[104] *See, e.g.*, Elizabeth Wilmshurst, *Ukraine: Debunking Russia's Legal Justifications*, Chatham House (Feb. 24, 2022, updated Feb. 25, 2022), https://www.chathamhouse.org/2022/02/ukraine-debunking-russias-legal-justifications [https://perma.cc/9ZLW-2Q2L].
[105] Statement by Secretary of Defense Lloyd J. Austin III on Coalition Strikes in Houthi-Controlled Areas of Yemen, U.S. Dept. of Defense (Feb. 3, 2024), https://www.defense.gov/News/Releases/Release/Article/3665867/statement-by-secretary-of-defense-lloyd-j-austin-iii-on-coalition-strikes-in-ho/.
[106] *Id.*

support these operations. It has intimated that the use of military force against the Houthis is not subject to the authorization or reporting requirements in the resolution because U.S. forces are not being "introduced . . . into hostilities."[107] Rather, they are already present, because U.S. naval and other military forces were already located in the region. This interpretation of the War Powers Resolution effectively reads Congress out of any role in U.S. use of force decisions short of full-scale ground invasions. After all, today the United States has forces located around the globe. The Department of Defense maintains over 4,790 military sites worldwide.[108] Under this newest interpretation of international and U.S. legal authorities, it seems, each of those sites is authorized to act in its region in collective defense of any state or non-state actor the executive branch decides ought to be defended against any state or non-state threat.

A Way Forward

The long-standing debate over reforming war powers and reasserting Congress's authority over decisions to use force does not simply have stakes for U.S. constitutional law and separation of powers within the United States. The debate has global consequences. Reasserting congressional war powers is important to ensuring that the expansion of self-defense claims made by successive presidents does not continue. It is not simply a matter of constitutional law, it is a matter of international law as well. And, as such, it has implications not only for the scope of future U.S. actions but for the behavior of other states that may rely on the same legal theories to take action that may be antithetical to U.S. national security interests.

The connection between the erosion of war powers and the erosion of international law limits on the use of force should therefore add urgency to the debate over whether and how to reassert congressional war powers. If the United States is going to lead the charge in softening the limits on the use of military force globally—in ways that foreign states inevitably will emulate—that should be done not simply by the president and his lawyers acting on their own, but by the president in consultation with—and with the approval of—Congress.

There is a further reason to address the problem now: With the war waging in Ukraine, the United States has repeatedly (and rightly) condemned the Russian war of aggression.[109] It has for the first time endorsed accountability for the crime of

[107] War Powers Resolution § 4.

[108] *Where Are US Military Members Stationed, and Why?*, USAFACTS (Feb. 2, 2024), https://usafacts.org/articles/where-are-us-military-members-stationed-and-why/ [https://perma.cc/5WDD-2C2A].

[109] *See, e.g.*, Joseph Biden, President of the U.S., Remarks by President Biden on Russia's Unprovoked and Unjustified Attack on Ukraine (Feb. 24, 2022), https://www.whitehouse.gov/briefing-room/speeches-remarks/2022/02/24/remarks-by-president-biden-on-russias-unprovoked-and-unjustified-attack-on-ukraine/ [https://perma.cc/3NSQ-BWYG].

aggression—that is, the crime of waging a war that violates the U.N. Charter's prohibition on force.[110] And the United States has helped create a coalition of states that have supported Ukraine through providing financial and military assistance while sanctioning Russia for its illegal acts.[111] But the capacity of the United States to rally others to the Ukrainian cause has been hampered by concerns that the United States is applying a double standard—holding Russia to account for violating the prohibition on force that it has itself undermined in its invasion of Iraq in 2003, which is widely regarded in much of the world as a manifestly illegal war, but also through its decades-long global counterterrorism campaign.

While comprehensive war powers reform may be out of reach in the near term, there are a number of reforms that could be made individually or collectively that would make a real difference in the capacity of Congress to exercise effective oversight over the use of military force and thus reduce the likelihood that the United States will use force in ways that violate international law. These include the following.[112]

Define hostilities. As noted earlier, one of the reasons the War Powers Resolution has been ineffectual is that it turns on "hostilities," a term that is not defined in the law. Any revision to the War Powers Resolution should define the term, to respond to the executive branch's repeated interpretations of the term "hostilities" in ways that allow the executive branch to act without congressional consent. As of this writing, the most recent legislation proposed in Congress to reform war powers defined hostilities as "any situation involving any continuous or intermittent use of lethal or potentially lethal force by or against United States forces (or, for purposes of paragraph (3)(B), foreign regular or irregular forces) carried out through land, sea, air, space, or cyber operations, or through any other domain, including whether or not such force is deployed remotely."[113]

[110] Beth Van Schaak, Ambassador-at-Large for Global Criminal Justice, U.S. Dep't of State, Ambassador Van Schaack's Remarks on the U.S. Proposal to Prosecute Russian Crimes of Aggression (Mar. 27, 2023), https://2021-2025.state.gov/ambassador-van-schaacks-remarks/ [https://perma.cc/BJR5-44R8].

[111] Fact Sheet: One Year of Supporting Ukraine, The White House (Feb. 21, 2023), https://www.whitehouse.gov/briefing-room/statements-releases/2023/02/21/fact-sheet-one-year-of-supporting-ukraine/ [https://perma.cc/2GE9-G4RJ].

[112] For more proposals, *see* Oona A. Hathaway, *How to Revive Congress' War Powers, in Policy Roundtable: The War Powers Resolution*, Tex. Nat'l Sec. Rev. (Nov. 14, 2019), https://tnsr.org/roundtable/policy-roundtable-the-war-powers-resolution/ [https://perma.cc/X63Y-NKYB]; Oona A. Hathaway & Geoffrey Block, *How to Recover a Role for Congress and the Courts in Decisions to Wage War*, Just Security (Jan. 10, 2020), https://www.justsecurity.org/68001/how-to-recover-a-role-for-congress-and-the-courts-in-decisions-to-wage-war/ [https://perma.cc/U8MS-8LYG].

[113] This was the House version. *See* National Security Reforms and Accountability Act, H.R. 5410, 117th Cong. (2021). The Senate version was slightly different: "The term 'hostilities' means any situation involving any use of lethal or potentially lethal force by or against United States forces (or, for purposes of paragraph 4(B), by or against foreign regular or irregular forces), irrespective of the domain, whether such force is deployed remotely, or the intermittency thereof. The term does not include activities undertaken pursuant to section 503 of the National Security Act of 1947 (50 U.S.C.

Any definition should make clear that it applies broadly to modern warfare operations—including cyber operations, operations involving remotely piloted vehicles, and operations involving partnered operations. It should also clarify the meaning of "introduce into . . . hostilities" to make clear that the mere presence of U.S. forces in the region does not constitute an advance authorization of the use of military force by those forces.

Automatic funding cutoff. There should be an automatic funding cutoff for operations that do not comply with the War Powers Resolution, without requiring further action by Congress. As noted earlier, Congress not only has the constitutional authority to "declare war" but also possesses the power of the purse. And yet that power has been largely ineffectual. Due to the massive defense budgets, most military operations, even large ones, do not require separate appropriations. This means that members of Congress who disapprove must affirmatively enact a law to prohibit the use of funds—and this is subject to a veto by the very president seeking to use those funds for the military operation in question. This has had the effect of turning the constitutional order upside down. A law that would prohibit, *ex ante*, any use of funds that would violate the war powers act would reassert Congress's constitutional authority to control both the exercise of war powers and appropriations. Senators Chris Murphy, Mike Lee, and Bernie Sanders have introduced legislation that would do just that.[114] Their National Security Powers Act would require the president to consult congressional leaders and obtain congressional authorization before initiating military force, emergency powers, or arms exports. Any activities lacking authorization will face an automatic funding cutoff. The failure to abide by that cutoff would subject those involved to penalties under the Anti-Deficiency Act, which can include criminal penalties for those involved in unauthorized use of funds.

Enhance congressional standing to challenge unlawful uses of force. Recent D.C. Circuit and Supreme Court decisions indicate that the courts may be increasingly open to institutional standing.[115] Consistent with these decisions, each

5093) if such action is intended to have exclusively non-lethal effects." National Security Powers Act of 2021, S. 2391, 117th Cong. (2021).

114 S. 2391, *supra* note 113.

115 Comm. on Judiciary of U.S. House of Representatives v. McGahn, 968 F.3d 755, 765–66 (D.C. Cir. 2020) (en banc) (finding that a Committee of the House had standing to sue); *see also* U.S. House of Representatives v. Mnuchin, 976 F.3d 1, 13 (D.C. Cir. 2020) ("When the injury alleged is to the Congress as a whole, one chamber does not have standing to litigate. When the injury is to the distinct prerogatives of a single chamber, that chamber does have standing to assert the injury."), *cert. granted, judgment vacated sub nom.* Yellen v. United States House of Representatives, 142 S. Ct. 332 (2021) (mem.) (remanded with instructions to vacate as moot); *cf.* Raines v. Byrd, 521 U.S. 811, 829–30 (1997) (suggesting that individual members of Congress may have standing if they were authorized to represent their respective chambers); Va. House of Delegates v. Bethune-Hill, 587 U.S. 658, 667 (2019) (holding that a single house of a bicameral legislature does not have standing to sue to enforce interests that belong to the whole legislature).

house of Congress could enact a Simple Resolution to authorize key members of each chamber—likely the Chair and Ranking member of the House Foreign Affairs Committee or Senate Foreign Relations Committee or the Speaker or House Minority Leader—to sue to challenge a decision by the executive branch that has concrete and particular injuries to Congress's war powers. In this way, Congress might encourage the courts to re-engage on national security matters. A similar technique could be applied to address the political question doctrine, to the extent it is prudential and therefore discretionary.

Repeal the existing AUMFs. The authorizations for use of military force that remain in effect were enacted by past Congresses for purposes that have long since been achieved. The 1991 AUMF permitted then-President George H.W. Bush to use military force pursuant to U.N. Security Council Resolution 678, a resolution that required Iraq, then led by Saddam Hussein, to withdraw from Kuwait, which it had invaded and occupied, no later than January 15, 1991.[116] The 2002 AUMF was enacted primarily in response to fears that Saddam Hussein's Iraq possessed weapons of mass destruction that posed a direct threat to the United States and its allies.[117] It authorized the president "to use the Armed Forces of the United States as he determines to be necessary and appropriate in order to—(1) defend the national security of the United States against the continuing threat posed by Iraq; and (2) enforce all relevant United Nations Security Council resolutions regarding Iraq."[118] The purposes of these authorities have long ago been met. The government of Iraq was long ago expelled from Kuwait, the U.N. resolutions referred to in the resolutions have long since expired, and Iraq does not pose a threat to the United States or its allies. The Biden administration has endorsed repeal of the 2002 AUMF, explaining that it no longer relies on it for any authorities.[119] Leaving these AUMFs on the books simply leaves the door open to their misuse without giving presidents any additional legitimate basis for military action.

The AUMF that the executive branch does continue to rely on—the 2001 AUMF[120]—has long been in need of reform. Enacted mere days after the

[116] Authorization for the Use of Military Force Against Iraq Resolution, Pub. L. No. 102-1, 105 Stat. 3 (1991). Though no one has sought to rely on it or suggested it is still effective, it may nonetheless be wise to also repeal the 1957 Middle East Force Resolution. Pub. L. No. 85-7, § 2, 71 Stat. 5, 5 (1957) (codified at 22 U.S.C § 1962). The 1957 Resolution authorized the president to use military force in the Middle East to "assist any such nation or group of such nations requesting assistance against armed aggression from any country controlled by international communism." *Id.* For further context, *see* Matthew Waxman, *Remembering Eisenhower's Middle East Force Resolution*, LAWFARE (Mar. 9, 2019), https://www.lawfareblog.com/remembering-eisenhowers-middle-east-force-resolution [https://perma.cc/6934-Z2C2].

[117] 2002 AUMF, *supra* note 4.

[118] *Id.*

[119] Tess Bridgeman, *Biden's Support of 2002 AUMF Repeal: The Start of a Long Overdue Conversation*, JUST SECURITY (June 16, 2021), https://www.justsecurity.org/76949/bidens-support-of-2002-aumf-repeal-the-start-of-a-long-overdue-conversation/ [https://perma.cc/CV4B-YV8H].

[120] 2001 AUMF, *supra* note 5.

September 11, 2001, attacks in the United States, it authorized the president to use "necessary and appropriate force against those nations, organizations, or persons he determines planned, authorized, committed, or aided the terrorist attacks that occurred on September 11, 2001, or harbored such organizations or persons, in order to prevent any future acts of international terrorism against the United States by such nations, organizations or persons."[121] The clear intent was to allow the use of force against those who carried out the attacks and those who had harbored them. Today, more than two decades later, that authority has been stretched beyond any reasonable limits. It is far past time to repeal the authorization and replace it with one more narrowly focused on the threats that the United States currently faces. That new AUMF, moreover, should contain a periodic reauthorization requirement, so that Congress can retain control over decisions to use force in the future and restrain overreading of the resolution in ways that Congress does not support. Because agreeing on a replacement is likely to be a time-consuming process that will require a theater-by-theater assessment of current military needs, Congress could simply pass a law now repealing the AUMF, but making that repeal effective in two years. Doing so would give ample time to agree on a replacement, while making clear that continuing to rely on the outdated authorization will no longer be an option.

Internal congressional reforms. With the exception of enhancing congressional standing, the reforms outlined here all would require passage of legislation that would be subject to a veto by the president. That makes reform an uphill battle. But there are internal reforms that Congress could adopt that could make it more effective in its oversight role that would not be subject to a presidential veto. First, Congress could take steps to address siloing of information in individual committees, including expanding cross-committee membership and holding more frequent joint briefings and hearings, particularly for cross-cutting, high-stakes issues that implicate the equities of multiple committees. It could even create a Congressional National Security Council (C-NSC)—a counterpart to the executive branch National Security Council (NSC), which was formed in 1947 to allow better coordination in the executive branch on national security matters. A C-NSC (or it could be called a "working group"; the name is unimportant) could bring together the leadership of each of the committees involved in national security matters to coordinate on cross-cutting matters, just as the NSC brings together the leadership of the agencies that have equities in planning certain operations or activities. Second, Congress could modify rules to allow for sharing of classified information with members and staff when necessary for effective oversight. When information is classified, it can only be shared on a need-to-know basis

[121] *Id.*

as determined by the executive branch. Classification can prevent members of Congress from sharing certain information with other congressional representatives, and it prevents staff from sharing information across committees. Third, Congress could create a Congressional Office of Legal Counsel (C-OLC). As noted earlier, one reason that the executive branch almost always wins war powers debates is that the Justice Department's Office of Legal Counsel (OLC) is too often the only body that opines on legal issues relating to war powers. Congress should create its own C-OLC to analyze the law in ways that take account of congressional interests. To do this, Congress could constitute a new office that serves a role for Congress comparable to the role of the OLC for the executive branch. Like the Congressional Research Service, the new office should be placed under the leadership of the Library of Congress, a nonpartisan entity created to serve Congress. A modest version of this proposal would simply be to expand the role of legal analysts at the Congressional Research Service so that they could offer more frequent and timely legal opinions on war powers matters.[122]

If adopted, these reforms would not only affirm domestic legal limits on the use of military force but they would also help prevent further erosion of the international prohibition on the use of force.

Conclusion

President Biden, speaking before the United Nations on September 21, 2022, declared: "Russia has shamelessly violated the core tenets of the United Nations Charter—no more important than the clear prohibition against countries taking the territory of their neighbor by force . . . This world should see these outrageous acts for what they are. Putin claims he had to act because Russia was threatened. But no one threatened Russia, and no one other than Russia sought conflict."[123] He continued: "[S]tanding up for those principles for the U.N. Charter is the job of every responsible member state . . . . I reject the use of violence and war to conquer nations or expand borders through bloodshed."[124]

[122] Several of these proposals are elaborated at greater length in Hathaway et al., *supra* note 32. The General Accounting Office produced a report in late 2023 on the C-OLC proposal: U.S. Gov't Accountability Off., GAO-24-105870, Legislative Branch: Options for Enhancing Congressional Oversight of Rulemaking and Establishing an Office of Legal Counsel (2023, reissued with revisions 2024), https://www.gao.gov/products/gao-24-105870 [https://perma.cc/56RQ-9AWA].

[123] Joseph Biden, President of the U.S., Remarks by President Biden Before the 77th Session of the United Nations General Assembly (Sept. 21, 2022), https://www.whitehouse.gov/briefing-room/speeches-remarks/2022/09/21/remarks-by-president-biden-before-the-77th-session-of-the-united-nations-general-assembly/ [https://perma.cc/QZA2-XY5B].

[124] *Id.*

These are powerful words. Yet there was a shadow in the room as the president spoke. The capacity of the United States to rally others to the Ukrainian cause has been hampered by concerns that the United States is applying a double standard—holding Russia to account for violating the prohibition on force that it has itself undermined in its invasion of Iraq in 2003, which is widely regarded in much of the world as a manifestly illegal war, but also through its decades-long global counterterrorism campaign. The United States' own actions over the last several decades—including during President Biden's own tenure—have stretched the limits of the U.N. Charter up to, and sometimes past, their breaking point. President Biden was right to affirm the importance of the Charter and reject the use of violence in violation of its core legal principles. But these words would have more force if the United States acknowledged its own role in the erosion of the Charter's protections and pledged to repair that harm.

This chapter has aimed to show that the long-standing debate on reforming war powers and reasserting Congress's authority over decisions to use force does not simply have stakes for U.S. constitutional law and separation of powers within the United States. The debate has global consequences. Reasserting congressional war powers is important to ensuring that the expansion of self-defense claims made by successive presidents does not continue. It is not simply a matter of constitutional law, it is a matter of international law as well. And, as such, it has implications not only for the scope of future U.S. actions but for the behavior of other states that may rely on the same legal theories to take actions that undermine global peace and security.

The connection between the erosion of war powers and the erosion of international law limits on the use of force should add urgency to the debate on whether and how to reassert congressional war powers. If the United States is going to lead the charge in softening the limits on the use of military force globally—in ways that other states inevitably will seek to emulate—that should be done not simply by executive branch lawyers but by the president in consultation with, and with the approval of, Congress.

Just as the erosion of Congress's constitutional war powers have aided and abetted the erosion of constraints on Article 51's exception for actions taken in self-defense, the opposite can also be true: reaffirming Congress's constitutional war powers could help reduce the likelihood that the United States will undertake military operations that are difficult, if not impossible, to square with the Charter. While taking steps to strengthen democratic checks on war is no guarantee that the United States will only use force consistent with international law in the future, it would create more effective checks on unilateral presidential decisions to go to war and thereby make all wars, including those in violation of the Charter, less likely. Moreover, a revised and revived War Powers Resolution that provides Congress real capacity to check presidential decisions to use force could serve a powerful symbolic function, demonstrating the United States' commitment to the rule of law and serving as a counterpoint to the Russian state, which, it appears, has waged a disastrous illegal war of aggression on the whim of a single man.

VI

ENDING PERPETUAL WAR

16

Alternative Approaches to Counterterrorism

*Fionnuala Ní Aoláin KC (Hon)**

The Shifting Counterterrorism Landscape

Terrorism and counterterrorism have long and intersecting histories which I will not recount here.[1] Suffice to note that for as long as indiscriminate violence targeting civilians motivated by political intent has proliferated, states have relied on both law and force in response. Shifting to a more recent historical frame beginning in 1973, states began adopting sectoral treaties regulating certain acts of terrorism, culminating in the adoption of nineteen specialized treaties.[2] Notably absent, however, is a general terrorism treaty, which continues to elude broad international consensus.[3] Conveniently, the lack of a comprehensive definition has served other purposes, offering no constraint on the relentless proliferation of counterterrorism law and practice. In parallel to this international treaty framework, states across all continents—often with international and bilateral incentives—have for decades extended their regulation of terrorism at the national level, using various exceptional legislative measures designed to define, regulate, and punish acts of terrorism.[4] Such legislation has frequently

* Fionnuala Ní Aoláin served as United Nations Special Rapporteur on Counter-Terrorism and Human Rights (2017–23). The views expressed in this chapter are personal and do not reflect any institutional position by the United Nations. I thank Professor Laura Dickinson, Pablo de Greiff, and Ambassador Stephen Rapp for thoughtful and insightful comments on an earlier draft of this chapter.

[1] The Oxford Handbook of the History of Terrorism (Carola Dietze & Claudia Verhoeven eds., 2021).

[2] *See e.g.*, U.N. Convention on the Prevention and Punishment of Crimes against Internationally Protected Persons, Including Diplomatic Agents, Dec. 14, 1973, 28 U.S.T. 1975.

[3] Alex Schmid, *Terrorism—The Definitional Problem*, 36 Case W. Res. J. Int'l L. 375 (2004).

[4] *See, e.g.*, Prevention of Terrorism Act 2005, c. 2 (U.K.); Northern Ireland (Emergency Provisions) Act 1973, c. 53 (U.K.); Loi 2021-998 du 30 juillet 2021 relative à la prévention d'actes de terrorisme et au renseignement [Law 2021-998 of July 30, 2021, on the Prevention of Acts of Terrorism and Intelligence], Journal Officiel de la République Française [J.O] [Official Gazette of France], July 31, 2021; Decreto Ley No. 25475, May 5, 1992, Establecen la penalidad para los delitos de terrorismo y los procedimientos para la investigación, la instrucción y el judicio [Decree Establishing the Penalties, Investigations, and Judicial Procedures for Crimes of Terrorism] (Peru); Decreto No. 108, Oct. 17, 2006, Ley Especial Contra Actos de Terrorismo [Special Law Against Terrorist Acts] (El Salvador); Anti-Terrorism Bill 12 of 2003 (S. Afr.); Protection of Constitutional Democracy

Fionnuala Ní Aoláin KC (Hons), *Alternative Approaches to Counterterrorism* In: *Perpetual War and International Law*. Edited by: Brianna Rosen, Oxford University Press. © Oxford University Press 2026.
DOI: 10.1093/oso/9780197748992.003.0016

been passed as emergency law, operating as an alternative to the "normal" or regular criminal law, and often triggering derogations as well as limitations from human rights treaty obligations.[5] As counterterrorism expanded, legal exceptionalism has flourished both nationally and internationally. Expansion and exceptionalism are intrinsic to the contemporary model of perpetual warfare underpinned by counterterrorism. Undoing this perpetual warfare requires two simultaneous moves: dismantling its global supremacy and shifting from exceptional law back to ordinary law as the framework for addressing complex violence.

The international counterterrorism architecture has grown exponentially in the two decades since 9/11.[6] In the aftermath of the attacks, counterterrorism experienced extraordinary institutional and normative growth, with a surge in the production of legal and policy norms at multilateral and regional levels. The United Nations (U.N.) Security Council has played an outsized role in shaping global, regional, and national regulation of counterterrorism.[7] An extraordinary

against Terrorist and Related Activities Amendment Act 23 of 2022 (S. Afr.); Federal'nyi Zakon RF Federatsii o vnesenii izmeneniy v Federal'nyy zakon "O protivodeystvii terrorizmu" [Federal Law of the Russian Federation on Amendments to the Federal Law on Combatting Terrorism] SOBRANIE ZAKONODATEL'STVA ROSSIYSKOY FEDERATSII [SZ RF] [Russian Federation Collection of Legislation] 2016, No. 374 & No. 375; Counter-Terrorism Law (promulgated by the Standing Comm. Nat'l People's Cong., Dec. 27, 2015, amended Apr. 4, 2018) 2018 STANDING COMM. NAT'L PEOPLE'S CONG. GAZ. (China); Security Offences (Special Measures) Act 2012 (Act No. 747) (Malay.); Prevention of Terrorism Act 2015 (Act No. 769) (Malay.). *See* as regards U.K. derogations R. (Anderson) v. Secretary of State for the Home Department [2002] UKHL 46 *per* Lord Bingham; and Brannigan & McBride v. United Kingdom, App. Nos. 14553/89 and 14554/89, 258 Eur. Ct. H.R. (ser. A) (1993).

[5] *Id.*

[6] Fionnuala Ní Aoláin, *The Datification of Counter-Terrorism*, *in* BIG DATA AND ARMED CONFLICT: LEGAL ISSUES ABOVE AND BELOW THE ARMED CONFLICT (Laura Dickinson & Edward Berg eds., 2023); Fionnuala Ní Aoláin (Special Rapporteur on the Promotion and Protection of Human Rights and Fundamental Freedoms while Countering Terrorism), *Rep. of the Special Rapporteur on the Promotion and Protection of Human Rights and Fundamental Freedoms while Countering Terrorism on the Impact of Counterterrorism on Peacemaking, Peacebuilding, Sustaining Peace, and Conflict Prevention and Resolution*, U.N. Doc. A/77/345 (Sept. 16, 2022); Fionnuala Ní Aoláin (Special Rapporteur on the Promotion and Protection of Human Rights and Fundamental Freedoms while Countering Terrorism), *Rep. of the Special Rapporteur on the Promotion and Protection of Human Rights and Fundamental Freedoms while Countering Terrorism on Advancing Human Rights Through the Mainstreaming of Human Rights in Counterterrorism Capacity-Building and Technical Assistance at the National, Regional and Global Levels*, U.N. Doc. A/76/261 (Aug. 3, 2021); Fionnuala Ní Aoláin (Special Rapporteur on the Promotion and Protection of Human Rights and Fundamental Freedoms while Countering Terrorism), *Rep. of the Special Rapporteur on the Promotion and Protection of Human Rights and Fundamental Freedoms while Countering Terrorism*, U.N. Doc. A/75/337 (Sept. 3, 2020); Fionnuala Ní Aoláin (Special Rapporteur on the Promotion and Protection of Human Rights and Fundamental Freedoms while Countering Terrorism), *Rep. of the Special Rapporteur on the Promotion and Protection of Human Rights and Fundamental Freedoms while Countering Terrorism*, U.N. Doc. A/74/335 (Aug. 29, 2019); Fionnuala Ní Aoláin (Special Rapporteur on the Promotion and Protection of Human Rights and Fundamental Freedoms while Countering Terrorism), *Rep. of the Special Rapporteur on the Promotion and Protection of Human Rights and Fundamental Freedoms while Countering Terrorism*, U.N. Doc. A/73/361 (Sept. 3, 2018).

[7] Fionnuala Ní Aoláin (Special Rapporteur on the Promotion and Protection of Human Rights and Fundamental Freedoms while Countering Terrorism), *Rep. of the Special Rapporteur on the*

counterterrorism architecture has since emerged both within the United Nations and outside of it. Following the U.N. Security Council's invocation of Chapter VII of the U.N. Charter in 2001, which qualified international terrorism as a threat to international peace and security,[8] member states were required to adopt a broad set of preventive and suppressive measures. This created an anchoring framework for global action on counterterrorism and preventing violent extremism that continues to inform and legitimize exceptional national policies and legislation. Member states' counterterrorism obligations have been continually refined and expanded since the adoption of the Security Council's seminal Resolution 1373 in 2001.[9] Of particular importance here is the Council's broadening of the types of national measures required against suspected "terrorists," "foreign terrorist fighters," and associated categories. This move—one of many expansionist actions— significantly widened the scope of who could be labeled a terrorist and what situations could be classified as terrorism contexts. The result has been an incentive structure for terrorism legislation and practice that has had calamitous effects on the rule of law and global governance. The chapter proceeds to assess post-9/11 counterterrorism exceptionalism by first addressing the expansion and associated costs of institutional and normative counterterrorism. Using Mali as an example, the chapter follows, by illustrating governance and rule of law costs for ascendent counterterrorism in complex and fractured political contexts. The chapter follows by addressing the sustained and negative impact of counterterrorism on civic space, and shows how counterterrorism measures have been weaponized against civil society globally. Thereafter, the chapter highlights the ways in which counterterrorism has reshaped armed conflict regulation, distorting the nature and form of conflict classification, as well as preventing conflict management and ending sequences. The chapter concludes by offering a fundamentally different approach to post-9/11 counterterrorism regulation.

Promotion and Protection of Human Rights and Fundamental Freedoms while Countering Terrorism on the Human Rights Challenge of States of Emergency in the Context of Countering Terrorism, 65, U.N. Doc. A/HRC/37/52 (Mar. 1, 2018). S.C. Res. 1368 (Sept. 12, 2001).

[8] *Id.*

[9] In the resolution, the Council decided that states should take measures to prevent acts of terrorism and to bring terrorists to justice, assisting each other with respect to criminal prosecutions of terrorist offenders, instituting effective border security measures and exchanging information related to movements of terrorist persons or networks and forged or falsified travel documents. Subsequent resolutions include S.C. Res. 1267 (Oct. 15, 1999), S.C. Res. 1390 (Jan. 16, 2002); S.C. Res. 1988 (June 17, 2011); S.C. Res. 1989 (June 17, 2011); S.C. Res. 2170 (Aug. 15, 2014); S.C. Res. 2178 (Sept. 24, 2014); S.C. Res. 2253 (Dec. 17, 2015); S.C. Res. 2368 (July 20, 2017).

Identifying the Pathways and Costs of Prevailing Counterterrorism Frameworks

There are multiple entry points for measuring the costs of the untrammeled expansion of counterterrorism norms and architecture. Counterterrorism's approach, both historically and contemporaneously, remains essentially repressive, necessitating a range of military, law enforcement, and criminal measures against individuals even vaguely suspected of involvement in, or accused of acts of, terrorism.[10] Despite the Security Council affirming that human rights law maintains regime primacy in the peacetime assessment of the application of counterterrorism regulation—and that, in the event of an armed conflict, counterterrorism measures must be read in the context of the *lex specialis* of international humanitarian law (IHL)[11]—the untrammeled growth of counterterrorism, allied with its profound rule of law and human rights deficits, mean that, in practice, this rhetoric has had little effect on mitigating the perniciousness or costs of counterterrorism entrenchment.[12]

The expansion of the counterterrorism architecture has come with extraordinary costs for the integrity of international law, particularly evident in the pushback against the classification and regulation of non-international armed conflicts under a laws of war framework. For many states, a counterterrorism legal framework is highly preferable to any alternative, precisely because of its inherently malleable application to a range of actors self-defined by the state's narrow (read: political) and security interests. In line with an expansionist and securitizing trend, there is a palpable tendency by many states to classify any act of violence—and many nonviolent acts—carried out by a non-state armed group in a non-international armed conflict as "terrorist" by definition. This sidesteps the legal assessment of lawfulness under IHL and obscures the legal and political significance of non-international armed conflicts occurring on state territories. Given the proliferation of such conflicts, and the historical unwillingness of states to acknowledge the full applicability of IHL to them[13]—including Common Article 3 of the Geneva Conventions—it is precisely in this context that the categorization of acts as "terrorism" may be seen as a means of displacing the applicability of essentially protective legal norms. The dangers of such displacement are not merely formalistic; they have tangible effects on humanitarian action, the provision of humanitarian assistance, the protection of humanitarian personnel,

[10] G.A. Res. 60/288, The United Nations Global Counter-Terrorism Strategy (Sept. 20, 2006).

[11] *See* S.C. Res. 2462 (Mar. 28, 2019); S.C. Res. 2482 (July 19, 2019); Ní Aoláin, *supra* note 7, paras. 15, 16.

[12] G.A. Res. 72/284, The United Nations Global Counter-Terrorism Strategy Review (July 2, 2018).

[13] Including in conflicts involving groups designated as "terrorist."

the safeguarding of non-derogable rights and essential judicial guarantees, as well as the principle of nondiscrimination. Counterterrorism's pernicious norm displacement has adverse consequences for the integrity of human rights and humanitarian law because the institutional and political interests represented by counterterrorism seek to displace these norms and reframe complex conflict and fragile spaces as primarily subject to exceptional, nationally defined counterterrorism legal regimes. It is, again, the traction and entrenchment of exceptional counterterrorism norms and institutions—viewed through the lens of the declining authority of IHL and human rights—that helps explain why the grasp of legal exceptionalism has proven so enduring.

This chapter now turns to address a select number of these fissures, examining the impacts on the rule of law, governance, and democracy. The consequences of regulating armed conflict through a counterterrorism lens are also considered. By illuminating the pathways of exceptionalism and their associated costs, the methods and means to undo the status quo will be better revealed.

Governance Costs of Entrenched Counterterrorism Regimes

The trends outlined in this chapter intersect with the rise and popularity of populism; the strengthening of nationalistic politics in national settings tied to discourses of "othering," xenophobia and racism; the proliferation of coups and military-led governments (often using the tools and institutions of the security state to rise); the weakening of democracy and the emergence of governance forms that prioritize control, centralizing of power in executives and a lack of civilian oversight of the security sector. While it would be an overreach to claim a linear relationship between every particular country context where these trends exhibit (for example, Mali, Burkina Faso, Egypt, Turkey, and Niger),[14]

[14] Federica Paddeu & Niko Pavlopoulos, *Between Legitimacy and Control: The Taliban's Pursuit of Governmental Status*, Just Security (Sept. 7, 2021), https://www.justsecurity.org/78051/between-legitimacy-and-control-the-talibans-pursuit-of-governmental-status/; Florian Weigand, *Why Did the Taliban Win (Again) in Afghanistan?*, 2 LSE Pub. Pol'y Rev. 1 (2022); *Mali, A Coup within a Coup*, Int'l Crisis Group (May 27, 2021), https://www.crisisgroup.org/africa/sahel/mali/mali-un-coup-dans-le-coup; Susanna D. Wing, Mali's Precarious Democracy and the Causes of Conflict (United States Inst. of Peace 2013); Africa Center for Strategic Studies, *Understanding Burkina Faso's Latest Coup* (Oct. 28, 2022), https://africacenter.org/spotlight/understanding-burkina-faso-latest-coup/; Evan Horn, *Civil Society, Coups, and the Future of Burkina Faso*, The SAIS Rev. of Int'l Affairs (Aug. 25, 2022), https://saisreview.sais.jhu.edu/civil-society-coups-burkina-faso/; Viljar Haavik, Morten Boas, & Alessio Iocchi, *The End of Stability: How Burkina Faso Fell Apart*, 15 Afr. Sec. J. 317 (2022); Méryl Demuynck & Mathis Bohm, *Unravelling the Niger Coup and Its Implications for Violent Extremism in the Sahel*, International Centre for Counter-Terrorism (Aug. 4, 2023),

this chapter in part explores co-relational trends in order to better understand the overarchingly negative effects of a permanent counterterrorism architecture, and the normative consolidation of counterterrorism regulatory regimes at national, regional, and global nodal points.

Mali illustrates a striking convergence of governance challenges, excessive reliance on counterterrorism frameworks, and external support that prioritized security over democratic accountability. This approach highlights the confluence of multiple governance challenges including overuse and reliance on counterterrorism as the overarching frame of reference on the country's challenges. This facilitated direct supply of weapons, technical assistance, and capacity-building efforts to a state where democratic institutions and the judiciary were weak, and where security sector reform and civilian oversight were largely ignored. In a universe where the continued human rights violations by the military became unacceptable to western and other states supporting the G5 Sahel initiative, the military dismantled and overthrew the civilian government, substituting military rule for civilian administration.[15] It then sought and secured support from mercenaries to ensure its "counterterrorism" operations could continue.[16] This circularity of counterterrorism governance—and its relationship to rising authoritarianism and the inversion of civil-military relations[17]—provides evidence of the persistent underestimation of threat assessment in the practice of counterterrorism responses. The costs to governance from ascendant counterterrorism have yet to be fully reckoned, and the protection of inclusive and representative government is one of the clearest and most viable alternatives to the normalization of counterterrorism.

[15] In parallel, the United Nations Multidimensional Integrated Stabilization Mission in Mali (MINUSMA) was given a direct stabilization role in a country engaged in various conflicts with non-state armed groups, some designated as terrorist by the United Nations. Through an evolution in its mandate, MINUSMA has assisted in restoring state authority and deterring violent extremist groups. It has also played more specific counterterrorism roles, such as formal and informal cooperation with counterterrorism operations deployed in the region, thirty-five taking "direct action" to mitigate and respond to the asymmetric threats that the terrorist groups in Mali represent, and to support the U.N. counterterrorism sanctions committees. Possibly as a consequence of the closeness of MINUSMA to both the government and other counterterrorism operations, it has been the target of attacks from varied groups, with significant fatalities. As of February 2022, MINUSMA has lost, in the course of eleven years, a total of 462 U.N. and associated personnel.

[16] Special Procedures Comm. dated Dec. 30, 2022, from the Working Group on Mercenaries, the Working Group on Enforced Disappearances, the Independent Expert on the Situation of Human Rights in Mali, the Special Rapporteur on Minority Issues, the Special Rapporteur on the Promotion and Protection of Human Rights and Fundamental Freedoms While Countering Terrorism, the Special Rapporteur on Torture, and Other Cruel, Inhuman or Degrading Treatment or Punishment, and the Special Rapporteur on Violence Against Women and Girls, its Causes and Consequences addressed to the Government of Mali, U.N. Doc. AL MLI 3/2022 (Dec. 30, 2022).

[17] Rethinking Civil-Military Relations in Africa: Beyond the Coup d'État (Moses Khisa & Christopher Day eds., 2022).

The Cost to Civil Society of Normalized and Perpetual Counterterrorism

Directly relevant to the trajectory and relationship of weak or abusive governance to counterterrorism is the health of civil society. Since 2001, civil society space has been shrinking globally.[18] Civil society as a whole is frequently stigmatized and, in some cases, discriminated against. Its actors are subjected to smear campaigns, defamation, and physical harassment, and are often spuriously charged and sentenced under various laws—particularly under counterterrorism, national security, and extremism legislation. The shrinking space for civil society is a structural global challenge, directly connected to the rise and consolidation of counterterrorism regimes.[19] As of March 2023, the CIVICUS Monitor[20] rated just thirty-eight countries and territories as having open civic space,[21] forty as obstructed, forty-two as narrowed, twenty-seven as closed (up from twenty-three in 2020), and fifty as repressed (up from forty-four in 2020).[22] This means that there are "severe" attacks on civil society in 117 countries and territories.[23]

This trend has accelerated in recent years, with the International Center for Not-for-Profit Law recording the adoption of sixty-four restrictive laws on civil society between the beginning of 2015 and into 2016 alone.[24] Impunity flourishes for the killing, injury, maiming, torture, detention, and disappearance of civil society actors—often carried out in a widespread and systematic manner.[25] Other key violations contributing to the closing of civic

[18] U.N. Human Rights Special Procedures, *Global Study on the Impact of Counter-Terrorism on Civil Society & Civic Space*, Study produced by the Special Rapporteur on the Promotion and Protection of Human Rights and Fundamental Freedoms while Countering Terrorism, at 90–93 (June 21, 2023).

[19] International Center for Not-for-Profit Law, *Survey of Trends Affecting Civic Space: 2015–16*, Global Trends in NGO Law, 2016, at 1; Fionnuala Ní Aoláin (Special Rapporteur on the Promotion and Protection of Human Rights and Fundamental Freedoms while Countering Terrorism), *Rep. of the Special Rapporteur on the Promotion and Protection of Human Rights and Fundamental Freedoms while Countering Terrorism on the Impact of Measures to Address Terrorism and Violent Extremism on Civic Space and the Rights of Civil Society Actors and Human Rights Defenders*, U.N. Doc. A/HRC/40/52 (Mar. 1, 2019).

[20] CIVICUS, Civic Space on a Downward Spiral (2020), found at https://findings2020.monitor.civicus.org/downward-spiral.html.

[21] Consistent with 2020 figures.

[22] CIVICUS Monitor, last updated on March 16, 2023, https://monitor.civicus.org/facts/. Noting the widespread use of the CIVICUS Monitor for the United Nations as well as OECD figures.

[23] CIVICUS Monitor, last updated on March 16, 2023, https://monitor.civicus.org/globalfindings/.

[24] International Center for Not-for-Profit Law, *Survey of Trends Affecting Civic Space: 2015–16*, Global Trends in NGO Law, 2016, at 1.

[25] UN Human Rights Special Procedures, Global Study on the Impact of Counter-Terrorism on Civil Society & Civic Space, Study produced by the Special Rapporteur on the Promotion and Protection of Human Rights and Fundamental Freedoms while Countering Terrorism (June 21, 2023).

space include arbitrary detention and arrests, legal harassment, intimidation, threats, smear campaigns and verbal abuse, physical attacks, excessive use of force, censorship, and the adoption of restrictive counterterrorism and related legislation. For example, between 2001 and 2018, at least 140 governments adopted counterterrorism legislation.[26] New and multiple legislative and administrative measures continue to be justified by reference to real or perceived threats, or simply to comply with ever evolving international counterterrorism requirements. According to Human Rights Watch, at least forty-seven countries passed laws relating to foreign (terrorist) fighters between 2013 and 2017—the largest wave of counterterrorism legislation since the immediate aftermath of September 11, 2001. These pervasive and sustained attacks on civil society are symptomatic of how post-9/11 counterterrorism logic has been domesticated in national settings, as discussed further in the following. Using civil society as a barometer of how counterterrorism operates provides not only a measure of its harm but also a potential route toward undoing some of its worst excesses.

The Nexus of Armed Conflict to Counterterrorism: Why Critical Reframing Is Necessary

Counterterrorism measures are frequently taken in the context of armed conflict, in which IHL is applied.[27] That reality is further illustrated by multiple non-international armed conflicts involving non-state armed groups subject to terrorist designation by the United Nations and its targeted sanctions regime, or included on regional and national terrorist sanctions lists. The widening net of counterterrorism regulation and practice is being applied to numerous national contexts where the threshold requirements for armed conflict may be formally met under international law, but are not applied in practice. It is also occurring in contexts where the threshold for armed conflict is formally acknowledged, yet counterterrorism management and discourse play an increasingly dominant role in shaping responses to violence. These situations are routinely defined as contexts of terrorism rather than complex conflicts in which acts of terrorism

[26] Center for Strategic and Int'l Studies, Counterterrorism Measures and Civil Society: Changing the Will, Finding the Way (2018).

[27] Fionnuala Ní Aoláin (Special Rapporteur on the Promotion and Protection of Human Rights and Fundamental Freedoms while Countering Terrorism), *Rep. of the Special Rapporteur on the Promotion and Protection of Human Rights and Fundamental Freedoms while Countering Terrorism*, U.N. Doc. A/73/361 (Sept. 3, 2018); Fionnuala Ní Aoláin (Special Rapporteur on the Promotion and Protection of Human Rights and Fundamental Freedoms while Countering Terrorism), *Rep. of the Special Rapporteur on the Promotion and Protection of Human Rights and Fundamental Freedoms while Countering Terrorism*, U.N. Doc. A/75/337 (Sept. 3, 2020).

occur but should, in fact, be properly regulated as situations of armed conflict to which both human rights and humanitarian law apply.[28]

What does it mean for a situation to be defined in counterterrorism rather than armed conflict terms? The answer has multiple dimensions. First, IHL comprises a well-established body of treaty and customary law standards which frame both state and non-state actor obligations in situations of armed conflict. This includes, but is not limited to, provisions on detention, protection of civilians, combatant status, means and methods of warfare, and the conduct of humanitarian action. By contrast, terrorism lacks an agreed-upon definition in international law and is characterized by significant imprecision in its application. Applying a vague, often politically expedient, set of legal regulations and policy guidance to a highly complex phenomenon results in the absence of consistent standards for state conduct, no clear consensus on constitutes a breach, and substantial ambiguity that enables ongoing abuse. Second, as a conceptual matter, the fundamental logic of counterterrorism discourse is centered on the destruction of the terrorist group, the elimination of its support networks, and the dismantling of its leadership and structures that enable the production of violence. The widespread political mantra of "not negotiating with terrorists," present across many national contexts, means that once a situation or group is labeled as "terrorist," dialogue and negotiation are often formally prohibited and politically unacceptable. Armed conflict, by contrast, does not prohibit or preclude negotiation with the "enemy," and in practice offers multiple pathways to bring an end to conflict—whether by amnesty[29] or the exchange of prisoners.[30] Third, embracing a counterterrorism framework generally brings a number of its regulatory preferences into play, including proscription of groups and individuals, sanctions, emergency powers that restrict due process, limitations on legal proceedings and freedom of movement, counterterrorism financing measures, and constraints on freedoms of expression. Many of these measures function to exacerbate fundamental grievances that drive violence and have been repeatedly associated with systematic human rights violations in multiple countries. As a result, the capacity to resolve violence or address grievances through political means, such as ceasefires or peace agreements, is undermined.

Moreover, armed conflicts continue to emerge, intensify, and reignite, while the maintenance of peace in societies marked by cyclical violence remains elusive. The conditions that sustain long-term violence—continued human

[28] *Id.*

[29] Protocol Additional to the Geneva Conventions of 12 August 1949, and relating to the Protection of Victims of Non-International Armed Conflicts (Protocol II), art. 6(5), International Committee of the Red Cross, Study on Customary International Humanitarian Law, rule 64 (2005).

[30] International Committee of the Red Cross, Study on Customary International Humanitarian Law, rule 128 (2005).

rights violations, weak rule of law, and the absence of justice or accountability institutions—remain largely unaddressed. Other persistent drivers of armed conflict include climate change, grinding inequality, unresolved questions of self-determination, the lack of meaningful political participation, and inadequate representation in fragile, complex, and contested sovereignties. These dynamics remain peripheral, if not entirely absent, in global discussions on the failures and limitations of counterterrorism. Instead, conflicts that are fundamentally political and structural in nature are reframed, in whole or in part, as problems of terrorism. In short, it is the failure to define complex conflict as such—and the haphazard application of permissive and exceptional counterterrorism standards—that has entrenched and sustained the unhealthy growth of counterterrorism, at the expense of exposing the underlying dynamics of violence, exclusion, commodification, and facilitation of violence in national contexts. Only through a willingness to render visible the misuse of counterterrorism, and to disaggregate the beneficiaries of this legal and apolitical apparatus, will space for alternative approaches emerge. Counterterrorism, as politically entrenched practice, does not exist in a neutral universe; its opposite can only be constructed by confronting the harms it has produced and identifying those who have benefited from its two-decade dominance.

Alternative Approaches to Counterterrorism

Imagining alternative approaches to counterterrorism requires a fundamental shift in national and global approaches to regulating complex and entrenched violence. It mandates asking both simple and difficult questions about the very nature of violence itself, along with a marked commitment to departing from the routine labeling of violence and other phenomena as "terrorism" across diverse societies. It means less counterterrorism and downsizing existing institutions, ending normative and exceptional legal augmentations that expand the nomenclature of terrorism to apply to more things,[31] and defunding counterterrorism infrastructures in order to fundamentally reorient priorities. Fundamentally—and provocatively—a sizable portion of the phenomena currently labeled by states as "terrorism" would no longer rightfully fall into that category. An alternative requires a different mindset for assessing what constitutes a "threat" in national security terms. It demands critical and sustained reflection on both the recent and long past of counterterrorism. If we do not identify the failures that enable, sustain, and facilitate abusive counterterrorism—and that contribute to

[31] S.C. Res. 2482 (July 19, 2019).

the conditions conducive for violence—we should be resigned to a Groundhog Day of recurring violence.

An alternative approach must begin by addressing the structural conditions that foster violence. This is not a novel proposal.[32] There is a circularity and predictability in the international community's calls for states to address the root causes of fragility and violence. These include profound rule of law deficits, lack of judicial independence, social systems that fail to meet basic human needs, economic disenfranchisement, widespread poverty, insecurity, and a chronic underinvestment in marginalized communities that have experienced systemic discrimination based on race, ethnicity, nationality, or religious belief. None of this is new. The weight of social science and policy research demonstrating the connection between these conditions conducive to violence and the rise of insecurity, politically motivated violence, and armed conflict is overwhelming.[33] The real issue is not lack of knowledge about the causes of violence including terrorism, but our sustained failure to integrate that knowledge into actual prevention practices.

In my analysis, the principal challenge lies in the absence of commitment to holistic terrorism prevention. Rhetoric around counterterrorism prevention and action is readily adopted by states, and even by U.N. counterterrorism entities, when it maps onto such hot topics such as the protecting critical infrastructure,[34] preventing access to drones by non-state actors,[35] or restricting terrorist use of the Internet.[36] But such after-the-fact management misses a more fundamental point: the need to reorient investment and discourse toward the basic obligations of states to uphold their side of the social contract. Prevention must begin with unrelenting scrutiny of states that fail to deliver basic justice, inclusion, and security for their populations. Ultimately, diagnosing a viable alternative requires broad consensus among a sizable number of states that the parasitic deployment of counterterrorism by security-driven regimes—often

[32] UNDP, JOURNEY TO EXTREMISM IN AFRICA: PATHWAYS TO RECRUITMENT AND DISENGAGEMENT 40 (2023); Fionnuala Ní Aoláin (Special Rapporteur on the Promotion and Protection of Human Rights and Fundamental Freedoms while Countering Terrorism), *Rep. of the Special Rapporteur on the Promotion and Protection of Human Rights and Fundamental Freedoms while Countering Terrorism*, 18, U.N. Doc. A/75/337 (Sept. 3, 2020).

[33] UNDP, *Unearthing the Human Dimension of Violent Conflict*, *in* NEW THREATS TO HUMAN SECURITY IN THE ANTHROPOCENE 78 (2022); U.N. TRUST FUND FOR HUMAN SECURITY, HUMAN SECURITY HANDBOOK (2016); OHCHR, Human Rights, Terrorism and Counter-terrorism: Fact Sheet No. 32; SECRETARY-GENERAL HIGH-LEVEL PANEL ON THREATS, CHALLENGES, AND CHANGE, A MORE SECURE WORLD: OUR SHARED RESPONSIBILITY (2004).

[34] S.C. Counter-Terrorism Comm. Executive Directorate & UN Office of Counter-Terrorism, The Protection of Critical Infrastructure Against Terrorist Attacks: Compendium of Good Practices (2018).

[35] S.C. Counter-Terrorism Comm., *Delhi Declaration on Countering the Use of New and Emerging Technologies for Terrorist Purposes*, 4, 26 (Oct. 29, 2022).

[36] Global Internet Forum to Counter Terrorism, https://gifct.org/.

to advance authoritarian interests and narrow security agendas—can no longer be tolerated under the tacit approval of global and bilateral support frameworks.

First, this means undoing the language we use and being consistently critical of the term "terrorism"—interrogating who defines it, and identifying against whom it is deployed. Second, it entails learning from geographies and communities where holistic approaches have been utilized and have shown success. Third, it involves addressing the entrenched misuse of counterterrorism and security practices against civil society and recognizing that a vibrant, diverse civil society is not a threat but rather a cornerstone of alternative governance that coexists with open societies. Fourth, it requires serious pruning of the ambition and scope of counterterrorism—in particular challenging the narrative that armed conflict is simply a vector of terrorism—and returning to the difficult but essential work of making peace in divided societies.

Thus, a profound rethinking of counterterrorism as the central pillar of global security is needed. Building on the growing disenchantment among some states with the misuse of counterterrorism, there is now an opportunity for a fundamentally different conversation about what "security" constitutes within the global counterterrorism agenda.

Changing the Language, the Discourse Matters

One clear and critical consequence of the contemporary wholesale approach to the overcategorization of complex conflict situations is that the simple use of the qualifiers "terrorist" or "violent extremist" applied to conflicts and actors—and the ensuing acceptance that repressive government action constitutes "counterterrorism" or the "prevention of violent extremism"—means that counterterrorism frameworks underpin fundamental policy choices regarding conflict analysis. These include the determination of the causes of violence and the management and resolution of conflict situations. The use of the terms "terrorism" and "violent extremism" imposes a unitary lens on harms and drivers, providing an oversimplified analytical framing that often fails to grasp the complexity of conflict and crisis situations. As a result, this tends to: (1) lock actors into categories of legitimate (the government) and illegitimate (non-state armed groups designated as terrorist or violent extremist); (2) reinforce the legitimacy and sovereignty of existing regimes; (3) call for a securitized response that contributes to the long-term ("perpetual") nature of the conflicts by feeding ongoing patterns of violence; and (4) drive a simplified understanding of causes of crises and conflicts that seriously impairs any ability to end them and prevent their recurrence.

In contrast, analyzing the underlying legal, political, economic, and social causes of violence through a broader peace and security lens—including transitional justice—can offer a more nuanced and contextualized understanding of origins and drivers. Understanding the internal motives and external factors leading to crises and conflicts can help address the real or perceived grievances and needs of those involved in conflict, as well as the needs of all victims—a highly politically complex exercise in conflicts framed as "terrorism."[37] Transitional justice approaches,[38] ideally involving short-, medium-, and long-term measures such as institutional reforms, improved public policy, delivery of good governance, and accountability of institutions,[39] represent a far more effective policy response for countering terrorism and preventing violent extremism than the continued overconcentration on security-focused interventions.[40]

By allowing governments to frame their own counterterrorism responses as a legitimate form of violence, indiscriminate U.N. and regional counterterrorism frameworks in fact reinforce, support, protect, and strengthen regimes in power against groups using illegitimate forms of violence. The counterterrorism framework acts as a whiteout to any legitimate claims that non-state armed groups designated as terrorists may have, including claims of self-determination formally protected by international law.[41] International counterterrorism intervention and support is therefore usually aimed at reinforcing the sovereignty and power of governments, re-establishing political order, or strengthening territorial control in areas where state presence is weak. This is often diametrically opposed to the fundamentally oppositional logic that drives broader peace and justice interventions and discourses. With power concentrated in the hands of the same governments, elites, law enforcement, and militaries that may have contributed to grievances, discrimination, and injustice—or to creating or fueling conflicts—counterterrorism can reinforce poor governance and corrupt or failed regimes. This can lead to the specific investment and funding of failed security sectors implicated in human rights violations, the repression of political protest, torture, and corruption.

[37] Ronald Slye & Mark Freeman, The Limits of Punishment: Transitional Justice and Violent Extremism 23 (May 2018).

[38] *See* Chapter 17 of this volume, "Beyond Redress: Rethinking Transitional Justice," by Pablo de Greiff.

[39] *See* UN Secretary-General, Sustainable Development Goal 16, on the promotion of peaceful and inclusive societies for sustainable development, access to justice for all, and effective, accountable and inclusive institutions at all levels (2022).

[40] Fionnuala Ní Aoláin (Special Rapporteur on the Promotion and Protection of Human Rights and Fundamental Freedoms while Countering Terrorism), *Human Rights Impact of Policies and Practices Aimed at Preventing and Countering Violent Extremism*, 2, U.N. Doc. A/HRC/43/46 (Feb. 21, 2020).

[41] Tony Honoré, *The Right to Rebel*, 8 Oxford J. Legal Stud. 34 (1988); Ralph Wilde, *Using the Master's Tools to Dismantle the Master's House: International Law and Palestinian Liberation*, 22 Palestine Y.B. Int'l L. 3, 5 (2021).

In this context, a related step is to acknowledge and prevent the undermining of IHL through the ascendency of counterterrorism. It is essential to revisit practical mechanisms to deepen state engagement with IHL and ensure respect by all states consistent with Common Article 1 of the Geneva Conventions in times of conflict, including those affected by terrorism. Concrete steps are needed to avoid the broad interpretation of "association with terrorist organizations," which leads to the stigmatization of entire communities, cycles of revictimization, undermines the presumption of innocence, and limits individual criminal responsibility. This requires global, regional, and national action to limit the growth of counterterrorism law and practice, while also establishing practical ways to call out abuse and ensure that core international law regimes (IHL and international human rights law) are applied consistently and not undermined by counterterrorism normative displacement.

The example of Mali, discussed earlier, demonstrates the pitfalls of expanded investment in security-sector kinetic capacity-building, which resulted in a military coup enabled by the very counterterrorism assistance directly provided to the military.[42] More insidiously, where counterterrorism funding is used by corrupt governments, it can give the impression that such funds aim primarily to prop up governments, security sectors, and elites that lack public legitimacy. The overall risks from a commitment to narrow security imperatives—absent a focus on governance, rule of law, and human rights—create conditions in which conflict erupts with few institutional constraints to prevent egregious violations of international law. This has identifiable consequences for how conflict ends, the peace negotiations, and the terms on which hostilities cease.

A New Agenda for Peace Is Essential

At the heart of this analysis is a critical stance toward the commodification of counterterrorism for the nefarious and diverse political agendas of security-abusing states. Nowhere has this commodification been more evident than in the marginalization of global peace practice while the language and institutions of counterterrorism have thrived. For example, despite the announcement by the United Nations' Secretary-General of a New Agenda for Peace in 2021, fiscal

[42] Fabien Offner, *New Sahel Anti-Terror Force: Risks and Opportunities*, The New Humanitarian (Oct. 30, 2017), https://www.thenewhumanitarian.org/2017/10/30/new-sahel-anti-terror-force-risks-and-opportunities; FIDH, *The Crisis in Mali Must Be a Wake-Up Call for New Responses in the Sahel* (Feb. 9, 2020), https://www.fidh.org/en/region/Africa/mali/the-crisis-in-mali-must-be-a-wake-up-call-for-a-new-response-in-the.

and institutional support to that agenda has waned even as support for the entrenchment of a gargantuan counterterrorism architecture deepens.[43]

Consider, in this regard, the funding deficits and needs within the United Nations' peace architecture, and the fragility of peacebuilding architecture and the human rights pillar, which rely heavily on voluntary contributions, despite commitments to their centrality in U.N. reforms. In 2022, the human rights pillar received just 3 percent of the total U.N. regular budget. The Peacebuilding Fund is still under consideration for inclusion in the regular budget and approved assessed contributions as of 2022. Meanwhile, the U.N. Office of Counter-Terrorism (UNOCT) saw its budget increase to $9.462 million (up from $5.4 million), supporting 57 staff posts (up from 33)—a substantial 74.1 percent increase compared to the 2023 allocation. By contrast, the Department of Political and Peacebuilding Affairs, responsible for peacebuilding and conflict prevention and resolution, was allocated $26.158 million in 2024, which merely maintains rather than increases staffing levels from 2023. This is in the context of the ongoing war in Ukraine, a series of military coups in the Sahel, and persistent armed conflicts in the Middle East, Yemen, Somalia, and Libya.[44] Comparing staffing allocations, while UNOCT was allocated fifty-seven staff posts, the Peacebuilding Support Office was allocated only seventeen staff posts for the same fiscal year.[45]

How can we remedy what appears to be sustained investment in failing expansion of counterterrorism at the United Nations? As a starting point, the Executive Office of the Secretary-General must be reprimed and tasked with consolidating and elevating a public, principled, and official stance aimed at advancing human rights and rule of law compliance in countering terrorism and violent extremism by both the United Nations and its member states. Without clear signaling from this Office, the untrammeled growth of ill-fitting counterterrorism will continue to fuel a global crisis of counterterrorism abuses unabated. The Secretary-General's Office can play a vital role in balancing the lack of visibility for these issues outside the unrelenting advocacy of human rights mechanisms and can politically clarify where global priorities should lie.

In parallel, governments and the United Nations must prioritize investments in rule- of-law-based approaches to counterterrorism and the prevention and countering of violent extremism, alongside investments focused on addressing the conditions conducive to terrorism and violence. This includes supporting

[43] U.N. Secretary-General, *Our Common Agenda*, 4 (2021); U.N. Secretary-General, *A New Agenda for Peace*, Policy Brief 9 (July 2023).

[44] Council on Foreign Relations, *Global Conflict Tracker*, https://www.cfr.org/global-conflict-tracker.

[45] Budgetary Impact: UNOCT vs. OHCHR: The budget increase of 74.1% for the Office of Counter-Terrorism contrasts with an 18.8% decrease in funding for the UN Office of the High Commissioner for Human Rights (OHCHR).

legal and security sector reform, good governance, peacebuilding, and broader community-based violence prevention. These kinds of "bread and butter" issues and investments are neither glamorous nor often considered essential to effective counterterrorism and prevention, as evidenced by the stark lack of financial investment in them. A more fundamental "hearts and minds" strategy is needed—a reckoning with the global costs of harmful and ineffective counterterrorism and prevention/countering violent extremism policies that can form the basis for advancing a normative and institutional shift. It is not enough that human rights and civil society actors speak about these costs and failures. Other institutional actors, including those in peace and security sectors, must articulate a clearer vision of what is failing and why the perpetuation of outdated and ill-fitting counterterrorism practices is incompatible with the complex challenges of insecurity and violence today.

Learning from Examples of Where We Have Done Better

Before the consolidation of the global counterterrorism architecture post-9/11, some states shifted from framing sustained communal violence through the language and practice of counterterrorism to acknowledging a broader framework centered on conflict, peacemaking, and transitional justice. The success of these shifts—and the "lessons learned" model that emerged—can inform how we assess evidence of viable alternatives and develop proof-of-concept approaches to doing things differently.

Northern Ireland provides one such relevant example. Beginning with the modern version of the "Troubles" in 1969, and despite early recognition of the situation as a de facto armed conflict,[46] the state quickly moved to frame and regulate the sustained violence as a "terrorism" problem. This approach was formalized inter alia through the Emergency Powers Act (1973) and the Prevention of Terrorism Act (1974). The conflict was marked by systemic violence carried out by non-state actors—including the targeting of civilians and civilian objects—as well as state practices such as targeted killings, proscription, the use of exceptional (non-jury) courts, travel bans, exclusion orders, and a range of military and policing measures emblematic of a classic kinetic response to terrorism and non-state violence. Despite multiple efforts to resolve aspects of the conflict through selective negotiations, most failed.[47] In 1998, following an

[46] Best illustrated by the decision to allow persons arrested and detained for certain offenses before 1973 to wear their own clothing in prison and be separated from the regular prison population. *See* Fionnuala Ní Aoláin, The Politics of Force (2000).

[47] Michael Connolly & John Loughlin, *Reflections on the Anglo-Irish Agreement*, 21 Gov't & Opp. 146, 241–42 n.2 (1985).

extraordinary series of "confidence-building measures," the Good Friday/Belfast Peace Agreement was signed.[48] The Agreement encompasses many dimensions, but most salient for current purposes are its peacemaking and transitional justice components, which reframed the conflict from a counter "terrorism" problem to one requiring a conflict-ending methodology.

The Agreement redefined the roles and responsibilities of conflict actors, including non-state actors; provided for demilitarization and the decommissioning of all weapons; implemented a de facto amnesty; and institutionalized a broad range of human rights and equality measures aimed at redressing historical discrimination and exclusion—the push and pull factors of violence. It also engaged directly with root causes of violence, such as political exclusion, minority rights, and disputed sovereignty.[49] In this focus on addressing the root causes of violence lies one of the key takeaways for developing counterterrorism alternatives: without directly confronting the root causes of violence, there can be no durable end to violence. Equally critical was the sustained engagement of civil society in holding the "middle ground" within a deeply divided and sectarian context. While the term "transitional justice" did not appear in the Good Friday/Belfast Peace Agreement, many of its most innovative aspects map onto the four core pillars of transitional justice. This illustrates how a comprehensive peace agreement, applied to a context long defined as a "terrorism" problem, was instead reframed as a complex conflict requiring far more than kinetic or counterterrorism measures to address the conditions conducive to violence. The lessons from this case carry broader implications for how we think about resetting global and bilateral "solutions" to complex conflict settings, particularly those involving acts of terrorism or designated terrorist groups.

A Zero Tolerance Approach on the Misuse of Counterterrorism

Some significant work has been undertaken to collect global, disaggregated data on the misuse and abuse of counterterrorism measures.[50] However, more sustained action is urgently needed—and this will require multilateral and regional organizations to take such abuse seriously.[51]

[48] Agreement Reached in the Multi-Party Negotiation, Apr. 10, 1998, Eng.-Ir., 37 I.L.M. 751.

[49] Colm Campbell, Fionnuala Ní Aoláin, & Colin Harvey, *The Frontiers of Legal Analysis: Reframing the Transition in Northern Ireland*, 66 Mod. L. Rev. 317, 341 (2003); Colm Campbell, Christine Bell, & Fionnuala Ní Aoláin, *Justice Discourses in Transition*, 13 Soc. & Legal Stud. 305, 318 (2004).

[50] U.N. Human Rights Special Procedures, *Global Study on the Impact of Counter-Terrorism on Civil Society & Civic Space*, Study produced by the Special Rapporteur on the Promotion and Protection of Human Rights and Fundamental Freedoms while Countering Terrorism (June 21, 2023).

[51] This includes agreeing to a way to collect these data, in line with principles of do no harm, informed consent, and human rights due diligence, to identify discriminatory and group-based

A clear pattern has emerged, rooted in the political dynamics of the post-9/11 era of rendition and torture: the practice of naming and shaming states for the misuse of counterterrorism has generally been avoided, both bilaterally and internationally. Yet no meaningful reform or effective response to these deficiencies is possible until the prevailing culture of silence around counterterrorism abuse is dismantled. Within the U.N. system, oversight bodies such as UNOCT, UNCTED, and the UNCTC must find effective mechanisms to identify and address patterns of discriminatory counterterrorism misuse by states, including those that provide substantial financial support to the existing global counterterrorism infrastructure. Where consistent and cumulative misuse is identified, it should be publicly named, and the provision of technical assistance and capacity-building support should be suspended or terminated. One potential approach would be for regional and international counterterrorism bodies to develop political and legal accountability mechanisms, such as the creation of "greylists" to track and flag states engaged in systematic misuse.

At present, the only mechanism for addressing the misuse of counterterrorism against civil society actors is the U.N. Secretary-General's Annual Reprisals Report. Yet this report is insufficient to capture the scope, frequency, and severity of abuses carried out under the guise of counterterrorism. A more robust and targeted option would be for the Secretary-General to establish a publicly available annual list identifying member states that engage in consistent patterns of targeting and sanctioning civil society as a whole—or specific vulnerable national, social, legal, or religious groups—under the pretext of counterterrorism.

In sum, abuse is not just costly in terms of human rights abuses—it lies at the heart of the repetitive and cyclical interplay of terrorism and counterterrorism that continues to afflict societies from Afghanistan to Mali. Addressing such abuse must be redefined and implemented not merely as a human rights imperative but as a core strategy in the prevention of terrorism itself.

Conclusion

Alternative approaches are often invoked by scholars and policymakers as necessary to address persistent problems—here, the reality of perpetual war in the post-9/11 era. Yet far less imaginative, scholarly, or policy energy is devoted to

patterns of misuse of counterterrorism and countering and preventing violent extremism measures in a sustained way utilizing the template provided by the *Global Study on the Impact of Counter-Terrorism on Civil Society & Civic Space*, *id.*

articulating and investing in what such alternatives might in fact involve. To get there, the diagnosis of past failure must be deliberate, unflinching, and honest. With diagnosis in hand, we are only halfway there to end a cycle of repetitive behavior, and we must in a fundamental manner reorder priorities and spending to change the path-dependency of post-9/11 counterterrorism efforts.

17

Beyond Redress

Rethinking Transitional Justice

*Pablo de Greiff**

Introduction

The idea that transitional justice may have something to contribute to countries that face terrorism issues is one that is far from obvious,[1] but part of a general tendency of many actors, including some in the international community, to think of the polysemic "transitional justice" as akin to a "universal policy tool" without much regard for functional adequacy.[2] Despite the fact that I am not a cynic—I have devoted the largest part of my now no longer so short professional life to the promotion of transitional justice—I am not a romantic either; I do not believe in easy fixes, or in the existence of "all-purpose" policy tools that are good to resolve all sorts of problems, under just any circumstances. So, while defending the utility of transitional justice measures in some contexts that differ from those in which the "paradigm" took shape,[3] I have always been serious about both preconditions of success and about the notion of "functional adequacy." I have thus been critical of the unreflective extension of the domain of application of transitional justice tools, which took shape in strongly institutionalized, post-authoritarian contexts, in, for example, weakly institutionalized, post-conflict—or even more so, ongoing conflict—contexts, taking this as a manifestation of what some economists and organizational sociologists call

* I am grateful to the participants in the workshop organized by the editors to discuss earlier versions of the drafts of the papers for valuable comments, and particularly to Fionnuala Ní Aoláin KC (Hons) and Ambassador Stephen Rapp, who read and commented insightfully on the penultimate version of the paper. Remaining infelicities, both substantive and linguistic, are mine alone.

[1] As I will argue later, part—but only part—of the difficulty of clarifying the potential usefulness of transitional justice measures in contexts where terrorism is an issue is that the term "terrorism" is even more polysemic than "transitional justice." I will return to this problem later in the chapter.

[2] *See, e.g.*, Elena Sciandra, *Facing States of Fear: The Emerging Issues of Terrorism and Counterterrorism in Transitional Justice*, *in* The Palgrave Handbook of Global Counterterrorism Policy (Scott Nicholas Romaniuk et al., eds., 2017); Pierre Hazan, *Transitional Justice After September 11—A New Rapport with Evil*, *in* Localizing Transitional Justice (Rosalind Shaw, Lars Waldorf, & Pierre Hazan eds., 2010).

[3] *See, e.g.*, Pablo de Greiff, *The Applicability of Transitional Justice in Pre-Conflict Settings*, Center on International Cooperation (2021), https://cic.nyu.edu/wp-content/uploads/2023/02/The-Applicability-of-Transitional-Justice-Pablo-de-Greiff-2021.pdf [https://perma.cc/6YYU-2TSS].

Pablo de Greiff, *Beyond Redress* In: *Perpetual War and International Law*. Edited by: Brianna Rosen, Oxford University Press. © Oxford University Press 2026. DOI: 10.1093/oso/9780197748992.003.0017

"isomorphic mimicry": the tendency to think that the same institutional formation will work equally well regardless of background conditions.[4] This is not to say that I am completely opposed to the application of the lessons learned during the last twenty to thirty years of work on transitional justice, or even of its tools in "novel" contexts, that is to say, to the "vernacularization" of transitional justice (to use the felicitous term that our late colleague Sally Engle Merry popularized), as long as this is done reflectively, in full awareness of both contextual differences and of plausible transcontextual means-to-ends adequacy (which, in the case of justice-related measures, will never be devoid of considerations of legitimacy, and hence will be irreducible to purely consequentialist considerations).[5]

So, to start by problematizing the point that I have been asked to address here, the usefulness of transitional justice in the context of the "war on terror" at the highest level of generality, transitional justice and counterterrorism seem to occupy different spatial and temporal horizons. Spatially, transitional justice, up to now, has been almost exclusively a state-based, essentially nationally delimited initiative (the failures of efforts to apply the measures even in contexts where the cross-border nature of the violations and the abuses are obvious—the Balkans, the Great Lakes region, Israel/Occupied Palestinian Territories, even Indonesia/Timor Leste—are notorious).[6] Temporally, transitional justice, as its very name suggests, is not only meant to be applied at a particular juncture, but it is also a temporary endeavor. Counterterrorism these days, although not definitionally, but in practice, seems to be, in both senses the opposite: it is spatially global, both in the sense that its object knows no boundaries, and moreover, it is transnational, in being a heavily internationally networked activity, both formally and "informally" (at the height of the war on terror the United States and several countries, some of them in Europe reached informal agreements for purposes of "rendition" and other illegal practices; also now, counterterrorism has been formalized through the various agreements between countries for intelligence sharing, and so forth).[7] Temporally, in its form of the war

[4] *See, e.g.*, Lant Pritchett & Frauke de Weijer, *Fragile States: Stuck in a Capability Trap?*, World Bank (2011), https://documents1.worldbank.org/curated/en/681031468337197655/pdf/620080WP0Fragi0BOX0361475B00PUBLIC0.pdf [https://perma.cc/UEF4-AYMC]. For some of the challenges that the transposition of the model from post-authoritarian to weakly institutionalized post-conflict contexts involves, see my report to the Human Rights Council. Pablo de Greiff, Rep. of the Special Rapporteur on the promotion of truth, justice, reparation and guarantees of non-recurrence to the Human Rights Council, U.N. Doc. A/HRC/36/50 (Aug. 21, 2017).

[5] *See, e.g.*, Sally Engle Merry, *Transnational Human Rights and Local Activism: Mapping the Middle*, 2 World Bank Legal Rev. 185 (2006); Pablo de Greiff, *The Vernacularization of Transitional Justice: Is Transitional Justice Useful in Pre-conflict Settings?*, *in* The Complexity of Human Rights (Philip Alston ed., 2024).

[6] The failures in question refer to the implementation of cross-border comprehensive transitional justice policies. Of course, there have been quite successful prosecutorial efforts by international tribunals, both the ad hoc ones and the International Criminal Court, as well as efforts under universal jurisdiction. I thank Ambassador Stephen Rapp for asking for this clarification.

[7] *See, e.g.*, Fiona de Londras, The Practice and Problems of Transnational Counter-Terrorism (2022) (noting especially Chapter 1, for a compelling description of what she calls the "institutional density" of the counterterrorism architecture).

on terror, counterterrorism is described as an "endless war."[8] But even leaving aside the (rhetorically although not always factually) rejected war on terror, the mentioned institutionalization gives counterterrorism a permanence that transitional justice does not have.

More importantly, in terms of aims, counterterrorism and transitional justice seem to work at cross purposes to each other. The oft-mentioned but seldomly articulated "holism" of transitional justice,[9] I have explained in terms both of the mutually reinforcing potential of the measures as well as of the *shared aims* arguably attributable to the four basic components of a comprehensive transitional justice policy (truth, justice, reparations, and guarantees of nonrecurrence). I will not rehearse the arguments in detail here, but the first point is that the comprehensive implementation of the measures can reinforce the sense that they are part of a multipronged effort to achieve justice, so that despite the individual weakness of the measures, "beneficiaries" can interpret them in the key of justice rather than expedience, and hence a pragmatic argument acquires semantic significance. The second (convergent) argument is that while each of the four measures can be thought to have its distinct purpose, collectively they also share two "mediate aims"—namely, to recognize victims not only as victims but as rights-holders, and to foster civic trust. These, in turn, support two "final" ends: strengthening the rule of law and contributing to social cohesion or reconciliation.[10] It is important to note that these are not merely desirable ends but are closely connected with justice in being both essential conditions and consequences of formal, rights-based systems of law. Each of the measures, then,

[8] *See, e.g.*, MARY DUDZIAK, WAR TIME: AN IDEA, ITS HISTORY, ITS CONSEQUENCES 4–5 (2012) (tracing the temporal extension of American attitudes toward war, which, factually, would require abandoning the idea that war is essentially a temporary "exception to normal life," in the face of the realization that "war is not an exception to peacetime, but instead, an enduring condition"). War, in Dudziak's terms, has become both spatially and temporally "boundless." *See id.*; *see also* Frédéric Mégret, *Transitional Justice for the "War on Terror?,"* 22 J. HUM. RTS. 643 (2023).

[9] *See* U.N. Secretary-General, *The Rule of Law and Transitional Justice in Conflict and Post-Conflict Societies*, U.N. Doc. S/2004/616 (Aug. 23, 2004).

[10] I am using the vocabulary of immediate, mediate, and final aims, not primarily in virtue of their temporal connotations (that is, to refer to proximity or distance in time), but rather, to causal sufficiency or insufficiency. Hence, the "immediate" goal of a particular measure is one that in theory can be brought about by that intervention (regardless of how much time this might take). So, for example, those who think of deterrence as the immediate goal of criminal prosecutions think that prosecutions *can* bring about this effect (even if not in a short time). "Mediate" and "final," therefore, refer to degrees of separation from this position. The mediate aims of a measure are aims that it is reasonable to think the measure's implementation may further, but whose accomplishment may also require a number of additional measures. For example, reparations may contribute to making victims feel recognized but almost certainly cannot satisfy victims' claims for recognition on their own. That will require the implementation of a variety of measures, including those in the typical transitional justice portfolio. "Final ends" in the way I am using the term here are not the ends "for sake of which everything else is done," as Aristotle would have it in Book I of the *Nicomachean Ethics*, but ends whose attainment is causally even more distant, and therefore whose realization really depends upon the contribution of an even larger number of factors, whose role, relatively speaking, increases in importance. *See* Pablo de Greiff, *Theorizing Transitional Justice*, *in* TRANSITIONAL JUSTICE (Melissa Williams, Rosemary Nagy, & Jon Elster eds., 2012).

is more than a token in a random collection of initiatives; rather, each is part of a whole where they reinforce each other and, together, are functionally fit-to-purpose (that is, adequate means for achieving the aims in question—which of course does not mean fail-safe), and oriented to restoring or establishing anew the currency of basic rights precisely by *doing justice* in the aftermath of systemic injustice. So while far from perfect—no country has ever criminally prosecuted each and every perpetrator of human rights violations, let alone convicted them in proportion to the harm they caused; no truth commission has disclosed the whereabouts of each and every victim or accounted for all the institutional dimensions that made the violations possible; no country has offered reparations benefits to each and every victim, much less benefits that satisfy the principle of *restitutio in integrum*; and of course, no country, especially in the short run, has engaged in the complicated reform project that would be required to truly be able to guarantee nonrecurrence—transitional justice holds the great virtue of "unpacking" different dimensions of justice and advocating for the implementation of measures in all of them.[11] Although its offer, along each "pillar," typically differs from what would be expected in terms of redress in an isolated violation by a well-functioning system of justice, the coordinated implementation of a comprehensive, multidimensional transitional justice policy allows people to read the measures, despite their shortcomings, in the key of justice, rather than mere expediency.[12]

Counterterrorism seems to be very different in terms of ends. Without further specification of what the essential elements of a counterterrorism policy are, or ought to be, counterterrorism, *in practice*, is more easily seen as a *security*[13] (or even as "stability"), rather than a *justice* policy.[14]

Definitional Challenges

The question of whether transitional justice has anything to contribute to counterterrorism would, of course, be easier to answer if there was consensus around a definition of the term "terrorism." But despite great and long-standing

[11] *See, e.g.*, Pablo de Greiff, Rep. of the Special Rapporteur on the promotion of truth, justice, reparation and guarantees of non-recurrence to the Human Rights Council on his global study of transitional justice, U.N. Doc. A/HRC/36/50/Add.1 (Aug. 7, 2017).

[12] *See* de Greiff, *supra* note 11; and Pablo de Greiff, *Some Thoughts on the Development and Present State of Transitional Justice*, 5 Zeitschrift für Menschenrechte 2 (2011).

[13] "Security" in a narrow, militaristic sense, often indifferent to human rights, and to that extent, orthogonal to the aims of transitional justice as I described the latter. There are, of course, broader conceptions of "security," such as "human security," which integrate human rights considerations. *See, e.g.*, Comm'n on Hum. Sec., *Human Security Now: Protecting and Empowering People* (2003).

[14] The qualifier "in practice" is important for reasons that will become apparent later.

efforts, no universally accepted definition exists.[15] Some basic distinctions, however, may be helpful. Numerous typologies of terrorism have been articulated (despite the definitional problem):[16] some are *actor-based* (starting with the distinction between state and non-state actors);[17] some are based on *political orientation* (distinguishing, for example, ethnic, religious, and nationalist groups—including national or anticolonial movements, regional or separatist groups, social-revolutionary movements, and opposition movements, among others); some are *purpose-based* (distinguishing terrorist aims into "morale-building, advertising, disorientation, elimination of opposing forces, and provocation of countermeasures by incumbents"[18]); and some are based on scope, aspiration, and magnitude (allowing for distinctions between, for example, individual terrorism, subnational terrorism, and transnational terrorism). These also reflect differences in the frequency and magnitude of "terrorist activity," ranging from isolated acts to the use of terrorism as one among several tactics in asymmetrical conflicts, with aims varying from changes in local power dynamics to the broader, more diffuse global objectives associated with "super terrorism," as seen in the cases of al-Qaeda, ISIS, and jihadist movements more generally.[19] Some of these typologies are, appropriately, multidimensional.[20]

[15] On the definitional problem generally, *see* Alex P. Schmid, *The Definition of Terrorism*, *in* The Routledge Handbook of Terrorism Research (Alex P. Schmid ed., 2011); in the same collection and with a telling title, *see* Joseph J. Easson & Alex P. Schmid, *Appendix 2.1: 250-Plus Academic, Governmental and Intergovernmental Definitions of Terrorism*, *in* The Routledge Handbook of Terrorism Research (Alex P. Schmid ed., 2011); *see also* Alice Martini & Emeka T. Njoku, *The Challenges of Defining Terrorism for Counter-Terrorism Policy*, *in* The Palgrave Handbook of Global Counterterrorism Policy (Scott Nicholas Romaniuk et al., eds., 2017); Timothy Shanahan, *The Definition of Terrorism*, *in* The Routledge Handbook of Critical Terrorism Studies (Richard Jackson ed., 2016). Within the United Nations, and for practical purposes, the conception of terrorism articulated by Martin Scheinin while he was Special Rapporteur in his report and the narrow definition in Chapter VI of the U.N. Charter are also influential, as are the nineteen sectoral terrorism treaties, some of which more explicitly than others, offer an understanding of terrorism. *See* Martin Scheinin, Rep. of the Special Rapporteur on the promotion and protection of human rights and fundamental freedoms while countering terrorism, U.N. Doc. E/CN.4/2006/98, 26–50, 72 (Dec. 28, 2005); U.N. Charter arts. 33–38. I thank Fionnuala Ní Aoláin KC (Hons) for suggesting this last remark.

[16] For what follows, see the very useful review in Sarah V. Marsden & Alex P. Schmid, *Typologies of Terrorism and Political Violence*, *in* The Routledge Handbook of Terrorism Research (Alex P. Schmid ed., 2011).

[17] *See, e.g.*, William L. Waugh, International Terrorism: How Nations Respond to Terrorists (1982).

[18] Sarah V. Marsden & Alex P. Schmid, *Typologies of Terrorism and Political Violence*, *in* The Routledge Handbook of Terrorism Research (Alex P. Schmid ed., 2011); *see also* T.P. Thompson, *Terror as a Weapon of Political Agitation*, *in* Internal War: Problems and Approaches (Harry Eckstein ed., 1964).

[19] *See, e.g.*, Ekaterina Stepanova, Terrorism in Asymmetrical Conflict: Ideological and Structural Aspects (2008); Marsden & Schmid, *supra* note 19, at 160. It is worth remarking that "super terrorism" is a contested category, with some observers noting that it captures organizations with particular structures and tactics, and others arguing that the term simply designates those groups that become particularly worrisome to some governments, especially those who happen to be influential in setting counterterrorism policy internationally.

[20] *See* Marsden & Schmid, *supra* note 19, at 167, 173, and 180 (charts summarizing Reed's "generational typology of war and conflict," Lökinger's "typological tree of terrorism," and Ross's "structural

Keeping this broad-brush stroke summary of the typologies of terrorism (and their implications for counterterrorism) as background, the following conclusions seem to me to be justified. First, and at the highest level of generality, while the term "terrorism" may gesture toward a core idea—namely, the use of violence against civilians and noncombatants (and their basic interests and rights, which may include the integrity of infrastructure and property) by either state or by non-state actors, with the expectation that such violence will have spillover effects beyond those directly affected, and with the aim of changing balances of power, decision-making, either directly or indirectly (that is, by changing attitudes toward the contending groups), or as an "expressive act" (retributive, vengeful, or intended to "even the score")—it may be time to acknowledge that the term is not only "essentially contested" but that it either refers to multiple, distinct phenomena, or to a phenomenon that has grown too complex to be meaningfully captured by a single category.

Second, and bearing in mind the nature of transitional justice instruments and experiences, it is perhaps reasonable to assume that transitional justice will have more to offer in relation to terrorism in its more "local," subnational, and national manifestations—particularly, where groups use terrorism tactically, as part of broader agendas that are not entirely divorced from rational calculation. In such contexts, transitional justice's "socially integrative mechanisms," grounded in shared conceptions of rights or justice, will, predictably, have a harder time showing results beyond certain thresholds of "radicalism" in the pursuit of "reformist" agendas, be they politically, ethnically, religiously, or ideologically motivated.

Abstracting from factors that make purely national conflicts increasingly rare,[21] transitional justice measures—such as those implemented in Colombia—can offer, at least temporarily, a degree of social integration through the familiar combination of justice initiatives, truth-seeking and truth-telling measures, reparations, and reforms aimed at preventing recurrence. Northern Ireland, South Africa, and Sierra Leone, among others, exemplify countries that experienced internal conflicts in which some groups were designated as "terrorist," but which nonetheless benefited—at least to some extent—by the implementation

causes of oppositional political terrorism," respectively, and the references therein, which are especially illustrative of these multidimensional approaches).

[21] These factors include, on the side of "insurgents"—presumed to be the only side that exercises "terrorism"—connections with international organized crime, including drug-trafficking, illegal arms trade, trafficking of persons, and so forth. On the side of states, transnational economic arrangements that, in turn, lead to defense agreements indifferent not just to questions of governance but also to respect for the rights of citizens, geopolitical alliances that often lead to similar indifference to how certain governments exercise their power and especially whether they respect the rights of their citizens, and so forth.

of such measures, and where the "problem of terrorism" has been largely solved, at least in part through the implementation of transitional justice measures.[22] In all these cases, the terminology of "terrorism" was eventually set aside, and a peace agreement or other arrangements were made to address the core causes of conflict.[23]

But, of course, the "terrorism" that afflicted these countries—if that is the proper characterization of the (undeniable) violence exercised not only by insurgents but also by state forces or their proxies—differs significantly from the kind that is the central concern of this volume. In these contexts, violence often took "extralegal" forms on both sides, though I set aside for now the complex legal questions regarding applicable regimes.

Regarding the more transnational,[24] "expressivist,"[25] frequent, and "normalized"[26] use of terror, transitional justice may be overtaxed. Even here, given the complexity of the phenomenon in question, there may be limited and discrete uses of transitional justice tools that may be considered. For example, regarding the reintegration of national "ex-combatants," who either voluntarily or through larger-scale agreements end up abandoning the fight. Similarly, it may be that there are aspects of the struggle that would profit from the implementation of transitional justice measures, rather than leaving them in total impunity or

[22] *See* Fionnuala Ní Aoláin's contribution to this volume, Chapter 16, "Alternative Approaches to Counterterrorism."

[23] Peru is a case worth bearing in mind. Sendero Luminoso was defeated militarily, and its leader Abimael Guzmán, imprisoned. The group never ceased to be called "terrorist," even by the Truth and Reconciliation Commission (CVR), and members of Sendero, for example, were not eligible for reparations, even if they had been the victims of human rights violations by the authorities. The term "terrorist" and the (informal) verb "terruqueo" has become a form of attack on anyone espousing positions that are considered socially progressive (including the implementation of some of the recommendations of the CVR). Here, one can find an example of the noxious effects of the use of a term (even in a situation in which the designated group was militarily defeated) illustrating the aim to maintain privileges rather than reform institutions with a view to the generation of public goods. Peru is now suffering deep democratic regression, historical revisionism, and denialism—portraying the violations committed in the course of the conflict at most as "necessary evils," and more positively as the means of salvation from Sendero—and, not surprisingly, high degrees of social conflict. For an excellent analysis, see the essays compiled by Salomón Lerner Febres (President of the CVR) and Elizabeth Salmón on the twentieth anniversary of the presentation of the CVR's Final Report. *Legados de un pasado irresuelto El Informe Final de la CVR y la crisis de la democracia veinte años después* (Salomón Lerner Febres & Elizabeth Salmón eds., 2023).

[24] Not forgetting that even the more "transnational" cases more often than not have deep roots in local grievances.

[25] By which I mean here, the use of violence that is not necessarily linked with the success in the achievement of given goals, but that is seen as having "value" in its own terms, to "score a point," attract attention, and create hazards regardless of whether doing so is likely to fulfill a group's (including a state's) longer-term agenda.

[26] Using the term instead of "systematic," for the latter term may connote strategic considerations, whereas here the referent is the adoption of violence as a habitual modus operandi, independent of strategic considerations of success.

only the weakest forms of accountability.[27] Frédéric Mégret is correct (although not "hermeneutically generous") in asserting that the emphasis of this proposal as well as the International Center for Transitional Justice's U.S. Accountability Project "was tellingly provincial and concerned with American policy and reconciliation after the Bush years rather than a form of engagement with foreign victims."[28] And yet, while acknowledging the significant political challenges and the limited experience with the transnational application of the relevant mechanisms,[29] even these modest proposals, had they been implemented, may have had beneficial effects—such as complicating the defense of torture during the 2016 U.S. presidential campaign[30]—and could have marked a meaningful starting point. After all, the pursuit of justice must start somewhere.[31]

Finally, perhaps the main concern here does not lie as much with the *nature* of terrorist groups as with the *methods* of fighting them. That is, to use an expression to summarize the concern, if counterterrorism is understood as a temporally and spatially open-ended war, which almost by necessity would have multiple, simultaneous targets, fought with very few normative constraints the contribution of transitional justice (as of virtually any other policy) to the solution of this war would be marginal at best.

[27] Senator Leahy's proposal in March 2009 for the establishment of a truth commission to investigate the Bush administration's policies on detention and interrogation would have been an instance of this use of a transitional justice measure. *See, e.g.*, Neil A. Lewis, *Senator Pushes Idea of Truth Commission*, N.Y. Times (Mar. 4, 2009), https://www.nytimes.com/2009/03/05/us/politics/05brfs-SENATORPUSHE_BRF.html.

[28] Mégret, *supra* note 9.

[29] The only element of transitional justice that has received wide cross-border application is criminal prosecutions, including in international, hybrid, and even national tribunals under the principle of universal jurisdiction, which is something to celebrate (I thank Ambassador Stephen Rapp for insisting on the importance of highlighting this point). But these efforts have rarely been fully integrated in wider transitional justice policies. Additionally, the number of international prosecutions for terrorist acts is, comparatively speaking, small. Indeed, as Helen Duffy argues, one of the negative consequences of the war on terror has been the disincentive to use criminal justice as a counterterrorism tool. *See* Helen Duffy, The "War on Terror" and the Framework of International Law 119–245 (2d ed. 2015).

[30] *See, e.g.*, Jenna Johnson, *Trump Says "Torture Works," Backs Waterboarding and "Much Worse,"* Wash. Post (Feb. 17, 2016), https://www.washingtonpost.com/politics/trump-says-torture-works-backs-waterboarding-and-much-worse/2016/02/17/4c9277be-d59c-11e5-b195-2e29a4e13425_story.html.

[31] In saying this, I want to insist on the importance of avoiding romanticism. The sort of tendencies that have led the United States to adopt the position on the war on terror that would need to be disclosed, socialized, transformed, and held those responsible accountable for, are deeply rooted. *See* John W. Dower, Cultures of War: Pearl Harbor/Hiroshima/9-11/Iraq (2010). On the other hand, the fact that so much information is available and that there is so little *institutional* risk in calling for accountability for these practices (compared to other countries that have gone through the efforts to establish accountability, understood in the broad sense in which transitional justice understands the notion, that is, including criminal justice but also truth, reparations, and guarantees of nonrecurrence) also buttresses the case for avoiding the cynicism that is expressed in not even trying.

Understanding the Drivers of Terrorism

There is, of course, nothing necessary in this way of thinking about how to combat terrorism. To illustrate the alternative, I will, perhaps ironically, appeal to United Nations (U.N.) documents on counterterrorism (with the caveat that in appealing, to some degree approvingly, to the texts, I am not similarly approving the United Nations' *practice*). It is well known that since September 11, 2001, the United Nations has established a complex and far-reaching counterterrorism architecture, whose workings have come in for very well deserved criticism, including by Fionnuala Ní Aoláin in her capacity as Special Rapporteur on the topic (which saves me from even trying to provide a full picture of the system, since I could never do so as well as she).[32] The system rests, crucially, on Security Council Resolution 1373 (2001), which requires member states to criminalize various acts of terrorism as serious criminal offenses in domestic laws, prevent and suppress the financing of terrorism, and freeze the assets of individuals linked to terrorism.[33] By imposing on all U.N. member states general, permanent obligations, unconnected to a specific conflict situation, the resolution establishes new binding rules of international law and is considered as the first "legislative" resolution of the Council.

Over time, and for various reasons—including a lack of results and pressure from the U.N. General Assembly, Special Rapporteurs, and High Commissioners for Human Rights—what began, without much exaggeration, as a purely security-focused enterprise has seen its guiding texts become more "complexified" (even though, I insist, these "textual" changes have not led to significant changes in practice). The texts, however, have come to acknowledge that while responses to terrorism can include military action, law enforcement, and intelligence operations, these measures alone are insufficient.[34] Although they may be effective in immediately halting violence, they primarily address symptoms rather than root causes. The very nature of such responses, with their emphasis on short-term security and correspondingly heavy resourcing needs, can sometimes "detract support and attention from achieving sustainable peace."[35] Military and security

[32] *See, again*, Fionnuala Ní Aoláin's contribution to this volume, Chapter 16, "Alternative Approaches to Counterterrorism," and her multiple reports to the Human Rights Council and the U.N. General Assembly. *See also* Anne Charbord, Transitional Justice in Contexts Where Terrorism and Counter-Terrorism Are Part of the Discourse (2023), https://www.ohchr.org/sites/default/files/documents/issues/transitionaljustice/sg-guidance-note/7th-tj-ct.pdf [https://perma.cc/63ER-E43V].

[33] In the resolution, the Council decided that states should take measures to prevent acts of terrorism and to bring terrorists to justice, assisting each other with respect to criminal prosecutions of terrorist offenders, instituting effective border security measures and exchange information related to movements of terrorist persons or networks and forged or falsified travel documents. *See* S.C. Res. 1373 (Sept. 28, 2001).

[34] S.C. Res. 1963 (Dec. 20, 2010).

[35] Rep. of the Advisory Group of Experts for the 2015 Review of the United Nations Peacebuilding Architecture: "The Challenge of Sustaining Peace," transmitted by Letter dated 29 June 2015 from the Chair of the Secretary-General's Advisory Group of Experts for the 2015 Review of the United

responses to the terrorism threat, including in situations of armed conflict, can exacerbate violence and prove counterproductive, not only by acting as a potent recruiting tool but also by allowing various groups to take root among and gain the perpetual support of disenfranchised and marginalized populations, rendering military "victory" illusory. It is essential to strengthen efforts to prevent and peacefully resolve prolonged conflict—alongside promoting the rule of law, human rights and fundamental freedoms, good governance, tolerance, and inclusiveness—to offer a viable alternative to those susceptible to terrorist recruitment and radicalization.[36]

At the end of 2015, then–U.N. Secretary-General Ban Ki-moon presented his "Plan of Action to Prevent Violent Extremism"[37] from which I will provide an extensive quote because it has the merit of illustrating well the "complexification" I was mentioning, one that also shows (textually, at least, unfortunately not in reality) a different way of reacting to terrorism.[38]

The text opens with a telling statement: "Nothing can justify violent extremism, but we must also acknowledge that it does not arise in a vacuum. Narratives of grievance, actual or perceived injustice, promised empowerment and sweeping change become attractive where human rights are being violated, good governance is being ignored and aspirations are being crushed."[39] And then it provides a useful summary of the trajectory that the textual discussions followed, showing that by 2006 the position was no longer pure security:

> The UN Global Counter-Terrorism Strategy, adopted unanimously by the General Assembly by its resolution 60/288, explicitly addresses prevention and foresees balanced implementation across all four of its pillars: (a) tackling conditions conducive to terrorism; (b) preventing and combating terrorism; (c) building countries' capacity to combat terrorism and to strengthen the role of the United Nations system in that regard; and (d) ensuring respect for human rights for all and the rule of law while countering terrorism. Over the last decade, there has been a strong emphasis on the implementation of measures under pillar II of the Global Strategy, while pillars I and IV have often been

Nations Peacebuilding Architecture Addressed to the Presidents of the Security Council and of the General Assembly, para 121 (June 29, 2015).

[36] S.C. Res. 1963, *supra* note 35; S.C. Res. 2178 (Sept. 24, 2014).

[37] U.N. Secretary-General, *Plan of Action to Prevent Violent Extremism*, U.N. Doc. A/70/674 (Dec. 24, 2015).

[38] A term that remains undefined within the system and that is the origin of a good number of the problems that afflict the operations of the system, despite the fact that this is well recognized. *See, e.g.*, Fionnuala D. Ní Aoláin, Rep. of the Special Rapporteur on the promotion and protection of human rights and fundamental freedoms while countering terrorism to the H.R.C., U.N. Doc. A/HRC/43/46 (Feb. 21, 2020); Ben Emmerson, Rep. of the Special Rapporteur on the promotion and protection of human rights and fundamental freedoms while countering terrorism to the H.R.C., U.N. Doc. A/HRC/31/65 (Apr. 29, 2016).

[39] *Plan of Action to Prevent Violent Extremism*, *supra* note 38, at 3.

> overlooked. Ahead of the tenth anniversary of the adoption of the Strategy, in 2016, I am launching this Plan of Action, with a focus on preventive measures for addressing violent extremism, including by reinvigorating those measures covered under pillars I and IV of the Strategy, ensuring a more comprehensive implementation of the Strategy in view of the lessons learned over the past decade and the challenges that may lie ahead. . . . We must refocus our priorities, strengthen our application of justice, and rebuild the social compact between the governing and governed. We need to pay attention to why individuals are attracted to violent extremist groups. I am convinced that the creation of open, equitable, inclusive and pluralist societies, based on the full respect of human rights and with economic opportunities for all, represents the most tangible and meaningful alternative to violent extremism and the most promising strategy for rendering it unattractive.[40]

The text offers quite a comprehensive analysis of the drivers of violent extremism, including, at the structural level, inequality and lack of economic opportunities, marginalization and discrimination, poor governance, violations of human rights and the rule of law,[41] prolonged and unresolved conflict, and inhumane prison conditions and inhumane treatment of inmates.[42] At the individual level, the report mentions "witnessing torture, the death of a relative or friend at the hands of the security forces or a foreign power, unfair trials, the loss of property and the humiliation of a parent—and even the refusal of a personal loan."[43] At the collective level, the Plan of Action mentions as drivers of extremism "[h]istorical legacies of, or collective grievances stemming from, domination, oppression, subjugation or foreign intervention"[44] and their instrumentalization to create narratives of victimization. Politically, the text is concerned about the polarization that results from the divisive use of "religious beliefs, ethnic differences and political ideologies"[45] and from the work of "political entrepreneurs" and social networks.[46]

In other words, without saying so explicitly, naturally, the text conforms with the very old sociological argument according to which sustainable social change is not merely a matter of clever institutional engineering—even less of sheer coercion—but that it also requires changes in the domain of the economy, societal relations, and even personal and cultural dispositions and convictions.

Not bad for a U.N. document, I would say. Alas, not much of this has been translated into action. Had this been adopted seriously, I believe that it would

[40] *Id.* at 7.
[41] *Id.* at 27, 31, and 33 (emphasizing those carried out in the name of security).
[42] *Id.* at. 27–31.
[43] *Id.* at 33.
[44] *Id.* at 35.
[45] *Id.* at 36.
[46] *Id.* at 37.

have made a difference. And for purposes of this discussion, here transitional justice would have "lent a hand" with its broad understanding of accountability and its (not always sufficiently remembered) preventive intent.[47] Of course, it would not have been a "magic bullet"—there is no such thing. But the combination of its measures would have addressed in some cases, and mitigated or prevented in others, the drivers or the effects of radicalization.

Moving from Redress to Prevention

Perhaps we are looking for help from transitional justice and approaching it from the wrong angle, one that sees the policy more as a technocratic policy of *redress* (of different degrees of "softness"). I would like to encourage a more systematic exploration of the other side of transitional justice, one that does not forsake redress but that concentrates more on *prevention*. Like human rights in general, which are both crucial tools for *ex post* redress—and also *ex ante*—anti-grievance measures (the latter underattended), we should think about transitional justice as an opportunity to consider the conditions that would make terrorism less likely to arise in the first place. Taking prevention seriously requires moving beyond crisis prevention, for crisis prevention always arrives "too late" and tends to narrow our understanding of the causes, solutions, and actors involved in conflict. It often overemphasizes the role of international actors and relies heavily on familiar peacemaking and peacekeeping tools as solutions, thereby failing to address enabling factors and drivers of conflict). Broadening and "upstreaming" prevention work—a project long discussed but repeatedly postponed at the United Nations—holds far more promise than the reactive, *ex post* approaches to conflict resolution that remain dominant, even eight years after the U.N.-World Bank report *Pathways for Peace* sought to make the "business case" for comprehensive prevention.[48] Some of us, however, still insist on the need to

[47] *See* Thomas Unger, *Interview with Pablo de Greiff, Making Prevention a Reality*, 14 ZEITSCHRIFT FÜR MENSCHENRECHTE 1 (2020).

[48] PATHWAYS FOR PEACE: INCLUSIVE APPROACHES TO PREVENTING VIOLENT CONFLICT, U.N. & THE WORLD BANK (2017), https://openknowledge.worldbank.org/handle/10986/28337. Consensus about the need to broaden and upstream prevention long preceded this report. The importance of broadening and "upstreaming" prevention measures had been one of the points of convergence of the three important reviews of 2014–15. *See* Identical letters dated 17 June 2015 from the Secretary-General addressed to the President of the General Assembly and the President of the Security Council, U.N. Doc. A/70/95–S/2015/446 (June 17, 2015); *see also* Identical letters dated 29 June 2015 from the Chair of the Advisory Group of Experts on the Review of the Peacebuilding Architecture addressed to the President of the General Assembly and the President of the Security Council, U.N. Doc. A/69/968–S/2015/490 (June 29, 2015) (producing the so-called AGE Report, ten years of work since the establishment of the Peacebuilding Commission and Support Office); *see also* PREVENTING CONFLICT, TRANSFORMING JUSTICE, SECURING THE PEACE, A GLOBAL STUDY ON THE IMPLEMENTATION OF UNITED NATIONS SECURITY COUNCIL RESOLUTION 1325, U.N. WOMEN (2015), https://wps.unwomen.org/pdf/en/GlobalStudy_EN_Web.pdf [https://perma.cc/EFD9-GC68] (a review evaluating fifteen years of implementation of Resolution 1325).

develop a "framework" approach to prevention—one that moves beyond isolated initiatives in times of "emergency" and instead embraces systematic, long-term efforts. This approach focuses on building strong state and governance institutions, strengthening civil society and social cohesion, promoting norms and capacities for peaceful dispute resolution, and shaping cultures and personal dispositions. All of these elements are essential to giving prevention a real chance.[49] Transitional justice, of course, is only part of the broader agenda. But if we stop conceiving it merely as a redress mechanism and instead recognize its multiple preventive functions, we might see it as a policy that, to the extent it works, operates through two key "social mechanisms"[50]: (a) norm-affirmation, and (b) its capacity to articulate and disarticulate some social groups. Seen this way, transitional justice can be deployed more strategically to address the underlying challenges that give rise to terrorism[51]—not bad instruments to apply to the problem at hand.

[49] For a summary description of this large-scale project, *see* PABLO DE GREIFF, A FRAMEWORK APPROACH TO MAKING PREVENTION A REALITY (2024), https://app.box.com/s/9p9oildfxgk3fsd3gxsbfzoo16zq466q.

[50] For a useful collection of papers on this notion, *see* SOCIAL MECHANISMS: AN ANALYTICAL APPROACH TO SOCIAL THEORY (Peter Hedstrom & Richard Swedberg eds., 1998).

[51] *See* PABLO DE GREIFF, TRANSITIONAL JUSTICE, SECURITY, AND DEVELOPMENT: SECURITY AND JUSTICE THEMATIC PAPER, THE WORLD BANK (2010), https://documents1.worldbank.org/curated/en/937211468151160151/pdf/620610WP0Trans0BOX0361475B00PBLIC0.pdf [https://perma.cc/D3RW-JXDC]; *see also* GUIDANCE NOTE OF THE SECRETARY GENERAL ON TRANSITIONAL JUSTICE: A STRATEGIC TOOL FOR PEOPLE, PREVENTION AND PEACE, U.N. (2023), https://www.ohchr.org/sites/default/files/documents/issues/transitionaljustice/sg-guidance-note/2023_07_guidance_note_transitional_justice_en.pdf [https://perma.cc/42LF-XGVL]. The argument also converges with Adil Ahmed Haque's contribution to this volume, Chapter 12, Filling the Void: Law, Policy, and Morality at War."

18
Risk and Ending War

Elad Uzan

Introduction

Traditional just war theory distinguishes between *jus ad bellum* (norms governing the resort to war—essentially, whether making war is justified) and *jus in bello* (norms governing the conduct of war—whether a particular military action is justified). According to traditional just war theory, as long as the predicates of a war are just and the means by which it is prosecuted necessary and proportionate, a belligerent may continue fighting until it attains victory.[1]

This vision of just war developed over the course of centuries and as such tends to fit most neatly the contours of historical conflicts.[2] Yet contemporary wars do not necessarily follow in the footsteps of their predecessors. Importantly, the old criterion of victory—overt surrender by a well-defined army or state—has dissolved into the ambiguity of endless, shifting objectives, often against non-state enemies. Syria and Somalia have been wracked by civil wars since 2011 and the 1980s, respectively, and decades-old conflicts between states and terrorist organizations continue to unfold, from Kashmir to the Gaza Strip. Such conflicts now comprise the most prevalent form of war. Researchers at Uppsala University counted 254 armed conflicts between 1946 and 2014, only 24 of which were characterized as interstate conflicts.[3] Where terrorist organizations are involved, they may surrender, but there is often no central, organized entity that could conceivably lay down arms. And in many cases, states are not willing to negotiate with any such entities. When terrorist groups do falter, other violent actors soon emerge.

What do we do about conflicts that "have no clear end-state," as Gabriella Blum puts it? Conflicts that "blur the traditional lines between war and peace"?[4]

[1] The most important advocate of this view is MICHAEL WALZER, JUST AND UNJUST WARS (1977). For criticism of Walzer's just war theory, *see* JEFF MCMAHAN, KILLING IN WAR (2009).

[2] For discussion of the origins of modern just war theory, *see* Pablo Kalmanovitz, *Early Modern Sources of the Regular War Tradition*, *in* THE OXFORD HANDBOOK OF ETHICS AND WAR 145–59 (Seth Lazar & Helen Frowe eds., 2015).

[3] Therése Pettersson & Peter Wallensteen, *Armed Conflicts, 1946–2014*, 52 J. PEACE RES. 4 (2015).

[4] *See* Gabriella Blum, *The Fog of Victory*, 24 EUR. J. INT'L L. 1 (2013).

Elad Uzan, *Risk and Ending War* In: *Perpetual War and International Law*. Edited by: Brianna Rosen, Oxford University Press. © Oxford University Press 2026. DOI: 10.1093/oso/9780197748992.003.0018

Permanent war is untenable. The state of war undermines the possibility of maintaining free societies; war entails not only the moral catastrophe of mass death but also exceptional legal regimes incompatible with freedom. If changing aims and technologies of war have made victory unattainable, then we have no choice but to end wars without victory.

Considering that terrorism will always pose a threat and that the risk of attack can never be reduced to zero, when do states have a moral obligation to end counterterrorism wars? I argue that such wars should end when their crucial objective is met: when the terrorist risk to the defender's population is reduced to an acceptable level.[5] The war should end once this goal is achieved or else when achieving it becomes impossible without disproportionate violence. After providing some more general remarks on the ethics of ending wars, I argue for a risk-based approach for the conclusion of just wars against terrorist organizations. I define the relevant notion of risk and explore the concept of minimizing the risk posed by the terrorist organization to various reference classes within the population of the defending state. (I will discuss reference classes in more detail, but briefly they are groups of objects, persons, or events used for probability assessment.) I contend that a war on terror should conclude when the average risk to each relevant reference class falls below its specific acceptable threshold.

Normative Considerations in War Termination

The literature on war termination has scarcely considered when and how conflicts should end, instead focusing on what should be done after war ends. As Cécile Fabre notes, "There is hardly any work on the transition from war to peace, and more specifically on the ethics of war termination."[6] David Rodin suggests that we need a regime *jus terminatio* alongside *jus ad bellum*, *jus in bello*, and *jus post bellum*, as a "fourth and independent component of the morality of war."[7] These "four components of the morality of war are sometimes treated as consecutive temporal components of war," but "a better way of conceiving them is as articulating moral reasons appropriate to distinctive forms of moral problem generated by different aspects of conflict."[8] Darrel Moellendorf's "distinct morality" of ending wars is encompassed in the notion of *jus ex bello*.[9] His

[5] While the morality of risk is a significant consideration, ending a war against a terrorist organization involves considerations that extend beyond risk alone. For a discussion, *see* STEPHEN NATHANSON, TERRORISM AND THE ETHICS OF WAR (2010); Max Abrahms, *Does Terrorism Really Work? Evolution in the Conventional Wisdom since 9/11*, DEF. & PEACE ECON. 22 (2011).

[6] Cécile Fabre, *Ending Wars*, *in* COSMOPOLITAN PEACE (2016).

[7] David Rodin, *The War Trap: Dilemmas of* Jus Terminatio, 125 ETHICS 674, 675 (2015).

[8] *Id.*

[9] Darrel Moellendorf, *Two Doctrines of* Jus Ex Bello, 125 ETHICS 653, 653 (2015).

support for separate moral regimes stems from the fact that "after a war begins circumstances change very dramatically, so much so that a reconsideration of the application of the criteria appropriate for evaluating the morality of the war may be required."[10]

It follows that we need an ethics of ending war, which must be sensitive to conditions of war in an advanced state.[11] There may be differences in the proper moral calculations surrounding resort to force, the continued use of force, and cessation of the use of force. For example, how should "sunk costs"—in particular, the losses a force has accrued in fighting—affect moral calculations about ending wars?[12] Terminating a war might also foster moral costs that outweigh the moral wrong of fighting even after the just cause is satisfied. Mechanistically applying *ad bellum* principles to ongoing conflicts, demanding the war end whenever one of the *ad bellum* conditions is no longer satisfied, could lead to morally perverse situations. *Ad bellum* conditions can be useful in providing a first approximation as to whether an ongoing war is still just, but they do not tell us all we might need to know.

As we will see in the next section, the moral considerations guiding the end of a war are even more complex when the aggressor is a terrorist organization rather than a state. Consequently, determining when a counterterrorism war should end involves special moral considerations.

War Termination and the Goals of War

Current philosophical thinking on war justification focuses on a central moral question: What are the legitimate goals of war, and is the achievement of these goals proportionate to the cost incurred in achieving them? As Henry Shue observes, "One must both ask prior to going to war, would the evil to be prevented by military action in this case be worth engaging in a war overall, and ask throughout any war engaged in, would this particular military engagement make a sufficiently great contribution to potential victory to be worth the death and destruction likely to result?"[13]

There is a deep connection between the goals of war and decisions about when to end it. Put succinctly, the answer to the question "when should war end?" depends to a considerable measure on what the goals of war are and whether

[10] *Id.* at 654.

[11] Seth Lazar, *War's Endings and the Structure of Just War Theory*, *in* THE ETHICS OF WAR: ESSAYS 227–43 (Saba Bazargan & Samuel C. Rickless eds., 2017).

[12] Seth Lazar, *Moral Sunk Costs*, 68 PHIL. Q. 841 (2018); Elad Uzan, *Moral Sunk Costs in War and Self-Defence*, 71 PHIL. Q. 359 (2021).

[13] Henry Shue, *War*, *in* THE OXFORD HANDBOOK OF PRACTICAL ETHICS 734–61, 748 (Hugh LaFollette ed., 2005).

they have been fulfilled. It is notoriously complicated, however, to identify when defensive goals are fulfilled and thus when the right of self-defense is exhausted. As Seth Lazar notes, "Although common-sense morality and international law view national defence as the paradigm case of justified warfare, grounding this consensus is surprisingly difficult."[14] Positive international law does not clearly indicate the scope of lawful self-defense, nor does it delineate what are lawful goals of defensive force. Chris O'Meara summarizes the situation accurately when he writes that "the legitimate purposes of the right of self-defense remain highly controversial."[15]

Theorists offer a range of proposals concerning the legitimate scope of self-defense. Some believe that, in most circumstances, even invasion by another state does not warrant resorting to defensive force.[16] Others believe national self-defense is justified only to halt and repel an invasion.[17] Still others allow defending states wider latitude, arguing there are legitimate self-defense aims beyond halting and repelling invasion.[18] They argue that repeat aggressors are liable to suffer greater harm than might otherwise be proportionate in response to a single attack, in order to establish deterrence.[19] Or, if a state is facing genocidal aggression, it may be justified in pursuing the attacker's unconditional surrender, even if surrender is not necessary in the immediate defensive context.[20]

In war against a terrorist organization, goals that would not be countenanced by traditional just war theory must be considered. For instance, according to traditional just war theory, establishing a functioning polity is a concern of the postwar period. But in a war against a terrorist organization, the establishment of stable administration is often less a postwar policy than a military strategy, part of an effort to defeat an organization operating within the borders of a "failed state."[21]

Another consideration involves the goals of terrorist organizations themselves. In interstate wars, the aggressor seeks to achieve a specific goal, such as

[14] Seth Lazar, *National Defence, Self-Defence, and the Problem of Political Aggression*, *in* The Morality of Defensive Wars 11–39, 12 (Cécile Fabre & Seth Lazar eds., 2014).

[15] Chris O'Meara, Necessity and Proportionality and the Right of Self-Defence in International Law 20 (2021).

[16] David Rodin, *The Myth of National Self-Defence*, *in* The Morality of Defensive War 69–89 (Cécile Fabre & Seth Lazar eds., 2014).

[17] As Anna Stilz notes, "Both just war theory and international law recognize the defence of one's own state and its territory as the core example of just cause for war." *See* Anna Stilz *Territorial Rights and National Defence*, *in* The Oxford Handbook of Ethics and War 241–57, 242 (Seth Lazar & Helen Frowe eds., 2015).

[18] Jeff McMahan, *Aggression and Punishment*, *in* War: Essays in Political Philosophy 67–84, 79 (Larry May ed., 2008); Thomas Hurka, *Proportionality in the Morality of War*, 33 Phil. & Pub. Aff. 34 (2005).

[19] Yitzhak Benbaji & Daniel Statman, War by Agreement: A Contractarian Ethics of War 71 (2019).

[20] Walzer, *supra* note 1, at 121.

[21] *See* Gary Bass, Jus Post Bellum, 32 Phil. & Pub. Aff. 384 (2004).

the conquest of a territory. Terrorist organizations typically pose a different kind of threat. Instead of taking territory, they maximize individual deaths in order to demoralize the citizenry of the state attacked. The question then arises what a state may legitimately do when its citizens are placed at risk, but its sovereignty is not.

A further complication is the disparity between military victory (defeat of the enemy) and political victory (realizing political gains). Traditional interstate wars end when military goals (for instance, defeating invading armed forces) achieve legitimate political *ad bellum* goals (for instance, protecting territorial integrity). However, in counterterrorism wars, there may be no easy translation between military and political victory. Defeating a terrorist organization in battle neither ensures defeat of associated political movements nor secures the state from those movements' influence.

Since the threat posed by terrorist organizations will never be zero, the most a state can do is hope to reduce that threat sufficiently. For this reason, I suggest that the point at which states have a moral obligation to stop fighting terrorists is not the point of their defeat—which, again, can never be achieved with certainty—but rather is the point at which the terrorist risk is tolerable. To assess when this point might arise, we need to know something about the morality of risk.

Risk and Normativity

Broadly, theories on the morality of risk fall into objective, subjective, and hybrid camps.[22] Objectivists posit that risk can be determined solely from objective facts. One such account is the relative-frequency account, prevalent in economics and decision theory.[23] According to this account, we can, for example, assess the risk of any given American man dying in a car accident on the basis of facts about the world. Specifically, if we divide the average number of American men who die in car crashes annually by the total number of American men, we will know the risk to any one member of this class (American men) of dying in a car accident in a given year.[24]

[22] *See* Ian Hacking, An Introduction to Probability and Inductive Logic 133 (2001). For the distinction between objective and subjective accounts of risk in a normative context, *see* Stephen Perry, *Risk, Harm, and Responsibility*, *in* Philosophical Foundations of Tort Law 322–29 (David G. Owen ed., 1995).

[23] For the frequency theory of probability, *see* Donald Gillies, *Repeatability and Independence*, *in* Philosophical Theories of Probability 94, 94–118 (2000).

[24] The relative frequency account is the oldest account of probability. For a brief historical overview, *see* David Freedman, *Some Issues in the Foundation of Statistics*, 1 Foundations of Science 19 (1995).

Subjective accounts, by contrast, propose that risk is determined not by facts of the world but by what we know.[25] To illustrate the distinction, consider the spin of a roulette wheel. Every fact necessary to predict the outcome of the spin is knowable: if we possessed complete knowledge about the spin—details like the ball's trajectory and the wheel's angular momentum—we could state with certainty where the ball would land. On the other hand, if we knew nothing about the spin, then any outcome would seem to us equally probable. Here, then, the probability we assign to winning or losing—that is, the likelihood of victory and the risk of defeat—comes down to epistemic conditions, not observer-independent facts.

A final account holds that risk blends the other two. According to this hybrid account, risks and probabilities are determined by beliefs about causal facts.[26] Consider the reasonable-person standard employed in areas of law. To convict a murder suspect, one does not calculate the objective probability that the suspect did it. Nor does one poll random individuals for their subjective determination based on their knowledge of the case. Instead, what matters is whether a reasonable person, with access to a set of facts determined by the court, would consider the suspect guilty beyond a reasonable doubt—that is, with a very high probability.

Which of these three accounts should we adopt? Any account of risk must fulfill two essential functions. Descriptively, it must establish relevant causal factors—for instance, it must establish that consuming alcohol and driving fast increase the risk of being involved in a car accident. Normatively, an account of risk must be able to differentiate between morally relevant and irrelevant acts leading to heightened risk, enabling assignment of responsibilities for risk reduction. For instance, if increased risk to Dean is his own doing—for instance, because he speeds on the highway—then it is his responsibility to reduce the risk to himself. If risk to Dean is a result of poor roads, then responsibility falls to the government to fix the roads.

I adopt the hybrid account of risk for two primary reasons. First, it fulfills both descriptive and normative functions. Second, partly owing to the first reason, hybrid accounts are frequently employed in practical cases. They are commonly utilized to comprehend how the state or other entities, such as corporations, should address risks encountered by populations they serve, for instance, risks posed by natural disasters.[27]

[25] For a discussion about the differences between objective and subjective accounts of risk, *see* Sven Ove Hansson, *Risk: Objective or Subjective, Facts or Values*, 13 J. Risk Res. 231 (2010).

[26] For a defense of a hybrid account of risk, *see* John Oberdiek, *Moralizing Risk*, *in* Imposing Risk: A Normative Framework 35, 35–58 (2017).

[27] *Id.* at 15–32.

In the next section, I argue that a crucial objective of a just war against a terrorist organization is to reduce the terrorist risk to the defender's population to an acceptable level. We will find that the acceptable level varies across different sectors of the population. We will also find that some sectors can be protected while causing no more than proportionate harm, while reducing risk sufficiently for other sectors is impossible without engaging in disproportionate harm.

Risk in the Termination of Counterterrorism Wars

It seems common-sensical that the state's duty to reduce risk from terrorist attacks is at least comparable to its duty to protect individuals from other hazards: from road accidents, medical emergencies, natural disasters, and so on. That is, the state is responsible for ensuring some minimum level of protection from harms generally, hence it must assure that level of protection from terrorism. For simplicity, I consider road accidents as a representative case. Consider one version of how we might then characterize the state's responsibility to reduce the risk due to terrorism:

> *Version I*: The goal of a counterterrorism war is achieved when the average risk of harm to a citizen is less than a specified threshold, being the acceptable risk of a road accident. The war should end once this goal is achieved or when achieving it becomes disproportionate.[28]

Per Version I, the counterterrorism war should end when the goal of reducing risk is achieved or else when achieving it becomes disproportionate. But Version I fails to acknowledge that the moral duty of the state to safeguard citizens from risk can vary in stringency, contingent on the nature of the threat. Most people believe that the state's duty to protect them from terrorist attacks outstrips its duty to protect them from car accidents or other risks of daily life, even as the latter risks are, in numerical terms, far greater.

Why is this so? First, we need to recognize that the public perception of the risk of death from a terrorist attack is exaggerated due to cognitive biases.[29] For instance, the availability bias, which occurs when people rely on information that is readily available to them, rather than seeking out all relevant information when making decisions or forming judgments. This bias can lead individuals

[28] That is, if there are N civilians and the risk of individual *i* being killed by a terrorist attack is r_i, the condition for ending the war is that $\frac{\sum_{i=1}^{N} r_i}{N} < p$.

[29] *See* Åsa Boholm, *Comparative Studies of Risk Perception: A Review of Twenty Years of Research*, 1 J. Risk Res. 135 (1998); Baruch Fischhoff et al., *How Safe Is Safe Enough? A Psychometric Study of Attitudes Toward Technological Risks and Benefits*, 9 Pol'y Sci. 127 (1978).

to give disproportionate weight to information that comes to mind easily, often because that information is vivid or personally relevant or because it relates to recent events. Importantly, the mental harm associated with exaggerated risk perception is real and consequential, even if the risk itself is actually low. This mental harm is worth mitigating.

Second, we also need to recognize that public willingness to tolerate risk from terrorist attacks is low because terrorism is perceived as a source of involuntary risk, whereas death from road accidents is viewed as voluntary—at least when it comes to drivers and passengers, the great majority of those killed or injured in road accidents. There exists a psychological inclination to tolerate voluntary risks to a much higher degree than involuntary ones.[30]

Finally, terrorism, akin to crime, is perceived by the public as violating the fundamental function of the state.[31] Some citizens believe the state is responsible for protecting citizens from any harm, but this is controversial. What is not controversial is that states have responsibility to secure citizens against harms due to violence. Consequently, acts of terrorism are seen as demanding an especially vigorous government response.

These reasons at least arguably justify governments acting more robustly in response to the low risk of terrorist violence than they do in response to the relatively high risk of death due to car accidents. However, these reasons do not, in themselves, justify taking unlimited action to reduce the risk of terrorism to zero, no matter what the public demands. That people are more willing to accept voluntary than involuntary risk does not entail that it is rational to accept voluntary risks one thousand times greater than that of involuntary risks, as demonstrated by the classic studies of Chauncey Starr.[32]

Still, in democratic societies, governments should respect citizens' wishes to consider some risks as more significant than others. The preceding caveats only demonstrate that there is no moral obligation for the government to reduce this risk to zero or to view the risk of terrorism as *sui generis*. There exists a level of terrorism risk so low that the government has fulfilled its duty to protect citizens from terrorist attacks, even if that level must be significantly lower than the level of risk due to road accidents.

[30] John Mueller & Mark G. Stewart, *The Terrorism Delusion: America's Overwrought Response to September 11*, 37 Int'l Sec. 81 (2012); T.R Lee, *The Public's Perception of Risk and the Question of Irrationality*, 376 Proc. Royal Soc'y London 5 (1981).

[31] Arie W. Kruglanski et al., *What Should This Fight Be Called? Metaphors of Counterterrorism and Their Implications*, 8 Psychol. Sci. Pub. Int. 97 (2007); Heinz Steinert, *The Indispensable Metaphor of War: On Populist Politics and the State's Monopoly of Force*, 7 Theoretical Criminology 265 (2003).

[32] Chauncey Starr, *Social Benefit versus Technological Risk*, 165 Science 1232 (1969).

With respect to self-defense, Gabriella Blum and David Luban have called this risk level "*morally legitimate bearable risk*."[33] They argue that this is the greatest degree of risk a state can be required to accept before it can claim justification in defending its citizens, given that it must do so by military force, which means that others will themselves be placed at risk.[34] This view assumes that states and their citizens can reasonably prioritize security risks without being irrational.[35]

While I agree with Blum and Luban that it is morally acceptable to distinguish risk from terrorism and risk from more common causes, and that it is not morally justified to demand that states reduce terror risk to zero, I think that their approach is not wholly satisfying. The trouble is that, implicitly, Blum and Luban consider morally legitimate bearable risk to be a point rather than a range. Once this goal is reached, the goal of the war is achieved, and any further use of force is presumptively disproportionate.

This results in challenges, for two reasons. First, it risks undervaluing the lives of citizens in large countries. To illustrate, consider Iceland with a population of about 400,000 people and China with approximately 1,400,000,000. Now suppose the point of morally legitimate bearable risk is set at 0.1 percent of the population killed by terrorists, per decade. In this case, once 400 Icelanders are killed in terrorist attacks in the course of a decade, Iceland is justified in the use of force. Must China endure 1,400,000 deaths by terrorism per decade before it is justified in using force? This is highly counterintuitive. It seems obviously wrong that a Chinese person's life is worth less than an Icelander's—that it is less worthy of protection—simply because the Chinese person has many more fellow citizens than does the Icelander.

Second, the risk of harm from terrorist attacks is not evenly distributed. It is significantly higher in certain areas, such as those near war zones or particular prominent civilian sites. It seems clearly unacceptable that some people should be left constantly to suffer a high risk of harm just because the average risk across the population of their state is low. This principle is obvious by analogy. Imagine a case in which economically disadvantaged people face a significantly higher risk of being killed in road accidents because they cannot afford safer new cars. Even if the overall risk of citizens being killed in a road accident is low, the state has not fulfilled its protective duty unless and until the risk to the economically disadvantaged is also acceptably low. This might involve implementing measures such as ensuring that even old and inexpensive cars meet stringent safety standards.

[33] Gabriella Blum & David Luban, *Unsatisfying Wars: Degrees of Risk and the* Jus ex Bello, 125 Ethics 751 (2015) (emphasis added).
[34] *Id.* at 763.
[35] *Id.*

A revision of Blum and Luban's position should acknowledge that the state's responsibility is to take appropriate care to protect all its citizens from harm, rather than solely focusing on lowering the average risk. Consider:

> *Version II*: The goal of a counterterrorism war is achieved when the risk to the most at-risk person falls below a specified threshold. The war should end once this goal is achieved or when achieving it becomes disproportionate.[36]

While Version II offers heightened protection to individual civilians, its practical implementation poses significant challenges. Drawing a parallel with road accidents, ensuring that the maximal risk anyone faces from driving remains below the acceptable threshold would necessitate drastic measures. These might include alcohol prohibition and installed speed governors that restrict driver behavior without possibility of user override. It may well be necessary to simply ban cars altogether to ensure that the risk to all would be below the threshold.

Version II also is unrealistic as a goal of a counterterrorism war. The reduction of risk to all of the defender's citizens to the necessarily low level may require inflicting great harm on nonliable persons and thus would be grossly disproportionate. For example, demanding that frontline troops face no greater risk than noncombatants in the rear would necessitate very permissive rules of engagement, allowing an army to fire at targets on the basis of even slight suspicion that the targets pose risk to troops. Or consider another scenario, in which the state attempts to ensure near-zero risk to every noncombatant on its frontier. The state might have to forbid all entry from countries in which a particular terrorist organization originates, or engage in indefinite bombing campaigns in those countries. Because achieving the goal in Version II imposes a high risk of harm to nonliable persons, the war contemplated here would surely become disproportionate before its aims are achieved.[37] Version II therefore also fails.

Versions I and II fail because they both employ the wrong *reference classes*. A reference class is a group of objects, persons, or events used for probability assessment. For example, one estimates the probability of a combatant being killed in war by considering the percentage of similar combatants, in similar units facing similar risks—the reference class—who were killed in war.

In Version I, the reference class used is overly broad, encompassing all of the defender's citizens, which overlooks morally relevant distinctions among subgroups, particularly the critical difference between combatants and

[36] That is, if there are N civilians and the risk of individual x_i being killed by a terrorist attack is r_i, the condition for ending the war is that $\frac{\sum_{i=1}^{N} r_i}{N} < p$.

[37] The moral significance of risk imposition and the ethical standards governing such imposition is complex. For an excellent overview of the moral problems of risk imposition, *see* Madeleine Hayenhjelm & Jonathan Wolff, *The Moral Problem of Risk Impositions: A Survey of the Literature*, 20 Eur. J. Phil. 26 (2012).

noncombatants. For its part, Version II considers too many reference classes—specifically, all subgroups consisting of one individual citizen.

The solution lies in a middle way. The relevant reference classes are neither the broadest (all of the defender's citizens) nor the narrowest (each individual citizen). I suggest that the correct interpretation of the state's duty to reduce risk involves minimizing the risk to relevant reference classes of civilians, particularly those at highest risk.

> *Version III*: The goal of a counterterrorism war is achieved when the average risk to all relevant reference classes falls below a specified threshold. The war should end once this goal is achieved or when achieving it becomes disproportionate.[38]

In Version III, the challenge lies in determining what the relevant reference classes are, and in ensuring they are appropriately tailored to the level of risk. We can see how this works in the context of road safety, in which policymakers routinely identify a range of reference classes based on which groups face higher or lower levels of risk. High-risk groups include young drivers, those driving impaired by alcohol, those sharing roads with impaired drivers, and those driving unsafe vehicles. States address these disparities through specific rules and regulations. For example, they mandate that young people drive with a companion and impose penalties that deter impaired driving. These measures strategically allocate resources, reducing risk to members of relevant reference classes.

These reference classes are tailored to be neither overly specific nor overly broad. Reducing the risk of a road accident for *every* driver by requiring an experienced companion to join them on every trip is clearly impractical. At the same time, it is clearly impermissible for the government to allow the economically disadvantaged to suffer a high risk of road accidents merely because the average risk to citizens generally is low.

Similar dynamics emerge in war, in which certain groups face elevated risks. Combatants are an obvious example, but others at high risk may include those residing near conflict areas, in proximity to strategic targets, or belonging to a particular population group (for instance, an ethnic group) targeted by terrorists. The reference classes must not be overly specific, preventing the need for drastic measures like endless war to reduce the risk of terrorism to each individual citizen below an acceptable threshold. At the same time, the reference classes cannot be overly broad, as it is impermissible for the state to allow, say, ethnic minorities to be persecuted by terrorist organizations merely because the average overall risk to citizens is low.

[38] That is, if there are N civilians and the risk of individual x_i being killed by a terrorist attack is r_i, the condition for ending the war is that $max\,\{r_1, r_2, \ldots r_N\} < p_0$.

Version III has a significant advantage over Version II: it is easier to satisfy the demand that the average risk to every reference class be lower than the threshold than to ensure that the actual risk to every individual citizen be lower than the threshold, if only because there are far fewer reference classes than individual citizens. Achieving the latter is very costly and therefore likely disproportionate, while achieving the former requires less costly, and therefore potentially proportionate, means. For instance, stricter security control in ports of entry may well be sufficient to ensure low-enough average risk to those in the reference class of civilians. Such controls impose only small costs on nonliable persons—longer lines at airports, say—and therefore are likely proportionate.

Version III still faces problems in the case of reference classes whose members face a high risk of harm, such as combatants. Ensuring that every frontline soldier faces no more than the threshold level of risk requires greater harm to nonliable persons than does ensuring that the average frontline soldier faces no more than the threshold level of risk. However, reducing the average risk a frontline soldier faces below the threshold would still demand permissive rules of engagement. It would still likely necessitate allowing troops to fire on targets even on a slight suspicion that they pose a risk. Consequently, Version III, too, requires revision.

To revise Version III, note an important difference between risk of death from road accidents and from terrorist attacks. Nearly every driver or passenger has the right to be equally protected from the risk of being killed in a road accident. There are exceptions, as in the cases of race car or ambulance drivers. But these exceptions are rare and prove the rule.

In contrast, in the context of counterterrorism war, not only do different reference classes face substantial differences in risks, but there are also variations in the maximal risk the state may demand these groups face. Importantly, combatants are generally assumed to be capable of facing relatively high risk, given their training and preparation. Consequently, the maximal risk they may be required to incur could be higher than that legitimately faced by most civilians. The state has no right to send soldiers on missions with a very high chance of being killed, but it does have the right to demand that soldiers face much higher risk in combat than, say, when driving alongside fellow civilians. So Version III is revised as follows:

> *Version IV*: The goal of a counterterrorism war is achieved when the average risk of harm to each relevant reference class is below the threshold risk assumed by the reference class members. The war should end once this goal is achieved or when achieving it becomes disproportionate.[39]

[39] This criterion translates to the following: for every $1 < i < n$, if reference class R_i has N_i members $x_{i1}, x_{i2}, \ldots x_{iNi}$, the average risk per reference class, $\frac{\Sigma_{j=1}^{N_i} x_{ij}}{N_i} < p_i$.

Version IV addresses both the problem of the acceptable harm from terrorism being too high, on par with death from road accidents, and the opposing issue of setting the acceptable risk level so low that achieving it is impossible without disproportionate use of force. The first problem is resolved by recognizing that many, if not most, citizens may rightly demand that the state use force to ensure a very low risk of death from terrorism. Thus, significant force may be employed to prevent attacks posing a threat to particular noncombatants on the home front, even if the average risk to noncombatants posed by such an attack is low. The second problem is mitigated by the understanding that the state is not obliged to use force to ensure an extremely low risk for every individual citizen, or even for every reference class. Combatants, for example, are a reference class that may legitimately be exposed to relatively high average risk.

Version IV defines an achievable goal because the defender can realize its aims while inflicting only proportionate harm on the nonliable. Consider that reducing to a very low level the average risk to civilians in the rear requires much less use of force than reducing to a similar level the average risk to soldiers at the front—stricter border controls versus permissive rules of engagement. Strict border controls reduce risk to the defender's civilians without imposing significant harm on anyone. Meanwhile, at the front, conservative rules of engagement may be sufficient to keep the average risk to soldiers below the maximal level of risk that *soldiers* are required to endure. Soldiers do not cause disproportionate harm in order that they face sufficiently low risk; this is in the nature of soldiering. Version IV allows us to defend each reference class according to its legitimate risk expectations, without engaging in disproportionate use of force.

Conclusion: Ending Wars on Terror

A crucial objective of a just war in our moment is to reduce the risk to civilians of terrorist violence to a morally acceptable level consistent with the state's duty to protect civilians from harm. But because terrorists typically cannot be defeated in a traditional sense, there is great risk that just defensive wars against them will go on endlessly, becoming disproportionate.

The tools of just war theory can help us to establish at what point even a justified war on terror should cease lest it become disproportionate and therefore no longer just. I have laid out a framework that can help us determine what this point is—a framework based on the careful consideration of risks. By taking seriously the differential risk tolerance of various sectors of the population, we can ascertain risk thresholds whose achievement constitutes a legitimate goal of war.

Preventing wars against terrorism from spiraling endlessly means giving up on the unrealistic proposition that the whole population could ever enjoy zero risk by legitimate—that is, proportionate—means. Justice demands proportionality, which in this case necessitates proper assessment of risk thresholds among different reference classes within a population. These thresholds establish the point at which the state has fulfilled its protective duty and therefore must stop using force for protective purposes. Yet it is entirely possible that disproportionate harm will occur before these thresholds are achieved. In these cases as well, such wars must, as a matter of justice, come to an end.

19

Forever War and the *Jus Ex Bello*

Tom Dannenbaum

Introduction

On September 21, 2021, then-President Joe Biden announced that the United States' was finally "not at war" after its withdrawal from Afghanistan.[1] Days later, Acting Solicitor General Brian Fletcher argued, "notwithstanding the withdrawal . . . we continue to be engaged in hostilities with al-Qaeda and, therefore, the detention under law of war remains proper."[2] The doublespeak continued through the 2024 election campaign,[3] but there is little doubt that Fletcher's statement is more faithful to the government's long-standing legal position. The posited conflict remains the legal predicate for detention at Guantánamo, "over-the-horizon" strikes in Afghanistan and elsewhere, and military operations against an array of groups, many of whose links to the war's origins are tenuous at best.

In 2012, then–General Counsel of the U.S. Department of Defense Jeh Johnson predicted a "tipping point" at which al-Qaeda's capabilities will have been so degraded as to preclude a strategic attack against the United States, thereby terminating the "'armed conflict' against al-Qaeda and its associated forces."[4] The statement was significantly more measured than former President George W. Bush's rallying cry to Congress in September 2001, when he proclaimed that the "war on terror begins with al Qaeda, but it . . . will not end until every terrorist group of global reach has been found, stopped and defeated."[5] However, even

[1] Remarks by President Biden Before the 76th Session of the United Nations General Assembly, New York, NY (Sept. 21, 2021), https://www.whitehouse.gov/briefing-room/speeches-remarks/2021/09/21/remarks-by-president-biden-before-the-76th-session-of-the-united-nations-general-assembly/.

[2] United States v. Zubaydah, No. 20-827 Supreme Court of the United States, Oral Argument Transcript, 79–80 (Oct. 6, 2021), https://www.supremecourt.gov/oral_arguments/argument_transcripts/2021/20-827_m6hn.pdf.

[3] *See, e.g., Full Transcript of Biden's Speech on Ending His Run for Re-election*, N.Y. Times (July 24, 2024).

[4] Jeh Charles Johnson Jr., "The Conflict Against Al Qaeda and its Affiliates: How Will It End?," Speech to the Oxford Union (Nov. 30, 2012), http://www.lawfareblog.com/2012/11/jeh-johnson-speech-atthe-oxford-union/.

[5] President George W. Bush, Address to a Joint Session of Congress and the American People, Washington, D.C. (Sept. 20, 2001), https://georgewbush-whitehouse.archives.gov/news/releases/2001/09/20010920-8.html.

Tom Dannenbaum, *Forever War and the* Jus Ex Bello In: *Perpetual War and International Law*. Edited by: Brianna Rosen, Oxford University Press. © Oxford University Press 2026.
DOI: 10.1093/oso/9780197748992.003.0019

adopting Johnson's approach, the problem of perpetuity is clear. Particularly given expansive assessments of belligerent participation ("affiliates" or "associated forces"), the statement presaged an apparently chronic posture of armed conflict—the "Forever War."[6]

As Mary L. Dudziak and Cheyney Ryan emphasize in this volume, perpetual war is not new.[7] However, the United States' sprawling temporal and geographic projection of military force in the decades since 9/11 has provoked multidimensional law and policy debates, many of which are revisited in this volume. Focusing on one of the less-explored legal issues, this chapter evaluates whether there is a point at which international law requires a state belligerent to stop fighting—or, more precisely, to cease its contributions to the perpetuation of an armed conflict. This parallels the moral question identified by just war theorists as *jus ex bello* or *jus terminatio* (the justice of ending or terminating war).[8]

The importance of this question inheres in the fact that war involves the infliction of death, destruction, and suffering through methods that would be impermissible in any other context. Partly for that reason, contemporary international law is structured around a comprehensive prohibition on the resort to force, with permissions defined by their exceptionality in relation to that ban.[9] This *jus ad bellum* framework is the central component of a system that aspires to "save succeeding generations from the scourge of war."[10] Could it be that once an exception to the prohibition has been activated, and armed conflict initiated, the morally urgent question of whether to perpetuate the war lacks a legal equivalent?

Drawing on necessity and proportionality in the *jus ad bellum* and human rights law, as well as underlying legal principles relating to the pursuit of peace, this chapter contends that international law includes the foundations of an obligation to cease fighting beyond a certain point. Underdeveloped though it may be, an elemental *jus ex bello* exists in international law today.

Of course, decisions relating to the resort to, and perpetuation of, force are among those on which deference to executive decision makers is greatest and the enforcement of law is most complicated. However, even assuming nonjusticiability (a topic beyond this chapter's scope), the identification of relevant international legal obligations can provide a normative framework for

[6] I use the singular to capture the United States' framing, not to obscure the multiplicity of conflicts and other engagements.

[7] *See* Chapter 2, "How Law, History, and Culture Enabled Perpetual War," and Chapter 3, "Endless War as Aimless War," of this volume, respectively.

[8] *Symposium on Ending Wars* 125(3) ETHICS (2015).

[9] *See, e.g.*, Tom Dannenbaum, *Why Have We Criminalized Aggressive War?*, 126 YALE L.J. 1242 (2017); Jens David Ohlin, *The Crime of Bootstrapping*, in THE CRIME OF AGGRESSION: A COMMENTARY 1454 (Claus Kreß & Stefan Barriga eds., 2017); Frédéric Mégret, *What Is the Specific Evil of Aggression?*, in *id.* 1398.

[10] U.N. Charter, T.S. 993 (1945), Preamble.

political action, thus helping to shape public and intragovernmental discourse, as well as third state evaluation and response.

Part one of this chapter distinguishes the topic at hand from the aspects of perpetual armed conflict that have drawn most legal attention. Part two details the ways in which existing legal sources—*jus ad bellum*, human rights law, and foundational imperatives to pursue peace—provide the intersecting basis for an elemental *jus ex bello*. Part three responds to objections that this framework demands state self-abandonment or suffers fatal ambiguity.

Foreverness and the Law

Domestically, the foreverness of what was initially termed the "Global War on Terror" has motivated debates regarding the 2001 Authorization for Use of Military Force (AUMF) and its possible repeal.[11] Although critically important, these arguments diverge from the issue addressed here. AUMF repeal advocates argue not that there is a legal obligation to end the war but that Congress should exercise its discretion to replace the existing AUMF with an authorization of narrower scope.[12] Quite apart from the absence of an identified international legal obligation in this discourse, congressional politics exclude the voices of those most acutely affected by the U.S. projection of force abroad.[13]

Internationally, the dominant analytical frame has been international humanitarian law (IHL). IHL provides specialized rules that apply only in international or non-international armed conflict (IAC/NIAC) or in belligerent occupation (a species of IAC).[14] Under commonly invoked approaches to the relationship between IHL and human rights law,[15] whether conduct falls within the scope of

[11] Authorization for Use of Military Force, 115 Stat. 966 – Public Law No. 107-40 (Sept. 18, 2001), https://www.congress.gov/bill/107th-congress/senate-joint-resolution/23/text. On repeal and replacement, Tess Bridgeman, *Now Is the Time to Repeal the 2002 AUMF*, Just Security (July 11, 2019); Brian Finucane, *Putting AUMF Repeal into Context*, Just Security (June 24, 2021).

[12] *See, e.g.*, Luke Hartig, *Five Principles to End the Forever War*, Just Security (Sept. 7, 2021); Brian Finucane, *Still at War*, Just Security (Apr. 7, 2022). H.J. Res. 52, 118th Congress, 1st Session, To Repeal and Replace the Authorization for Use of Military Force (Apr. 6, 2023), https://democrats-foreignaffairs.house.gov/index.cfm?a=Files.Serve&File_id=3A1EB5F8-C3BF-4026-B460-5E64C88C04E8.

[13] This is neither to downplay the burdens of participating as an agent of violence (Tom Dannenbaum, The Crime of Aggression, Humanity, and the Soldier ch.1 (2018)), nor to deny that risking one's own forces in resorting to war implicates human rights. Frédéric Mégret, *To Surrender or to Fight On? A Human Rights Perspective*, 5 Jus Cogens 32 (2023).

[14] *See, e.g.*, Geneva Convention Relative to the Protection of Civilian Persons in Time of War arts. 2–3, Aug. 12, 1949, 75 U.N.T.S. 287.

[15] When human rights law and IHL bear on the same issue, legal authorities have addressed tensions using various tools: *lex specialis* (the notion that the more specialized regime—IHL—ought to be definitive), coordinated interpretation (the notion that the rules should be interpreted harmoniously in light of one another), and cumulative application (the notion that unless they require

an armed conflict determines inter alia who can be detained or targeted with lethal force, for what reasons, and pursuant to what procedures, as well as whether that conduct is subject to the external jurisdiction associated with war crimes. Unsurprisingly, in a context of multidimensional sprawl, the reach of armed conflict has become a focal point of IHL debate. In addition to controversy regarding geographic[16] and participatory scope,[17] there is increasing attention to the question of when a NIAC terminates legally.[18] Jeh Johnson's "tipping point" sounds in this register.

Here, however, IHL is fact-responsive rather than normative; whether armed conflict obtains is orthogonal to whether a given party has the legal *right* to contribute to its perpetuation. This fact-responsiveness reflects the regime's legal limits and doctrinal independence.[19] IHL aims to limit the harms of war as much as possible, *given* the parties' presumed mutual commitment to fight. Performing that function is understood to require agnosticism as to which if any of the parties has a right to be in the fight.[20] From that perspective, the foreverness of the Forever War is a fact determining IHL's applicability, rather than a reality that any belligerent is required to change.

In interstate conflict, the *jus ad bellum* helps to close the normative gap left by IHL's agnosticism regarding the resort to force, including specifically as it pertains to human protection. Thus understood, the *jus ad bellum* is not simply a regime for protecting sovereignty or abstract states' rights. It also incorporates the wrongfulness of the IHL-compliant death, destruction, and suffering inflicted by a state that lacks a legal basis for being in the fight.[21] This is reflected in the Human Rights Committee's General Comment 36, which reasoned that all the killing inflicted in an aggressive war—IHL-compliant or not—is *ipso facto*

contradictory things, they should be applied independently, with the more demanding rule therefore dominating—sometimes described as *pro homine* or *lex protector*).

16 ICRC, International Humanitarian Law and the Challenges of Contemporary Armed Conflicts, 32IC/15/11, 32nd International Conference of the Red Cross and Red Crescent (Dec. 8–10, 2015), at 7–11.

17 Rebecca Ingber, *Co-Belligerency*, 42 Yale J. Int'l L. 67 (2017); Kevin Jon Heller, *The Use and Abuse of Analogy in IHL*, *in* Theoretical Boundaries of Armed Conflict & Human Rights (Jens Ohlin ed., 2016).

18 Dustin A. Lewis, Gabriella Blum, & Naz K. Modirzadeh, Indefinite War § 8 (Feb. 2017).

19 Protocol Additional to the Geneva Conventions of 12 August 1949, and Relating to the Protection of Victims of International Armed Conflicts (Protocol I), June 8, 1977, 1125 U.N.T.S. 3, preamble [hereinafter AP I] (the Geneva Conventions and "this Protocol must be fully applied . . . without any adverse distinction based on the nature or origin of the armed conflict or on the causes espoused by or attributed to the Parties to the conflict").

20 *See, e.g.*, Janina Dill & Henry Shue, *Limiting the Killing in War*, 26 Ethics & Int'l Affs. 311 (2012).

21 *See supra* note 10.

a violation of the right to life (a point that can be extended straightforwardly to other affected rights).[22]

Of course, except during the early stages of the war in Afghanistan, most U.S. military activity in the Forever War has involved fighting non-state armed groups. When such operations lack host state consent, as in the case of U.S. attacks on ISIS in Syria or IS-Khorasan in Afghanistan after the U.S. withdrawal, the *jus ad bellum* remains relevant, albeit contested in its substantive content.[23] However, when a state acts on its own territory or with territorial state consent, as in the case of U.S. attacks on ISIS targets in Iraq or on Taliban and IS-Khorasan targets in Afghanistan before September 2021, there is no *jus ad bellum* restraint on the resort to force.

Here, the gap left by IHL's agnosticism demands a different solution. Persuasively, Anthony Dworkin, Eliav Lieblich, and others have identified international human rights law (IHRL) as a relevant, if largely untapped, source in this respect.[24] It is now relatively uncontroversial that human rights law applies in armed conflict. On questions relating to how the war is conducted, many take the view that IHL holds interpretive dominance, either as *lex specialis*[25] or through a process of coordinated interpretation that reaches a similar result.[26] However, the primary area related to war in which IHL is very clearly not *lex specialis* is the lawfulness of the resort to force.[27] The human rights stakes associated with that question are undeniable, as reflected in the notion that the *jus ad bellum* determines the meaning of IHRL on harms arising from the resort to force between states. It follows that on issues with respect to which neither IHL nor the *jus ad bellum* provides a specialized legal framework, human rights law necessarily stands as *lex generalis* unmodified by any *lex specialis*. The resort to force between states and non-state armed groups on their (or a consenting state's) territory is precisely such an issue.

Less clear is what this entails. Absent an organized armed insurgency, human rights law precludes resort to status-based killing, administrative security

[22] Human Rights Committee, General Comment 36, U.N. Doc. CCPR/C/GC/36 (Sept. 3, 2019), para. 70.

[23] Debate centers on whether self-defense can be invoked only if the state on whose territory force is used can be attributed with the armed attack or (as some states assert) also if the territorial state is "unable or unwilling" to prevent imminent or ongoing armed attacks by the targeted non-state group. Ashley Deeks, *Unwilling or Unable*, 52 Va. J. Int'l L. 483 (2012); Olivier Corten, *The "Unwilling or Unable" Test*, 29 Leiden J. Int'l L. 777 (2016); Craig Martin, *Challenging and Refining the "Unwilling or Unable" Doctrine*, 52 Vand. J. Transnat'l L. 387 (2019).

[24] Anthony Dworkin, *Individual, Not Collective*, 93 Int'l L. Stud. 476 (2017); Eliav Lieblich, *Internal Jus ad Bellum*, 67 Hastings L.J. 687 (2016).

[25] Advisory Opinion on the Legality of the Threat or Use of Nuclear Weapons, International Court of Justice (July 8, 1996), para. 25.

[26] Hassan v. U.K., ECtHR [GC] App. No. 29750/09 (2014), paras. 96–111.

[27] Eliav Lieblich, *The Facilitative Function of* Jus in Bello, 30 Eur. J. Int'l L. 321 (2019).

detention, and other ordinary methods of war.[28] Such actions would impair human rights without being necessary and proportionate to the pursuit of a legitimate aim (the key criteria for lawful rights limitation). A state's widespread or systematic resort to military violence in such a situation would likely constitute a crime against humanity.[29]

Once an armed insurgency exists, the more conservative interpretation of human rights law is that the state may resort to force to quell it. However, it has also been argued that states sometimes lack the basis to resort to war methods in response to organized armed uprising. For Dworkin, this is because IHL does not directly authorize such methods in NIACs, so their use would need to be assessed individually in each encounter, pursuant to a human rights analysis of whether the state could have used less harmful means to suppress the threat—a test that may be satisfied by ordinary methods of war in areas of intense fighting, but not elsewhere.[30] Alternatively, per Lieblich, the state may lack the authority to resort to force if the adversary organized armed group itself acts pursuant to a legal right to use force.[31] Notably, in assessing Russian actions against Chechen rebels, the European Court of Human Rights identified the state's legitimate aim in impairing the right to life as the suppression of "*illegal* armed insurgency," thus hinting at the possibility of a *lawful* armed insurgency.[32] Several states' constitutions allow for precisely that possibility.[33] Furthermore, Additional Protocol I recognizes the lawful belligerency of those waging wars of self-determination against colonial domination, alien occupation, or racist regimes.[34] These concepts could inform IHRL limits on the state's authority to resort to internal force.

Ultimately, however, missing from each line of analysis outlined in the preceding (U.S. law, IHL, *jus ad bellum*, and human rights) is a legal framework for analyzing the normative question implicated by foreverness—namely, when, and pursuant to what criteria, a belligerent must stop fighting. Absent such a requirement, one or more warring parties may seek to perpetuate armed conflict to take advantage of IHL's more relaxed constraints on killing, detention, and other practices.[35] That moral hazard may be particularly perilous as applied to

[28] *Id.* at 740–43; Tom Dannenbaum, *War Crimes and Just War Theory*, in The Palgrave Handbook of Applied Ethics and the Criminal Law 775, 785–90 (2019).

[29] Dannenbaum, *supra* note 9, at 1272–73;

[30] Dworkin, *supra* note 24.

[31] Lieblich, *supra* note 24, at 743–46.

[32] Isayeva v. Russia, ECtHR, App. No. 57950/00 (Feb. 24, 2005), para. 180.

[33] Chiara Redaelli, *Revolution*, Max Planck Encyclopedia of Comparative Constitutional Law (2021).

[34] AP I, *supra* note 19, art 1(4).

[35] Dannenbaum, *supra* note 28, at 788–90; Derek Jinks, *International Human Rights Law in Time of Armed Conflict, in* The Oxford Handbook of International Law in Armed Conflict 656, 669 (Andrew Clapham & Paola Gaeta eds., 2014); Lieblich, *supra* note 24, at 735.

state action against non-state armed groups abroad, where the political costs of acknowledging a lack of territorial control or elevating the status of armed opponents are minimal.

Jus Ex Bello in International Law

Two distinct *jus ex bello* questions must be distinguished. First, *whether* (and, if so, *when*) a belligerent has a legal obligation to cease contributing to conflict perpetuation. Second, *how* any such obligation is to be discharged.[36] The focus here is on the first. Three frameworks provide potentially intersecting legal sources of such an obligation: the *jus ad bellum*, inclusive of necessity and proportionality; human rights law, also inclusive of necessity and proportionality; and United Nations (U.N.) Charter and human rights imperatives to pursue peace.

Continuing Rules Governing the Resort to Force

Properly understood, *jus ad bellum* rules continue to apply after conflict initiation. The crimes against peace convictions of Karl Dönitz and Mamoru Shigemitsu after World War II were rooted exclusively in their contributions to waging aggressive war after those wars' initiation.[37] Many of their co-defendants were convicted in part on that basis, with the identified criminal conduct persisting to the wars' final days.[38] The International Criminal Court (ICC) Statute criminalizes not only "prepar[ing]" and "initiat[ing]" aggressive war but also "execut[ing]" it,[39] while codifying acts of aggression that are, in some cases, necessarily subsequent to conflict initiation, such as "military occupation . . . *resulting from* [an illegal] invasion or attack."[40] Regarding state responsibility, the Human Rights Committee has affirmed that *all* killings in an aggressive war violate the right to life,[41] and the International Court of Justice (ICJ) has

[36] The chaotic U.S. withdrawal from Afghanistan in 2021 underscored the stakes of this question. U.S. Department of State, After Action Review on Afghanistan January 2020–August 2021 (March 2022).

[37] United States v. Göring et al., Judgment, *in* 22 Trial of the Major War Criminals before the International Military Tribunal 411, 556–57 (1948); United States v. Araki et al., Judgment of 12 November 1948, *in* 20 The Tokyo War Crimes Trial 48,413, 49,831–32 (R. John Pritchard & Sonia Magbanua Zaide eds., 1981).

[38] United States v. Göring, *supra* note 37, at 467, 524–87; United States v. Araki, *supra* note 37, at 48,421–48,423, 49,774–49,858. *See also* United States v. von Leeb et al., *in* Trial War Criminals before the Nuremberg Military Tribunals under Control Council Law No. 10, at 462, 490 (1949).

[39] Rome Statute of the International Criminal Court, art. 8 *bis* (1), July 17, 1998, 2187 U.N.T.S. 90 (as amended Nov. 29, 2010, depository notification C.N.651.2010.TREATIES-8) [ICC Statute].

[40] ICC Statute, *id.*, art. 8bis(2)(a) [emphasis added].

[41] *Supra* note 22.

specified similarly "that, as a matter of principle, the loss of life caused by these internationally wrongful acts [including a *jus ad bellum* violation] gives rise to the obligation of Uganda to make full reparation."[42] Subsequently, the Court predicated its determination that Israel is under an "obligation to bring to an end its unlawful presence in the Occupied Palestinian Territory" on the enduring application of the *jus ad bellum* (specifically the component prohibiting forcible territorial acquisition) to a decades-long belligerent occupation (in which IHL governs).[43]

Uniting these determinations is a basic principle: even IHL-compliant actions in furtherance of aggressive war are unlawful at the *ad bellum* level. Absent a separate justification, the only way to avoid compounding the *ad bellum* violation in such a scenario is to cease fighting.[44] Intricate belligerent entanglement may complicate *how* to withdraw in a way that minimizes harm. However, regarding *whether* to stop, the aggressor has an immediate and continuing legal obligation to do so, unless the war has changed so fundamentally that it is no longer properly characterized as a war of aggression at all.[45]

As explained earlier, in internal or consensual uses of force, human rights law provides the most plausible resort-to-force framework. Were the notion of lawful insurgency to gain traction, it might imply that the state that initiates

[42] Armed Activities on the Territory of the Congo (DRC v. Uganda) 2022 I.C.J. Rep. 13 (Feb. 9, 2022), para. 145.

[43] Legal Consequences arising from the Policies and Practices of Israel in the Occupied Palestinian Territory, including East Jerusalem, 2024 I.C.J. Rep. (July 19, 2024), paras. 174–79, 251, 253, 261, 267, 285(4).

[44] Morally, Cécile Fabre has advocated separating *jus ex bello* from *jus ad bellum*: we must sever the ethics of war termination from the ethics of war initiation: a belligerent who embarks on a just war (from its point of view) at time t1 might have a duty to sue for peace at t2 before it has achieved its ex hypothesi just war aims; conversely, a belligerent who embarks on an unjust war at t1 might acquire a justification for continuing at t2. Moreover, when assessing whether a belligerent must exit or continue with its war, we must pay attention to the various ways in which it might do so and to the goods and bads which a particular exit strategy would bring about relative to other strategies. Cécile Fabre, *War Exit*, 125 ETHICS 631, 652 (2015). Reflecting on the legal analogue of this issue, a couple of observations bear emphasis. Fabre's first scenario can be understood through the legal lens of *jus ad bellum* necessity and proportionality. In that respect, her argument is compatible with the analysis advanced here. Fabre's second scenario may appear more challenging. However, even if a scenario could arise in which an aggressor would have a legal basis for providing urgent military protection to a population facing atrocity, that would not justify the perpetuation *of aggression*. To the extent the protective act constitutes part of the aggressive war at all, its circumstances may entail a criminal defense against responsibility *for that particular component* of the aggression. ICC Statute, *supra* note 39, art. 31(1)(c). Alternatively, were the defensive war to transition into an overarching war of atrocity, the *jus ad bellum* status of the war may transform, such that fighting against that atrocity would no longer be properly understood as criminally aggressive. Dannenbaum, *supra* note 9, at 1295–1301. *See also infra* note 45. Finally, Fabre's scenario may bear on *how* the aggressive war is to be ended. For example, positive human rights obligations may preclude war exit that would abandon a population to atrocity.

[45] In certain circumstances, the original aggressor being forced into a posture of existential self-defense could ground a credible legal basis for its resort to force. However, this would entail not a right to continue the aggression, but a distinct right of self-defense, defined and limited by the defensive objective.

and perpetuates a conflict against such a group lacks a legitimate aim and therefore engages in a continuing human rights violation. On the more conservative, and likely dominant, understanding of existing law, even when a state resorts to force initially in violation of human rights law, once an armed insurgency exists, the question of fault in initiation is likely to dissipate in favor of the state's legal authority to restore its monopoly on the legitimate use of violence. On a common understanding of the interaction between IHL and IHRL, the state's compliance with the former would be sufficient, despite its responsibility for the condition triggering IHL's applicability, and thus the loosening of human rights constraints.[46] On that interpretation, states have greater freedom to bootstrap their way into a framework permissive of violence vis-à-vis non-state armed groups than they do vis-à-vis state forces. Conversely, as discussed earlier, most non-state armed groups have little legal basis for building an insurgency and perpetuating armed conflict, even if they were initially attacked.[47] Were more nuanced interpretations on this point to prevail, the range of contexts in which states would have a duty to cease perpetuating a NIAC for lack of a legitimate aim would grow.

In short, interstate aggressors have a clear continuing legal duty to cease perpetuating their wars of aggression, whereas states' authority to resort to force to suppress armed insurgencies is less clearly precluded by responsibility for the eruption of conflict. Across contexts, the more complicated question is whether there is a point at which even states that had a *lawful* basis for resorting to force must stop fighting. Here, necessity and proportionality are central, both in defining that point and in enabling analysis of perpetuation notwithstanding contestation regarding the legality of initiation.[48]

Ad Bellum Necessity and Proportionality

Just as it is unlawful to perpetuate (and not only to initiate) aggression, it must also be unlawful to perpetuate the use of defensive force beyond what is necessary and proportionate to the defensive objective (and not only to initiate defensive war when doing so is unnecessary or foreseeably disproportionate). This reflects international law's orientation toward peace and the reality that even

[46] *But see* Dworkin, *supra* note 24.

[47] For rare exceptions, *see supra* notes 33–34.

[48] The ICJ often invokes necessity and proportionality in the alternative in decisions relying primarily on the lack of an armed attack to ground self-defense. *See, e.g., Case Concerning Military and Paramilitary Activities in and Against Nicaragua (Merits) (Nicaragua v. United States)* 1986 I.C.J. Rep. 14 (June 27, 1986), paras. 176, 237; *Case Concerning Oil Platforms (Iran v. US)*, 2003 I.C.J. Rep. 161 (Nov. 6, 2003), para. 77; *Armed Activities on the Territory of the Congo (DRC v. Uganda)*, 2005 I.C.J. Rep. 168 (Dec. 19, 2005), para. 147.

IHL-compliant armed conflict diminishes human rights. It is, moreover, the logical implication of the function of necessity and proportionality, which define the resort to force as an exceptional response to an overwhelming imperative and deny that suffering an armed attack grants the attacked state unchecked belligerent authority. Aptly, there is broad support for those principles' continuing application.[49]

On *jus ad bellum* necessity, Chris O'Meara has usefully distinguished general and specific necessity.[50] The first relates to whether the resort to force is required to address the armed attack. The second asks whether the force under consideration is necessary to pursuing the war's defensive objective. As Noam Lubell and Amichai Cohen emphasize, "Both of these questions should be considered part of the necessity test."[51] Precision on this is essential to avoiding the common conflation of necessity and proportionality.

General necessity is particularly salient to the question of when to stop fighting. However, to what necessity must attach is debated. Answers span a spectrum from repelling the current attack to eliminating any prospect of future attack, with seemingly greater state tolerance for the latter (maximalist) standard in actions against non-state armed groups abroad than in wars between state forces.[52] Needless to say, the greater the range of interpretively viable positions, the weaker necessity's contribution to defining clear *jus ex bello* obligations. That problem of legal ambiguity is exacerbated by inevitable factual uncertainty regarding what is required to achieve even a clearly defined objective.[53]

Although resolving the interpretive question is beyond this chapter's scope, it is worth emphasizing that necessity attaches to the legal basis for resorting to force, which is defined not as the elimination of any possible threat but as defense against an armed attack.[54] The notion that the necessity component might allow whatever it takes to preclude even the possibility of a future attack by the initial aggressor is difficult to reconcile with that limited grounding. In any event, both the difficulty (perhaps impossibility) of total threat elimination and the relatively proximate value of significant threat reduction are such that perpetuating war toward the former objective would very likely be disproportionate.

[49] *See, e.g.*, Chris O'Meara, *Necessity and Proportionality and the Right of Self-Defence, in* International Law (2021); Eliav Lieblich, *On the Continuous and Concurrent Application of Ad Bellum and In Bello Proportionality, in* Necessity and Proportionality in International Peace & Security Law 41 (Claus Kreß & Robert Lawless eds., 2020); Judith Gardam, Necessity, Proportionality and the Use of Force by States 166–68 (2004); Adil Ahmad Haque, *Enough*, Just Security (Nov. 6, 2023). *But see* Ruth Wedgwood, *Proportionality and Necessity in American National Security Decision Making*, 86 Am. Soc. Int'l L. 59–61 (1992).

[50] O'Meara, *supra* note 49, ch. 2.

[51] Noam Lubell & Amichai Cohen, *Strategic Proportionality*, 96 Int'l L. Stud. 159, 168 (2020).

[52] O'Meara, *supra* note 49.

[53] *See* part three, "Objections," *infra*.

[54] U.N. Charter, T.S. 993 (1945) art. 51.

Jus ad bellum proportionality is also contested. It has been invoked as a quantitative (or tit-for-tat) test (reflected in notable respects in the ICJ's jurisprudence), as a means-end or teleological test (on which proportionality is defined by the imperative to halt and repel the aggressive threat), and as just war theory's balance of harms and benefits test.[55]

In assessing these alternatives, it is helpful to begin with a point of conceptual clarity. Lubell and Cohen correctly observe, "Proportionality, as a general principle of law, is concerned with measuring the effects of X in relation to Y, and is a separate step that follows from the necessity question."[56] In other words, whatever its ingredients, to perform its function, proportionality must remain distinct from the "question of whether the force used was more than actually required to achieve the aim." Therefore, the only conceptually viable version of the teleological approach is one that does not reduce to necessity but instead entails weighing the harm associated with defensive action (the means) against the expected value of the goal that justifies it (the end). This is different from (and more plausible than) both the backward-looking tit-for-tat analysis and the all-encompassing balance of benefits and harms approach.

In this vein, Gabriella Blum and David Luban frame *ad bellum* proportionality analysis as an effort to define the point at which it is appropriate to shift risk from one community to another.[57] Aptly, this focuses on the legitimate *purpose* of perpetuating war and *weighs* it against the key harms associated with doing so. Similarly, the International Law Association's Use of Force Committee asserts that *ad bellum* proportionality should be assessed according to "whether the harmful effects of the force taken in self-defence are outweighed by achieving the legitimate aims."[58] Adil Haque and Chris O'Meara have distilled relevant state practice and *opinio juris* indicating an obligation to weigh such considerations, at least if the defensive force goes beyond the immediate halt-and-repel objective (and toward some form of threat neutralization).[59]

Here, too, legal (and typically factual) disagreement limits the degree to which *ad bellum* proportionality analysis will produce clear *jus ex bello* thresholds. That difficulty and the significant challenge of how to evaluate proportionality over time are discussed further in the final section of this chapter.

[55] *See generally* David Kretzmer, *The Inherent Right to Self-Defence and Proportionality in* Jus Ad Bellum, 24 Eur. J. Int'l L. 235 (2013); Lieblich, *supra* note 49; Gardam, *supra* note 49; O'Meara, *supra* note 49.

[56] Lubell & Cohen, *supra* note 51, at 168.

[57] Gabriella Blum & David Luban, *Unsatisfying Wars*, 125 Ethics 751 (2015).

[58] International Law Association, Use of Force Committee, Final Report 12 (2018), https://www.ila-hq.org/en_GB/documents/conference-report-sydney-2018. *See also* Kretzmer, *supra* note 55, at 276–79; Gardam, *supra* note 49, at 166–67.

[59] Haque, *supra* note 49; Adil Ahmad Haque, *Proportionality in Self-Defense*, Just Security (Nov. 14, 2023); O'Meara, *supra* note 49, at 145.

Necessity and Proportionality in Human Rights

The human rights analogues of these principles can further equip legal analysis of conflict perpetuation. Necessity manifests in the form of a least harmful means test in human rights limitation analysis, as well as via an analogous test regarding the exigency of derogation. Proportionality involves balancing the value of the legitimate aim of a rights-limiting measure against the diminution of the right, whether in ordinary rights limitation or derogation analysis (although the latter function is less developed).

It is true, of course, that General Comment 36 did not supplement its affirmation of the human rights implications of aggression with a similarly explicit recognition of the parallel implications of *ad bellum* necessity and proportionality.[60] However, the latter association follows logically from the former. Notably, General Comment 36 *did* emphasize that "[e]fforts to avert the risks of war and any other armed conflict, and to strengthen international peace and security, are among the most important safeguards of the right to life."[61] Ultimately, however, it is in contexts to which the *jus ad bellum* does *not* apply that human rights law is indispensable to analyzing the perpetuation of armed conflict. Here, just as IHL's inapplicability to the question of internal resort entails that IHRL (as *lex generalis*) is the key interpretive framework for evaluating that question, so too IHL's inapplicability to the normative questions of *jus ex bello* implies IHRL's applicability as *lex generalis* on that point.

The aptness of turning to IHRL necessity and proportionality here is exemplified by their parallel roles in derogation analysis. The latter involves assessing emergency measures in contexts in which full human rights realization is temporarily impaired by the context of emergency, but where certain obligations endure and the emergency and its prolongation are themselves appropriate objects of human rights analysis. War is recognized explicitly as the kind of emergency that can ground derogation.[62]

Human rights derogation in armed conflict does not entail simple deference to IHL. In General Comment 29, the Human Rights Committee specified that, in addition to complying with other relevant regimes (such as IHL), derogations must *also* be of an "exceptional and temporary nature," be undertaken pursuant to a "public emergency which threatens the life of the nation," and be limited to

[60] HRC General Comment 36, *supra* note 22, para. 70.
[61] *Id.* para. 69.
[62] *See, e.g.*, Convention for the Protection of Human Rights and Fundamental Freedoms, 213 U.N.T.S. 221 (Nov. 4, 1950), art. 15(1); American Convention on Human Rights, 1144 U.N.T.S. 123 (Nov. 22, 1969), art. 27; Human Rights Committee, General Comment 29, U.N. Doc. CCPR/C/21/Rev.1/Add.11 (Aug. 31, 2001), para. 3; *Armed Activities*, *supra* note 48, para. 106; Legal Consequences of the Construction of a Wall in the Occupied Palestinian Territory, 2004 I.C.J. Rep. 136 (July 9, 2004), para. 106.

what is "strictly required by the exigencies" of that emergency, including with appropriate geographic, material, *and temporal* limits.[63] At the very least, this indicates a strict necessity test regarding the use of warfighting methods. The Committee has also invoked the concept of "proportionality" in this regard, reasoning that "no provision . . . will be entirely inapplicable" even under a valid derogation.[64]

The European Court of Human Rights specifies that rights derogation analysis must give "appropriate weight to such relevant factors as the *nature of the rights* affected by the derogation and the circumstances leading to, and the *duration* of, the emergency situation."[65] In short, all else equal, including the nature of the emergency, the derogability of the right, and the necessity of the derogation, a longer and more severely rights-impairing derogation would be more likely to breach human rights requirements as disproportionate. Similarly, the Court standardly tightens its margin of appreciation (narrowing the scope of state discretion) as the derogation lengthens. This reflects the insufficiency of asking merely whether the relevant rights adjustments are necessary in service of a particular end without also asking whether that end can justify the accumulated rights impairment.

Certain state belligerents have eschewed derogation, particularly in extraterritorial conflicts.[66] For others, derogation is absent from the treaty framework or inapplicable to the relevant right. Through treating IHL either as *lex specialis* or as interpretively dominant in a process of coordinated interpretation, certain courts and other bodies faced with such scenarios have allowed action that, but for a condition of armed conflict, would have impermissibly diminished human rights.[67] Dworkin has powerfully questioned this approach as applied to NIACs.[68] However, even if IHL *is* to play such an interpretive role, the fact that its rules are wholly insulated from whether the state is legally justified in resorting to the practices that sustain IHL's applicability precludes reducing human rights protection entirely to the IHL framework.

In other words, even accepting that non-derogating states may nonetheless invoke IHL's adjustment of human rights to the exigencies of armed conflict,[69] it

[63] HRC General Comment 29, *supra* note 62, paras. 2, 4–5.

[64] *Id.* para. 4.

[65] A v. United Kingdom, ECtHR App. No. 3455/05 (Feb. 19, 2009), para. 173. *See also* Brannigan and McBride v. United Kingdom, ECtHR App. Nos. 14553/89 & 14554/89 (May 26, 1993), para. 43; *id.* (Pettiti, J. dissenting); Aksoy v. Turkey, App. No. 21987/93 (Dec. 18, 1996), para. 68.

[66] Hassan v. UK, *supra* note 26, paras. 40–42, 101.

[67] *Id.* paras. 96–111; HRC General Comment 36, *supra* note 22, para. 64; Cruz Sánchez v. Peru, IACtHR Ser. C 292 (Apr. 17, 2015), paras. 257–79; African Commission on Human and Peoples' Rights, General Comment 3 (2015), paras. 27–35.

[68] Dworkin, *supra* note 24, at 497–504. In this volume, *see* Anthony Dworkin, Chapter 9, "Europe's Role in Perpetual War: From Counterpoint to Convergence."

[69] Hassan v. UK, *supra* note 26, paras. 96–111.

is implausible to permit that adjustment without reference to principles (necessity and proportionality) that (i) bear on questions to which IHL has no answer; (ii) have direct *jus ad bellum* analogues; (iii) frame rights-limitation and derogation analysis; and (iv) inform analysis of the emergency itself. The role of IHL as an interpretive tool can be justified with reference to the object and purpose of human rights law only if human rights doctrines pertaining to issues entirely outside the scope of IHL retain autonomous force, safeguarding against states perpetuating the very condition that loosens the constraints on their action.

This is not to determine justiciability or the appropriate standard of review on these matters. Nor is it to deny the challenges associated with concretizing such an analysis. However, recognizing the applicability of necessity and proportionality is the essential first step toward such concretization.

Peace and International Law

The legal imperative to pursue peace supports this line of analysis. That imperative is manifest inter alia in the asserted right of all persons "to enjoy peace such that all human rights are promoted and protected,"[70] and in U.N. member states' commitments to "save succeeding generations from the scourge of war," to "live together in peace," to ensure "that armed force shall not be used, save in the common interest," and to maintain "international peace and security," "friendly relations," and "universal peace."[71] Article 28 of the Universal Declaration of Human Rights asserts the entitlement "to a social and international order in which the rights and freedoms set forth in this Declaration can be fully realized," while the Human Rights Committee has reasoned that "[e]fforts to avert the risks of war and any other armed conflict, and to strengthen international peace and security, are among the most important safeguards of the right to life."[72] As Frédéric Mégret argues, this must include assessments not only of the state's obligations vis-à-vis the rights of those against whom it uses force but also its own citizens' right not to be sacrificed pointlessly.[73]

Of course, as Mégret acknowledges, the human rights duties of a state to its own people may also entail duties to (continue to) fight in certain contexts, such as when the human right to self-determination is implicated.[74] Similarly, Lieblich has emphasized that General Comment 36's articulation of states' duty

[70] G.A. Res. 71/189: Declaration on the Right to Peace, U.N. Doc. A/RES/71/189 (Dec. 19, 2016), art. 1. *See also* G.A. Res. 39/11: Declaration on the Right of Peoples to Peace (Nov. 12, 1984).

[71] U.N. Charter, T.S. 993 (1945), Preamble; arts. 1–2.

[72] G.A. Res. 271 A: Universal Declaration of Human Rights (Dec. 10, 1948), art. 28; HRC General Comment 36, *supra* note 22, para. 69.

[73] Mégret, *supra* note 13.

[74] *Id.* at 17–18.

to "protect lives and to oppose widespread or systematic attacks on the right to life, including acts of aggression" could drive conflict perpetuation.[75] For these reasons, caution is warranted in defining the implications of human rights analysis for resort-to-force decision-making. However, many of the identified pressures to fight (whether or not attributed to human rights) are already politically salient in most decisions to initiate or perpetuate war. The human rights reasons to *cease*, on the other hand, tend to be marginalized.

Objections

Two objections warrant consideration. First, the notion that a state could be required to stop fighting a defensive war might be thought to imply a politically, psychologically, and perhaps morally inconceivable duty of self-abandonment. Second, disagreement as to the ingredients and weights applicable to necessity and proportionality might be thought to nullify their *jus ex bello* utility, particularly when compounded by factual uncertainty regarding war's trajectory. Especially thorny as a legal question is how to count harms that have already occurred when assessing the proportionality of continuing the action that produced them.[76]

Self-Abandonment

Neither the notion that aggressors must cease perpetuating aggression nor the notion that defensive states must stop once fighting ceases to be defensively necessary imply a legal duty of self-abandonment. The concern arises instead with respect to the notion that a state could be required to stop waging a defensive war because the harm associated with its perpetuation would be disproportionate to the defensive goal. Responding to the notion that, at a certain point, continuing self-defense would be prohibited even in response to a "significant armed attack," Lieblich describes the approach as potentially "morally virtuous," but "doubtful" in its acceptability to states. He questions whether "any state ever refrained from responding to an armed attack because of the results of a universal harm-benefit analysis."[77] Janina Dill has argued that international law is ill-placed to sustain

[75] HRC General Comment 36, *supra* note 22, para. 70; Eliav Lieblich, *The Humanization of Jus ad Bellum*, 32 Eur. J. Int'l L. 579, 604–05 (2021).

[76] *See, e.g.*, Seth Lazar, *Moral Sunk Costs*, 68 Phil. Q. 841 (2018); Victor Tadros, *Past Killings and Proportionality in War*, 46 Phil. & Pub. Affs. 9 (2018); Elad Uzan, *Moral Sunk Costs in War and Self-Defence*, 71 Phil. Q. 359 (2020); *Symposium on Ending Wars* 125(3) Ethics (2015).

[77] Lieblich, *supra* note 49.

demands of self-abandonment due to its dependency on sovereign self-help.[78] Were the regime endowed with robust enforcement mechanisms, "the best way to uphold the rule of international law would be to constrain states' self- defense with absolute, justiciable limits."[79] However, absent such mechanisms, Dill argues, there is an extent to which, international law, unlike domestic law, "needs to retreat to sustain the rule of law in an emergency."[80]

Clearly, any law requiring self-abandonment is unlikely to motivate its addressee in the moment of that demand. However, this problem is not unique to international law. It applies equally to domestic legal demands that require individual self-abandonment prior to the availability of centralized enforcement.[81] Systems of security and enforcement within the state reduce the probability of this scenario arising for individuals as compared to states, but that does not mitigate the severity of the demand when it does arise. And yet such rules exist. This is not because law is oblivious to psychological or political reality. It is instead because eschewing a rule that could conceivably demand self-abandonment in an extreme case risks opening the door to a dangerous lack of constraint in other cases. In such circumstances, extreme cases may be addressed more effectively through excuse, mitigation, or non-enforcement, rather than through the eschewal of regulation. Far more commonly, what might be framed as a requirement of self-abandonment is in fact a requirement to bear certain risks or costs—a burden that is demanding but far from psychologically or politically absurd.

Indeed, international law frequently precludes states from fully vindicating their rights. The absence of any viable nonforcible alternative does not justify the use of force to remedy interstate rights-infringements below the threshold of an armed attack.[82] For the many states that reject the unable and unwilling theory of self-defense against non-state actors, this is also true of cross-border attacks by non-state armed groups that cannot be attributed to the state in which they are based and cannot be halted except through extraterritorial force.[83] In those scenarios in which defensive force *is* permitted, IHL violations are prohibited even if they would advance the legitimate defensive end.[84] During conflict, using

[78] Janina Dill, *Threats to State Survival as Emergencies in International Law*, 15 INT'L THEORY 155 (2023).

[79] *Id.* at 3.

[80] *Id.*

[81] R v. Dudley & Stephens, 14 QBD 273 (Dec. 9, 1884).

[82] *Military and Paramilitary Activities in and Against Nicaragua, supra* note 48, paras. 191–95; TALLINN MANUAL 2.0 ON THE INTERNATIONAL LAW APPLICABLE TO CYBER OPERATIONS 11–29, 301–48 (Michael N. Schmitt ed., 2017); TOM RUYS, "ARMED ATTACK," AND ARTICLE 51 OF THE U.N. CHARTER ch. 3 (2013).

[83] Elena Chachko & Ashley Deeks, *Which States Support the "Unwilling and Unable" Test*, LAWFARE (Oct. 10, 2016); Alex Moorehead, *Brazil's Robust Defense of the Legal Prohibition on the Use of Force and Self Defense*, JUST SECURITY (Apr. 20, 2018); Ruys, *supra* note 82, at 419–510.

[84] AP I, *supra* note 19, Preamble.

involuntary human shields to immunize a key military objective from attack is illegal, but that does not alleviate the adversary's obligation not to attack that objective if the expected civilian harm would be disproportionate.[85]

Of course, none of these constraints entails self-*abandonment*. In contrast, were Ukraine required to cease fighting against Russia's aggression due to the disproportionate costs of continuing, that would arguably entail a legal requirement to succumb to conquest and forgo self-determination. That, it might be thought, is past the point of normative plausibility.

This, however, is not a persuasive argument against the use of proportionality in *jus ex bello* analysis. First, unlike many of the other doctrines noted earlier, proportionality weighs and incorporates the value pursued. In other words, when ceasing to fight would entail self-abandonment, the profundity of that burden would elevate the threshold of permissible harm associated with continuing the defensive fight. Therefore, proportionality is rarely, if ever, likely to demand surrender in a genuinely existential war of self-defense.

Second, most defensive wars are not existential. All-out wars of territorial conquest have been a minority of aggressive uses of force in the U.N. Charter era. In the U.S. counterterrorism wars, for example, even the purported justification for perpetuation is not state survival. Wars of that kind are instead about the transfer of risk from one population to another.[86] As the risks imposed through defensive action escalate in relation to the risks avoided, how could the viability of claiming *ad bellum* or human rights proportionality in perpetuating conflict *not* be affected? To require the state to bear some security risks due to the severe harms associated with mitigating those risks is not to require self-abandonment; it is to impose a standard legal demand.

Third, with the exception of highly controversial language in the ICJ's *Nuclear Weapons* advisory opinion, defensive necessity in even existential conflicts is not generally thought to justify violating IHL.[87] Even more strikingly, criminal law sometimes demands that individuals accept the near certainty of their own deaths when there is no way for them to survive without engaging in grave criminal conduct.[88] In such extreme cases, the law's normativity is weak and enforcement may be eschewed or mitigated. And yet the rule is maintained to avoid the slippery slope of introducing an exception.

Ultimately, notwithstanding her observations regarding the international law's limits in contexts implicating state survival, Dill argues against a legal retreat

[85] *Id.* art. 51(8).

[86] Blum & Luban, *supra* note 57. *See also* in this volume, Brianna Rosen, Chapter 1, "Still at War: Law and the Erosion of Restraint," and Elad Uzan, Chapter 18, "Risk and Ending War."

[87] *Nuclear Weapons* Advisory Opinion, *supra* note 25, paras. 1, 95–97, 105(2)(E).

[88] R v. Dudley & Stephens, *supra* note 81; Prosecutor v. Erdemović, Case No. IT-96-22-A (7 October 1997), paras. 1–8, 20; *id.* (McDonald & Vorah, JJ sep. op.), paras. 32, 47–50, 55–66, 72, 75, 78–87.

from *jus ad bellum* proportionality. Specifically, she contends, "International law should preclude that a community emergency for the victim state becomes an 'international community emergency', that is, a threat to the survival of the international community," with the law properly "treat[ing] any escalation beyond the states at war as a first step toward an international community emergency."[89] For Dill, any such risk would be "disproportionate even to an aim as important as state survival."[90] Necessarily, the threshold of disproportionality would be lower for aims that do not reach that existential level.

Ambiguity

Additional challenges arise from dissensus regarding the object of necessity (from halt-and-repel to threat-elimination) and the components of proportionality (tit-for-tat, teleological, or harm-benefit). These are exacerbated by uncertainty regarding the likelihood of success and the costs of its pursuit. Proportionality is further hamstrung by both the lack of an agreed exchange rate for balancing incommensurate values and uncertainty regarding how to evaluate harm over time.

These ambiguities are real, but they should not prompt fatalism regarding the utility of necessity and proportionality as *jus ex bello* keystones. Rather, recognizing their importance ought to motivate demands that states clarify their positions on the meaning of the principles and defend their actions accordingly. At a minimum, this would facilitate holding states to political account pursuant to their own standards (itself a step forward from a discourse in which *jus ex bello* questions barely figure). More ambitiously, it could catalyze the coalescence of *opinio juris*.

This chapter does not purport to perform that harmonization. There is, however, one substantive issue that demands analysis here—namely, the legal analogue of what just war theorists have termed the problem of "moral sunk costs."[91] Ordinarily, proportionality entails a prospective analysis from the point of view of the law's addressee. *Jus ex bello* analysis, however, occurs in the ongoing war that is its object, raising the question of how to weigh the war's history in assessing the proportionality of continuing.

In just war theory, the sunk costs debate has settled into four camps, categorized by Victor Tadros as the Prospect, Quota, Discount, and Addition views.[92] On the Prospect view, war damage up to the point of analysis is straightforwardly

[89] Dill, *supra* note 78, at 22–23.
[90] *Id.* at 23.
[91] *See supra* note 76.
[92] Tadros, *supra* note 76.

sunk and thus irrelevant to whether to continue. Here, the decision to continue becomes functionally equivalent to a decision to initiate, evaluated in isolation from the preceding chain of similar decisions. The Quota approach, on the other hand, requires evaluating the war in its totality at any point in that chain. On this view, a war becomes disproportionate as soon as the aggregate harm exceeds the proportionality threshold defined at the point of initiation,[93] even if continuing to fight would promise gains exceeding *future* harms. The Discount view offers a middle ground, according to which the weight of legitimate reasons for continuing ought to be discounted progressively (but asymptotically) as the harms accumulate.[94] Finally, on the Addition view, sacrifices made over time are thought to *strengthen* the reasons for continuing due to the importance of ensuring that they were not in vain. Given the limited doctrinal attention to diachronic proportionality analysis, it is unclear how the question of sunk costs will be resolved legally. Nonetheless, a few observations can be offered.

The Addition view, although often politically motivating, lacks legal merit. Exceptions to the general prohibition on the use of force are limited to certain *kinds*: defense against armed attack and peace and security maintenance under Security Council authority. Fundamental rights are at stake in those limits. There is no legal basis for introducing reasons that are not of the requisite kind to warrant the initiation of war in assessing whether to perpetuate it.

The Quota view, on the other hand, might be thought to contradict the legal (and moral) principle that truly defensive action must be continually forward-looking, so as not to lapse into reprisal. Presuming a consistent quota for any given war also risks ossifying *jus ex bello* analysis, leaving it ill-equipped to adjust as the nature of the threat changes.

Given epistemic constraints and the interrelatedness of harm over time, a straightforward legal adoption of the Prospect view would also be problematic.[95] Epistemically, purely prospective analyses of (i) the ongoing attacks and threats that justify defensive action; (ii) the military imperatives arising from those threats; and (iii) the harms likely to be inflicted in pursuing defensive action are all inevitably speculative. Once a war is underway, however, a record starts to develop. Thus, even assuming the Prospect view is directionally correct, the fact that a war is approaching the proportionality limit as determined at the outset should prompt humility regarding predictions of success and the viability of containing associated harms. It should also improve public deliberation on

[93] Assuming lawful initiation, this would most likely be because the harms associated with the war exceeded initial expectations.

[94] Lazar, *supra* note 76.

[95] On deep morality: Jeff McMahan, *The Ethics of Killing in War*, 114 Ethics 693 (2004); Jeff McMahan, *The Morality of War and the Law of War*, *in* Just and Unjust Warriors 19 (David Rodin & Henry Shue eds., 2010). For a critique: Henry Shue, *Do We Need a "Morality of War"?*, in Fighting Hurt (2016).

the continuing resort to force, with publicly available data mitigating epistemic asymmetry in a context of informational classification. Along these lines, recent analysis of the effects of the U.S. targeted killing program ought to weigh heavily in deliberations regarding the legality of perpetuating the claimed armed conflict that underpins it.[96]

However, the deeper *ex bello* significance of the past burdens of war is that many of the relevant harms are not simply sunk. On the contrary, their reverberation through time is perhaps the most significant way in which proportionality in continuing war is distinct from the proportionality of initiation. The terror associated with life under the surveillance of weaponized drones, the suffering associated with long-term detention, and the anguish of deprivation due to encirclement or displacement are cumulative.[97] Enduring such harms after having suffered them already for two decades is not equivalent to enduring them for the first time. Similarly, the suffering associated with the prospect of their indeterminate continuation is likely to be shaped by the length of time for which they have already been borne. Past suffering shapes the meaning and severity of future suffering. Recognizing this may militate in favor of something closer to the Discount view.

Here, human rights jurisprudence on Guantánamo is instructive. Particularly striking is the Inter-American Commission on Human Rights' (IACHR's) evolving perspective over time. Having argued initially for IHL's applicability,[98] the Commission held a decade into the conflict that "although international humanitarian law is the *lex specialis* for determining states' obligations in these situations, in certain circumstances, its norms may not provide sufficient protection for the rights of the persons affected."[99] It emphasized that, notwithstanding the "duty of states to protect the security of their citizens," including sometimes through "the extension of normal periods of preventive or administrative detention," it is also the case that "extraordinary circumstances 'cannot serve as a pretext for the indefinite detention of individuals, without any charge

[96] MITT REGAN, DRONE STRIKE (2022).

[97] Tom Dannenbaum, *Siege Starvation: A War Crime of Societal Torture*, 22 CHI. J. INT'L L. 368 (2021); STANFORD LAW SCHOOL INTERNATIONAL HUMAN RIGHTS AND CONFLICT RESOLUTION CLINIC, LIVING UNDER DRONES (2012); Ioannis Kalpouzos, *The Armed Drone*, in INTERNATIONAL LAW'S OBJECTS (J. Hohmann & D. Joyce eds., 2018); M. von Werthern et al., *The Impact of Immigration Detention on Mental Health*, 18 BMC PSYCHIATRY 382 (2018).

[98] Inter-American Commission on Human Rights, Precautionary Measures 259/02, Detainees held by the United States in Guantanamo Bay, Cuba (Mar. 12, 2002); Committee Against Torture, Conclusions and Recommendations: United States, CAT/C/USA/CO/2 (July 25, 2006), para. 22 [hereinafter CAT, US Conclusions & Recommendations].

[99] IACHR, Resolution No. 2/11, Regarding the Situation of Detainees at Guantanamo Bay (July 22, 2011). *See also* Ameziane v. United States, IACHR Report No. 17/12 (Mar. 20, 2012), para. 28; Ameziane v. United States, IACHR Report No. 29/20, OEA/Ser.L/V/II Doc. 39 (Apr. 22, 2020), para. 122; IACHR, Press Release 3/12, *10 Years After Detentions in Guantanamo Began, the IACHR Repeats Its Call to Close the Detention Center* (Jan. 11, 2012).

whatever.' "[100] This led the Commission to deem the continued detention of at least seventy-eight persons at the time a violation of their fundamental rights.[101] Other bodies have reached similar conclusions, albeit through a variety of interpretive routes. In 2017, the U.N. Working Group on Arbitrary Detention reasoned that IHL "was never conceived to apply to detention of . . . . more than 11 years," thus concluding, like the IACHR, that "such cases must be considered with reference to international human rights law."[102] The Committee Against Torture determined that indefinite detention, such as at Guantánamo manifests cruel, inhuman, and degrading treatment and thus "constitutes per se a violation of the UN Convention Against Torture."[103] A similar position was adopted by the IACHR, the U.N. Working Group on Arbitrary Detention, the U.N. Rapporteur on Torture, the U.N. Rapporteur on Human Rights and Counter-Terrorism, and the U.N. Rapporteur on Health in 2013.[104]

From this perspective, as purportedly IHL-compliant rights limitations accumulate over time, they can reach a severity that exceeds what can be justified from the perspective of human rights law, even assuming a state of armed conflict (although analyses of Guantánamo typically also contest the latter). As with the relevance of emergency duration in derogation analysis, this entails evaluating perpetuation with reference to the accumulation and interconnectedness of harm over time.

A separate question regarding sunk costs is how to determine when military operations should be evaluated through the lens of perpetuation rather than initiation, particularly given sporadic patterns of military activity and the related invocation of concepts such as unit self-defense. At a minimum, states can be held to their own assertions in that respect. When they rely on conflict continuity to establish the NIAC intensity criterion, to justify continuous detention, or to frame their operations as responsive to an ongoing armed attack, they cannot plausibly invoke discontinuity to avoid *jus ex bello* analysis. Conversely, when the initial claims or presumptions regarding continuity are themselves untenable, the operations in question ought to be evaluated through the prism of ordinary human rights law, without IHL adjustment, and without need for *jus ex*

[100] IACHR, Resolution No. 2/11, *supra* note 99. *See also* IACHR, Press Release, *supra* note 99; IACHR, Annual Report 1976, OAS Doc. OEA/Ser.L/V/II.40, Doc. 5 corr. 1 (June 7, 1977), Section II, Part I.

[101] IACHR, Resolution No. 2/11, *supra* note 99.

[102] Working Group on Arbitrary Detention, Opinion No. 89/2017 concerning Ammar al Baluchi (United States of America), 80th session, November 20–24, 2017 (Jan. 24, 2018), para. 43.

[103] CAT, US Conclusions & Recommendations, *supra* note 98, para. 22.

[104] Press Release: *IACHR, UN Working Group on Arbitrary Detention, UN Rapporteur on Torture, UN Rapporteur on Human Rights and Counter-Terrorism, and UN Rapporteur on Health Reiterate Need to End the Indefinite Detention of Individuals at Guantánamo Naval Base in Light of Current Human Rights Crisis* (May 1, 2013).

bello evaluation, unless a new armed conflict obtains and a new *ad bellum* justification proves viable.

Ultimately, unambiguous legal direction on when to end war is not yet realistic. However, this does not mean the law is silent. The first step toward a viable *jus ex bello* in international law involves identifying existing resources, specifying their gaps and ambiguities, and pushing states to clarify and articulate their views on those areas of contestation.

Conclusion

Law alone cannot end war any more than it can prevent its initiation. However, it can provide a framework for analyzing and mobilizing politically, and it can underpin certain forms of enforcement and sanction. This chapter has identified existing doctrinal resources regarding *when* to stop fighting. Further analysis is warranted on the question of *how* to stop, particularly in conflicts with deep military entanglements. In contexts such as the United States' largely remote projection of force in the Forever War, the answer to the latter may be relatively straightforward. Building on the approach of human rights bodies vis-à-vis Guantánamo, a key step would be to hold the United States to a human rights standard unmodified by IHL, not simply because the conditions of armed conflict have ended (although they plausibly have) but because even assuming *arguendo* that those conditions endure, the basis for perpetuating them has lapsed.

20

How to Finally End America's Forever War

*Harold Hongju Koh**

Introduction

The United States has now been at war for more than two decades: nearly all this millennium, fifteen years longer than the Revolutionary War, and nineteen years longer than the Civil War or World War II. This "Forever War" began before a generation of today's adults was born. Many of my current students are military veterans, a group that in the United States now numbers in the millions. Countless Americans—to say nothing of those overseas who have borne the brunt of these interventions—have lived only in a state of war. But if peace is meant to be the norm, and war is the aberration, how did this happen and how do we finally end it?

I come to these questions wearing three hats. First, for more than forty years, I have taught international law and foreign relations law, primarily as a professor at Yale Law School since 1985. In leading several different law school clinics, I have sued several presidential administrations in foreign affairs cases and filed dozens of amicus briefs against the U.S. government in human rights and national security litigation. Second, over the last five decades, I have served in the U.S. government in four different administrations of both political parties,

* This chapter is a lightly edited and footnoted version of a keynote address delivered in London at the Just Security/Oxford Center for Ethics, Law and Armed Conflict (ELAC) workshop on *Perpetual War and International Law: Legacies of the War on Terror* on June 1, 2023. This piece was previously excerpted in Harold Hongju Koh, *Finally Ending America's Forever War, Part I: Diagnosis*, Just Security (Sept. 11, 2023), https://www.justsecurity.org/88131/finallyending-americas-forever-war-part-i-diagnosis/ [https://perma.cc/7HRG-NMKC], and Harold Hongju Koh, *Finally Ending America's Forever War, Part II: Prescription*, Just Security (Sept. 12, 2023), https://www.justsecurity.org/88164/finally-ending-americasforever-war-part-ii-prescription/ [https://perma.cc/BP34-JL4B]. I am grateful to Brianna Rosen, Executive Director of the Oxford Programme for Cyber and Technology Policy at the University of Oxford and Senior Fellow at *Just Security*; and my friends and colleagues Ryan Goodman, Co-Editor-in-Chief at *Just Security*, and Shaheed Fatima KC, Barrister, Blackstone Chambers, and Editor at *Just Security* for their support and insightful comments. Some of the ideas in it are drawn from and developed in Harold Hongju Koh, The National Security Constitution in the 21st Century (2024) [hereinafter Koh, 21st Century], summarized in Harold Hongju Koh, *The 21st Century Nation Security Constitution*, 91 Geo. Wash. L. Rev. 1391 (2023). I am grateful to Connor Brashear, Grace Kier, and Mary Szarkowicz of Yale Law School for their outstanding research assistance.

Harold Hongju Koh, *How to Finally End America's Forever War* In: *Perpetual War and International Law*. Edited by: Brianna Rosen, Oxford University Press. © Oxford University Press 2026.
DOI: 10.1093/oso/9780197748992.003.0020

serving in the 1980s as an attorney-adviser in the Office of Legal Counsel in the Reagan Justice Department; in the late 1990s and early 2000s as Assistant Secretary for Democracy, Human Rights, and Labor in the Clinton State Department under Secretary Madeleine Albright; in the early 2010s as Legal Adviser in the Obama State Department under Secretary Hillary Clinton; and most recently, during 2021, as Senior Adviser, the senior political appointee, in that same Legal Adviser's Office under President Joe Biden and Secretary Antony Blinken. Third, since 2016, I have also served as Ukraine's legal counsel in three different international lawsuits proceeding against Russia before the International Court of Justice and the Permanent Court of Arbitration.[1]

These different roles have given me varying perspectives on the questions raised here, which this chapter addresses in two parts. Part one offers a diagnosis of the societal, legal, and political factors that got us here. Part two offers prescriptions for how, finally, to end this Forever War by developing micro-strategies for reform to address specific challenges that must be overcome.

Diagnosis

When I went to the State Department as Legal Adviser in 2009, I had no idea so much of my time and energy on the job would be spent thinking through the domestic and international law issues that underlie the Forever War.[2] But many of the legal questions I faced during the next four years grew out of a single issue: How can domestic and international law restrain a powerful state (here, the United States) from pursuing armed conflict indefinitely against perceived external threats?

By the time I had left government in January 2013, I had thought long and hard about what could be done to bring the state of perpetual war to an end. In May 2013, I summarized my conclusions in a speech at the Oxford Union entitled "How to End the Forever War?," which argued that the United States should execute President Barack Obama's plan to end the Forever War by taking four steps: leaving Afghanistan, closing Guantánamo, disciplining drones, and

[1] *See* Allegations of Genocide Under the Convention on the Prevention and Punishment of the Crime of Genocide (Ukr. v. Russ. Fed'n), Provisional Measure, 2022 I.C.J. 182 (March 23); Application of the International Convention for the Suppression of the Financing of Terrorism and of the International Convention on the Elimination of All Forms of Racial Discrimination (Ukr. v. Russ. Fed'n), Provisional Measure, 2021 I.C.J. 166 (October 8); Dispute Concerning Coastal State Rights in the Black Sea, Sea of Azov, and Kerch Strait (Ukr. v. Russ. Fed'n), 2017-06, Procedural Order 9 (Perm. Ct. Arb. 2022).

[2] Harold Hongju Koh, *The Emerging Law of 21st Century War*, 66 EMORY L.J. 487 (2017).

defeating al-Qaeda on the battlefield.[3] A few weeks later, in a major speech at the National Defense University, President Obama embraced all four objectives.[4]

At this writing, each of these objectives seems to have been largely, if not entirely, achieved. The United States left Afghanistan, albeit sloppily, in August 2021.[5] Of the 780 detainees held at Guantánamo at its height, only forty were left on January 21, 2023, the day Joe Biden became president; at the time of this writing, only fifteen detainees remain.[6] With regard to disciplining drones, first President Obama and then-President Biden issued "Playbooks," now largely declassified, to govern out-of-theater targeting, in the form of Presidential Policy Guidance (PPG) and a stricter Presidential Policy Memorandum (PPM), issued in October 2022.[7] And the goal of defeating al-Qaeda on the battlefield, raised publicly by former U.S. Department of Defense General Counsel Jeh Johnson in his own 2012 speech at the Oxford Union, now has been largely achieved, at least with respect to al-Qaeda Core.[8]

But if these goals have been achieved, why does the Forever War appear to persist? The primary reason is that societal, legal, and other institutional drivers have created pressures for continuing the war paradigm, as opposed to shifting to a law enforcement paradigm. In particular, the bureaucratic internalization of a war culture and the quiet normalization of "GWOT (Global War on Terror) Lite" have combined with a sense of public apathy about whether the United States is, in fact, in a perpetual state of war. As a legal matter, overly broad interpretations of domestic and international laws, as well as government inertia to repeal outdated domestic laws, have contributed to making war the default paradigm.

The changing character of conflict has contributed to this state of affairs. Armed conflict is now waged by an array of state and non-state actors fighting

[3] Harold Hongju Koh, *How to End the Forever War?: Address at Oxford Union* (May 7, 2013), https://law.yale.edu/sites/default/files/documents/pdf/Faculty/KohOxfordSpeech.pdf [https://perma.cc/B82U-9CH4].

[4] Barack Obama, *Remarks by the President at the National Defense University*, White House (May 23, 2013), https://obamawhitehouse.archives.gov/the-press-office/2013/05/23/remarks-president-national-defense-university [https://perma.cc/D3VC-98TT].

[5] David Zucchino, *The U.S. War in Afghanistan: How It Started, and How It Ended*, N.Y. Times (Oct. 21, 2022), https://www.nytimes.com/article/afghanistan-war-us.html [https://perma.cc/E3VT-49L5].

[6] Carol Rosenberg, *Pentagon's Repatriation of Algerian Leaves 30 Prisoners at Guantánamo*, N.Y. Times (Apr. 22, 2023), https://www.nytimes.com/2023/04/20/us/politics/repatriation-prisoner-guantanamo-bakush.html [https://perma.cc/VNC3-NB2N]; Sacha Pfeiffer, *Biden Administration Releases Guantánamo Inmate, Its Fourth Transfer in a Month*, NPR (Mar. 9, 2023), https://www.npr.org/2023/03/09/1162424158/biden-administration-releases-guantanamo-inmate-its-fourth-transfer-in-a-month [https://perma.cc/LP5P-9QG7].

[7] Charlie Savage, *White House Tightens Rules on Counterterrorism Drone Strikes*, N.Y. Times (Oct. 7, 2022), https://www.nytimes.com/2022/10/07/us/politics/drone-strikes-biden-trump.html [https://perma.cc/U93W-JSTE].

[8] Benjamin Wittes, *Jeh Johnson Speech at the Oxford Union*, Lawfare (Nov. 30, 2012), https://www.lawfaremedia.org/article/jeh-johnson-speech-oxford-union[https://perma.cc/4DCN-BHCN].

on ill-defined battlefields and employing nontraditional uses of force, including through special operations, cyber tools, autonomous weapons systems, and artificial intelligence (AI). Rapidly evolving technologies have enabled conflicts to start, mutate, and persist at lower thresholds than full-scale war, making them more difficult to end.

Add in the evolving nature of the terrorist threat, which we now understand far better than we did on September 11, 2001. We now know that transborder terrorist groups splinter and spin off. They use social media and the "Dark Web" to recruit imitators around the world, who are usually not bona fide members of the original group, but take pride in being associated with it in name. Their political aims are predominantly local, so they only rarely launch the kinds of attacks on major foreign capitals that are likely to trigger massive retaliation. And they do not surrender or concede defeat. Instead, as their membership gets depleted, less fervent members withdraw and cross borders as foreign fighters to join or form different groups with new names, which often pay homage to their progenitor.

All these realities make outdated Jeh Johnson's idea of a "tipping point," where the United States conclusively defeats a terrorist group like al-Qaeda. When belonging to al-Qaeda Core became a losing proposition, members of that group did not simply quit; instead, they dispersed to other regions and splintered into new subentities.[9] Even when a terrorist group is effectively defeated on the battlefield, the core leadership of that group migrates and operates within a new armed group that constitutes a mobile threat from its new location.

The U.S. departure from Afghanistan and partial withdrawal from Iraq also raise the issue of "over-the-horizon" threats. Even when the United States or other countries withdraw from a military invasion—which may not have been lawfully undertaken in the first place—they still must protect small military and civilian deployments left behind from local terrorist actors. These deployments must retain kinetic capacity for "unit self-defense" against imminent attacks. Thus, continuous military deployments become an irreducible residue of past interventions, many of which may have been misguided from the start (most notably, the 2003 U.S.-led invasion of Iraq). In several countries—Iraq, Afghanistan, Syria, Yemen, and Somalia, to name just a few—the constant fighting has created chaos and effectively destroyed meaningful governance in significant parts of the country. Once chaos reigns in a particular region within a failed or failing state, zones of anarchy or "no-man's lands" may become grounds for terrorist bases, particularly when the local sovereign is "unable or unwilling" to address

[9] A.M. Vasiliev & N.A. Zherlitsyna, *The Evolution of Al-Qaeda: Between Regional Conflicts and a Globalist Perspective*, 92 (Suppl. 13) Her. Russ. Acad. Sci. S1240–6 (2022), https://www.ncbi.nlm.nih.gov/pmc/articles/PMC10036157 [https://perma.cc/5CLT-WENP]; Clayton Thomas, Cong. Rsch. Serv., IF11854, Al Qaeda: Background, Current Status, and U.S. Policy 2 (May 6, 2022), https://crsreports.congress.gov/product/pdf/IF/IF11854 [https://perma.cc/JDT3-6QPY].

the threat. And so, a distant state that nevertheless perceives itself to be vulnerable to attack may feel obliged to extend its self-defense rationale to taking continuing military action to address these over-the-horizon threats, which helps perpetuate Forever War.[10]

A swelling national security bureaucracy built to be laser-focused on these threats has fostered continuing financial and institutional incentives for entrenching the war paradigm. Within the executive branch, national security bureaucracies have grown steadily richer, more powerful, and opaque relative to their diplomatic and justice counterparts. I personally witnessed this transformation over four stints in five decades in the U.S. government. On each return, I observed how military and intelligence budgets have swelled since 9/11.[11] The 9/11 mentality has reshaped the foreign relations bureaucracy, with each agency replicating subunits that mirror and multiply a persistent focus on foreign counterterrorism.[12] The resulting bureaucratic structure too often resists new priorities in favor of combating more familiar threats. This institutional fixation on past threats has resisted the Biden administration's efforts to turn the page to address newly pressing challenges. Yet the continuing march toward executive unilateralism has been met by congressional acquiescence and judicial tolerance, ensuring that no branch will develop a strong enough incentive to check the trend toward perpetual war.[13]

All these changes have blurred traditional lines in legal doctrine: between offense and lawful self-defense, both individual and collective; between uses of force and threats thereof; between proximate threats that trigger a lawful right of self-defense and remote threats that would not; between state and non-state actors; and between noncombatant civilians and individuals who are lawfully targetable.

This line-blurring also has dramatically affected governments' perceptions of whether and when they have a legal right or moral duty to act to prevent serious harm. It has made international humanitarian law elastic, expanding the law of *jus ad bellum*.[14] It has globalized the battlefield.[15] And as Sir Daniel Bethlehem

[10] *See* Brianna Rosen, *The Longest War Is Over the Horizon*, Just Security (Nov. 1, 2021), https://www.justsecurity.org/78818/the-longest-war-is-over-the-horizon/.

[11] Linda J. Bilmes provides an in-depth examination of such budgetary matters in this volume. *See* Chapter 5 of this volume, "The 'Ghost Budget': How America Pays for Endless Wars."

[12] *See, e.g., Terrorism and Illicit Finance*, U.S. Department of the Treasury, https://home.treasury.gov/policy-issues/terrorism-and-illicit-finance [https://perma.cc/HMA2-H39Y]; *Counterterrorism Section*, National Security Division, U.S. Department of Justice (July 23, 2014), https://www.justice.gov/nsd/counterterrorism-section [https://perma.cc/LK8R-WDZV]; *Commerce Control List Overview and the Country Chart*, U.S. Department of Commerce (Aug. 11, 2023), https://www.bis.doc.gov/index.php/documents/regulations-docs/federal-register-notices/federal-register-2014/1033-738-supp-1/file [https://perma.cc/HPX3-N9F4].

[13] *See generally* Koh, 21st Century, *supra* note 1.

[14] *See* Chapter 19 of this volume, "Forever War and the *Jus Ex Bello*," by Tom Dannenbaum.

[15] *See* Chapter 15 of this volume, "The Rise of 'Self-Defense'—And the Fall of Constraints on the Use of Force," by Oona A. Hathaway.

has suggested, and both the U.S. and U.K. governments have acknowledged, it has elongated the notion of "imminence" that is legally sufficient to trigger a national right to self-defense against terrorist actors.[16]

The Forever War that began on 9/11 has thus joined other "frozen conflicts" around the world that appear never to truly end.[17] Domestic political actors have begun to adapt so that war can now be waged remotely with manageable domestic consequence. When there are continuing hostilities but no surrenders, battlefield stalemate may lead to uneasy ceasefires, without ever ending in full-scale armistices, much less fully negotiated peace treaties. Some situations simply never progress all the way to peace: for example, in Kashmir; Nagorno-Karabakh; South Ossetia and Abkhazia; and most famously, North and South Korea.[18] As bombs continue to fall in Gaza and Ukraine, some have begun to ask whether the Israel-Hamas and Russia-Ukraine wars will join this list.

Prescription

With this clearer understanding of why conflicts persist, we can build on current developments to identify practical ways to end the Forever War. While the picture painted thus far is discouraging, we should not overlook the positive signs that lay the needed groundwork for future progress.

Significantly, the last three U.S. presidents opposed draining foreign military interventions. While President Obama made progress in that direction, President Donald Trump had no visible strategy for implementing his opposition. President Biden made ending Forever War a hallmark of his campaign and took concrete steps to implement that goal, although he did not revoke the outdated legal interpretations and authorizations underpinning the Forever War.[19]

[16] Daniel Bethlehem, *Principles Relevant to the Scope of a State's Right of Self-Defense Against an Imminent or Actual Armed Attack by Nonstate Actors*, 106 Am. J. Int'l. L. 770 (2012).

[17] Nahal Toosi, *Ukraine Could Join Ranks of "Frozen" Conflicts, U.S. Officials Say* (May 18, 2023), https://www.politico.com/news/2023/05/18/ukraine-russia-south-korea-00097563 [https://perma.cc/G43L-9MYB].

[18] *See, e.g.*, Center for Preventive Action, *Conflict Between India and Pakistan*, Council on Foreign Relations (updated June 28, 2023), https://www.cfr.org/global-conflict-tracker/conflict/conflict-between-india-and-pakistan [https://perma.cc/9LQ8-QREX]; Center for Preventive Action, *Nagorno-Karabakh Conflict*, Council on Foreign Relations (updated Aug. 10, 2023), https://www.cfr.org/global-conflict-tracker/conflict/nagorno-karabakh-conflict [https://perma.cc/V8QC-K3E3]; Emil Avdaliani, *Playing with Fire: Georgia's Cautious Rapprochement with Russia*, Carnegie Politika (July 21, 2023), https://carnegieendowment.org/politika/90246 [https://perma.cc/KDX5-GH3P]; Center for Preventive Action, *North Korea Crisis*, Council on Foreign Relations (updated Aug. 7, 2023), https://www.cfr.org/global-conflict-tracker/conflict/north-korea-crisis [https://perma.cc/5BXB-3ZNA].

[19] Harold Hongju Koh, The Trump Administration and International Law 105–26 (2018).

Rather than dismissing these steps as inadequate, however, we should seek to build on them by pursuing four micro-reform strategies, which for shorthand purposes I will call: "seizing the inch," "moving their food," "watching where the puck is going," and "changing the lightbulb." If we pursue these micro-strategies, keeping commonsense considerations to the forefront, we can make progress by overcoming legal, political, and practical obstacles as they arise, with the broader goal of orchestrating a sea change over time.

Seizing the Inch: Piecemeal Reform

More than three decades ago, I urged Congress to enact a comprehensive charter of national security reforms.[20] If the political will could be mustered for such sweeping reforms, recent bipartisan legislative proposals—like the Senate's National Security Powers Act and its House counterpart, the National Security Reforms and Accountability Act—would lay the necessary foundation for broader structural changes to rebalance the institutional allocation of war-making powers.[21] Until then, we should instead "seize the inch" and embrace a collection of possible changes by all three federal branches that could be implemented either collectively or piecemeal over time. A pragmatic approach would start by acknowledging and building upon the halting progress that has been made, focusing more on what is genuinely broken than on areas where the Obama, Trump, and Biden administrations endorsed, but have not fully implemented, the right principles. Securing and building on piecemeal reforms when they can be achieved will keep us making progress, while staying

[20] Some of the ideas elaborated here were first presented in Harold Hongju Koh, The National Security Constitution: Sharing Power After the Iran-Contra Affair 156–84 (1990) (urging a national security charter that would re-enact, in five separate titles, the War Powers Resolution, the International Emergency Economic Powers Act, the arms export control laws, the Intelligence Oversight Act, and the National Security Council provisions of the National Security Act of 1947; address modes of congressional-executive consultation in international agreement making, internal and external agency control procedures, and provisions for judicial review of executive action; and create new congressional structures and effect revisions in internal House and Senate rules).

[21] *See* National Security Powers Act of 2021, S. 2391, 117th Cong. (2021), https://www.congress.gov/bill/117th-congress/senate-bill/2391/text [https://perma.cc/22U8-GWES]; National Security Reforms and Accountability Act, H.R. 5410, 117th Cong. (2021), https://www.congress.gov/bill/117th-congress/house-bill/5410 [https://perma.cc/P3L2-FDSF]. For an analysis of this legislation, *see* Tess Bridgeman & Stephen Pomper, *A Giant Step Forward for War Powers Reform*, Just Security (July 20, 2021), https://www.justsecurity.org/77533/a-giant-step-forward-for-war-powers-reform [https://perma.cc/VJ83-WNLN]; Tess Bridgeman & Stephen Pomper, *Good Governance Paper No. 14: War Powers Reform & 2022 Update*, Just Security (Jan. 21, 2022), https://www.justsecurity.org/79933/2022-update-good-governance-paper-no-14-war-powers-reform [https://perma.cc/XSA7-6C5C]; and Tess Bridgeman, *In Support of Sunsets: Easy Yes Votes on AUMF Reform*, Just Security (July 13, 2022), https://www.justsecurity.org/82312/in-support-of-sunsets-easy-yes-votes-on-aumf-reform [https://perma.cc/872E-PAC2].

transparent and candid about the moral hazards involved in living with an unsatisfactory and unstable status quo.

Perhaps the prime example of this is the continuing tragedy at Guantánamo. At the time of this writing, fifteen detainees remain, despite Obama's and Biden's repeated, vocal pledges to close the prison.[22] Perversely, the need to claim that "law-of-war detainee" status justifies keeping Guantánamo open has itself become an obstacle to removing the armed conflict framework. This is backward: the war was supposed to justify long-term detention without charges, not the other way around. A painfully unwieldy interagency bureaucracy now determines who can be released from Guantánamo detention, with virtually every agency participant holding a de facto veto. Consequently, even when nearly every knowledgeable actor agrees that a detainee no longer presents a current threat, almost anyone who fears being blamed for that detainee's release can block it from happening.

To end this extended tragedy, this process should be dramatically streamlined and driven by the Deputy National Security Adviser for Homeland Security and Counterterrorism Affairs. But since Trump's second term shows no interest in closing Guantanamo, a future administration must devote more resources and diplomatic incentives, driven from the White House, to persuade foreign countries to take the twenty who have already been cleared for transfer. A United Nations (U.N.) Special Rapporteur has issued a blistering report that makes clear why the status quo is unacceptable.[23] Amid competing policy priorities, it should be the job of someone senior in the White House to ask, every single day: "And what did we do today to close Guantánamo?" Many of those remaining are so old and sick, physically and mentally, that they presumably could be released on humanitarian grounds without genuine elevation of threat to the public. Finally, a military court ruling bars using as evidence before military commissions "voluntary" confessions made after the torture that many detainees undeniably

[22] Barack Obama, President of the United States, Remarks by the President on Plan to Close the Prison at Guantanamo Bay (Feb. 23, 2016), https://obamawhitehouse.archives.gov/the-press-office/2016/02/23/remarks-president-plan-close-prison-guantanamo-bay [https://perma.cc/6TWK-HP9M] ("When I first ran for President, it was widely recognized that this facility needed to close.... There was bipartisan support to close it.... I've been working for seven years now to get this thing closed. As President, I have spent countless hours dealing with this.... Our closest allies have raised it with me continually.... I don't want to pass this problem on to the next President, whoever it is. And if, as a nation, we don't deal with this now, when will we deal with it?"); Ellie Kaufman, *Biden Administration Says It Intends to Close Guantanamo Prison*, CNN (Feb. 12, 2021), https://edition.cnn.com/2021/02/12/politics/biden-guantanamo-bay/index.html [https://perma.cc/ZF5Q-VK4F].

[23] *See* Technical Visit to the United States and Guantánamo Detention Facility by the Special Rapporteur on the Promotion and Protection of Human Rights and Fundamental Freedoms while Countering Terrorism, June 14, 2023, https://www.ohchr.org/sites/default/files/documents/issues/terrorism/sr/2023-06-26-SR-terrorism-technical-visit-US-guantanamo-detention-facility.pdf.

endured.[24] Given that this evidentiary ruling jeopardizes future military commission convictions, the Chief Prosecutor of Military Commissions should negotiate plea bargains based on time served with the detainees' pro bono counsel. Given that the Guantanamo population now stands at only fifteen, the President could simply announce the closure of the offshore prison and bring the remaining detainees out on a single airplane, if necessary, to secure detention facilities within the continental United States. Congressional restrictions should not bar such actions. President Obama made a related claim of presidential authority to release six members of the Taliban in exchange for the Taliban's release of prisoner Bowe Bergdahl in 2013.[25] For all of its saber-rattling, Congress's response was mild, and no legislation was enacted in protest. But in his second tumultuous term, Donald Trump has announced the opposite intent: to expand Guantanamo, and worse yet, to send detainees without assurances against torture to offshore prisons like CECOT in El Salvador or as a kind of political theater, to irregular domestic prisons like the so-called "Alligator Alcatraz" in the Florida Everglades.

Under international law, the United States has acknowledged an obligation to follow both international humanitarian law, both *jus ad bellum* (the laws of initiating war) and *jus in bello* (the laws applied during wartime), particularly the Four Geneva Conventions of 1949 and those elements of Additional Protocols I and II that the United States has accepted as controlling domestically. We should demand greater rigor for the interpretation of *jus ad bellum* relating to armed conflict, self-defense, collective self-defense, and state consent. As two colleagues have noted, "the growing reliance upon self-defense as a justification for using force . . . threatens to make self-defense the exception that swallows the rule against war."[26] Efforts to expand the concept have come from three different directions: growing pressure to relax the "imminence" requirement with respect to well-known terrorist operational leaders; using the notion of "unable or unwilling" as a proxy or workaround for state consent; and the increasing elasticization of the concept of collective self-defense in an age of over-the-horizon threats.

Article 51 of the U.N. Charter speaks of an "inherent right of individual or collective self-defense if an armed attack occurs against a Member of the United Nations," but those words leave many questions open, that demand doctrinal clarification through state practice, normative development, and legal declaration

[24] Carol Rosenberg, *How a Judge's Ruling on Torture Imperils a Guantánamo Prosecution Strategy*, N.Y. Times (Aug. 26, 2023), https://www.nytimes.com/2023/08/26/us/politics/torture-uss-cole-september-11.html [https://perma.cc/JJN5-TM4U].

[25] Eric Schmitt & Charlie Savage, *Bowe Bergdahl, American Soldier, Freed by Taliban in Prisoner Trade*, N.Y. Times (May 31, 2014), https://www.nytimes.com/2014/06/01/us/bowe-bergdahl-american-soldier-is-freed-by-taliban.html [https://perma.cc/C7LA-HXW8].

[26] Oona Hathaway & Scott Shapiro, The Internationalists 416 (2017).

and agreement.[27] How serious must the military incursion be to qualify as an armed attack (a particularly urgent issue with respect to cyberwarfare)? What are the sources of an actionable "armed attack"? When, exactly, do attacks from non-state actors give the target state a right to respond against the non-state actor and against the territorial state on whose soil the non-state actor operates? When may a state lawfully respond in collective self-defense, and who may be protected by this collective self-defense? In Trump 2.0, the Administration has offered either no or elastic answers to all of these questions to justify repeated lethal drone strikes on claimed Venezuelan drug cartel boats traveling on the high seas, where there is no territorial sovereign.

A related question is whether the use of defensive force against a non-state actor located on the territory of a foreign state is forbidden if that foreign state is self-evidently unwilling or unable to resolve the threat itself (as was the case when President Obama ordered a deadly attack on Osama bin Laden at Abbottabad)?[28] Although the "unable-or-unwilling" test remains controversial among international law scholars,[29] it has proven less controversial among leading states, and it is unclear what a better alternative would be. If the unable-or-unwilling test is invalid, the critics of the test should clarify what better legal rule should take its place.[30]

With respect to targeted killings, there is growing acceptance that the traditional *Caroline* test for "imminence" has been overtaken by technology and the need for immediate response, at least in the counterterrorism domain. But considerable debate remains about how imminent the next armed attack must be when there has been a history of armed attacks by the threatening actor. U.S. Attorney General Eric Holder argued that "[t]he evaluation of whether an individual presents an 'imminent threat' incorporates considerations of the relevant window of opportunity to act, the possible harm that missing the window would cause to civilians, and the likelihood of heading off future disastrous attacks against the United States."[31] U.K. Attorney General Jeremy Wright clarified that the "window of opportunity to act" means the defending state must wait to strike

[27] U.N. Charter art. 51.

[28] Harold Hongju Koh, *The Lawfulness of the U.S. Operation Against Osama bin Laden*, Opinio Juris (May 19, 2011), http://opiniojuris.org/2011/05/19/the-lawfulness-of-the-us-operation-against-osama-bin-laden [https://perma.cc/XRX2-RGK7].

[29] *See, e.g.*, Ashley S. Deeks, *"Unwilling or Unable": Toward a Normative Framework for Extraterritorial Self-Defense*, 52 Va. J. Int'l L. 483 (2012).

[30] *See, e.g.*, Letter from the Chargé d'affaires a.i. of the Permanent Mission of Canada to the United Nations addressed to the President of the Security Council, U.N. Doc. S/2015/221 (Mar. 31, 2015), https://digitallibrary.un.org/record/790832?ln=en [https://perma.cc/SWZ8-QRKE].

[31] Eric Holder, Att'y Gen., U.S. Dep't of Just., Speech at Northwestern University School of Law (Mar. 5, 2012), https://www.justice.gov/opa/speech/attorney-general-eric-holder-speaks-northwestern-university-school-law [https://perma.cc/75LF-F86T].

until its "last clear chance" to address the threat.[32] At the same time, there is comparable acceptance that the doctrine of "preemptive self-defense" pressed by Presidents George W. Bush and Donald Trump cannot be squared with either the U.N. Charter or international humanitarian law (IHL).[33]

This suggests that what is wrong in this area is not the legal standards per se, but their overly elastic application in certain cases. Given that, in controversial cases, diligent oversight should demand facts and assign a rigorous burden of proof, rather than reject wholesale the legal standard being applied. When, for example, in 2020, the Trump administration claimed that it had targeted Iranian Major General Qassem Soleimani in "elongated self-defense" because of his past bad acts, Congress, U.S. allies, and the public all appropriately pressed the administration for its factual basis for five claims: necessity, proportionality, sovereignty, and imminence: in particular, that killing Soleimani prevented an unavoidable and imminent attack on U.S. territory or critical American interests. In response, the Trump administration failed to produce or share any persuasive evidence to support its claim that the strike was aimed at disrupting ongoing attacks, leaving little doubt that the attack was, in fact, illegal.[34] The same is true with respect to Trump 2.0's lawless 2025 attacks on Venezuelan drug boats on the high seas.

In 1981, President Ronald Reagan issued Executive Order 12333, which, as amended, remains in effect today and limits application of that prohibition to individuals "acting on behalf of" the U.S. government. That executive order should now be clarified to reinforce the ban on preemptive assassinations.[35]

Under domestic law, the Obama-Biden legal theory regarding use of force has acknowledged that its war-making must follow Article II of the U.S. Constitution, the statutory Authorizations for Use of Military Force (AUMFs), and presidential policy guidance on direct action—the latest iteration of which is the 2023 PPM. As a matter of executive policy, the Biden administration has also tightened the rules originally found in the 2016 PPG on detention and targeting outside of ongoing theaters of armed conflict. Those rules state a clear preference for

[32] Jeremy Wright, U.K. Att'y Gen., Speech at the International Institute for Strategic Studies: The Modern Law of Self-defence (Jan. 11, 2017), https://www.justsecurity.org/wp-content/uploads/2017/01/United-Kingdom-Attorney-General-Speech-modern-law-of-self-defense-IISS.pdf [https://perma.cc/5KUA-CKU6].

[33] *See, e.g.*, Harold Hongju Koh, *Is Preemptive Assassination the New Trump Doctrine?*, Foreign Pol'y (Jan. 9, 2020), https://foreignpolicy.com/2020/01/09/preemptive-assassination-suleimani-new-trump-doctrine-legal [https://perma.cc/6XXR-NT9K].

[34] *See* Andrew Chung, *U.S. "Self-Defense" Argument for Killing Soleimani Meets Skepticism* (Jan. 3, 2020), https://www.reuters.com/article/us-iraq-security-blast-legal-analysis-idCAKBN1Z301R/. *See, e.g.*, Koh, *supra* note 33.

[35] Exec. Order No. 11,905, 3 C.F.R. § 90 (1976); Exec. Order No. 12,333, 3 C.F.R. § 200 (1981); *see also* Michael N. Schmitt, *Assassination in the Law of War*, Lieber Inst., West Point (Oct. 15, 2021), https://lieber.westpoint.edu/assassination-law-of-war [https://perma.cc/D4LS-EY7F].

capture, using lethal force only when necessary, and showing genuine respect for state sovereignty, rather than simply reciting that the host state is unable and unwilling to address the threat on its soil. So again, this is a foundation that can be built upon. Congress should press the second Trump administration to reissue and strengthen Obama's Executive Order 13732, which, among other things, required all U.S. government agencies to publicly disclose the number of civilians killed in drone strikes, particularly if those killings occur outside of "areas of active hostilities."[36] In 2019, the first Trump administration quietly revoked that reporting requirement, which should be clearly and publicly reinstated.

If the whole world is not a battleground, greater precision is needed to define exactly where are the zones outside of "areas of active hostilities" to which the rules of the PPM should apply. Afghanistan and adjoining areas? Iraq? Somalia? Yemen? The real question here is an operational one: Exactly where should military commanders have broad discretion to decide when and where to attack without prior political approval or civilian oversight? This question implicates proper civilian control of the military. As Franklin Foer has reported, the inevitable "dynamic . . . that kept the United States entangled in Afghanistan [was that] politicians who hadn't served in the military could never summon the will to overrule the generals, and the generals could never admit that they were losing. So the war continued indefinitely, a zombie campaign. Biden believed that he could break this cycle," which the president correctly saw as crucial to ending the Forever War.[37]

To wind down the conflict, the first and most obvious legislative step is to finally repeal and, if necessary, replace the 1991, 2001, and 2002 AUMFs, which have become principal facilitators of the Forever War. These statutes have no sunset clauses and are elastically worded Accordingly, so long as the "enemy" keeps mutating, government lawyers will try to extend these force authorizations to new enemies and situations never considered by the Congresses that enacted them nor affirmatively endorsed by any Congress since. This creates a vicious circle: if we keep acquiring new enemies and can fight them under the same laws, we will never repeal those laws. Instead, we will keep using those laws—as Trump 2.0 seems intent to do—to extend warfare to new arenas. But if we are always fighting in new theaters against "associated forces," there will always be new enemies and the war will never end.

Add to this toxic mix rigid textualism, the interpretive philosophy that now commands a majority of the U.S. Supreme Court. To give just one example,

[36] Exec. Order No. 13,732, 81 Fed. Reg. 44485 (2016), https://irp.fas.org/offdocs/eo/eo-13732.htm [https://perma.cc/WF8B-FJBB].

[37] Franklin Foer, *The Final Days*, ATLANTIC (Aug. 29, 2023), https://www.theatlantic.com/magazine/archive/2023/10/afghanistan-withdrawal-biden-decision/675116 [https://perma.cc/L4Y3-CMRU].

under the October 10, 2002, AUMF, the president is authorized to use U.S. armed forces as he determines to be "necessary and appropriate" in order to defend the national security of the United States against "the continuing threat posed by Iraq."[38] Even though that law was historically passed to address the threat posed by the long-departed Saddam Hussein, Scalian textualists working at the Office of Legal Counsel during the Trump administration later argued that this language authorized the 2020 strike against Soleimani.[39]

So, we cannot end the Forever War, unless we end forever war legislation. President Biden's legislative successes in his second and third years offered some hope that under the right circumstances, foreign affairs reform legislation could be passed.[40] The Biden administration, alongside Senators Tim Kaine and Jeff Merkley, all favored adopting a narrow approach, substituting an ISIS-specific/mission-specific AUMF that included a sunset clause, with transparency and reporting provisions, and possibly third-party *ex post* review of drone strikes.[41] Regarding Iran, after the 2020 Soleimani strike, the Senate passed the Kaine War Powers Resolution by a bipartisan vote of 55–45, specifying that the president must obtain congressional approval to attack Iran but can act in self-defense against an imminent attack. However, no companion House legislation materialized. For Iraq, there has been bipartisan legislation to repeal the 1991 and 2002 AUMFs to formally end the Gulf and Iraq wars, and reassert Congress's constitutional role in deciding whether and when to commit U.S. troops to future conflicts. But again, after the Senate passage, related efforts stalled in the House.[42] Regarding Yemen, a bipartisan group of Senators—Tim Kaine, Todd

[38] Authorization for Use of Military Force Against Iraq, Pub. L. No. 107-243, 115 Stat. 1498 (2002).

[39] The highly redacted public version of the OLC opinion justifying the strike against Soleimani states. *See, e.g.*, "Although the President had independent constitutional authority under Article II to direct the January 2 airstrike, we also advised that he could rely on the 2002 AUMF. Congress has authorized the President 'to use the Armed Forces of the United States as he determines to be necessary and appropriate in order to . . . defend the national security of the United States against the continuing threat posed by Iraq.'" Although the primary focus of the 2002 AUMF was the threat posed by Saddam Hussein's regime, the statute has long been read, in accordance with its express goals, to authorize the use of force for the related purposes of helping to establish a stable, democratic Iraq and addressing terrorist threats emanating from Iraq. https://www.justice.gov/d9/2023-04/2020-03-10_soleimani_airstrike_redacted_2021.pdf (emphasis added); https://www.documentcloud.org/documents/6776446-Section-1264-NDAA-Notice.html.

[40] *See, e.g.*, Inflation Reduction Act of 2022, H.R. 5376, 117th Cong.; Chips and Science Act, H.R. 4346, 117th Cong. (2022), A Resolution Expressing the Senate's Support for Finland and Sweden's Accession into the North Atlantic Treaty Organization (NATO) and the Expedited Ratification of Accession Protocols, S. Res. 646, 117th Cong. (2022).

[41] Alex Ward, *White House Signals Support for Replacing Decades-long Authorizations for Military Force* (Mar. 5, 2021), https://www.vox.com/2021/3/5/22315258/white-house-biden-authorization-military-force-forever-wars [https://perma.cc/G8VT-7CNK]; A Joint Resolution to Repeal the Authorizations for Use of Military Force Against Iraq, and for Other Purposes, S.J. Res. 10, 117th Cong. (2021).

[42] A Bill to Repeal the Authorizations for Use of Military Force Against Iraq., S. 316, 118th Cong. (2023).

Young, Mike Lee, and Rand Paul— all introduced a bill similar to the 2019 bill vetoed by Trump that would end U.S. logistical and personnel support and intelligence-sharing enabling offensive strikes by the Saudi-led coalition fighting the Houthis in Yemen.[43] At this writing new bipartisan legislation would restrict military adventurism in Venezuela. In brief, promising legislative proposals exist, missing only the necessary congressional majorities.

Until such legislation can be passed, we should work harder to clarify the international law standards that are internalized within the AUMFs. The statute authorizes the "necessary and appropriate use of force" against those states, organizations, or persons who "planned, authorized, committed, or aided the terrorist attacks . . . or harbored such organizations or persons."[44] The Biden and Obama administrations both committed themselves to reading the 2001 AUMF as "informed by" international law, in effect applying the famous *Charming Betsy* Principle.[45] Nevertheless, in the twenty-two years since it was first passed, the 9/11 AUMF has been read by the executive branch to authorize the use of force in a wider and wider set of conflicts without clear geographic, temporal, or citizenship-based limitations.

To counter this trend, State Department lawyers, in particular, should argue for application of international human rights law to check overly self-serving readings of international humanitarian law. In its 1996 *Nuclear Weapons* opinion, the International Court of Justice made clear that the International Covenant on Civil and Political Rights (ICCPR) does not cease to operate in times of war "except by operation of Article 4," which governs derogation in a time of national emergency. The Court's 2004 Advisory Opinion in the *Palestinian Wall* case further enunciated that "the Court will have to take into consideration both these branches of international law."[46]

Finally, we should be frank that some U.S. laws have just become obsolete. A prime candidate is the 1973 War Powers Resolution, which in my view has run its course. To its credit, the resolution tried to define the respective roles of each political branch in a realm of shared constitutional power in a framework statute that aimed to promote interbranch communication, consultation, and cooperation. It has succeeded in forcing presidents to report regularly, albeit cryptically,

[43] Julie Hirschfeld Davis & Eric Schmitt, *Senate Votes to End Aid for Yemen Fight Over Khashoggi Killing and Saudis' War Aims*, N.Y. TIMES (Dec. 13, 2018), https://www.nytimes.com/2018/12/13/us/politics/yemen-saudi-war-pompeo-mattis.html [https://perma.cc/XJ6G-6PF5].

[44] Authorization for Use of Military Force, Pub. L. No. 107-40, § 2, 115 Stat. 224 (2001) (to be codified at 50 U.S.C.A. § 1541).

[45] Murray v. Schooner Charming Betsy, 6 U.S. (2 Cranch.) 4 (18043) ("an act of Congress ought never to be construed to violate the laws of nations if any other possible construction remains.").

[46] Legality of the Threat or Use of Nuclear Weapons, Advisory Opinion, 1996 I.C.J. 226, 240 (July 8); Legal Consequences of the Construction of a Wall in the Occupied Palestinian Territory, Advisory Opinion, 2004 I.C.J. 136, 178 (July).

on foreign deployments and to shorten sustained foreign interventions. But successive administrations have increasingly skirted the resolution's textual restrictions on the sustained introduction of U.S. "armed forces . . . into the territory, airspace or waters of a foreign nation," by resorting to limited uses of force in the form of special forces, drones, and cyberattacks.[47]

Apart from that, the resolution has largely failed to promote the interbranch dialogue and cooperation it was designed to produce. This failure is because the resolution was based on a gimmick: it "promotes" interbranch dialogue only indirectly, by threatening the president and Congress with a sixty-day statutory time limit to force them to talk to one another. But because the practice of all three branches has essentially rendered this "deadline" non-self-executing, that time limit has lost its power either to push the president toward consultation or to push Congress toward a prompt vote of approval or disapproval of the president's troop commitments. The resolution's legislative-veto provision runs afoul of the Supreme Court's decision invalidating legislative vetoes in *INS v. Chadha*.[48] At the same time, the substantive provisions of the resolution derogate from Congress's war-making powers by allowing the president too much freedom to make covert and short-term war and to commit military forces overseas without a clear purpose or exit strategy. And as John Hart Ely elaborated in *War and Responsibility*, the resolution glaringly defines no role for the courts in forcing the political branches to engage in dialogue with one another about the reasons for engaging in armed conflict.[49]

When the resolution was first enacted, Charles Black pointed out its most glaring omission: it defines how many months U.S. troops may stay abroad, but "utterly refus[es] even to begin the task of defining the conditions under which the president should not commit troops for even ten minutes—the really crucial matter."[50] As the Libya episode in 2011 showed, the resolution, as currently worded, does not encourage meaningful interbranch dialogue regarding the wisdom of any particular presidential troop commitment, for example, for urgent humanitarian intervention. Instead, the current law entrenches existing institutional inertia by condoning what Professor Richard Pildes has called "policymaking-by-silence." "By design," he explained, the resolution "makes Congress's silence . . . tantamount to a decision by Congress to prohibit the United States from continu[ing] to participate in 'hostilities' that the

[47] War Powers Resolution, Pub. L. No. 93-148, § 4(a), 87 Stat. 555 (1973).

[48] INS v. Chadha, 462 U.S. 919 (1983); 50 U.S.C.A. § 1544(c) (1982) (legislative veto in War Powers Resolution).

[49] *See generally* JOHN HART ELY, WAR AND RESPONSIBILITY: CONSTITUTIONAL LESSONS OF VIETNAM AND ITS AFTERMATH (1993).

[50] Charles L. Black, *The Working Balance of the American Political Departments*, 1 HASTINGS CONST. L.Q. 13, 18 (1980).

United States has initiated."[51] It thereby frees Congress to take no position on the wisdom of any proposed conflict, to say nothing if the military action succeeds, but then to blame the president if it fails.

As the twenty-first century proceeds, this kind of war powers law will become increasingly obsolete. Russia's invasion of Ukraine in 2022 notwithstanding, large-scale manned interventions like Vietnam or Operation Desert Storm will become increasingly rare. As armed conflict is conducted not by massive airstrikes or ground invasions but by the sporadic use of special operations, drones, cyberwarfare, and AI, the War Power Resolution's durational limit will become entirely ineffective in forcing thoughtful interbranch dialogue about the goals of military operations.

The first-best option would obviously be general reform of the War Powers Resolution.[52] A war powers bill should create a consultative congressional group or Joint Committee on National Security that would function as a centralized repository of political expertise in Congress with continuing responsibility to deal with the war powers problem.

Second, by requiring the president to consult regularly with that core consultative group, the bill should directly foster interbranch dialogue and attempt to equalize access to sensitive information that would otherwise lie exclusively within the president's control. Thicker consultation requirements would promote congressional involvement earlier in the decision-making process so that the president could not simply commit troops first and then present Congress with a fait accompli.

Third, any new war powers bill should also grant individual members of Congress statutory standing to seek judicial enforcement of the act in the D.C. federal courts, which would develop a judicial counter-arena of legal expertise in that circuit with regard to war powers issues. Ely wryly observed that the same courts that have claimed separation-of-powers or judicial-incompetence reasons for refusing to decide whether "hostilities" exist for the purpose of triggering the War Powers Resolution have routinely decided whether hostilities exist in insurance-contract cases. At the same time as judges have abstained from deciding whether our own government and officials have violated international

[51] *See* Richard Pildes, *Power Wars Symposium: What Role Should Law Play in Areas of Vital National and International Affairs?*, Just Security (Nov. 13, 2015) ("Thus, Congress's failure to act has all the consequences, as a practical matter, of an affirmative decision by Congress to cut off the . . . operation, though without Congress actually making such a decision or having to take direct responsibility, through the act of voting, for such a decision and its ensuing consequences."), https://www.justsecurity.org/27583/role-should-law-play-areas-vital-national-international-affairs/ [https://perma.cc/QGM6-6PXP].

[52] *See, e.g.*, War Powers Consultation Act of 2014, S. 1939, 113th Cong. (2014). For a now-classic proposal explaining how Congress could broadly modify the War Powers Resolution to make it more effective, *see generally* Ely, *supra* note 49.

law and the constitutional law of foreign affairs, they have regularly passed judgment on whether foreign government officials have violated international and domestic law in transnational commercial and human rights cases.[53]

Simply put, executive practice has gained undue predominance as the prime source of customary constitutional law in war-making. Over time, we must restore a process whereby all three branches work together: a presidency that will accept internal and external constraints; a Congress that will enact laws clarifying institutional responsibilities; and courts that will fulfill their duty to declare conduct illegal.

Moving Their Food: Changing Incentives

As difficult as it is to herd cats, you can still change their incentives by moving their food. The same reasoning applies to institutional reform: over the long term, the best way to change institutions is to alter organizational and individual incentives. The goal of institutional reform proposals should be to reduce the isolation that currently surrounds executive branch activities, to enhance internal executive branch deliberations, and to increase congressional-executive dialogue while national security objectives are being set and initiatives implemented. By doing so, even piecemeal reform could modify normative expectations *within* foreign-policy institutions, reduce cynicism about the possibilities for balanced institutional decision-making, and generate a more virtuous policy cycle over time.

First, and most obviously, the executive branch should recast its current structure to incorporate more reliable mechanisms to ensure *internal* checks and balances. Three changes should be made to ensure that the president receives loyal but impartial national security legal advice. First, the White House counsel's office should shrink in size, and the National Security Council (NSC) legal adviser should no longer function as a "double-hatted" deputy White House counsel vulnerable to political oversight and influence. Instead, the NSC legal adviser, advised by a group of foreign-relations lawyers from the general counsels' offices of the participating agencies, should give independent advice directly to the national security adviser and deputy.[54]

[53] Ely, *supra* note 49, at 61. For rulings in the human rights area, *see, e.g.*, Filartiga v. Pena-Irala, 630 F.2d 876 (2d Cir. 1980); Forti v. Suarez-Mason, 672 F. Supp. 1531 (N.D. Cal. 1987); Von Dardel v. U.S.S.R., 623 F. Supp. 246 (D.D.C. 1985). For commercial rulings under the act-of-state doctrine and the Foreign Sovereign Immunities Act, *see generally* Gary B. Born & Peter B. Rutledge, International Civil Litigation in United States Courts (7th ed. 2022).

[54] Harold Hongju Koh, *National Security Legal Advice in the New Administration*, Just Security (Nov. 16, 2016), https://www.justsecurity.org/34507/national-security-legal-advice-administration/ [https://perma.cc/HX5Z-B9J6].

Second, an adversarial process inside and outside the executive branch should test the legality of all proposed foreign policy initiatives. To ensure that executive initiatives will not commence without genuine consensus, or on the basis of one general counsel's secret and self-serving invocation of "find the statute," a formal executive order should make permanent the requirement of the type of interagency lawyers group convened during the Clinton, Obama, and Biden administrations, but truncated in the George W. Bush era (especially his first term) and abandoned in the Trump era.[55] Such interagency review would mimic the centralized review of agency rulemaking that the Office of Management and Budget has conducted since the Reagan administration. The task of obtaining and coordinating competing legal analyses could be confided to the NSC's legal adviser. As in earlier times, the NSC legal adviser should rarely generate his own written opinions; instead, he should see his role as discerning consensus, breaking ties, and deriving the best advice available from the detailed analyses of the expert agencies. The participants in the interagency legal process must press the NSC legal adviser to ensure that public written rationales are offered for all major legal decisions.[56]

Third, we should return to the more efficient and effective system that functioned in the 1980s, when most detailed foreign-affairs legal advice came from two large, established foreign policy offices with expertise in both foreign-affairs law and international and humanitarian law: the Legal Adviser's Office at the State Department and the General Counsel's Office at the Defense Department.[57] The role of the Office of Legal Counsel at Justice (OLC) should be accordingly reduced. In fact, in most of the interagency national-security meetings that I attended since 2009, the Justice Department input came not

[55] Rebecca Ingber, *Good Governance Paper No. 17: How to Use the Bureaucracy to Govern Well*, Just Security (Oct. 31, 2020) ("When the question on the table is the legality of action, and there are differing views on the appropriate legal rationale, this may result in a decision to act but with no clear consensus on why it is lawful. *In fact, this may mean that the government takes action even when a majority of the relevant officials are opposed to any one legal rationale for doing so.*" (emphasis added)), https://www.justsecurity.org/73126/good-governance-paper-no-17-how-to-use-the-bureaucracy-to-govern-well/ [https://perma.cc/U6VT-BQEX].

[56] Harold Hongju Koh, *The Legal Adviser's Duty to Explain*, 41 Yale J. Int'l L. 189, 195 (2016) ("Providing a public justification is a necessary step to explain why others should agree that actions taken by those government officials are consistent with international law. As a prudential matter, such public explanations prove to be critically important in bringing along the rest of the country and prospective allies in establishing the legitimacy of a public action."); Ingber, *supra* note 55 ("[M]aking the [legal] output *public* (or as much of it as possible) incentivizes clarity of output and allows for broader debate and accountability when the legal rationale for government action is overly generalized or otherwise weak." (emphasis in original)).

[57] *See* Ingber, *supra* note 55 ("Group decisionmaking is often hailed for bringing together all the relevant players with expertise and interest, and for allowing the full airing of views. But it can also stifle dissent, promote group think, and . . . dilute the relevant expertise in the room, for example, when the entire group is asked to weigh in on a matter on which only a small subset have expertise—such as a question of international law.").

from OLC, but from the National Security Division, which was created after September 11. Many of the OLC opinions generated since the George W. Bush administration have greatly exaggerated the breadth of presidential power in foreign affairs, and so should accordingly be systematically reviewed for their correctness, published if believed correct, and withdrawn when found incorrect.[58] In addition to formally adopting public internal principles of "best practices" to apply to this review, the office should publicly overrule a number of plainly incorrect OLC opinions from previous eras, like the 2020 Soleimani opinion, some of which were apparently generated as post hoc justifications for controversial national security decisions.[59]

This is an equally ripe area for congressional reforms. Congress's three top priorities should be building the core consultative group (or Joint Committee on National Security) mentioned earlier; building a central repository within Congress of *legal advice* regarding international and foreign relations law; and developing *better tools to counter executive overreach.*

Congress should create a joint committee on national security, akin to the Joint Committee on Taxation, that would become a core group of expert members on national security matters generally, and war powers matters in particular.[60] This

[58] For discussion of articles about OLC, *see* Trevor W. Morrison, *Stare Decisis in the Office of Legal Counsel*, 116 COLUM. L. REV. 1448, 1450–51 nn.4–7 (2010). In the 1980s, I had the privilege of serving in that fine office, but I have long expressed hesitations about the ways in which its actual and desired prominence is exaggerated by its academic alumni from both parties. *See, e.g.*, Harold Hongju Koh, *Protecting the Office of Legal Counsel from Itself*, 15 CARDOZO L. REV. 513 (1993). For example, OLC attorneys may have expertise in constitutional law, but they generally have far less expertise in international law. *Cf.* Harold Hongju Koh, *Can the President Be Torturer in Chief?*, 81 IND. L.J. 1145 (2006) (analyzing OLC's infamous torture memo).

[59] For such a "best practices" statement, *see* Walter Dellinger et al., *Principles to Guide the Office of Legal Counsel* (2004), *reprinted in* Dawn E. Johnsen, *Faithfully Executing the Laws: Internal Legal Constraints on Executive Power*, 54 UCLA L. REV. 1559, 1603 app. 2 (2007) (drafted by attorneys who worked in OLC during the Clinton, George W. Bush, and Obama administrations); Morrison, *supra* note 58; and Memorandum from David J. Barron, Acting Assistant Att'y Gen., Office of Legal Counsel, to Attorneys of the Office (July 16, 2010) (*"This memorandum updates a prior memorandum, 'Best Practices for OLC Opinions,' issued May 16, 2005."), https://www.justice.gov/sites/default/files/olc/legacy/2010/08/26/olc-legal-advice-opinions.pdf [https://perma.cc/VV9K-TJK7]. Prime candidates for disavowal are the legal opinions that justified, after the fact, the killing of Iranian general Qassem Soleimani, which was illegal when ordered. *See supra* note 39; Koh, *supra* note 33; Brian Finucane, *Time for the Biden Administration to Disavow the Dangerous Soleimani Legal Opinions*, JUST SECURITY (Jan. 3, 2022), https://www.justsecurity.org/79700/time-for-the-biden-administration-to-disavow-the-dangerous-soleimani-legal-opinions/ [https://perma.cc/8RTR-ETPQ].

[60] The Joint Committee on Taxation, which has existed since 1926, is a nonpartisan committee of Congress with five members from the Senate Finance Committee and five from the House Ways and Means Committee. It is supported by a nonpartisan staff of economists, lawyers, and other tax professionals. The committee staff "enjoys a high-level of trust from both sides of the political aisle and in both houses of Congress . . . . Because the . . . staff is independent, [expert,] and involved in all stages of the . . . legislative process, the staff is able to ensure consistency" as bills move through Congress. *About the Joint Committee on Taxation*, JOINT COMMITTEE ON TAXATION, https://www.jct.gov/about-us/overview/ [https://perma.cc/M95C-VA56. A number of thoughtful bills, never enacted, sought to achieve such centralization by requiring the president, before using force, to

new committee would have eight to twelve members, drawn from the leaders of the foreign affairs, armed services, and intelligence committees in the House and Senate. The four congressional leaders—the Speaker and minority leader of the House and the majority and minority leaders of the Senate—would sit on the committee, *ex officio*, as needed. The committee would hire a bipartisan, expert, professional staff to consult, investigate, write reports and legislative histories, and meet regularly with staff from foreign affairs agencies and the National Security Council to discuss national security matters. Through this core consultative group, Congress would provide the executive with the benefit of its deliberative judgments without demanding unacceptable sacrifices in flexibility, secrecy, or dispatch.

The creation of a core consultative group would serve the long-term interests not only of Congress but also of the executive. It would eliminate the president's chronic complaint that in emergencies, statutory consultation requirements impose an intolerable burden on the president to find members with whom to consult.[61] In the most extreme situations, the number of members consulted could even be reduced to the subgroup consisting of the four ranking minority and majority leaders in each house. Were Congress to mandate regular confidential meetings between its core consultative group and the president or his principal cabinet officers at the start of each new administration, we might return to true consultative decision-making between the branches.[62]

To encourage presidential signature, a revised law could define areas of legislative pre-authorization for war-making activity. The original Senate version of the War Powers Resolution laid out various circumstances under which Congress would approve in advance the introduction of U.S. armed forces into actual or imminent hostilities without a declaration of war.[63] The core consultative group,

consult with a "permanent consultative group" composed of the majority and minority leaders of both houses of Congress, plus the chairs and ranking minority members of the armed services, foreign affairs, and intelligence committees of each house. The bills required that this group be consulted to design legislative remedies to terminate or approve particular military involvements. Under the proposed bills, the group would have had formal authority to invoke the War Powers Resolution even if the president chose not to do so; its legislative proposals would have been accorded a special fast-track status in the legislative process.

[61] *See, e.g.*, GERALD R. FORD, A TIME TO HEAL: THE AUTOBIOGRAPHY OF GERALD R. FORD 252 (1979) (describing how the president could not consult with key congressional leaders about 1975 Da Nang evacuation, because ten were abroad and twelve were scattered throughout the United States).

[62] *See* CYRUS VANCE, HARD CHOICES: CRITICAL YEARS IN AMERICA'S FOREIGN POLICY 14 (1983) (pointing out that during the Iranian hostage crisis, the secretary of state or his deputy spent up to two hours each day in meetings or briefing sessions with members of Congress).

[63] *See* War Powers Act, S. 440, 93rd Cong. (1973), *reprinted in* SEAN D. MURPHY, EDWARD T. SWAINE, & INGRID BRUNK, U.S. FOREIGN RELATIONS LAW: CASES, MATERIALS, AND PRACTICE EXERCISES 475–69 (6th ed. 2024); War Powers Act, S. 2956, 92d Cong., 117 CONG. REC. 44,794–95 (1971) (similar bill proposed by Sen. Javits).

familiar with the subtleties of past cases, could work with the executive branch to refine this provision for reinsertion into future legislation. In addition, the War Powers Resolution took no account of either covert warfare or short-term military strikes. Again, the core consultative group could redress that omission by treating covert warfare as both a war-making and an intelligence issue and address the currently unregulated problem of short-term military strikes. The revised law would expressly authorize the president to engage in certain activities for which he currently lacks legislative authorization: for example, committing troops overseas for such limited, short-term purposes as rescuing American citizens endangered abroad. Not only would such provisions eliminate existing ambiguities regarding the scope of the president's statutory authorities, but they would also render Congress's legislative package more attractive to the president by unambiguously elevating the pre-authorized activities into the zone of express congressional approval (category one of Justice Jackson's famous *Youngstown* concurrence).[64]

Because the core consultative group would be drawn from expert congressional leaders, its members would view themselves, like the president, as representing a broad national constituency and not just particular interest groups.[65] Over time, the group and its staff would develop a bipartisan view of the policy terrain comparable to that of the president or the Joint Committee on Taxation, without forsaking the expertise of the existing specialized committees and committee staffs. Given that members of Congress now experience far greater longevity in office than executive branch officials, the core legislative group could very well come to gain greater perspective and expertise than its executive branch counterparts.[66] Just as earlier presidents have selected secretaries of state and defense from the Senate—such as John Kerry, Hillary Clinton, Edmund Muskie, William Cohen, and Chuck Hagel—future presidents could draw upon this core

64 *See* Youngstown Sheet & Tube Co. v. Sawyer, 343 U.S. 579, 635 (1952) (Jackson, J., concurring) (defining three levels of congressional approval for presidential action, and noting as first category: "When the President acts pursuant to an express or implied authorization of Congress, his authority is at its maximum, for it includes all that he possesses in his own right plus all that Congress can delegate. . . .").

65 *See* Michael Fitts, *The Vices of Virtue: A Political Party Perspective on Civic Virtue Reforms of the Legislative Process*, 136 U. Pa. L. Rev. 1567, 1603–07 (1988) (because centralized institutions tend to represent broad constituencies and experience fewer collective action problems, they are more likely to promote public-regarding action).

66 *Compare* Roger Davidson, *Congress and the Dispersion of Powers*, *in* Mr. Madison's Constitution and the Twenty-First Century: A Report from the Williamsburg Conference 25, 25–28 (1988) ("The average tenure of senators and representatives is about 10.5 years," with some members serving several times that length), *with* Alton Frye, *Congress and President: The Balance Wheels of American Foreign Policy*, 49 Yale Rev. 1, 3–4 (1979) (cabinet officers historically average only two years' consecutive service, and assistant secretaries serve an average of only eighteen months).

group for future cabinet officers, bringing the two branches ever closer together.[67]

To obtain better legal advice, Congress should create, as legal counsel to this consultative group, a central legal staff headed by a Congressional Legal Adviser. This office would correspond to the Legal Adviser's Office in the State Department or the Office of Legal Counsel in the Justice Department and would also be comparable to the Congressional Budget Office (CBO) in the sense of independently monitoring and analyzing the legal output of the executive branch's national security apparatus.[68] The congressional legal adviser could be an elected officer of the House, like the clerk or the parliamentarian, or an attorney agreed upon by a consensus decision of both parties, similar to the director of the CBO. The congressional legal adviser's task would be to coordinate the work of the staff counsels to the various international-affairs committees, to act as a liaison between executive legal staffs, and to brief and advise the core consultative group on difficult legal questions.

The proposed congressional legal adviser would play a counseling function similar to that currently played by the staff counsels to the foreign affairs or intelligence committees (who need not be lawyers) but would not be beholden to any particular committee or chair. The congressional legal adviser would represent Congress as a whole and thus exercise a jurisdiction encompassing all of the issues of constitutional, foreign relations, national security, and international law that are currently scattered across a great many committees, including the judiciary, armed services, foreign affairs, intelligence, commerce, and government operations committees. The legal adviser's central task would be to render legal opinions to Congress regarding both presidential and congressional conduct. By internal rule, Congress could both authorize and require the legal adviser to issue a "counter-report" whenever the executive branch transmits a declaration of national emergency, a war powers report, or an intelligence finding. These counter-reports could then be subject to an immediate congressional vote (under the fast-track procedure described in greater detail later), which would establish a contemporaneous written record either accepting or rejecting the president's legal justification, against which any future executive claim of congressional acquiescence could be immediately tested.

[67] *See* Richard Lugar, Letters to the Next President 51 (1988) (six future presidents, nine vice presidents, and nineteen secretaries of state have served on the Senate Foreign Relations Committee).

[68] *See* Congressional Budget Off., Introduction to CBO, https://www.cbo.gov/about/overview [https://perma.cc/EAJ2-CDYC] (The Congressional Budget Office, which has existed since 1975, "is strictly nonpartisan; conducts objective, impartial analysis; . . . hires its employees solely on the basis of professional competence without regard to political affiliation"; and has a "commitment to objectivity and transparency."); Richard Falk, *Remarks*, *in* 5 Appendices to Commission on the Organization of the Government for the Conduct of Foreign Policy 29 (1975) (urging the creation of a similar congressional unit).

In effect, these reports would form legal analogues to the independent cost assessments of proposed administration programs that the CBO currently provides to the foreign affairs committees.[69] The long-term goal of the congressional legal adviser's office would be to promote continuing interbranch dialogue by encouraging congressional and executive legal staffs to foster common constitutional understandings regarding issues of foreign affairs that would rarely be resolved in court.

To ensure that Congress withholds statutory authority from executive acts that it does not wish to authorize, this legal team could develop established terms of art specifying Congress's intent to preempt presidential claims of inherent constitutional authority, to declare that a court may not read statutory silences or limited delegations as congressional endorsement of related presidential initiatives, and to require "clear statements" to prevent executive action taken under the statute from infringing upon individual rights. Congress could enhance external legal accountability by requiring that executive branch legal opinions justifying particularly controversial actions be submitted, confidentially, for adversarial review by the congressional legal adviser, or until one is created, by the committee legal staff. Each house of Congress could modify its internal rules to set forth special threshold circumstances under which a committee, house, or both houses could demand an executive branch legal opinion.

Finally, Congress should strengthen its toolkit by developing a constitutional substitute for the legislative veto and making more effective use of its appropriations power. One alternative that would largely preserve the veto's beneficial political compromise, without its accompanying disadvantages, is the "fast-track legislative approval procedure." Unlike the so-called legislative veto—which is not legislation jointly voted by the two houses and signed by the president—fast-track approval is a greatly expedited legislative process, found most prominently in the trade laws. Under this procedure, Congress authorizes the president to initiate a military action in exchange for a commitment that the president will submit the product of that action to Congress for final approval. Under modified House and Senate rules, Congress "promises" the president that it will require automatic discharge of the completed initiative from committee within a certain number of days, bar floor amendment of the submitted proposal, and limit floor debate, thereby ensuring that the package will be voted up or down as is, within a fixed period.[70]

[69] *See* Thomas Franck & Edward Weisband, Foreign Policy by Congress 245 (1979).

[70] *See* Trade Act of 1974, 19 U.S.C. §§ 2191–93 (1982); Harold Hongju Koh, *The Fast Track and United States Trade Policy*, 18 Brook. J. Int'l L. 143 (1992); Harold Hongju Koh, *Congressional Controls on Presidential Trade Policymaking After* INS v. Chadha, 18 N.Y.U. J. Int'l L. & Pol. 1191, 1211–21 (1986). The fast-track procedure has also been included in several other foreign-affairs statutes, including the foreign-assistance and war powers legislation. *See* Jeffrey Meyer, *Congressional*

The fast-track procedure allows Congress to overcome both the political inertia and the procedural obstacles that most frequently prevent a controversial measure from coming to a vote at all. Furthermore, because one-fifth of the members present in each house retain constitutional power to require a roll-call vote on any matter, an individual member's vote on any particular fast-track approval resolution would almost invariably be made visible to the public.[71] If triggered by objectively determinable circumstances—for example, "exchanges of hostile fire"—fast-track procedures could be used to privilege certain joint resolutions introduced by any interested member and thereby to compel Congress to vote up or down quickly on resolutions that challenge executive acts. An alternative would be for the president and Congress to agree, for example, to a joint resolution that amends the War Powers Resolution so that Congress authorizes the president to carry on military actions in particular countries for, say, one year. But in addition, the law could state that that action shall cease upon a concurrent resolution of the House and Senate—that is, a bicameral vote not subject to presidential veto—and the president would agree *ex ante*, in the joint resolution, to abide by that concurrent resolution. The bill could also authorize Congress to declare its opposition to a presidential troop commitment by less than a two-thirds vote in each house, and combine a fast-track procedure with an automatic appropriations-cutoff device and a judicial-review provision.[72] Such a procedure would force Congress to vote on each particular troop commitment and thereby make a swift specific public judgment approving or disapproving each proposed presidential military action by action, not silence. [73]

Control of Foreign Assistance, 13 YALE J. INT'L L. 69, 78–79 & n.38, 86–88 (1988) (citing statutes). For proposals to incorporate fast-track provisions into other foreign affairs statutes, *see, e.g.*, Note, *Reinterpreting Advice and Consent: A Congressional Fast Track for Arms Control Treaties*, 98 YALE L.J. 885 (1989); Note, *Congress and Arms Sales: Tapping the Potential of the Fast-Thick Guarantee Procedure*, 97 YALE L.J. 1439, 1448, 1453–57 (1988).

[71] *See* U.S. CONST. art. I, § 5, cl. 3 ("[T]he Yeas and Nays of the Members of either House on any question shall, at the Desire of one fifth of those Present, be entered on the Journal.").

[72] For a similar proposal, *see* Charles Tiefer, *Can the President and Congress Establish a Legislative Veto Mechanism for Jointly Drawing Down a Long and Controversial War?*, 6 J. NAT'L SEC'Y L. & POL'Y 131 (2012); S.J. Res. 323, 100th Cong., 134 CONG. REC. S6,239 (daily ed. May 19, 1988) (reintroduced in 101st Congress as S.J. Res. 2, 135 CONG. REC. S167, S184–85 (daily ed. Jan. 25, 1989)). Former Secretary of State Cyrus Vance had earlier proposed that Congress amend the War Powers Resolution to declare that "no funds made available under any law may be obligated or expended for any presidential use of force not authorized by Congress" under the terms of the amended act. *See* Cyrus Vance, *Striking the Balance: Congress and the President Under the War Powers Resolution*, 133 U. PA. L. REV. 79, 93–94 (1984).

[73] The current War Powers Resolution already provides expedited fast-track procedures for considering certain joint resolutions introduced after a presidential report on "hostilities" is submitted or "required to be submitted" to Congress. *See* 50 U.S.C. §§ 1544(b), 1545 (1982, 1973). Reasoning that a presidential report was required to be submitted after U.S. forces had destroyed an Iranian oil platform, Senator Brock Adams attempted in 1988 to invoke this procedure to force a vote on the president's compliance with the War Powers Resolution in the Persian Gulf. *See* Allan Adler, *Senator Adams' Gambit Paves the Way for Vote on Tanker-Escort in the Persian Gulf*, FIRST PRINCIPLES, Feb.–Mar. 1988, at 4.

Finally, it will not be enough simply to strengthen the checking power of the coordinate branches of the federal government. Reforms are also needed to empower an additional set of counterweights capable of acting against a unilateralist executive. Elsewhere, I have chronicled the role of these counterweights, individually and collectively, in supporting many effective "resistance measures" taken to challenge the Trump administration's illegal initiatives through participation in "transnational legal process."[74] These include the courts (as discussed earlier); activist states and localities engaged in foreign affairs federalism; an aggressive and persistent mainstream and social media; private-public partnerships; and alliance politics.

Watching Where the Puck Is Going

Hockey star Wayne Gretzky once explained his success by saying, "I skate to where the puck is going to be, not where it has been."[75] As technology evolves, a state of perpetual conflict may strike policymakers as the best way to deal with future threats, thus perpetuating the Forever War.

Where the puck seems to be going is "video game wars": cyber-assisted AI fighting other AI, with much if not most kinetic work being done by "expendable mercenaries," such as the Wagner Group. This mode of fighting would appear to reduce the financial and physical risks that aggressor states face, while leading to increased civilian harm.[76]

Any new war powers resolution must consider targeted killing conducted by autonomous or semi-autonomous weapons systems, as well as cyberattacks. President Obama's speech at the National Defense University in May 2013 acknowledged that if Congress saw the need for judicial oversight as a more effective check on executive conduct than committee oversight, it could create a court to review targeted killing *ex post*, along the lines of the Foreign Intelligence Surveillance Court.[77] Congress could require intelligence officials to make ex parte, in camera submissions to the court of their evidence and justifications for action, with the court having discretion

[74] Harold Hongju Koh, The Trump Administration and International Law 105–26 (2018).

[75] Generally attributed to Wayne Gretzky, *see also* Clayton M. Christensen et al., *Skate to Where the Money Will Be*, Harv. Bus. Rev. (2001).

[76] *See* Brianna Rosen, *AI and the Future of Drone Warfare: Risks and Recommendations*, Just Security (Oct. 3, 2023).

[77] *See* 50 U.S.C. §§ 1801–11 (1982). *See generally* Jack Boeglin & Julius Taranto, *Stare Decisis and Secret Law: On Precedent and Publication in the Foreign Intelligence Surveillance Court*, 124 Yale L.J. 2189 (2015); Andrew Nolan & Richard M. Thompson II, Cong. Rsch. Serv., R43362, Reform of the Foreign Intelligence Surveillance Courts: Procedural and Operational Changes 2 (2014), [https://perma.cc/2U92-YMPU].

to deny that submission and order the release of the classified information to the oversight committees. Over time, such a court could become an expert referee between the intelligence agencies and the committees, while reducing the likelihood of leaks and offering greater protection of classified information.

It may be some time before the emerging fields of cyberwarfare, AI, and private security contractors are ready for statutory codification. But in each area, even without new legislation, the executive branch can continue to translate best practices into codes of conduct. Cyber conflict is currently under active discussion in a variety of public and private lawmaking forums: the Group of Government Experts (GGE), the Open-Ended Working Group (OEWG), the *Tallinn Manual*, and the Oxford Process on International Legal Protections in Cyberspace.[78] Rules that are being negotiated have already become important reference points for U.S. interagency and allied legal discussions.[79] With respect to private security contractors or Private Security Offensive Actors (PSOAs), public-private arrangements like the Montreux Document—a nonbinding statement of principles and practices approved by fifty-eight states participating (including the United States, the European Union, NATO, and the OSCE) have produced an International Code of Conduct (ICoC) to govern the private security practices of more than five hundred global corporations.[80] That code of conduct can be internalized into private behavior through contracts that govern the conduct of private security contractors, as well as domestic criminal and contract law.[81]

[78] Rep. of the Group of Governmental Experts on Advancing responsible State behaviour in cyberspace in the context of international security (2021), transmitted by Letter dated 28 May 2021 from the Chairman of the Group of Governmental Experts. Established Pursuant to Resolution 73/266 (2019), U.N. Doc. A/76/135 (July 14, 2021); Rep. of the Open-Ended Working Group on Information and Communication Technologies (2018). Established Pursuant to Resolution 73/27 (2018), U.N. Doc. A/AC.290/2021/CRP.2 (Mar. 12, 2021); TALLINN MANUAL 2.0 ON THE INTERNATIONAL LAW APPLICABLE TO CYBER WARFARE (Michael N. Schmitt ed., 2017); OXFORD INSTITUTE FOR ETHICS, LAW, AND ARMED CONFLICT, THE OXFORD PROCESS ON INTERNATIONAL LAW PROTECTIONS IN CYBERSPACE (2022), [https://perma.cc/Q4JC-9E75].

[79] *E.g.*, Michael Schmitt, *Germany's Positions on International Law in Cyberspace Part II*, JUST SECURITY (Mar. 10, 2021), https://www.justsecurity.org/75278/germanys-positions-on-international-law-in-cyberspace-part-ii/ [https://perma.cc/7XZW-7LZ3]; Przemysław Roguski, *Poland's Position on International Law and Cyber Operations: Sovereignty and Third-Party Countermeasures*, JUST SECURITY (Jan. 18, 2023), https://www.justsecurity.org/84799/polands-position-on-international-law-and-cyber-operations-sovereignty-and-third-party-countermeasures/ [https://perma.cc/JN3L-75GM].

[80] Montreux Document on pertinent international legal obligations and good practices for States related to operations of private military and security companies during armed conflict Montreux, 17 September 2008, https://www.europarl.europa.eu/meetdocs/2004_2009/documents/dv/droi_090209_33/droi_090209_33en.pdf.

[81] *See* U.N. General Assembly Security Council, Annex to the Letter Dated Oct. 2, 2008 from the Permanent Representative of Switzerland to the Secretary-General: Montreux Document on Pertinent International Legal Obligations and Practices for States Related to Operations of Private Military and Security Companies During Armed Conflict, U.N. Doc. A/63/467-S/2008/636 (2008); International Code of Conduct for Private Security Service Providers, Int'l Code of Conduct Ass'n, https://perma.cc/B7JV-TZZQ.

As recent U.S. policy declarations and executive orders on AI demonstrate, global laws regulating the use of AI in warfare are being intensely debated.[82] The laws of war do not yet treat autonomous robots as per se illegal weapons. To the extent that many such weapons are only semi-autonomous, the human operators of such robots can program in controlling principles analogous to those stated in the PPM to foster compliance with international humanitarian, human rights, and criminal law. Following the Montreux model for private security contractors, the president could issue an executive order, to be reinforced later by statute, directing purchase-contract terms, and updating policies, contracts, and regulations to ensure producer liability for legal violations by "killer robots."

The main concern in this field should be weapon systems which, once activated, can—*independently of human interference or supervision*—acquire and engage targets, and adapt to a changing environment. Fully autonomous robots that do not have a human operator "in the loop" when they select, acquire, and engage targets should be considered per se illegal weapons of war. The laws of war do not yet explicitly prohibit use of such weapons even as they are being widely developed. To be clear, the problem is not the technology itself, but the *exclusion* of human beings from algorithmic decisions to engage in offensive selection of targets that are then attacked with lethal force. Even with full human control, however, special care still must be taken to ensure the underlying algorithms are unbiased and that AI-enabled technology is used in transparent, just, and equitable ways.[83]

A global consensus is emerging that relevant governmental personnel must require appropriate levels of human judgment in the development, deployment, and use of such AI for military purposes. Two possible models of an AI treaty have been discussed: a flat prohibition or ban akin to the Ottawa landmines ban, or a rule of nonproliferation of the kind that exists with respect to nuclear weapons. There is currently so much AI currently being used in conflict that the prospect of a flat ban seems already to have been overtaken by events, at

[82] Bureau of Arms Control, *Verification & Compliance, U.S. State Dep't, Political Declaration on Responsible Military Use of Artificial Intelligence and Autonomy* (Feb. 16, 2023), https://perma.cc/T299-PEXL; Charlie Dunlap, *The Law and the U.S.'[s] New Declaration on Military Uses of AI: Some Observations*, LAWFARE (Feb. 18, 2023), https://perma.cc/U2QN-AR2P; The White House, Executive Order on the Safe, Secure, and Trustworthy Development and Use of Artificial Intelligence (Oct. 30, 2023), https://www.whitehouse.gov/briefing-room/presidential-actions/2023/10/30/executive-order-on-the-safe-secure-and-trustworthy-development-and-use-of-artificial-intelligence/ (ordering development of a National Security Memorandum directing further actions on AI and security, to ensure that the United States military and intelligence community will use AI safely, ethically, and effectively in their missions, and will direct actions to counter adversaries' military use of AI).

[83] *See* Brianna Rosen, *How to Make Military AI Governance More Robust*, WAR ON THE ROCKS (Aug. 6, 2024), https://warontherocks.com/2024/08/how-to-make-military-ai-governance-more-robust/.

least with respect to semi-autonomous weapons. So the only legally pragmatic approach going forward would seem to be a nonproliferation regime, coupled with a flat ban on fully autonomous weapons. Such a regime could be negotiated at either the U.N. Convention on Certain Conventional Weapons (CCW) in Geneva, or failing that, in a stand-alone forum of the kind that negotiated the Ottawa Landmines Convention.[84] The CCW has stated general principles for maintaining meaningful human control in compliance with international humanitarian law and establishing a responsible chain of command with humans in the loop,[85] which the United States' political declaration on the matter tracks.[86] Both of these should be developed and made more detailed. But the evolution of these legal standards remains at a relatively early stage. As these standards mature and crystallize, they too can be embedded into private contracts, codes of conduct, political declarations, executive orders and statutes, and eventually intergovernmental legal agreements.

Even if all of this were done, however, we would not be spared hard moral choices. As the 2021 Afghanistan withdrawal painfully illustrates, war termination also poses significant risks in the form of egregious human rights violations, the resurgence of terrorism, and the betrayal of loyal allies and local actors. When brutal dictators like Syrian President Bashar al-Assad commit widespread war crimes, would humanitarian intervention or Responsibility to Protect (R2P) be illegal under all circumstances, or—as I have argued—a policy option legally available under certain narrow, carefully defined conditions?[87]

Ending the Forever War would hardly spare us further painful moral dilemmas. As the book-cum-movie, *Oppenheimer*, reveals, leaders decide almost every day that one group of lives is more important to them than another: for President Harry Truman, for example, American lives mattered more than the civilian lives taken in Hiroshima and Nagasaki. Such horrific choices will inevitably be made, but at least we want them to *be made by human beings* who face political accountability and who will bear the moral and legal consequences when they are wrong.

[84] *See, e.g.*, Harold Hongju Koh, *Bringing International Law Home*, 35 Hous. L. Rev. 623 (1998–99) (discussing evolution of the Ottawa regime).

[85] U.N. Institute for Disarmament Research, *The Weaponization of Increasingly Autonomous Technologies* (2014).

[86] Press Release, *U.S. Dep't of State, Political Declaration on Responsible Military Use of Artificial Intelligence and Autonomy* (Feb. 16, 2023).

[87] *See, e.g.*, Harold Hongju Koh, *The War Powers and Humanitarian Intervention*, 53 Hous. L. Rev. 971 (2016); Harold Hongju Koh, *Humanitarian Intervention: Time for Better Law*, 111 AJIL Unbound 287, 287–91 (2017).

Changing the Lightbulb

How many psychiatrists does it take to change a lightbulb? The answer to this familiar joke is, of course: "the lightbulb must want to change." The same goes for the national security bureaucracy: when its hammer is waging war against terrorism, everything looks like a nail. The overriding goal should be to make perpetual war a less attractive default option by attacking "the normalization mindset"—the notion that a powerful nation must continuously maintain military deployments overseas to protect its national security, even if doing so inevitably gives rise to new threats, harms foreign civilians, and undermines the rule of law at home or abroad. Over several decades, this mindset has become too entrenched in the American public consciousness and must be dislodged.

Executive branch reforms must address the growing autonomy of the national security bureaucracy. On the one hand, bureaucratic inertia frustrated many extreme political initiatives during the first Trump era; in response, the second Trump era has largely purged the resistant career bureaucracy. On the other hand, during the Biden era, such resistance has stymied reforms such as closing Guantánamo, reversing draconian immigration policies, and issuing stricter guidance for drone strikes.[88] When I returned to the government in 2021—at a time when thousands of Americans were dying from COVID-19 and feeling the ever-greater impact of climate change, and just weeks after an angry domestic mob had attacked the U.S. Capitol seeking to undo a presidential election—I found countless hours still being spent contemplating the continued detention of a few dozen aging detainees at Guantánamo and potential terrorist threats originating in distant theaters. At interagency meetings, military and security interests were regularly double- and triple-counted and kinetic solutions privileged over diplomatic ones. Even if today's sprawling national security agencies cannot be quickly downsized, they must be better structured and their legal marching orders clarified to reflect current policy imperatives.

The main challenge here is for conscientious political appointees to take more deliberate, long-term steps to reframe elements of what Rebecca Ingber calls "intentional bureaucratic architecture," with the goal of promoting better national-security governance.[89] Successive political leaders of cabinet agencies have found it consistently easier to answer today's short-term fire drills, while leaving untouched the longer-term specification of how the bureaucracy should give, receive, and incorporate foreign-affairs legal advice. This has led to a shared bias among both politically appointed and career executive branch lawyers in

[88] *See generally* Rebecca Ingber, *Bureaucratic Resistance and the National Security State*, 104 Iowa L. Rev. 139 (2018).

[89] Ingber, *supra* note 55.

favor of legal positions that preserve and extend the impulse toward executive warmaking.

Citing internal executive *stare decisis*, the bureaucracy tends to entrench even legal decisions that were reached outside a well-functioning interagency legal process. Plainly, the national security bureaucracy can respond better to lawful political direction without becoming obstructionist. New political appointees to agency general counsel positions should press for the internal overruling of defective prior positions. These political appointees should especially demand change when bureaucracies seek to preserve, on grounds of executive *stare decisis*, past legal analyses "that are not reached through cautious, deliberative, forward-looking processes, that do not appropriately buffer law enforcement or intelligence decisions from partisan politics, that do not appropriately marry expertise to authority, and that do not reflect well-considered rules for addressing conflict and reaching a clear output."[90]

This volume is about highlighting the costs and opposing the continuation and normalization of perpetual war. To do so, we must promote alternatives to war that allow us to turn the page and change the generational mindset. In their chapters in this volume, Mary L. Dudziak and Cheyney Ryan each draw important historical parallels comparing the institutional mindsets that enabled previous "never-ending" wars to the perpetual counterterrorism wars that continue today.[91] Fionnuala Ní Aoláin's chapter considers how global and regional counterterrorism architectures further entrench and sustain perpetual war, exposing the dangers of relying on force as the primary tool for responding to violent extremism.[92] Building on this analysis, Pablo de Greiff's chapter applies a transitional justice lens to counterterrorism that shifts the policy focus from militarized responses to prevention.[93]

Ultimately, ending perpetual war requires ending the mindset that enables it. This challenge is about winning the hearts and minds of a rising generation that is tired of endless war. We need more public education on why war—as opposed to diplomacy and dispute resolution—is ultimately a grievously costly means of achieving national ends. We need to remind younger people of Paul Kennedy's historical lesson about the decline and fall of the Great Powers, an inevitable by-product of endless war and imperial overstretch.[94] In the long run, our best hope

[90] *Id.*

[91] *See* Chapter 2 of this volume, "How Law, History, and Culture Enabled Perpetual War," by Mary L. Dudziak, and Chapter 3, "Endless War as Aimless War," by Cheyney Ryan.

[92] *See* Chapter 16 of this volume, "Alternative Approaches to Counterterrorism," by Fionnuala Ní Aoláin KC (Hon).

[93] *See* Chapter 17 of this volume, "Beyond Redress: Rethinking Transitional Justice," by Pablo de Greiff.

[94] PAUL KENNEDY, THE RISE AND FALL OF THE GREAT POWERS (1989).

for ending the Forever War is to win over the rising generation that does not want to keep fighting it.

Conclusion

In sum, a perpetual war mentality has taken hold within the United States due to social, legal, and political factors. The first year of the second Trump term shows that Trump 2.0 is determined to extend, not contract, the "Forever War" paradigm. Thus, the long-term prescription must be to adopt micro-strategies for reform that seek wholesale reform in the long term, while seizing piecemeal legal and institutional reforms whenever possible.

Clearly, some will warn that too many reforms enacted too quickly could hamstring a president at a time of crisis. Similar concerns were expressed in the 1980s, following the barrage of post-Vietnam and post-Watergate reforms. But in my experience, whenever real threats emerge, the executive finds a way to respond. Undeniable proof of genuine national security threats empowers presidents to act decisively despite these accumulated constraints. In such crises, the president leads, Congress acknowledges the emergency, and the courts defer for understandable reasons. The resulting institutional interaction inevitably creates the necessary play in the joints to permit the required robust American response.

Over the longer term, institutional change requires new incentive structures. Most fundamentally, comprehensive public education is needed to demonstrate why perpetual war invariably results in diminishing returns for national security. When all is said and done, America's "lightbulb will not change" unless and until we recognize that Forever War is an unacceptable default position for a country committed to global leadership in times of peace.

Index

For the benefit of digital users, indexed terms that span two pages (e.g., 52–53) may, on occasion, appear on only one of those pages.

Tables and figures are indicated by an italic *t* and *f*.

www.ingramcontent.com/pod-product-compliance
Ingram Content Group UK Ltd.
Pitfield, Milton Keynes, MK11 3LW, UK
UKHW040930210926
475773UK00001BA/6

9 780197 748992